D0082547

www.wadsworth.com

wadsworth.com is the World Wide Web site for Wadsworth Publishing Company and is your direct source to dozens of online resources.

At *wadsworth.com* you can find out about supplements, demonstration software, and student resources. You can also send e-mail to many of our authors and preview new publications and exciting new technologies.

wadsworth.com
Changing the way the world learns®

The Place of Mind

Brian Cooney
Centre College

Australia • Canada • Denmark • Japan • Mexico • New Zealand • Philippines
Puerto Rico • Singapore • South Africa • Spain • United Kingdom • United States

Philosophy Editor: Peter Adams
Assistant Editor: Kerri Abdinoor
Editorial Assistant: Mindy Newfarmer
Marketing Manager: Dave Garrison
Print Buyer: Stacey Weinberger
Permissions Editor: Robert Kauser

Production: Matrix Productions Inc.
Copyeditor: John Blanpied
Cover Design: Cuttriss & Hambleton
Compositor: G&S Typesetters, Inc.
Printer: Custom Printing Co.

Printed in the United States of America

1 2 3 4 5 6 03 02 01 00 99

For permission to use material from this text, contact us by:
   Web: www.thomsonrights.com
   Fax: 1-800-730-2215
   Phone: 1-800-730-2214

Library of Congress
Cataloging-in-Publication Data
Cooney, Brian.
   The place of mind / Brian Cooney.
      p.   cm.
   Includes bibliographical references.
   ISBN 0-534-52825-2 (alk. paper)
   1. Philosophy of mind.   I. Title.
BD418.3.C657   1999
128'.2—dc21   99-12987

For more information, contact
Wadsworth/Thomson Learning
10 Davis Drive
Belmont, CA 94002-3098
USA
www. wadsworth.com

International Headquarters
Thomson Learning
290 Harbor Drive, 2nd Floor
Stamford, CT 06902-7477
USA

UK/Europe/Middle East
Thomson Learning
Berkshire House
168–173 High Holborn
London WC1V 7AA
United Kingdom

Asia
Thomson Learning
60 Albert Street #15-01
Albert Complex
Singapore 189969

Canada
Nelson/Thomson Learning
1120 Birchmount Road
Scarborough, Ontario M1K 5G4
Canada

Contents

Preface

Textbooks in the philosophy of mind are typically *either* works of a single author who combines a critical survey of the various theories and controversies in the field with arguments for a particular viewpoint, *or* anthologies of influential readings for which the editor sometimes provides brief introductions. In two decades of teaching this subject I have come to prefer anthologies despite the availability of several fine monographs. As in other areas of philosophy, anthologies give the student an experience of the diversity of styles and viewpoints among philosophers and, I believe, a better awareness of the scope and intensity of the controversies. However, anthologies in the philosophy of mind have this drawback: Many important writings are very hard for a student to read. Since much of the material was originally written by philosophy professors for a readership of peers, it is filled with difficult terminology and brief mentions of complex issues and concepts in both philosophy and other areas such as neurobiology or cognitive science. As a result, the instructor has to spend a good deal of class time bringing students to a level of reading comprehension at which discussion of the issues can begin in earnest. I have tried to alleviate this problem by several means:

1. Each reading is framed by introductory and concluding comments. The former briefly present the main thesis of the reading and supply any needed background information; the latter usually provide a critical perspective for the student's assessment of the argument in the reading. Both will often relate the reading to others in the book.

2. Where passages are especially difficult or terms and references need explanation, there are explanatory footnotes.

3. There is a glossary in back of the book. The terms explained in the glossary are bold-faced the first time they occur in the text.

4. There are one or two substantial review questions at the end of each reading.

5. Readings 4 and 15 are primers in the subjects of neuroscience and theory of computation respectively. Both try to provide an accessible but careful introduction to the basic ideas students need in order to make intelligible frequently used terms such as "brain events" and "Turing machine."

I hope that the components of this pedagogical infrastructure will make it easier for students to get involved in the collection of fascinating and important philosophical questions that is called philosophy of mind.

I am grateful to my colleague Bruce White for his many helpful comments and suggestions during the preparation of this book.

INTRODUCTION

The Place of Mind in
a Scientific Universe

Suppose you are out of doors in the countryside one autumn evening. Countless stars and a reddish yellow full moon shine vividly in the crisp, dry air. The moon looks about the size of a large medallion if you held it up in front of you. Now ask yourself what may seem a silly question: Exactly where is this heavenly scene located? Of course, you know that the moon is over 200,000 miles away, and that the nearest star is 27 trillion miles (4.5 light-years) from us. The stars in the night sky are flickering images of ancient events, of vast conflagrations that burnt years or even millennia ago. But that won't do as an answer, because the question was about the location of the *scene,* of what you are experiencing, not its remote causes. If you had rocketed with the Apollo astronauts toward the moon, the scene would be constantly changing as the moon grew in immensity and detail. You would soon reach the moon, but you could never get to the scene you started with. This scene just isn't "out there" to get to. Nor is it "in here," if you mean the inside of your head or brain (ask any brain surgeon). Where is it then?

You can ask this question about any *scene,* about how anything appears to you. (Try it for yourself, using any set of objects in front of you. The closer you get, the larger they seem. Yet what's out there isn't really changing in size.) *Scenes* are *of* what is out there, but they themselves seem not to be in physical space. They are somehow "in me" as experiences. Without my brain tissue I couldn't experience a scene, but the scenes I experience can't be found in this tissue or any other body part of mine. Am I then some nonphysical place (a mind or consciousness) *in addition to* being a body that takes up physical space? If so, how do these two ingredients of me relate to each other? This was a question that preoccupied René Descartes, the great philosopher-mathematician-scientist of the seventeenth century.

1. DESCARTES AND THE SCIENTIFIC REVOLUTION

Descartes was struck by what he saw as the stark differences between the mental and bodily components of human nature. Bodies are observable and measurable, while minds seem quite otherwise—after all, does it make any sense to ask what is the width, velocity, or location of a *thought* or *sensation* or *decision?* As we will see in Part I, he argued that humans were composed of a material body and immaterial mind that could exist separately from each other, even though they happened to come together and interact in human beings. This view is known as *dualism*. Descartes thought that his dualism would be congenial to Christians and others who believed that they would survive the death of their bodies. If one's self is a mind that *can* exist apart from its body, then the hope of personal immortality seems to make more sense.

Descartes' dualism was also an early response to the scientific revolution that was gaining momentum in seventeenth-century Europe and would culminate in the publication of Newton's *Mathematical Principles of Natural Philosophy* in 1687. Newton's book exemplified and vindicated what we now take for granted as "scientific method." After Newton it was accepted that scientific claims were to be hypotheses (1) that are based on experiment or observation, and (2) that are expressed in the language of mathematics. When Newton, building on the observations and calculations of Copernicus, Brahe, Kepler, and Galileo, was able to express in a single mathematical formula the law of gravitational attraction governing every last particle of matter in the universe, science was well on its way to becoming the dominant intellectual force of our civilization. Pope's couplet of 1728 expressed an admiration for Newton that has since extended to science itself:

Nature and Nature's laws lay hid in night;
God said, "Let Newton be," and all was light.

However, science could shed its light only on what can be observed and measured. It could deal with only those aspects of nature that were part of a public world and that could be analyzed into homogeneous units of measurement. What about the "inner" world of feelings, thoughts, and "scenes" or appearances? I seem to be conscious of such things occurring in my mind, but I can't observe them in someone else—they aren't part of the public world. Therefore they can't be measured—I can't apply a ruler or caliper to a thought. The light of science seemed to leave the mind in darkness.

It was easy to conclude that if the science of nature dealt only with what was observable and measurable, and the mind was neither, then the mind was not a part of nature. The world seemed to divide into two domains with contradictory attributes: the physical, which was spatial, observable, and measurable; and the mental, which was *non*spatial, *un*observable, and *un*measurable. Dualism, in some form or other, was a typical view among seventeenth-century thinkers reflecting on the implications of the success of the new science of nature. However, dualism is a profoundly unsatisfactory worldview. It frustrates our intellectual thirst for unity by forever splitting the world into two irreconcilable domains. It seems to make unintelligible the interaction we regularly experience in ourselves between thought and action, between events "out there" and the sensations or feelings arising "in us."

Moreover, as the readings in Part II explain, dualism seems to project into the human body a ghostly counterpart of that body, one whose nonphysical doings supposedly explain the physical doings or behavior that we observe in ourselves and others. How can we get to know other people if they (their "real" selves) are imperceptible ghosts? Imagine a house that is haunted by a ghost with predictable behavior and responses (banging doors at midnight, turning on lights when the house is empty, and the like). Although this ghost never appears, we could begin to form a notion of its personality. Are humans haunted bodies? We perceive these bodies and their behavior, but dualism seems to say that the real person doesn't appear to us. Only in our own cases do we have a supposedly special self-awareness called "introspection."

Although many philosophers before Descartes had much to say about the mind or soul and its relation to the body, it is primarily Descartes' formulation of the the issue that has been at the core of a subdiscipline of philosophy called the philosophy of mind. Other disciplines, such as psychology, neuropsychology, sociology, and computer science, also have a great deal to say about the human mind and related notions such as consciousness and self. There is a growing dialogue between these disciplines and the philosophy of mind. Nevertheless, there is a specifically philosophical set of questions about these notions, and our scientific and technological culture that originated in the seventeenth-century scientific revolution makes these questions especially urgent and fascinating.

2. MATERIALISM

In the three centuries since the publication of Newton's *Principles,* science has cast its light far, wide, and deep. It is penetrating the vast reaches of intergalactic space and time and the infinitesimal gaps between elementary particles in bodies close at hand. Even more importantly for our subject, it is exposing the molecular mechanisms by which living systems maintain and reproduce themselves, and by which the cells of the nervous system carry out sensory and cognitive functions in humans and other animals. It is as if science, in turning its attention to the system that includes the human brain, is trying to illuminate its own source of light. Part III presents an overview of some of the important structures and functions of the human nervous system, and points to some of the philosophical issues arising from brain science.

For a dualist like Descartes, the human brain is an instrument used by the nonspatial, immaterial mind to observe and act on the external world. Studying an instrument may tell you something about what its user can do, but the instrument should not be confused with the user. The brain, like any body, can be observed, measured, and analyzed. But a dualist must say that the mind itself is forever closed to scientific investigation. This implication is a further reason why dualism is so unacceptable to most philosophers (and brain researchers, for that matter). As we will see in Part III, although brain science is still only in its infancy, what we now know about brain functions suggests that the brain is more of an agent than an instrument of our perceiving, knowing, and acting on the world around us. Or it is an instrument only in the sense that it is that part of the body which the physical human organism uses when *it* carries out mental functions, just as it uses its legs for walking.

Given the rapid progress of brain science in the last fifty years, it also seems plausible to many that we will have before too long a science of mental functions as refined and well established as biology or even physics and chemistry. Yet, how could there even be a science of mental functions if, as many seventeenth-century thinkers believed, the mind is inaccessible to observation and measurement? Moved by such considerations, and by their general admiration for science, a majority of philosophers of mind have adopted a philosophical position known as materialism (or physicalism). Here, for instance, is the manifesto with which D. M. Armstrong begins in Reading 10 of Part IV:

> For me, then, and for many philosophers who think like me, the moral is clear. We must try to work out an account of the nature of mind which is compatible with the view that man is nothing but a physico-chemical mechanism.

At the core of materialism is the denial that there exists any mental reality of the Cartesian kind—unobservable, unmeasurable, and inaccessible to scientific analysis. The claim that a human is "nothing but a physico-chemical mechanism" suggests that materialism admits as real only those entities (e.g., particles and energies of various kinds) that are included in, or indispensable to, the description of the world in the language and theories of physical science. It implies a bias toward the microscopic over the macroscopic, toward simple and very small entities over larger and more complex ones. Desks, humans, cats and other inhabitants of the macroworld exist, of course, but only as more or less complex aggregates of their lower-level components (molecules, atoms, and so on down to ultimate particles).

3. FUNCTIONALISM

It may seem from the preceding discussion of materialism that, whatever the objections to which it is liable, materialism is at least clear about what it's trying to *say*. But it's not that easy. Materialism rejects anything like a dualistic mind—an unobservable, unmeasurable inner reality lurking in the brain and its workings. Okay, then materialists must be claiming that the mind *is* nothing but the brain, or that conscious mental states *are* nothing but certain sorts of brain processes. This claim is usually called the *mind-brain identity* thesis. Two of the earliest versions of this thesis are put forward by Place and Smart in Part IV-A. Yet most materialists now agree that they don't want to say that.

The trouble with the identity thesis is that it seems to restrict arbitrarily the scope of the term *mind*. There is a parallel here with the term *person*. If we limit this term to the class of human beings, then we are excluding such beings as God or the members of an extraterrestrial civilization that may become known to us. The restriction of such terms to human organisms is often called **human chauvinism.** Presumably, any being that we classified as a person would be assumed to have a mind. So we don't want to identify having a mind with having a human brain.

It might seem that a quick fix could save the identity thesis from chauvinism. Instead of saying that *the* mind is the brain, or that consciousness is a brain process, just put the word "human" in front of "mind" or "consciousness," to leave room for the nonhuman cases. But this change in wording doesn't help; it only makes the thesis rather uninformative. Suppose I were to tell you that all the human beings on earth are persons. If the word "persons" is to convey any information, it has to be telling you something more about humans than that they have those features that make them human. They must have certain attributes that make them members of a potentially broader class or community than the human, attributes they would share with non-human persons. Similarly, to say that the human mind is the human brain raises the question of what it is about the human brain that makes it a mind.

Most materialists have addressed this question by embracing a view called **functionalism,** which claims that the mind should be conceived as a *functional system.* To understand this claim let's begin with the term *function.* The entity to which a function is attributed is a *system* (a collection of components). Loosely speaking, the function of a system is what that system *does* or how it interacts with its environment. The most familiar cases of functional systems are artifacts with which we regularly interact. A chair, for instance, is an assembly of components (i.e., a system) that supports the human body in a sitting position. Unless you're reading this book in the wilderness, you're probably surrounded by objects to which you can give functional definitions like that of "chair." Try it. As you define these objects, you will notice that you need not be very specific about the kinds of components or the materials from which they are made. Many different arrangements of parts, and many different materials, can go into the making of a chair or table, as long as they enable the object as a whole to do what a chair or table does. Insofar as the description of a system is functional, it does not specify the component materials and inner details of that system. It is restricted to the interaction of the system with its environment. To the extent that two systems (e.g., a metal chair and a wooden chair) made of different materials and structural components interact with their environments in the same way, they are *functional equivalents.* Functionalists such as Fodor (Part IV, Reading 11) advocate such a definition of mind in order to avoid limiting it to the human brain. Such a limitation would be as arbitrary as limiting the term *chair* to what is made of wood. As long as a system *does* what a mind does, it *is* a mind.

What does a mind do? What are its typical activities, and what attribute(s) do these activities have in common, in virtue of which they are all *mental?* These are hard questions. We want to avoid a circular definition of mind as a system that performs mental operations. One approximation to a noncircular definition is biological in its orientation: Minds are functional *sub*systems within organisms, contributing to the organism's overall function of self-maintenance. The life of an organism consists of responding to changes in its environment in such a way as to retain the capacity to respond in the same ways to the same kinds of changes. Self-preservation at the biological level pretty much consists in preserving a body with a repertoire of adaptive behavior. The mind's contribution to this function is to receive sensory input from various kinds of sensory receptors (such as human eyes, ears, and skin), and by a variety of intermediate processes selecting and causing adaptive responses (such as various muscular contractions in humans) to the environmental changes signaled by the sensory input. This functional definition of the mind is, of course, very rough and probably too broad (since it seems to apply to plants). But it does illustrate the functionalist goal of avoiding human chauvinism. This definition doesn't require a human body, and allows for an indefinite variety of material and structural components in the system we call a mind. It opens the way to thinking of computer-like systems as having minds or performing mental operations. Perceiving, thinking and deciding are *functions* that could be embodied in "hardware" other than human brain cells (sometimes jokingly called "wetware").

How can a functionalist be a materialist if she abandons the identity thesis, if she refuses to *identify* our mental processes with the electrochemical workings of our brains? In avoiding human chauvinism, has functionalism committed dualism? If mental processes and brain events aren't one and the same, don't they become separate realities? Not necessarily. Consider the example of hip-replacement surgery. As you grow older, arthritis may cause so much degeneration of the joint that a surgeon will recommend a synthetic replacement. This is now a rather routine procedure. The metal hip joint is a functional equivalent of the original; it certainly does, far better than your arthritic joint, what a hip joint does. And you can walk, in exactly the same sense of "walk," as you did before. A materialist could ask whether you want to claim that walking is a separate reality in addition to the working of the various parts (natural and/or synthetic) of the skeletal system. What could such a statement mean? The nonidentity of function and embodiment is no more dualistic than the nonidentity of the shape of a statue with the material that embodies it. Philosophers use the term *supervenience* for the relation between a function and its embodiment or physical realization. Supervenience is a dependency relation of the sort expressed by the formula: no difference in function without a difference in the physical embodiment. This relation is the topic of the readings in Part IV-D.

4. COMPUTERS AND MINDS

Late twentieth-century humans in advanced industrial societies regularly interact with computers whose operations are the functional equivalents of various human mental processes (such as mathematical calculation, pattern recognition, and playing chess, to name just a few). From a functionalist perspective, it is as if we have managed to construct working fragments of what we call mind. Suppose (as many researchers in artificial intelligence do) that we will be able to assemble all these existing fragments, as well as ones yet to be invented, into a single integrated system. In the not-too-distant future we may find ourselves interacting with computers housed in artificial, functional near-equivalents of a human body, capable of interacting with our environment in ways that may make it hard for us to deny them the attributes of mind and personhood. In Reading 14, a panel of writers and researchers discusses the implications of this scenario for our sense of the worth and role of human beings.

Many philosophers, such as Hilary Putnam and Jerry Fodor (Readings 16 and 17), and researchers in **cognitive science** and **artificial intelligence,** have proposed that the functional equivalence between human mental processes and what computers can or might do is much deeper than just sensory input and behavioral output relations with an external environment. They claim that what intervenes between input and output, what is going on *inside* the brains of humans and other animals, is *computation.* In Reading 15 Bruce White explains the basics of computational processes. John Searle, in Reading 18, attacks the computational model of the mind.

His most famous (or, depending on what side you're on, infamous) argument against this model involves a fictional scenario called the Chinese Room.

What goes on inside the room is supposed to resemble what would go on inside a computer running a program for responding in strings of Chinese characters to questions posed in such strings. The input of a typical personal computer consists of sequences of symbols entered via the keyboard, and its output consists of such strings on a screen. Similarly, question strings would be handed to the people inside the Chinese Room. These persons know only English. Their task is to follow rules (their "program") written in English on what sorts of output strings are called for by the input strings. Suppose the program works as intended, and speakers of Chinese put questions to the people in the room. They get back appropriate answers. The Chinese Room is, from the point of view of those who pose questions to the room, the functional equivalent of a Chinese speaker. Searle claims that neither the person(s) inside the room nor the entire setup *understands* Chinese. Nor would a computer executing such a program understand what it was doing. The computational model seems to leave out some essential characteristic of mental processes involved in language.

Moreover, Searle's argument against this model suggests a problem for functionalism in general. *Functional* analyses of mental processes seem to miss something important about what goes on *inside* the mind. They adopt the third-person, external point of view (e.g., that of a Chinese speaker inputting questions to the Chinese Room), and seem to neglect the first-person or "inner" point of view, one we all have of ourselves as we perform our mental operations. By treating mental processes as nothing but very complex *mechanisms,* functionalism seems to leave out some essential features of our mental lives, ones that will be discussed in Parts VI and VII.

5. INTENTIONALITY

One of those features is *intentionality,* the topic of the readings in Part VI. The precise definition of intentionality is a matter of debate among philosophers, but the core idea is something like this: most, if not all, of our mental states seem to involve a "directedness" or "aboutness" in relation to some object or content. You don't just become conscious when you wake up in the morning; in fact, you can't be conscious at all unless you are conscious *of* something or other such as your surroundings, body position, or feelings. The intentional relation can occur both in the physical presence and in the absence of the object(s). For instance, I am sitting on a bench in the park watching people stroll by and appreciating the beauty of the flower beds lining the walkways. I assume that the people and flowers would be there even if I weren't experiencing them. But they have also become a *scene* for me, a content of my consciousness. They have somehow become part of the reality that is me as a conscious being. But their presence in me seems not to be physical. Instead, they have what Brentano (see Reading 19) called "intentional inexistence." I could be dreaming that I'm sitting here in the park. The scene could have the same vividness as now, but it would be occurring in the *absence* of the corresponding physical objects. Or I could simply be thinking about such a scene. It would be less vivid and clear than when I was in the park or dreaming, but my consciousness would still be directed upon *it*—a content or intentional object occurring in the absence of the corresponding physical objects.

It is very hard to understand how the intentional relation can occur between one physical thing and another. It doesn't seem to be a spatial, temporal, or causal relation. Happening *before,* lying *near,* or *moving* something just aren't the kinds of relations that make one thing be *of* another in the intentional sense. Insofar as a brain or a computer is understood as a physical system, it is difficult to conceive of it or anything in it having this special "of" relation to something else. Daniel Dennett, an intensely materialist philosopher of mind, argues in Reading 20 that the attribution of intentional states to others is a useful, even indispensable, fiction without which we could not make the predictions we need to make about others. But such attributions should not be understood as describing anything going on inside the heads of others. Fred Dretske in Reading 21 attempts to describe in outline the construction of a physical system that could be said to have intentional states.

6. CONSCIOUSNESS

Science necessarily adopts the external, third-person point of view toward mental events. The seventeenth-century revolution in scientific method recognized that science should deal only with what is observable, measurable, and thereby expressible in mathematical language. Let's understand the word "observable" as applying only to phenomena that are part of the public world, able to be perceived by more than one person. You can't observe the pain that I *feel,* although you can hear my grunt or see my grimace. You can see what I refer to as this red wall, but you can't observe how I *experience* what I call red; you can't have *my* sensation any more than I can have *yours.* Because we're both humans with similar bodies and sensory apparatus, each of us assumes that what it is like for one of us to experience toothaches and colors is the same as what it is like for the other. But we can't verify this assumption.

Measurement rests on the possibility of comparing what is to be measured with some standard (like the units marked off on a caliper or measuring tape) in the public world. But we can't measure what is unobservable. Toothaches and sensations of redness therefore can't be quantified and expressed in the language of science. It would seem that a blind person could understand all that science has to say about visual stimuli and the neurobiology of the human visual system, yet have no idea *what it is like* to see a certain color, or to see at all. In current philosophy of mind, the term *consciousness* is often used to refer to this first-person, what-it-is-like aspect of mental events. Closely related to *consciousness* in this sense are what philosophers call *qualia* (the plural of *quale*). These are the specific, intrinsic contents of sensations and feelings, such as the painfulness of pain or the difference between the painfulness of a toothache and a headache, or between something feeling cool rather than warm to the touch. It is through *consciousness,* in the sense just specified, that we are aware of, and differentiate, *qualia.* Hence the title of Part VII.

There is an obvious problem here for a materialist functionalist. If qualia are unintelligible from a third-person perspective, then there would seem to be more to the world than what materialism allows and more to mental events than what functionalism can admit. There is a very lively debate these days over the implications of this problem, and some of the range of opinions is reflected in the readings of Part VII. Nagel and McGinn give reasons for concluding that the problem is insoluble. The Churchlands argue that qualia *can* be accommodated by functionalism. Campbell, Jackson, and Chalmers maintain that only some form of dualism can do justice to consciousness and qualia. Finally, Brian Loar in Reading 29 defends physicalism by arguing that one can accept the "antiphysicalist" intuition about qualia and still be a physicalist.

7. SELVES

In explaining the topic of Part VI, I described intentionality as a "directedness" toward some object or content. That phrase suggests a question: Just *what* is directed in this way, what is the *subject* of the intentional relation and of the consciousness discussed in Part VII? Given the strongly first-person inner perspective from which we've been discussing intentionality and consciousness, you may be inclined to answer simply: a *self*—what people refer to with the pronoun "I." To think of minds as selves is to think of them not only from a first-person perspective, but also as having a special, strong sense of unity both in the present and over time. I like to think that if there's anything that I am just *one* of now, it's my *self,* and I believe I've been *that one* all my life. However, like so many of our familiar beliefs, this one tends to look murkier in the light of philosophical reflection, and it too is a source of controversy in the philosophy of mind, as the readings in Part VIII will show.

When Socrates was in jail awaiting execution he had a long conversation with some friends about what is likely to happen to our souls when we die. In an effort to console his grieving companions, he argued in several ways that the soul is something so different from the body that it is unlikely to suffer the body's fate at death. One of his arguments concluded that souls are recycled into new bodies after each death. In one form or another over the ages belief in the transmigration of souls has been a comfort to many persons as they contemplated their own deaths. What do you think about the *consolation* offered by this prospect? (I'm not asking whether you find the belief plausible.) Is it a case of *my* surviving my death? My reincarnated soul would cease to have my memories, and would acquire a new history of experiences in its new body. Is it still me or just a thing that was once part of me? For many people this scenario would not be survival in the *important* sense, since my personality and memories would cease.

So perhaps it is the *psychological* continuity that we value most in the prospect of life after death. If so, then the traditional Christian story about survival could be altered. Instead of a soul that survives the death of the body, one could allow that the entire person (body *and* mind or soul, if one rejects materialism) ceases to exist at death, but that God replicates the dead person (the replica would be psychologically continuous with the deceased, but perhaps would have a younger, healthier body). Would *I,* the one who died, *be* that replica?

The underlying issue in the preceding scenarios is the *criterion* of what philosophers call *personal identity* or sameness of self over time. The degree of psychological continuity between myself at age five and at age seventy is far less than the continuity I have with myself yesterday. There's been a lot of growing up and a lot of forgetting over the decades. Similarly, over any period of several years there is a large turnover in the chemical constituents of my body. Nearly all the atoms and molecules that were there at the beginning have now been replaced. What is the basis for my believing that I am the *same* person over these periods of time?

Is there any problem with the assumption that I am *now* a single, undivided self, exactly and no more than one? My brain (like the rest of my body) is an assembly or community of cells acting in concert as tissues and organs. Where in that seething mass of neurons do I discern anything like a self? Do we have to resort to dualism to get a unified self? Parallelling the bilateral symmetry of the human body as a whole (two legs, two arms, etc.) are two halves or hemispheres of the brain, each (like arms) capable of doing most of what the other does. Are there two streams of consciousness, then, one in each hemisphere?

The readings in the final part of the book remind us quite vividly that the philosophy of mind, like any other part of philosophy, has major implications for our understanding of ourselves and our place in nature.

PART I

CARTESIAN DUALISM

Raise a glass to René Descartes, who was born 400 years ago in the village of La Haye below the vineyards of the Loire. If provocation is a test of great philosophy, Descartes belongs with the elect. By the time he died of pneumonia in Stockholm in 1650 he had bequeathed the modern version of two deep but simple questions. Are minds and bodies distinct? If so, how do they interact? There are still no good answers. But spurred by recent work in neuroscience and artificial intelligence today's philosophers are trying harder than ever to find some. (*The Economist* July 20, 1996)

1

Human Minds and Animal Machines

René Descartes

René Descartes (1596–1650) was a French mathematician, scientist, and philosopher. His major works include the *Discourse on Method* (1637), *Principles of Philosophy* (1644), and *Meditations on First Philosophy* (1641), from which the first two selections below are taken.

In his *First Meditation* (not included in this reading) Descartes attempts to call into question all his previous beliefs in order to get a fresh start in his search for certain and lasting knowledge. He uses two main arguments for doubting whatever he has come to believe based on the evidence of his senses. His *first* argument is that I (he writes in the first person) have no clear indication that the experience I am now having is not merely a dream. During a dream I usually experience what goes on as really happening, just as really as what's going on around me now (which is why nightmares are frightening). However, what I experience is happening only in my mind, and not in the external, public world. It is true that, after I wake up, I can usually judge that what I experienced was only a dream because it doesn't fit into the web of the rest of my experience (e.g., the effects that a nightmarish event should have caused are not there). Yet this sorting of experiences into a large set of consistent ones (which I call "reality") and a smaller set of unruly ones doesn't answer the questions raised by the phenomenon of dreaming: Why couldn't it be the case that the contents of *all* my experiences are the stuff that dreams are made of—purely mental stuff without any correlate in the external world? How can I know that there is an external world at all? And that I am not *alone* with my experiences?

Descartes' *second* argument asks how I can know that I am not being acted on by a powerful and malevolent divine being—a demon—who is sending me experiences to snare me into falsely believing in the world they present? Until I can know otherwise, I must resist the temptation to believe, and admit that, for all I know, the external world may be a demonically induced illusion.

In the *Second Meditation,* Descartes argues that even though I continue to doubt the existence of everything I can perceive with my senses (including my own body), I still can know the truth of the statement that "I exist." Since the existence of my body is in doubt and yet I know that I exist, the self whose existence is so certain must have a nonbodily or immaterial aspect. I know of my existence only insofar as I am a mental being or what Descartes calls a "thinking thing." Moreover, my self-awareness can't be sensory, since I still doubt the existence of everything that my senses seem to perceive. So I have this nonsensory or supersensory perception of my self, an entirely intellectual kind of awareness that Descartes refers to as "mind alone" and "purely mental scrutiny." Descartes maintains that this sort of consciousness is at work even in our everyday perceptions of the most ordinary objects. In his analysis of the melting beeswax, he goes so far as to claim that (contrary to what I may believe) my perception is *not* the work of any of my senses or even of my imagination; instead, it is accomplished by the mind alone.

Second Meditation

The Nature of the Human Mind,
and How It Is Better Known Than the Body

So serious are the doubts into which I have been thrown as a result of yesterday's meditation that I can neither put them out of my mind nor see any way of resolving them. It feels as if I have fallen unexpectedly into a deep whirlpool which tumbles me around so that I can neither stand on the bottom nor swim up to the top. Nevertheless I will make an effort and once more attempt the same path which I started on yesterday. Anything which admits of the slightest doubt I will set aside just as if I had found it to be wholly false; and I will proceed in this way until I recognize something certain, or, if nothing else, until I at least recognize for certain that there is no certainty. Archimedes used to demand just one firm and immovable point in order to shift the entire earth; so I too can hope for great things if I manage to find just one thing, however slight, that is certain and unshakeable.

I will suppose then, that everything I see is spurious. I will believe that my memory tells me lies, and that none of the things that it reports ever happened. I have no senses.[1] Body, shape, extension, movement and place are chimeras. So what remains true? Perhaps just the one fact that nothing is certain.

Yet apart from everything I have just listed, how do I know that there is not something else which does not allow even the slightest occasion for doubt? Is there not a God, or whatever I may call him, who puts into me[2] the thoughts I am now having? But why do I think this, since I myself may

perhaps be the author of these thoughts? In that case am not I, at least, something? But I have just said that I have no senses and no body. This is the sticking point: what follows from this? Am I not so bound up with a body and with senses that I cannot exist without them? But I have convinced myself that there is absolutely nothing in the world, no sky, no earth, no minds, no bodies. Does it now follow that I too do not exist? No: if I convinced myself of something[3] then I certainly existed. But there is a deceiver of supreme power and cunning who is deliberately and constantly deceiving me. In that case I too undoubtedly exist, if he is deceiving me; and let him deceive me as much as he can, he will never bring it about that I am nothing so long as I think that I am something. So after considering everything very thoroughly, I must finally conclude that this proposition, *I am, I exist,* is necessarily true whenever it is put forward by me or conceived in my mind.

But I do not yet have a sufficient understanding of what this 'I' is, that now necessarily exists. So I must be on my guard against carelessly taking something else to be this 'I', and so making a mistake in the very item of knowledge that I maintain is the most certain and evident of all. I will therefore go back and meditate on what I originally believed myself to be, before I embarked on this present train of thought. I will then subtract anything capable of being weakened, even minimally, by the arguments now introduced, so that what is left at the end may be exactly and only what is certain and unshakeable.

What then did I formerly think I was? A man. But what is a man? Shall I say 'a rational animal'? No; for then I should have to inquire what an animal is, what rationality is, and in this way one question would lead me down the slope to other harder

From René Descartes, *The Philosophical Writings of Descartes,* trans. John Cottingham, Robert Stoothoff, Dugald Murdoch, and (for vol. 3) Anthony Kenny, 3 volumes (Cambridge: Cambridge University Press, 1984 and [Vol. 3] 1991), Vol. 2, pp. 16–23, 54–61, Vol. 3, pp. 365–366. © Cambridge University Press, 1984 and 1991. Reprinted with the permission of Cambridge University Press. Some footnotes renumbered.

[1]Descartes is not doubting that he is having various sensations or sensory experiences; he is merely recalling that, for all he knows, he may not have a body with sensory organs. Ed.

[2]'. . . puts into my mind' (French version). Trans.

[3]'. . . or thought anything at all' (French version). Trans.

ones, and I do not now have the time to waste on subtleties of this kind. Instead I propose to concentrate on what came into my thought spontaneously and quite naturally whenever I used to consider what I was. Well, the first thought to come to mind was that I had a face, hands, arms and the whole mechanical structure of limbs which can be seen in a corpse, and which I called the body. The next thought was that I was nourished, that I moved about, and that I engaged in sense-perception and thinking; and these actions I attributed to the soul. But as to the nature of this soul, either I did not think about this or else I imagined it to be something tenuous, like a wind or fire or ether, which permeated my more solid parts. As to the body, however, I had no doubts about it, but thought I knew its nature distinctly. If I had tried to describe the mental conception I had of it, I would have expressed it as follows: by a body I understand whatever has a determinable shape and a definable location and can occupy a space in such a way as to exclude any other body; it can be perceived by touch, sight, hearing, taste or smell, and can be moved in various ways, not by itself but by whatever else comes into contact with it. For, according to my judgement, the power of self-movement, like the power of sensation or of thought, was quite foreign to the nature of a body; indeed, it was a source of wonder to me that certain bodies were found to contain faculties of this kind.

But what shall I now say that I am, when I am supposing that there is some supremely powerful and, if it is permissible to say so, malicious deceiver, who is deliberately trying to trick me in every way he can? Can I now assert that I possess even the most insignificant of all the attributes which I have just said belong to the nature of a body? I scrutinize them, think about them, go over them again, but nothing suggests itself; it is tiresome and pointless to go through the list once more. But what about the attributes I assigned to the soul? Nutrition or movement? Since now I do not have a body, these are mere fabrications. Sense-perception? This surely does not occur without a body, and besides, when asleep I have appeared to perceive through the senses many things which I afterwards realized I did not perceive through the senses at all. Thinking? At last I have discovered it—thought; this alone is inseparable from me. I am, I exist—that is

certain. But for how long? For as long as I am thinking. For it could be that were I totally to cease from thinking, I should totally cease to exist. At present I am not admitting anything except what is necessarily true. I am, then, in the strict sense only a thing that thinks;[4] that is, I am a mind, or intelligence, or intellect, or reason—words whose meaning I have been ignorant of until now. But for all that I am a thing which is real and which truly exists. But what kind of a thing? As I have just said—a thinking thing.

What else am I? I will use my imagination.[5] I am not that structure of limbs which is called a human body. I am not even some thin vapour which permeates the limbs—a wind, fire, air, breath, or whatever I depict in my imagination; for these are things which I have supposed to be nothing. Let this supposition stand;[6] for all that I am still something. And yet may it not perhaps be the case that these very things which I am supposing to be nothing, because they are unknown to me, are in reality identical with the 'I' of which I am aware? I do not know, and for the moment I shall not argue the point, since I can make judgements only about things which are known to me.[7] I know that I exist; the question is, what is this 'I' that I know? If the 'I' is understood strictly as we have been taking it, then it is quite certain that knowledge of it does not depend on things of whose existence I am as yet unaware; so it cannot depend on any of the things which I invent in my imagination. And this very word 'invent' shows me my mistake. It would indeed be a case of fictitious invention if I used my imagination to establish that I was something or

---

[4] The word 'only' is most naturally taken as going with 'a thing that thinks,' and this interpretation is followed in the French version. When discussing this passage with Gassendi, however, Descartes suggests that he meant the 'only' to govern 'in the strict sense'. TRANS.

[5] '. . . to see if I am not something more' (added in French version). TRANS.

[6] Lat. *maneat* ('let it stand'), first edition. The second edition has the indicative *manet*: 'The proposition still stands, *viz.* that I am nonetheless something.' The French version reads: 'without changing this supposition, I find that I am still certain that I am something'. TRANS.

[7] The two preceding sentences are an important reminder that Descartes does *not,* at this stage of his argument, claim that the mind and the body are two distinct things which can exist apart from one another. At this point, as far as he *knows,* the thinking thing that he is may be "identical" with a body. All he can say with certainty is that he can know that he exists as a thinking thing even though he does not know whether any body, including his own, exists. ED.

other; for imagining is simply contemplating the shape or image of a corporeal thing. Yet now I know for certain both that I·exist and at the same time that all such images and, in general, everything relating to the nature of body, could be mere dreams <and chimeras>. Once this point has been grasped,[8] to say 'I will use my imagination to get to know more distinctly what I am' would seem to be as silly as saying 'I am now awake, and see some truth; but since my vision is not yet clear enough, I will deliberately fall asleep so that my dreams may provide a truer and clearer representation.' I thus realize that none of the things that the imagination enables me to grasp is at all relevant to this knowledge of myself which I possess, and that the mind must therefore be most carefully diverted from such things[9] if it is to perceive its own nature as distinctly as possible.

But what then am I? A thing that thinks. What is that? A thing that doubts, understands, affirms, denies, is willing, is unwilling, and also imagines and has sensory perceptions.

This is a considerable list, if everything on it belongs to me. But does it? Is it not one and the same 'I' who is now doubting almost everything, who nonetheless understands some things, who affirms that this one thing is true, denies everything else, desires to know more, is unwilling to be deceived, imagines many things even involuntarily, and is aware of many things which apparently come from the senses? Are not all these things just as true as the fact that I exist, even if I am asleep all the time, and even if he who created me is doing all he can to deceive me? Which of all these activities is distinct from my thinking? Which of them can be said to be separate from myself? The fact that it is I who am doubting and understanding and willing is so evident that I see no way of making it any clearer. But it is also the case that the 'I' who imagines is the same 'I'. For even if, as I have supposed, none of the

objects of imagination are real, the power of imagination is something that really exists and is part of my thinking. Lastly, it is also the same 'I' who has sensory perceptions, or is aware of bodily things as it were through the senses. For example, I am now seeing light, hearing a noise, feeling heat. But I am asleep, so all this is false. Yet I certainly *seem* to see, to hear, and to be warmed. This cannot be false; what is called 'having a sensory perception' is strictly just this, and in this restricted sense of the term it is simply thinking.[10]

From all this I am beginning to have a rather better understanding of what I am. But it still appears—and I cannot stop thinking this—that the corporeal things of which images are formed in my thought, and which the senses investigate, are known with much more distinctness than this puzzling 'I' which cannot be pictured in the imagination. And yet it is surely surprising that I should have a more distinct grasp of things which I realize are doubtful, unknown and foreign to me, than I have of that which is true and known—my own self. But I see what it is: my mind enjoys wandering off and will not yet submit to being restrained within the bounds of truth. Very well then; just this once let us give it a completely free rein, so that after a while, when it is time to tighten the reins, it may more readily submit to being curbed.

Let us consider the things which people commonly think they understand most distinctly of all; that is, the bodies which we touch and see. I do not mean bodies in general—for general perceptions are apt to be somewhat more confused—but one particular body. Let us take, for example, this piece of wax. It has just been taken from the honeycomb; it has not yet quite lost the taste of the honey; it retains some of the scent of the flowers from which it was gathered; its colour, shape and size are plain to see; it is hard, cold and can be handled without

---

[8] Imagination differs from sense perception insofar as it allows us to have or summon a sensory image of an object without having the experience of actually perceiving the object. Descartes shared the widely held assumption that all the images of imagination, directly or indirectly (through their components or elements), were derived from sense perception. On this assumption the dream problem and demon hypothesis of the *First Meditation* undermine our belief in the reality not only of what we sense, but also of what we can imagine. ED.

[9] '. . . from this manner of conceiving things' (French version). TRANS.

[10] In the two preceding paragraphs Descartes appears to claim that a core attribute of what he calls "thinking" is an implicit self-awareness such that if I am seeing or willing or analyzing something, whether or not the *object* really exists (as part of the external, public world), I can have no doubt that *I* am really having a visual experience of it, or willing, or analyzing it. This indubitable self-presence is a common feature of the otherwise very diverse array of acts or processes that I engage in as a "thinking thing." In the rest of the *Second Meditation* and in the *Sixth*, Descartes will argue that *sensory* content is *not* essential to our functioning as thinking things, that it is present in our minds only because we are united with bodies. ED.

difficulty; if you rap it with your knuckle it makes a sound. In short, it has everything which appears necessary to enable a body to be known as distinctly as possible. But even as I speak, I put the wax by the fire, and look: the shape is lost, the size increases; it becomes liquid and hot; you can hardly touch it, and if you strike it, it no longer makes a sound. But does the same wax remain? It must be admitted that it does; no one denies it, no one thinks otherwise. So what was it in the wax that I understood with such distinctness? Evidently none of the features which I arrived at by means of the senses; for whatever came under taste, smell, sight, touch or hearing has now altered—yet the wax remains.

Perhaps the answer lies in the thought which now comes to my mind; namely, the wax was not after all the sweetness of the honey, or the fragrance of the flowers, or the whiteness, or the shape, or the sound, but was rather a body which presented itself to me in these various forms a little while ago, but which now exhibits different ones. But what exactly is it that I am now imagining? Let us concentrate, take away everything which does not belong to the wax, and see what is left: merely something extended, flexible and changeable. But what is meant here by 'flexible' and 'changeable'? Is it what I picture in my imagination: that this piece of wax is capable of changing from a round shape to a square shape, or from a square shape to a triangular shape? Not at all; for I can grasp that the wax is capable of countless changes of this kind, yet I am unable to run through this immeasurable number of changes in my imagination, from which it follows that it is not the faculty of imagination that gives me my grasp of the wax as flexible and changeable. And what is meant by 'extended'? Is the extension of the wax also unknown? For it increases if the wax melts, increases again if it boils, and is greater still if the heat is increased. I would not be making a correct judgement about the nature of wax unless I believed it capable of being extended in many more different ways that I will ever encompass in my imagination. I must therefore admit that the nature of this piece of wax is in no way revealed by my imagination, but is perceived by the mind alone. (I am speaking of this particular piece of wax; the point is even clearer with regard to wax in general.) But what is this wax which is perceived by the mind alone?[11] It is of course the same wax which I see, which I touch, which I picture in my imagination, in short the same wax which I thought it to be from the start. And yet, and here is the point, the perception I have of it[12] is a case not of vision or touch or imagination—nor has it ever been, despite previous appearances—but of purely mental scrutiny; and this can be imperfect and confused, as it was before, or clear and distinct as it is now, depending on how carefully I concentrate on what the wax consists in.[13]

But as I reach this conclusion I am amazed at how <weak and> prone to error my mind is. For although I am thinking about these matters within myself, silently and without speaking, nonetheless the actual words bring me up short, and I am almost tricked by ordinary ways of talking. We say that we see the wax itself, if it is there before us, not that we judge it to be there from its colour or shape; and this might lead me to conclude without more ado that knowledge of the wax comes from what the eye sees, and not from the scrutiny of the mind alone. But then if I look out of the window and see men crossing the square, as I just happen to have done, I normally say that I see the men themselves, just as I say that I see the wax. Yet do I see any more than hats and coats which could conceal automatons? I *judge* that they are men. And so something

---

[11] '. . . which can only be conceived by the understanding or the mind' (French version). TRANS.

[12] '. . . or rather the act whereby it is perceived' (add in French version). TRANS.

[13] These paragraphs present a rather sketchy and incomplete argument for the following claims: (1) *What "belongs" to the nature or concept of this piece of wax in itself is nothing but extension* (in three dimensions), *flexibility* (of shape) *and being changeable* (e.g., in size and in position). Those are the only attributes left once you leave out of your concept of this body the temporary states (e.g., this or that actual shape) it can exist without, and the features (such as color or odor) that it appears to have only insofar as it interacts with your sensory organs. (2) *Your awareness of the melting wax is a perception by your "mind alone" or "intellect alone."* You can't get the idea of something being *flexible* or *changeable* through your senses or imagination because these ideas represent "countless" possible states, something you can't do in a sensory image. (Although Descartes doesn't say so, you can't even form a sensory image of one body having, or able to have, as few as two shapes in succession; you wouldn't get *an* image, but two successive ones instead.) As far as your senses are concerned, the melting wax is a succession of different objects. Only through a purely intellectual perception do you "see" the melting as going on in a single body. (3) Thus *the self whose existence you discovered by "mind alone" at the beginning of the meditation is just as well known as familiar material objects.* In both cases you understand what you're talking about only when your mind operates independently of sense and imagination. ED.

which I thought I was seeing with my eyes is in fact grasped solely by the faculty of judgement which is in my mind.

However, one who wants to achieve knowledge above the ordinary level should feel ashamed at having taken ordinary ways of talking as a basis for doubt. So let us proceed, and consider on which occasion my perception of the nature of the wax was more perfect and evident. Was it when I first looked at it, and believed I knew it by my external senses, or at least by what they call the 'common' sense—that is, the power of imagination? Or is my knowledge more perfect now, after a more careful investigation of the nature of the wax and of the means by which it is known? Any doubt on this issue would clearly be foolish; for what distinctness was there in my earlier perception? Was there anything in it which an animal could not possess? But when I distinguish the wax from its outward forms—take the clothes off, as it were, and consider it naked—then although my judgement may still contain errors, at least my perception now requires a human mind.

But what am I to say about this mind, or about myself? (So far, remember, I am not admitting that there is anything else in me except a mind.) What, I ask, is this 'I' which seems to perceive the wax so distinctly? Surely my awareness of my own self is not merely much truer and more certain than my awareness of the wax, but also much more distinct and evident. For if I judge that the wax exists from the fact that I see it, clearly this same fact entails much more evidently that I myself also exist. It is possible that what I see is not really the wax; it is possible that I do not even have eyes with which to see anything. But when I see, or think I see (I am not here distinguishing the two), it is simply not possible that I who am now thinking am not something. By the same token, if I judge that the wax exists from the fact that I touch it, the same result follows, namely that I exist. If I judge that it exists from the fact that I imagine it, or for any other reason, exactly the same thing follows. And the result that I have grasped in the case of the wax may be applied to everything else located outside me. Moreover, if my perception of the wax seemed more distinct[14] after it was established not just by sight or touch but by many other considerations, it must be admitted that I now know myself even more distinctly. This is because every consideration whatsoever which contributes to my perception of the wax, or of any other body, cannot but establish even more effectively the nature of my own mind. But besides this, there is so much else in the mind itself which can serve to make my knowledge of it more distinct, that it scarcely seems worth going through the contributions made by considering bodily things.

I see that without any effort I have now finally got back to where I wanted. I now know that even bodies are not strictly perceived by the senses or the faculty of imagination but by the intellect alone, and that this perception derives not from their being touched or seen but from their being understood; and in view of this I know plainly that I can achieve an easier and more evident perception of my own mind than of anything else. But since the habit of holding on to old opinions cannot be set aside so quickly, I should like to stop here and meditate for some time on this new knowledge I have gained, so as to fix it more deeply in my memory.

---

[14] The French version has 'more clear and distinct' and, at the end of this sentence, 'more evidently, distinctly and clearly'. TRANS.

Descartes has now concluded that he exists as a thinking thing, and that the only clear and accurate awareness he has of his own mind and of bodies occurs when his mind operates independently of sense and imagination. Yet there is still very little that he can claim to know. He exists, but (for all he knows) he may still be alone in the universe with nothing but his ideas or mental contents. He must now establish that there is a reality outside himself. In his *Third* and *Fifth Meditations* Descartes argues from the fact that he has in his mind the idea of an infinitely perfect Being to the conclusion that such a Being (God) exists. Instead of the deceitful demon that he had supposed in the *First Meditation,* there is an all-powerful, benevolent and truthful God acting (directly or indirectly) on Descartes' mind. With this reassurance, Descartes will argue in his *Sixth Meditation* from the fact that he has 1 certain kinds of sensory experiences to the conclusion that there must be a world of bodies "out there," among which is one that he, as a thinking thing, can call "his own." However much it may seem to his senses that he is one with his body, his clear and accurate (nonsensory) awareness of the nature of mind and body tells him that they are essentially different and that each could exist apart from the other. This meditation closes with a brief discussion of how the human mind and body interact through the brain and nervous system.

Sixth Meditation

The Existence of Material Things,
and the Real Distinction Between Mind and Body

. . . But now, when I am beginning to achieve a better knowledge of myself and the author of my being, although I do not think I should heedlessly accept everything I seem to have acquired from the senses, neither do I think that everything should be called into doubt.

First, I know that everything which I clearly and distinctly understand is capable of being created by God so as to correspond exactly with my understanding of it. Hence the fact that I can clearly and distinctly understand one thing apart from another is enough to make me certain that the two things are distinct, since they are capable of being separated, at least by God.[15] The question of what kind of power is required to bring about such a separation does not affect the judgement that the two things are distinct. Thus, simply by knowing that I exist and seeing at the same time that absolutely nothing else belongs to my nature or essence except that I am a thinking thing,[16] I can infer cor-

rectly that my essence consists solely in the fact that I am a thinking thing. It is true that I may have (or, to anticipate, that I certainly have) a body that is very closely joined to me. But nevertheless, on the one hand I have a clear and distinct idea of myself, in so far as I am simply a thinking, non-extended thing; and on the other hand I have a distinct idea of body,[17] in so far as this is simply an extended, non-thinking thing. And accordingly, it is certain that I[18] am really distinct from my body, and can exist without it.

Besides this, I find in myself faculties[19] for certain special modes of thinking,[20] namely imagination and sensory perception. Now I can clearly and distinctly understand myself as a whole without these faculties; but I cannot, conversely, understand these faculties without me, that is, without an intellectual substance to inhere in.[21] This is because

[15] The kind of real distinction or separability to which Descartes is referring here occurs only between *substances*—things that can exist on their own: e.g., between two bodies but not between two shapes or between a body and its shape. Descartes' *dualism* is the doctrine that a real distinction, in this sense, exists between me and my body. ED.

[16] It's unclear where we are supposed to have "seen" this. The fact that I can know that I exist without yet knowing that my body exists is not a sufficient warrant (see footnote 7 in the previous meditation). Perhaps Descartes would want to say that his analysis of the melting wax, by showing that our perception is the work of "mind alone," also establishes that the mind could *exist* alone, since it doesn't need the body (in the form of sensory organs) to *function* as a thinking thing. It is certainly important to Descartes that he has (in the *Third* and *Fifth Meditations*) concluded that an all-powerful and truthful God exists. He can now trust his power of understanding because he knows that it was given to him by this truthful God. Descartes might then argue this way: Since (1) God can create (make exist) whatever I can clearly and distinctly conceive as an existent,

and (2) (in the *Second Meditation*) I can understand "clearly and distinctly" *that I exist* without needing to know that my body exists, I can infer that my nonbodily aspect, my thinking, is *enough* for me to exist. ED.

[17] The Latin term *corpus* as used here by Descartes is ambiguous as between 'body' (i.e., corporeal matter in general) and 'the body' (i.e., this particular body of mine). The French version preserves the ambiguity. TRANS.

[18] '. . . that is, my soul, by which I am what I am' (added in French version). TRANS.

[19] The word "faculty" in this context can be understood as "power" or "capacity." ED.

[20] '. . . certain modes of thinking which are quite special and distinct from me' (French version). TRANS.

[21] Descartes is here invoking a distinction, that traces back to Aristotle, between two kinds of beings: substances and "accidents" or "modes." Substances (e.g., rocks or persons) can exist on their own or be understood "clearly and distinctly" by themselves. Modes, by contrast, can exist or be fully understood only *in* something else as their subject (e.g., walking or being tall). Thus *walking* exists or "inheres" in a bipedal

there is an intellectual act included in their essential definition;[22] and hence I perceive that the distinction between them and myself corresponds to the distinction between the modes of a thing and the thing itself.[23] Of course I also recognize that there are other faculties (like those of changing position, of taking on various shapes, and so on) which, like sensory perception and imagination, cannot be understood apart from some substance for them to inhere in, and hence cannot exist without it. But it is clear that these other faculties, if they exist, must be in a corporeal or extended substance and not an intellectual one; for the clear and distinct conception of them includes extension, but does not include any intellectual act whatsoever. Now there is in me a passive faculty of sensory perception, that is, a faculty for receiving and recognizing the ideas of sensible objects; but I could not make use of it unless there was also an active faculty, either in me or in something else, which produced or brought about these ideas. But this faculty cannot be in me, since clearly it presupposes no intellectual act on my part,[24] and the ideas in question are produced without my cooperation and often even against my will.[25] So the only alternative is that it is in another substance distinct from me—a substance which contains either formally or eminently all the reality which exists objectively in the ideas produced by this faculty (as I have just noted).[26] This substance is

either a body, that is, a corporeal nature, in which case it will contain formally <and in fact> everything which is to be found objectively <or representatively> in the ideas; or else it is God, or some creature more noble than a body, in which case it will contain eminently whatever is to be found in the ideas. But since God is not a deceiver, it is quite clear that he does not transmit the ideas to me either directly from himself, or indirectly, via some creature which contains the objective reality of the ideas not formally but only eminently. For God has given me no faculty at all for recognizing any such source for these ideas; on the contrary, he has given me a great propensity to believe that they are produced by corporeal things. So I do not see how God could be understood to be anything but a deceiver if the ideas were transmitted from a source other than corporeal things. It follows that corporeal things exist. They may not all exist in a way that exactly corresponds with my sensory grasp of them, for in many cases the grasp of the senses is very obscure and confused. But at least they possess all the properties which I clearly and distinctly understand, that is, all those which, viewed in general terms, are comprised within the subject-matter of pure mathematics.

What of the other aspects of corporeal things which are either particular (for example that the sun is of such and such a size or shape), or less clearly understood, such as light or sound or pain, and so on? Despite the high degree of doubt and uncertainty involved here, the very fact that God is not a deceiver, and the consequent impossibility of there being any falsity in my opinions which cannot be corrected by some other faculty supplied by God, offers me a sure hope that I can attain the truth even in these matters. Indeed, there is no doubt that everything that I am taught by nature contains

---

substance such as a human being. Depending on the kind of mode, the subject will be either an extended or a thinking thing. Imagination and sense-perception, insofar as they are kinds of awareness, must inhere in a thinking subject. However, the complete account of these "faculties" involves sensory organs and a brain. Thus imagination and sense perception are hybrid cases, inhering in both kinds of substance, in a way that is symptomatic of the dualism of human nature. ED.

[22] The "intellectual act" is, of course, the self-transparent functioning of "mind/intellect alone," the same sort of "act" that Descartes in the *Second Meditation* claimed to be the sole source of my knowledge of my own existence and of whatever I could know about the melting wax. ED.

[23] '. . . between the shapes, movements and other modes or accidents of a body and the body which supports them' (French version). TRANS.

[24] '. . . cannot be in me in so far as I am merely a thinking thing, since it does not presuppose any thought on my part' (French version). TRANS.

[25] When I open my eyes, I see what is there to see, whether it's what I want to see or not. The content happens to me, as it were; I experience it as a *given* rather than as my doing. This passivity in sensory experience implies that I am undergoing an *alien* influence. ED.

[26] Take as an example your perception of the extension of the book in front of you. The "formal" or literal reality of this extension is what is present in the book itself. The "objective" reality of the same extension is the *content* of your perception—the extension that is present in your

mind. Since Descartes hasn't yet argued his way out of his doubt concerning the external world, he is in effect asking whether there is a formal reality corresponding to, or resembling, the objective reality in his sense-perceptions. Descartes assumes that (1) there is nothing in the effect that is not somehow in its cause (since something can't come from nothing), and (2) the adequate cause of any objective reality must contain that reality either formally or "eminently" (in some higher form). So the cause of the objective reality of the book's extension will have to be either a book "out there " or some other being that contains the book's extension "eminently" (e.g., the way God must contain all the reality of the universe that comes from God as Creator). ED.

some truth. For if nature is considered in its general aspect, then I understand by the term nothing other than God himself, or the ordered system of created things established by God. And by my own nature in particular I understand nothing other than the totality of things bestowed on me by God.

There is nothing that my own nature teaches me more vividly than that I have a body, and that when I feel pain there is something wrong with the body, and that when I am hungry or thirsty the body needs food and drink, and so on. So I should not doubt that there is some truth in this.

Nature also teaches me, by these sensations of pain, hunger, thirst and so on, that I am not merely present in my body as a sailor is present in a ship,[27] but that I am very closely joined and, as it were, intermingled with it, so that I and the body form a unit.[28] If this were not so, I, who am nothing but a thinking thing, would not feel pain when the body was hurt, but would perceive the damage purely by the intellect, just as a sailor perceives by sight if anything in his ship is broken. Similarly, when the body needed food or drink, I should have an explicit understanding of the fact, instead of having confused sensations of hunger and thirst. For these sensations of hunger, thirst, pain and so on are nothing but confused modes of thinking which arise from the union and, as it were, intermingling of the mind with the body.[29]

I am also taught by nature that various other bodies exist in the vicinity of my body, and that some of these are to be sought out and others avoided. And from the fact that I perceive by my senses a great variety of colours, sounds, smells and tastes, as well as differences in heat, hardness and the like, I am correct in inferring that the bodies which are the source of these various sensory perceptions possess differences corresponding to them, though perhaps not resembling them.[30] Also, the fact that some of the perceptions are agreeable to me while others are disagreeable makes it quite certain that my body, or rather my whole self, in so far as I am a combination of body and mind, can be affected by the various beneficial or harmful bodies which surround it.

There are, however, many other things which I may appear to have been taught by nature, but which in reality I acquired not from nature but from a habit of making ill-considered judgements; and it is therefore quite possible that these are false. Cases in point are the belief that any space in which nothing is occurring to stimulate my senses must be empty; or that the heat in a body is something exactly resembling the idea of heat which is in me; or that when a body is white or green, the selfsame whiteness or greenness which I perceive through my senses is present in the body; or that in a body which is bitter or sweet there is the selfsame taste which I experience, and so on; or, finally, that stars and towers and other distant bodies have the same size and shape which they present to my senses, and other examples of this kind. But to make sure that my perceptions in this matter are sufficiently distinct, I must more accurately define exactly what I mean when I say that I am taught something by nature. In this context I am taking nature to be something more limited than the totality of things bestowed on me by God. For this includes many things that belong to the mind alone—for example my perception that what is done cannot be undone, and all other things that are known by the natural light;[31] but at this stage I am not speaking of these matters. It also includes much that relates to the body alone, like the tendency to move in a downward direction, and so on; but I am not speaking of these matters either. My sole concern here is with what God has bestowed on me as a combination of mind and body. My nature, then, in this limited sense, does indeed teach me to avoid

---

[27] ‘. . . as a pilot in his ship’ (French version). TRANS.

[28] Take the case of pain: If your finger is cut, you could say with equal readiness: "I hurt (there)" or "My finger hurts." When I experience the pain, I experience my finger as (part of) *myself*. Compare this with the experience of simply looking at your finger. ED.

[29] Pain, hunger and thirst are "confused" in two related ways: (1) Like all sensation, they lack the clarity and intelligibility that the mind finds when it operates independently of the senses, such as when it focuses on the nonsensory idea of extension in its perception of the melting wax. (2) They are also "confused" insofar as they confound mind with body in letting me experience my body as my*self*. The clear and distinct (nonsensory) ideas of mind and body present these two entities as utterly distinct. ED.

[30] The "corresponding differences" would be analyzed with mathematical ideas, just as we now have mathematical measures of the electromagnetic frequencies corresponding to visible colors, and frequencies corresponding to the differences of pitch that we hear. ED.

[31] ‘. . . without any help from the body’ (added in French version). TRANS.

what induces a feeling of pain and to seek out what induces feelings of pleasure, and so on. But it does not appear to teach us to draw any conclusions from these sensory perceptions about things located outside us without waiting until the intellect has examined[32] the matter. For knowledge of the truth about such things seems to belong to the mind alone, not to the combination of mind and body.[33] Hence, although a star has no greater effect on my eye than the flame of a small light, that does not mean that there is any real or positive inclination in me to believe that the star is no bigger than the light; I have simply made this judgement from childhood onwards without any rational basis. Similarly, although I feel heat when I go near a fire and feel pain when I go too near, there is no convincing argument for supposing that there is something in the fire which resembles the heat, any more than for supposing that there is something which resembles the pain. There is simply reason to suppose that there is something in the fire, whatever it may eventually turn out to be, which produces in us the feelings of heat or pain. And likewise, even though there is nothing in any given space that stimulates the senses, it does not follow that there is no body there. In these cases and many others I see that I have been in the habit of misusing the order of nature. For the proper purpose of the sensory perceptions given me by nature is simply to inform the mind of what is beneficial or harmful for the composite of which the mind is a part; and to this extent they are sufficiently clear and distinct. But I misuse them by treating them as reliable touchstones for immediate judgements about the essential nature of the bodies located outside us; yet this is an area where they provide only very obscure information.

I have already looked in sufficient detail at how, notwithstanding the goodness of God, it may happen that my judgements are false. But a further problem now comes to mind regarding those very things which nature presents to me as objects which I should seek out or avoid, and also regarding the internal sensations, where I seem to have detected errors[34]—e.g., when someone is tricked by the pleasant taste of some food into eating the poison concealed inside it. Yet in this case, what the man's nature urges him to go for is simply what is responsible for the pleasant taste, and not the poison, which his nature knows nothing about. The only inference that can be drawn from this is that his nature is not omniscient. And this is not surprising, since man is a limited thing, and so it is only fitting that his perfection should be limited.

And yet it is not unusual for us to go wrong even in cases where nature does urge us towards something. Those who are ill, for example, may desire food or drink that will shortly afterwards turn out to be bad for them. Perhaps it may be said that they go wrong because their nature is disordered, but this does not remove the difficulty. A sick man is no less one of God's creatures than a healthy one, and it seems no less a contradiction to suppose that he has received from God a nature which deceives him. Yet a clock constructed with wheels and weights observes all the laws of its nature just as closely when it is badly made and tells the wrong time as when it completely fulfils the wishes of the clock maker. In the same way, I might consider the body of a man as a kind of machine equipped with and made up of bones, nerves, muscles, veins, blood and skin in such a way that, even if there were no mind in it, it would still perform all the same movements as it now does in those cases where movement is not under the control of the will or, consequently, of the mind.[35] I can easily see that if such a body suffers from dropsy,[36] for example, and is affected by the dryness of the throat which normally

---

[32] ' . . . carefully and maturely examined' (French version). TRANS.

[33] This is how Descartes resolves an apparent contradiction between his dualism and what he says about the experience of pain, hunger, and thirst in his discussion of the sailor simile above. Since God is not a deceiver, there must be some truth in what my sense-perception teaches me. One of the most insistent teachings of my senses is that I must avoid what causes pain, eat when I am hungry, and drink when I am thirsty. The sensations through which God sends these messages give me the experience of my body as myself—they incline me to identify myself with my body and thus take care of it as if it were myself. That I should do so is the *practical* "truth" delivered by the senses. But I am not entitled to draw from my sensations any *theoretical* truths about the way things really are. For such truths God has given me clear and distinct ideas, such as those of mind and body as utterly distinct. ED.

---

[34] ' . . . and thus seem to have been directly deceived by my nature' (added in French version). TRANS.

[35] ' . . . but occurs merely as a result of the disposition of the organs' (French version). TRANS.

[36] "Dropsy" is more commonly referred to as *edema,* a condition in which there is an excess of intercellular fluid due to abnormal output of water from capillaries. Edema is commonly manifested in observable swelling of the affected tissue. ED.

produces in the mind the sensation of thirst, the resulting condition of the nerves and other parts will dispose the body to take a drink, with the result that the disease will be aggravated. Yet this is just as natural as the body's being stimulated by a similar dryness of the throat to take a drink when there is no such illness and the drink is beneficial. Admittedly, when I consider the purpose of the clock, I may say that it is departing from its nature when it does not tell the right time; and similarly when I consider the mechanism of the human body, I may think that, in relation to the movements which normally occur in it, it too is deviating from its nature if the throat is dry at a time when drinking is not beneficial to its continued health. But I am well aware that 'nature' as I have just used it has a very different significance from 'nature' in the other sense. As I have just used it, 'nature' is simply a label which depends on my thought; it is quite extraneous to the things to which it is applied, and depends simply on my comparison between the idea of a sick man and a badly-made clock, and the idea of a healthy man and a well-made clock. But by 'nature' in the other sense I understand something which is really to be found in the things themselves; in this sense, therefore, the term contains something of the truth.

When we say, then, with respect to the body suffering from dropsy, that it has a disordered nature because it has a dry throat and yet does not need drink, the term 'nature' is here used merely as an extraneous label. However, with respect to the composite, that is, the mind united with this body, what is involved is not a mere label, but a true error of nature, namely that it is thirsty at a time when drink is going to cause it harm.[37] It thus remains to inquire how it is that the goodness of God does not prevent nature, in this sense, from deceiving us.

The first observation I make at this point is that there is a great difference between the mind and the body, inasmuch as the body is by its very nature always divisible, while the mind is utterly indivisible. For when I consider the mind, or myself in so far as I am merely a thinking thing, I am unable to distinguish any parts within myself; I understand myself to be something quite single and complete. Although the whole mind seems to be united to the whole body,[38] I recognize that if a foot or arm or any other part of the body is cut off, nothing has thereby been taken away from the mind. As for the faculties of willing, of understanding, of sensory perception and so on, these cannot be termed parts of the mind, since it is one and the same mind that wills, and understands and has sensory perceptions. By contrast, there is no corporeal or extended thing that I can think of which in my thought I cannot easily divide into parts; and this very fact makes me understand that it is divisible. This one argument would be enough to show me that the mind is completely different from the body, even if I did not already know as much from other considerations.

My next observation is that the mind is not immediately affected by all parts of the body, but only by the brain, or perhaps just by one small part of the brain,[39] namely the part which is said to contain the

---

[37] The human being, as a natural composite of mind and body, has a natural, conscious goal or purpose of preserving the integrity of its body. This goal is manifest to each of us in the appetites, desires, and aversions that are part of our human nature. A mindless body such as a clock cannot in itself have a goal; it simply does what it does according to the laws that govern all material beings. Having no intrinsic purpose or goal, it has no *good* in terms of which it can be harmed. One of our natural appetites—thirst—in the case of dropsy inclines us to behavior that is harmful or contrary to our natural goal. Dropsical thirst seems, then, to be a deception on the part of the divine Author of our nature and appetites. ED.

[38] Superficial pain sensations and, even more clearly, temperature and tactile sensations map onto our visual image of the surface of our bodies to create the appearance of a precise *extent* of our*selves*. ED.

[39] The image at the right is from Descartes' *Treatise of Man* (published posthumously in 1664). It represents his analysis of the withdrawal reflex activated by the foot coming too close to the fire. All of the responses (withdrawal of the foot, turning of the head and gaze, and orientation of arm and hand) are purely *reflexive*—they are not caused by any conscious mental event such as a choice. To emphasize the mechanical nature of the reflex, Descartes refers to the young male body as "this machine." The physical locus of the "common sense" is in the cavity labeled *F,* which we now call the third ventricle. Descartes thought that the cerebrospinal fluid which fills the ventricle was "animal spirits" heated by the heart and pumped into the cavity from various arteries in the brain. He thought that the pineal gland (which he incorrectly located on the inside roof of the ventricle) was the site of mind-body interaction.

According to Descartes, each nerve, like the one labeled *C* in the image, is a hollow tubule whose outer sheath is continuous with the meninges—the layer of protective tissue encasing the brain. Inside each

'common' sense.[40] Every time this part of the brain is in a given state, it presents the same signals to the mind, even though the other parts of the body may be in a different condition at the time.[41] This is established by countless observations, which there is no need to review here.

I observe, in addition, that the nature of the body is such that whenever any part of it is moved by another part which is some distance away, it can always be moved in the same fashion by any of the parts which lie in between, even if the more distant part does nothing. For example, in a cord ABCD,

---

nerve is a bundle of fibrils originating in sensory receptors (such as skin surface) and terminating at the inside wall of the cavity. (The matter of brain tissue is composed of fibrils projecting out from nerve openings at the meninges and ending at the inner wall of the cavity.) These fibrils are bathed in animal spirits. A sensory stimulus, such as the heat affecting the surface of the boy's foot, causes a pull on the fibril at that site, which immediately (like a rope ringing a bell) alters the texture and permeability of the inner cavity surface. This sensory input in turn alters the flow of animal spirits out from the cavity, through the interfibrillar spaces of the brain tissue, and into nerves such as *C*. This altered flow causes the muscular contractions that execute the withdrawal reflex.

In the preceding mechanical sequence, *consciousness* would fit in as follows: The altered flow of animal spirits in the cavity would affect the pineal gland and generate a sensation in the mind. The kind or modality of the sensation, and the locus to which the mind would refer it (e.g., burning sensation in foot) is determined by the character of the flow change in the pool of animal spirits; and that in turn is a function of exactly which site(s) on the cavity's inner wall are altered by fibril displacement(s). If the withdrawal were a *voluntary* rather than a reflex action, a conscious decision would cause the pineal gland to direct a stream of animal spirits to the relevant site(s) on the cavity wall, resulting finally in the chosen response. In this way the pineal gland is the site of mind-body interaction insofar as it is the insertion point for conscious sensation and choice between the purely physical events of sensory input (fibrillar displacement) and motor output (flow of animal spirits). Nonhuman animals are merely machines, all of whose adaptive behavior is reflexive. ED.

[40] The supposed faculty which integrates the data from the five specialized senses (the notion goes back ultimately to Aristotle). 'The seat of the common sense must be very mobile, to receive all the impressions coming from the senses, but must be moveable only by the spirits which transmit these impressions. Only the *conarion* [pineal gland] fits these conditions' (letter to Mersenne, 21 April 1641). TRANS.

[41] Descartes is claiming that the immediate cause and **sufficient condition** for my having a particular sense-perception (whether of a pain in my foot or of the stars in the night sky) is the occurrence of the relevant *brain* events. Although our scientific account of brain events is now very different from Descartes', his claim is still plausible. It suggests a variation on the demon hypothesis of the *First Meditation:* I could suppose that I might be only a *brain,* or else a "thinking thing" joined to nothing but a brain, which is being directly stimulated by a malevolent super-scientist in immensely complex ways that would be sufficient to generate the sensory experience I am now having. This "synthetic" experience would include apparent muscle contractions and motions of my body responding to my will as I "interact" with what I am deceived into regarding as an external world. ED.

---

if one end D is pulled so that the other end A moves, the exact same movement could have been brought about if one of the intermediate points B or C had been pulled, and D had not been moved at all. In similar fashion, when I feel a pain in my foot, physiology tells me that this happens by means of nerves distributed throughout the foot, and that these nerves are like cords which go from the foot right up to the brain. When the nerves are pulled in the foot, they in turn pull on inner parts of the brain to which they are attached, and produce a certain motion in them; and nature has laid it down that this motion should produce in the mind a sensation of pain, as occurring in the foot. But since these nerves, in passing from the foot to the brain, must pass through the calf, the thigh, the lumbar region, the back and the neck, it can happen that, even if it is not the part in the foot but one of the intermediate parts which is being pulled, the same motion will occur in the brain as occurs when the foot is hurt, and so it will necessarily come about that the mind feels the same sensation of pain. And we must suppose the same thing happens with regard to any other sensation.

My final observation is that any given movement occurring in the part of the brain that immediately affects the mind produces just one corresponding sensation; and hence the best system that could be devised is that it should produce the one sensation which, of all possible sensations, is most especially and most frequently conducive to the preservation of the healthy man. And experience shows that the sensations which nature has given us are all of this kind; and so there is absolutely nothing to be found in them that does not bear witness to the power and goodness of God. For example, when the nerves in the foot are set in motion in a violent and unusual manner, this motion, by way of the spinal cord, reaches the inner parts of the brain, and there gives the mind its signal for having a certain sensation, namely the sensation of a pain as occurring in the foot. This stimulates the mind to do its best to get rid of the cause of the pain, which it takes to be harmful to the foot. It is true that God could have made the nature of man such that this particular motion in the brain indicated something else to the mind; it might, for example, have made the mind aware of the actual motion occurring in the brain, or in the foot, or in any of the intermediate regions; or it might have indicated something else entirely.[42] But there is nothing else which would have been so conducive to the continued well-being of the body. In the same way, when we need drink, there arises a certain dryness in the throat; this sets in motion the nerves of the throat, which in turn move the inner parts of the brain. This motion produced in the mind a sensation of thirst, because the most useful thing for us to know about the whole business is that we need drink in order to stay healthy. And so it is in the other cases. . . .

It is quite clear from all this that, notwithstanding the immense goodness of God, the nature of man as a combination of mind and body is such that

it is bound to mislead him from time to time. For there may be some occurrence, not in the foot but in one of the other areas through which the nerves travel in their route from the foot to the brain, or even in the brain itself; and if this cause produces the same motion which is generally produced by injury to the foot, then pain will be felt as if it were in the foot. This deception of the senses is natural, because a given motion in the brain must always produce the same sensation in the mind; and the origin of the motion in question is much more often going to be something which is hurting the foot, rather than something existing elsewhere. So it is reasonable that this motion should always indicate to the mind a pain in the foot rather than in any other part of the body. Again, dryness of the throat may sometimes arise not, as it normally does, from the fact that a drink is necessary to the health of the body, but from some quite opposite cause, as happens in the case of the man with dropsy. Yet it is much better that it should mislead on this occasion than that it should always mislead when the body is in good health. And the same goes for the other cases. . . .

---

[42] Just as Descartes relies on a truthful God to guarantee a resemblance between our purely intellectual ideas of bodies and real bodies of which we can have no direct awareness, so he needs this all-powerful Being to make the inexplicable happen: At the point of interaction between mind and body changes in the flow of animal spirits *present* to the mind not themselves or anything else in the brain, but instead specific objects, events and associated affects (such as a pain in the foot), none of which we could even guess at from an analysis of the attributes of the brain events themselves. ED.

In the Duc de Luynes' 1647 translation of the *Meditations* (approved by Descartes) the French *pilote* is substituted for the Latin *nauta* (sailor) in the first sentence of Descartes' discussion of "pain, hunger and thirst" (see p. 21 above). The sentence then reads: "Nature also teaches me, by these sensations of pain, hunger, thirst and so on, that I am not merely present in my body as a *pilot* is present in his ship, but that I am very closely joined and, as it were, intermingled with it, so that I and the body form a unit." For reasons I will now explain, it seems to me that this change of wording was appropriate for the doctrine of the *Sixth Meditation*.

Descartes has argued that the experience of mind-body unity afforded by pain, hunger, and thirst is truthful only insofar as it combines with other kinds of sensation to give me generally correct guidance in maintaining the well-being of my body. From a *theoretical* perspective, this experience is "confused." My "clear and distinct" ideas of mind and body tell me that I, as a human being, am composed of two radically different substances and that I, as thinking thing, could exist apart from my body. Since my mind is not extended, it doesn't occupy space; so it doesn't have a place or location the way my body does. However, we speak not only of where bodies are but also of where events happen. Events that happen to or in bodies are located where those bodies are. In this second sense, Descartes locates the mind in the pineal gland inside the ventricular cavity of the brain, because that is where mind and body "meet" to interact. Descartes believed that there had to be a common destination ("common sense") for the various kinds of sensory input the mind must integrate in order to formulate and initiate a coordinated behavioral response to changes in its body's environment. It is not surprising that the combination of this **functional** consideration and what he knew of the anatomical structure of the brain and nervous system led Descartes to the ventricle and pineal gland as the locus of the mind within the body.

Although pilots of ships, unlike human minds, don't have the experience of being one with their "vessels" there is nevertheless a strong resemblance in their roles. Like the ship's pilot, the mind must constantly monitor the status of its "vessel" and the vessel's environment in order to steer it safely in a chosen direction. To further assimilate the pilot/ship analogy to Descartes' neurophysiological sketch of mind-body interaction, let's suppose a modern ship's pilot closeted inside a control room with devices for controlling the engines and the direction of the ship, and a panel of instruments measuring such things as wind speed and direction, and the speed, list, and direction of the ship. The room is windowless, but it has television screens linked to cameras scanning the ship and sea in many directions.

A major disanalogy between such pilots and Cartesian minds is that the pilots would be aware that they are inside a room with images and symbols of what's going on in the ship and its environment—they would see the control panel *as* a control panel; whereas a Cartesian mind doesn't perceive the "control panel" it's using—the ventricle-pineal gland system. Instead, it seems to the Cartesian mind that its body and environment are immediately present to it when in fact it is interfacing with the inside of its brain. The "objective reality" of the entire universe is somehow present in or through the "formal reality" of "animal spirits" and brain tissue. Because pilots can leave their control rooms and become directly acquainted with the world outside, they can consciously relate what they observe on the instruments and displays to the external reality they represent. A Cartesian mind can't adopt this stance toward its "panel" because it can never leave its "control room."

Thus we have a double layer of obscurity in Descartes' account. First, it is hard to understand *interaction* between observable and measurable brain matter and an unobservable and unmeasurable mind. (In the ship analogy we at least have the body of the pilot interacting with the control panel.) Second, the mind has to somehow unconsciously look past or through brain events to the external events they signal. Descartes would insist that all this *does* happen and would be the first to admit that only God knows *how* it can happen.

The next selection is from a letter of Descartes to the English philosopher and poet Henry More (1614–87). In this letter Descartes makes explicit the doctrine implied by the *Sixth Meditation* that animals are no more than very complex machines.

To More, 5 February 1649

5. But there is no preconceived opinion to which we are all more accustomed from our earliest years than the belief that dumb animals think. Our only reason for this belief is the fact that we see that many of the organs of animals are not very different from ours in shape and movement. Since we believe that there is a single principle within us which causes these movements—namely the soul, which both moves the body and thinks—we do not doubt that some such soul is to be found in animals also. I came to realize, however, that there are two different principles causing our movements: The first is purely mechanical and corporeal, and depends solely on the force of the spirits [43] and the structure of our organs, and can be called the corporeal soul. The other, an incorporeal principle, is the mind or that soul which I have defined as a thinking sub-

stance. Thereupon I investigated more carefully whether the movements of animals originated from both these principles or from one only. I soon perceived clearly that they could all originate from the corporeal and mechanical principle, and I regarded it as certain and demonstrated that we cannot at all prove the presence of a thinking soul in animals. I am not disturbed by the astuteness and cunning of dogs and foxes, or by all the things which animals do for the sake of food, sex, and fear; I claim that I can easily explain all of them as originating from the structure of their bodily parts.

But though I regard it as established that we cannot prove there is any thought in animals, I do not think it can be proved that there is none, since the human mind does not reach into their hearts. But when I investigate what is most probable in this matter, I see no argument for animals having thoughts except this one: since they have eyes, ears,

---

[43] I.e., the "animal spirits" described in footnote 41 above. ED.

tongues, and other sense-organs like ours, it seems likely that they have sensation like us; and since thought is included in our mode of sensation, similar thought seems to be attributable to them. This argument, which is very obvious, has taken possession of the minds of all men from their earliest age. But there are other arguments, stronger and more numerous, but not so obvious to everyone, which strongly urge the opposite. One is that it is more probable that worms, flies, caterpillars and other animals move like machines than that they all have immortal souls.[44]

In the first place, it is certain that in the bodies of animals, as in ours, there are bones, nerves, muscles, animal spirits, and other organs so arranged that they can by themselves, without any thought, give rise to all the movements we observe in animals. This is very clear in convulsions when the mechanism of the body moves despite the mind, and often moves more violently and in a more varied manner than usually happens when it is moved by the will.

Second, since art copies nature, and people can make various automatons which move without thought, it seems reasonable that nature should even produce its own automatons, much more splendid than artificial ones—namely the animals. This is especially likely since we know no reason why thought should always accompany the sort of arrangement of organs that we find in animals. It is much more wonderful that a mind should be found in every human body than that one should be lacking in every animal.

But in my opinion the main reason for holding that animals lack thought is the following. Within a single species some of them are more perfect than others, as humans are too. This can be seen in horses and dogs, some of which learn what they are taught much better than others; and all animals easily communicate to us, by voice or bodily movement, their natural impulses of anger, fear, hunger and so on. Yet in spite of all these facts, it has never yet been observed that any brute animal has attained the perfection of using real speech, that is to say, of indicating by word or sign something relating to thought alone and not to natural impulse. Such speech is the only certain sign of thought hidden in a body. All human beings use it, however stupid and insane they may be, even though they may have no tongue and organs of voice; but no animals do. Consequently this can be taken as a real specific difference between humans and animals.

For brevity's sake I here omit the other reasons for denying thought to animals. Please note that I am speaking of thought, and not of life or sensation. I do not deny life to animals, since I regard it as consisting simply in the heat of the heart; and I do not deny sensation, in so far as it depends on a bodily organ.[45] Thus my opinion is not so much cruel to animals as indulgent to human beings—at least to those who are not given to the superstitions of Pythagoras [46]—since it absolves them from the suspicion of crime when they eat or kill animals.

---

[44]Descartes has adopted an all-or-nothing meaning of "soul" here: *Either* animals have the human kind of soul—immaterial, immortal (capable of existing without a body) and thinking—*or* they are soul-less machines. *Life* has nothing to do with soul in Descartes' theory; it is a purely mechanical function (in animals it is primarily a matter of the heart working as a heat engine pumping "spirits" through a circulatory system). This meaning of "soul" was restrictive by seventeenth-century standards. Some of Descartes' contemporaries attributed to animals a *sub*rational soul that bestowed not only life but also sentience (consciousness or awareness *without* thought); while others gave the word a material interpretation (cf. Descartes' description, in the *Second Meditation,* of how he formerly understood the soul as "something tenuous, like a wind or fire or ether, which permeated my solid parts"). ED.

[45]"Insofar as it depends on a bodily organ," sensation is *unconscious;* it is merely the brain event mediating stimulus and response in a purely mechanical sequence such as the withdrawal reflex. ED.

[46]Pythagoras was a Greek philosopher of the sixth century B.C.E. He and his followers were supposed to have believed that the souls of humans could migrate, at death, into the bodies of animals. For that reason, it is said, the Pythagoreans forbade the killing of animals and the eating of meat. ED.

The preceding selection should caution us against exaggerating the contrast between Descartes' robust dualism and the scientifically inspired **materialism** that is common in contemporary anglophone philosophy of mind. For most citizens of seventeenth-century Europe, like most of us today, the world contained four broad categories of beings: inanimate bodies; living things such as plants; living, sentient organisms such as fish and deer; and us living, sentient, and "rational" animals. Materialism seeks to reduce the four categories to one—that of bodies or the domain of physical science. Descartes, in going nearly as far by leaving us with only two categories, was perceived as radical in his day. In a way, his dualism was more jarring to "common sense" than materialism because it placed an abyss between conscious humans and unconscious animals whereas materialism draws attention to the complex brain and nervous system which are remarkably similar in human and nonhuman mammals and are inherited from common ancestors. Part of the interest and pleasure in keeping dogs and cats, for those of us so inclined, is the *empathy* we feel as we interact with animals so similar to us and yet so different. To be sure, some of that empathy involves projecting onto our pets human cognitive abilities such as understanding our conversation. In our saner moments we know this. However, our relationship to these animals would probably be fundamentally different if we genuinely believed what Descartes is telling us: that they have no consciousness whatsoever, no feelings or sensations.

Descartes' confidence that no mere machine would be capable of "real speech" was no doubt strongly influenced by the complete inadequacy for such a task of any machine or concept of a machine in the seventeenth century. He could not have imagined the combination of minuscule size and energy level with great speed that characterizes electronic microcircuitry today and permits immense complexity of function within small spaces and short times. It's now far from obvious that we won't soon have machines that can converse with us and each other.

In the next reading, Gilbert Ryle will argue that it is unhelpful to the point of being nonsensical for us to postulate an unobservable "inner" source of what we are pleased to call intelligent behavior.

REVIEW QUESTIONS

1. How much does Descartes' analysis of the perception of melting beeswax really prove? Has he gone too far when he infers that the nature of the wax is "in no way revealed" by the senses, and that the perception is by the "mind alone"? Does he have a better argument for his similar conclusion about his awareness of himself as a thinking thing earlier in the Second Meditation?

2. Descartes' dualism is *interactionist*—mind and body can act on each other (through the pineal gland). Some philosophers have opted for a different kind of dualism called **epiphenomenalism,** according to which bodily (including brain) events can cause mental events, but mental events are causally inert—they cannot themselves cause a physical event. Suppose that you are a philosophically inclined neuroscientist. Which sort of dualism might you find more acceptable? Why?

3. Let's think again about Descartes' discussion of awareness of one's body in terms of pain, hunger, and thirst. Try this thought-experiment: Suppose that *all* your sensory awareness of your body is like vision rather than like pain, hunger, or thirst. (You might have the capacity to form visual images of the inside of your body like those generated by magnetic resonance imagers (MRIs) and other advanced imaging machines today.) Instead of feeling pain when you perceive damage to a part of your body, you would "see" the damage and immediately *know* that you had to tend to it with an appropriate urgency. How would this sort of awareness of one's body relate to the sailor/ship simile? How would it affect the experience of your body as *yours*? Would your *self*-awareness be different in some major way?

PART II

THE GHOST IN THE MACHINE

The philosopher's treatment of a question is like the treatment of an illness.
                                        —Ludwig Wittgenstein

2

Descartes' Myth

Gilbert Ryle

Gilbert Ryle (1900–1976) was a professor of philosophy at Oxford University from 1945 to 1968 and editor of the influential philosophical journal *Mind* from 1947 to 1971. His most famous work was *The Concept of Mind* (1949), of which this reading is the first chapter. The clashing viewpoints of Descartes' *Sixth Meditation* and this reading vividly present the "mind-body problem" as a central and even foundational question for the philosophy of mind.

As Ryle makes clear in the introduction to his book, his analysis of the concept of mind is intended as a demonstration of the proper task of a philosopher. As he sees it, philosophers have always concerned themselves with subjects (like right and wrong, mind, freedom, and truth) which are also the topics of much of our ordinary discourse as we go about the business of living in human society. Most people have no problem making sense *with* these concepts; but it takes special care and skill to make sense *about* them. This second, reflective use of language, this talk about talk, is philosophy. It can be done more or less well, with more or less awareness of exactly what sort of thing one is doing. A typical philosophical mistake is to place an important term such as *mind* in the wrong "category." Categories are very broad classes such as *event, action, concrete thing* and *abstraction* into which fall the words we use to talk about the world. Categories determine which kinds of statements it is meaningful to make about various kinds of things. For instance, we can say in the same grammatical breath: "Put your signature on that document" and "Put the cup on that document." But it doesn't make sense to ask where the signature was before you put it on the document, because a signature is not a concrete thing like a cup. Words such as "signature" and "cup" can seem to belong to the same category because they are used in grammatically the same way in certain types of sentence. We need to see beyond these superficial resemblances to the underlying difference in the "logic" or "logical geography" of the words. Categories are the national and continental boundaries of our map of the world of discourse, marking off from each other areas in which different rules and conventions apply. Ryle believes that persistent and apparently intractable philosophical problems (such as the mind-body relation) can be diagnosed as arising from category mistakes. A successful diagnosis "solves" a problem by showing that it should not have arisen.

This "ordinary language" agenda, a legacy of the compelling presence in England of the transplanted Austrian philosopher Ludwig Wittgenstein (1889–1951), was very fashionable in anglophone philosophical circles during the two decades after Ryle's book. It survives today mostly as an increased awareness among philosophers of the degree to which language, especially when it goes unwatched, can shape or distort philosophical issues.

(1) THE OFFICIAL DOCTRINE

There is a doctrine about the nature and place of minds which is so prevalent among theorists and even among laymen that it deserves to be described as the official theory. Most philosophers, psychologists and religious teachers subscribe, with minor reservations, to its main articles and, although they admit certain theoretical difficulties in it, they tend to assume that these can be overcome without serious modifications being made to the architecture of the theory.[1] It will be argued here that the central principles of the doctrine are unsound and conflict with the whole body of what we know about minds when we are not speculating about them.[2]

The official doctrine, which hails chiefly from Descartes, is something like this. With the doubtful exceptions of idiots and infants in arms every human being has both a body and a mind. Some would prefer to say that every human being is both a body and a mind. His body and his mind are ordinarily harnessed together, but after the death of the body his mind may continue to exist and function.

Human bodies are in space and are subject to the mechanical laws which govern all other bodies in space. Bodily processes and states can be inspected by external observers. So a man's bodily life is as much a public affair as are the lives of animals and reptiles and even as the careers of trees, crystals and planets.

But minds are not in space, nor are their operations subject to mechanical laws. The workings of one mind are not witnessable by other observers; its career is private. Only I can take direct cognisance of the states and processes of my own mind. A person therefore lives through two collateral histories, one consisting of what happens in and to his body, the other consisting of what happens in and to his mind. The first is public, the second private. The events in the first history are events in the physical world, those in the second are events in the mental world.

It has been disputed whether a person does or can directly monitor all or only some of the episodes of his own private history; but, according to the official doctrine, of at least some of these episodes he has direct and unchallengeable cognisance. In consciousness and introspection he is directly and authentically apprised of the present states and operations of his mind. He may have great or small uncertainties about concurrent and adjacent episodes in the physical world, but he can have none about at least part of what is momentarily occupying his mind.

It is customary to express this bifurcation of his two lives and of his two worlds by saying that the things and events which belong to the physical world, including his own body, are external, while the workings of his own mind are internal. This antithesis of outer and inner is of course meant to be construed as a metaphor, since minds, not being in space, could not be described as being spatially inside anything else, or as having things going on spatially inside themselves. But relapses from this good intention are common and theorists are found speculating how stimuli, the physical sources of which are yards or miles outside a person's skin, can generate mental responses inside his skull, or how decisions framed inside his cranium can set going movements of his extremities.

Even when 'inner' and 'outer' are construed as metaphors, the problem how a person's mind and body influence one another is notoriously charged

---

Reprinted from Gilbert Ryle, *The Concept of Mind,* by permission of Random House UK Limited.

[1] There is a great deal of exaggeration in this sentence. Among many of the prominent philosophers of the first half of the twentieth century one can find dualistic elements or assumptions; but the set of claims Ryle uses to characterize Cartesian dualism simply was not at that time the "official doctrine" of philosophy as a discipline and was not professed by most philosophers. Nor did it have any such status in psychology by 1949. It is true that in the late nineteenth and early twentieth centuries major experimental psychologists such as Wundt, Ebbinghaus, and Titchener did assume that the subject matter of psychology prominently included unobservable conscious experience, reported by subjects trained to **introspect** what was going on "in" their minds. However, this methodology had been vigorously rejected by the **behaviorist** school in America, beginning with the publication in 1913 of a manifesto by J. B. Watson titled "Psychology as the Behaviorist Views It." He and other behaviorists such as Clark Hull and B. F. Skinner insisted in the name of science that psychology confine itself to observable and measurable phenomena (which they understood as behavior). Such a complete abandonment of the first-person viewpoint in studying the mind is about as anti-Cartesian as one can get. ED.

[2] Ryle and like-minded "ordinary-language" philosophers tended to equate the ordinary person's facility in everyday use of words such as "mind" with the possession of a bedrock of *knowledge* about the referents of those words. Some philosophers would have very much the opposite view—that everyday usage, if it is even consistent, is often a reflection of outworn theories, popular prejudice, and passing fashions. ED.

with theoretical difficulties. What the mind wills, the legs, arms and the tongue execute; what affects the ear and the eye has something to do with what the mind perceives; grimaces and smiles betray the mind's moods and bodily castigations lead, it is hoped, to moral improvement. But the actual transactions between the episodes of the private history and those of the public history remain mysterious, since by definition they can belong to neither series. They could not be reported among the happenings described in a person's autobiography of his inner life, but nor could they be reported among those described in some one else's biography of that person's overt career. They can be inspected neither by introspection nor by laboratory experiment. They are theoretical shuttlecocks which are forever being bandied from the physiologist back to the psychologist and from the psychologist back to the physiologist.

Underlying this partly metaphorical representation of the bifurcation of a person's two lives there is a seemingly more profound and philosophical assumption. It is assumed that there are two different kinds of existence or status. What exists or happens may have the status of physical existence, or it may have the status of mental existence. Somewhat as the faces of coins are either heads or tails, or somewhat as living creatures are either male or female, so, it is supposed, some existing is physical existing, other existing is mental existing. It is a necessary feature of what has physical existence that it is in space and time; it is a necessary feature of what has mental existence that it is in time but not in space. What has physical existence is composed of matter, or else is a function of matter; what has mental existence consists of consciousness, or else is a function of consciousness.

There is thus a polar opposition between mind and matter, an opposition which is often brought out as follows. Material objects are situated in a common field, known as 'space', and what happens to one body in one part of space is mechanically connected with what happens to other bodies in other parts of space. But mental happenings occur in insulated fields, known as 'minds', and there is, apart maybe from telepathy, no direct causal connection between what happens in one mind and what happens in another. Only through the me-

dium of the public physical world can the mind of one person make a difference to the mind of another. The mind is its own place and in his inner life each of us lives the life of a ghostly Robinson Crusoe. People can see, hear and jolt one another's bodies, but they are irremediably blind and deaf to the workings of one another's minds and inoperative upon them.[3]

What sort of knowledge can be secured of the workings of a mind? On the one side, according to the official theory, a person has direct knowledge of the best imaginable kind of the workings of his own mind. Mental states and processes are (or are normally) conscious states and processes, and the consciousness which irradiates them can engender no illusions and leaves the door open for no doubts. A person's present thinkings, feelings and willings, his perceivings, rememberings and imaginings are intrinsically 'phosphorescent'; their existence and their nature are inevitably betrayed to their owner. The inner life is a stream of consciousness of such a sort that it would be absurd to suggest that the mind whose life is that stream might be unaware of what is passing down it.

True, the evidence adduced recently by Freud seems to show that there exist channels tributary to this stream, which run hidden from their owner. People are actuated by impulses the existence of which they vigorously disavow; some of their thoughts differ from the thoughts which they acknowledge; and some of the actions which they think they will to perform they do not really will. They are thoroughly gulled by some of their own hypocrisies and they successfully ignore facts about their mental lives which on the official theory ought to be patent to them. Holders of the official theory tend, however, to maintain that anyhow in normal circumstances a person must be directly and authentically seized of the present state and workings of his own mind.

---

[3] The isolation of the individual mind in Descartes' theory is even more radical than depicted by Ryle. At the end of the *Sixth Meditation,* I remain as alone with *my* content or "ideas" (the stuff that my dreams are made of) as I was at the end of the *First Meditation.* But now I know that, beyond the perimeter of my consciousness (where, by definition, I cannot be), there are God, bodies that partly resemble my images of them, and ("inside" some of these bodies) other selves of which I can't even form an image. ED.

Besides being currently supplied with these alleged immediate data of consciousness, a person is also generally supposed to be able to exercise from time to time a special kind of perception, namely inner perception, or introspection.[4] He can take a (non-optical) 'look' at what is passing in his mind. Not only can he view and scrutinize a flower through his sense of sight and listen to and discriminate the notes of a bell through his sense of hearing; he can also reflectively or introspectively watch, without any bodily organ of sense, the current episodes of his inner life. This self-observation is also commonly supposed to be immune from illusion, confusion or doubt. A mind's reports of its own affairs have a certainty superior to the best that is possessed by its reports of matters in the physical world. Sense-perceptions can, but consciousness and introspection cannot, be mistaken or confused.

On the other side, one person has no direct access of any sort to the events of the inner life of another. He cannot do better than make problematic inferences from the observed behaviour of the other person's body to the states of mind which, by analogy from his own conduct, he supposes to be signalised by that behaviour. Direct access to the workings of a mind is the privilege of that mind itself; in default of such privileged access, the workings of one mind are inevitably occult to everyone else. For the supposed arguments from bodily movements similar to their own to mental workings similar to their own would lack any possibility of observational corroboration. Not unnaturally, therefore, an adherent of the official theory finds it difficult to resist this consequence of his premises, that he has no good reason to believe that there do exist minds other than his own. Even if he prefers to believe that to other human bodies there are harnessed minds not unlike his own, he cannot claim to be able to discover their individual characteristics, or the particular things that they undergo and do. Absolute solitude is on this showing the ineluctable destiny of the soul. Only our bodies can meet.[5]

As a necessary corollary of this general scheme there is implicitly prescribed a special way of construing our ordinary concepts of mental powers and operations. The verbs, nouns and adjectives, with which in ordinary life we describe the wits, characters and higher-grade performances of the people with whom we have to do, are required to be construed as signifying special episodes in their secret histories, or else as signifying tendencies for such episodes to occur. When someone is described as knowing, believing or guessing something, as designing this or being amused at that, these verbs are supposed to denote the occurrence of specific modifications in his (to us) occult stream of consciousness. Only his own privileged access to this stream in direct awareness and introspection could provide authentic testimony that these mental-conduct verbs were correctly or incorrectly applied. The onlooker, be he teacher, critic, biographer or friend, can never assure himself that his comments have any vestige of truth. Yet it was just because we do in fact all know how to make such comments, make them with general correctness and correct them when they turn out to be confused or mistaken, that philosophers found it necessary to construct their theories of the nature and place of minds. Finding mental-conduct concepts being regularly and effectively used, they properly sought to fix their logical geography. But the logical geography officially recommended would entail that there could be no regular or effective use of these

---

[4] The first sort of self-awareness is merely implicit in, or concomitant with, awareness of an object. Thus, when I look inside a room and see that someone is there, my consciousness is directed entirely toward that fact. Yet, I later remember not merely the fact that someone was there, but also *my seeing* that someone was there. By contrast, *introspection* is explicit self-awareness, when I take my mental state as object, as when I try to explain what particular sensation I'm having or when I reflect on the difference between my visual experience of my body and pain, hunger, or thirst. ED.

[5] The preceding paragraph states quite succinctly what is known as the "other minds" problem—one that has a special relevance to dualism. Since I can observe only the behavior of other humans, and not their mental states, it is *only in my own case* that I can be aware of regular correlations between someone's behaving in a certain way or their body's being affected in a certain way, and a specific sort of mental event taking place. This limitation raises two questions: (1) How can I know that there are mental events of *any* sort correlated with what I can observe in *other* humans? In other words, how can I know that they have minds? Would a world in which other humans had no minds (in the Cartesian sense) be observably different from the world as I now experience it? (2) Even if I can know that there are mental events of some sort correlated with the observable behavior of other humans, how can I know that the mental correlates for a type of behavior or physical stimulus are of the same sort in them as in me? For instance, how can I know that what it feels like when I'm angry is similar to what it's like for you? ED.

mental-conduct concepts in our descriptions of, and prescriptions for, other people's minds.[6]

(2) THE ABSURDITY OF THE OFFICIAL DOCTRINE

Such in outline is the official theory. I shall often speak of it, with deliberate abusiveness, as the 'dogma of the Ghost in the Machine'. I hope to prove that it is entirely false, and false not in detail but in principle. It is not merely an assemblage of particular mistakes. It is one big mistake and mistake of a special kind. It is, namely, a category-mistake. It represents the facts of mental life as if they belonged to one logical type or category (or range of types or categories), when they actually belong to another. The dogma is therefore a philosopher's myth. In attempting to explode the myth I shall probably be taken to be denying well-known facts about the mental life of human beings, and my plea that I aim at doing nothing more than rectify the logic of mental-conduct concepts will probably be disallowed as mere subterfuge.

I must first indicate what is meant by the phrase 'Category-mistake'. This I do in a series of illustrations.

A foreigner visiting Oxford or Cambridge for the first time is shown a number of colleges, libraries, playing fields, museums, scientific departments and administrative offices. He then asks 'But where is the University? I have seen where the members of the Colleges live, where the Registrar works, where the scientists experiment and the rest. But I have not yet seen the University.' It has then to be explained to him the University is not another collateral institution, some ulterior counterpart to the colleges, laboratories and offices which he has seen. The University is just the way in which all that he has already seen is organized. When they are seen and when their co-ordination is understood, the University has been seen. His mistake lay in his innocent assumption that it was correct to speak of Christ Church, the Bodleian Library, the Ashmolean Museum *and* the University, to speak, that is, as if 'the University' stood for an extra member

of the class of which these other units are members. He was mistakenly allocating the University to the same category as that to which the other institutions belong.

The same mistake would be made by a child witnessing the march-past of a division, who, having had pointed out to him such and such battalions, batteries, squadrons, etc., asked when the division was going to appear. He would be supposing that a division was a counterpart to the units already seen, partly similar to them and partly unlike them. He would be shown his mistake by being told that in watching the battalions, batteries and squadrons marching past he had been watching the division marching past. The march-past was not a parade of battalions, batteries, squadrons *and* a division; it was a parade of the battalions, batteries and squadrons *of* a division.

One more illustration. A foreigner watching his first game of cricket learns what are the functions of the bowlers, the batsmen, the fielders, the umpires and the scorers. He then says 'But there is no one left on the field to contribute the famous element of team-spirit. I see who does the bowling, the batting and the wicket-keeping; but I do not see whose role it is to exercise *esprit de corps*'. Once more, it would have to be explained that he was looking for the wrong type of thing. Team-spirit is not another cricketing-operation supplementary to all of the other special tasks. It is, roughly, the keenness with which each of the special tasks is performed, and performing a task keenly is not performing two tasks. Certainly exhibiting team-spirit is not the same thing as bowling or catching, but nor is it a third thing such that we can say that the bowler first bowls *and* then exhibits team-spirit or that a fielder is at a given moment *either* catching *or* displaying *esprit de corps*.

These illustrations of category-mistakes have a common feature which must be noticed. The mistakes were made by people who did not know how to wield the concepts *University, division* and *team-spirit*. Their puzzles arose from inability to use certain items in the English vocabulary.

The theoretically interesting category-mistakes are those made by people who are perfectly competent to apply concepts, at least in the situations with which they are familiar, but are still liable in their abstract thinking to allocate those concepts to

---

[6] The conclusion Ryle wants us to draw here is that, precisely because we do know how to use words referring to mental states and processes, these words can't be referring to what is unobservable. Ed.

logical types to which they do not belong. An instance of a mistake of this sort would be the following story. A student of politics has learned the main differences between the British, the French and the American Constitutions, and has learned also the differences and connections between the Cabinet, Parliament, the various Ministries, the Judicature and the Church of England. But he still becomes embarrassed when asked questions about the connections between the Church of England, the Home Office and the British Constitution. For while the Church and the Home Office are institutions, the British Constitution is not another institution in the same sense of that noun. So inter-institutional relations which can be asserted or denied to hold between the Church and the Home Office cannot be asserted or denied to hold between either of them and the British Constitution. 'The British Constitution' is not a term of the same logical type as 'the Home Office' and 'the Church of England'. In a partially similar way, John Doe may be a relative, a friend, an enemy or a stranger to Richard Roe; but he cannot be any of these things to the Average Taxpayer. He knows how to talk sense in certain sorts of discussions about the Average Taxpayer, but he is baffled to say why he could not come across him in the street as he can come across Richard Roe.

It is pertinent to our main subject to notice that, so long as the student of politics continues to think of the British Constitution as a counterpart to the other institutions, he will tend to describe it as a mysteriously occult institution; and so long as John Doe continues to think of the Average Taxpayer as a fellow-citizen, he will tend to think of him as an elusive insubstantial man, a ghost who is everywhere yet nowhere.

My destructive purpose is to show that a family of radical category-mistakes is the source of the double-life theory. The representation of a person as a ghost mysteriously ensconced in a machine derives from this argument.[7] Because, as is true, a person's thinking, feeling and purposive doing cannot be described solely in the idioms of physics, chemistry and physiology, therefore they must be de-

scribed in counterpart idioms. As the human body is a complex organised unit, so the human mind must be another complex organised unit, though one made of a different sort of stuff and with a different sort of structure. Or, again, as the human body, like any other parcel of matter, is a field of causes and effects, so the mind must be another field of causes and effects, though not (Heaven be praised) mechanical causes and effects.

(3) THE ORIGIN OF THE CATEGORY-MISTAKE

One of the chief intellectual origins of what I have yet to prove to be the Cartesian category-mistake seems to be this. When Galileo showed that his methods of scientific discovery were competent to provide a mechanical theory which should cover every occupant of space, Descartes found in himself two conflicting motives. As a man of scientific genius he could not but endorse the claims of mechanics, yet as a religious and moral man he could not accept, as Hobbes accepted, the discouraging rider to those claims, namely that human nature differs only in degree of complexity from clockwork. The mental could not be just a variety of the mechanical.

He and subsequent philosophers naturally but erroneously availed themselves of the following escape-route. Since mental-conduct words are not to be construed as signifying the occurrence of mechanical processes, they must be construed as signifying the occurrence of non-mechanical processes; since mechanical laws explain movements in space as the effects of other movements in space, other laws must explain some of the non-spatial workings of minds as the effects of other non-spatial workings of minds. The difference between the human behaviours which we describe as intelligent and those which we describe as unintelligent must be a difference in their causation; so, while some movements of human tongues and limbs are the effects of mechanical causes, others must be the effects of non-mechanical causes, i.e. some issue from movements of particles of matter, others from workings of the mind.

The differences between the physical and the mental were thus represented as differences inside

---

[7] The conclusions in the sentences that follow in this paragraph are all what Ryle regards as category-mistakes of the sort leading to the mind-body problem. ED.

the common framework of the categories of 'thing', 'stuff', 'attribute', 'state', 'process', 'change', 'cause' and 'effect'. Minds are things, but different sorts of things from bodies; mental processes are causes and effects, but different sorts of causes and effects from bodily movements. And so on. Somewhat as the foreigner expected the University to be an extra edifice, rather like a college but also considerably different, so the repudiators of mechanism represented minds as extra centres of causal processes, rather like machines but also considerably different from them. Their theory was a para-mechanical hypothesis.

That this assumption was at the heart of the doctrine is shown by the fact that there was from the beginning felt to be a major theoretical difficulty in explaining how minds can influence and be influenced by bodies. How can a mental process, such as willing, cause spatial movements like the movements of the tongue? How can a physical change in the optic nerve have among its effects a mind's perception of a flash of light? This notorious crux by itself shows the logical mould into which Descartes pressed his theory of the mind. It was the self-same mould into which he and Galileo set their mechanics. Still unwittingly adhering to the grammar of mechanics, he tried to avert disaster by describing minds in what was merely an obverse vocabulary. The workings of minds had to be described by the mere negatives of the specific descriptions given to bodies; they are not in space, they are not motions, they are not modifications of matter, they are not accessible to public observation. Minds are not bits of clockwork, they are just bits of not-clockwork.

As thus represented, minds are not merely ghosts harnessed to machines, they are themselves just spectral machines. Though the human body is an engine, it is not quite an ordinary engine, since some of its workings are governed by another engine inside it—this interior governor-engine being one of a very special sort. It is invisible, inaudible and it has no size or weight. It cannot be taken to bits and the laws it obeys are not those known to ordinary engineers. Nothing is known of how it governs the bodily engine.[8]

A second major crux points the same moral. Since, according to the doctrine, minds belong to the same category as bodies and since bodies are rigidly governed by mechanical laws, it seemed to many theorists to follow that minds must be similarly governed by rigid non-mechanical laws. The physical world is a deterministic system, so the mental world must be a deterministic system. Bodies cannot help the modifications that they undergo, so minds cannot help pursuing the careers fixed for them. *Responsibility, choice, merit* and *demerit* are therefore inapplicable concepts—unless the compromise solution is adopted of saying that the laws governing mental processes, unlike those governing physical processes, have the congenial attribute of being only rather rigid. The problem of the Freedom of the Will was the problem [of] how to reconcile the hypothesis that minds are to be described in terms drawn from the categories of mechanics with the knowledge that higher-grade human conduct is not of a piece with the behaviour of machines.

It is an historical curiosity that it was not noticed that the entire argument was broken-backed. Theorists correctly assumed that any sane man could already recognise the differences between, say, rational and non-rational utterances or between purposive and automatic behaviour. Else there would have been nothing requiring to be salved from mechanism. Yet the explanation given presupposed that one person could in principle never recognise the difference between the rational and the irrational utterances issuing from other human bodies, since he could never get access to the postulated immaterial causes of some of their utterances. Save for the doubtful exception of himself, he could never tell the difference between a man and a Robot.[9] It would have to be conceded, for example, that, for all that we can tell, the inner lives of persons who are classed as idiots or lunatics are as rational as those of anyone else. Perhaps only

---

[8] Thomas Nagel (1986) makes a similar point: "The main objection to dualism is that it postulates an additional, non-physical substance with-

out explaining how *it* can support subjective mental states whereas the brain can't. Even if we conclude that mental events are not simply physical events, it doesn't follow that we can explain their place in the universe by summoning up a type of substance whose only function is to provide them with a medium" (29). Ed.

[9] Descartes would, of course, reject this claim and insist that "real speech" is a "certain [i.e., sure] sign of thought hidden in a body" ("Descartes to More" in Reading 1). Ed.

their overt behaviour is disappointing; that is to say, perhaps 'idiots' are not really idiotic, or 'lunatics' lunatic. Perhaps, too, some of those who are classed as sane are really idiots. According to the theory, external observers could never know how the overt behaviour of others is correlated with their mental powers and processes and so they could never know or even plausibly conjecture whether their applications of mental-conduct concepts to these other people were correct or incorrect. It would then be hazardous or impossible for a man to claim sanity or logical consistency even for himself, since he would be debarred from comparing his own performances with those of others.[10] In short, our characterisations of persons and their performances as intelligent, prudent and virtuous or as stupid, hypocritical and cowardly could never have been made, so the problem of providing a special causal hypothesis to serve as the basis of such diagnoses would never have arisen. The question, 'How do persons differ from machines?' arose just because everyone already knew how to apply mental-conduct concepts before the new causal hypothesis was introduced. This causal hypothesis could not therefore be the source of the criteria used in those applications. Nor, of course, has the causal hypothesis in any degree improved our handling of those criteria. We still distinguish good from bad arithmetic, politic from impolitic conduct and fertile from infertile imaginations in the ways in which Descartes himself distinguished them before and after he speculated how the applicability of these criteria was compatible with the principle of mechanical causation.

He had mistaken the logic of his problem. Instead of asking by what criteria intelligent behaviour is actually distinguished from non-intelligent behaviour, he asked 'Given that the principle of mechanical causation does not tell us the difference, what other causal principle will tell it us?' He re-

alised that the problem was not one of mechanics and assumed that it must therefore be one of some counterpart to mechanics. Not unnaturally psychology is often cast for just this role.

When two terms belong to the same category, it is proper to construct conjunctive propositions embodying them. Thus a purchaser may say that he bought a left-hand glove and a right-hand glove, but not that he bought a left-hand glove, a right-hand glove and a pair of gloves. 'She came home in a flood of tears and a sedan-chair' is a well-known joke based on the absurdity of conjoining terms of different types. It would have been equally ridiculous to construct the disjunction 'She came home either in a flood of tears or else in a sedan-chair'. Now the dogma of the Ghost in the Machine does just this. It maintains that there exist both bodies and minds; that there occur physical processes and mental processes; that there are mechanical causes of corporeal movements and mental causes of corporeal movements. I shall argue that these and other analogous conjunctions are absurd; but, it must be noticed, the argument will not show that either of the illegitimately conjoined propositions is absurd in itself. I am not, for example, denying that there occur mental processes. Doing long division is a mental process and so is making a joke. But I am saying that the phrase 'there occur mental processes' does not mean the same sort of thing as 'there occur physical processes', and, therefore, that it makes no sense to conjoin or disjoin the two.

If my argument is successful, there will follow some interesting consequences. First, the hallowed contrast between Mind and Matter will be dissipated, but dissipated not by either of the equally hallowed absorptions of Mind by Matter or of Matter by Mind, but in quite a different way. For the seeming contrast of the two will be shown to be as illegitimate as would be the contrast of 'she came home in a flood of tears' and 'she came home in a sedan-chair'. The belief that there is a polar opposition between Mind and Matter is the belief that they are terms of the same logical type.

It will also follow that both Idealism and Materialism are answers to an improper question. The 'reduction' of the material world to mental states and processes, as well as the 'reduction' of mental

---

[10] If I use a word such as "logical" or "smart" to characterize someone else's mental operations, and yet there is no shared awareness of these operations, how can I know that you and I are using the word in the same way? And if I can't know that I am using the word the way others use it, how can I know that I am using it correctly in talking about my own mental life? As Ryle sees it, these problems can be avoided only if mental terms are about behavior in the shared space of the public world rather than about the radically private performances of a Cartesian mind. ED.

states and processes to physical states and processes, presuppose the legitimacy of the disjunction 'Either there exist minds or there exist bodies (but not both)'. It would be like saying, 'Either she bought a left-hand and a right-hand glove or she bought a pair of gloves (but not both)'.

It is perfectly proper to say, in one logical tone of voice, that there exist minds and to say, in another logical tone of voice, that there exist bodies. But these expressions do not indicate two different species of existence, for 'existence' is not a generic word like 'coloured' or 'sexed'. They indicate two different senses of 'exist', somewhat as 'rising' has different senses in 'the tide is rising', 'hopes are rising', and 'the average age of death is rising'. A man would be thought to be making a poor joke who said that three things are now rising, namely the tide, hopes and the average age of death. It would be just as good or bad a joke to say that there exist prime numbers and Wednesdays and public opinions and navies; or that there exist both minds and bodies. In the succeeding chapters I try to prove that the official theory does rest on a batch of category-mistakes by showing that logically absurd corollaries follow from it. The exhibition of these absurdities will have the constructive effect of bringing out part of the correct logic of mental-conduct concepts.

(4) HISTORICAL NOTE

It would not be true to say that the official theory derives solely from Descartes' theories, or even from a more widespread anxiety about the implications of seventeenth century mechanism. Scholastic and Reformation theology had schooled the intellects of the scientists as well as of the laymen, philosophers and clerics of that age. Stoic-Augustinian theories of the will were embedded in the Calvinist doctrines of sin and grace; Platonic and Aristotelian theories of the intellect shaped the orthodox doctrines of the immortality of the soul. Descartes was reformulating already prevalent theological doctrines of the soul in the new syntax of Galileo. The theologian's privacy of conscience became the philosopher's privacy of consciousness,

and what had been the bogy of Predestination reappeared as the bogy of Determinism.[11]

It would also not be true to say that the two-worlds myth did no theoretical good. Myths often do a lot of theoretical good, while they are still new. One benefit bestowed by the para-mechanical myth was that it partly superannuated the then prevalent para-political myth. Minds and their Faculties had previously been described by analogies with political superiors and political subordinates. The idioms used were those of ruling, obeying, collaborating and rebelling.[12] They survived and still survive in many ethical and some epistemological discussions. As, in physics, the new myth of occult Forces[13] was a scientific improvement on the

---

[11] *Predestination* is the notion that God's will has ordained in advance everything that will happen in time, especially the salvation of only some humans. *Determinism* is the notion that every event is caused, i.e., necessarily occurs because of the existence of some other event or set of events. The necessity in a deterministic sequence of events is strongly connected with a belief that nature is law-abiding—that all events occur according to laws of nature to which there can be no exception. Armed with this faith, the scientist undertakes the arduous task of discovering these laws. ED.

[12] In Plato's *Republic,* for instance, the structure of the soul is compared to that of a city-state, and the proper relation of our various kinds of desires and appetites to reason is analyzed in terms of the harmonious subordination of the working class to the "guardian" and ruling classes. ED.

[13] What Isaac Newton had to say about gravity would be an example of the "new myth of occult Forces." He discovered that the tendency of any two bodies to accelerate toward each other (as when things fall to earth) was directly proportional to the product of their masses and inversely proportional to the square of their distance from each other. His law of gravitation gives a precise correlation among the masses of the two bodies, the rate of change in their velocity, and the distance between them, so that we can infer or predict any one of these if we know the other three. Newton *also* postulated a *force* he called gravity that was the "inner" source of the attractive "influence" of one body on another. He didn't understand *how* gravity worked (how, for instance, it apparently acted without the bodies being in contact directly or through a medium); only *that* bodies behaved in accordance with his law. That was enough for Newton to confidently assert the existence of this otherwise unobservable "occult" entity, even while modestly refraining from any guesses as to what gravity was in itself: "And to us it is enough that gravity does really exist, and act according to the laws which we have explained and abundantly serves to account for all the motions of the celestial bodies, and of our sea" (From the General Scholium to *Philosophiae Naturalis Principia Mathematica,* trans. Andrew Motte).

For Ryle it is the predictive power of the law of gravitation that "accounts for all the motions," and not the alleged existence of an occult force. Similarly, it is the predictive power of our ordinary discourse about mental acts and processes that "accounts for" what we call intelligent or logical behavior, and not the unobservable operation of an occult Cartesian mind. ED.

old myth of Final Causes,[14] so, in anthropological and psychological theory, the new myth of hidden operations, impulses and agencies was an improvement on the old myth of dictations, deferences and disobediences.

---

[14] Final causes act like the purposes or goals of a conscious being, influencing the behavior of that being. Aristotle and many of his followers down through the centuries thought that unconscious, and even inanimate, bodies had natural goals or states to which they tended. For instance, earth, which they believed to be one of the four terrestrial elements, had its natural place at the center of the universe (where they believed the Earth was located). Falling bodies were merely "seeking" their natural place. ED.

Ryle claims that, instead of trying to understand the nature of mind by asking what sort of *cause* could give rise to what we call intelligent behavior, Descartes should have been "asking by what criteria intelligent behaviour is actually distinguished from non-intelligent behaviour . . ." (p. 38 above). Why so? we want to ask. Why not do both? If "criteria" for a term such as "mental" are those properties that it is both necessary and sufficient for something to have in order that we can call it mental, why shouldn't a study of mental phenomena concern itself *both* with the criteria that define its subject matter *and* with the causes of such phenomena?

Ryle's response seems to be something like this: There are, of course, inner causes of mental phenomena, including complex sequences of events in the brain and nervous system. Whether you think these inner causes include ghostly events that are unobservable in principle, or just neural events that are unobservable in practice, don't imitate Descartes' category mistake of calling the inner events "mental." What makes events mental is their having those *observable* properties that are criterial for applying the term "mental." Since we can't have been observing the properties of neural or ghostly Cartesian events as we have gone about correctly using "mental," no such events can belong to the domain of the mental.

This response relies on the premise that a term such as "mental" can be applied only to those items that can possess the criterial properties for that term. (This premise is often referred to as **verificationism:** To observe that an item has the relevant property is to *verify* the application of the term.) The only items that can have the observable properties relevant to mental terms are kinds of *behavior,* and not the doings of Descartes' "ghost" or even brain events. For instance, if the criterion for "knowing how to ride a bike" is the actual riding of one, then the being or knower to whom one would apply that phrase is the rider and not a small organ within her head or a nonspatial "pilot" within that organ. **Behaviorism** is a doctrine that limits the domain of the mental or psychological to that of behavior. *Methodological* behaviorism claims that the subject matter of psychology is behavior and not inner subjective events. (The opposite view is often called *mentalism.*) Since this sort of behaviorism restricts its claim to how psychology should be done, a methodological behaviorist could even be a philosophical dualist. Ryle's verificationism leads to a *philosophical* behaviorism, a denial that there is a mind or a domain of mental events distinct from the behavior which it causes. Because his behaviorism follows from his analysis of the concept of mind (i.e., the "logic" of "mind"), it is often called *logical behaviorism.*

A common criticism of logical behaviorism is that it sometimes badly misinterprets what people are saying in the ordinary mental language that Ryle professes to be analyzing. For instance, when we ask the doctor to give us something that will take away the pain, we're not usually asking to be rid of the behavior we exhibit when in pain, but rather of the *inner* state that *causes* us to behave that way and from which we suffer. If we manage to make sense when talking about pain that way, then so much the worse for verificationism if it implies that we can't. Another major problem with logical behaviorism is what Dennett (1978) calls its "conceptual conservatism." Since "mind" and other mental terms have their criteria already firmly established in ordinary discourse, and since these criteria are behavioral, a neuropsychologist researching the brain mechanisms involved in detecting visible patterns cannot claim to be studying how we *see* since these mechanisms are not criterial for the application of the verb "see." A concept of seeing that included neural mechanisms would be about something entirely different from the original concept. Ryle's theory labels as nonsense what seems to be a perfectly intelligible way to talk about what is going on in neuroscience, and it seems to forbid ordinary discourse from evolving in response to what gets established in scientific discourse.

REVIEW QUESTION

Ryle has argued that materialism is based on the same category mistake that leads to dualism: Since mind and body are not "counterparts," since they don't belong to the same logical type (e.g., stuff, concrete thing, substance), claiming that mind is body or a body part makes as much sense as claiming that someone's coming home in a car is the same as their coming home in a mood. If you were a materialist philosopher or neuroscientist, would you be convinced by this argument? Does accepting Ryle's claim about the difference in logical types between mind and body really make it hard to be a materialist?

3

Knowledge of Other Minds

Norman Malcolm

Norman Malcolm (1911–1990) was an American philosopher who taught at Cornell University during most of his professional career. He and Gilbert Ryle were among the most prominent exponents of the "ordinary language" school of philosophy.

In this reading Malcolm discusses in greater detail the "other minds" problem which Ryle sees as a fatal implication of Cartesian dualism. Here's a way to enter again into the puzzle: Other minds are *other selves*. To know a self *as* a self I need to have access to it the way that I, and only I, have access to *my* thoughts, feelings and other mental processes. Thus, to know a self *as* a self is to know it as *my*self. The notion of an *other* self seems contradictory, and the prospect of getting to know another self or mind seems hopeless. Yet we all firmly believe that we do come to know others, despite the tangle we get into when we think of others in the Cartesian way—as observable bodies housing unobservable selves or minds.

Many philosophers have used the so-called argument from analogy in attempting to solve or get around the "other minds" problem without rejecting the Cartesian premises that give rise to it. These premises are (1) that I have a unique awareness of my own mental states in "introspection," and (2) that I can only *infer* the existence of the unobservable minds of others from their observable behavior. (As Descartes wrote to More: "Speech is the only sure sign of thought hidden in a body.") The argument from analogy (expanded in the quotation from Mill below) is that since I know (introspectively) in my own case that certain sorts of mental states regularly accompany certain sorts of behavior or changes in my body, I can infer that the same sorts of mental states accompany the same kinds of bodily events in other human beings. Malcolm will argue against these two premises from an ordinary language and verificationist perspective.

I

I believe that the argument from analogy for the existence of other minds still enjoys more credit than it deserves, and my first aim in this paper will be to show that it leads nowhere. J. S. Mill[1] is one of many who have accepted the argument and I take his statement of it as representative. He puts to himself the question, "By what evidence do I know, or by what considerations am I led to believe, that there exist other sentient creatures; that the walking and speaking figures which I see and hear, have sensations and thoughts, or in other words, possess Minds?" His answer is the following:

I conclude that other human beings have feelings like me, because, first, they have bodies like me, which I know, in my own case, to be the antecedent condition of feelings; and because, secondly, they exhibit

From Norman Malcolm, "Knowledge of Other Minds," *The Journal of Philosophy* LV, 23 (Nov. 6, 1958): 969–78. Reprinted with permission of the publisher.

[1]Mill (1806–1873) was a British philosopher and social reformer. ED.

the acts, and other outward signs, which in my own case I know by experience to be caused by feelings. I am conscious in myself of a series of facts connected by an uniform sequence, of which the beginning is modifications of my body, the middle is feelings, the end is outward demeanor. In the case of other human beings I have the Evidence of my senses for the first and last links of the series, but not for the intermediate link. I find, however, that the sequence between the first and last is as regular and constant in those other cases as it is in mine. In my own case I know that the first link produces the last through the intermediate link, and could not produce it without. Experience, therefore, obliges me to conclude that there must be an intermediate link; which must either be the same in others as in myself, or a different one; I must either believe them to be alive, or to be automatons; and by believing them to be alive, that is, by supposing the link to be of the same nature as in the case of which I have experience, and which is in all other respects similar, I bring other human beings, as phenomena, under the same generalizations which I know by experience to be the true theory of my own existence.[2]

I shall pass by the possible objection that this would be very *weak* **inductive** reasoning, based as it is on the observation of a single instance. More interesting is the following point: Suppose this reasoning could yield a conclusion of the sort "It is probable that the human figure" (pointing at some person other than oneself) "has thoughts and feelings." Then there is a question as to whether this conclusion can *mean* anything to the philosopher who draws it, because there is a question as to whether the sentence "That human figure has thoughts and feelings" can mean anything to him. Why should this be a question? Because the assumption from which Mill starts is that he has *no criterion* for determining whether another "walking and speaking figure" does or does not have thoughts and feelings. If he had a criterion he could apply it, establishing with certainty that this or that human figure does or does not have feelings (for the only plausible criterion would lie in behavior and circumstances that are open to view),[3] and there

would be no call to resort to tenuous analogical reasoning that yields at best a probability. If Mill has no criterion for the existence of feelings other than his own then in that sense he does not understand the sentence "That human figure has feelings" and therefore does not understand the sentence "It is *probable* that that human figure has feelings."

There is a familiar inclination to make the following reply: "Although I have no criterion of verification still I *understand,* for example, the sentence 'He has a pain.' For I understand the meaning of 'I have a pain,' and 'He has a pain' means that he has the same thing I have when I have a pain." But this is a fruitless maneuver. If I do not know how to establish that someone has a pain then I do not know how to establish that he has the *same* as I have when I have a pain.[4] You cannot improve my understanding of "He has a pain" by this recourse to the notion of "the same," unless you give me a criterion for saying that someone *has* the same as I have. If you can do this you will have no use for the argument from analogy: and if you cannot then you do not understand the supposed conclusion of that argument. A philosopher who purports to rely on the analogical argument cannot, I think, escape this dilemma.

There have been various attempts to repair the argument from analogy. Mr. Stuart Hampshire has argued[5] that its validity as a method of inference can be established in the following way: Others sometimes infer that I am feeling giddy from my behavior. Now I have direct, non-inferential knowledge, says Hampshire, of my own feelings. So I can check inferences made about me against the facts, checking thereby the accuracy of the "methods" of inference.

> All that is required for testing the validity of any method of factual inference is that each one of us should sometimes be in a position to confront the conclusions of the doubtful method of inference about the feelings of persons other than ourselves, in virtue of the fact that each one of us is constantly

---

[2] J. S. Mill, *An Examination of Sir William Hamilton's Philosophy,* 6th edition (London, 1889), pp. 243–244.

[3] See footnote 10 in the previous reading, and the comments at the end of that reading. ED.

[4] "It is no explanation to say: the supposition that he has a pain is simply the supposition that he has the same as I. For *that* part of the grammar is quite clear to me: that is, that one will say that the stove has the same experience as I, *if* one says: it is in pain and I am in pain" (Wittgenstein, *Philosophical Investigations* [New York, 1953], § 350).

[5] "The Analogy of Feeling," *Mind,* January, 1952, pp. 1–12.

able to compare the results of this type of inference with what he knows to be true directly and non-inferentially; each one of us is in the position to make this testing comparison, whenever he is the designated subject of a statement about feelings and sensations. I, Hampshire, know by what sort of signs I may be misled in inferring Jones' and Smith's feelings, because I have implicitly noticed (though probably not formulated) where Jones, Smith and others generally go wrong in inferring my feelings. [pp. 4–5]

Presumably I can also note when the inferences of others about my feelings do not go wrong. Having ascertained the reliability of some inference-procedures I can use them myself, in a guarded way, to draw conclusions about the feelings of others, with a modest but justified confidence in the truth of those conclusions.

My first comment is that Hampshire has apparently forgotten the purpose of the argument from analogy, which is to provide some probability that "the walking and speaking figures which I see and hear, have sensations and thoughts" (Mill). For the reasoning that he describes involves the assumption that other human figures *do* have thoughts and sensations: for they are assumed to *make inferences* about me from *observations* of my behavior. But the philosophical problem of the existence of other minds *is* the problem of whether human figures other than oneself do, among other things, make observations, inferences, and assertions. Hampshire's supposed defense of the argument from analogy is an *ignoratio elenchi*.[6]

If we struck from the reasoning described by Hampshire all assumption of thoughts and sensations in others we should be left with something roughly like this: "When my behavior is such and such there come from nearby human figures the sounds 'He feels giddy.'" And generally I do feel giddy at the time. Therefore when another human

figure exhibits the same behavior and I say 'He feels giddy,' it is probable that he does feel giddy." But the reference here to the sentence-like sounds coming from other human bodies is irrelevant, since I must not assume that those sounds express inferences. Thus the reasoning becomes simply the classical argument from analogy: "When my behavior is such and such I feel giddy; so probably when another human figure behaves the same way he feels the same way." This argument, again, is caught in the dilemma about the criterion of the *same*.

The version of analogical reasoning offered by Professor H. H. Price[7] is more interesting. He suggests that "one's evidence for the existence of other minds is derived primarily from the understanding of language" (p. 429). His idea is that if another body gives forth noises one understands, like "There's the bus," and if these noises give one new information, this "provides some evidence that the foreign body which uttered the noises is animated by a mind like one's own. . . . Suppose I am often in its neighborhood, and it repeatedly produces utterances which I can understand, and which I then proceed to verify for myself. And suppose that this happens in many different kinds of situation. I think that my evidence for believing that this body is animated by a mind like my own would then become very strong" (p. 430). The body from which these informative sounds proceed need not be a human body. "If the rustling of the leaves of an oak formed intelligible words conveying new information to me, and if gorse-bushes made intelligible gestures, I should have evidence that the oak or the gorse-bush was animated by an intelligence like my own" (p. 436). Even if the intelligible and informative sounds did not proceed from a body they would provide evidence for the existence of a (disembodied) mind (p. 435).

Although differing sharply from the classical analogical argument, the reasoning presented by Price is still analogical in form: I know by introspection that when certain combinations of sounds come from me they are "symbols in acts of spontaneous thinking"; therefore similar combinations of

---

[6] *Ignoratio elenchi* is the fallacy of arguing for a conclusion other than what is called for—in other words, missing the point. What Malcolm is accusing Hampshire of doing is more like a *petitio principii* or begging the question: If *inferring* and *observing* are understood as performances in and by an *unobservable* mind, then Hampshire cannot use such performances *by others* as a premise for an argument that seeks to establish the existence of *other* minds. On the other hand, if referring and observing *are observable* performances, then there is no problem of other minds, and no need for the argument from analogy. ED.

[7] "Our Evidence for the Existence of Other Minds," *Philosophy*, Vol. 13, 1938, pp. 425–456.

sounds, not produced by me, "probably function as instruments to an act of spontaneous thinking, which in this case is not my own" (p. 446). Price says that the reasoning also provides an *explanation* of the otherwise mysterious occurrence of sounds which I understand but did not produce. He anticipates the objection that the hypothesis is nonsensical because unverifiable. "The Hypothesis is a perfectly conceivable one," he says, "in the sense that I know very well what the world would have to be like if the hypothesis were true—what sorts of entities there must be in it, and what sorts of events must occur in them. I know from introspection what acts of thinking and perceiving are and I know what it is for such acts to be combined into the unity of a single mind . . . " (pp. 446–447).

I wish to argue against Price that no amount of intelligible sounds coming from an oak tree or a kitchen table could create any probability that it has sensations and thoughts. The question to be asked is: What would show that a tree or table *understands* the sounds that come from it? We can imagine that useful warnings, true descriptions and predictions, even "replies" to questions, should emanate from a tree, so that it came to be of enormous value to its owner. How should we establish that it understood those sentences? Should we "question" it? Suppose that the tree "said" that there was a vixen in the neighborhood, and we "asked" it "what is a vixen?," and it "replied," "A vixen is a female fox." It might go on to do as well for "female" and "fox." This performance might incline us to say that the tree understood the words, in contrast to the possible case in which it answered "I don't know" or did not answer at all. But would it show that the tree understood the words in the same sense that a person could understand them? With a person such a performance would create a presumption that he could make correct *applications* of the word in question: but not so with a tree. To see this point think of the normal teaching of words (e.g., "spoon," "dog," "red") to a child and how one decides whether he understands them. At a primitive stage of teaching one does not require or expect definitions, but rather that the child should *pick out* reds from blues, dogs from cats, spoons from forks. This involves his looking, pointing, reaching for and going to the right things and not the wrong ones.

That a child says "red" when a red thing and "blue" when a blue thing is put before him, is indicative of a mastery of those words *only* in conjunction with the other activities of looking, pointing, trying to get, fetching and carrying. Try to suppose that he says the right words but looks at and reaches for the wrong things. Should we be tempted to say that he has mastered the use of those words? No, indeed. The disparity between words and behavior would make us say that he does not understand the words. In the case of a tree there could be no disparity between its words and its "behavior" because it is logically incapable of behavior of the relevant kind.

Since it has nothing like the human face and body it makes no sense to say of a tree, or an electronic computer, that it is looking or pointing at or fetching something. (Of course one can always *invent* a sense for these expressions.) Therefore it would make no sense to say that it did or did not understand the above words. Trees and computers cannot either pass or fail the tests that a child is put through. They cannot even take them. That an object was a source of intelligible sounds or other signs (no matter how sequential) would not be enough by itself to establish that it had thoughts or sensations. How informative sentences and valuable predictions could emanate from a gorse-bush might be a grave scientific problem, but the explanation could never be that the gorse-bush has a mind. Better no explanation than nonsense!

It might be thought that the above difficulty holds only for words whose meaning has a "perceptual content" and that if we imagined, for example, that our gorse-bush produced nothing but pure mathematical propositions we should be justified in attributing thought to it, although not sensation. But suppose there was a remarkable "calculating boy" who could give right answers to arithmetical problems but could not apply numerals to reality in empirical propositions, i.e., he could not *count* any objects. I believe that everyone would be reluctant to say that he *understood* the mathematical signs and truths that he produced. If he could count in the normal way there would not be this reluctance. And "counting in the normal way" involves looking, pointing, reaching, fetching, and so on. That is, it requires the human face and body, and human behavior—or something similar. Things which do not have the human form, or anything like it, not merely do not but *cannot* satisfy the criteria for thinking.[8] I am trying to bring out part of what Wittgenstein meant when he said, "We only say of a human being and what is like one that it thinks" (*Investigations,* section 360), and "The human body is the best picture of the human soul" (*ibid.,* p. 178).

I have not yet gone into the most fundamental error of the argument from analogy. It is present whether the argument is the classical one (the analogy between my body and other bodies) or Price's version (the analogy between my language and the noises and signs produced by other things). It is the mistaken assumption that *one learns from one's own case* what thinking, feeling, sensation are. Price gives expression to this assumption when he says: "I know from introspection what acts of thinking and perceiving are . . . " (*op. cit.,* p. 447). It is the most natural assumption for a philosopher to make and indeed seems at first to be the only possibility. Yet Wittgenstein has made us see that it leads first to solipsism[9] and then to nonsense. I shall try to state as briefly as possible how it produces those results.

A philosopher who believes that one must learn what thinking, fear, or pain is "from one's own case," does not believe that the thing to be observed is one's behavior, but rather something "inward." He considers behavior to be related to the inward states and occurrences merely as an accompaniment or possibly an effect. He cannot regard behavior as a *criterion*[10] of psychological phenomena: for if he did he would have no use for the analogical argument (as was said before) and also the priority given to "one's own case" would be pointless. He believes that he notes something in himself that he calls

"thinking" or "fear" or "pain," and then he tries to infer the presence of the *same* in others. He should then deal with the question of what his criterion of the *same* in others is. This he cannot do because it is of the essence of his viewpoint to reject circumstances and behavior as a criterion of mental phenomena in others. And what else could serve as a criterion?[11] He ought, therefore, to draw the conclusion that the notion of thinking, fear, or pain in others is in an important sense meaningless. He has no idea of what would count for or against it.[12] "That there should be thinking or pain other than my own is unintelligible," he ought to hold. This would be a rigorous solipsism, and a correct outcome of the assumption that one can know only from one's own case what the mental phenomena are. An equivalent way of putting it would be: "When I say 'I am in pain,' by 'pain' I mean a certain inward state. When I say '*He* is in pain,' by 'pain' I mean *behavior.* I cannot attribute pain to others *in the same sense* that I attribute it to myself."

Some philosophers before Wittgenstein may have seen the solipsistic result of starting from "one's own case." But I believe he is the first to have shown how that starting point destroys itself. This may be presented as follows: One supposes that one inwardly picks out something as thinking or pain and thereafter identifies it whenever it presents itself in the soul. But the question to be pressed is, Does one make *correct* identifications? The proponent of the "private" identifications has nothing to say here. He feels sure that he identifies correctly the occurrences in his soul; but feeling sure is no guarantee of being right. Indeed he has no idea of what being *right* could mean. He does not know how to distinguish between actually making correct identifications and being under the impression that he does. (See *Investigations,* section 258–9.) Suppose that he identified the emotion of anxiety as the sensation of pain? Neither he nor

---

[8] This is another example of the "conceptual conservatism" in logical behaviorism (see the comments at the end of the previous reading) and of what functionalist philosophers of mind a decade later would call *human chauvinism.* ED.

[9] *Solipsism* is the view that the self is all that exists or can be known. Although Descartes rejects solipsism, many philosophers have remarked on the solipsistic quality of the situation of a Cartesian mind, insofar as it is *directly* aware only of itself and *its* ideas or contents. ED.

[10] Again, a "criterion" for a mental attribute establishes (in Malcolm's words on p. 46 above) "with certainty that this or that human figure does or does not have" the attribute in question. Having the criterial properties is both (a) a necessary condition and (b) a sufficient condition for something having the mental attribute. If (a) something doesn't have the criterial properties, then it doesn't have the mental attribute, and if (b) it does have the former, then it has the latter. ED.

[11] For your mental state and mine to be the same would be, criterially, for each of them to exhibit the same set of properties. However, I can't know what it is for your or any other person's mental state to exhibit properties at all; by definition, I'm aware only of my own mental states. The comparison needed to verify the application of "same" is impossible in principle. ED.

[12] One reason why philosophers have not commonly drawn this conclusion may be, as Wittgenstein acutely suggests, that they assume that they have "an infallible paradigm of identity in the identity of a thing with itself" (*Investigations,* § 215).

anyone else could know about this "mistake." Perhaps he makes a mistake *every* time! Perhaps all of us do! We ought to see now that we are talking nonsense. We do not know what a *mistake* would be. We have no standard, no examples, no customary practice, with which to compare our inner recognitions. The inward identification cannot hit the bull's-eye, or miss it either, because there is no bull's-eye. When we see that the ideas of correct and incorrect have no application to the supposed inner identification, the latter notion loses its appearance of sense.[13] Its collapse brings down both solipsism and the argument from analogy.

II

This destruction of the argument from analogy also destroys the *problem* for which it was supposed to provide a solution. A philosopher feels himself in a difficulty about other minds because he assumes that first of all he is acquainted with mental phenomena "from his own case." What troubles him is how to make the transition from his own case to the case of others. When his thinking is freed of the illusion of the priority of his own case, then he is able to look at the familiar facts and to acknowledge that the circumstances, behavior, and utterances of others actually are his *criteria* (not merely his evidence) for the existence of their mental states. Previously this had seemed impossible.

But now he is in danger of flying to the opposite extreme of behaviorism, which errs by believing that through observation of one's own circumstances, behavior, and utterances one can find out that one is thinking or angry. The philosophy of "From one's own case" and behaviorism, though in a sense opposites, make the common assumption that the first-person, present-tense psychological statements are verified by self-observation. According to the "one's own case" philosophy the self-observation cannot be checked by others; according to behaviorism the self-observation would be by means of outward criteria that are available to all. The first position becomes unintelligible; the second is false for at least many kinds of psychological statements. We are forced to conclude that the first-

person psychological statements are not (or hardly ever) verified by self-observation. It follows that they have no verification at all; for if they had a verification it would have to be by self-observation.

But if sentences like "My head aches" or "I wonder where she is" do not express observations then what do they do? What is the relation between my declaration that my head aches and the fact that my head aches, if the former is not the report of an observation? The perplexity about the existence of *other* minds has, as the result of criticism, turned into a perplexity about the meaning of one's own psychological sentences about oneself. At our starting point it was the sentence "*His* head aches" that posed a problem; but now it is the sentence "*My* head aches" that puzzles us.

One way in which this problem can be put is by the question, "How does *one know when to say* the words 'My head aches'?" The inclination to ask this question can be made acute by imagining a fantastic but not impossible case of a person who has survived to adult years without ever experiencing pain. He is given various sorts of injections to correct this condition, and on receiving one of these one day, he jumps and exclaims, "Now I feel pain!" One wants to ask, "How did he *recognize* the new sensation as a *pain?*"

Let us note that if the man gives an answer (e.g., "I knew it must be pain because of the way I jumped") then he proves by that very fact that he has not mastered the correct use of the words "I feel pain." They cannot be used to state a *conclusion*.[14] In telling us *how* he did it he will convict himself of a misuse. Therefore the question "How did he recognize his sensation?" requests the impossible. The inclination to ask it is evidence of our inability to grasp the fact that the use of this psychological sentence has nothing to do with recognizing or identifying or observing a state of oneself.

The fact that this imagined case produces an especially strong temptation to ask the "How?" question shows that we have the idea that it must be more difficult to give the right name of one's sensation *the first time*. The implication would be that it is not so difficult *after* the first time. Why should this be? Are we thinking that then the man

---

[13] See footnote 10 in the prior reading. ED.

[14] It isn't clear what Malcolm's reason or argument is for this "cannot." ED.

would have a paradigm of pain with which he could compare his sensations and so be in a position to know right off whether a certain sensation was or was not a pain? But the paradigm would be either something "outer" (behavior) or something "inner" (perhaps a memory impression of the sensation). If the former then he is misusing the first-person sentence. If the latter then the question of whether he compared *correctly* the present sensation with the inner paradigm of pain would be without sense. Thus the idea that the use of the first-person sentences can be governed by paradigms must be abandoned. It is another form of our insistent misconception of the first-person sentence as resting somehow on the identification of a psychological state.

These absurdities prove that we must conceive of the first-person psychological sentences in some entirely different light. Wittgenstein presents us with the suggestion (to which philosophers have not been sufficiently attentive) that the first-person sentences are to be thought of as similar to the natural non-verbal, behavioral expressions of psychological states. "My leg hurts, " for example, is to be assimilated to crying, limping, holding one's leg.

This is a bewildering comparison and one's first thought is that two sorts of things could not be more unlike. By saying the sentence one can make a *statement;* it has a *contradictory;* it is *true* or *false;* in saying it one *lies* or *tells the truth;* and so on. None of these things, exactly, can be said of crying, limping, holding one's leg. So how can there by any resemblance? But Wittgenstein knew this when he deliberately likened such a sentence to "the primitive, the natural, expressions" of pain, and said that it is "new pain-behavior" (*ibid.,* section 244). Although my limits prevent my attempting it here, I think this analogy ought to be explored. For it has at least two important merits: first, it breaks the hold on us of the question "How does one *know when to say* "'My leg hurts'?" for in the light of the analogy this will be as nonsensical as the question "How does one know when to cry, limp, or hold one's leg?"; second, it explains how the utterance of a first-person psychological sentence by another person can have *importance* for us, although not as an identification—for in the light of the analogy it will have the same importance as the natural behavior which serves as our pre-verbal criterion of the psychological states of others.

Although Malcolm, in his analysis of mental language, seems intent on appealing to the facts of ordinary experience and everyday English usage, one could argue that his grasp of those facts is strongly affected, and even distorted, by *verificationism.* He concludes his argument against the possibility of introspective self-observation (on which the argument from analogy depends) by claiming that when I say "My head aches" I am not reporting a fact, but merely engaging in verbal pain behavior. Thus, had you asked me why I wasn't coming to the party, and I had answered "Because I have a headache," I would not have been telling you anything about my condition at the time; I would merely have engaged in an acceptable alternative to stating a fact or giving a reason, rather like looking thoughtful while searching for what to say.

Suppose you were to object that this analysis is a blatant misrepresentation of what is going on: there is a clear difference between my excuse being a lie and being the truth, a difference that could not obtain unless my excuse did report a fact. Malcolm would remind you that what the occurrence of an inner psychological state such as "headache" seems to designate cannot have criterial properties, since these would have to be observable. So the sentence "I have a headache" can't be about an inner state, and it is usually not about behavior. Therefore it's usually not about anything.

This response invites the following objection: Why must the inner psychological state be the *bearer* of the criterial properties? Why isn't it meaningful to think of the inner state as standing in a constant relation (such as cause or effect) to the behavior that bears the relevant properties? Even if we know nothing else about the inner state except its causal relation to the behavior, isn't that enough to give sense to the mental term? Why can't "headache" designate the inner state that causes me (among other things) to point to my head when asked "Where does it hurt?" It is this sort of objection that lead many philosophers to reject logical behaviorism.

In the 1950s the progress of neuroscience accelerated rapidly. It seemed that we were on the verge of a scientific understanding of the inner events that stood in a causal relation to psychological behavior. Because logical behaviorism asserted that it was nonsense to speak of brain research as dealing with human *mental* functions, it was unacceptable to philosophers impressed with developments in this field.

REVIEW QUESTION

Malcolm says, on p. 46 above, that "Things which do not have the human form, or anything like it, not merely do not but *cannot* satisfy the criteria for thinking. I am trying to bring out part of what Wittgenstein meant when he said, 'We only say of a human being and what is like one that it thinks' (*Investigations,* section 360), and 'The human body is the best picture of the human soul' (ibid., p. 178). Why does he say so? "Like" is a key word in Malcolm's assertion and in the first quotation from Wittgenstein. *In what respects* would it be necessary that a body be "like" a human one in order to satisfy the criteria for such words as "thinking? Would a very alien looking extraterrestrial necessarily fail the criteria?

PART III

THE HUMAN BRAIN

4

Brain Events

Brian Cooney

1. INTRODUCTION

In an operation to remove diseased or damaged brain tissue it is not always necessary or desirable for the patient to undergo general anesthesia. Instead, the surgeon can administer a local anesthetic to an area of the skull and then open it to expose the underlying part of the brain. Figure 4.1 shows the result of such a procedure (craniotomy) as performed by the famous neurosurgeon Wilder Penfield (1891–1976) and his team. What you see in this photograph is the organ of perception, thought, and choice in a patient who is still conscious. Before proceeding with the operation, the surgeons needed to determine the extent of diseased or damaged tissue. One of the techniques they used was to insert at various sites a thin wire (electrode) that delivered a very small electric current at its tip. Since there are no pain or sensory **receptors** in brain tissue, and such patients are unable to see what the surgeon is doing, they don't feel or perceive the insertion of the electrode *as* an event in the brain. However, they do frequently experience sensations or find some part of their bodies moving as a result of the stimulation. And, as Descartes foresaw three centuries ago,[1] the *kind* of sensation or body motion induced is determined rather precisely by the *site* of the brain stimulation. The numbered tags in Figure 4.1 indicate points at which this stimulation elicited positive responses such as tactile sensation on the inside of the right upper lip (17), tingling on the right side of the tongue at the tip (16), and pulling of the jaw to the right (13). Repeated stimulation at the same numbered point results in the same response each time.

What's happening in the brain tissue affected by the mild current from the electrode? An easy but uninformative answer is that what the electrode makes happen is rather like what goes on when we normally have such a sensation or move that body part. In this chapter we'll look in a basic and summary way at what brain science tells us about the cellular components of brain tissue, and how these components interact, often in immense numbers and very complex ways, to *make possible* our conscious and unconscious mental processes. I italicized "make possible" because we should be careful to understand that phrase in a way that doesn't jump to philosophical conclusions. From the fact that stimulation of a certain brain site regularly produces a certain kind of conscious experience, it does *not* follow that the experience is *nothing but* the brain process induced by the electrode. In fact, many philosophers (and brain scientists) would claim that the experience is a *non*physical event that is regularly caused by the physical brain process, or is somehow correlated with it. The former is Descartes' view. It may surprise you to learn that Penfield also came to hold something like this view.

Penfield began his scientific career with the belief that a complete explanation of the brain mechanisms underlying our various mental functions would amount to an understanding of the mind

---

[1] See Descartes' description of brain functions toward the end of Meditation 6 in Reading 1.

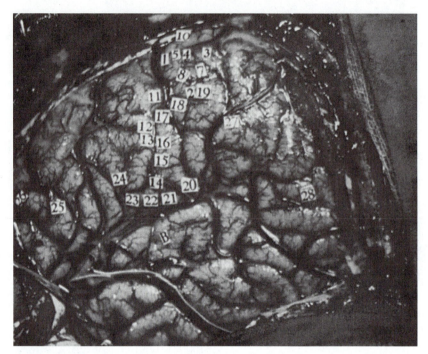

Figure 4.1 Photograph of the left hemisphere exposed prior to surgery. From Penfield and Roberts (1959).

itself. In 1975, a year before his death, he published a book significantly titled *The Mystery of the Mind*. In that book, after reflecting on what he had learnt about brain mechanisms after decades of research, he declared that "it comes as a surprise now to discover, during this final examination of the evidence, that the dualist hypothesis seems the more reasonable" (85). Why did Penfield think that the *scientific* evidence suggested that the mind was something *other* than the brain? After all, he did a lot to show where exactly brains are active when certain kinds of mental processes are occurring. He was a pioneer in the development of functional maps of the human brain—diagrams like figure 4.2 in which specific mental functions are localized in specific parts of the brain. These "maps" rely on evidence such as the effects of stimulating electrodes, data gathered from electrodes that record activity in specific areas of the brain while subjects interact with their environment or report their mental states, and the sensory, behavioral, or other deficits observed in subjects with damage to specific areas. Penfield was drawn to the "dualist hypothe-

sis" because not once in countless surgeries did artificial stimulation of brain tissue ever "cause a patient to believe or to decide" (1975, 77). Furthermore, he knew of no cases in which the initial brain activity associated with an **epileptic seizure** induced a belief or decision. So he concluded that believing and deciding are not brain mechanisms; rather, they are acts of a mind that uses its brain the way a human operator uses a computer. Such an argument is provocative, but incomplete and open to major objections (see if you can think of one). It's a good example of how philosophical issues are closely intertwined with brain research.

2. THE NERVOUS SYSTEM

Descartes thought of human minds as immaterial spirits acting from within the central cavity of the brain. Many contemporary philosophers think of humans as special sorts of computational mechanisms housed in the "wetware" of the brain and its enclosing body. Whatever we may think of such claims, it is an undeniable and hugely important

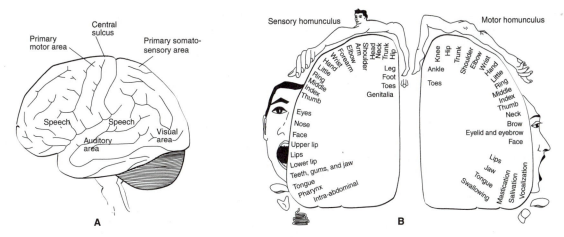

Figure 4.2 A: General functional map of the human neocortex, with horizontal lines in the primary motor area, and vertical lines in the primary somatosensory area. **B:** Simplified functional maps of the primary motor and primary somatosensory areas separated by sectioning through the central sulcus. These maps are in the forms of sensory and motor "homunculi." *Homunculus* is Latin for "little man." Each homunculus is composed of representations of the body parts in which (for the sensory homunculus) somatic sensations (such as touch and pressure) are felt when the corresponding cortical tissue is stimulated, or in which (for the motor homunculus) muscle contractions occur when the corresponding tissue is stimulated.

fact about us that we are *animals.* A human brain—the mind's organ—is, in the average adult, about three pounds of soft tissue bathed in fluid and laced with blood vessels (look again at figure 4.1). It belongs together with other components such as nerves, eyes, and spinal cord—to an organ system called the nervous system. Like other animal organ systems such as the digestive or circulatory, the nervous system has a major role to play in the organism's ceaseless task of staying alive. Its special contribution is to coordinate and regulate the behavior of the body's other parts and systems.

To stay alive in a constantly changing environment, an animal needs to be able to respond to events that can affect its well-being—for example, the sound or smell of a predator or prey, a sharp change in temperature, or the waning of daylight. We can give the term "well-being" a functional meaning: What affects well-being is whatever promotes or hinders the animal's continuing capacity to behave like the sort of animal it is. The phrase "staying alive" refers to this sort of continuity. For us humans staying alive in this sense includes eating, sleeping, personal hygiene, "earning a living," and a great deal else that we do on a daily or regular

basis. In very general terms we can say that an animal's unceasing task of staying alive consists in responding to relevant events in such a way as to preserve its capacity to respond in the same ways to the same sorts of events. A response that promotes this continuity is called *adaptive.* Insofar as the nervous system coordinates adaptive responses, we can call it an **adaptive control system.**

Let's examine the concept of such a system to see what sorts of operations and subsystems it involves. Since the system's overall function is adaptive interaction with an environment, it must enable the animal to *detect* relevant events, *select* and *effect* adaptive responses, and be guided by the effects of the responses (this last element is called *feedback*). Figure 4.3 diagrams the operation of a generalized control system, of which an adaptive system is a special case. The sensor subsystem executes the function of detecting, and the modulator subsystem does the selecting of responses. The function of this generalized system is to keep one or more aspects of another system (its "environment") within optimal limits. Although it is easy to see what the human anatomical correlates would be for the subsystems in the diagram, we should keep in mind that it is a

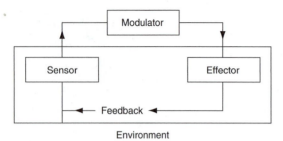

Figure 4.3 Functional diagram of a control system. The large box containing the sensor and effector represents the environment.

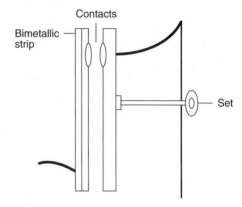

Figure 4.4 Thermostat with bimetallic strip.

functional diagram which need not correspond to the *spatial* parts of any physical system. A climate-control system illustrates this point.

A thermostat linked to a furnace often consists of a bimetallic strip with one end anchored and the other at a small distance from an electrical contact (see fig. 4.4). When this gap is closed, the resulting electrical current causes the furnace to deliver a fixed amount of heated air through the ducts to the vents in the building. Because the two thin layers of the strip are different metals which expand or contract at different rates as the air temperature changes, the strip bends to close the gap as the temperature drops, and bends away again as it rises. We can see how in this case there is no clear spatial distinction between the sensor and modulator despite the clear conceptual difference in the two functions. A modulator must do the functional equivalent of comparing the current state of its environment against a standard, in order to select a response that will bring the environment into conformity with the standard. This standard is introduced into the thermostat by "setting" it, i.e., by varying the initial distance of the strip from the electrical contact. The greater the gap, the colder the building will have to get in order to bend the strip far enough to activate the furnace. (You can further articulate the climate-control system for yourself by applying the concept of feedback to its operation.)

When there is a spatial interval between functional subsystems of a control system, one will activate the other by means of an intervening event or set of events that spans the interval. Let's call such events *signals*. Since the thermostat's bimetallic strip is both sensor and modulator, the sensor need not

signal the modulator in this case, but the modulator does send a signal to the furnace (effector) in the form of an electric current. Although terms such as *signal, detect,* and *select* have overtones of consciousness and purpose, they are nevertheless useful and probably indispensable in understanding control systems. We need to talk about such systems *as if* they operate **intentionally.** Examples like the thermostat remind us just how *as if.*

The modulator works as if it were following a pair of hypothetical prescriptions: *If* the temperature of the environment is less than x (the setting), *then* activate the furnace; and, *if* the temperature is equal to or greater than x, *then* do not activate. The sensor (bimetallic strip) "tells" the modulator which of the two antecedent conditions obtains, the modulator (bimetallic strip) "selects" the relevant response, and the effector (furnace) executes the response (coming on or not).

To keep alive an animal that moves about and thereby constantly changes the features of its environment, an *adaptive* control system must monitor not just temperature but all the constantly changing aspects of the environment that are relevant to the animal's well-being. (Keep in mind that the environment regulated by an adaptive control system includes both the inside and outside of the organism.) For *detection* to occur, something in the environment must act on the sensor. Energy in some form must be transferred from the environment to the sensor, like the heat in the air that causes expansion of the metals in the thermostat's bimetallic strip. This energy comes in different forms and embodiments such as heat, light, sound waves, and the pressure of an external body against the animal. A sensor must be able to detect not merely the occurrence of an energy transfer, but must also enable it to be measured or analyzed in various ways. The bimetallic strip detects not only that warming or cooling is occurring, but also whether it exceeds or falls short of the optimal temperature (the setting). Similarly, the sensors in an adaptive control system must be able to measure duration, frequency, intensity, location, direction and other dimensions of the impinging energy. All of these have a bearing on how the animal can respond *adaptively*. For instance, it makes a big difference to an animal whether sounds made by a predator are increasing or decreasing in volume, and in which direction the source is shifting. So an animal will need a variety of sensors with physical structures and materials suited to a specific kind of energy input and to the dimensions of that input that need to be measured.

The animal's modulator (its brain) will be barraged with **signals** from different kinds of sensors (called "sensory receptors") distributed over the surface and inside of its body. Its selection of an adaptive response will often be determined by the *combination* of signals from different kinds of receptors measuring different kinds of input—for instance, by the joint input from a prey to ears, eyes, and nose. Just as you can't compare apples with oranges or count one as the other, so a brain needs the signals from its different kinds of sensory receptors to be composed of a common unit so that it can measure, compare, or otherwise integrate them. Insofar as sensory receptors perform this function of converting energy from one form or embodiment into another, they act as *transducers* (see fig. 4.5). Also, the time between sensory stimulus and resulting adaptive response will usually have to be very short to enable an animal to respond to events as quickly as they happen. Signals to the brain from sensory receptors and from the brain to its effectors (muscles) will have to travel very rapidly. Furthermore, sensory signals, as events within the animal body, usually need to be precisely *scaled down* to a micro-level from the macro-dimensions of the environmental events they detect. Otherwise, their energy and magnitude would destroy the animal. By contrast, ("motor") signals reaching muscles

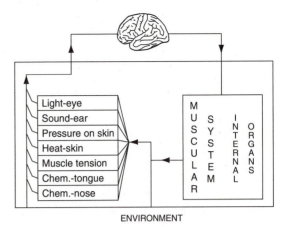

Figure 4.5 Diagram of neural control system showing transduction of varieties of input from environment into standardized sensory signal.

from the brain will have to be *amplified,* in muscular contractions, back to the macro-level of the environment on which the animal must act.

In the last few pages I've been comparing the nervous system to the very much simpler case of a thermostatic control system. However, the nervous system differs not only in complexity but also in kind—it is an *adaptive* control system. We can see this difference most clearly if we look at what corresponds in it to the thermostat's setting. The initial gap between the tip of the bimetallic strip and the contact makes the thermostat behave as if it were following a pair of hypothetical prescriptions (if $<x,$ then activate; if $\geq x,$ then don't activate). How are we to think of the "setting" in the brain-module of the nervous system? The hypothetical prescriptions embodied in the brain and jointly defining its "staying-alive setting" will be vast in number and in the complexity of their interrelations.[2] Simpler tasks may be only very small parts of more inclusive ones such as maintaining a circle of friends or pursuing a career. Human life is full of such complexity at every level, from the trivial to

---

[2] As in the case of the thermostat's "detecting," "hypothetical prescription" is part of the *as-if* analysis of the human brain. I am not claiming that these prescriptions are consciously held or invoked beliefs, but only that humans behave as if they were following such prescriptions. Even in cases where we plan our behavior with conscious reference to some of our practical beliefs, there could never be time enough to rehearse all the beliefs that are implied by our behavior.

the momentous. Since humans seek more than biological survival, we should perhaps be talking not about a setting for staying alive, but about an "identity setting": a conjunction of prescriptions that enables me to continue to be not only the kind of animal I am, but also the kind of individual I am.

Another important difference between the simple setting of the thermostat and what we find in the brain is the effect of *learning.* One way to think of the brain as a system capable of learning is to include in its "setting" (its structure as determined by human genes) a tendency to select behavior as if following very general prescriptions such as: *If behavior y upon stimulus x is followed by state z, then avoid/repeat the y response to x.* If the result is avoidance, state z is, in the language of psychologists, a *punisher;* if the result is repetition, z is a *reinforcer.* For instance, if one's seeing a cheesecake is followed by one's eating the entire cheesecake and then by indigestion, one will henceforth avoid eating an entire cheesecake on sight. The kind of learning described here (in overly simple terms) is often called "**conditioning,**" and is very important in the lives of humans and other animals. It is a mechanism that gives rise to indefinitely many learned responses which can be described as obeying prescriptions specific to the different values of *x, y,* and *z.*

3. NEURONS

An average adult human is a community of a trillion or so cells. Cells are the smallest units of life on earth—the smallest naturally occurring bodies possessing adaptive control systems. Their diameters are in the $10-30$ μm (micron = millionth of a meter) range. Each of these micro-organisms individually carries out most of the functions that we associate with life at the macro-level: adaptive control,[3] taking in nutrients and expelling wastes, **metabolism,** and replication. *Unicellular* organisms such as protozoa and certain types of algae and fungi have a behavioral repertoire that enables them to stay alive in an *external* environment (one not constituted by

an enclosing organism). The component cells of a *multicellular* organism or *metazoon* are typically differentiated into types. The members of each type have, in addition to their self-maintenance activities, a specialized function by which they contribute to the maintenance of the internal environment within the enclosing organism. They usually perform their special task(s) in clusters called *tissues.* For instance, muscle fibers are long, cylindrical, and highly contractile cells that bundle and act together as muscle. Several kinds of tissue frequently are joined together as an *organ* to carry out one or more functions. And, of course, at a still higher level of organization, there are *organ systems* such as the nervous or digestive.

3.1 Interneurons

We are now going to "zoom in" from the macro-image of brain tissue in fig. 4.1 to the cells that make up this tissue. These cells are called *neurons,* and different kinds of neurons have evolved to carry out, singly or in tissue, specific functions of an adaptive control system such as detecting, transducing, signaling, selecting, and effecting. Figure 4.6 is a simplified drawing of a typical cell in the tissue exposed in figure 4.1. Because such a cell belongs to a type that interacts primarily with other neurons rather than with sensory organs or muscles, it is classified as an *interneuron.* It has, like nearly all cells in the body, a nucleus with protein-encased **DNA** in the form of **chromosomes.** As in other cell types, this DNA (in conjunction with other **organelles** not represented) regulates the metabolic processes that maintain the cell as a living system and synthesize chemical products (such as the transmitter substance shown in fig. 4.6B) which contribute to the function of the enclosing cortical tissue. The neuron has numerous branch-like extensions of its body called *dendrites* (from the Greek for *tree*) as well as a larger and more uniform extension called an *axon.* In neurons within the brain an axon is typically no longer than a few microns, but it can stretch a meter or more in spinal neurons which send motor signals to leg or hand muscles. An axon often divides into *collaterals* before sending out thin extensions called *telodendria,* at the ends of which are little knobs called *terminals.* The presynaptic membrane of a terminal is usually $10-20$ nm (nanometer = one thousandth of a micron) away

---

[3]Many will remember from their biology courses how various large molecules such as DNA and protein act as sensors, modulators and effectors within the cell.

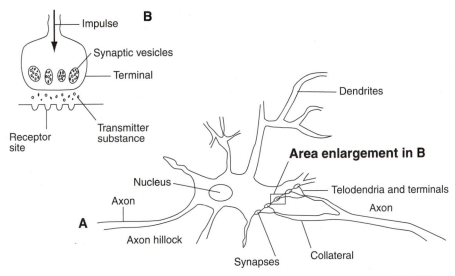

Figure 4.6 A: Simplified drawing of a neuron in the cerebral cortex with axodendritic and axosomatic synapses with the axon of another neuron. **B:** Simplified drawing of a synapse with discharge of transmitter substance from synaptic vesicles through terminal membrane into synaptic cleft.

from the postsynaptic membrane of the cell with which it junctions. This gap is the *synaptic cleft*.

Having glanced at the *structure* of a neuron, let's turn to what it *does*. What it does, when sufficiently stimulated, is to send an impulse along the full length of its axon. This impulse consists of a very brief and rapidly shifting alteration in the electric charge near the inner surface of the axon membrane. When this impulse reaches the axon's terminals, it causes the synaptic vesicles there to release a chemical known as a *transmitter substance,* which traverses the synaptic cleft (see fig. 4.6B) to a receptor site on the membrane of another neuron. The effect of this emission on the postsynaptic membrane is ultimately to move the electric charge at the axon hillock of the other cell closer to or further from the threshold for starting an impulse down the axon. When philosophers ask such questions as whether "brain events" are the same as, or nothing but, or somehow different from, the mental events with which they are correlated, the brain events referred to are what I have just described—sequences linking transmitter stimulations to axonal impulses in a single neuron or, more commonly, in large numbers of neurons. Since we will spend so much

time in later readings thinking about the relation between brain and mental events from a philosophical point of view, we should now look more closely at the biochemistry of a "brain event" to get a better idea of what we're talking about.

Among the principal ingredients of brain events are currents of ions (electrically charged atoms). An atom is electrically neutral if it has the same number of protons as electrons; its charge is negative if it has one or more electrons than protons, and positive if it has an excess of protons over electrons. Like other types of cells, neurons have high internal concentrations of potassium ions ($K+$) and low concentrations of sodium ions ($NA+$) relative to the fluid just outside their membranes. Furthermore, the combination of ions in the fluid just inside the membrane creates a negative charge of -70 millivolts in relation to the fluid just outside. This negative internal charge exerts a force that attracts positively charged particles and repels negatively charged ones. Insofar as the charge has this capacity to move particles, it is called a *potential*. Because this unequal charge is stable, it is called the *resting potential*. If these differences in concentration and potential were to occur without a barrier between the unequal areas, or with a membrane that was completely permeable to the ions, the inequalities would quickly be eliminated. The opposite charges would attract oppositely charged particles, and the random motion and collisions of NA+ and K+ would result in a more even distribution of the two.

However, the cellular membrane is only *semipermeable*—it allows some ions to enter freely, some in limited amounts or under certain conditions, and some not at all. (The combination of skin, mouth, and nose gives human bodies a "semipermeability.") NA+, K+, and other molecules that are given limited or controlled access to the inside of the cell typically pass through specific channels in the membrane. Some of these channels have molecular "gates" that open and close under certain conditions, while other channels are ungated. NA+ and K+ have both gated and ungated channels, but K+ has more ungated ones than NA+. Since there are ungated channels for both these ions, the −70 mv inside potential should be unstable. However, according to current theory there is a cellular mechanism—the so-called sodium-potassium pump—that actively takes in K+ and extrudes NA+. This pump maintains the resting potential.

Neurons have evolved so as to put this general property of body cells in the service of an animal's adaptive control system. If, for reasons we will look at shortly, the inside of the membrane at the axon hillock gets *depolarized* (becomes less negative) by about 20 mv, there immediately occurs a 2-millisecond sequence of events called the *action potential*. This event is all-or-nothing—it either occurs in its full magnitude or not at all. The progression of the action potential is diagrammed in figure 4.7. At about −50 mv at the axon hillock, the NA+/K+ pump shuts down and sodium ions pour into the cell through now open channels, driving the internal charge to about +40 mv. Almost immediately, the gated potassium channels open up and potassium ions stream outside and the sodium gates shut again, quickly repolarizing the inside space and often hyperpolarizing it for a millisecond or two to about −80 mv. The effect of hyperpolarization is to make that space less susceptible than normal to the initiation of an action impulse. Then the pump reactivates and the resting potential is re-

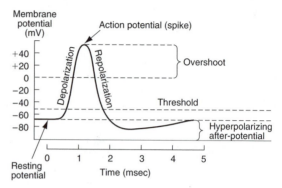

Figure 4.7 Diagram of the action potential. The brief interval of positive internal charge is labeled "overshoot."

stored. The effect of depolarization during the action potential at any point along the inside of the axon is to bring the immediately adjacent area up to the threshold for an action impulse. In this way, the impulse is self-propagating all the way from the axon hillock to the synaptic terminals where it causes the release of transmitter substance.

Neurotransmitter substances released across the synaptic cleft briefly bind to receptor proteins on the postsynaptic membrane of a dendrite or cell body. This alters the permeability of the membrane at that site, allowing specific ions to enter or leave, and thereby changing the electric potential of the inside. The change can go two ways, depending on how the molecular mechanism of the receptor affects the membrane: If, for instance, NA+ channels get opened, then the sodium influx causes *depolarization*; if K+ channels open up, then the outflow of positive ions leaves the inside potential even more negative (*hyper*polarization). Unlike what happens at the axon hillock, depolarization in the dendrite or cell body does not trigger an action potential there. Instead, when there is an *influx* of ions, they will spread out from the receptor site, their local effect on electric potential diminishing as the initial cloud of ions thins out over time and distance. If there is an *outflow* of ions, adjacent concentrations of ions will shift somewhat toward the affected area, to a degree that diminishes with time and distance. Because they are not all-or-nothing-like action potentials, these gradual, small (1–3 mv) postsynaptic effects are called *graded* potentials. A cerebral interneuron typically has thousands of synapses, a large number of which will be active at nearly the same time. Whether the neuron will "fire" depends on the combined effect at the axon hillock of all the graded potentials, depolarizing and hyperpolarizing, spreading toward the hillock from hundreds or thousands of receptor sites. Each of these, weakening as it spreads, combines with others, increasing or reducing the depolarization. If net depolarization at the hillock reaches the threshold of -50 mv, an action impulse ensues. Because a postsynaptic *de*polarization makes the neuron more likely to fire, it is called an *excitatory* postsynaptic potential (EPSP); whereas a postsynaptic *hyper*polarization is an *inhibitory* postsynaptic potential (IPSP). A particular neurotransmitter such as acetylcholine or adrenaline can be either excitatory or inhibitory, depending on the action of the receptors with which it binds.[4]

Each neuron is a microscopically small analytical engine. Its cell body-dendrite complex enables it in milliseconds to integrate and measure hundreds or even thousands of signals received from other neurons, and select a response (impulse or not). It can be understood as carrying out hypothetical prescriptions of great logical complexity. To see this let's look first at figure 4.8, which represents a simple disjunction circuit of a sort that could be built into electronic equipment. The circuit embodies a pair of prescriptions: *If* at least one signal occurs, *then* transmit; *if* none occurs, *then* don't transmit. The output of the circuit, like that of a neuron, is **digital:** it is a fixed quantity of current that occurs entirely or not at all. However, unlike the neuron, the input for the circuit is also digital, whereas the signal reaching the axon hillock is **analog**—a continuously variable quantity summing the graded potentials induced by synaptic transmissions. Not just two, but hundreds or even thousands of inputs determine a neuron's output. The conditional clause in a neuronal prescription will have a complexity of the sort suggested by this fragment of a clause: *If a and b and . . . n, and any two of q, r, s, and t, unless x, y, or z. . . .* Since

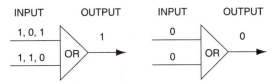

Figure 4.8 A disjunction circuit converting two inputs into one output. "1" represents the occurrence of a signal, and "0" the nonoccurrence of a signal. The pairing of inputs is the top digit plus the one directly below.

there are a hundred billion neurons in the brain, and about ten trillion synapses, the degree of complexity in the interconnections of neurons and in the resulting prescriptions they embody is hard to underestimate. However, the complexity is not as confusing as these numbers might suggest. As we will see shortly, neurons are not randomly interconnected throughout the brain. Instead, they interact to a large extent within discrete areas of tissue that are strongly correlated to specific functions. Clusters of these richly interconnected neural analytical engines perform the *selecting* function of an adaptive control system by receiving patterned signals from sensory receptors, performing various levels of analysis of these signals, and engaging other clusters that generate patterned motor signals going from the brain to musculature. Having looked at the structure and activity of *inter*neurons in the brain, let's turn our attention now to neurons that have specialized in the *motor* and *sensory* functions of the nervous system.

3.2 Motor Neurons

The cell body of the typical motor neuron shown in figure 4.9 resides in the spine, while its axon can stretch a meter or more to form a synapse with muscle fibers at the periphery of the body. Its cell body and dendrites are covered with thousands of terminals from interneurons whose input comes from neurons in the brain, the body and other parts of the spine. Notice that the axon is sheathed in a series of Schwann cells separated from one another by gaps of exposed axonal membrane called nodes of Ranvier. Each Schwann cell wraps its portion of the axon with layers of *myelin*, a fatty substance laced with protein. The myelin sheath prevents an

---

[4]Although most synapses utilize a chemical messenger, some are electrical: Ion channels physically connect the presynaptic to the postsynaptic membrane, and an impulse reaching the synapse causes an ionic current to cross through the channel, giving rise to a postsynaptic potential.

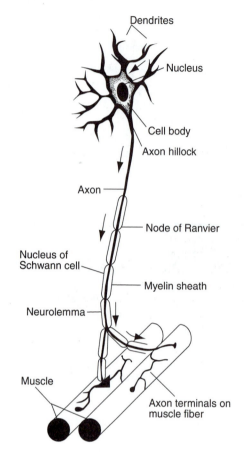

Figure 4.9 Neuromuscular junction.

ceive the *amplification* discussed in section 2.[5] We go from micro- to macro-dimensions in the transition *from* the electrochemical energy expended in the molecular events preceding muscle contraction *to* the mechanical energy in the contraction itself.

One axon of a motor neuron can synapse with anywhere from three to one hundred fifty muscle fibers. All the fibers with synapses from a single axon contract at the same time, forming what is called a *motor unit*. A muscle can contain hundreds of such units that are able to contract independently. Other things being equal, the fewer fibers per motor unit, the more motor units there will be for the muscle as a whole, and the more finely the muscle action can be graded by varying the phasing and frequency of impulses into its motor units.

3.3 Sensory Receptors

To keep this section to an appropriate length, I will discuss in some (but not great) detail only the visual system and, to a lesser extent, the auditory system.

The function of sensory receptors is to *transduce* various forms of energetic input from the environment into standard nerve impulses. The receptors get these inputs to play a stimulus role similar to that of transmitter substances for interneurons: the inputs satisfy the complex sets of conditions under which neurons will initiate an action potential or not. Like the ear, the eye (fig. 4.10A) is an *accessory apparatus* that focuses or otherwise alters energetic inputs so that they can appropriately stimulate the receptor. The retina, the innermost of three tissue layers encasing the eye, is the actual receptor for vision. Light entering the eye through the pupil (fig. 4.10B) manages to pass through the mostly transparent gel inside the eye and through the upper layers of retinal cells until it reaches the back of the retina. There the photons are absorbed by *rods* and *cones* (fig. 4.10C), two kinds of photoreceptor cells that convert photic energy into graded potentials. Rods are sensitive to dim light and are inactivated by bright light. Their primary function is night vision. Cones are sensitive to bright light, and belong to three types, each of which is maximally responsive to light waves with frequencies corresponding to either blue, green, or red. Cones are

exchange of ions across the axonal membrane. As an action potential moves down the axon, it jumps from node to node as the depolarization at one node moves the next to the impulse threshold. This kind of conduction, by going much faster than one involving the entire axonal membrane, compensates for the distance that motor signals must travel.

When the nerve impulse reaches the axon terminals, it causes the release of acetylcholine across the synaptic cleft onto receptors on the membrane of the muscle fiber, the principal **effector** of the neural control system (see figs. 4.3 and 4.5). Sodium and potassium channels in the membrane open, creating a spreading depolarization that releases calcium ions from inside the muscle cell, which in turn trigger an all-or-nothing contraction of the muscle fiber. It is at this point that motor signals re-

---

[5] See p. 57 above.

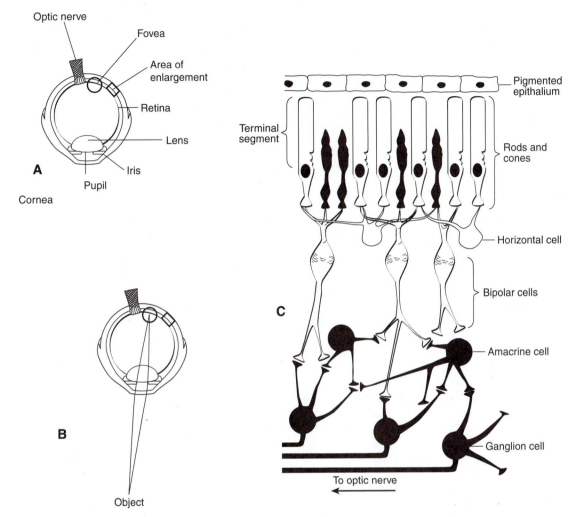

Figure 4.10 A: Schematic drawing of human eye. **B:** Light diverging outward from a focal point ("object") passes through the transparent cornea and pupil. The lens makes it converge onto a point on the fovea. If the diameter of the eye is too short or too long, the point of convergence will be behind or in front of the retinal surface, and there will be a scattering of "hits" on that surface by light from one focal point, resulting in the blurred vision of "farsightedness" or "nearsightedness" respectively. **C:** Section of retina. Axons from ganglion cells spread across inner retinal surface to converge on optic nerve. Rods are differentiated from cones (drawn with dark fill) by the conic shape of their light-absorbent terminal segments.

for daytime vision and color detection. Light from a focal point (see fig. 10B) converges onto the fovea, a part of the retina thick with cones but lacking rods. It is from this part of the retina that signals to the brain yield the sharpest image. The *pigmented epithelium* absorbs photons that make it past the photoreceptors, thereby preventing reflection of light from the back of the eye.

There is no sodium-potassium pump in the terminal segments of rods and cones, and sodium channels there are open as long as the cell is in darkness. This permits a NA+ current to enter across the terminal membrane and spread into the lower segment of the cell. This influx combines with the pump in the lower segment to create a resting potential of about -40 mv. The first phase of the retina's *transduction* of photic energy goes like this: Absorption of light by pigment molecules in the terminal segment initiates a series of chemical reactions which ends in the closing of NA+ channels in the membrane of the terminal. Although the influx of NA+ from the terminal then ceases, the sodium pump in the lower segment continues to function, *hyper*polarizing the interior from -40 mv to as much as -80 mv. This hyperpolarization is only the first step in the *transduction* of photic input into action potentials, the coin of the neural realm. Let's now jump to the end of the process and look back.

The retina's output of action potentials is conveyed to the brain by the axons of *ganglion* cells. As you can see from figure 4.10C, there are three kinds of interneurons linking photoreceptors to ganglion cells. *Bipolar* cells are the only kind that actually synapse with both. Although the other two kinds (*horizontal* and *amacrine*) play a role in shaping the signals from photoreceptors to ganglion cells, I will have to omit it for the sake of brevity.

To understand the interaction between photoreceptors and ganglion cells, we need to introduce the notion of a **receptive field.** The area of the receptor surface within which stimulation affects the firing rate of a neuron, by excitation or inhibition, is that neuron's receptive field. There's a great deal of overlap among the receptive fields of different neurons because stimulation of a particular receptor cell usually affects more than one neuron. A single receptor cell can excite one neuron and inhibit another, depending on the kind of synaptic site involved. It can also be part of the receptor fields of downstream neurons at different levels: For instance, the receptive field of an interneuron in the visual cortex of the brain could overlap with that of a ganglion cell. The *visual field,* understood as the entire set of objects available to an eye directed at a given focal point, is *mapped* in orderly fashion onto the retina. Light from any two points in the visual field will stimulate corresponding points on the retinal surface. As we will see in section 4, there is also a mapping relationship between the retinal surface and the sheets of neurons that carry out various levels of the brain's analysis of visual signals.

Ganglion cells, and the bipolar cells that link them with photoreceptors, have circular receptive fields. Moreover, these receptive fields have a center-surround structure (a smaller circle within the larger one). *On-center* bipolar and ganglion cells are excited by stimulation within the center, and inhibited by stimulation in the surround. *Off-center* cells have the opposite property. Diffuse illumination over its entire center-surround receptive field evokes only a weak response from a cell because excitation is matched by inhibition. Thus the center-surround structure makes ganglion cells maximally sensitive to *contrasting intensity* within receptive fields rather than degrees of diffuse illumination. They are good *edge* detectors within their tiny fields, which enables them to function jointly as shape detectors.

Now back to the second stage of the transduction process—to what happens after photoreceptor cells gets hyperpolarized: Rods and cones in their resting state constantly release transmitter substance at their synapses with bipolar cells. When rods and cones are hyperpolarized by stimulation, the rate of release at their synapses is lessened. This rate reduction will have the opposite of the excitatory or inhibitory effect[6] brought about by the normal rate. Because bipolar cells are very short neurons, the polarizations they undergo at synapses with rods or cones easily reach their synapses with ganglion cells and alter the release rates there. Ganglion cells in turn, like the interneurons described in section 3.1 above, initiate impulses or not, depending on the degree of depolarization induced by the sum of graded potentials reaching the hillock from synapses.

What the retina does with light is remarkable not merely for the fact that it converts light into neural impulses, but even more because it faithfully translates into the language of impulses the dimensions of so many properties of the light stimulus. I will refer to this aspect of transduction as **encoding.** We have already seen how the working of center-surround receptive fields encodes bound-

---

[6]I.e., reduced excitation = inhibition, and reduced inhibition = excitation.

aries of contrasting illumination. Color is another good example of encoding. At any site along the retinal surface there are populations of the three kinds of cones, each kind firing more often as the light it absorbs approaches its preferred frequency (corresponding to blue or yellow or red). These cones synapse with types of ganglion cells that also differ in their preferred frequencies. Each of these ganglion cells has an axon that bundles with the others leading away from that site (see fig. 10C), ultimately joining millions more to form the optic nerve going to the brain. Within the bundle from a particular site impulses will be occurring with different frequencies in different fibers, and this spatiotemporal pattern of impulses in the bundle encodes with great precision the color of the light absorbed at that site. Furthermore, the *locus* of the light source in the visual field is encoded in the locus of stimulation on the retina, and this locus in turn is encoded in the segregation of fibers in the optic nerve, and then by the termination of those fibers at a particular spot on the sheet of brain neurons that receives visual input. The original retinal locus is in the receptive field for that spot in the brain tissue.

The auditory system provides us with another striking example of transduction and encoding. The canal of the outer ear directs sound waves against the eardrum (see fig. 4.11A), causing it to vibrate with corresponding frequencies. A network of three small bones conducts these vibrations to the fluid in the cochlea (inner ear). The waves induced in that fluid will peak at different distances along the basilar membrane depending on their amplitude (see fig. 4.11B). High amplitude, low-frequency waves will peak farther down toward the tip, whereas shallower, higher frequency waves will peak near the base of the membrane (think of what happens when you flick a rope slowly or quickly). The basilar membrane has a band of hair cells along its length. The hairs vibrate maximally where the fluid wave peaks, and their vibrations give rise to graded potentials that affect synapses between the hair cells and sensory neurons. The latter send impulses toward the brain. A sound composed of many frequencies, such as a musical chord, will produce waves with peaks at different sites along the basilar membrane. Thus the chord is transduced

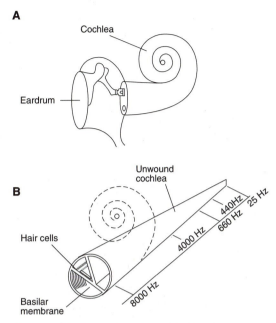

Figure 4.11 A: Simplified drawing of the eardrum and the bones connecting it with the cochlea. **B:** Diagram of the cochlea as if unwound. Waves induced in its fluid peak at different points along the basilar membrane corresponding to their frequencies. Adapted from Churchland (1986). © 1986 by the Massachusetts Institute of Technology.

and encoded as a set of impulses simultaneously traveling along frequency-specific fibers from these different sites and terminating at corresponding sites on sheets of neurons in the auditory zone of the cerebral cortex.

It isn't just the variables *within* one modality (such as different colors in vision or different frequencies of sounds) that are encoded in the patterns of impulses moving along bundles of fibers to specific sites in the brain. The same code also renders what we experience as the qualitative difference between color and sound, or between heat and pain. In these cases there are separate cables (nerves) and brain terminal sites for what is otherwise the same sort of content: patterned impulses. This neural code can be exhaustively analyzed in the mathematical language of spatial relations, energy, duration, frequency, and so on; but the subjective "transduction" of this code into qualitatively different sensations leaves us with items that are *not* observable or mathematically analyzable and which seem, therefore, to be beyond scientific understanding (rather like the situation created by the seventeenth-century distinction of **primary** and **secondary qualities**). In short, we are brought face to face with the nagging question of the relation between consciousness and brain events.

3.4. The Withdrawal Reflex Revisited

Look again at Descartes' drawing of the boy-machine retracting his foot from the fire (see fn. 41 of Reading 1). We want now to see why his guess was wrong when he depicted the sensory signal as traveling all the way from foot to brain before the boy could respond. When your foot is in contact with a fire, or your finger is pressing on the point of a tack as in figure 4.12, there's nearly always one thing that needs to be done *instantly:* withdraw. You don't need to think first, or even look. Impulses can travel very fast along the myelinated axons of sensory and motor neurons (see fig. 4.9). The slowest components of the loop between sensory stimulus and adaptive response are synaptic transmissions. So your nervous system doesn't wait until the signals of tissue damage reach your brain and its array of synapses across which they would have to travel in order to elicit motor signals. Instead, as indicated in figure 4.12, the penetration of the tack into the skin activates a two-synapse circuit[7] resulting in rapid withdrawal of the hand. The sensory neuron involved is somewhat different in structure from interneurons and motor neurons. It appears to have a single axonal process going both directions from the cell body. Its receptor component consists of free filaments that function like dendrites (fig. 4.12A). Contents escaping from cells ruptured by the tack alter the chemistry of the intercellular fluid around the receptor endings. This initiates a sequence of chemical reactions that induce graded potentials in the endings. These potentials are summed further down the axon where myelination begins and action potentials are initiated. (This site does what a

hillock does for interneurons). On the other side of the cell body (B), the axon synapses with an interneuron that acts on a motor neuron. As a result of this action, impulses travel out from the spine along the myelinated motor fiber (C) to the terminals of a neuromuscular synapse (D). There the release of acetylcholine brings about muscle contractions that withdraw the hand and forearm.

The same interneurons that mediate between sensory and motor neurons in the withdrawal reflex also influence motor neurons controlling muscles on the other side of the body. This arrangement enables a compensatory reflex movement of the other arm in the opposite direction, which stabilizes the body. Sensory axons entering the spine from the dorsal root (top of figure 4.12) also synapse with neurons that relay sensory signals to the brain where they result in the perception of pain. If you decided in advance to show how tough you are by allowing the tack to go on penetrating your skin, your brain would send motor signals that would tighten the muscles extending your arm, hand, and finger so as to override the withdrawal reflex. This, like pressing your finger over your upper lip to stop a sneeze, is an example of voluntary control over a reflex action.

It's easier to give examples of reflex action than to define the term. Further examples include coughing, blinking in response to a close, sudden movement, and the compensatory limb adjustments made in response to a slip of the foot or a misstep. All of these are automatic, stereotyped, genetically determined immediate responses to specific stimuli. Some of them involve brain as well as spinal circuits. They can be *conditioned* as in the example of Pavlov's dog: If a bell is rung or a light flashed each time a hungry dog is presented with food, the dog will salivate not only with the natural ("unconditioned") stimulus, but also with presentation of the *conditioned stimulus* (bell or light) alone. Much of the ambiguity in the term *reflex* comes from its variable relation to *voluntariness.*

There is a maximum of *involuntariness* about examples like salivation. One cannot *train* a dog *not* to salivate by withholding food if it does salivate in the presence of food. However, dogs and humans can be trained not to promptly urinate in response to sensations of bladder pressure, although urination is purely involuntary or reflexive in the earliest stage

---

[7]Some reflexes have only one synapse, for example, the patellar or "knee-jerk" reflex tested when your doctor taps the tendon below your knee. Other reflexes have many synapses. A reflex action almost never involves only one sensory or motor neuron. The description speaks as if there is just one in order to concentrate on the steps or synapses in the pathway ("reflex arc") between stimulus and response.

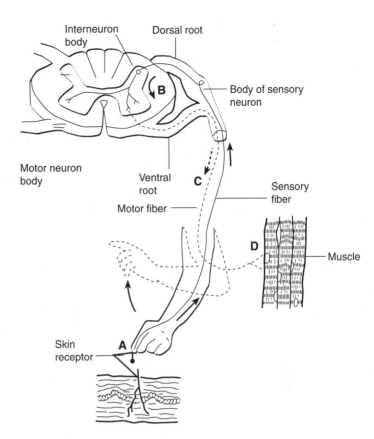

Figure 4.12 Diagram of the reflex arc for the withdrawal or flexor reflex. The center of the spinal cord contains a grey, butterfly-shaped mass consisting of cell bodies and unmyelinated fibers. The surrounding white matter consists of myelinated fibers.

of life for both dogs and humans. While urination is considered a voluntary act in adults not afflicted with incontinence, coughing is a mixed case rather like the withdrawal reflex. I can voluntarily suppress either of them if I know the relevant stimulus is about to occur and I make appropriate muscular adjustments.

Many reflexes are low-level components of complex behavioral repertoires that we can acquire with practice and guidance. For instance, playing tennis involves constant reflexive postural adjustments as we start/stop running or swing at a ball. These reflexes are incorporated into more complex behaviors (such as follow-through on a stroke) that are consciously executed by novice players, but quickly become unconscious routines. The latter are incorporated into still larger behavioral units such as the execution of various tactics designed to score points or defend against opponents' maneuvers. This is the domain of conscious perception

and voluntary activity carried out by what are, in evolutionary terms, the most distinctively human tissues in the brain. Let's turn our attention to them now.

4. THE NEOCORTEX

The tissue in the photograph of figure 4.1 and the simplified drawings of figure 4.13 below is called the *neocortex* (from the Greek prefix for *new* and the Latin word for *rind, bark,* or *shell*). It has a surface of about 2500 cm.[2] (comparable to a 19″ × 20″ sheet), but it is only 1.5–3 mm. thick. Just as a bandanna or large handkerchief gets bunched when it is stuffed inside a pocket, so the neocortex has had to develop undulations in order to fit inside the relatively small space of the upper cranium. The ridge of an undulation is called a *gyrus* and the cleft between gyri is called a *sulcus* (see figure 4.13A, in

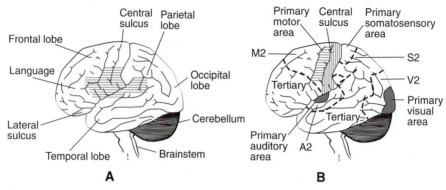

Figure 4.13 A: The four principal lobes and two major sulci of the human neocortex. The cerebellum, an organ of motor coordination, is not part of the cortex. The lined areas on either side of the lateral sulcus represent zones in which electrical stimulation interferes with speech. Damage to this zone produces lasting speech impairment, except for the tissue coinciding with the primary or secondary motor area in 13B, where the impairment is usually temporary. **B:** Functional map of the human neocortex. M2 = secondary motor area; S2 = secondary somatosensory area; V2 = secondary visual area; A2 = secondary auditory area. Tertiary cortex lies outside the single-modality areas of the parietal and temporal lobes and is involved in cross-modal perception. There is also tertiary cortex anterior to the secondary motor area of the frontal lobe. It is involved in the production of language and the planning and execution of complex behavioral sequences.

which the central sulcus is sandwiched by the pre-central and postcentral gyri). The prefix *neo-* refers to the evolutionary novelty of this layer of cortex; when it is not being contrasted with older cortical layers, it is often referred to simply as (the) cortex. As the mammalian brain evolved in the direction of *homo sapiens* there was a dramatic growth in the bulk and functional importance of the neocortex. In early mammals it was smooth and proportionally much smaller than ours, and this difference persists in contemporary descendants such as rodents.

The neocortex is almost entirely dedicated to the reception and analysis of visual, auditory, and somatosensory (touch, pressure, and kinesthetic) input; and to the initiation and coordination of movement based on this input. Since it is vision, hearing, and somatic sensation that enable us to perceive the speech of others and to monitor our own speech production, it is not surprising that the neocortex plays a principal role in the comprehension and production of speech. Damage to the frontal lobe just in front of the lower secondary motor area immediately above the lateral sulcus, or to the temporal-parietal area at the end of the lateral sulcus (see fig. 4.13A), produces lasting impair-

ment of speech (*aphasia*), sometimes without any other major sensory or motor dysfunction.

The demarcation of the neocortex in figure 4.13B into various primary and secondary sensory areas picks up on what we discussed at the end of section 3.3: that the qualitative differences between what we experience as sound and as color, for instance, are *encoded* in the segregation of sensory nerves leading to the brain and in the separate locations of cortical areas to which these nerves project. As Descartes pointed out 350 years ago, if the relevant nerve or brain site is appropriately stimulated downstream from the receptor site, you will experience pain as localized in a body part even if that part (with its receptor site) has been amputated.[8] Everywhere in the neocortex and the rest of the brain there is the same "stuff" (various ions, transmitter substances, neuronal membranes) embodying the same sorts of events (synaptic transmissions, graded potentials, action potentials). Despite the great variety of perceptions, feelings, thoughts, and behaviors which they generate, most brain events are remarkably similar at the cellular level. What,

---

[8]See p. 25 above.

then, does the fact that a set of impulses occurs in the occipital rather than the temporal lobe have to do with the difference between color and sound as experienced? The diversity of neural events comes mainly from their spatiotemporal patterning, and the resulting input/output relations of neurons, singly and in groups, with each other and with the external environment. *That* diversity, according to the functionalist theory,[9] is enough to make intelligible the experiential diversity of color, sound, and other qualities.

One of the most striking features of the neural code is the *mapping* of receptor surfaces onto cortical surfaces. Consider first what enables one surface (of whatever sort) to be a map of the other. Each surface must constitute a grid, a system of fixed points. There must also be a point-for-point correspondence between a point on one surface and only one point on the other, and the mapping process must situate the points on the map surface such that they have the same neighborhood relations to each other as do the corresponding points on the surface being mapped. One obvious way to meet these conditions is to draw the two-dimensional boundaries of an area's features according to a simple scale such as 1 in. = 1 mi. However, since the earth is a sphere, it isn't possible to map all or a large part of the earth's surface onto a flat sheet with a simple scale. Instead, cartographers must systematically transform (and distort) the areas of a spherical surface into areas of a plane surface in a way that still represents clearly the spatial relations between points on the earth that are of interest to the map's user. One of the most common of these projection techniques was invented by Mercator in 1569. In effect it converts the Earth's sphere into a cylinder, and then flattens the surface of the cylinder. This results in some major distortions in the apparent size of land masses as one approaches the poles (e.g., Greenland). The complexity of the projection from receptor surface to neocortical surface is far greater since both surfaces are more irregular. For instance, cortical maps will extend over gyri *and* sulci.

The "cartographic" projection from receptor sheet to cortical area is executed by a physiological projection from cells in a *receptive field* to the cortical neurons activated by stimulation within that field. This projection establishes a patch-for-patch correspondence: Stimulation at any point in a receptive field (e.g., on the surface of your hand) will affect the impulse rate of a patch of cortical neurons one or two millimeters across. When the stimulus shifts a tiny distance across the receptor sheet, it will affect a new cortical patch having almost no overlap with the original. However, the division of receptive fields into excitatory and inhibitory zones[10] makes the correspondences between receptor and cortical sheet far pointier or sharper than the word "patch" suggests.

As the "homunculi" in figure 4.2B demonstrate, cortical maps don't always represent the entire receptor surface as one continuous area. In the primary somatosensory cortex, various parts of the body surface such as the leg, sole, or arm are mapped as separate wholes within which the neighborhood relations of one point to another are preserved, while the neighborhood relations of these parts to each other are distorted by the overall form of the homunculus. Moreover, the relative sizes of the somatosensory subareas do not correspond with the sizes of the surfaces they map. For instance, the lips, tongue, and hand have far more cortex devoted to them than comparable areas of skin on the back or chest. This disproportionate representation is a function of the greater sensitivity in the former due to a higher density of sensory receptors. Because somatosensory sensation provides essential feedback for the control of motor functions, it is easy to see why the surfaces of our hands need to be much more sensitive than our chests or backs. For similar reasons, the hands of the *motor* homunculus are larger than its chest or back, and the fovea (onto which light converges from the focal point of the visual field[11] gets a disproportionately large area in the visual cortex.

A further complication in the mapping relation between cortex and receptor sheet is the presence of multiple maps in the secondary sensory areas with different sizes and shapes, and different receptive fields. The cells in these areas are usually responsive to different aspects of the stimulus than cells in the primary area, and these aspects are

---

[9] See Section 3 of the Introduction.

[10] See the discussion of retinal receptive fields on p. 64 above.
[11] See p. 63 above.

frequently more complex and abstract, as we will now see in the case of vision.

The size and complexity of **receptive fields** tends to grow as one moves from the periphery to the center of the nervous system. For instance, as we saw in sec. 3.3, the receptive field of a ganglion cell is constituted by a population of photoreceptors occupying a tiny area of the retinal surface with a circular center-surround structure. The preferred stimulus of a ganglion cell is a spot of light. Impulses from ganglion cells are relayed to neurons in the middle layer of the visual cortex. They too have circular fields. However, the cells in the layers above and below are most responsive to lines or bars of light with a specific axis of orientation. Their receptive fields appear to be a linear array of circular receptive fields at a particular angle across a small part of the retina. Their behavior suggests that each receives input from a set of middle-layer cells. Their fields have a *rectangular* center and surround, making them most responsive to a line or bar at a precise location in the field. Other cells in the primary visual area have even larger rectangular fields *without* a center-surround structure. Their preferred stimulus is a line or bar at a particular angle *anywhere* in the receptive field. These cells can serve as motion detectors insofar as they continue to fire as the line or edge moves across their fields. Cells in the secondary visual area (see fig. 4.13B) have even larger receptive fields and more complex stimuli such as corners or lines at a particular orientation moving in a specific direction.

There is a striking degree of vertical organization in the two-millimeter thickness of the sensory cortical sheets, as the second and third panels of figure 4.14 suggest. Beneath a square millimeter of visual cortex surface there are columns thirty to one hundred micrometers in width and consisting of thousands of cells sorted into six layers. Except for layer IV, the cells in these columns all have fields with a specific axis of orientation. The orientation preference of cells in any one column differs from that of cells in an adjacent column by about ten degrees. Underneath any square millimeter there will be columns enough to cover the entire 180 degrees of orientation. Interspersed among the orientation columns are cylindrical groupings (called "blobs") of frequency-sensitive cells with circular fields for color detection. In effect, each 1 mm.^{2} patch of the

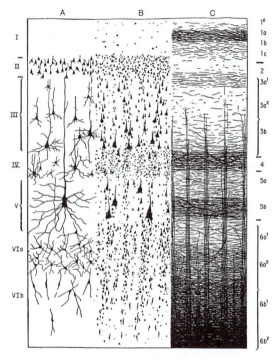

Figure 4.14 The different staining techniques used in each panel highlight different aspects of the cellular architecture in the neocortex. Each technique images only a small fraction of the neuron population. The first panel exhibits the complete extent of a few typical cells in each layer. The second panel shows alignments of cell bodies, while the third shows fiber patterns. Adapted, with permission of the publisher, from S. W. Ranson and S. L. Clark, *The Anatomy of the Nervous System* (Philadelphia: W. B. Saunders Co., 1959).

visual area is the top of an analytical engine for detecting color, line, and motion in the segment of the visual field corresponding to its receptive field.

The visual cortex, like the rest of the brain, is not a single entity doing one thing at a time. It does not, as we have just seen, assemble one part of the visual image after another (what is called *serial processing* in computer language). Instead, a large number of subsystems simultaneously extract features from their own small parts of the visual field (*parallel processing*). It is not easy to relate this picture of large numbers of **weakly-coupled** parallel processors to the unitary self that each of us seems to ourselves to be, the self Descartes described as "utterly indivisible":

> For when I consider the mind, or myself insofar as I am merely a thinking thing, I am unable to distinguish any parts within myself; I understand myself to be something quite single and complete. (*Meditation 6*)

As the final topic in this all-too-brief and selective treatment of the neocortex I want to discuss one of the functions of what is labelled *tertiary* cortex in figure 4.13B. Tertiary ("association") cortex is the most recently evolved component of the neocortex. The temporal-parietal association area is crucial to *intermodal perception*. We don't have visual and *also* auditory and *also* tactile experience of the world around us. Instead, we're conscious of a single world that we can see, hear, and touch. If you were blindfolded and asked to *handle* three differently shaped pieces of wood and then remove the blindfold, you would have no trouble recognizing by sight alone which object you had been handling. The shape you see *is* (recognizably) the same shape that you felt. You can *hear* in the music the orchestra is playing the tempo that you *see* the conductor's baton signalling. When you dance to music, your muscles and tendons are sending a flood of impulses to the somatosensory areas of your brain as feedback that let's you know whether your motions are synchronized with the music. You are "mapping" patterns of sounds into patterns of somatosensory sensation, and feeling what you hear. Similarly, when you draw a shape you see, you are "mapping" a visible form into a pattern of somatosensory feedback from your hand and arm. When you imitate a rhythmic sound by repeated foot or arm motions, or the curve of a hill by the sweep of your brush as you paint it, you are extracting the measurable features of your experience and rendering them in *units* of movement in a way that is not tied to a particular sensory modality. You are perceiving the **primary qualities** of objects, the quantifiable aspects that are the content of scientific analysis. Intermodal perception is the basis for much of what we call *thinking*. Rhesus monkeys and chimpanzees can be trained to do intermodal matching like what we do when we handle objects blindfolded and then visually distinguish them. But we are the only terrestrial species for whom complex intermodal perception pervasively structures normal behavior.

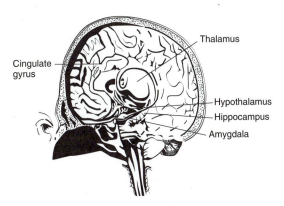

Figure 4.15 A medial view (as if the brain were opened up at the longitudinal fissure between the two hemispheres) of some components of the limbic system.

5. THE LIMBIC SYSTEM

Beneath the *neo*cortex are more ancient cortical layers (such as the cingulate cortex) strongly interconnected with various subcortical structures such as the hypothalamus, hippocampus, amygdala, and the anterior nuclei of the thalamus (see figure 4.15 above). Collectively, these components are often called the *limbic system* (from *limbus*, the Latin word for "hem"; the limbic system forms a kind of hem around the forward end of the brainstem). As the mammalian brain evolved in the direction of our species, it was the neocortex, but not the limbic system, that greatly expanded in function and proportional size.

The limbic system is a major player in the brain's generation of emotional experience and behavior. Electrical stimulation of the hypothalamus, amygdala, or cingulate cortex can elicit in humans and other mammals behaviors such as eating, displays of rage, and aggression, as well as what humans describe as a variety of emotional experiences. Although the human neocortex is much more recently evolved than the limbic system, we should not infer that specifically human kinds of perception and behavior made possible by the neocortex are simply yoked to "animal" feelings and behaviors inherited intact from ancestral species via the limbic system. If the *neo*cortex is an evolutionary novelty, then so is its interaction with the limbic system. As an example of how this interaction can affect the quality of our experience, consider the effect of frontal lobotomies. This surgical procedure severs the fibers linking the limbic system with the prefrontal association cortex—one of the most recently evolved areas of the neocortex. This procedure used to be employed as a last resort in treating otherwise unmanageable pain. After surgery, the patients still had pain sensations (at lower thresholds), but they no longer *suffered* from their pain. The quality of pain in the intact patients seems to have been the *joint* effect of the limbic system and prefrontal cortex.

Lobotomies were often performed, with some success, in the 1940s and 1950s to relieve not only pain, but also severe anxiety, agitation, and violence in psychiatric patients. However, the neuropsychiatric community no longer favors prefrontal lobotomy because it does lasting and fundamental damage to the personality, including apathy, disinhibition of criminal or socially unacceptable behavior, and perseverance in unsuccessful behavior. Paul D. MacLean (1958), the researcher who coined the term "limbic system," has suggested that the suffering of subjects with chronic pain is reduced by prefrontal lobotomy because these persons no longer react to *anticipated* pain after surgery.

Two of the most important functions of the limbic system are (1) what could be described from a subjective point of view as registering the *hedonic* tone of a stimulus (its position on a continuum of pain/pleasure) or, in more objective language, assessing the relevance of the stimulus to the organism's well-being; and (2) linking that stimulus with an adaptive response such as avoidance or aggression. For instance, if I am very thirsty, the temperature is high, and I am drinking a glass of ice water, I am strongly inclined to continue my drinking behavior for as long as my thirst continues. The inclination toward this adaptive behavior in response to the taste and feel of the drink readily transfers to the visual stimulus—the sight of the drink under similar circumstances. This example illustrates the hypothetical imperative discussed at the end of section 2 for an **adaptive control system** with a capacity for learning[12]: *If* behavior y upon stimulus x is followed by state z, *then* avoid/repeat the y response to x. The limbic system plays a major role in the brain-modulator's function of *selecting* adaptive responses to sensory input.

Certain manifestations of *psychomotor epilepsy* provide striking evidence of the pervasive contribution that the limbic system makes to our everyday rational processes. In this form of epilepsy, the wave of electrical activity causing the seizure usually originates in the temporal lobe on the inside of the lateral sulcus (see fig. 4.13A), in an area that includes the amygdala. Before the onset of major symptoms, subjects usually experience *auras:* sensations or affects that warn them of the imminent seizure. As in other kinds of epilepsy, the content of an aura is strongly correlated with the function of the tissue where the seizure originates. The auras of psychomotor epilepsy include sexual feelings, fear, sadness, nausea, hunger, thirst, and other types of affect that are also induced by electrode stimulation in the amygdalar region of the limbic system. Once the wave of electrical activity has spread through the limbic system, that system is temporarily "down." Although these persons retain consciousness of a sort, they usually have no memory from the time between the aura and the end of the seizure. During the seizure they typically engage in random repetitive behavior such as lip-smacking or picking at clothing. Sometimes, however, the behavior can be of longer duration and quite elaborate.

Wilder Penfield (1954) and John Hughlings Jackson[13] (1958) have described interesting cases of the elaborate sort. Jackson's subject (whom he referred to as Z) was a young British doctor who maintained a diary of his epileptic episodes. One day Z had his stethoscope out to examine the chest of a patient with a history of lung problems. Feeling the onset of a seizure, he turned away to avoid conversation. He later found himself in the same examining room with another patient. Remembering the previous patient, he later found out that he had correctly diagnosed him and admitted him to the hospital! Penfield's patient, P. Ge., was married to a woman who had just quit her job as a domestic. She asked P. Ge. to retrieve her belongings

---

[12]See p. 58 above.

[13]Jackson (1835-1911), one of the founders of modern neurological medicine, made lasting contributions to our understanding of epilepsy and **aphasia.** He did his research and practice in London, England from 1859 to 1906.

from the house of her former employer. On the way there he had a seizure. Finding the house locked, he gained entry by breaking a window. Having carried out his mission, he then went to the hospital to get treatment for the cuts his hands sustained from broken window glass. He later had no memory of all this.

The clinical term for the behavior just described is psychomotor *automatism*. The meaning of this word is not entirely clear from its usage in the literature, since it applies to a wide range of behaviors from simple to complex, with varying degrees of responsiveness to events in the immediate environment during the seizure. However, two common attributes of automatic behavior seem to be diminished awareness and subsequent amnesia. Persons in this condition will occasionally become very violent if their activity is interfered with. There is controversy in the American and English legal systems over the extent to which criminal acts performed during these seizures allow a plea of insanity or diminished guilt. The case of Jackson's doctor *Z* demonstrates how intellectually complex the behavior of a psychomotor automaton can be. Both cases involve continuation of a task undertaken prior to the onset of the seizure. P. Ge. demonstrated a curious mixture of strategic rigidity and tactical flexibility. When he found the house unoccupied and locked, he could not let go of his pre-seizure intention to get his wife's things. Yet, when he couldn't gain entry the usual way, he did make a tactical adjustment by switching to breaking and entering. However, the injury to his hands did not deflect him, or jolt him into a recognition of the inappropriateness of his behavior. It seems that without a functioning limbic system he couldn't hurt enough from his injury, or be concerned enough about social and legal consequences, to abandon his

goal. It's as if his relation to his body became more like that of a sailor to his ship[14]: He noticed, but didn't hurt (enough), where *it* was damaged; and he got *it* repaired after completing his task.

There is an imbalance between the uniquely human perceptual, cognitive, and motor capacities of our neocortex and the paleo-mammalian repertoire of the limbic components of our motivational system; and much about the human condition reflects this imbalance. Although we often need to be calm and think or converse intelligently when dealing with a bad or dangerous situation, our ancestral reflexes have us tensing our muscles in readiness for fighting or fleeing—which is what most other animals do in such situations. We even tend to remain in this stressful and uselessly tiring state in response to long-range chronic concerns and worries that are the inevitable effect of our neocortical capacity to think *ahead*. Our *moral* progress seems not to keep pace with our *cognitive* progress in science and technology, so that our increasing power over natural forces threatens to destroy us in the service of irrational hatreds and fears. Aristotle, the greatest of the Greek philosophers, defines happiness, or the highest good for humankind, as the harmonious subordination of the desires and appetites within us to reason, so that we come to want spontaneously to do the right thing in the right way at the right time. We're to achieve this good by practice, by acting rationally until it becomes a habit and we *like* acting that way. This is also much of what we mean by the phrase "growing up." I think Aristotle would agree that part of the reason why growing up is so hard for individuals and societies is the evolutionary imbalance between the human neocortex and limbic system.

---

[14] See the discussion of Descartes' simile on pp. 25–26 above.

PART IV

MATERIALISM

5

Is Consciousness
a Brain Process?

U. T. Place

Place adopts the useful device, common to scientific papers, of providing an introductory abstract of his argument. The first sentence of the abstract is very important. He tells us that he is not himself putting forward a scientific hypothesis. Instead, he is claiming that (1) the assertion, "Consciousness is a brain process," is an *intelligible* thesis that can be confirmed or refuted by the same kind of scientific reasoning and evidence that is used for such claims as "Water is H_2O"; and that (2) the usual sorts of philosophical or "logical" objections against the *intelligibility* of this thesis are not valid. The scope of Place's claim is narrower than that of later supporters of mind-brain identity. His claim is about only what he calls acts of "consciousness." He uses this word to designate the kind of mental process going on when I make an "introspective report"—a report about how something appears or feels to me.

[Abstract]

The thesis that consciousness is a process in the brain is put forward as a reasonable scientific hypothesis, not to be dismissed on logical grounds alone. The conditions under which two sets of observations are treated as observations of the same process, rather than as observations of two independent correlated processes, are discussed. It is suggested that we can identify consciousness with a given pattern of brain activity, if we can explain the subject's introspective observations by reference to the brain processes with which they are correlated. It is argued that the problem of providing a physiological explanation of introspective observations is made to seem more difficult than it really is by the "phenomenological fallacy," the mistaken idea that descriptions of the appearances of things are descriptions of the actual state of affairs in a mysterious internal environment.

1. INTRODUCTION

The view that there exists a separate class of events, mental events, which cannot be described in terms of the concepts employed by the physical sciences no longer commands the universal and unquestioning acceptance among philosophers and psychologists which it once did.[1] Modern physicalism,[2] however,

---

Reprinted from U.T. Place, "Is consciousness a brain process?" *British Journal of Psychology* 47 (1956): 44–50, with permission of The British Psychological Society.

[1] Remember that Place is writing in 1956. If there ever was such "universal and unquestioning acceptance," it stopped decades ago. ED.

[2] As they are used by philosophers, "physicalism" and "materialism" usually have the same or a strongly similar meaning. ED.

unlike the materialism of the seventeenth and eighteenth centuries, is behavioristic.[3] Consciousness on this view is either a special type of behavior, "sampling" or "running back-and-forth" behavior as Tolman has it,[4] or a disposition to behave in a certain way, an itch for example being a temporary propensity to scratch. In the case of cognitive concepts like "knowing," "believing," "understanding," "remembering," and volitional concepts like "wanting" and "intending" there can be little doubt, I think, that an analysis in terms of dispositions to behave is fundamentally sound.[5] On the other hand, there would seem to be an intractable residue of concepts clustering around the notions of consciousness, experience, sensation, and mental imagery, where some sort of inner process story is unavoidable. It is possible, of course, that a satisfactory behavioristic account of this conceptual residuum will ultimately be found. For our present purposes, however, I shall assume that this cannot be done and that statements about pains and twinges, about how things look, sound, and feel, about things dreamed of or pictured in the mind's eye, are statements referring to events and processes which are in some sense private or internal to the individual of whom they are predicated. The question I wish to raise is whether in making this assumption we are inevitably committed to a dualist position in which sensations and mental images form a separate category of processes over and above the physical and physiological processes with which they are known to be correlated. I shall argue that an acceptance of inner processes does not entail dualism and that the thesis that consciousness is a process in the brain cannot be dismissed on logical grounds.

2. THE "IS" OF DEFINITION AND THE "IS" OF COMPOSITION

I want to stress from the outset that in defending the thesis that consciousness is a process in the brain, I am not trying to argue that when we describe our dreams, fantasies, and sensations we are talking about processes in our brains. That is, I am not claiming that statements about sensations and mental images are reducible to or analyzable into statements about brain processes, in the way in which "cognition statements" are analyzable into statements about behavior. To say that statements about consciousness are statements about brain processes is manifestly false. This is shown (a) by the fact that you can describe your sensations and mental imagery without knowing anything about your brain processes or even that such things exist, (b) by the fact that statements about one's consciousness and statements about one's brain processes are verified in entirely different ways, and (c) by the fact that there is nothing self-contradictory about the statement "X has a pain but there is nothing going on in his brain."[6] What I do want to assert, however, is that the statement "Consciousness is a process in the brain," although not necessarily true, is not necessarily false. "Consciousness is a process in the brain," on my view is neither self-contradictory nor self-evident; it is a reasonable scientific hypothesis, in the way that the statement "Lightning is a motion of electric charges" is a reasonable scientific hypothesis. The all but universally accepted view that an assertion of identity between consciousness and brain processes[7] can be ruled out on logical grounds alone, derives, I suspect, from a failure to distinguish between what we may call the

---

[3] Again, this was 1956. Very few philosophers today are adherents of philosophical or logical behaviorism. However, it is still the case today that most philosophers of mind believe there is a strong conceptual connection between the concepts of *mind* and *behavior*. For a discussion of behaviorism, see my remarks following Ryle's essay (reading 2). Ed.

[4] E. C. Tolman, *Purposive Behavior in Animals and Men* (Berkeley: University of California Press, 1932).

[5] A logical behaviorist would analyze the statement "She believes the intersection is dangerous" as attributing to her a "disposition," or strong degree of likelihood, to be unusually cautious when crossing the intersection, looking often each way, going slowly, and so on. Ed.

[6] "This is a square that has uneven sides" *is* self-contradictory because any statement about a square is a statement about a figure that is equilateral. The sentence is *necessarily* false, whereas "A square is equilateral" is "self-evident" or necessarily true. Ed.

[7] Strictly speaking, "Consciousness is a brain process" does *not* assert an *identity* between consciousness and brain processes any more than the statement "Humans are mammals" asserts an identity between humans and mammals. There are plenty of *non*human mammals and *unconscious* brain processes. The identity claim about consciousness would be more properly phrased as "Consciousness is a brain process of a certain kind," which would make it like "Humans are bipedal mammals." In both these revised sentences, the subject phrase designates all and only those entities that the predicate phrase designates; in other words, the subject and predicate concepts are *coextensive*. Ed.

"is" of definition and the "is" of composition. The distinction I have in mind here is the difference between the function of the word "is" in statements like "A square is an equilateral rectangle," "Red is a color," "To understand an instruction is to be able to act appropriately under the appropriate circumstances,"[8] and its function in statements like "His table is an old packing case," "Her hat is a bundle of straw tied together with string," "A cloud is a mass of water droplets or other particles in suspension." These two types of "is" statements have one thing in common. In both cases it makes sense to add the qualification "and nothing else." In this they differ from those statements in which the "is" is an "is" of predication; the statements "Toby is 80 years old and nothing else," "Her hat is red and nothing else" or "Giraffes are tall and nothing else," for example, are nonsense. This logical feature may be described by saying that in both cases both the grammatical subject and the grammatical predicate are expressions which provide an adequate characterization of the state of affairs to which they both refer.

In another respect, however, the two groups of statements are strikingly different. Statements like "A square is an equilateral rectangle" are necessary statements which are true by definition. Statements like "His table is an old packing case," on the other hand, are contingent statements which have to be verified by observation. In the case of statements like "A square is an equilateral rectangle" or "Red is a color," there is a relationship between the meaning of the expression forming the grammatical predicate and the meaning of the expression forming the grammatical subject, such that whenever the subject expression is applicable the predicate must also be applicable. If you can describe something as red then you must also be able to describe it as colored. In the case of statements like "His table is an old packing case," on the other hand, there is no such relationship between the meanings of the expressions "his table" and "old packing case"; it merely so happens that in this case both expressions are applicable to and at the same time provide an adequate characterization of the

same object. Those who contend that the statement "Consciousness is a brain process" is logically untenable base their claim, I suspect, on the mistaken assumption that if the meanings of two statements or expressions are quite unconnected, they cannot both provide an adequate characterization of the same object or state of affairs: if something is a state of consciousness, it cannot be a brain process, since there is nothing self-contradictory in supposing that someone feels a pain when there is nothing happening inside his skull. By the same token we might be led to conclude that a table cannot be an old packing case, since there is nothing self-contradictory in supposing that someone has a table, but is not in possession of an old packing case.

3. THE LOGICAL INDEPENDENCE OF EXPRESSIONS AND THE ONTOLOGICAL INDEPENDENCE OF ENTITIES

There is, of course, an important difference between the table/packing case case and the consciousness/brain process case in that the statement "His table is an old packing case" is a particular proposition which refers only to one particular case, whereas the statement "Consciousness is a process in the brain" is a general or universal proposition applying to all states of consciousness whatever. It is fairly clear, I think, that if we lived in a world in which all tables without exception were packing cases, the concepts of "table" and "packing case" in our language would not have their present logically independent status. In such a world a table would be a species of packing case in much the same way that red is a species of color. It seems to be a rule of language that whenever a given variety of object or state of affairs has two characteristics or sets of characteristics, one of which is unique to the variety of object or state of affairs in question, the expression used to refer to the characteristic or set of characteristics which defines the variety of object or state of affairs in question will always entail the expression used to refer to the other characteristic or set of characteristics. If this rule admitted of no exception it would follow that any expression which is logically independent of another

---

[8] For a logical behaviorist, mental terms can be *defined* or analyzed by statements about behavior. ED.

expression which uniquely characterizes a given variety of object or state of affairs, must refer to a characteristic or set of characteristics which is not normally or necessarily associated with the object or state of affairs in question. It is because this rule applies almost universally, I suggest, that we are normally justified in arguing from the logical independence of two expressions to the ontological independence of the states of affairs to which they refer. This would explain both the undoubted force of the argument that consciousness and brain processes must be independent entities because the expressions used to refer to them are logically independent and, in general, the curious phenomenon whereby questions about the furniture of the universe are often fought and not infrequently decided merely on a point of logic.

The argument from the logical independence of two expressions to the ontological independence of the entities to which they refer breaks down in the case of brain processes and consciousness, I believe, because this is one of a relatively small number of cases where the rule stated above does not apply. These exceptions are to be found, I suggest, in those cases where the operations which have to be performed in order to verify the presence of the two sets of characteristics inhering in the object or state of affairs in question can seldom if ever be performed simultaneously. A good example here is the case of the cloud and the mass of droplets or other particles in suspension. A cloud is a large semitransparent mass with a fleecy texture suspended in the atmosphere whose shape is subject to continual and kaleidoscopic change. When observed at close quarters, however, it is found to consist of a mass of tiny particles and nothing else. But there is no logical connection in our language between a cloud and a mass of tiny particles; there is nothing self-contradictory in talking about a cloud which is not composed of tiny particles in suspension. There is no contradiction involved in supposing that clouds consist of a dense mass of fibrous tissue; indeed, such a consistency seems to be implied by many of the functions performed by clouds in fairy stories and mythology. It is clear from this that the terms "cloud" and "mass of tiny particles in suspension" mean quite different things. Yet we do not conclude from this that there must be two things, the mass of particles in suspension and the cloud. The

reason for this,[9] I suggest, is that although the characteristics of being a cloud and being a mass of tiny particles in suspension are invariably associated, we never make the observations necessary to verify the statement "That is a cloud" and those necessary to verify the statement "This is a mass of tiny particles in suspension" at one and the same time. We can observe the microstructure of a cloud only when we are enveloped by it, a condition which effectively prevents us from observing those characteristics which from a distance lead us to describe it as a cloud. Indeed, so disparate are these two experiences that we use different words to describe them. That which is a cloud when we observe it from a distance becomes a fog or mist when we are enveloped by it.

4. WHEN ARE TWO SETS OF OBSERVATIONS OBSERVATIONS OF THE SAME EVENT?

The example of the cloud and the mass of tiny particles in suspension was chosen because it is one of the few cases of a general proposition involving what I have called the "is" of composition which does not involve us in scientific technicalities. It is useful because it brings out the connection between the ordinary everyday cases of the "is" of composition like the table/packing case example and the more technical cases like "Lightning is a motion of electric charges" where the analogy with the consciousness/brain process case is most marked. The limitation of the cloud/tiny particles-in-suspension case is that it does not bring out sufficiently clearly the crucial problem of how the identity of the states of affairs referred to by the two expressions is established. In the cloud case the fact that something is a cloud and the fact that something is a mass of tiny particles in suspension are both verified by the normal processes of visual observation. It is arguable, moreover, that the identity of the entities referred to by the two expressions is established by the continuity between the two sets of observations as the observer moves towards or away from the cloud. In the case of brain processes

---

[9]"This" seems to refer not to the immediately preceding sentence, but to the one before. ED.

and consciousness there is no such continuity between the two sets of observations involved. A closer introspective scrutiny will never reveal the passage of nerve impulses over a thousand synapses in the way that a closer scrutiny of a cloud will reveal a mass of tiny particles in suspension. The operations required to verify statements about consciousness and statements about brain processes are fundamentally different.

To find a parallel for this feature we must examine other cases where an identity is asserted between something whose occurrence is verified by the ordinary processes of observation and something whose occurrence is established by special scientific procedures. For this purpose I have chosen the case where we say that lightning is a motion of electric charges.[10] As in the case of consciousness, however closely we scrutinize the lightning we shall never be able to observe the electric charges, and just as the operations for determining the nature of one's state of consciousness are radically different from those involved in determining the nature of one's brain processes, so the operations for determining the occurrence of lightning are radically different from those involved in determining the occurrence of a motion of electric charges. What is it, therefore, that leads us to say that the two sets of observations are observations of the same event? It cannot be merely the fact that the two sets of observations are systematically correlated such that whenever there is lightning there is always a motion of electric charges. There are innumerable cases of such correlations where we have no temptation to say that the two sets of observations are observations of the same event. There is a systematic correlation, for example, between the movement of the tides and the stages of the moon, but this does not lead us to say that records of tidal levels are records of the moon's stages or vice versa. We speak rather of a causal connection between two independent events or processes.

The answer here seems to be that we treat the two sets of observations as observations of the same event in those cases where the technical scientific observations set in the context of the appropriate body of scientific theory provide an immediate explanation of the observations made by the man in the street. Thus we conclude that lightning is nothing more than a motion of electric charges, because we know that a motion of electric charges through the atmosphere, such as occurs when lightning is reported, gives rise to the type of visual stimulation which would lead an observer to report a flash of lightning. In the moon/tide case, on the other hand, there is no such direct causal connection between the stages of the moon and the observations made by the man who measures the height of the tide. The causal connection is between the moon and the tides, not between the moon and the measurement of the tides.

5. THE PHYSIOLOGICAL EXPLANATION OF INTROSPECTION AND THE PHENOMENOLOGICAL FALLACY

If this account is correct, it should follow that in order to establish the identity of consciousness and certain processes in the brain, it would be necessary to show that the introspective observations reported by the subject can be accounted for in terms of processes which are known to have occurred in his brain. In the light of this suggestion it is extremely interesting to find that when a physiologist as distinct from a philosopher finds it difficult to see how consciousness could be a process in the brain, what worries him is not any supposed self-contradiction involved in such an assumption, but the apparent impossibility of accounting for the reports given by the subject of his conscious processes in terms of the known properties of the central nervous system. Sir Charles Sherrington[11] has posed the problem as follows:

> The chain of events stretching from the sun's radiation entering the eye to, on the one hand, the

---

[10] "A motion of electric charges" applies to any electric current, and is therefore too broad to serve as a definition or as one side of an identity claim about lightning. More precisely, lightning is a visible discharge of electricity that occurs when there is a **potential difference** between a part of the atmosphere and a site on the ground or in a cloud sufficient to overcome the resistance of the air to the passage of an electric current.

[11] Sir Charles Scott Sherrington (1857–1952) was a professor of physiology at the Universities of London, Liverpool, and Oxford. He ranks among the founders of modern neurophysiology and was the originator of the terms *neuron* and *synapse*. He won (with Edgar Adrian) the Nobel prize in physiology or medicine in 1932. His greatest contributions were to the physiology of reflexes and perception. ED.

contraction of the pupillary muscles, and on the other, to the electrical disturbances in the brain-cortex are all straightforward steps in a sequence of physical "causation" such as, thanks to science, are intelligible. But in the second serial chain there follows on, or attends, the stage of brain-cortex reaction an event or set of events quite inexplicable to us, which both as to themselves and as to the causal tie between them and what preceded them science does not help us; a set of events seemingly incommensurable with any of the events leading up to it. The self "sees" the sun; it senses a two-dimensional disc of brightness, located in the "sky," this last a field of lesser brightness, and overhead shaped as a rather flattened dome, coping the self and a hundred other visual things as well. Of hint that this is within the head there is none. Vision is saturated with this strange property called "projection," the unargued inference that what it sees is at a "distance" from the seeing "self." Enough has been said to stress that in the sequence of events a step is reached where a physical situation in the brain leads to a psychical, which however contains no hint of the brain or any other bodily part. . . . The supposition has to be, it would seem, two continuous series of events, one physico-chemical, the other psychical, and at times interaction between them.[12]

Just as the physiologist is not likely to be impressed by the philosopher's contention that there is some self-contradiction involved in supposing consciousness to be a brain process, so the philosopher is unlikely to be impressed by the considerations which lead Sherrington to conclude that there are two sets of events, one physicochemical, the other psychical. Sherrington's argument for all its emotional appeal depends on a fairly simple logical mistake, which is unfortunately all too frequently made by psychologists and physiologists and not infrequently in the past by the philosophers themselves. This logical mistake, which I shall refer to as the "phenomenological fallacy,"[13] is the mistake of supposing that when the subject describes his experience, when he describes how things look, sound, smell, taste, or feel to him, he is describing the literal properties of objects and events on a peculiar sort of internal cinema or television screen, usually referred to in the modern psychological literature as the "phenomenal field." If we assume, for example, that when a subject reports a green after-image[14] he is asserting the occurrence inside himself of an object which is literally green, it is clear that we have on our hands an entity for which there is no place in the world of physics. In the case of the green after-image there is no green object in the subject's environment corresponding to the description that he gives. Nor is there anything green in his brain; certainly there is nothing which could have emerged when he reported the appearance of the green after-image. Brain processes are not the sort of things to which color concepts can be properly applied.

The phenomenological fallacy on which this argument is based depends on the mistaken assumption that because our ability to describe things in our environment depends on our consciousness of them, our descriptions of things are primarily descriptions of our conscious experience and only secondarily, indirectly, and inferentially descriptions of the objects and events in our environments. It is assumed that because we recognize things in our environment by their look, sound, smell, taste, and feel, we begin by describing their phenomenal properties, i.e., the properties of the looks, sounds, smells, tastes, and feels which they produce in us, and infer their real properties from their phenomenal properties. In fact, the reverse is the case. We begin by learning to recognize the real properties of things in our environment. We learn to recognize them, of course, by their look, sound, smell, taste, and feel; but this does not mean that we have to learn to describe the look, sound, smell, taste, and

---

[12] Sir Charles Sherrington, *The Integrative Action of the Nervous System* (Cambridge: Cambridge University Press, 1947), pp. xx–xxi.

[13] The term *fallacy* properly refers to a type of argument that seems valid but is not. Common examples of fallacious reasoning are *begging the question,* in which an argument assumes as a premise what it is trying to prove, and *post hoc, propter hoc,* in which one concludes that B is the effect of A simply because B follows A. Labeled fallacies such as these are a kind of erroneous reasoning which is easily and frequently committed. "Phenomenological fallacy" is not a commonly accepted label; it is more of a rhetorical device on the part of Place. You're at an advantage if you can claim not only that an opposing argument is unsound or invalid, but also that it commits a common error that is obvious once exposed. This de-

vice has been used so frequently that it now has its own joking label: the fallacy fallacy. Ed.

[14] The term *after-image* is usually applied to visual content, and is a species of *after-sensation* or *after-effect* in which the sensation continues after removal of the stimulus. The most familiar example of an after-image is what happens after we look at a lit electric bulb or a camera bulb flashing. Even as we look away, an image of the light persists in the same part of our visual field. The image is the same color for a moment, and then assumes a complementary color (going, for instance, from pale yellow to dark blue-violet). This phenomenon is due initially to after-discharge of retinal cells and then to brief loss of sensitivity in the same cells. Ed.

feel of things before we can describe the things themselves. Indeed, it is only after we have learned to describe the things in our environment that we can learn to describe our consciousness of them. We describe our conscious experience not in terms of the mythological "phenomenal properties" which are supposed to inhere in the mythological "objects" in the mythological "phenomenal field," but by reference to the actual physical properties of the concrete physical objects, events, and processes which normally, though not perhaps in the present instance, give rise to the sort of conscious experience which we are trying to describe. In other words when we describe the after-image as green, we are not saying that there is something, the after-image, which is green; we are saying that we are having the sort of experience which we normally have when, and which we have learned to describe as, looking at a green patch of light.

Once we rid ourselves of the phenomenological fallacy we realize that the problem of explaining introspective observations in terms of brain processes is far from insuperable. We realize that there is nothing that the introspecting subject says about his conscious experiences which is inconsistent with anything the physiologist might want to say about the brain processes which cause him to describe the environment and his consciousness of that environment in the way he does. When the subject describes his experience by saying that a light which is in fact stationary, appears to move, all the physiologist or physiological psychologist has to do in order to explain the subject's introspective observations, is to show that the brain process which is causing the subject to describe his experience in this way, is the sort of process which normally occurs when he is observing an actual moving object and which therefore normally causes him to report the movement of an object in his environment. Once the mechanism whereby the individual describes what is going on in his environment has been worked out, all that is required to explain the individual's capacity to make introspective observations is an explanation of his ability to discriminate between those cases where his normal habits of verbal description are appropriate to the stimulus situation and those cases where they are not and an explanation of how and why, in those cases where the appropriateness of his normal descriptive habits is in doubt, he learns to issue his ordinary descriptive protocols preceded by a qualificatory phrase like "it appears," "seems," "looks," "feels," etc.[15]

[15] I am greatly indebted to my fellow-participants in a series of informal discussion on this topic which took place in the Department of Philosophy, University of Adelaide, in particular to Mr. C. B. Martin for his persistent and searching criticism of my earlier attempts to defend the thesis that consciousness is a brain process, to Prof. D. A. T. Gasking, of the University of Melbourne, for clarifying many of the logical issues involved, and to Prof. J. J. C. Smart for moral support and encouragement in what often seemed a lost cause.

There is a great deal at stake in Place's rejection of the "mythological" phenomenal field. This field is the focus of what he calls the "phenomenological fallacy"—the belief that "when [the subject] describes his experience, when he describes how things look, sound, smell, taste, or feel to him, he is describing the literal properties of objects and events on a peculiar sort of internal cinema . . . usually referred to in the modern psychological literature as the 'phenomenal field'" (p. 82). Why would presumably intelligent persons such as the authors of "modern psychological literature" be so convinced that there are such things as phenomenal fields? Their reasoning appears to be that there must be something in which *appearances* occur, and this something must have its own (quasi) spatiotemporal structure: The phenomenal field of a particular person is the world-as-it-is-being-experienced, or the world-as-it-is-appearing to that person. It is the world of what I called "scenes" at the beginning of the Introduction. It is a world in which appear or occur not only after-images, but also nearby objects that *seem* far bigger than distant ones which we know are *really* just as big or bigger; and where the stick under water really does look bent. Stare at a lighted bulb briefly and then look away. The after-image will continue to occupy the same position in your visual (phenomenal) field that the bulb occupied even though you're no longer looking in the direction of the bulb. Where is this space in which the after-image is located? It can't be part of the physical space of the room or of your brain. Is it then a nonphysical space, a phenomenal space? If so, then the goings-on within that space can't be brain processes. They would be mental events that are neither observable behavior nor brain processes. The materialist thesis would then be falsified.

What is Place's alternative to interpreting reports of after-images and the like as occurring in a phenomenal field? He suggests we can understand these phenomena as being nothing but brain processes. An after-image looks like an object not because it is a special sort of object in a special domain of being, but because the brain process that causes us to report the experience of an after-image is the sort of brain process that usually causes us to report seeing the object that the image resembles. In making this proposal, Place is assuming that it is a specific brain process that "normally causes" a person to make an observation report about a specific physical object. However, this explanation seems inconsistent with his account of how we arrive at identity statements such as the one about lightning being an electric discharge. According to Place, we identify lightning with a certain type of electric discharge because "the technical scientific observations [of lightning] set in the context of the appropriate body of scientific theory provide an immediate explanation of the observations made by the man in the street." However, if the "technical scientific observations" of certain kinds of brain processes, set in the context of neuroscientific theory, "provide an immediate explanation" not only for our introspective observations, but also for our observations of the external world (as he claims they do in the case of objects resembling after-images), then it would seem to follow that *all we ever observe is brain processes.* Yet Place wants to identify only appearances or purely phenomenal occurrences with brain processes.

Place has brought us up against what looks like a tough dilemma for the philosophy of mind: *Either A:* There is a phenomenal field, a domain of apparent objects in a nonphysical space-time, and materialism is false. *Or B:* There is no phenomenal field. If we accept *A,* we seem to invite an infinite regress of *homunculi*—little humans positioned inside bigger humans in order to explain how the bigger humans can do what they do. The phenomenal field is like an internal screen and the mind must be like an audience of one for what projects onto that screen. Such a picture merely pushes onto the homunculus and the inner screen the problem of how the big human can perceive the physical world. Does the homunculus also have an inner screen? The materialist tries to prevent this regress by asserting *B.* On this account there is no inner screen; there is just the sequence of sensory stimulus, brain event, and production of (or readiness to produce) a speech act such as "There it is" or "I think I see it." However, this option seems to have the awkward result of converting our awareness of the external world into a relationship between one part of the brain and another, between the part that deals with sensory input and the part which formulates a relevant linguistic or other response. We then wonder how awareness of what is external to the brain can be a relation internal to the brain. As Sherrington put it: "Of hint that this is within the head there is none."

REVIEW QUESTIONS

1. Look again at the passage from Sherrington. Where in that passage would Place say that Sherrington is committing the phenomenological fallacy? Can one describe better or differently the facts he is trying to describe, so as to avoid the fallacy? How?

2. According to the description of the world that physics provides, every body large enough for us to see is nothing but a swarm of imperceptibly small particles of various kinds occupying a mostly empty space. The visible solidity of such bodies is in every case merely apparent, and due to the limitations of our senses. The apparent continuity of the stuff making up the wall and table in front of me is no more a part of the world described by physics than is the after-image seeming to float in front of me. Can Place say the same sort of thing about the wall and table's solidity that he said about the after-image, so as to avoid resorting to an internal screen on which to locate these appearances?

6

Sensations and Brain Processes

J. J. C. Smart

J. J. C. Smart is an Australian philosopher who has taught at several Australian and American universities, and is currently Professor Emeritus at the Australian National University. He has written extensively in the philosophy of science, ethics and philosophy of mind. The reading which follows is one of the most frequently reprinted papers in the philosophy of mind. U. T. Place was a member of Smart's philosophy department at the University of Adelaide when he wrote "Is Consciousness a Brain Process?" As Smart makes clear in the opening of his paper, he is doing battle for Place's thesis, continuing to give the support for which Place expresses gratitude in a final endnote to the previous reading—support for "what often seemed a lost cause." As it turned out, the cause was far from lost.

This paper[1] takes its departure from arguments to be found in U. T. Place's "Is consciousness a brain process?"[2] I have had the benefit of discussing Place's thesis in a good many universities in the United States and Australia, and I hope that the present paper answers objections to his thesis which Place has not considered and that it presents his thesis in a more nearly unobjectionable form. This paper is meant also to supplement the paper 'The "Mental" and the "Physical"' by H. Feigl,[3] which in part argues for a similar thesis to Place's.

Suppose that I report that I have at this moment a roundish, blurry-edged after-image which is yel-lowish towards its edge and is orange towards its centre. What is it that I am reporting? One answer to this question might be that I am not reporting anything, that when I say that it looks to me as though there is a roundish yellowy-orange patch of light on the wall I am expressing some sort of *temptation*, the temptation to say that there is a roundish yellowy-orange patch on the wall (though I may know that there is not such a patch on the wall). This is perhaps Wittgenstein's view in the *Philosophical Investigations* (see sections 367, 370). Similarly, when I "report" a pain, I am not really re-porting anything (or, if you like, I am reporting in a queer sense of "reporting"), but am doing a sophisticated sort of wince. (See section 244: "The verbal expression of pain replaces crying and does not describe it." Nor does it describe anything else?)[4] I prefer most of the time to discuss an

Reprinted with permission from the *Philosophical Review* LXVIII (1959) 141–156. © 1959 Cornell University.

[1] This is a very slightly revised version (which first appeared in *The Philosophy of Mind*, ed. V. G. Chappell (Englewood Cliffs, N.J., 1962) of a paper which was first published in the *Philosophical Review*, LXVIII (1959), pp. 141–56. Since that date there have been criticisms of my paper by J. T. Stevenson [*The Philosophical Review* LXIX (1960) 505–510], to which I have replied in [*The Philosophical Review* LXX (1961) 406–407], and by G. Pitcher and by W. D. Joske, *Australasian Journal of Philosophy*, XXXVIII (1960), pp. 150–60, to which I have replied in the same volume of that journal, pp. 252–4.

[2] *British Journal of Psychology*, XLVII (1956) pp. 44–50; reprinted in this volume as Paper II. (Page references are to the reprint in this volume.)

[3] *Minnesota Studies in the Philosophy of Science*, II, pp. 370–497.

[4] Some philosophers of my acquaintance, who have the advantage over me in having known Wittgenstein, would say that this interpretation of him is too behaviouristic. However, it seems to me a very natural interpretation of his printed words, and whether or not it is Wittgenstein's real view it is certainly an interesting and important one. I wish to consider it here as a possible rival both to the 'brain-process' thesis and to straight-out old-fashioned dualism.

after-image rather than a pain, because the word "pain" brings in something which is irrelevant to my purpose: the notion of "distress." I think that "he is in pain" entails "he is in distress," that is, that he is in a certain agitation-condition.[5] Similarly, to say, "I am in pain" may be to do more than "replace pain behaviour": it may be partly to report something, though this something is quite non-mysterious, being an agitation-condition, and so susceptible of behaviouristic analysis.[6] The suggestion I wish if possible to avoid is a different one, namely that "I am in pain" is a genuine report, and that what it reports is an irreducibly psychical something. And similarly the suggestion I wish to resist is also that to say "I have a yellowish-orange after-image" is to report something irreducibly psychical.

Why do I wish to resist this suggestion? Mainly because of **Occam's razor.** It seems to me that science is increasingly giving us a viewpoint whereby organisms are able to be seen as physico-chemical mechanisms:[7] it seems that even the behaviour of man himself will one day be explicable in mechanistic terms. There does seem to be, so far as science is concerned, nothing in the world but increasingly complex arrangements of physical constituents.[8] All except for one place: in consciousness. That is, for a full description of what is going on in a man you would have to mention not only the physical processes in his tissues, glands, nervous system, and so forth, but also his states of consciousness: his visual, auditory, and tactual sensations, his aches and pains. That these should be *correlated* with brain processes does not help, for to say that they are *correlated* is to say that they are something "over and above". You cannot correlate something with itself. You correlate footprints with burglars, but not Bill Sikes the burglar with Bill Sikes the burglar. So sensations, states of consciousness, do seem to be the one sort of thing left outside the physicalist picture, and for various reasons I just cannot believe that this can be

so. That everything should be explicable in terms of physics (together of course with descriptions of the ways in which the parts are put together—roughly, biology is to physics as radio-engineering is to electromagnetism) except the occurrence of sensations seems to me to be frankly unbelievable. Such sensations would be "nomological danglers," to use Feigl's expression.[9] It is not often realized how odd would be the laws whereby these nomological danglers would dangle. It is sometimes asked, "Why can't there be psycho-physical laws which are of a novel sort, just as the laws of electricity and magnetism were novelties from the standpoint of Newtonian mechanics?" Certainly we are pretty sure in the future to come across new ultimate laws of a novel type, but I expect them to relate simple constituents: for example, whatever ultimate particles are then in vogue. I cannot believe that ultimate laws of nature could relate simple constituents to configurations consisting of perhaps billions of neurons (and goodness knows how many billion billions of ultimate particles) all put together for all the world as though their main purpose in life was to be a negative feedback mechanism of a complicated sort. Such ultimate laws would be like nothing so far known in science. They have a queer "smell" to them. I am just unable to believe in the nomological danglers themselves, or in the laws whereby they would dangle.[10] If any philosophical arguments seemed to compel us to believe in such things, I would suspect a catch in the argument. In any case it is the object of this paper to show that

---

[5] See Ryle, *The Concept of Mind,* p. 93.

[6] Like Place, Smart conceded, at the time of writing, that an adequate behaviorist analysis could be given of many terms referring to mental states. He later changed his mind. ED.

[7] On this point, see Paul Oppenheim and Hilary Putnam, "Unity of Science as a Working Hypothesis", in *Minnesota Studies in the Philosophy of Science,* II, pp. 3–36.

[8] For a discussion of the mentality behind such a declaration of faith, see sec. 2 ("Materialism") of the Introduction. ED.

[9] Feigl, *Minnesota Studies in the Philosophy of Science,* II, p. 428. Feigl uses the expression "nomological danglers" for the laws whereby the entities dangle: I have used the expression to refer to the dangling entities themselves.

[10] This paragraph is not easy to interpret. It begins by rejecting (mere) "correlation" between sensations and brain processes, because correlates are distinct entities, whereas (he would claim) sensations are *not* distinct from the relevant brain processes. But he then goes on to attack the very notion of a *psycho-physical* correlation or *law:* In such laws, the psychic or psychological correlate would "dangle." Unlike the usual physical law, such "laws" would relate physical with nonphysical items. As science progressed all the refinements in such laws would be on the physical side of the psycho-physical correlation, as brain processes get analyzed in terms of more "ultimate" laws dealing with lower-level, more fundamental particles. The psychological side would just "dangle" in its original, unanalyzed state. However, later in the paragraph, Smart talks about the "danglers" not as sensations but rather as large configurations of neurons. The laws correlating the simpler constituents in the domain of physical science with these large neural configurations don't pass Smart's smell test. ED.

there are no philosophical arguments which compel us to be dualists.

The above is largely a confession of faith, but it explains why I find Wittgenstein's position (as I construe it) so congenial. For on this view there are, in a sense, no sensations. A man is a vast arrangement of physical particles, but there are not, over and above this, sensations or states of consciousness. There are just behavioural facts about this vast mechanism, such as that it expresses a temptation (behaviour disposition) to say "there is a yellowish-red patch on the wall" or that it goes through a sophisticated sort of wince, that is, says "I am in pain." Admittedly Wittgenstein says that though the sensation "is not a something," it is nevertheless "not a nothing either" (section 304), but this need only mean that the word "ache" has a use. An ache is a thing, but only in the innocuous sense in which the plain man, in the first paragraph of Frege's *Foundations of Arithmetic,* answers the question "What is the number one?" by "A thing." It should be noted that when I assert that to say "I have a yellowish-orange after-image" is to express a temptation to assert the physical-object statement "There is a yellowish-orange patch on the wall," I mean that saying "I have a yellowish-orange after-image" is (partly) the exercise of the disposition[11] which is the temptation. It is not to *report* that I have the temptation, any more than is "I love you" normally a report that I love someone. Saying "I love you" is just part of the behaviour which is the exercise of the disposition of loving someone.

Though for the reasons given above I am very receptive to the above "expressive" account of sensation statements, I do not feel that it will quite do the trick. Maybe this is because I have not thought it out sufficiently, but it does seem to me as though, when a person says "I have an after-image," he *is* making a genuine report, and that when he says "I have a pain," he *is* doing more than "replace pain-behaviour" and that this "more" is not just to say that he is in distress. I am not so sure, however, that

to admit this is to admit that there are non-physical correlates of brain processes. Why should not sensations just be brain processes of a certain sort? There are, of course, well-known (as well as lesser-known) philosophical objections to the view that reports of sensations are reports of brain processes, but I shall try to argue that these arguments are by no means as cogent as is commonly thought to be the case.

Let me first try to state more accurately the thesis that sensations are brain processes. It is not the thesis that, for example, "after-image" or "ache" means the same as "brain process of sort X" (where "X" is replaced by a description of a certain sort of brain process). It is that in so far as "after-image" or "ache" is a report of a process, it is a report of a process that *happens to be* a brain process. It follows that the thesis does not claim that sensation statements can be *translated* into statements about brain processes.[12] Nor does it claim that the logic of a sensation statement is the same as that of a brain-process statement. All it claims is that in so far as a sensation statement is a report of something, that something is in fact a brain process. Sensations are nothing over and above brain processes. Nations are nothing "over and above" citizens, but this does not prevent the logic of nation statements being very different from the logic of citizen statements, nor does it ensure the translatability of nation statements into citizen statements. (I do not, however, wish to assert that the relation of sensation statements to brain-process statements is very like that of nation statements to citizen statements. Nations do not just *happen to be* nothing over and above citizens, for example.[13] I bring in the "nations" example merely to make a negative point: that the fact that the logic of A-statements is different from that of B-statements does not ensure that A's are anything over and above B's.)

---

[11] Wittgenstein did not like the word "disposition." I am using it to put in a nutshell (and perhaps inaccurately) the view which I am attributing to Wittgenstein. I should like to repeat that I do not wish to claim that my interpretation of Wittgenstein is correct. Some of those who knew him do not interpret him in this way. It is merely a view which I find myself extracting from his printed words and which I think is important and worth discussing for its own sake.

[12] See Place, p. [78 of this book Ed.] and Feigl, in *Minnesota Studies in the Philosophy of Science,* II, p. 390.

[13] A nation is by definition a whole composed of citizens, whereas it is not the case that sensations are by definition brain processes. Smart seems to take for granted that a nation is by definition not only composed of citizens, but is also "nothing over and above" them. Many philosophers would not agree. For a population to be a nation, there must be a highly complicated set of relations among them. To assume that these relations are "nothing over and above" the citizens reflects the more general belief that relations have no other reality than that of the entities related. This more general view is commonly, but not universally, held. ED.

REMARKS ON IDENTITY

When I say that a sensation is a brain process or that lightning is an electric discharge, I am using "is" in the sense of strict identity. (Just as in the—in this case necessary—proposition "7 is identical with the smallest prime number greater than 5.") When I say that a sensation is a brain process or that lightning is an electric discharge I do not mean just that the sensation is somehow spatially or temporally continuous with the brain process or that the lightning is just spatially or temporally continuous with the discharge. When on the other hand I say that the successful general is the same person as the small boy who stole the apples I mean only that the successful general I see before me is a time slice of the same four-dimensional object of which the small boy stealing apples is an earlier time slice.[14] However, the four-dimensional object which has the general-I-see-before-me for its late time slice is identical in the strict sense with the four-dimensional object which has the small-boy-stealing-apples for an early time slice. I distinguish these two senses of "is identical with" because I wish to make it clear that the brain-process doctrine asserts identity in the *strict* sense.

I shall now discuss various possible objections to the view that the processes reported in sensation statements are in fact processes in the brain. Most of us have met some of these objections in our first year as philosophy students. All the more reason to take a good look at them. Others of the objections will be more recondite and subtle.

Objection 1. Any illiterate peasant can talk perfectly well about his after-images, or how things look or feel to him, or about his aches and pains, and yet he may know nothing whatever about neurophysiology. A man may, like Aristotle, believe that the brain is an organ for cooling the body without any impairment of his ability to make true statements about his sensations. Hence the things we are talking about when we describe our sensations cannot be processes in the brain.

Reply. You might as well say that a nation of slug-abeds, who never saw the Morning Star or knew of its existence, or who had never thought of the expression "the Morning Star," but who used the expression "the Evening Star" perfectly well, could not use this expression to refer to the same entity as we refer to (and describe as) "the Morning Star."[15]

You may object that the Morning Star is in a sense not the very same thing as the Evening Star, but only something spatio-temporally continuous with it. That is, you may say that the Morning Star is not the Evening Star in the strict sense of "identity" that I distinguished earlier.[16]

There is, however, a more plausible example. Consider lightning.[17] Modern physical science tells us that lightning is a certain kind of electrical discharge due to ionisation of clouds of water vapour in the atmosphere. This, it is now believed, is what the true nature of lightning is. Note that there are not two things: a flash of lightning and an electrical discharge. There is one thing, a flash of lightning, which is described scientifically as an electrical discharge to the earth from a cloud of ionised water molecules. The case is not at all like that of explaining a footprint by reference to a burglar. We say that what lightning really is, what its true nature as revealed by science is, is an electrical discharge. (It is not the true nature of a footprint to be a burglar.)

To forestall irrelevant objections, I should like to make it clear that by "lightning" I mean the publicly observable physical object lightning, not a visual sense-datum[18] of lightning. I say that the pub-

---

[14] See J. H. Woodger, *Theory Construction,* International Encyclopedia of Unified Science, II, No. 5 (Chicago, 1939) p. 38. I here permit myself to speak loosely. For warnings against possible ways of going wrong with this sort of talk, see my note "Spatialising Time," *Mind,* LXIV (1955), pp. 239–41.

[15] Cf. Feigl in *Minnesota Studies in the Philosophy of Science,* II, p. 439. [The *morning star* is a bright star or planet conspicuous in the east just before sunrise, and the *evening star* is the same sort of object in the western sky just before sunset. Once we understand the orbit of the planet Venus, we can predict that it will be visible as the morning and evening stars. Thus *morning star* and *evening star* have different meanings, but have the same referent. Therefore, although it is true that the morning star is the evening star because both are Venus, you could be acquainted with one or other star and be perfectly clear about the meaning of the phrase for that star without knowing the meaning or reference of the other phrase. So with the phrases *sensation* and *brain process.* ED.]

[16] I.e., they are related as different "time slices" of the same planet. ED.

[17] See Place, p. [81 in this book Ed.] above; also Feigl in *Minnesota Studies in the Philosophy of Science,* II, p. 438.

[18] A "sense-datum" in this context is the immediately given sense-impression, what is directly present to our perception, apart from any interpretation we put on it in the process of assigning it a place in a world of objects. Examples would include intense light upon opening my eyes,

licly observable physical object lightning is in fact the electrical discharge, not just a correlate of it. The sense-datum, or rather the having of the sense-datum, the "look" of lightning, may well in my view be a correlate of the electrical discharge. For in my view it is a brain state *caused* by the lightning. But we should no more confuse sensations of lightning with lightning than we confuse sensations of a table with the table.

In short, the reply to Objection 1 is that there can be contingent statements of the form "A is identical with B", and a person may well know that something is an A without knowing that it is a B. An illiterate peasant might well be able to talk about his sensations without knowing about his brain processes, just as he can talk about lightning though he knows nothing of electricity.

Objection 2. It is only a contingent fact (if it is a fact) that when we have a certain kind of sensation there is a certain kind of process in our brain. Indeed it is possible, though perhaps in the highest degree unlikely, that our present physiological theories will be as out of date as the ancient theory connecting mental processes with goings on in the heart. It follows that when we report a sensation we are not reporting a brain process.

Reply. The objection certainly proves that when we say "I have an after-image" we cannot *mean* something of the form "I have such and such a brain process." But this does not show that what we report (having an after-image) is not *in fact* a brain process. "I see lightning" does not *mean* "I see an electrical discharge." Indeed, it is logically possible (though highly unlikely) that the electrical discharge account of lightning might one day be given up. Again, "I see the Evening Star" does not *mean* the same as "I see the Morning Star," and yet "The Evening Star and the Morning Star are one and the same thing" is a contingent proposition. Possibly Objection 2 derives some of its apparent strength from a "Fido"-Fido theory of meaning. If the meaning of an expression were what the expression

named, then of course it *would* follow from the fact that "sensation" and "brain process" have different meanings, that they cannot name one and the same thing.[19]

Objection 3.[20] Even if Objections 1 and 2 do not prove that sensations are something over and above brain processes, they do prove that the qualities of sensations are something over and above the qualities of brain processes. That is, it may be possible to get out of asserting the existence of irreducibly psychic processes, but not out of asserting the existence of irreducibly psychic *properties*. For suppose we identify the Morning Star with the Evening Star. Then there must be some properties which logically imply that of being the Morning Star, and quite distinct properties which entail that of being the Evening Star. Again, there must be some properties (for example, that of being a yellow flash) which are logically distinct from those in the physicalist story.

Indeed, it might be thought that the objection succeeds at one jump. For consider the property of "being a yellow flash." It might seem that this property lies inevitably outside the physicalist framework within which I am trying to work (either by "yellow" being an objective emergent property[21] of physical objects, or else by being a power to produce yellow sense-data, where "yellow" in this second instantiation of the word, refers to a purely phenomenal or introspectible quality). I must therefore digress for a moment and indicate how I deal with secondary qualities. I shall concentrate on colour.

First of all, let me introduce the concept of a normal percipient. One person is more a normal percipient than another if he can make colour discriminations that the other cannot. For example, if A can pick a lettuce leaf out of a heap of cabbage leaves, whereas B cannot though he can pick a lettuce leaf out of a heap of beetroot leaves, then A is

---

or an unfamiliar sound in the distance. Many philosophers would argue that there are no such things as sense-data because we are always aware of sensory content as being something or other. They argue, in other words, that the sensory data are never raw, but always classified or interpreted. ED.

[19] As we saw in the case of morning star/evening star, we must distinguish the meaning or sense of an expression from its reference. ED.

[20] I think this objection was first put to me by Professor Max Black. I think it is the most subtle of any of those I have considered, and the one which I am least confident of having satisfactorily met.

[21] By "emergent" Smart seems to mean something which can't be deduced from or predicted from or understood in terms of the physical properties of the object (lightning). ED.

more normal than B. (I am assuming that A and B are not given time to distinguish the leaves by their slight difference in shape, and so forth.) From the concept of "more normal than" it is easy to see how we can introduce the concept of "normal." Of course, Eskimos may make the finest discriminations at the blue end of the spectrum, Hottentots at the red end. In this case the concept of a normal percipient is a slightly idealised one, rather like that of "the mean sun"[22] in astronomical chronology. There is no need to go into such subtleties now. I say that "This is red" means something roughly like "A normal percipient would not easily pick this out of a clump of geranium petals though he would pick it out of a clump of lettuce leaves." Of course it does not exactly mean this: a person might know the meaning of "red" without knowing anything about geraniums, or even about normal percipients. But the point is that a person can be *trained* to say "This is red" of objects which would not easily be picked out of geranium petals by a normal percipient, and so on. (Note that even a colour-blind person can reasonably assert that something is red, though of course he needs to use another human being, not just himself, as his "colour meter.") This account of secondary qualities explains their unimportance in physics. For obviously the discriminations and lack of discriminations made by a very complex neurophysiological mechanism are hardly likely to correspond to simple and non-arbitrary distinctions in nature. I therefore elucidate colours as powers, in Locke's sense,[23] to evoke certain sorts

of discriminatory responses in human beings. They are also, of course, powers to cause sensation in human beings (an account still nearer Locke's). But these sensations, I am arguing, are identifiable with brain processes.

Now how do I get over the objection that a sensation can be identified with a brain process only if it has some phenomenal property, not possessed by brain processes, whereby one half of the identification may be, so to speak, pinned down?

Reply. My suggestion is as follows. When a person says, "I see a yellowish-orange after-image," he is saying something like this: "*There is something going on which is like what is going on when* I have my eyes open, am awake, and there is an orange illuminated in good light in front of me, that is, when I really see an orange." (And there is no reason why a person should not say the same thing when he is having a veridical sense-datum,[24] so long as we construe "like" in the last sentence in such a sense that something can be like itself.) Notice that the italicised words, namely "there is something going on which is like what is going on when," are all quasi-logical or topic-neutral words.[25] This explains why the ancient Greek peasant's reports about his sensa-

---

[22] The apparent speed of the real sun varies slightly with the seasons. The "mean sun" is an imaginary sun traveling at uniform apparent speed. The real and mean suns may be as much as sixteen minutes apart. Most clocks keep mean solar time, the time that would be measured by observation of the position of the mean sun. ED.

[23] [ED.] Here is how Locke, in *An Essay Concerning Human Understanding,* explains the terms *idea, quality,* and *primary/secondary qualities:*

> Whatsoever the mind perceives in itself, or is the immediate object of perception, thought, or understanding, that I call *idea;* and the power to produce any *idea* in our mind, I call *quality* of the subject wherein that power is.
>
>   ★ ★ ★
>
> Qualities thus considered in bodies are:
> First, such as are utterly inseparable from the body, in what state soever it be; such as in all the alterations and changes it suffers, all the force can be used upon it, it constantly keeps; and such as sense constantly finds in every particle of matter which has bulk enough to be perceived; and the mind finds inseparable from every particle of matter, though less than to make itself singly be perceived by our senses. . . . These I call *original* or *primary* qualities of body; which I think we may observe to produce simple *ideas* in us, viz. solidity, extension, figure, motion or rest, and number.
>   Secondly, such *qualities* which in truth are nothing in the objects themselves but powers to produce various sensations in us by their *primary*

qualities, i.e. by the bulk, figure, texture, and motion of their insensible parts, as colours, sounds, tastes, etc. These I call *secondary qualities.* (II, VIII, 8–9).

[24] A "veridical" sense-datum is one that is being caused in us in the usual way, by the presence of the relevant physical object interacting with a sensory organ. ED.

[25] "Topic-neutral" is the label commonly used for the kind of analysis of sensation reports proposed by Smart, an analysis that is neutral between dualism and materialism. "Something going on which is like what is going on when" refers to an inner process without specifying that this process is physical or not. There are two dualistic perils which Smart's materialist account of sensation seeks to avoid by the topic-neutral analysis: (1) admitting as a real occurrence, presumably in a phenomenal field, an after-image with phenomenal properties such as yellowish-orange color and spatial position that cannot be assigned to the world as described by physical science; and (2) admitting that when I look at an orange it causes me to have a sensation with a phenomenal property—orange—that doesn't belong to the observable and measurable fruit as described in the language of science. He fends off the first peril by analyzing an after-image report as referring to something going on (in me) like what goes on when I'm actually perceiving the relevant object. And he defends against the second peril by interpreting "orange" in "I see a fruit with an orange surface" as referring to a property whereby fruits that we call oranges are distinguishable when illuminated against certain backgrounds, or as referring to something going on in me that is like what goes on when I look at other examples of what are called oranges. *Orange* is what he calls a secondary quality, and these two interpretations of "orange" correspond to the two definitions he gives (two paragraphs above) of a secondary quality. ED.

tions can be neutral between dualistic metaphysics or my materialistic metaphysics. It explains how sensations can be brain processes and yet how a man who reports them need know nothing about brain processes. For he reports them only very abstractly as "something going on which is like what is going on when. . . ." Similarly, a person may say "someone is in the room," thus reporting truly that the doctor is in the room, even though he has never heard of doctors. (There are not two people in the room: "someone" *and* the doctor.) This account of sensation statements also explains the singular elusiveness of "raw feels"[26]—why no one seems to be able to pin any properties on them.[27] Raw feels, in my view, are colourless for the very same reason that *something* is colourless. This does not mean that sensations do not have plenty of properties, for if they are brain processes they certainly have lots of neurological properties. It only means that in speaking of them as being like or unlike one another we need not know or mention these properties.

This, then, is how I would reply to Objection 3. The strength of my reply depends on the possibility of our being able to report that one thing is like another without being able to state the respect in which it is like. I do not see why this should not be so. If we think cybernetically about the nervous system we can envisage it as able to respond to certain likenesses of its internal processes without being able to do more. It would be easier to build a machine which would tell us, say on a punched tape, whether or not two objects were similar, than it would be to build a machine which would report wherein the similarities consisted.

Objection 4. The after-image is not in physical space. The brain process is. So the after-image is not a brain process.

Reply. This is an *ignoratio elenchi.*[28] I am not arguing that the after-image is a brain process, but that the experience of having an after-image is a brain process. It is the *experience* which is reported in the introspective report. Similarly, if it is objected that the after-image is yellowy-orange, my reply is that it is the experience of seeing yellowy-orange that is being described, and this experience is not a yellowy-orange something. So to say that a brain process cannot be yellowy-orange is not to say that a brain process cannot in fact be the experience of having a yellowy-orange after-image. There is, in a sense, no such thing as an after-image or a sense-datum, though there is such a thing as the experience of having an image, and this experience is described indirectly in material object language, not in phenomenal language, for there is no such thing.[29] We describe the experience by saying, in effect, that it is like the experience we have when, for example, we really see a yellowy-orange patch on the wall. Trees and wallpaper can be green, but not the experience of seeing or imagining a tree or wallpaper. (Or if they are described as green or yellow this can only be in a derived sense.)

Objection 5. It would make sense to say of a molecular movement in the brain that it is swift or slow, straight or circular, but it makes no sense to say this of the experience of seeing something yellow.

Reply. So far we have not given sense to talk of experiences as swift or slow, straight or circular. But I am not claiming that "experience" and "brain process" mean the same or even that they have the same logic. "Somebody" and "the doctor" do not have the same logic, but this does not lead us to suppose that talking about somebody telephoning is talking about someone over and above, say, the doctor. The ordinary man when he reports an experience is reporting that something is going on, but he leaves it open as to what sort of thing is going on, whether in a material solid medium or

---

[26] The term is used by the famous American psychologist, E. C. Tolman (1886–1959), an advocate of the behaviorist approach to mental phenomena. "Raw feels" were what got *left out* of a behaviorist analysis of such things as perception, motivation, and discriminatory responses— the unobservable what-it-is-like-for-the-subject side of what the psychologists attempt to measure and predict. Ed.

[27] See B. A. Farrell, "Experience," *Mind,* LIX (1950), pp. 170–98, especially p. 174.

[28] *Ignoratio elenchi* is the fallacy of arguing to an irrelevant conclusion, or more loosely, of missing the point. In this case Smart says he is not claiming what the objector is arguing against: that an after-image is a brain process. Ed.

[29] Dr. J. R. Smythies claims that a sense-datum language could be taught independently of the material object language ('A Note on the Fallacy of "Phenomenological Fallacy"', *British Journal of Psychology,* XLVIII (1957), pp. 141–4). I am not so sure of this: there must be some public criteria for a person having got a rule wrong before we can teach him the rule. I suppose someone might *accidentally* learn colour words by Dr. Smythies' procedure. I am not, of course, denying that we can learn a sense-datum language in the sense that we can learn to report our experience. Nor would Place deny it.

perhaps in some sort of gaseous medium, or even perhaps in some sort of non-spatial medium (if this makes sense). All that I am saying is that "experience" and "brain process" may in fact refer to the same thing, and if so we may easily adopt a convention (which is not a change in our present rules for the use of experience words but an addition to them) whereby it would make sense to talk of an experience in terms appropriate to physical processes.

Objection 6. Sensations are private, brain processes are *public.* If I sincerely say "I see a yellowish-orange after-image," and I am not making a verbal mistake, then I cannot be wrong. But I can be wrong about a brain process. The scientist looking into my brain might be having an illusion. Moreover, it makes sense to say that two or more people are observing the same brain process but not that two or more people are reporting the same inner experience.

Reply. This shows that the language of introspective reports has a different logic from the language of material processes. It is obvious that until the brain-process theory is much improved and widely accepted there will be no *criteria* for saying "Smith has an experience of such-and-such a sort" *except* Smith's introspective reports.[30] So we have adopted a rule of language that (normally) what Smith says goes.

Objection 7. I can imagine myself turned to stone and yet having images, aches, pains, and so on.

Reply. I can imagine that the electrical theory of lightning is false, that lightning is some sort of purely optical phenomenon. I can imagine that lightning is not an electrical discharge. I can imagine that the Evening Star is not the Morning Star. But it is. All the objection shows is that "experience" and "brain process" do not have the same meaning. It does not show that an experience is not in fact a brain process.

This objection is perhaps much the same as one which can be summed up by the slogan: "What can

be composed of nothing cannot be composed of anything."[31] The argument goes as follows: on the brain-process thesis the identity between the brain process and the experience is a contingent one. So it is logically possible that there should be no brain process, and no process of any other sort either (no heart process, no kidney process, no liver process). There would be the experience but no "corresponding" physiological process with which we might be able to identify it empirically.

I suspect that the objector is thinking of the experience as a ghostly entity. So it is composed of something, not of nothing, after all. On his view it is composed of ghost stuff, and on mine it is composed of brain stuff. Perhaps the counter-reply will be[32] that the experience is simple and uncompounded, and so it is not composed of anything after all. This seems to be a quibble, for, if it were taken seriously, the remark "What can be composed of nothing cannot be composed of anything" could be recast as an *a priori* argument against Democritus and atomism and for Descartes and infinite divisibility.[33] And it seems odd that a question of this sort could be settled *a priori.* We must therefore construe the word "composed" in a very weak sense, which would allow us to say that even an indivisible atom is composed of something (namely, itself). The dualist cannot really say that an experience can be composed of nothing. For he holds that experiences are something over and above material processes, that is that they are a sort of ghost stuff. (Or perhaps ripples in an underlying ghost stuff.) I say that the dualist's hypothesis[34] is a perfectly intelligible one. But I say that experiences

---

[30] The improvement in neuroscience would have to be that we would have learnt which specific kinds of brain processes regularly occur when a human subject reports having a specific type of experience. Then the occurrence of those kinds of brain processes could serve as a criterion for the occurrence of that type of experience. ED.

[31] I owe this objection to Dr. C. B. Martin. I gather that he no longer wishes to maintain this objection, at any rate in its present form.

[32] Martin did not make this reply, but one of his students did.

[33] This and the preceding paragraph are not easy to read. The disagreement between the Cartesian and atomist positions is over the connection between having extension (taking up space, which is what "stuff" does) and divisibility. For Descartes, divisibility is an essential property of whatever is extended, whereas the atomists claimed that an atom, although *indivisible* and imperceptibly small, was nevertheless a piece of the same stuff that was in every other atom. In this context, then, the objection "What can be composed of nothing cannot be composed of anything" can be paraphrased as "What is indivisible cannot be composed of anything." The objector would go on to say that an experience is indivisible and so cannot be composed of anything, and therefore cannot be a brain process. ED.

[34] Descartes would not, of course, accept Smart's formula for the dualist position. As he says in the beginning of Meditation 6: "I have a clear idea of myself insofar as I am simply a thinking, non-extended thing. . . ." There can't be a non-extended stuff. ED.

are not to be identified with ghost stuff but with brain stuff. This is another hypothesis, and in my view a very plausible one. The present argument cannot knock it down *a priori*.

Objection 8. The "beetle in the box" objection (see Wittgenstein, *Philosophical Investigations,* section 293).[35] How could descriptions of experiences, if these are genuine reports, get a foothold in language? For any rule of language must have public criteria for its correct application.[36]

Reply. The change from describing how things are to describing how we feel is just a change from uninhibitedly saying "this is so" to saying "this looks so." That is, when the naive person might be tempted to say "There is a patch of light on the wall which moves whenever I move my eyes" or "A pin is being stuck into me," we have learned how to resist this temptation and say "It *looks as though* there is a patch of light on the wallpaper" or "It *feels as though* someone were sticking a pin into me." The introspective account tells us about the individual's state of consciousness in the same way as does "I see a patch of light" or "I feel a pin being stuck into me": it differs from the corresponding perception statement in so far as it withdraws any claim about what is actually going on in the external world. From the point of view of the psychologist, the change from talking about the environment to talking about one's perceptual sensations is simply a matter of disinhibiting certain reactions. These are reactions which one normally suppresses because one has learned that in the prevailing circumstances they are unlikely to provide a good indication of the state of the environment.[37] To say that something looks green to me is simply to say that my ex-

perience is like the experience I get when I see something that really is green. In my reply to Objection 3, I pointed out the extreme openness or generality of statements which report experiences. This explains why there is no language of private qualities. (Just as "someone," unlike "the doctor," is a colourless word.)[38]

If it is asked what is the difference between those brain processes which, in my view, are experiences and those brain processes which are not, I can only reply that it is at present unknown. I have been tempted to conjecture that the difference may in part be that between perception and reception (in D. M. MacKay's terminology)[39] and that the type of brain process which is an experience might be identifiable with MacKay's active "matching response."[40] This, however, cannot be the whole story, because sometimes I can perceive something unconsciously, as when I take a handkerchief out of a drawer without being aware that I am doing so. But at the very least we can classify the brain processes which are experiences as those brain processes which are, or might have been, causal conditions of those pieces of verbal behaviour which we call reports of immediate experience.

I have considered a number of objections to the brain-process thesis. I wish now to conclude with some remarks on the logical status of the thesis itself. U. T. Place seems to hold that it is a straight-out scientific hypothesis.[41] If so, he is partly right and partly wrong. If the issue is between (say) a brain process thesis and a heart thesis, or a liver

---

[35] Wittgenstein asks what it would be like if there were a community in which each person had a box into which only she could look. Suppose that it was part of the community's language to call what was in the box "the beetle." "Beetle" in this case would not be like words that "designate" an object—the words (such as "chair") that we have for designating publicly observable objects. For all we could know, every beetle might be different. Wittgenstein says that "pain" in our language is like "beetle" in its usage. In talking about this scenario Wittgenstein seems to assume, without saying, that what each person calls a "beetle" could not be described by means of predicates that would also apply to publicly accessible objects. What kind of thing is it? One could only say "It is the sort of thing that I find when I look into my box." ED.

[36] See fn. 10 in Reading 2 and my remarks at the end of Reading 2 for an explanation of "criteria" of usage. ED.

[37] I owe this point to Place, in correspondence.

[38] The "beetle in the box" objection is, *if it is sound,* an objection to *any* view, and in particular the Cartesian one, that introspective reports are genuine reports. So it is no objection to a weaker thesis that I would be concerned to uphold, namely, that if introspective reports of "experiences" are genuinely reports, then the things they are reports of are in fact brain processes.

[39] In MacKay's terminology, "reception" is the occurrence of sensory signals capable of eliciting reflexive responses such as withdrawal, whereas "perception" is the result of the sorts of analytical operations which the visual cortex, for example, performs on signals incoming from the retina, highlighting those features (such as edges and direction of movement of edges) that are relevant to the organism's adaptive or "matching" response. In other words, "perception" adds to "reception" the element of representation.

Obviously more is needed to respond adequately to the important question of just what is it about some brain processes (and not others) that enables them to be experiences. ED.

[40] See his article "Towards an Information-Flow Model of Human Behaviour," *British Journal of Psychology,* XLVII (1956), pp. 30–43.

[41] See Place's Abstract on p. 77 above. Ed.

thesis, or a kidney thesis, then the issue is a purely empirical one, and the verdict is overwhelmingly in favour of the brain. The right sorts of things don't go on in the heart, liver, or kidney, nor do these organs possess the right sort of complexity of structure. On the other hand, if the issue is between a brain-or-liver-or-kidney thesis (that is, some form of materialism) on the one hand and epiphenomenalism on the other hand, then the issue is not an empirical one. For there is no conceivable experiment which could decide between materialism and epiphenomenalism. This latter issue is not like the average straight-out empirical issue in science, but like the issue between the nineteenth-century English naturalist Philip Gosse [42] and the orthodox geologists and palaeontologists of his day. According to Gosse, the earth was created about 4000 B.C. exactly as described in Genesis, with twisted rock strata, "evidence" of erosion, and so forth, and all sorts of fossils, all in their appropriate strata, just as if the usual evolutionist story had been true. Clearly this theory is in a sense irrefutable: no evidence can possibly tell against it. Let us ignore the theological setting in which Philip Gosse's hypothesis had been placed, thus ruling out objections of a theological kind, such as "what a queer God who would go to such elaborate lengths to deceive us." Let us suppose that it is held that the universe just *began* in 4004 B.C. with the initial conditions just everywhere as they were in 4004 B.C., and in particular that our own planet began with sediment in the rivers, eroded cliffs, fossils in the rocks, and so on. No scientist would ever entertain this as a serious hypothesis, consistent though it is with all possible evidence. The hypothesis offends against the principles of parsimony and simplicity. There would be far too many brute and inexplicable facts. Why are pterodactyl bones just as they are? No explanation in terms of the evolution of pterodactyls from earlier forms of life would any longer be possible. We would have millions of facts about the world as it was in 4004 B.C. that just have to be *accepted*.

The issue between the brain-process theory and epiphenomenalism seems to be of the above sort. (Assuming that a behaviouristic reduction of introspective reports is not possible.) If it be agreed that there are no cogent philosophical arguments which force us into accepting dualism, and if the brain-process theory and dualism are equally consistent with the facts, then the principles of parsimony and simplicity seem to me to decide overwhelmingly in favor of the brain-process theory. As I pointed out earlier, dualism involves a large number of irreducible psycho-physical saws (whereby the "nomological danglers" dangle) of a queer sort, that just have to be taken on trust, and are just as difficult to swallow as the irreducible facts about the palaeontology of the earth with which we are faced on Philip Gosse's theory.

---

[42] See the entertaining account of Gosse's book *Omphalos* by Martin Gardner in *Fads and Fallacies in the Name of Science*, 2nd ed. (New York, 1957), pp. 124–7.

As you can see from many of his objections and replies, Smart shares Place's determination not to be forced into dualism by a phenomenal field populated with after-images, patches or flashes of color, and other items that can't be included in the world as described by physical science. Like Place, he stresses that just as lightning is not a second thing in addition to the electric discharge with which it is identical, so (the having of) a sensation or the experience of an after-image is not a second thing in addition to the brain process with which it is identical. If either of these were "second things," there would be a "phenomenal object" or a nonphysical process needing to be housed in an immaterial mind. In his reply to Objection 4, Smart says "There is, in a sense, no such thing as an after-image or a sense-datum, though there is such a thing as the experience of having an image. . . ." The sense in which there is no such thing is the sense in which there *is* such a thing as lightning or a rock. By "sense-datum" he means such items as the look of the lightning (its flashy yellowness). In his reply to Objection 2, he carefully distinguishes the look or sense-datum of lightning from "the publicly observable object." He would certainly not want to say about *publicly* observable objects that there are no such things, but only experiences of them. This distinction between the *look* of a publicly observable object and the *object* itself is of central importance to his materialist thesis, but it's not easy to maintain. To see the difficulty, let's shift our example to something more stable than lightning, for instance the iron stove described by Reichenbach (1938):

> We see the iron stove before us as a model of rigidity, solidity, immovability; but we know that its particles perform a violent dance, and that it resembles a swarm of dancing gnats more than the picture of solidity we attribute to it. . . . We do not see things, not even the concreta, as they objectively are but in a distorted form; we see a *substitute world*—not the world as it is, objectively speaking. (219–220)

The language Reichenbach uses to describe the vibratory motions of the atoms and molecules making up the walls of the stove is somewhat fanciful, but his point is straightforward: the *real* (scientifically described) stove is a vast assembly of shaking particles in mostly empty space. Notice that the *un*real "substitute" stove is described not in terms of *secondary qualities* such as color, but of *primary qualities* like solidity and continuous extension in three dimensions. I can't observe the "look" that the stove has for you, and I can't feel what it's like for you to touch it with your hands. But the both of us can see and measure with a ruler the width and height of its continuous front surface. What we both see (in the ruler and the stove) is decidedly *not* busy particles in mostly empty space. The "substitute" stove is, in Smart's language, a "publicly observable object," just like the "substitute" lightning that a group of us could point to in the night sky (a brief, spatially continuous, jagged and narrow illuminated path between cloud and earth, most unlike a stream of particles). But it is publicly observed to be other than how it is described in physical science. I don't mean to question the claim that lightning *is* an electric discharge. But such scientific identity claims are not as easy to understand as Smart and Place assume when they use them as models for the identity of experiences with brain processes.

There surely *are* such things as "publicly observable objects" which are very unlike their scientifically described counterparts. Can they fit into the world as described by science? For a materialist there's nowhere else.

REVIEW QUESTION

Look again at Smart's statement that "There is, in a sense, no such thing as an after-image or a sense-datum, though there is such a thing as the experience of having an image. . . ." (p. 91 above) To be a consistent materialist, does Smart have to say that the after-image is *nothing*—a nonentity? Can there be an experience of nothing? What should be said about the experience of a sunset?

7

The Identity Relation:
Selections from
Naming and Necessity

Saul Kripke

Saul Kripke is a professor of philosophy at Princeton University. His papers in logic, most notably those in modal logic which he published between the ages of nineteen and twenty-three, have been very influential. He is the author of two widely read books: *Naming and Necessity,* from which the selections in this reading are taken, and *Wittgenstein on Rules and Private Language* (1983).

Kripke's argument aims straight at the heart of the claim by Place and Smart that the identity of a conscious process with a brain process is, as Place says in his abstract, "a reasonable scientific hypothesis, not to be dismissed on logical grounds alone." Kripke's thesis is that there *are* logical grounds for regarding the identity theory as very implausible.

Place and Smart point out that despite the difference in *meaning* between subject and predicate phrases in scientific identities such as "Water = H_2O," or "Heat = average kinetic energy of molecules," each phrase has the same *referent*. Identities between neural and psychological terms would be like this too. So the great difference in meaning between such terms as "sensation" and "brain process" doesn't imply that they are two different things. Furthermore, since there is no contradiction in denying that water = H_2O, or heat = the average kinetic energy of molecules, Place and Smart infer that such identities are *contingent*. So with psychological and neural processes: as Smart puts it, "in so far as 'after-image' or 'ache' is a report of a process, it is a report of a process that *happens to be* a brain process" (p. 87). This contingency is supposed to explain the strong intuition many people claim to have that there is no intelligible relation between a brain process (as described in neuroscience) and what we introspectively recognize as an ache, so that it seems perfectly conceivable that one could occur without the other.

Kripke will argue that identities such as those about water and heat are in fact *necessary,* even though they are discovered **a posteriori;** and therefore psychophysical identities would also have to be necessary and thus strongly counter-intuitive.

I wish at this point to introduce something which I need in the methodology of discussing the theory of names that I'm talking about. We need the notion of 'identity across possible worlds' as it's usually and, as I think, somewhat misleadingly called,[1] to explicate one distinction that I want to make now. What's the difference between asking whether it's necessary that 9 is greater than 7 or whether it's necessary that the number of planets is greater than 7? Why does one show anything more about essence than the other? The answer to this might be intuitively 'Well, look, the number of planets might have been different from what it in fact is. It doesn't make any sense, though, to say that 9 might have been different from what it in fact is'. Let's use some terms quasi-technically. Let's call something *rigid designator* if in every possible world it designates the same object, a *nonrigid* or *accidental designator* if that is not the case. Of course we don't require that the objects exist in all possible worlds. Certainly Nixon might not have existed if his parents had not gotten married, in the normal course of things. When we think of a property as essential to an object we usually mean that it is true of that object in any case where it would have existed. A rigid designator of a necessary existent can be called *strongly rigid*.

One of the intuitive theses I will maintain in these talks is that *names* are rigid designators. Certainly they seem to satisfy the intuitive test mentioned above: although someone other than the U.S. President in 1970 might have been the U.S. President in 1970 (e.g., Humphrey might have), no one other than Nixon might have been Nixon. In the same way, a designator rigidly designates a certain object if it designates that object wherever the object exists; if, in addition, the object is a neces-

sary existent, the designator can be called *strongly rigid*. For example, 'the President of the U.S. in 1970' designates a certain man, Nixon; but someone else (e.g., Humphrey) might have been the President in 1970, and Nixon might not have; so this designator is not rigid.

In these lectures, I will argue, intuitively, that proper names are rigid designators, for although the man (Nixon) might not have been the President, it is not the case that he might not have been Nixon (though he might not have been *called* 'Nixon'). Those who have argued that to make sense of the notion of rigid designator, we must antecedently make sense of 'criteria of transworld identity' have precisely reversed the cart and the horse; it is *because* we can refer (rigidly) to Nixon, and stipulate that we are speaking of what might have happened to *him* (under certain circumstances), that 'transworld identifications' are unproblematic in such cases.[2]

* * *

To me Aristotle's most important properties consist in his philosophical work, and Hitler's in his murderous political role; both, as I have said, might have lacked these properties altogether. Surely there was no logical fate hanging over either Aristotle or Hitler which made it in any sense inevitable that they should have possessed the properties we regard as important to them; they could have had careers completely different from their actual ones. *Important* properties of an object need not be essential, unless 'importance' is used as a synonym for essence; and an object could have had properties very different from its most striking actual properties, or from the properties we use to identify it.

To clear up one thing which some people have asked me: When I say that a designator is rigid, and designates the same thing in all possible worlds, I mean that, as used in *our* language, it stands for that thing, when *we* talk about counterfactual[3] situations. I don't mean, of course, that there mightn't be counterfactual situations in which in the other possible worlds people actually spoke a different

---

From: Saul A. Kripke, *Naming and Necessity* (Cambridge, MA: Harvard University Press, 1980), pp. 47–49, 77–78, 97–100, 139–55. Copyright © 1972, 1980 by Saul A. Kripke. Reprinted with permission of the publisher.

[1] Misleadingly, because the phrase suggests that there is a special problem of 'transworld identification', that we cannot trivially stipulate whom or what we are talking about when we imagine another possible world. The term 'possible world' may also mislead; perhaps it suggests the 'foreign country' picture. I have sometimes used 'counterfactual situation' in the text; Michael Slote has suggested that 'possible state (or history) of the world' might be less misleading than 'possible world'. It is better still, to avoid confusion, not to say, 'In some possible world, Humphrey would have won' but rather, simply, 'Humphrey might have won'. The apparatus of possible worlds has (I hope) been very useful as far as the set-theoretic model-theory of quantified modal logic is concerned, but has encouraged philosophical pseudo-problems and misleading pictures.

---

[2] Of course I don't imply that language contains a name for every object. Demonstratives can be used as rigid designators, and free variables can be used as rigid designators of unspecified objects. Of course when we specify a counterfactual situation, we do not describe the whole possible world, but only the portion which interests us.

[3] A possible world is "counterfactual" insofar as it is an alternative to the actual world, the world that is factual. ED.

language. One doesn't say that 'two plus two equals four' is contingent because people might have spoken a language in which 'two plus two equals four' meant that seven is even. Similarly, when we speak of a counterfactual situation, we speak of it in English, even if it is part of the description of that counterfactual situation that we were all speaking German in that counterfactual situation. We say, 'suppose we had all been speaking German' or 'suppose we had been using English in a nonstandard way'. Then we are describing a possible world or counterfactual situation in which people, including ourselves, did speak in a certain way different from the way we speak. But still, in describing that world, we use *English* with *our* meanings and *our* references. It is in this sense that I speak of a rigid designator as having the same reference in all possible worlds. I also don't mean to imply that the thing designated exists in all possible worlds, just that the name refers rigidly to that thing. If you say 'suppose Hitler had never been born' then 'Hitler' refers here, still rigidly, to something that would not exist in the counterfactual situation described.

* * *

I think the next topic I shall want to talk about is that of statements of identity. Are these necessary or contingent? The matter has been in some dispute in recent philosophy. First, everyone agrees that descriptions can be used to make contingent identity statements. If it is true that the man who invented bifocals was the first Postmaster General of the United States—that these were one and the same—it's contingently true. That is, it might have been the case that one man invented bifocals and another was the first Postmaster General of the United States. So certainly when you make identity statements using descriptions—when you say 'the x such that ϕx and the x such that φx are one and the same'—that can be a contingent fact. But philosophers have been interested also in the question of identity statements between names. When we say 'Hesperus is Phosphorus' or 'Cicero is Tully', is what we are saying necessary or contingent? Further, they've been interested in another type of identity statement, which comes from scientific theory. We identify, for example, light with electromagnetic radiation between certain limits of wavelengths, or with a stream of photons. We identify heat with the motion of molecules; sound with

a certain sort of wave disturbance in the air; and so on. Concerning such statements the following thesis is commonly held. First, that these are obviously contingent identities: we've found out that light is a stream of photons, but of course it might not have been a stream of photons. Heat is in fact the motion of molecules; we found that out, but heat might not have been the motion of molecules. Secondly, many philosophers feel damned lucky that these examples are around. Now, why? These philosophers, whose views are expounded in a vast literature, hold to a thesis called 'the identity thesis' with respect to some psychological concepts. They think, say, that pain is just a certain material state of the brain or of the body, or what have you—say the stimulation of C-fibers. (It doesn't matter what.) Some people have then objected, 'Well, look, there's perhaps a *correlation* between pain and these states of the body; but this must just be a contingent correlation between two different things, because it was an empirical discovery that this correlation ever held. Therefore, by "pain" we must mean something different from this state of the body or brain; and, therefore, they must be two different things.'

Then it's said, 'Ah, but you see, this is wrong! Everyone knows that there can be contingent identities.' First, as in the bifocals and Postmaster General case, which I have mentioned before. Second, in the case, believed closer to the present paradigm, of theoretical identifications, such as light and a stream of photons, or water and a certain compound of hydrogen and oxygen. These are all contingent identities. They might have been false. It's no surprise, therefore, that it can be true as a matter of contingent fact and not of any necessity that feeling pain, or seeing red, is just a certain state of the human body. Such psychophysical identifications can be contingent facts just as the other identities are contingent facts. And of course there are widespread motivations—ideological, or just not wanting to have the 'nomological dangler' of mysterious connections not accounted for by the laws of physics, one to one correlations between two different kinds of thing, material states, and things of an entirely different kind, which lead people to want to believe this thesis.

I guess the main thing I'll talk about first is identity statements between names. But I hold the following about the general case. First, that characteristic theoretical identifications like 'Heat is the motion of molecules', are not contingent truths but necessary truths, and here of course I don't mean just physically necessary, but necessary in the highest degree—whatever that means. (Physical necessity *might* turn out to be necessity in the highest degree. But that's a question which I don't wish to prejudge. At least for this sort of example, it might be that when something's physically necessary, it always is necessary *tout court*.) Second, that the way in which these have turned out to be necessary truths does not seem to me to be a way in which the mind-brain identities could turn out to be either necessary or contingently true. So this analogy has to go. It's hard to see what to put in its place. It's hard to see therefore how to avoid concluding that the two are actually different.

* * *

According to the view I advocate, then, terms for natural kinds are much closer to proper names than is ordinarily supposed. The old term 'common name' is thus quite appropriate for predicates marking out species or natural kinds, such as 'cow' or 'tiger'. My considerations apply also, however, to certain mass terms for natural kinds, such as 'gold', 'water', and the like. It is interesting to compare my views to those of Mill. Mill counts both predicates like 'cow', definite descriptions, and proper names as names. He says of 'singular' names that they are connotative[4] if they are definite descriptions but non-connotative if they are proper names. On the other hand, Mill says that *all* 'general' names are connotative; such a predicate as 'human being' is defined as the conjunction of certain properties which give necessary and sufficient conditions for humanity—rationality, animality, and certain physical features.[5] The modern logical tradition, as represented by Frege[6] and Russell,[7] seems to hold that

Mill was wrong about singular names, but right about general names. More recent philosophy has followed suit, except that, in the case of both proper names and natural kind terms, it often replaces the notion of defining properties by that of a cluster of properties, only some of which need to be satisfied in each particular case. My own view, on the other hand, regards Mill as more-or-less right about 'singular' names, but wrong about 'general' names. *Perhaps* some 'general' names ('foolish', 'fat', 'yellow') express properties.[8] In a significant sense, such general names as 'cow' and 'tiger' do not, unless *being a cow* counts trivially as a property. Certainly 'cow' and 'tiger' are *not* short for the conjunction of properties a dictionary would take to define them, as Mill thought. Whether science can discover empirically that certain properties are *necessary* of cows, or of tigers, is another question, which I answer affirmatively.

Let's consider how this applies to the types of identity statements expressing scientific discoveries that I talked about before—say, that water is H_2O. It certainly represents a discovery that water is H_2O. We identified water originally by its characteristic feel, appearance and perhaps taste, (though the taste may usually be due to the impurities). If there were a substance, even actually, which had a completely different atomic structure from that of water, but resembled water in these respects, would we say that some water wasn't H_2O? I think not. We would say instead that just as there is a fool's gold there could be a fool's water; a substance which, though having the properties by which we originally identified water, would not in fact be water. And this, I think, applies not only to the actual world but even when we talk about counterfactual situations. If there had been a substance, which was a fool's water, it would then be fool's

[4]The pair "connotation/denotation" in Mill parallels the distinction of intension and extension more commonly used today. The *denotation* of a term is the object or set of objects to which it applies, and the *connotation* is the general meaning or aspect or condition under which an object is picked out as being denoted by the term. ED.

[5]Mill, *A System of Logic*.

[6]Gottlob Frege (1848–1925), a German mathematician and philosopher of mathematics, was one of the originators of modern symbolic or mathematical logic. ED.

[7]Bertrand Russell (1872–1970) was a prominent British philosopher, social commentator, and political activist. His philosophical output was enormous and influential, including seminal work in mathematical logic. ED.

[8]I am not going to give any criterion for what I mean by a 'pure property', or Fregean intension. It is hard to find unquestionable examples of what is meant. Yellowness certainly expresses a manifest physical property of an object and, relative to the discussion of gold above, can be regarded as a property in the required sense. Actually, however, it is not without a certain referential element of its own, for on the present view yellowness is picked out and rigidly designated as that external physical property of the object which we sense by means of the *visual impression of yellowness*. It does in this respect resemble the natural kind terms. The phenomenological quality of the sensation itself, on the other hand, can be regarded as a *quale* in some pure sense. Perhaps I am rather vague about these questions, but further precision seems unnecessary here.

water and not water. On the other hand if this substance can take another form—such as the polywater allegedly discovered in the Soviet Union, with very different identifying marks from that of what we now call water—it is a form of water because it is the same substance, even though it doesn't have the appearances by which we originally identified water.

Let's consider the statement 'Light is a stream of photons' or 'Heat is the motion of molecules'. By referring to light, of course, I mean something which we have some of in this room. When I refer to heat, I refer not to an internal sensation that someone may have, but to an external phenomenon which we perceive through the sense of feeling; it produces a characteristic sensation which we call the sensation of heat. Heat *is* the motion of molecules. We have also discovered that increasing heat corresponds to increasing motion of molecules, or, strictly speaking, increasing average kinetic energy of molecules. So temperature is identified with mean molecular kinetic energy. However I won't talk about temperature because there is the question of how the actual scale is to be set. It might just be set in terms of the mean molecular kinetic energy.[9] But what represents an interesting phenomenological discovery is that when it's hotter the molecules are moving faster. We have also discovered about light that light is a stream of photons; alternatively it is a form of electromagnetic radiation. Originally we identified light by the characteristic internal visual impressions it can produce in us, that make us able to see. Heat, on the other hand, we originally identified by the characteristic effect on one aspect of our nerve endings or our sense of touch.

Imagine a situation in which human beings were blind or their eyes didn't work. They were unaffected by light. Would that have been a situation in which light did not exist? It seems to me that it would not. It would have been a situation in which our eyes were not sensitive to light. Some creatures may have eyes not sensitive to light. Among such creatures are unfortunately some people, of course; they are called 'blind'. Even if all people had had

awful vestigial growths and just couldn't see a thing, the light might have been around; but it would not have been able to affect people's eyes in the proper way. So it seems to me that such a situation would be a situation in which there was light, but people could not see it. So, though we may identify light by the characteristic visual impressions it produces in us, this seems to be a good example of fixing a reference. We fix what light is by the fact that it is whatever, out in the world, affects our eyes in a certain way. But now, talking about counterfactual situations in which let's say, people were blind, we would not then say that since, in such situations, nothing could affect their eyes, light would not exist; rather we would say that that would be a situation in which light—the thing we have identified as that which in fact enables us to see—existed but did not manage to help us see due to some defect in us.

Perhaps we can imagine that, by some miracle, sound waves somehow enabled some creature to see. I mean, they gave him visual impressions just as we have, maybe exactly the same color sense. We can also imagine the same creature to be completely *insensitive* to light (photons). Who knows what subtle undreamt of possibilities there may be? Would we say that in such a possible world, it was sound which was light, that these wave motions in the air were light? It seems to me that, given our concept of light, we should describe the situation differently. It would be a situation in which certain creatures, maybe even those who were called 'people' and inhabited this planet, were sensitive not to light but to sound waves, sensitive to them in exactly the same way that we are sensitive to light. If this is so, once we have found out what light is, when we talk about other possible worlds we are talking about *this* phenomenon in the world, and not using 'light' as a phrase *synonymous* with 'whatever gives us the visual impression—whatever helps us to see'; for there might have been light and it not helped us to see; and even something else might have helped us to see. The way we identified light *fixed a reference*.

And similarly for other such phrases, such as 'heat'. Here heat is something which we have identified (and fixed the reference of its name) by its giving a certain sensation, which we call 'the sensation of heat'. We don't have a special name for

---

[9] Of course, there is the question of the relation of the statistical mechanical notion of temperature to, for example, the thermodynamic notion. I wish to leave such questions aside in this discussion.

this sensation other than as a sensation of heat. It's interesting that the language is this way. Whereas you might suppose it, from what I am saying, to have been the other way. At any rate, we identify heat and are able to sense it by the fact that it produces in us a sensation of heat. It might here be so important to the concept that its reference is fixed in this way, that if someone else detects heat by some sort of instrument, but is unable to feel it, we might want to say, if we like, that the concept of heat is not the same even though the referent is the same.

Nevertheless, the term 'heat' doesn't *mean* 'whatever gives people these sensations'. For first, people might not have been sensitive to heat, and yet the heat still have existed in the external world. Secondly, let us suppose that somehow light rays, because of some difference in their nerve endings, *did* give them these sensations. It would not then be heat but light which gave people the sensation which we call the sensation of heat.

Can we then imagine a possible world in which heat was not molecular motion? We can imagine, of course, having discovered that it was not. It seems to me that any case which someone will think of, which he thinks at first is a case in which heat—contrary to what is actually the case—would have been something other than molecular motion, would actually be a case in which some creatures with different nerve endings from ours inhabit this planet (maybe even we, if it's a contingent fact about us that we have this particular neural structure), and in which these creatures were sensitive to that something else, say light, in such a way that they felt the same thing that we feel when we feel heat. But this is not a situation in which, say, light would have been heat, or even in which a stream of photons would have been heat, but a situation in which a stream of photons would have produced the characteristic sensations which *we* call 'sensations of heat'.

Similarly for many other such identifications, say, that lightning is electricity. Flashes of lightning are flashes of electricity. Lightning is an electrical discharge. We can imagine, of course, I suppose, other ways in which the sky might be illuminated at night with the same sort of flash without any electrical discharge being present. Here too, I am inclined to say, when we imagine this, we imagine something with all the visual appearances of lightning but which is not, in fact, lightning. One could be told: this appeared to be lightning but it was not. I suppose this might even happen now. Someone might, by a clever sort of apparatus, produce some phenomenon in the sky which would fool people into thinking that there was lightning even though in fact no lightning was present. And you wouldn't say that that phenomenon, because it looks like lightning, was in fact lightning. It was a different phenomenon from lightning, which is the phenomenon of an electrical discharge; and this is not lightning but just something that deceives us into thinking that there is lightning.

What characteristically goes on in these cases of, let's say, 'heat is molecular motion'? There is a certain referent which we have fixed, for the real world and for all possible worlds, by a contingent property of it, namely the property that it's able to produce such and such sensations in us. Let's say it's a contingent property of heat that it produces such and such sensations in people. It's after all contingent that there should ever have been people on this planet at all. So one doesn't know *a priori* what physical phenomenon, described in other terms—in basic terms of physical theory—is the phenomenon which produces these sensations. We don't know this, and we've discovered eventually that this phenomenon is in fact molecular motion. When we have discovered this, we've discovered an identification which gives us an essential property of this phenomenon. We have discovered a phenomenon which in all possible worlds will be molecular motion—which could not have failed to be molecular motion, because that's what the phenomenon *is*.[10] On the other hand, the property by which we identify it originally, that of producing such and

---

[10] Some people have been inclined to argue that although certainly we cannot say that sound waves 'would have been heat' if they had been felt by the sensation which we feel when we feel heat, the situation is different with respect to a possible phenomenon, not present in the actual world, and distinct from molecular motion. Perhaps, it is suggested, there might be another form of heat other than 'our heat', which was not molecular motion; though no actual phenomenon other than molecular motion, such as sound, would qualify. Similar claims have been made for gold and for light. Although I am disinclined to accept these views, they would make relatively little difference to the substance of the present lectures. Someone who is inclined to hold these views can simply replace the terms 'light', 'heat', 'pain', etc., in the examples by 'our light', 'our heat', 'our pain', and the like. I therefore will not take the space to discuss this issue here.

such a sensation in us, is not a necessary property but a contingent one.

* * *

Usually, when a proper name is passed from link to link, the way the reference of the name is fixed is of little importance to us. It matters not at all that different speakers may fix the reference of the name in different ways, provided that they give it the same referent. The situation is probably not very different for species names, though the temptation to think that the metallurgist has a different concept of gold from the man who has never seen any may be somewhat greater. The interesting fact is that the way the reference is fixed seems overwhelmingly important to us in the case of sensed phenomena: a blind man who uses the term 'light', even though he uses it as a rigid designator for the very same phenomenon as we, seems to us to have lost a great deal, perhaps enough for us to declare that he has a different concept. ('Concept' here is used non-technically!) The fact that we identify light in a certain way seems to us to be *crucial,* even though it is not necessary; the intimate connection may create an *illusion* of necessity. I think that this observation, together with the remarks on property-identity above, may well be essential to an understanding of the traditional disputes over primary and secondary qualities.[11]

---

[11] To understand this dispute, it is especially important to realize that yellowness is not a dispositional property, although it is related to a disposition. Many philosophers for want of any other theory of the meaning of the term 'yellow', have been inclined to regard it as expressing a dispositional property. At the same time, I suspect many have been bothered by the 'gut feeling' that yellowness is a manifest property, just as much 'right out there' as hardness or spherical shape. The proper account, on the present conception is, of course, that the reference of 'yellowness' is fixed by the description 'that (manifest) property of objects which causes them, under normal circumstances, to be seen as yellow (i.e., to be sensed by certain visual impressions)'; 'yellow', of course, does not *mean* 'tends to produce such and such a sensation'; if we had had different neural structures, if atmospheric conditions had been different, if we had been blind, and so on, then yellow objects would have done no such thing. If one tries to revise the definition of 'yellow' to be, 'tends to produce such and such visual impressions under circumstances C', then one will find that the specification of the circumstances C either circularly involves yellowness or plainly makes the alleged definition into a scientific discovery rather than a synonymy. If we take the 'fixes a reference' view, then it is up to the physical scientist to identify the property so marked out in any more fundamental physical terms that he wishes.

Some philosophers have argued that such terms as 'sensation of yellow', 'sensation of heat', 'sensation of pain', and the like, could not be in the language unless they were identifiable in terms of external observable phenomena, such as heat, yellowness, and associated human behavior. I think that this question is independent of any view argued in the text.

Let us return to the question of theoretical identification. Theoretical identities, according to the conception I advocate, are generally identities involving two rigid designators and therefore are examples of the necessary *a posteriori*.[12] Now in spite of the arguments I gave before for the distinction between necessary and *a priori* truth, the notion of *a posteriori* necessary truth may still be somewhat puzzling. Someone may well be inclined to argue as follows: 'You have admitted that heat might have turned out not to have been molecular motion, and that gold might have turned out not to have been the element with the atomic number 79. For that matter, you also have acknowledged that Elizabeth II might have turned out not to be the daughter of George VI, or even to originate in the particular sperm and egg we had thought, and this table might have turned out to be made from ice made from water from the Thames. I gather that Hesperus might have turned out not to be Phosphorus. What then can you mean when you say that such eventualities are impossible? If Hesperus might have *turned out* not to be Phosphorus, then Hesperus might not have *been* Phosphorus. And similarly for the other cases: if the world could have *turned out* otherwise, it could have *been* otherwise. To deny this fact is to deny the self-evident modal principle that what is entailed by a possibility must itself be possible. Nor can you evade the difficulty by declaring the "might have" of "might have turned out otherwise" to be merely epistemic, in

---

[Keep in mind that Kripke's distinction between primary and secondary qualities, as originated by Locke (see fn. 23 on p. 90), is a distinction of qualities *in the object*. Qualities are causal powers of objects to produce in us certain sensations via their interactions with the kinds of sensory receptors and cognitive apparatus we happen to have. Primary qualities such as shape or speed are perceptible by us in more than one sensory modality (we can, for instance, both feel a sphere and see it). Thus primary qualities would tend to be less strongly associated with the way in which we "fix their reference" than would secondary qualities such as color or taste, which are restricted to one sensory modality. Nevertheless, as Kripke's theory implies, and as he insists above, our word for the *quality* of yellow, although fixed in its reference by visual experience, does not mean 'what causes us to have a certain sensation (yellow).' ED.]

[12] Reminder: Designators are said to be rigid insofar as they pick out the same object or set of objects in all possible worlds. 'Lightning (the flash of light associated with thunder)' and 'a stream of electrons between earth and some point in the sky' are both rigid designators. Therefore, if they are identical in any one case or world, they are identical in all possible ones. Thus their identity is necessary (without possible exception). However, since this identity was discovered by empirical, scientific methods, and could not have been deduced from the very concept of lightning, this necessity is *a posteriori*. ED.

the way that "Fermat's Last Theorem might turn out to be true and might turn out to be false" merely expresses our present ignorance, and "Arithmetic might have turned out to be complete" signals our former ignorance. In these mathematical cases, we may have been ignorant, but it was in fact mathematically[13] impossible for the answer to turn out other than it did. Not so in your favorite cases of essence and of identity between two rigid designators: it really is logically possible that gold should have turned out to be a compound, and this table might really have turned out not to be made of wood, let alone of a given particular block of wood. The contrast with the mathematical case could not be greater and would not be alleviated even if, as you suggest, there may be mathematical truths which it is impossible to know *a priori.*

Perhaps anyone who has caught the spirit of my previous remarks can give my answer himself, but there is a clarification of my previous discussion which is relevant here. The objector is correct when he argues that if I hold that this table could not have been made of ice, then I must also hold that it could not have turned out to be made of ice; *it could have turned out that P* entails that P could have been the case. What, then, does the intuition that the table might have turned out to have been made of ice or of anything else, that it might even have turned out not to be made of molecules, amount to? I think that it means simply that there might have been *a table* looking and feeling just like this one and placed in this very position in the room, which was in fact made of ice. In other words, I (or some conscious being) could have been *qualitatively in the same epistemic situation* that in fact obtains, I could have the same sensory evidence that I in fact have, about *a table* which was made of ice. The situation is thus akin to the one which inspired the counterpart theorists[14]; when I speak of the possibility of the table turning out to be made of various things, I am speaking loosely. *This* table itself could

not have had an origin different from the one it in fact had, but in a situation qualitatively identical to this one with respect to all the evidence I had in advance, the room could have contained *a table made of ice* in place of this one. Something like counterpart theory is thus applicable to the situation, but it applies only because we are *not* interested in what might have been true of *this particular* table, but in what might or might not be true of *a table* given certain evidence. It is precisely because it is *not* true that this table might have been made of ice from the Thames that we must turn here to qualitative descriptions and counterparts. To apply these notions to genuine *de re* modalities[15] is, from the present standpoint, perverse.

The general answer to the objector can be stated, then, as follows: Any necessary truth, whether *a priori* or *a posteriori,* could not have turned out otherwise. In the case of some necessary *a posteriori* truths, however, we can say that under appropriate qualitatively identical evidential situations,[16] an appropriate corresponding qualitative statement might have been false. The loose and inaccurate statement that gold might have turned out to be a compound should be replaced (roughly) by the statement that it is logically possible that there should have been a compound with all the properties originally known to hold of gold. The inaccurate statement that Hesperus might have turned out not to be Phosphorus should be replaced by the true contingency mentioned earlier in these lectures: two distinct bodies might have occupied, in the morning and the evening, respectively, the very positions actually occupied by Hesperus-Phosphorus-Venus.[17] The reason the example of Fermat's Last Theorem gives a different impression is that here no analogue suggests itself, except for

---

[13] "Mathematically" in this sentence, and "logically" in the next sentence, have roughly the same meaning. Ed.

[14] Counterpart theory, to which Kripke is opposed, holds that statements such as 'John, the retired actuary, might have been a professional race car driver' take the following possible-world analysis: There is a possible world in which some *counterpart* of John, resembling him in all respects except those respects that would enable him to be a race car driver rather than an actuary, is a race car driver. 'John', according to this theory and contrary to Kripke, is *not* a rigid designator picking out the identical individual in all possible worlds. Ed.

[15] *Modalities* such as possibility or necessity are *de re* insofar as they pertain to the object or situation referred to, and are *de dicto* insofar as they pertain to sentences. Ed.

[16] E.g. the sensory perceptions of water in certain situations (e.g., when drinking) could have been caused by something other than H_2O. But this does not imply that water itself (H_2O) could have been something chemically different. Ed.

[17] Some of the statements I myself make above may be loose and inaccurate in this sense. If I say, 'Gold *might* turn out not to be an element,' I speak correctly; 'might' here is *epistemic* and expresses the fact that the evidence does not justify *a priori* (Cartesian) certainty that gold is an element. I am also strictly correct when I say that the elementhood of gold was discovered *a posteriori*. If I say, 'Gold *might have* turned out not to be an element,' I seem to mean this metaphysically and my statement is subject to the correction noted in the text.

the extremely general statement that, in the absence of proof or disproof, it is possible for *a mathematical conjecture* to be either true or false.

I have not given any general paradigm for the appropriate corresponding qualitative contingent statement. Since we are concerned with how things might have turned out otherwise, our general paradigm is to redescribe both the prior evidence and the statement qualitatively and claim that they are only contingently related. In the case of identities, using two rigid designators, such as the Hesperus-Phosphorus case above, there is a simpler paradigm which is often usable to at least approximately the same effect. Let 'R$_1$' and 'R$_2$' be the two rigid designators which flank the identity sign. Then 'R$_1$' = 'R$_2$' is necessary if true. The references of 'R$_1$' and 'R$_2$', respectively, may well be fixed by nonrigid designators 'D$_1$' and 'D$_2$'. In the Hesperus and Phosphorus cases these have the form 'the heavenly body in such-and-such position in the sky in the evening (morning)'. Then although 'R$_1$' = 'R$_2$' is necessary, 'D$_1$' = 'D$_2$' may well be contingent, and this is often what leads to the erroneous view that 'R$_1$' = 'R$_2$' might have turned out otherwise.

I finally turn to an all too cursory discussion of the application of the foregoing considerations to the identity thesis. Identity theorists have been concerned with several distinct types of identifications: of a person with his body, of a particular sensation (or event or state of having the sensation) with a particular brain state (Jones's pain at 06:00 was his C-fiber stimulation at that time), and of *types* of mental states with the corresponding *types* of physical states (pain is the stimulation of C-fibers). Each of these, and other types of identifications in the literature, present analytical problems, rightly raised by Cartesian critics, which cannot be avoided by a simple appeal to an alleged confusion of synonymy with identity.[18] I should mention that there is of course no obvious bar, at least (I say cautiously) none which should occur to any intelligent thinker on a first reflection just before bedtime, to advocacy of some identity theses while doubting or denying others. For example, some philosophers have accepted the identity of particular sensations with particular brain states while denying the possibility of identities between mental and physical *types*.[19] I will concern myself primarily with the type-type identities, and the philosophers in question will thus be immune to much of the discussion; but I will mention the other kinds of identities briefly.

Descartes, and others following him, argued that a person or mind is distinct from his body, since the mind could exist without the body. He might equally well have argued the same conclusion from the premise that the body could have existed without the mind.[20] Now the one response which I regard as plainly inadmissible is the response which cheerfully accepts the Cartesian premise while denying the Cartesian conclusion. Let 'Descartes' be a name, or rigid designator, of a certain person, and let 'B' be a rigid designator of his body. Then if Descartes were indeed identical to B, the supposed identity, being an identity between two rigid designators, would be necessary, and Descartes could not exist without B and B could not exist without Descartes. The case is not at all comparable to the alleged analogue, the identity of the first Postmaster General with the inventor of bifocals. True, this

---

[18] These criticisms, in other words, are not based on the incorrect premise that the referents of any terms can be identical only if the terms have the same meaning. In Reading 5, U. T. Place alleges that this confusion is behind much of the intuitive resistance to identity claims about consciousness and brain processes. ED.

[19] Thomas Nagel and Donald Davidson are notable examples. Their views are very interesting, and I wish I could discuss them in further detail. It is doubtful that such philosophers wish to call themselves 'materialists'. Davidson, in particular, bases his case for his version of the identity theory on the supposed *impossibility* of correlating psychological properties with physical ones. The argument against **token-token identification** in the text *does* apply to these views.

[20] Of course, the body *does* exist without the mind and presumably without the person, when the body is a corpse. This consideration, if accepted, would already show that a person and his body are distinct. (See David Wiggins, 'On Being at the Same Place at the Same Time', *Philosophical Review*, Vol. 77 [1968], pp. 90–5.) Similarly, it can be argued that a statue is not the hunk of matter of which it is composed. In the latter case, however, one might say instead that the former is 'nothing over and above' the latter; and the same device might be tried for the relation of the person and the body. The difficulties in the text would not then arise in the same form, but analogous difficulties would appear. A theory that a person is nothing over and above his body in the way that a statue is nothing over and above the matter of which it is composed, would have to hold that (necessarily) a person exists if and only if his body exists and has a certain additional physical organization. Such a thesis would be subject to modal difficulties similar to those besetting the ordinary identity thesis, and the same would apply to suggested analogues replacing the identification of mental states with physical states. A further discussion of this matter must be left for another place. Another view which I will not discuss, although I have little tendency to accept it and am not even certain that it has been set out with genuine clarity, is the so-called functional state view of psychological concepts.

identity obtains despite the fact that there could have been a first Postmaster General even though bifocals had never been invented. The reason is that 'the inventor of bifocals' is not a rigid designator; a world in which no one invented bifocals is not ipso facto a world in which Franklin did not exist. The alleged analogy therefore collapses; a philosopher who wishes to refute the Cartesian conclusion must refute the Cartesian premise,[21] and the latter task is not trivial.

Let 'A' name a particular pain sensation, and let 'B' name the corresponding brain state, or the brain state some identity theorist wishes to identify with A. Prima facie, it would seem that it is at least logically possible that B should have existed (Jones's brain could have been in exactly that state at the time in question) without Jones feeling any pain at all, and thus without the presence of A. Once again, the identity theorist cannot admit the possibility cheerfully and proceed from there; consistency, and the principle of the necessity of identities using rigid designators, disallows any such course. If A and B were identical, the identity would have to be necessary. The difficulty can hardly be evaded by arguing that although B could not exist without A, being a pain is merely a contingent property of A, and that therefore the presence of B without pain does not imply the presence of B without A. Can any case of essence be more obvious than the fact that being a pain is a necessary property of each pain? The identity theorist who wished to adopt the strategy in question must even argue that being a sensation is a contingent property of A, for prima facie it would seem logically possible that B could exist without any sensation with which it might plausibly be identified. Consider a particular pain, or other sensation, that you once had. Do you find it at all plausible that that very sensation could have existed without being a sensation, the way a certain inventor (Franklin) could have existed without being an inventor?

I mention this strategy because it seems to me to be adopted by a large number of identity theorists. These theorists, believing as they do that the supposed identity of a brain state with the corresponding mental state is to be analyzed on the par-

adigm of the contingent identity of Benjamin Franklin with the inventor of bifocals, realize that just as his contingent activity made Benjamin Franklin into the inventor of bifocals, so some contingent property of the brain state must make it into a pain. Generally they wish this property to be one statable in physical or at least 'topic-neutral' language, so that the materialist cannot be accused of positing irreducible non-physical properties. A typical view is that being a pain, as a property of a physical state, is to be analyzed in terms of the 'causal role'[22] of the state,[23] in terms of the characteristic stimuli (e.g., pinpricks) which cause it and the characteristic behavior it causes. I will not go into the details of such analyses, even though I usually find them faulty on specific grounds in addition to the general modal considerations I argue here. All I need to observe here is that the 'causal role' of the physical state is regarded by the theorists in question as a contingent property of the state, and thus it is supposed to be a contingent property of the state that it is a mental state at all, let alone that it is something as specific as a pain. To repeat, this notion seems to me self-evidently absurd. It amounts to the view that the very pain I now have could have existed without being a mental state at all.[24]

I have not discussed the converse problem, which is closer to the original Cartesian consideration—namely, that just as it seems that the brain state could have existed without any pain, so it seems that the pain could have existed without the corresponding brain state. Note that being a brain state is evidently an essential property of B (the brain state). Indeed, even more is true: not only being a brain state, but even being a brain state of a specific type is an essential property of B. The configuration of brain cells whose presence at a

---

[21] I.e., that the mind and the body could exist apart from each other. Ed.

[22] This is the core idea of *functionalism*, which will be articulated in Readings 10 and 11. Ed.

[23] For example, David Armstrong, *A Materialist Theory of the Mind*, London and New York, 1968. See the discussion review by Thomas Nagel, *Philosophical Review*, 79 (1970), pp. 394–403; and David Lewis, 'An Argument for the Identity Thesis', *The Journal of Philosophy*, LXIII, 1 (Jan. 6, 1966), pp. 17–25.

[24] The mental, according to this theory, is by definition causal. Therefore, to say that a particular physical state is the pain I have now because this physical state just happens to be playing a certain kind of causal role amounts to the claim that the pain I now have not only might not have been a pain, but might not have been a mental state at all. Ed.

given time constitutes the presence of B at that time is essential to B, and in its absence B would not have existed. Thus someone who wishes to claim that the brain state and the pain are identical must argue that the pain A could not have existed without a quite specific type of configuration of molecules. If A = B, then the identity of A with B is necessary, and any essential property of one must be an essential property of the other. Someone who wishes to maintain an identity thesis cannot simply accept the Cartesian intuitions that A can exist without B, that B can exist without A, that the correlative presence of anything with mental properties is merely contingent to B, and that the correlative presence of any specific physical properties is merely contingent to A. He must explain these intuitions away, showing how they are illusory. This task may not be impossible; we have seen above how some things which appear to be contingent turn out, on closer examination, to be necessary. The task, however, is obviously not child's play, and we shall see below how difficult it is.

The final kind of identity, the one which I said would get the closest attention, is the type-type sort of identity exemplified by the identification of pain with the stimulation of C-fibers. These identifications are supposed to be analogous with such scientific type-type identifications as the identity of heat with molecular motion, of water with hydrogen hydroxide, and the like. Let us consider, as an example, the analogy supposed to hold between the materialist identification and that of heat with molecular motion; both identifications identify two types of phenomena. The usual view holds that the identification of heat with molecular motion and of pain with the stimulation of C-fibers are both contingent. We have seen above that since 'heat' and 'molecular motion' are both rigid designators, the identification of the phenomena they name is necessary. What about 'pain' and 'C-fiber stimulation'? It should be clear from the previous discussion that 'pain' is a rigid designator of the type, or phenomenon, it designates: if something is a pain it is essentially so, and it seems absurd to suppose that pain could have been some phenomenon other than the one it is. The same holds for the term 'C-fiber stimulation', provided that 'C-fibers' is a rigid designator, as I will suppose here. (The supposition is somewhat risky, since I know virtually nothing

about C-fibers, except that the stimulation of them is said to be correlated with pain.[25] The point is unimportant; if 'C-fibers' is not a rigid designator, simply replace it by one which is, or suppose it used as a rigid designator in the present context.) Thus the identity of pain with the stimulation of C-fibers, if true, must be *necessary*.

So far the analogy between the identification of heat with molecular motion and pain with the stimulation of C-fibers has not failed; it has merely turned out to be the opposite of what is usually thought—both, if true, must be necessary. This means that the identity theorist is committed to the view that there could not be a C-fiber stimulation which was not a pain nor a pain which was not a C-fiber stimulation. These consequences are certainly surprising and counterintuitive, but let us not dismiss the identity theorist too quickly. Can he perhaps show that the apparent possibility of pain not having turned out to be C-fiber stimulation, or of there being an instance of one of the phenomena which is not an instance of the other, is an illusion of the same sort as the illusion that water might not have been hydrogen hydroxide, or that heat might not have been molecular motion? If so, he will have rebutted the Cartesian, not, as in the conventional analysis, by accepting his premise while exposing the fallacy of his argument, but rather by the reverse—while the Cartesian argument, given its premise of the contingency of the identification, is granted to yield its conclusion, the premise is to be exposed as superficially plausible but false.

Now I do not think it likely that the identity theorist will succeed in such an endeavor. I want to

---

[25] I have been surprised to find that at least one able listener took my use of such terms as 'correlated with', 'corresponding to', and the like as already begging the question against the identity thesis. The identity thesis, so he said, is not the thesis that pains and brain states are correlated, but rather that they are identical. Thus my entire discussion presupposes the anti-materialist position that I set out to prove. Although I was surprised to hear an objection which concedes so little intelligence to the argument, I have tried especially to avoid the term 'correlated' which seems to give rise to the objection. Nevertheless, to obviate misunderstanding, I shall explain my usage. Assuming, at least *arguendo*, that scientific discoveries have turned out so as not to refute materialism from the beginning, both the dualist and the identity theorist agree that there is a correlation or correspondence between mental states and physical states. The dualist holds that the 'correlation' relation in question is irreflexive; the identity theorist holds that it is simply a special case of the identity relation. Such terms as 'correlation' and 'correspondence' can be used neutrally without prejudging which side is correct.

argue that, at least, the case cannot be interpreted as analogous to that of scientific identification of the usual sort, as exemplified by the identity of heat and molecular motion. What was the strategy used above to handle the apparent contingency of certain cases of the necessary *a posteriori?* The strategy was to argue that although the statement itself is necessary, someone could, *qualitatively* speaking, be in the same epistemic situation as the original, and in such a situation a *qualitatively* analogous statement could be false. In the case of identities between two rigid designators, the strategy can be approximated by a simpler one: Consider how the references of the designators are determined; if these coincide only contingently, it is this fact which gives the original statement its illusion of contingency. In the case of heat and molecular motion, the way these two paradigms work out is simple. When someone says, inaccurately, that heat might have turned out not to be molecular motion, what is true in what he says is that someone could have sensed a phenomenon in the same way we sense heat, that is, feels it by means of its production of the sensation we call 'the sensation of heat' (call it 'S'), even though that phenomenon was not molecular motion. He means, additionally, that the planet might have been inhabited by creatures who did not get S when they were in the presence of molecular motion, though perhaps getting it in the presence of something else. Such creatures would be, in some qualitative sense, in the same epistemic situation as we are, they could use a rigid designator for the phenomenon that causes sensation S in them (the rigid designator could even be 'heat'), yet it would not be molecular motion (and therefore not heat!), which was causing the sensation.

Now can something be said analogously to explain away the feeling that the identity of pain and the stimulation of C-fibers, if it is a scientific discovery, could have turned out otherwise? I do not see that such an analogy is possible. In the case of the apparent possibility that molecular motion might have existed in the absence of heat, what seemed really possible is that molecular motion should have existed without being *felt as heat,* that is, it might have existed without producing the sensation S, the sensation of heat. In the appropriate sentient beings is it analogously possible that a stimulation of C-fibers should have existed without being felt as pain? If this is possible, then the stimulation of C-fibers can itself exist without pain, since for it to exist without being *felt as pain* is for it to exist without there *being any* pain. Such a situation would be in flat out contradiction with the supposed necessary identity of pain and the corresponding physical state, and the analogue holds for any physical state which might be identified with a corresponding mental state. The trouble is that the identity theorist does not hold that the physical state merely *produces* the mental state, rather he wishes the two to be identical and thus *a fortiori* necessarily co-occurrent. In the case of molecular motion and heat there is something, namely, the sensation of heat, which is an intermediary between the external phenomenon and the observer. In the mental-physical case no such intermediary is possible, since here the physical phenomenon is supposed to be identical with the internal phenomenon itself. Someone can be in the same epistemic situation as he would be if there were heat, even in the absence of heat, simply by feeling the sensation of heat; and even in the presence of heat, he can have the same evidence as he would have in the absence of heat simply by lacking the sensation S. No such possibility exists in the case of pain and other mental phenomena. To be in the same epistemic situation that would obtain if one had a pain *is* to have a pain; to be in the same epistemic situation that would obtain in the absence of a pain *is* not to have a pain. The apparent contingency of the connection between the mental state and the corresponding brain state thus cannot be explained by some sort of qualitative analogue as in the case of heat.

We have just analyzed the situation in terms of the notion of a qualitatively identical epistemic situation. The trouble is that the notion of an epistemic situation qualitatively identical to one in which the observer had a sensation S simply *is* one in which the observer had that sensation. The same point can be made in terms of the notion of what picks out the reference of a rigid designator. In the case of the identity of heat with molecular motion the important consideration was that although 'heat' is a rigid designator, the reference of that designator was determined by an accidental property of the referent, namely the property of producing in us the sensation S. It is thus possible that a phenomenon should have been rigidly designated in the same way as a phenomenon of heat, with its reference also picked out by means of the sensation S, without that phenomenon being heat and therefore without its being molecular motion. Pain, on the other hand, is not picked out by one of its accidental properties; rather it is picked out by the property of being pain itself, by its immediate phenomenological quality. Thus pain, unlike heat, is not only rigidly designated by 'pain' but the reference of the designator is determined by an essential property of the referent. Thus it is not possible to say that although pain is necessarily identical with a certain physical state, a certain phenomenon can be picked out in the same way we pick out pain without being correlated with that physical state. If any phenomenon is picked out in exactly the same way that we pick out pain, then that phenomenon *is* pain.

Perhaps the same point can be made more vivid without such specific reference to the technical apparatus in these lectures. Suppose we imagine God creating the world; what does He need to do to make the identity of heat and molecular motion obtain? Here it would seem that all He needs to do is to create the heat, that is, the molecular motion itself. If the air molecules on this earth are sufficiently agitated, if there is a burning fire, then the earth will be hot even if there are no observers to see it. God created light (and thus created streams of photons, according to present scientific doctrine) before He created human and animal observers; and the same presumably holds for heat. How then does it appear to us that the identity of molecular motion with heat is a substantive scientific fact, that the mere creation of molecular motion still leaves God with the additional task of making molecular motion into heat? This feeling is indeed illusory, but what *is* a substantive task for the Deity is the task of making molecular motion felt as heat. To do this He must create some sentient beings to insure that the molecular motion produces the sensation S in them. Only after He has done this will there be beings who can learn that the sentence 'Heat is the motion of molecules' expresses an *a posteriori* truth in precisely the same way that we do.

What about the case of the stimulation of C-fibers? To create this phenomenon, it would seem that God need only create beings with C-fibers capable of the appropriate type of physical stimula-

tion; whether the beings are conscious or not is irrelevant here. It would seem, though, that to make the C-fiber stimulation correspond to pain, or be felt as pain, God must do something in addition to the mere creation of the C-fiber stimulation; He must let the creatures feel the C-fiber stimulation as *pain,* and not as a tickle, or as warmth, or as nothing, as apparently would also have been within His powers. If these things in fact are within His powers, the relation between the pain God creates and the stimulation of C-fibers cannot be identity. For if so, the stimulation could exist without the pain; and since 'pain' and 'C-fiber stimulation' are rigid, this fact implies that the relation between the two phenomena is not that of identity. God had to do some work, in addition to making the man himself, to make a certain man be the inventor of bifocals; the man could well exist without inventing any such thing. The same cannot be said for pain; if the phenomenon exists at all, no further work should be required to make it into pain.

In sum, the correspondence between a brain state and a mental state seems to have a certain obvious element of contingency. We have seen that identity is not a relation which can hold contingently between objects. Therefore, if the identity thesis were correct, the element of contingency would not lie in the relation between the mental and physical states. It cannot lie, as in the case of heat and molecular motion, in the relation between the phenomenon (= heat = molecular motion) and the way it is felt or appears (sensation S), since in the case of mental phenomena there is no 'appearance' beyond the mental phenomenon itself.

Here I have been emphasizing the possibility, or apparent possibility, of a physical state without the corresponding mental state. The reverse possibility, the mental state (pain) without the physical state (C-fiber stimulation) also presents problems for the identity theorists which cannot be resolved by appeal to the analogy of heat and molecular motion.

I have discussed similar problems more briefly for views equating the self with the body, and particular mental events with particular physical events, without discussing possible countermoves in the same detail as in the type-type case. Suffice it to say that I suspect that the considerations given indicate that the theorist who wishes to identify various particular mental and physical events will have to face problems fairly similar to those of the type-type theorist; he too will be unable to appeal to the standard alleged analogues.

That the usual moves and analogies are not available to solve the problems of the identity theorist is, of course, no proof that no moves are available. I certainly cannot discuss all the possibilities here. I suspect, however, that the present considerations tell heavily against the usual forms of materialism. Materialism, I think, must hold that a physical description of the world is a *complete* description of it, that any mental facts are 'ontologically dependent' on physical facts in the straight-forward sense of following from them by necessity. No identity theorist seems to me to have made a convincing argument against the intuitive view that this is not the case.[26]

---

[26] Having expressed these doubts about the identity theory in the text, I should emphasize two things: first, identity theorists have presented positive arguments for their view, which I certainly have not answered here. Some of these arguments seem to me to be weak or based on ideological prejudices, but others strike me as highly compelling arguments which I am at present unable to answer convincingly. Second, rejection of the identity thesis does not imply acceptance of Cartesian dualism. In fact, my view above that a person could not have come from a different sperm and egg from the ones from which he actually originated implicitly suggests a rejection of the Cartesian picture. If we had a clear idea of the soul or the mind as an independent, subsistent, spiritual entity, why should it have to have any necessary connection with particular material objects such as a particular sperm or a particular egg? A convinced dualist may think that my views on sperms and eggs beg the question against Descartes. I would tend to argue the other way; the fact the it is hard to imagine me coming from a sperm and egg different from my actual origins seems to me to indicate that we have no such clear conception of a soul or self. In any event, Descartes' notion seems to have been rendered dubious ever since Hume's critique of the notion of a Cartesian self. I regard the mind-body problem as wide open and extremely confusing.

According to Kripke, many identity theorists "cheerfully" accept Descartes' premise that mind and body could exist separately. But they deny his conclusion—that mind and body are different things. Instead, they say that there is increasing scientific evidence that mind and body (or some part thereof) happen not to be different things; they are contingently identical.

Strictly speaking, no identity theorist accepts Descartes' premise as it is found in the *Meditations*. There Descartes argues that we have "clear and distinct" ideas of mind (thinking substance) and body (extended substance) as separable, as having nothing in common. Whatever we can clearly and distinctly conceive as existing separately God can create that way. Hence, mind and body could have been created apart from each other, even if they happen to be linked by God's will in human beings. Arguably, Kripke has reversed the order of Descartes' argument. But this is not important to Kripke's argument. His point seems to be that there is a strong "intuition" (what Descartes would call a clear and distinct idea) that there is no intrinsic connection between what we are introspectively aware of as mental states, and what we describe as states of the brain. The conventional identity theory grants this intuition and attempts to satisfy it with the contingency of the identity between mental and brain states. Kripke then attacks the claim that these identities, whether understood as token or as type identities, are contingent. He argues this way:

Re token identity: Let P name a particular psychological state or process, and B a particular brain state or process.

1. P and B are rigid designators.
2. Identities between rigid designators are necessary.
3. Therefore, if 'P = B' is true, then it is necessarily true.

Re type identity: Let P_n name a type of psychological state or process, and B_n a type of brain state or process.

1. P_n and B_n are rigid designators.
2. Identities between rigid designators are necessary.
3. Therefore, if 'For any x, if x is P_n only if x is B_n and x is B_n only if x is P_n' is true, then it is necessarily true.

The bottom line for Kripke seems to be that identity theory fails to address the strong intuition that drives dualist arguments. Nevertheless, as he explains in his final note, Kripke rejects dualism. As far as he is concerned, the mind-body problem is still "wide open and extremely confusing."

REVIEW QUESTION

Imagine the following dialogue between a Kripkean (K) and an identity theorist (ID):

ID: In your final scenario about what God must do to create heat and to create pain, you say that in the case of heat, all that is needed is the kinetic energy of molecules, whereas in the case of pain "God must do something in addition to the mere creation of the C-fiber stimulation; He must let the creatures feel the C-fiber stimulation as *pain*." This is one of your all-too-frequent appeals to what you call "intuition," to show that the relation of pain to stimulation of C-fibers can't be identity.

K: But the intuition here isn't just a vague hunch. What we call heat behaves in a certain way out there in the world, quite apart from its effect on our sensory apparatus. It flows, conducts, and so on. And the kinetic theory explains that behavior. But the most exhaustive description of C-fiber activity doesn't tell me why there should be pain rather than pleasure or just not awareness at all.

ID: Of course it doesn't, because C-fiber activity in isolation is like a piston doing what a piston does apart from an engine. So, of course God must "do something in addition to the mere creation of the C-fiber stimulation," and it doesn't take someone with the intelligence of a deity to know that.

What do you think? Join the conversation.

8

Mind-Body Identity, Privacy, and Categories

Richard Rorty

Richard Rorty is an American philosopher who has taught at Princeton University from 1961 to 1982, and at the University of Virginia from 1982 to the present. He has published many books and papers covering a wide range of philosophical topics, including *Philosophy and the Mirror of Nature* (1979) and *Objectivity, Relativism and Truth* (1991).

Like Smart and Place, Rorty will argue for an Identity theory the scope of which extends only to sensations. However, he differs with Smart over how to handle this standard objection to the Identity theory:

> If sensations are brain processes of a certain sort, then the predicates that can be asserted of these brain processes must also be asserted of the corresponding sensations, and vice versa. But it is non-sense (a "conceptual confusion" or "category mistake") to speak of sensations having electric charges and brain processes being unmeasurable. Therefore, the Identity Theory is false.

Smart tries to avoid this objection by a topic-neutral translation of sensation reports into sentences about a "something going on" which is so void of predicates that it can safely be identified with a brain process. Rorty thinks the cause of materialism is better served by interpreting the identity claim not in the strict sense assumed by the above objection ("Sensations are certain brain processes), but rather in this sense: "What people now call 'sensations' are identical with certain brain processes." This second sense is like "What used to be called 'caloric fluid' is nothing but the motion of molecules." The "is" here is one of identity, but does not entail that the molecular motion should have all the attributes of caloric fluid. Furthermore, it makes perfect sense to make this identity statement about caloric fluid and also to say, as scientists now believe, that caloric fluid doesn't exist, and that we can get along perfectly well without even referring to it any more. Rorty concedes that the case of sensations is different because for the foreseeable future it seems overwhelmingly impractical to cease referring to them. However, he claims that no philosopher can rule out the possibility that with adequate progress in neuroscience we could get along quite well by replacing reference to sensations with reference to the relevant sorts of brain processes. We would then be likely to claim that there's no such thing as a sensation. So the only thing that prevents us *now* from saying that "There's no such thing as a sensation" is the sheer impracticality of never referring to them. Reference to sensations does not, therefore, imply a metaphysical commitment to there being anything more to sensation than the occurrence of a brain process.

Rorty calls Smart's version of the Identity theory the "translation" form, and his own the "disappearance" form. Rorty's position is now known as Eliminative Materialism.

1. INTRODUCTORY

Current controversies about the Mind–Body Identity Theory form a case-study for the investigation of the methods practiced by linguistic philosophers.[1] Recent criticisms of these methods question that philosophers can discern lines of demarcation between "categories"[2] of entities, and thereby diagnose "conceptual confusions" in "reductionist" philosophical theories.[3] Such doubts arise once we see that it is very difficult, and perhaps impossible, to draw a firm line between the "conceptual" and the "empirical," and thus to differentiate between a statement embodying a conceptual confusion and one that expresses a surprising empirical result. The proponent of the Identity Theory (by which I mean one who thinks it sensible to assert that empirical inquiry will discover that *sensations* (not thoughts) are identical with certain brain processes[4]) holds that his opponents' arguments' to the effect that empirical inquiry *could* not identify brain-processes and sensations are admirable il-

lustrations of this difficulty. For, he argues, the classifications of linguistic expressions that are the ground of his opponents' criticism are classifications of a language which is as it is because it is the language spoken at a given stage of empirical inquiry. But the sort of empirical results that would show brain processes and sensations to be identical would also bring about changes in our way of speaking. These changes would make these classifications out of date. To argue against the Identity Theory on the basis of the way we talk now is like arguing against an assertion that supernatural phenomena are identical with certain natural phenomena on the basis of the way in which superstitious people talk. There is simply no such thing as a method of classifying linguistic expressions that has results guaranteed to remain intact despite the results of future empirical inquiry. Thus in this area (and perhaps in all areas) there is no method which will have the sort of magisterial neutrality of which linguistic philosophers fondly dream.

In this paper I wish to support this general line of argument. I shall begin by pressing the claims of the analogy between mental events and supernatural events. Then I shall try to rebut the objection which seems generally regarded as fatal to the claims of the Identity Theory—the objection that "privacy" is of the essence of mental events, and thus that a theory which holds that mental events might *not* be "private" is *ipso facto* confused. I shall conclude with some brief remarks on the implications of my arguments for the more general metaphilosophical[5] issues at stake.

2. THE TWO FORMS OF THE IDENTITY THEORY

The obvious objection to the identity theory is that "identical" either means a relation such that

$$(x)\,(y)\,[(x = y) \supset (F)\,(Fx = Fy)]$$

From "Mind-Body Identity, Privacy, and Categories," *The Review of Metaphysics* XIX, 1 (September, 1965): 24–54. Reprinted with permission of the editor.

[1] "Linguistic" philosophers are also called "ordinary-language" philosophers. Ryle is a prominent example of this approach to philosophy. For an explanation of this philosophical method, see my opening remarks for Reading 2. ED.

[2] See the explanation of the term "category" in my opening remarks for Reading 2. ED.

[3] A Rylean behaviorist might argue that the identification of the mind with the brain is a category mistake, and thus a conceptual confusion, because it identifies something (mind) which belongs to the category of behavior or disposition/capacity for behavior with something (the brain) that belongs to the category of body or body part. According to this objection, the reductionist claim that the mind is *nothing but* the brain is a "conceptual" error, like supposing that a university is a building. ED.

[4] A proponent of the Identity Theory is usually thought of as one who predicts that empirical inquiry *will* reach this result—but few philosophers in fact stick their necks out in this way. The issue is not the truth of the prediction, but whether such a prediction makes sense. Consequently, by "Identity Theory" I shall mean the assertion that it does make sense.

I include only sensations within the scope of the theory because the inclusion of thoughts would raise a host of separate problems (about the reducibility of intentional and semantic discourse to statements about linguistic behavior), and because the form of the Identity Theory which has been most discussed in the recent literature restricts itself to a consideration of sensations.

[5] The prefix *meta-* in front of *philosophy* signifies "higher-order" or "second-order." Metaphilosophy is philosophical reflection or discourse about philosophy or philosophical method, just as a metalanguage is a language about a language. ED.

(the relation of "strict identity")[6] or it does not. If it does, then we find ourselves forced into

> saying truthfully that physical processes such as brain processes are dim or fading or nagging or false, and that mental phenomena such as after-images are publicly observable or physical or spatially located or swift,[7]

and thus using meaningless expressions, for

> we may say that the above expressions are meaningless in the sense that they commit a category mistake; i.e., in forming these expressions we have predicated predicates, appropriate to one logical category, of expressions that belong to a different logical category. This is surely a conceptual mistake.[8]

But if by "identical" the Identity Theory does not mean a relation of strict identity, then what relation *is* intended? How does it differ from the mere relation of "correlation" which, it is admitted on all sides, might without confusion be said to hold between sensations and brain-processes?[9]

Given this dilemma, two forms of the identity theory may be distinguished. The first, which I shall call the *translation* form, grasps the first horn, and attempts to show that the odd-sounding expressions mentioned above do not involve category-mistakes, and that this can be shown by suitable translations into "topic neutral" language of the sentences in which these terms are originally used.[10] The second, which I shall call the *disappearance* form, grasps the second horn, and holds that the relation in question is not strict identity, but rather the sort of relation which obtains between, to put it crudely, existent entities and non-existent entities when reference to the latter once served (some of) the purposes presently served by reference to the former—the sort of relation that holds,

e.g., between "quantity of caloric fluid" and "mean kinetic energy of molecules."[11] There is an obvious sense of "same" in which what used to be called "a quantity of caloric fluid" is *the same thing* as what is now called a certain mean kinetic energy of molecules, but there is no reason to think that all features truly predicated of the one may be sensibly predicated of the other.[12] The translation form of the theory holds that if we really understood what we were saying when we said things like "I am having a stabbing pain" we should see that since we are talking about "topic-neutral" matters, we might, for all we know, be talking about brain-processes. The disappearance form holds that it is unnecessary to show that statements about quantities of caloric fluid, when properly understood, may be seen to be topic-neutral statements.[13]

From the point of view of this second form of the theory, it is a mistake to assume that "X's are nothing but Y's" entails "All attributes meaningfully predictable of X's are meaningfully predicated of Y's," for this assumption would forbid us to ever express the results of scientific inquiry in terms of

---

when I have my eyes open, am awake, and there is an orange illuminated in good light in front of me, that is, when I really see an orange'" (p. 167). For criticisms of Smart's program of translation, see Cornman, op. cit.; Jerome Shaffer, "Could Mental States Be Brain Processes?," *Journal of Philosophy,* 60 (1963), pp. 160–166. See also the articles cited in the first footnote to Smart's own article.

[11] During the eighteenth century it was widely accepted that heat was a weightless fluid called *caloric,* and that heat conduction between bodies consisted in the flow of this fluid from one to another. This conception of heat was replaced by the notion that heat conduction is an energy transfer. Heat is now understood as the mean kinetic energy of the atoms and molecules making up a body, an energy they have in virtue of their vibratory, rotatory, or translational motion. ED.

[12] No statement of the disappearance form of the theory with which I am acquainted is as clear and explicit as Smart's statement of the translation form. See, however, Feyerabend, "Mental Events and the Brain," *Journal of Philosophy,* 60 (1963), pp. 295–296, and "Materialism and the Mind-Body Problem," *The Review of Metaphysics,* 17 (1963), pp. 49–67. See also Wilfrid Sellars, "The Identity Approach to the Mind-Body Problem," *ibid.,* 18 (1965). My indebtedness to this and other writings of Sellars will be obvious in what follows.

[13] Both forms agree, however, on the requirements which would have to be satisfied if we are to claim that the empirical discovery in question has been made. Roughly, they are (1) that one-one or one-many correlations could be established between every type of sensation and some clearly demarcated kind(s) of brain-processes; (2) that every known law which refers to sensations would be subsumed under laws about brain-processes; (3) that new laws about sensations be discovered by deduction from laws about brain-processes.

---

[6] I.e., if any two things, x and y, are identical, then for any property F, x is F if and only if y is F. ED.

[7] James Cornman, "The Identity of Mind and Body," *Journal of Philosophy,* 59 (1962), p. 490.

[8] Cornman, p. 490.

[9] Even Descartes would admit such a correlation. ED.

[10] Cf. J. J. C. Smart, "Sensations and Brain Processes," reprinted in *The Philosophy of Mind,* ed. by V. C. Chappell (Englewood Cliffs, 1962), pp. 160–172, esp. pp. 166–168, and especially the claim that "When a person says 'I see a yellowish-orange after-image' he is saying something like this: 'There is something going on which is like what is going on

(in Cornman's useful phrase) "cross-category identity."[14] It would seem that the verb in such statements as "Zeus's thunderbolts are discharges of static electricity" and "Demoniacal possession is a form of hallucinatory psychosis" is the "is" of identity, yet it can hardly express *strict* identity. The disappearance form of the Identity Theory suggests that we view such statement as elliptical for e.g., "What people used to call 'demoniacal possession' is a form of hallucinatory psychosis," where the relation in question *is* strict identity. Since there is no reason why "what people call 'X'" should be in the same category (in the Rylean sense) as "X," there is no need to claim, as the translation form of the theory must, that topic-neutral translation of statements using "X" are possible.

In what follows, I shall confine myself to a discussion and defense of the disappearance form of the theory. My first reason for this is that I believe that the analysis of "Sensations are identical with certain brain-processes" proposed by the disappearance form (viz., "What people now call 'sensations' are identical with certain brain-processes") accomplishes the same end as the translation form's program of topic-neutral translation—namely, avoiding the charge of "category-mistake," while preserving the full force of the traditional materialist position. My second reason is that I believe that an attempt to defend the translation form will inevitably get bogged down in controversy about the adequacy of the proposed topic-neutral translations of statements about sensations.[15] There is obviously a sense of "adequate translation" in which the topic-neutrality of the purported translations *ipso facto* makes them inadequate. So the proponent of the translation form of the theory will have to fall back on a weaker sense of "adequate translation." But the weaker this sense becomes, the less im-

pressive is the claim being made, and the less difference between the Identity Theory and the noncontroversial thesis that certain brain-processes may be constantly correlated with certain sensations.

3. THE ANALOGY BETWEEN DEMONS AND SENSATIONS

At first glance, there seems to be a fatal weakness in the disappearance form of the Identity Theory. For normally when we say "What people call 'X's' are nothing but Y's" we are prepared to add that "There are no X's." Thus when, e.g., we say that "What people call 'caloric fluid' is nothing but the motion of molecules" or "What people call 'witches' are nothing but psychotic women" we are prepared to say that there are no witches, and no such thing as caloric fluid. But it seems absurd to say that there might turn out to be no such thing as sensations.

To see that this disanalogy is not fatal to the Identity Theory, let us consider the following situation. A certain primitive tribe holds the view that illnesses are caused by demons—a different demon for each sort of illness. When asked what more is known about these demons than that they cause illness, they reply that certain members of the tribe—the witch doctors—can see, after a meal of sacred mushrooms, various (intangible) humanoid forms on or near the bodies of patients. The witch doctors have noted, for example, that the blue demon with a long nose accompanies epileptics, a fat red one accompanies sufferers from pneumonia, etc., etc. They know such further facts as that the fat red demon dislikes a certain sort of mold which the witch doctors give people who have pneumonia. (There are various competing theories about what demons do when not causing diseases, but serious witch doctors regard such speculations as unverified and profitless.)

If we encountered such a tribe, we would be inclined to tell them that there are no demons. We would tell them that the diseases were caused by germs, viruses, and the like. We would add that the witch doctors were not seeing demons, but merely having hallucinations. We would be quite right, but would we be right on *empirical* grounds? What empirical criteria, built into the demon-talk of the

---

[14] Cornman, p. 492.

[15] Take for example "I am having a bluish after-image." Place would want to translate it as "Something is going on like what goes on when I'm looking at a physical object with a blue surface." But it's also in an important way *unlike* what I experience when looking at a *physical* object: The after-image moves with my eyes. The colors "out there" in the public world stay put; if my eyes move, they lose sight of the colored surface. The topic-neutral translation needs to assert a resemblance between what after-image reports are about and what one is reporting when looking at a physical object under normal conditions. But after-images have a non-resembling residue which is *distinctive* and therefore, one might argue, the topic-neutral translation is inadequate. ED.

tribe, go unsatisfied? What predictions which the tribesmen make fail to come true? If there are none, a sophisticated witch-doctor may reply that all modern science can do is to show (1) that the presence of demons is constantly correlated with that of germs, viruses, and the like, and (2) that eating certain mushrooms sometimes makes people think they see things that aren't really there. This is hardly sufficient to show that there are no demons. At best, it shows that if we forgot about demons, then (a) a simpler account of the cause and cure of the disease and (b) a simpler account of why people make the perceptual reports they do, may be given.

What do we reply to such a sophisticated witch-doctor? I think all that we would have left to say is that the simplicity of the accounts which can be offered if we forget about the demons *is* an excellent reason for saying there are no such demons. Demon-discourse is one way of describing and predicting phenomena, but there are better ways. We *could* (as the witch-doctor urges) tack demon-discourse on to the modern science by saying, first, that the witch-doctors (unlike drunkards and psychotics) really do see intangible beings (about whom, alas, nothing is known save their visual appearances). If we did so, we would retain all the predictive and explanatory advantage of modern science. We would know as much about the cause and cure of disease, and about hallucinations, as we did before. We would, however, be burdened with problems which we did not have before: the problem of why demons are visible only to witch-doctors, and the problem of why germs cannot cause diseases all by themselves. We avoid both problems by saying that demons do not exist. The witch-doctor may remark that this use of Occam's Razor has the same advantage as that of theft over honest toil. To such a remark, the only reply could be an account of the practical advantages gained by the use of the Razor in the past.

Now the Identity Theorist's claim is that sensation may be to the future progress of psychophysiology as demons are to modern science. Just as we now want to deny that there are demons, future science may want to deny that there are sensations. The only obstacle to replacing sensation-discourse with brain-discourse seems to be that sensation-statements have a reporting as well as an explanatory function. But the demon case makes clear that

the discovery of a new way of explaining the phenomena previously explained by reference to a certain sort of entity, *combined with a new account of what is being reported by observation-statements about that sort of entity,* may give good reason for saying that there are no entities of that sort. The absurdity of saying "Nobody has ever felt a pain" is no greater than that of saying "Nobody has ever seen a demon," *if* we have a suitable answer to the question "What *was* I reporting when I said I felt a pain?" To this question, the science of the future may reply "You were reporting the occurrence of a certain brain-process, and it would make life simpler for us if you would, in the future, say 'My C-fibers are firing' instead of saying 'I'm in pain'." In so saying, he has as good a prima facie case as the scientist who answers the witch-doctor's question "What *was* I reporting when I reported a demon?" by saying "You were reporting the content of your hallucination, and it would make life simpler if, in the future, you would describe your experiences in those terms."

Given this prima facie analogy between demons and sensation, we can now attend to some disanalogies. We may note, first, that there is no simple way of filling in the blank in "What people called 'demons' are nothing but _____." For neither "hallucinatory contents" nor "germs" will do. The observational and the explanatory roles of "demon" must be distinguished. We need to say something like "What people explained by reference to demons can be explained better by reference to germs, viruses, etc." Because of the need for a relatively complex account of how we are to get along without reference to demons, we cannot *identify* "What we called 'demons'" with anything. So, instead, we simply deny their existence. In the case of sensations, however, we can give a relatively simple account of how to get along in the future. Both the explanatory *and* the reporting functions of statements about sensations can be taken over by statements about brain-processes. Therefore, we are prepared to identify "What we called 'sensations'" with brain-processes, and to say "What we called 'sensations' turn out to be nothing but brain-processes."

Thus this disanalogy does not have the importance which it appears to have at first. In both the demon case and the sensation case, the proposed reduction has the same pragmatic consequences: namely, that we should stop asking questions about the causal and/or spatio-temporal relationships holding between the "reduced" entities (demons, sensations) and the rest of the universe, and replace these with questions about the relationships holding between certain other entities (germs, hallucinatory experience, brain-processes) and the rest of the universe. It happens, for the reasons just sketched, that the proposed reduction is put in the form of a denial of existence in one case, and of an identification in another case. But "There are no demons" and "What people call 'sensations' are nothing but brain processes" can both equally well be paraphrased as "Elimination of the referring use of the expression in question ('demon,' 'sensation') from our language would leave our ability to describe and predict undiminished."

Nevertheless, the claim that there might turn out to be no such thing as a "sensation" seems scandalous. The fact that a witch-doctor might be scandalized by a similar claim about demons does not, in itself, do much to diminish our sense of shock. In what follows, I wish to account for this intuitive implausibility. I shall argue that it rests *solely* upon the fact that elimination of the referring use of "sensation" from our language would be in the highest degree *impractical*. If this can be shown, then I think that the Identity Theorist will be cleared of the charge of "conceptual confusion" usually leveled against him. Rather than proceeding directly to this argument, however, I shall first consider a line of argument which has often been used to show that he is guilty of this charge. Examining this line of argument will permit me to sketch in greater detail what the Identity Theorist is and is not saying.

4. THE ELIMINABILITY OF OBSERVATION TERMS

The usual move made by the opponents of the Identity Theory is to compare suggested reduction of sensations to brain-processes to certain other cases in which we say that "X's turn out to be nothing but Y's." There are two significantly different classes of cases and it might seem that the Identity Theorist confuses them. First, there is the sort of case in which both "X" and "Y" are used to refer to observable entities, and the claim that "What

people called 'X's' are nothing but Y's" is backed up by pointing out that the statement "This is an X" commits one to an empirically false proposition. For example, we say that "What people called 'unicorn horns' are nothing but narwhal horns," and urge that we cease to respond to a perceptual situation with "This is a unicorn horn." We do this because "This is a unicorn horn" commits one to the existence of unicorns. Let us call this sort of case *identification of observables with other observables*. Second, there is the sort of case in which "X" is used to refer to an observable entity and "Y" is used to refer to an unobservable entity. Here we do not (typically) back up the claim that "What people called 'X's' are nothing but 'Y's" by citing an empirically false proposition presupposed by "This is an X." For example, the statement that "What people call 'tables' are nothing but clouds of molecules" does not suggest, or require as a ground, that people who say "This is a table" hold false beliefs. Rather, we are suggesting that something *more* has been found out about the sort of situation reported by "This is a table." Let us call this second sort of case *identification of observables with theoretical entities*.

It seems that we cannot assimilate the identification of sensations with brain-processes to either of these cases. For, unlike the typical case of identification of observables with other observables, we do not wish to say that people who have reported sensations in the past have (necessarily) any empirically disconfirmed beliefs. People are not wrong about sensations in the way in which they were wrong about "unicorn horns."[16] Again, unlike the typical case of the identification of observables with theoretical entities, we do not want to say that brain-processes are "theoretical" or unobservable. Furthermore, in cases in which we identify an observable X with an unobservable Y, we are usually willing to accept the remark that "That does not show that there are no X's." The existence of tables is not (it would seem) impugned by their identification with clouds of electrons, as the existence of unicorn horns is impugned by their identification with narwhal horns. But a defender of the disappearance form of the Identity Theory *does* want to impugn the existence of sensations.

---

[16] Similarly, the belief of members of the "primitive tribe" in demons was not empirically disconfirmed. Ed.

Because the claim that "What people call 'sensations' may turn out to be nothing but brain-processes" cannot be assimilated to either of these cases, it has been attacked as trivial or incoherent. The following dilemma is posed by those who attack it: either the Identity Theorist claims that talk about sensations presupposes some empirically disconfirmed belief (and what could it be?) or the "identity" which he has in mind is the uninteresting[17] sort of identity which holds between tables and clouds of molecules (mere "theoretical replaceability").

The point at which the Identity Theorist should attack this dilemma is the premiss invoked in stating the second horn—the premiss that the identification of tables with clouds of molecules does not permit us to infer to the non-existence of tables. This premiss is true, but *why* is it true? That there is room for reflection here is apparent when we place the case of tables side-by-side with the case of demons. If there is any point to saying that tables are nothing but clouds of molecules it is presumably to say that, in principle, we could stop making a referring use of "table," and of any extensionally equivalent term, and still leave our ability to describe and predict undiminished. But this would seem just the point of (and the justification for) saying that there are no demons. Why does the realization that nothing would be lost by the dropping of "table" from our vocabulary still leave us with the conviction that there are tables, whereas the same realization about demons leaves us with the conviction that there are no demons? I suggest that the only answer to this question which will stand examination is that although we could *in principle* drop "table," it would be monstrously inconvenient to do so, whereas it is both possible in principle and convenient in practice to drop "demon." The reason "But there still are tables" sounds so plausible is that nobody would dream of suggesting that we stop reporting our experiences in table-talk and start reporting them in molecule-talk. The reason "There are no demons" sounds so plausible is that we are quite willing to suggest that the witch-doctors stop reporting their experiences in demon-

talk and start reporting them in hallucination-talk.

A conclusive argument that this practical difference is the *only* relevant difference would, obviously, canvass all the other differences which might be noted. I shall not attempt this. Instead, I shall try to make my claim plausible by sketching a general theory of the conditions under which a term may cease to have a referring use without those who made such a use being convicted of having held false beliefs.

Given the same sorts of correlations between X's and Y's, we are more likely to say "X's are nothing but Y's" when reference to X's is habitually made in non-inferential reports, and more likely to say "There are no X's" when such reference is never or rarely made. (By "non-inferential report" I mean a statement in response to which question like "How did you know?" "On what evidence do you say . . . ?" and "What leads you to think . . . ?" are normally considered misplaced and unanswerable, but which is nonetheless capable of empirical confirmation.) Thus we do not say that the identification of temperature with the kinetic energy of molecules shows that there is no such thing as temperature, since "temperature" originally (i.e., before the invention of thermometers) stood for something which was always reported non-inferentially, and still is frequently so reported. Similarly for all identifications of familiar macro-objects with unfamiliar micro-objects. But since in our culture-circle we do not *habitually* report non-inferentially the presence of caloric fluid, demons, etc., we do not feel unhappy at the bald suggestion that there are no such things.

Roughly speaking, then, the more accustomed we are to "X" serving as an observation-term (by which I mean a term habitually used in non-inferential reports) the more we prefer, when inquiry shows the possibility of accounting for the phenomena explained by reference to X's without such reference, to "identify" X's with some sort of Y's, rather than to deny existence to X's *tout court*. *But the more grounds we have for such identification, the more chance there is that we shall stop using "X" in non-inferential reports,* and thus the greater chance of our eventually coming to accept the claim that "there are no X's" with equanimity. This is why we find borderline cases, and gradual shifts from assimilations of X's to Y's to an assertion that X's do not

---

[17] It is "uninteresting" presumably because it doesn't allow what the "disappearance" form of the identity theory needs: an inference to the nonexistence of sensations. ED.

exist. For example, most people do not report the presence of pink rats non-inferentially (nor inferentially, for that matter), but some do. The recognition that they are in the minority helps those who do so to admit that there are no pink rats. But suppose that the vast majority of us had always seen (intangible and uncatchable) pink rats; would it not then be likely that we should resist the bald assertion that there are no pink rats and insist on something of the form "pink rats are nothing but . . . "? It might be a very long time before we came to drop the habit of reporting pink rats and began reporting hallucinations instead.

The typical case-history of an observation-term ceasing to have referring use runs the following course:[18] (1) X's are the subjects of both inferential and non-inferential reports;[19] (2) empirical discoveries are made which enable us to subsume X-laws under Y-laws and to produce new X-laws by studying Y's; (3) inferential reports of X's cease to be made; (4) non-inferential reports of X's are reinterpreted either (4a) as reports of Y's, or (4b) as reports of mental entities (thoughts that one is seeing an X, hallucinatory images, etc.); (5) non-inferential reports of X's cease to be made (because their place is taken by noninferential reports either of Y's or of thoughts, hallucinatory images, etc.); (6) we conclude that there simply are no such things as X's.

This breakdown of stages lets us pick out two crucial conditions that must be satisfied if we are to move from "X's are nothing but Y's" (stage 2) to "there are no X's" (stage 6). These conditions are:

(A) The Y-laws must be *better* at explaining the kinds of phenomena explained by the X-laws (not just equally good). Indeed, they must be sufficiently better so that *the inconvenience of changing one's linguistic habits by ceasing to make inferential reports about X's is less than the inconvenience of going through the routine of translating*

one's X-reports into Y-reports in order to get satisfactory explanations of the phenomena in question. If this condition is not satisfied, the move from stage (2) to stage (3) will not be made, and thus no later move will be made.

(B) Either Y-reports may themselves be made non-inferentially, or X-reports may be treated as reports of mental entities. For we must be able to have some answer to the question "What *am* I reporting when I non-inferentially report about an X?," and the only answers available are "you're reporting on a Y" or "you're reporting on some merely mental entity." If neither answer is available, we can move neither to (4a) nor to (4b), nor, therefore, on to (5) and (6).

Now the reason we move from stage (2) to stage (3) in the case of demons is that (A) is obviously satisfied. The phenomena which we explained by reference to the activity of demons are so much better explained in other ways that it is simpler to stop inferring the existence of demons altogether than to continue making such inferences, and then turning to laws about germs and the like for an explanation of the behavior of the demons. The reason why we do *not* move from (2) to (3)—much less to (6)—in the case of temperature or tables is that explanations formulated in terms of temperatures are so good, on the ground which they were originally intended to cover, that we feel no temptation to stop talking about temperatures and tables merely because we can, in some cases, get more precise predictions by going up a level to laws about molecules. The reason why we move on from (3) to (4) in the case of demons is that the alternative labeled (4b) is readily available—we can easily consign experiences of demons to that great dumping-ground of out-dated entities, the Mind. There were no experiences of demons, we say, but only experiences of mental images.

Now it seems obvious that, in the case of sensations, (A) will not be satisfied. The inconvenience of ceasing to talk about sensations would be so great that only a fanatical materialist would think it worth the trouble to cease referring to sensations. If the Identity Theorist is taken to be predicting that some day "sensation," "pain," "mental image," and the like will drop out of our vocabulary, he is al-

---

[18] It will help in following this rather abstract discussion if you keep in mind Rorty's prior example of "demon-discourse," in which demons were noninferentially referred to as being in the visions of shamans, and inferentially referred to as causes of certain diseases. He will soon pick up on this example again. ED.

[19] Note that if X's are *only* referred to in inferential reports—as in the case of "neutrons" and "epicycles"—no philosophically interesting reduction takes place. For in such cases there is no hope of getting rid of an explanandum; all we get rid of is a putative explanation.

most certainly wrong. But if he is saying simply that, at no greater cost than an inconvenient linguistic reform, we *could* drop such terms, he is entirely justified. And I take this latter claim to be all that traditional materialism has ever desired.

Before leaving the analogy between demons and sensations, I wish to note one further disanalogy which an opponent of the Identity Theory might pounce upon. Even if we set aside the fact that (A) would not be satisfied in the case of sensations, such an opponent might say, we should note the difficulty in satisfying (B). It would seem that there is no satisfactory answer to the question "What *was* I non-inferentially reporting when I reported on my sensations?" For neither (4a) nor (4b) seems an available option. The first does not seem to be available because it is counter-intuitive to think of, e.g., "I am having my C-fibers stimulated," as capable of being used to make a non-inferential report. The second alternative is simply silly—there is no point in saying that when we report a sensation we are reporting some "merely mental" event. For sensations are *already* mental events. The last point is important for an understanding of the prima facie absurdity of the disappearance form of the Identity Theory. The reason why most statements of the form "there might turn out to be no X's at all" can be accepted with more or less equanimity in the context of forecasts of scientific results is that we are confident we shall always be able to "save the phenomena" by answering the question "But what about all those X's we've been accustomed to observe?" with some reference to thoughts-of-X's, images of X's, and the like. Reference to mental entities provides non-inferential reports of X's with something to have been about. But when we want to say "There might turn out to be no mental entities at all," we cannot use this device. This result makes clear that if the analogy between the past disappearance of supernatural beings and the possible future disappearance of sensations is to be pressed, we must claim that alternative (4a) is, appearances to the contrary, still open. That is, we must hold that the question "What *was* I non-inferentially reporting when I non-inferentially reported a stabbing pain?" can be sensibly answered "You were reporting a stimulation of your C-fibers."

Now why should this *not* be a sensible answer? Let us begin by getting a bad objection to it out of

the way. One can imagine someone arguing that this answer can only be given if a stimulation of C-fibers is strictly identical with a stabbing pain, and that such strict identification involves category-mistakes.[20] But this objection presupposes that "A report of an X is a report of a Y" entails that "X's are Y's." If we grant this presupposition we shall not be able to say that the question "What was I reporting when I reported a demon?" is properly answered by "You were reporting the content of an hallucination which you were having."[21] However, if we ask why this objection is plausible, we can see the grain of truth which it embodies and conceals. We are usually unwilling to accept "You were reporting a Y" as an answer to the question "What *was* I non-inferentially reporting when I non-inferentially reported an X?" unless (a) Y's are themselves the kind of thing we habitually report on non-inferentially, and (b) there does not exist already an habitual practice of reporting Y's non-inferentially. Thus we accept "the content of an hallucination" as a sensible answer because we know that such contents, being "mental images," are just the sort of thing which does get non-inferentially reported (once it is recognized for what it is) and because we are not accustomed to making non-inferential reports in the form "I am having an hallucinatory image of. . . ."[22] To take an example of answers to this sort of question that are *not* sensible, we reject the claim that when we report on a table we are reporting on a mass of whirling particles, for

---

[20]Remember what Rorty said on p. 113 above, that the "disappearance" version of the Identity theory does *not* assert a "strict identity" between sensations and brain processes. Strict identity would require that all predicates of brain processes be applicable to sensations, and this would be a category mistake. ED.

[21]In his previous discussion of demon-discourse Rorty said that a *non*inferential report of a demon is (plausibly understood as) a noninferential report of the content of a hallucination. If we join to that statement the premise "A report of X is a report of Y" only if "X *is* Y," then it follows that the demons of demon-discourse are (nothing but) the contents of hallucinations. But that would be incorrect since the demons that were *inferentially* reported were identical with disease-causing factors such as germs, rather than with hallucinated entities. So the premise is false, and the objection on which it depends is invalid. ED.

[22]Note that people who *become* accustomed to making the latter sort of reports may no longer accept explanations of their erroneous non-inferential reports by reference to hallucinations. For they know what mental images are like, and they know that *this* pink rat was not an hallucinatory content. The more frequent case, fortunately, is that they just cease to report pink rats and begin reporting hallucinations, for their hallucinations no longer deceive them.

either we think we know under what circumstances we should make such a report,[23] and know that these circumstances do not obtain, or we believe that the presence of such particles can only be inferred and never observed.

The oddity of saying that when I think I am reporting on a stabbing pain I am actually reporting on a stimulation of my C-fibers is similar to these last two cases. We either imagine a situation in which we can envisage ourselves non-inferentially reporting such stimulation (periscope hitched up to a microscope so as to give us a view of our trepanned skull, overlying fibers folded out of the way, stimulation evident by change in color, etc., etc.), or else we regard "stimulation of C-fibers" as not the sort of thing which *could* be the subject of a non-inferential report (but inherently a "theoretical" state of affairs whose existence can only be inferred, and not observed). In either case, the assertion that we have been non-inferentially reporting on a brain-process all our lives seems absurd. So the proponent of the disappearance form of the Identity Theory must show that reports of brain-processes are neither incapable of being non-inferential nor, if non-inferential, necessarily made in the way just imagined (with the periscope-microscope gadget) or in some other peculiar way. But now we must ask who bears the burden of proof. Why, after all, should we think that brain-processes are *not* a fit subject-matter for non-inferential reports? And why should it not be the case that the circumstances in which we make non-inferential reports about brain-processes are just those circumstances in which we make non-inferential reports about sensations? For this will in fact be the case if, when we were trained to say, e.g., "I'm in pain" we were in fact being trained to respond to the occurrence within ourselves of a stimulation of C-fibers. If this is the case, the situation will be perfectly parallel to the case of demons and hallucinations. We *will*, indeed, have been making non-inferential reports about brain-processes all our lives *sans le savoir*.

This latter suggestion can hardly be rejected a priori, unless we hold that we can only be taught to

respond to the occurrence of A's with the utterance "A!" if we were able, prior to this teaching, to be aware, when an A was present, that it was present. But this latter claim is plausible only if we assume that there is an activity which can reasonably be called "awareness" prior to the learning of language. I do not wish to fight once again the battle which has been fought by Wittgenstein and many of his followers against such a notion of awareness.[24] I wish rather to take it as having been won,[25] and to take for granted that there is no a priori reason why a brain-process is inherently unsuited to be the subject of a non-inferential report. The distinction between observation-terms and non-observation-terms is relative to linguistic practices (practices which may change as inquiry progresses), rather than capable of being marked out once and for all by distinguishing between the "found" and the "made" elements in our experience.[26] I think that the recognition of the relativity is the first of the steps necessary for a proper appreciation of the claims of the Identity Theory. In what follows, I

---

[24]Rorty is trying to make plausible the scenario in which we are taught to speak of "stimulation of C-fibers" instead of "pain" when the inner events that generate what we now call "pain" are occurring in us. He is fending off an objection based on the following notion of pre-linguistic awareness: What "pain" means is also what we experience independently of knowing how to use the word "pain," so that we are ready to learn to apply "pain" to a certain experience because its meaning somehow fits the content of the pre-linguistic awareness. ED.

[25]This is not, of course, a settled issue among philosophers. It's not perfectly clear what the phrase "awareness prior to learning language" is about. In normal human development the onset of language occurs at the age of 18 months. Prior to this age, infants are already acquiring the elements of language, and presumably undergoing corresponding cognitive development. Some groups of deaf children may be an exception. Eric H. Lenneberg (1967) studied the cognitive development of deaf preschool children who had not yet begun language training and were effectively prelinguistic. From his own research and a survey of the literature he concluded that "The development of basic cognitive functions gives no evidence of impairment in congenitally deaf children at the the time they begin instruction in school and before they have acquired a natural language" (367). The question of prelinguistic awareness is a delicate one for a materialist account of mind. The materialist needs to be able to reduce experiences of inner events such as sensations and after-images to certain brain processes giving rise to "reports." It would be difficult for a materialist theory to accommodate the occurrence of an experience of an after-image, or a stick in water *looking* bent, apart from any capacity on the part of the subject to report such things. If the *look* of something isn't just a qualification of a reporting sentence (e.g., "The stick looks bent"), then what could it be? A materialist can't allow **phenomenal fields.** ED.

[26]Such a distinction would be like that between what is "given" by the normal operation of our sensory system and what is constructed out of that given as it interweaves with our speech and our behavior regarding it. ED.

---

[23]In other words, there already exists a practice of noninferential reporting of "whirling particles," and that practice is inappropriate in the context of just observing a table. ED.

want to show that this first step leads naturally to a second: the recognition that the distinction between *private* and *public* subject-matters is as relative as that between items signified by observation-terms and items not so signified.

The importance of this second step is clear. For even if we grant that reports of brain-processes may be non-inferential, we still need to get around the facts that reports of sensation have an epistemological peculiarity that leads us to call them reports of *private* entities, and that brain-processes are intrinsically *public* entities. Unless we can overcome our intuitive conviction that a report of a private matter (with its attendant infallibility) cannot be identified with a report of a public matter (with its attendant fallibility), we shall not be able to take seriously the claim of the proponents of the disappearance form of the Identity Theory that alternative (4a) is open, and hence that nothing prevents sensations from disappearing from discourse in the same manner, and for the same reasons, as supernatural beings have disappeared from discourse. So far in this paper I have deliberately avoided the problem of the "privacy" of sensations, because I wished to show that if this problem *can* be surmounted, the Identity Theorist may fairly throw the burden of proof onto his opponent by asking whether a criterion can be produced which would show that the identification of sensations and brain-processes involves a conceptual confusion, while absolving the claim that demons do not exist of such a confusion. Since I doubt that such a criterion *can* be produced, I am inclined to say that if the problem about "privacy" is overcome, then the Identity Theorist has made out his case.

5. THE "PRIVACY" OBJECTION

The problem that the privacy of first-person sensation reports presents for the Identity Theory has recently been formulated in considerable detail by Baier.[27] In this section, I shall confine myself to a discussion of his criticism of Smart's initial reply to this argument. Smart holds that the fact that "the language of introspective reports has a different logic from the logic of material processes" is no ob-

jection to the Identity Theory, since we may expect that empirical inquiry can and will change this logic:

> It is obvious that until the brain-process theory is much improved and widely accepted there will be no criteria for saying 'Smith has an experience of such-and-such a sort' except Smith's introspective reports. So we have adopted a rule of language that (normally) what Smith says goes.[28]

Baier thinks that this reply "is simply a confusion of the privacy of the subject-matter and the availability of external evidence."[29] Baier's intuition is that the difference between a language-stratum in which the fact that a report is sincerely made is sufficient warrant for its truth, and one in which this situation does not obtain, seems so great as to call for an explanation—and that the only explanation is that the two strata concern different subject-matters. Indeed Baier is content to let the mental-physical distinction stand or fall with the distinction between "private" subject-matters and "public" subject-matters, and he therefore assumes that to show that "introspective reports are necessarily about something private, and that being about something private is *incompatible with being* about something public"[30] is to show, once and for all, that the Identity Theory involves a conceptual confusion. Baier, in short, is undertaking to show that "once private, always private."

He argues for his view as follows:

> To say that one day our physiological knowledge will increase to such an extent that we shall be able to make absolutely reliable encephalograph-based claims about people's experiences, is only to say that, if carefully checked, our encephalograph-based claims about 'experiences' will always be *correct*, i.e. will make the *same claims* as a *truthful* introspective report. If correct encephalograph-based claims about Smith's experiences contradict Smith's introspective reports, we shall be entitled to infer that he is *lying*. In that sense, what Smith says will no longer go. But we cannot of course infer that he is making a

---

[27] Kurt Baier, "Smart on Sensations," *Australasian Journal of Philosophy*, 40 (1962), pp. 57–68.

[28] Smart, "Sensations and Brain Processes," p. 169.

[29] Baier, p. 63. [In other words, Baier is claiming that the *privacy* of the mental is *essential*; it belongs to the very nature of experience that it not be part of the public, observable, and measurable world. This privacy should not be confused with a *contingent* unavailability of publicly accessible evidence or a contingent obstacle to observation. ED.]

[30] Baier, p. 59.

mistake, for that is nonsense. . . . *However good the evidence may be, such a physiological theory can never be used to show to the sufferer that he was mistaken in thinking that he had a pain, for such a mistake is inconceivable.*[31] The sufferer's epistemological authority must therefore be better than the best physiological theory can ever be. Physiology can therefore never provide a person with more than *evidence* that someone else is having an experience of one sort or another. It can never lay down *criteria* for saying that someone is having an experience of a certain sort. Talk about brain processes therefore must be about something other than talk about experiences. Hence, introspective reports and brain-process talk cannot be merely different ways of talking about the same thing.[32]

Smart's own reply to this line of argument is to admit that

> No physiological evidence, say from a gadget attached to my skull, could make me withdraw the statement that I have a pain when as a matter of fact I feel a pain. For example, the gadget might show no suitable similarities of cerebral processes on the various occasions on which I felt a pain. . . . I must, I think, agree with Baier that if the sort of situation which we have just envisaged did in fact come about, then I should have to reject the brain process thesis, and would perhaps espouse dualism.[33]

But this is not the interesting case. The interesting case is the one in which suitable similarities are in fact found to occur—the same similarities in all subjects—until one day (long after all empirical generalizations about sensations *qua* sensations have been subsumed under physiological laws,[34] and long after direct manipulation of the brain has become the exclusive method of relieving pain) somebody (call him Jones) thinks he has no pain, but the encephalograph says that the brain-process correlated with pain did occur. (Let us imagine that Jones himself is observing the gadget, and that the problem about whether he might have made a mistake is a problem for Jones; this eliminates the possibility of lying.) Now in most cases in which one's observation throws doubt on a correlation which is so central to current scientific explanations, one tries to eliminate the possibility of observational error.[35] But in Baier's view it would be absurd for Jones to do this, for "a mistake is inconceivable." Actually, however, it is fairly clear what Jones' first move would be—he will begin to suspect that he does not know what pain is—i.e., that he is not using the word "pain" in the way in which his fellows use it.[36]

So now Jones looks about for independent verification of the hypothesis that he does not use "I am in pain" incorrectly. But here he runs up against the familiar difficulty about the vocabulary used in making introspective reports—the difficulty of distinguishing between "misuse of language" and "mistake in judgment," between (a) recognizing the state of affairs which obtains for what it is, but describing it wrongly because the words used in the description are not the right words, and (b) being able to describe it rightly once it is recognized for what it is, but not in fact recognizing it for what it is (in the way in which one deceived by an illusion does not recognize the situation for what it is).[37] If we do not have a way of determining which

---

[31] Although Rorty will go on to argue at length against Baier, there is an objection that he does not raise: In what sense is a mistaken judgment that one is in pain "inconceivable"? Is it contradictory, like "Rectangles have three interior angles"? Or is it "inconceivable" only in the sense that I can be certain it couldn't happen, like the prospect of my judging that "2 + 1 = 4"? If the latter, then the inconceivability is only a matter of degree, and does not suggest that the subject matter is essentially different from subject matters about which mistaken judgments *are* conceivable. It's quite conceivable that I might erroneously compute that "95 + 186 = 271." And it is also conceivable that I might mistake my feelings for someone, thinking that I love when I only admire. Furthermore, we are now accustomed to the idea that we may have feelings that are present at some level of consciousness/unconsciousness where we are incapable of correctly classifying them. Therefore, pain may be like "2 + 1 = 3": very simple cases which I'm certain I couldn't be mistaken about, even though I could easily misjudge more complex cases of the *same* sort. So the alleged infallibility of "I am in pain" doesn't mark any great metaphysical divide between the mental and the physical. ED.

[32] Baier, pp. 64–65; italics added.

[33] Smart, "Brain Processes and Incorrigibility—a Reply to Professor Baier," *Australasian Journal of Philosophy,* 40 (1962), p. 68.

[34] The hypothetical assumption here seems to be that neuroscience has progressed to the point of having precise correlations between types of sensation and types of brain processes, so that regularities in the occurrences of sensations can be adequately described as regularities in the occurrences of brain processes. ED.

[35] The "observational error" would be in introspection. Although this usage is clear enough in its context, many philosophers would not classify introspection as observation because it is not *inter*subjective and its content is not measurable. ED.

[36] This problem will remain, of course, even if Jones merely *thinks* about whether he is in pain, but does not say anything.

[37] The problem with distinguishing between misnaming and misjudging can be seen in the Wittgensteinian fiction of the beetle in the box discussed in footnote 34 of Reading 6. Suppose you're a recent arrival in this community and you think you've learned beetle-discourse. But then you find yourself speaking "deviantly" about *your* "beetle," failing to find

of these situations obtains, we do not have a genuine contrast between misnaming and misjudging. To see that there is no genuine contrast in this case, suppose that Jones was not burned prior to the time that he hitches on the encephalograph, but now he is. When he is, the encephalograph says that the brain-process constantly correlated with pain-reports occurs in Jones' brain. However, although he exhibits pain-behavior, Jones thinks that he does not feel pain. (But, now as in the past, he both exhibits pain-behavior and thinks that he feels pain when he is frozen, stuck, struck, racked, etc.) Now is it that he does not know that *pain* covers what you feel when you are burned as well as what you feel when you are stuck, struck, etc.? Or is it that he really does not feel pain when he is burned? Suppose we tell Jones that what he feels when he is burned is *also* called "pain." Suppose he then admits that he does feel *something,* but insists that what he feels is quite *different* from what he feels when he is stuck, struck, etc. Where does Jones go from here? Has he failed to learn the language properly, or is he correctly (indeed infallibly) reporting that he has different sensations than those normally had in the situation in question? (Compare the parallel question in the case of a man who uses "blue" in all the usual ways except that he refuses to grant that blue is a color—on the ground that it is so different from red, yellow, orange, violet, etc.)

The only device which would decide this question would be to establish a convention that anyone who sincerely denied that he felt a pain while exhibiting pain-behavior and being burned ipso facto did not understand how to use "pain." This denial would *prove* that he lacked such an understanding. But this would be a dangerous path to follow. For not to understand when to use the word "pain" in non-inferential reports is presumably to be unable to know which of one's sensations to call a "pain." And the denial that one felt pain in the circumstances mentioned would only prove such inability if one indeed *had* the sensation normally called a pain. So now we would have a public criterion, satisfaction of which would count as showing that the

subject had such a sensation—i.e., that he felt a pain even though he did not think that he did. But if such a criterion exists, its application over-rides any contradictory report that he may make—for such a report will be automatically disallowed by the fact that it constitutes a demonstration that he does not know what he is talking about. The dilemma is that either a report about one's sensations which violates a certain public criterion is a sufficient condition for saying that the reporter does not know how to use "pain" in the correct way, or there is no such criterion. If there is, the fact that one cannot be mistaken about pains does not entail that sincere reports of pain cannot be over-ridden. If there is not, then there is no way to answer the question formulated at the end of the last paragraph, and hence no way to eliminate the possibility that Jones may not know what pain is.[38] Now since the a priori probability that he does not is a good deal higher than the a priori probability that the psycho-physiological theory of Jones' era is mistaken, this theory has little to fear from Jones. (Although it would have a great deal to fear from a sizable accumulation of cases like Jones'.)

To sum up this point, we may look back at the italicized sentence in the above quotation from Baier. We now see that the claim that "such a mistake is inconceivable" is an ellipsis for the claim

---

[38] Perhaps a further summary would help in understanding this complex argument: Baier claimed that no neurophysiological evidence that she is not in pain can or should override a person's sincere belief that she is experiencing pain. The awareness that only she can have is also an infallible awareness, immune to any other person's denial that she is in pain, no matter how much evidence that other person may have. That makes pain, and sensations in general, importantly different from physical entities such as brain processes. The claim that a certain type of brain process is occurring is in principle, and in practice, *fallible*. One can always present decisive evidence that the claim is mistaken.

Rorty is arguing that for the claim of infallibility in my sensation-reports to have any importance in a situation in which all the evidence (neuroscientific and behavioral) indicates that I am in pain, but I sincerely believe I'm not, I must be able to decide between two possibilities: (1) I really am pain-free in this case, or (2) I'm not using the word "pain" correctly. To decide between these two alternatives, there must be a *criterion* for the correct use of "pain." (Notice that I couldn't even assert (1) sincerely unless I could also believe that I was using "pain" *correctly*.) However, such a criterion would have to be publicly accessible; it would be a statement of the "evidence" needed to apply the term "pain" (in the fictional scenario invoked by Baier, it could be pain behavior and/or encephalographic data). If "pain" *has* such a criterion, then a sincere first-person pain-report that violates the criterion would be rejected. Therefore, such reports don't have the infallibility that Baier alleges as a basis for rejecting materialism. ED.

---

it in circumstances in which others readily saw theirs when they looked into their boxes. How could you decide whether your problem was that you don't fully grasp the meaning of "beetle" or your problem was that you were missing something that was there in the box, perhaps because you weren't looking in the right place or way?

that a mistake, made *by one who knows what pain is,* is inconceivable, for only this expanded form will entail that when Jones and the encephalograph disagree, Jones is always right. But when formulated in this way our infallibility about our pains can be seen to be empty. Being infallible about something would be useful only if we could draw the usual distinction between misnaming and misjudging, and having ascertained that we were not misnaming, know that we were not misjudging. But where there are no criteria for misjudging (or to put it more accurately, where in the crucial cases the criteria for misjudging turn out to be the same as the criteria for misnaming) then to say that we are infallible is to pay ourselves an empty compliment. Our neighbors will not hesitate to ride roughshod over our reports of our sensations unless they are assured that we know our way around among them and we cannot satisfy them on this point unless, up to a certain point, we tell the same sort of story about them as they do. The limits of permissible stories are flexible enough for us to be able to convince them occasionally that we have odd sensations, but not flexible enough for us to use these surprising sensations to break down, at one blow, well-confirmed scientific theories. As in the case of other infallible pronouncements, the price of retaining one's epistemological authority is a decent respect for the opinions of mankind.

Thus the common-sense remark that first-person reports always will be a better source of information about the occurrence of pains than any other source borrows its plausibility from the fact that we normally do not raise questions about a man's ability to use the word "pain" correctly. Once we *do* raise such question seriously (as in the case of Jones), we realize that the question (1) "Does he know which sensations are called 'pains'?" and (2) "Is he a good judge of whether he is in pain or not?" are simply two ways of asking the same question: viz., "Can we fit his pain-reports into our scheme for explaining and predicting pains?" or, more bluntly, "Shall we disregard his pain-reports or not?" And once we see this we realize that if "always be a better source of information" means "will never be over-ridden on the sort of grounds on which presumed observational errors are over-ridden elsewhere in science," then our common-

sensical remark is probably false.[39] If "always be a better source of information" means merely "can only be over-ridden on the basis of a charge of misnaming, and never on the basis of a charge of misjudging," then our common-sensical remark turns out to depend upon a distinction that is not there.

This Wittgensteinian point that sensation-reports must conform to public criteria or else be disallowed may also be brought out in the following way. We determine whether to take a surprising first-person report of pain or its absence seriously (that is, whether to say that the sensation reported is something that science must try to explain) by seeing whether the reporter's overall pattern of pain-reporting is, by the usual behavioral and environmental criteria, normal. Now suppose that these public criteria (for "knowing how to use 'pain'") change as physiology and technology progress. Suppose, in particular, that we find it convenient to speed up the learning of contrastive observation predicates (such as "painful," "tickling," etc.) by supplying children with portable encephalographs-cum-teaching-machines which, whenever the appropriate brain-process occurs, murmur the appropriate term in their ears. Now "appropriate brain-process" will start out by meaning "brain process constantly correlated with sincere utterance of 'I'm in pain' by people taught the use of 'pain' in the old rough-and-ready way." But soon it will come to mean, "the brain-process which we have always programmed the machine to respond to with a murmur of 'pain.'" (A meter is [now, but not always] what matches the Standard Meter; intelligence is [now, but was not always] what intelligence tests test; pains will be [but are not now] what the Standard "Pain"-Training Program calls "pain.") Given this situation, it would make sense to say things like "You say you are in pain, and I'm sure you are sincere, but you can see for yourself that your brain is not in the state to which you were trained to respond to with "Pain," so apparently the training did not work, and you do not yet understand what pain is." In such a situa-

---

[39] If Jones reports having no pain when all neuroscientific information on his brain activity indicates pain, then his report is likely to be overridden, precisely because it is so contrary to well-established neuroscientific generalizations; just as an observation report about a solid piece of lead floating on water would be overridden. ED.

tion, our "inability to be mistaken" about our pains would remain, but our "final epistemological authority" on the subject would be gone, for there would be a standard procedure for overriding our reports. Our inability to be mistaken is, after all, no more than our ability to have such hypothetical statements as "If you admit that I'm sincere and that I know the language, you have to accept what I say" accepted by our fellows. But this assent can only be converted into final epistemological authority if we can secure both admissions. Where a clear-cut public criterion *does* exist for "knowing the language," inability to be mistaken does not entail inability to be over-ridden.

Now Baier might say that if such criteria did exist, then we should no longer be talking about what we presently mean by "pains." I do not think that this needs to be conceded,[40] but suppose that it is. Would this mean that there was now a subject-matter which was not being discussed—viz., the private subject-matter the existence of which Baier's argument was intended to demonstrate? That we once had contact with such a subject-matter, but lost it? These rhetorical questions are meant to suggest that Baier's explanation of the final epistemological authority of first-person reports of pains by the fact that this "logic" is "a function of this type of subject-matter"—rather than, as Smart thinks, a convention—is an explanation of the obscure by the more obscure. More precisely, it will not be an explanation of the epistemological authority in question—but only an unenlightening redescription of it—unless Baier can give a meaning to the term "private subject-matter" other than "kind of thing which is reported in reports which cannot be over-ridden." These considerations show the need for stepping back from Baier's argument and considering the criteria which he is using to demarcate distinct subject-matters.

6. "PRIVACY" AS A CRITERION OF CATEGORICAL DEMARCATION

The closest Baier comes to giving a definition of "private subject-matter" is to say that

> We must say that 'I have a pain' is about 'something private,' because in making this remark we report something which is (1) *necessarily owned* . . . (2) *necessarily exclusive and unsharable* . . . (3) *necessarily imperceptible by the senses* . . . (4) *necessarily asymmetrical,* for whereas it makes no sense to say 'I could see (or hear) that I had a pain,' it makes quite good sense to say 'I could see (or hear) that *he* had a pain';[41] (5) something about the possession of which the person who claims to possess it could not possibly examine, consider, or weigh any evidence, although other people could . . . and lastly (6) it is something about which the person whose private state it is has final epistemological authority, for it does not make sense to say 'I have a pain unless I am mistaken.'[42]

Now this definition of "something private" entails that nothing could be private except a state of a person, and is constructed to delimit all and only those states of a person which we call his "mental" states. To say that mental states are private is to say simply that mental states are described in the way in which mental states are described. But it is not hard to take *any* Rylean category of terms (call it C), list all the types of sentence-frames which do and do not make sense when their gaps are filled with terms belonging to this category, and say that "something C" is distinguished by the fact that it is "necessarily X," "necessarily Y," etc. where "X" and "Y" are labels for the fact that certain sentence-frames will or will not receive these terms as gap-fillers. For example, consider the thesis that:

> We must say that 'The devil is in that corner' is about 'something supernatural' because in making this report we report something which is *necessarily intangible,* since it makes no sense to ask about the texture of his skin, not *necessarily simply-located,* since it does not follow from the fact that a supernatural being is in the corner that the same supernatural being is not simultaneously at the other side of the globe,

---

40 My reasons for thinking this concession unnecessary are the same as those presented in some recent articles by Hilary Putnam: cf. "Minds and Machines," *Dimensions of Mind,* ed. S. Hook (New York, 1961), pp. 138–161, esp. pp. 153–160; "The Analytic and the Synthetic," *Minnesota Studies in the Philosophy of Science,* III, pp. 358–397; "Brains and Behavior," in *Analytic Philosophy,* II, ed. by R. J. Butler (Oxford, 1965).

---

41 For this to be consistent with (3), "see (or hear)" has to be understood *inferentially,* as in " I could see by his facial expression. . . ." ED.

42 Baier, "Smart on Sensations," p. 60; the numbers in parentheses have been added.

necessarily immortal, since it does not make sense to say that a supernatural being has died, *necessarily perceptible to exorcists,* since it would not make sense to say that a man was an exorcist and did not perceive the devil when he was present. . . .[43]

Are devils hallucinations? No, because when one reports an hallucination one reports something which, though intangible, is simply-located, is neither mortal nor immortal, and is not always perceptible to exorcists. Are reports of devils reports of hallucinations? No, because reports of devils are reports of something supernatural and reports of hallucinations are reports of something private. Is it simply because we lack further information about devils that we take exorcists' sincere reports as the best possible source for information about them? No, for this suggestion confuses the supernatural character of the subject-matter with the availability of external evidence. Those without the supernatural powers with which the exorcist is gifted may find ways of gathering *evidence* for the presence of supernatural beings,[44] but they can never formulate an overriding and independent *criterion* for saying that such a being is present. Their theories might become so good that we might sometimes say that a given exorcist was *lying,* but we could never say that he was *mistaken.*

If this pastiche of Baier's argument seems beside the point, it is presumably either (1) because the language-game[45] I have described is not in fact played, or else (2) because "necessarily intangible, not necessarily simply-located, necessarily immortal, and necessarily perceptible to exorcists" does not delimit a subject-matter in the way in which "necessarily owned, exclusive, imperceptible by the senses, asymmetrical, etc., etc." does. In (1) one has to ask "what if it *had* been played?" After all, if the technique of detecting distinct subject-matters which Baier uses is a generally applicable technique, and not just constructed *ad hoc* to suit our Cartesian intuitions, then it ought to work on imaginary as well as real language-games. But if it is, we ought to be able to formulate rules for applying it which would tell us *why* (2) is the case. For if we cannot, and if the language-game described once was played, then Baier's objection to the Identity Theory is an objection to the theory that reports of visible supernatural beings are reports of hallucinations.[46] Baier gives no more help in seeing what these rules would be. But I think that the root of Baier's conviction that "something private" is a suitable candidate for being a "distinct subject matter" is the thesis that certain terms are *intrinsically* observation predicates, and signify, so to speak, "natural explananda." When in quest of such predicates we look to the "foundations" of empirical knowledge, we tend to rapidly identify "observation predicate" with "predicate occurring in report about something private." This chain of identifications leaves us with the suspicion that if there were no longer a private subject-matter to be infallible about, the whole fabric of empirical inquiry about public matters would be left up in the air, unsupported by any absolute epistemological authority.[47] The suggestion that the distinction between items reportable in infallible reports and items not so reportable is "ultimate," or "irreducible," or

---

[43] It seems to me that this paragraph by Rorty about the devil and "supernatural" is not an accurate "pastiche" or fair imitation of what Baier writes in the quoted passage about pain being "private." What do you think? ED.

[44] Just as neuroscientists may arrive at very accurate correlations between reports of certain kinds of sensations and the occurrence of specific types of brain processes, so students of devil-discourse may arrive at very accurate correlations between exorcist's reports of demons being present and certain measurable, physical features of the place where the devil is said to be present. In both cases, there would be a public criterion for the unobservable, but (if we argue like Baier, or Rorty's rendition of Baier) this criterion has less authority than first-person reports of sensations or exorcist reports respectively. ED.

[45] I.e., devil-discourse. ED.

[46] Rorty is using a variety of *reductio ad absurdum* in which an argument of a certain form is shown to lead to an absurd or manifestly false conclusion. The absurdity in this case is that the claim that reports of devils were reports of hallucinations would be considered a conceptual confusion. ED.

[47] Rorty is linking the intuitive appeal of the notion that there is an irreducibly private subject-matter, via the supposed infallibility of our judgments about this subject matter, to the appeal of *foundationalism* in epistemology (theory of knowledge). Foundationalists believe that we can be said to have knowledge only if our beliefs about the world rest ultimately on claims that don't require any justification because they are infallible or self-evident. If we begin with such infallible judgments and validly infer a series of conclusions from them, the authority of the initial self-evident judgments will extend to the rest. Among the candidates for such foundational beliefs are statements about sense-data, about the unvarnished, pre-theoretical *given* in sensory awareness. However, many philosophers agree with Rorty in dismissing such infallibly given content as a myth. ED.

"categorical," owes its intuitive force to the difficulty of imagining a stage in the progress of inquiry in which there was not *some* situation in which absolute epistemological authority about *something* would be granted to *somebody*.

There probably could *not* be such a stage, for inquiry cannot proceed if everything is to be doubted at once, and if inquiry is even to get off the ground we need to get straight about what is to be questioned and what not. These practical dictates show the kernel of truth in the notion that inquiry cannot proceed without a foundation. Where we slide from truth into error is in assuming that certain items are *naturally* reportable in infallible reports, and thus assume that the items presently so reportable always were and always will be reportable (and conversely for items not presently so reportable). A pain looks like the paradigm of such an item, with the situation described by "seems to me as if I were seeing something red" almost as well-qualified. But in both cases, we can imagine situations in which we should feel justified in overriding sincere reports using these predicates. More important, we see that the device which we should use to justify ourselves in such situation—viz., "The reporter may not know how to use the word . . . "—is one which can apply in *all* proposed cases. Because this escape-hatch is always available, and because the question of whether the reporter does know how to use the word or not is probably not itself a question which could ever be settled by recourse to any absolute epistemological authority, the situation envisaged by Baier—namely, the body of current scientific theory foundering upon the rock of a single overriding report—can probably never arise. Baier sees a difference in kind between the weight of evidence produced by such a theory and the single, authoritative, *criterion* provided by such a report. But since there can be no overriding report until the ability of the speaker to use the words used in the report is established, and since this is to be established only by the weight of the evidence and not by recourse to any single criterion, this difference in kind (even though it may be indeed be "firmly embedded in the way we talk" for millennia) is always capable of being softened into a difference of degree by further empirical inquiry.

7. REDUCTIONIST PHILOSOPHICAL THEORIES AND CATEGORICAL DISTINCTIONS

In the preceding sections of this paper I have constantly invoked the fact that language changes as empirical discoveries are made, in order to argue that the thesis that "What people now call 'sensations' might be discovered to be brain-processes" is sensible and unconfused. The "deviance" of a statement of this thesis should not, I have been urging, blind us to the facts that (a) entities referred to in one Rylean category may also be referred to by expressions in another, (b) expressions in the first category may drop out of the language once this identity of reference is realized, and (c) the thesis in question is a natural way of expressing the result of this realization in the case of "sensation" and "brain-process." Now a critic might object that this strategy is subject to a *reductio ad absurdum*. For the same fact about linguistic change would seem to justify the claim that *any* statement of the form (S) "What people call 'X's' may be discovered to by Y's" is *always* sensible and unconfused. Yet this seems paradoxical, for consider the result of substituting, say "neutrino" for "X" and "mushroom" for "Y." If the resulting statement is not conceptually confused, what statement is?

In answer to this objection, I should argue that it is a mistake to attribute "conceptual confusions" to *statements*. No statement can be known to express a conceptual confusion simply by virtue of an acquaintance with the meanings of its component terms. Confusion is a property of people. Deviance is a property of utterance. Deviant utterances made by using sentences of the form (S) *may* betoken confusion on the part of the speaker about the meanings of words, but it may simply indicate a vivid (but unconfused) imagination, or perhaps (as in the neutrino-mushroom case) merely idle fancy. Although the making of such statements may be prima facie evidence of conceptual confusion—i.e., of the fact that the speaker is insufficiently familiar with the language to find a non-deviant way of making his point—this evidence is only prima facie, and questioning may bring out evidence pointing the other way. Such questioning may show that the speaker actually has some detailed suggestions about possible empirical results which would point to the discovery in question, or that he has no such suggestions, but is nevertheless not inclined to use the relevant words in any *other* deviant utterances, and to cheerfully admit the deviance of his original utterance. The possibility of such evidence, pointing to imagination or to fancy rather than to confusion, shows that from the fact that certain questions are typically asked, and certain statements typically made, by victims of conceptual confusion, it does not follow that all those who use the sentences used to ask these questions or to make these statements are thus victimized.

This confusion about confusion is due to the fact that philosophers who propound "reductionist" theories (such as "There is no insensate matter," "There are no minds," "There are no physical objects," etc.) often *have* been conceptually confused. Such theories are often advocated as solutions to pseudo-problems whose very formulation involves deviant uses of words—uses which in fact result from a confusion between the uses of two or more senses of the same term, or between two or more related terms (e.g., "name" and "word") or between the kind of questions appropriately asked of entities referred to by one set of terms and the kind appropriately asked of entities referred to by another. (That these deviant uses *are* the result of such confusion, it should be noticed, is only capable of being determined by questioning of those who use them—and we only feel *completely* safe in making this diagnosis when the original user has, in the light of the linguistic facts drawn to his attention, admitted that his putative "problem" has been dissolved.) Because reductionist theories may often be choked off at the source by an examination of uses of language, anti-reductionist philosophers have lately become prone to use "conceptual con-

fusion" or "category-mistake" as an all-purpose diagnosis for any deviant utterance in the mouth of a philosopher. But this is a mistake. Predictions of the sort illustrated by (S) may be turned to confused purposes, and they may be made by confused people. But we could only infer with certainty from the deviance of the utterance of a sentence of the form (S) to the conceptual confusion of the speaker if we had a map of the categories which are exhibited in all possible languages, and were thus in a position to say that the cross-category identification envisaged by the statement was eternally impossible. In other words, we should only be in a position to make this inference with certainty if we knew that empirical inquiry could *never* bring about the sort of linguistic change which permits the non-deviant use of "There are no X's" in the case of the "X's" to which the statement in question refers. But philosophers are in no position to say that such change is impossible. The hunt for categoreal confusions at the source of reductionist philosophical theories is an extremely valuable enterprise. But their successes in this enterprise should not lead linguistic philosophers to think that they can do better what metaphysicians did badly—namely, prove the irreducibility of entities. Traditional materialism embodied many confusions, but at its heart was the unconfused prediction about future empirical inquiry which is the Identity Theory.[48] The confusions may be eradicated without affecting the plausibility or interest of the prediction.[49]

---

[48] In the first paragraph of his essay, Rorty defines a proponent of the Identity theory as "one who thinks it sensible to assert that *sensations* (not thoughts) are identical with certain brain processes. . . ." ED.

[49] I have been greatly helped in preparing this paper by the comments of Richard Bernstein, Keith Gunderson, Amelie Rorty, and Richard Schmitt.

Just before section 5 ("The Privacy Objection") Rorty clearly indicates where he regards the argument of his essay as standing or falling. He claims that the only serious argument for the Identity Theory being a conceptual confusion is one that invokes the supposed privacy and consequent infallibility in reports of sensations: "I am inclined to say that if the problem about 'privacy' is overcome, then the Identity Theorist has made out his case."

Prior to making this claim he argued persuasively that it is insufficient to object against "What we used to call 'X' is nothing but 'Y'" that X and Y belong to different "categories." For instance, in the example of the demon-discourse of his fictional "primitive tribe" one can meaningfully and plausibly say that "The demons that the witch-doctors reported seeing were nothing but hallucinations." The fact that demons (if they exist) belong to a different category (supernatural beings) than hallucinations (private mental events) is not an adequate argument against identifying demons as hallucinations. For the objection to be adequate, Rorty seems to be saying, the category difference must point to a deeper difference between X and Y, such that what is being designated by "X" is necessarily, by its very nature, *not* Y. The only candidate for such a fundamental difference between sensations and brain processes, according to Rorty, is the opposition of private and public and the resulting contrast between infallibility and fallibility in reports. He goes on to argue that the latter contrast is a matter of linguistic convenience and the current status of brain science, and does not indicate a metaphysical gulf between the mental and the physical. Having disposed of the infallible/fallible contrast, and assuming that there is nothing else to worry about in the distinction between private and public, he rests the case for materialism.

However, as I indicated in footnote 31, it is far from obvious that reports of what is essentially private in experience must be infallible. My reports about my feeling states may seem infallible in simple cases such as "I am in pain" or "I feel hot." When you say such things, you don't expect someone to ask "Are you sure?" But suppose I were to ask you exactly what color your after-image was, or how long it took to fade. You might answer in a way that is different enough from most people's responses that I would ask "Are you sure?" You would then look again at the intense color patch or lit electric bulb and pay closer attention to the resulting after-image. You might then conclude (after several trials, perhaps) that you had been mistaken about the color or duration of the after-image. Of course, you're not looking at numerically the same after-image as the one you first reported, but you and I and any neuroscientist are convinced that people in general have qualitatively the same after-images in response to the same kind of stimulus. What's important to notice about this example is that, although you are motivated to check your after-image by my summary of the experimental data (other people's reports of after-images with this sort of stimulus), *your* checking of your after-image(s) is not a scientific observation; what you're focusing on is essentially private, though your judgment about it is *fallible.* For many philosophers the, or a, principal objection to the Identity Theory is that what is essentially private (even if fallibly reported) seems by its very nature *not to be identifiable with something (like a brain process) that is essentially public.*

REVIEW QUESTIONS

1. Look carefully at the ambiguous figure to the right and describe to yourself what you see, including the spatial relationships between elements of the image. Your description will be of the "look(s)" of the object on the page, something that is hard to accommodate in a world consisting only of what can be described in the language of physical science. Compare and contrast how Smart and Rorty would deal with this apparent difficulty for the materialist position.

2. Rorty maintains that in cases of the identification in science of observables (e.g., tables) with theoretical entities (e.g., "clouds" of elementary particles), we could cease to make a referring use of the word ("table") for the observable and of any other expression designating the same set of entities (e.g., "a piece of furniture with a flat top and one or more legs and serving a specified purpose"). In eliminating these expressions, we would "still leave our ability to describe and predict undiminished" (p. 117 above). What does he mean by this? Do you agree? Why?

9

Eliminative Materialism

Paul M. Churchland

Paul M. Churchland is a professor of philosophy at the University of California at San Diego. Among his many publications in the philosophy of mind and cognitive science are *Matter and Consciousness* (1988) and *The Engine of Reason, the Seat of the Soul* (1995).

In this reading Churchland argues that a pure, or at least radical, version of eliminative materialism is far likelier than a reductionism based on type identities to do justice to neuroscience. Surveying the history of scientific progress in other areas, and the kinds of perceptual and cognitive deficits that are caused by damage to specific areas of the brain, he concludes that our ordinary conceptual framework for characterizing minds is likely to become as out-of-date as references to heavenly spheres and phlogiston.

The identity theory was called into doubt not because the prospects for a materialist account of our mental capacities were thought to be poor, but because it seemed unlikely that the arrival of an adequate materialist theory would bring with it the nice one–to–one match-ups, between the concepts of folk psychology[1] and the concepts of theoretical neuroscience, that intertheoretic reduction requires.[2] The reason for that doubt was the great variety of quite different physical systems that could instantiate the required functional organization.[3] *Eliminative materialism* also doubts that the correct neuroscientific account of human capacities will produce a neat reduction of our common-sense framework, but here the doubts arise from a quite different source.

As the eliminative materialists see it, one–to–one match-ups will not be found and our common-sense psychological framework will not enjoy an intertheoretic reduction, *because our common-sense psychological framework is a false and radically misleading conception of the causes of human behavior and the nature of cognitive activity.* On this view, folk psychology is

---

From Paul M. Churchland, *Matter and Consciousness*, rev. ed. (Cambridge, MA: The MIT Press, 1988), pp. 43–49. © 1988 Massachusetts Institute of Technology. Reprinted with permission of the publisher.

[1] *Folk psychology* is the conceptual system we deploy in nonscientific contexts to attribute beliefs, knowledge, sensations, and other mental items to ourselves and others. ED.

[2] In *intertheoretic reduction* the explanatory work of one theory or conceptual framework gets done better by a more powerful theory in a way that mirrors the older one. As Churchland puts it earlier in his book, "The relevant principles entailed by the new theory have the same structure as the corresponding principles of the old framework, and they apply in exactly the same cases. The only difference is that where the old principles contained (for example) the notions of 'heat', 'is hot', and 'is cold', the new principles contain the notions of 'total molecular kinetic energy', 'has a high mean molecular kinetic energy', 'has a low mean molecular kinetic energy' (pp. 26–27).

[3] Readings 10 and 11 will introduce the philosophical theory called *functionalism*. According to this theory, mental states are functional states—they are to be defined not in terms of their physical constitution but rather in terms of the way in which they relate to one another and to input from sensory organs and behavioral output. In principle, these input-output relations could be realized by very different sorts of physical systems (such as computer hardware and brain wetware). Therefore, contrary to what seems to be implied by Place and Smart, one should not look for identities between types of mental states and types of neural events. ED.

not just an incomplete representation of our inner natures; it is an outright misrepresentation of our internal states and activities. Consequently, we cannot expect a truly adequate neuroscientific account of our inner lives to provide theoretical categories that match-up nicely with the categories of our common-sense framework. Accordingly, we must expect that the older framework will simply be eliminated, rather than be reduced, by a matured neuroscience.

HISTORICAL PARALLELS

As the identity theorist can point to historical cases of successful intertheoretic reduction, so the eliminative materialists can point to historical cases of the outright elimination of the ontology of an older theory in favor of the ontology of a new and superior theory. For most of the eighteenth and nineteenth centuries, learned people believed that heat was a subtle *fluid* held in bodies, much in the way water is held in a sponge. A fair body of moderately successful theory described the way this fluid substance—called "caloric"—flowed within a body, or from one body to another, and how it produced thermal expansion, melting, boiling and so forth. But by the end of the last century it had become abundantly clear that heat was not a substance at all, but just the energy of motion of the trillions of jostling molecules that make up the heated body itself. The new theory—the "corpuscular/kinetic theory of matter and heat"—was much more successful than the old in explaining and predicting the thermal behavior of bodies. And since we were unable to *identify* caloric fluid with kinetic energy (according to the old theory, caloric is a material *substance;* according to the new theory, kinetic energy is a form of *motion*), it was finally agreed that there is *no such thing* as caloric. Caloric was simply eliminated from our accepted **ontology.**

A second example. It used to be thought that when a piece of wood burns, or a piece of metal rusts, a spiritlike substance called "phlogiston" was being released: briskly in the former case, slowly in the latter. Once gone, that "noble" substance left only a base pile of ash or rust. It later came to be appreciated that both processes involve, not the loss of something, but the *gaining* of a substance taken from the atmosphere: oxygen. Phlogiston emerged, not as an incomplete description of what was going on, but as a radical misdescription. Phlogiston was therefore not suitable for reduction to or identification with some notion from within the new oxygen chemistry, and it was simply eliminated from science.

Admittedly, both these examples concern the elimination of something nonobservable, but our history also includes the elimination of certain widely accepted "observables". Before Copernicus' view became available, almost any human who ventured out at night could look up at the *starry sphere of the heavens,* and if he stayed for more than a few minutes he could also see that it turned, around an axis through Polaris. What the sphere was made of (crystal?) and what made it turn (the gods?) were theoretical questions that exercised us for over two millennia. But hardly anyone doubted the existence of what they could observe with their own eyes. In the end, however, we learned to reinterpret our visual experience of the night sky within a very different conceptual framework, and the turning sphere evaporated.[4]

Witches provide another example. Psychosis is a fairly common affliction among humans, and in earlier centuries its victims were standardly seen as cases of demonic possession, as instances of Satan's spirit itself, glaring malevolently out at us from behind the victims' eyes. That witches exist was not a matter of controversy. One would occasionally see them, in any city or hamlet, engaged in incoherent, paranoid, or even murderous behavior. But observable or not, we eventually decided that witches simply do not exist. We concluded that the concept of a witch is an element within a conceptual framework that misrepresents so badly the phenomenon to which it was standardly applied that literal application of the notion should be permanently withdrawn. Modern theories of mental dysfunction led to the elimination of witches from our serious ontology.

The concepts of folk psychology—belief, desire, fear, sensation, pain, joy, and so on—await a similar fate, according to the view at issue. And when neuroscience has matured to the point where

---

[4]A simpler example of this sort of case is the apparent motion of the sun from horizon to horizon. ED.

the poverty of our current conceptions is apparent to everyone, and the superiority of the new framework is established, we shall then be able to set about *reconceiving* our internal states as activities, within a truly adequate conceptual framework at last. Our explanations of one another's behavior will appeal to such things as our neuropharmacological states, the neural activity in specialized anatomical areas, and whatever other states are deemed relevant by the new theory. Our private introspection will also be transformed, and may be profoundly enhanced by reason of the more accurate and penetrating framework it will have to work with—just as the astronomer's perception of the night sky is much enhanced by the detailed knowledge of modern astronomical theory that he or she possesses.

The magnitude of the conceptual revolution here suggested should not be minimized: it would be enormous. And the benefits to humanity might be equally great. If each of us possessed an accurate neuroscientific understanding of (what we now conceive dimly as) the varieties and causes of mental illness, the factors involved in learning, the neural basis of emotions, intelligence, and socialization, then the sum total of human misery might be much reduced. The simple increase in mutual understanding that the new framework made possible could contribute substantially toward a more peaceful and humane society. Of course, there would be dangers as well: increased knowledge means increased power, and power can always be misused.

ARGUMENTS FOR ELIMINATIVE MATERIALISM

The arguments for eliminative materialism are diffuse and less than decisive, but they are stronger than is widely supposed. The distinguishing feature of this position is its denial that a smooth intertheoretic reduction is to be expected—even a species-specific reduction[5]—of the framework of folk psychology to the framework of a matured

neuroscience. The reason for this denial is the eliminative materialist's conviction that folk psychology is a hopelessly primitive and deeply confused conception of our internal activities. But why this low opinion of our common-sense conceptions?

There are at least three reasons. First, the eliminative materialist will point to the widespread explanatory, predictive, and manipulative failures of folk psychology. So much of what is central and familiar to us remains a complete mystery from within folk psychology. We do not know what *sleep* is, or why we have to have it, despite spending a full third of our lives in that condition. (The answer, "For rest," is mistaken. Even if people are allowed to rest continuously, their need for sleep is undiminished. Apparently, sleep serves some deeper functions, but we do not yet know what they are.) We do not understand how *learning* transforms each of us from a gaping infant to a cunning adult, or how differences in *intelligence* are grounded. We have not the slightest idea how *memory* works, or how we manage to retrieve relevant bits of information instantly from the awesome mass we have stored. We do not know what *mental illness* is, nor how to cure it.

In sum, the most central things about us remain almost entirely mysterious from within folk psychology. And the defects noted cannot be blamed on inadequate time allowed for their correction, for folk psychology has enjoyed no significant changes or advances in well over 2,000 years, despite its manifest failures. Truly successful theories may be expected to reduce, but significantly unsuccessful theories merit no such expectation.

This argument from explanatory poverty has a further aspect. So long as one sticks to normal brains, the poverty of folk psychology is perhaps not strikingly evident. But as soon as one examines the many perplexing behavioral and cognitive deficits suffered by people with damaged brains, one's descriptive and explanatory resources start to claw the air. . . .[6] As with other humble theories asked to op-

---

[5] This would involve identities not between types of mental and brain states in general, but between types of *human* mental states and human brain states. The restricted scope of such identities would avoid the accusation of "human chauvinism"—restricting the domain of the mental to subjects with our sort of brain tissue. ED.

[6] Here Churchland refers to a later part of his book that discusses various psychological deficits associated with damage to different part of the brain. His point is that the kinds of deficits that are observed in brain-damaged patients do not correspond to folk-psychology concepts of mental functions. For instance, damage to specific brain areas can result in the inability to comprehend written speech even though the subject can still write, and visual perception is intact. Or a person may become blind, los-

erate successfully in unexplored extensions of their old domain (for example, Newtonian mechanics in the domain of velocities close to the velocity of light, and the classical gas law in the domain of high pressures or temperatures)[7], the descriptive and explanatory inadequacies of folk psychology become starkly evident.

The second argument tries to draw an inductive lesson from our conceptual history. Our early folk theories of motion were profoundly confused, and were eventually displaced entirely by more sophisticated theories. Our early folk theories of the structure and activity of the heavens were wildly off the mark, and survive only as historical lessons in how wrong we can be. Our folk theories of the nature of fire, and the nature of life, were similarly cockeyed. And one could go on, since the vast majority of our past folk conceptions have been similarly exploded. All except folk psychology, which survives to this day and has only recently begun to feel pressure. But the phenomenon of conscious intelligence is surely a more complex and difficult phenomenon than any of those just listed. So far as accurate understanding is concerned, it would be a *miracle* if we had got *that* one right the very first time, when we fell down so badly on all the others. Folk psychology has survived for so very long, presumably not because it is basically correct in its representations, but because the phenomena addressed are so surpassingly difficult that any useful handle on them, no matter how feeble, is unlikely to be displaced in a hurry.

A third argument attempts to find an a priori advantage for eliminative materialism over the identity theory and functionalism. It attempts to counter the common intuition that eliminative materialism is distantly possible, perhaps, but is much less probable than either the identity theory or functionalism. The focus again is on whether the concepts of folk psychology will find vindicating match-ups in a matured neuroscience. The eliminativist bets no; the other two bet yes. (Even the functionalist bets yes, but expects the match-ups to be only species-specific, or only person specific. Functionalism, recall, denies the existence only of *universal* type/type identities.)

The eliminativist will point out that the requirements on a reduction are rather demanding. The new theory must entail a set of principles and embedded concepts that mirrors very closely the specific conceptual structure to be reduced. And the fact is, there are vastly many more ways of being an explanatorily successful neuroscience while *not* mirroring the structure of folk psychology. Accordingly, the a priori probability of eliminative materialism is not lower, but substantially *higher* than that of either of its competitors. One's initial intuitions here are simply mistaken.

Granted, this initial a priori advantage could be reduced if there were a very strong presumption in favor of the truth of folk psychology—true theories are better bets to win reduction. But according to the first two arguments, the presumptions on this point should run in precisely the opposite direction.

ARGUMENTS AGAINST ELIMINATIVE MATERIALISM

The initial plausibility of this rather radical view is low for almost everyone, since it denies deeply entrenched assumptions. That is at best a question-begging complaint, of course, since those assumptions are precisely what is at issue. But the following line of thought does attempt to mount a real argument.

Eliminative materialism is false, runs the argument, because one's introspection reveals directly the existence of pains, beliefs, desires, fears, and so forth. Their existence is as obvious as anything could be.

The eliminative materialist will reply that this argument makes the same mistake that an ancient or medieval person would be making if he insisted that he could just see with is own eyes that the heavens form a turning sphere, or that witches

---

ing their visual field in its entirety, yet be able accurately to indicate the location of a moving or illuminated object (so-called blindsight). These deficits suggest that the way mental functions are divided up by our brain "hardware" corresponds rather poorly with our folk concepts of the mental. ED.

[7] Newtonian mechanics is hardly a "humble" theory! As the velocity of a body approaches the speed of light, it begins to behave in ways that are inaccessible to Newtonian concepts. For instance, a body's mass will dramatically increase, and time will slow down for that body in relation to the time of a second body that remains at the point of departure of the first body. Boyle's Law (1662) stated that the pressure of a given gas varies inversely with its volume at a constant temperature ($pv = k$). However, at higher pressure, the product pv decreases somewhat. ED.

exist. The fact is, all observation occurs within some system of concepts, and our observation judgments are only as good as the conceptual framework in which they are expressed. In all three cases—the starry sphere, witches, and the familiar mental states—precisely what is challenged is the integrity of the background conceptual frameworks in which the observation judgments are expressed. To insist on the validity of one's experiences, *traditionally interpreted,* is therefore to beg the very question at issue. For in all three cases, the question is whether we should reconceive the nature of some familiar observational domain.

A second criticism attempts to find an incoherence in the eliminative materialist's position. The bald statement of eliminative materialism is that the familiar mental states do not really exist. But that statement is meaningful, runs the argument, only if it is the expression of a certain *belief,* and an *intention* to communicate, and a *knowledge* of the language, and so forth. But if the statement is true, then no such mental states exist, and the statement is therefore a meaningless string of marks or noises, and cannot be true. Evidently, the assumption that eliminative materialism is true entails that it cannot be true.

The hole in this argument is the premise concerning the conditions necessary for a statement to be meaningful. It begs the question. If eliminative materialism is true, then meaningfulness must have some different source. To insist on the 'old' source is to insist on the validity of the very framework at issue. Again an historical parallel may be helpful here. Consider the medieval theory that being biologically *alive* is a matter of being ensouled by an immaterial *vital spirit.* And consider the following response to someone who has expressed disbelief in that theory.

My learned friend has stated that there is no such thing as vital spirit. But this statement is incoherent.

For if it is true, then my friend does not have vital spirit, and must therefore be *dead.* But if he is dead, then his statement is just a string of noises, devoid of meaning or truth. Evidently, the assumption that antivitalism is true entails that it cannot be true! Q.E.D.

This second argument is now a joke, but the first argument begs the question in exactly the same way.

A final criticism draws a much weaker conclusion, but makes a rather stronger case. Eliminative materialism, it has been said, is making mountains out of molehills. It exaggerates the defects of folk psychology, and underplays its real successes. Perhaps the arrival of a matured neuroscience will require the elimination of the occasional folk-psychological concept, continues the criticism, and a minor adjustment in certain folk-psychological principles may have to be endured. But the large-scale elimination forecast by the eliminative materialist is just an alarmist worry or a romantic enthusiasm.

Perhaps this complaint is correct. And perhaps it is merely complacent. Whichever, it does bring out the important point that we do not confront two simple and mutually exclusive possibilities here: pure reduction versus pure elimination. Rather these are the end points of a smooth spectrum of possible outcomes, between which there are mixed cases of partial elimination and partial reduction. Only empirical research . . . can tell us where on that spectrum our own case will fall. Perhaps we should speak here, more liberally, of "revisionary materialism", instead of concentrating on the more radical possibility of an across-the-board elimination. Perhaps we should. But it has been my aim in this section to make at least intelligible to you that our collective conceptual destiny lies substantially toward the revolutionary end of the spectrum.

REVIEW QUESTIONS

1. Is Churchland being fair to folk psychology when he says that "the most central things about us remain almost entirely mysterious from within folk psychology" (p. 132)? Has folk psychology been useful to you today? How often? What do we learn from long experience in dealing with other people?

2. In predicting the demise of folk psychology, Churchland compares it with phlogiston theory, belief in witches, and astronomical theories invoking heavenly spheres. Compared to these other theories and beliefs, how many more believers and practitioners, past or present, does folk psychology have? Does this difference weaken Churchland's argument?

3. On p. 134, Churchland formulates this objection to eliminative materialism:

> A second criticism attempts to find an incoherence in the eliminative materialist's position. The bald statement of eliminative materialism is that the familiar mental states do not really exist. But that statement is meaningful, runs the argument, only if it is the expression of a certain *belief,* and an *intention* to communicate, and a *knowledge* of the language, and so forth. But if the statement is true, then no such mental states exist, and the statement is therefore a meaningless string of marks or noises, and cannot be true. Evidently, the assumption that eliminative materialism is true entails that it cannot be true.

By way of criticism, he recites a second argument, one which is now understood as a joke:

> My learned friend has stated that there is no such thing as vital spirit. But this statement is incoherent. For if it is true, then my friend does not have vital spirit, and must therefore be *dead*. But if he is dead, then his statement is just a string of noises, devoid of meaning or truth. Evidently, the assumption that antivitalism is true entails that it cannot be true! Q.E.D.

He claims that this argument is just as question-begging as the first one. Do you agree?

10

The Nature of Mind

David M. Armstrong

David Armstrong is an Australian philosopher who is currently Emeritus Professor at the University of Sydney where he has taught since 1964. He has written extensively in several areas of philosophy, including epistemology, metaphysics, philosophy of science, and philosophy of mind. Among his many books are *A Materialist Theory of Mind* (1968) and *The Nature of Mind and Other Essays* (1980), from which this reading is taken.

Echoing Smart, Armstrong begins by giving reasons for his faith in the "scientific vision of man" and its superiority to alternative visions. However he disagrees with the sharply limited scope of the mind-brain identity thesis in Place and Smart. They were ready to accept a Rylean behaviorist analysis of most mental language except for explicit reports of sensations, after-images, and the like. Armstrong will argue that the behaviorist analysis of ordinary mental language in general is incorrect because that language does intend to refer to *inner* mental processes distinct from behavior. He presents a topic-neutral, causal analysis of mental terms which, he claims, allows neuroscientists to step in and identify mental states with brain states.

Men have minds, that is to say, they perceive, they have sensations, emotions, beliefs, thoughts, purposes and desires. What is it to have a mind? What is it to perceive, to feel emotion, to hold a belief or to have a purpose? Many contemporary philosophers think that the best clue we have to the nature of mind is furnished by the discoveries and hypotheses of modern science concerning the nature of man.

What does modern science have to say about the nature of man? There are, of course, all sorts of disagreements and divergences in the views of individual scientists. But I think it is true to say that one view is steadily gaining ground, so that it bids fair to become established scientific doctrine. This is the view that we can give a complete account of man *in purely physico-chemical terms*.[1] This view has received a tremendous impetus in recent decades from the new subject of molecular biology, a subject that promises to unravel the physical and chemical mechanisms that lie at the basis of life. Before that time, it received great encouragement from pioneering work in neurophysiology pointing to the likelihood of a purely electro-chemical account of the working of the brain. I think it is fair to say that those scientists who still reject the physico-chemical account of man do so primarily

[1] The view in question may be a doctrine *about* science or about the synthesis of the various sciences that study the human being, but it can hardly be called a "scientific doctrine" since it is not a conclusion that could be established by what is usually regarded as scientific evidence. It is instead a philosophical doctrine about the roles of the various sciences (social, biological, and physical) which gives primacy to physical science over the others, and to scientific knowledge over other ways of understanding human beings. ED.

From: David Armstrong, "The Nature of Mind" in *The Nature of Mind and Other Essays* (University of Queensland Press, St. Lucia, Lld 1980; Cornell University Press, Ithaca, NY, 1981), pp. 1–15. Reprinted with permission of the publisher.

for philosophical, or moral or religious reasons, and only secondarily, and half-heartedly, for reasons of scientific detail. This is not to say that in the future new evidence and new problems may not come to light that will force science to reconsider the physico-chemical view of man. But at present the drift of scientific thought is clearly set towards the physico-chemical hypothesis. And we have nothing better to go on than the present.

For me, then, and for many philosophers who think like me, the moral is clear. We must try to work out an account of the nature of mind which is compatible with the view that man is nothing but a physico-chemical mechanism.

And in this paper, I shall be concerned to do just this: to sketch (in barest outline) what may be called a Materialist or Physicalist account of the mind.

THE AUTHORITY OF SCIENCE

But before doing this, I should like to go back and consider a criticism of my position that must inevitably occur to some. What reason have I, it may be asked, for taking my stand on science? Even granting that I am right about what is the currently dominant scientific view of man, why should we concede science a special authority to decide questions about the nature of man? What of the authority of philosophy, of religion, of morality, or even of literature and art? Why do I set the authority of science above all these? Why this "scientism"?[2]

It seems to me that the answer to this question is very simple. If we consider the search for truth, in all its fields, we find that it is only in science that men versed in their subject can, after investigation that is more or less prolonged, and which may in some cases extend beyond a single human lifetime, reach substantial agreement about what is the case. It is only as a result of scientific investigation that we ever seem to reach an intellectual consensus about controversial matters.

In the Epistle Dedicatory to *De Corpore,* Hobbes wrote of William Harvey, the discoverer of the circulation of the blood, that he was: "the only

man I know, that conquering envy, hath established a new doctrine in his life-time."

Before Copernicus, Galileo and Harvey, Hobbes remarks: "there was nothing certain in natural philosophy." And we might add, with the exception of mathematics, there was nothing certain in any other learned discipline.

These remarks of Hobbes are incredibly revealing. They show us what a watershed in the intellectual history of the human race the seventeenth century was. Before that time, enquiry proceeded, as it were, in the dark. Men could not hope to see their doctrine *established,* that is to say, accepted by the vast majority of those properly versed in the subject under discussion. There was no intellectual consensus. Since that time, it has become a commonplace to see new doctrines, sometimes of the most far-reaching kind, established to the satisfaction of the learned, often within the lifetime of their first proponents. Science has provided us with a method of deciding disputed questions. This is not to say, of course, that the consensus of those who are learned and competent in a subject cannot be mistaken. Of course such a consensus can be mistaken. Sometimes it has been mistaken. But, granting fallibility, what better authority have we than such a consensus?

Now this is of the utmost importance. For in philosophy, in religion, in such disciplines as literary criticism, in moral questions in so far as they are thought to be matters of truth and falsity, there has been a notable failure to achieve an intellectual consensus about disputed questions among the learned. Must we not then attach a peculiar authority to the discipline that can achieve a consensus? And if it presents us with a certain vision of the nature of man, is this not a powerful reason for accepting that vision?

I will not take up here the deeper question *why* it is that the methods of science have enabled us to achieve an intellectual consensus about so many disputed matters. That question, I think, could receive no brief or uncontroversial answer. I am resting my argument on the simple fact that, as a result of scientific investigation, such a consensus has been achieved.

It may be replied—it often is replied—that while science is all very well in its own sphere—the sphere of the physical, perhaps—there are matters

---
[2] See section 2 ("Materialism") of the Introduction for more discussion of this topic. ED.

of fact on which it is not competent to pronounce. And among such matters, it may be claimed, is the question: what is the whole nature of man? But I cannot see that this reply has much force. Science has provided us with an island of truths, or, perhaps one should say, a raft of truths, to bear us up on the sea of our disputatious ignorance. There may have to be revisions and refinements, new results may set old findings in a new perspective, but what science has given us will not be altogether superseded. Must we not therefore appeal to these relative certainties for guidance when we come to consider uncertainties elsewhere? Perhaps science cannot help us to decide whether or not there is a God, whether or not human beings have immortal souls, or whether or not the will is free. But if science cannot assist us, what can? I conclude that it is the scientific vision of man, and not the philosophical or religious or artistic or moral vision of man, that is the best clue we have to the nature of man. And it is rational to argue from the best evidence we have.[3]

DEFINING THE MENTAL

Having in this way attempted to justify my procedure, I turn back to my subject: the attempt to work out an account of mind, or, if you prefer, of mental process, within the framework of the physico-chemical, or, as we may call it, the Materialist view of man.

Now there is one account of mental process that is at once attractive to any philosopher sympathetic to a Materialist view of man: this is Behaviourism. Formulated originally by a psychologist, J. B. Watson, it attracted widespread interest and considerable support from scientifically oriented philosophers. Traditional philosophy had tended to think of the mind as a rather mysterious inward arena that lay behind, and was responsible for, the outward or physical behaviour of our bodies. Descartes thought of this inner arena as a *spiritual substance,* and it was this conception of the mind as spiritual object that Gilbert Ryle attacked, apparently in the interest of Behaviourism, in his important book *The Concept of Mind* (1949). He ridiculed the Cartesian view as the dogma of "the ghost in the machine".[4] The mind was not something behind the behaviour of the body, it was simply part of that physical behaviour. My anger with you is not some modification of a spiritual substance that somehow brings about aggressive behavior; rather it is the aggressive behaviour itself: my addressing strong words to you, striking you, turning my back on you, and so on. Thought is not an inner process that lies behind, and brings about, the words I speak and write: it is my speaking and writing. The mind is not an inner arena, it is outward act.

It is clear that such a view of mind fits in very well with a completely Materialistic or Physicalist view of man. If there is no need to draw a distinction between mental processes and their expression in physical behaviour, but if instead the mental processes are identified with their so-called "expressions", then the existence of mind stands in no conflict with the view that man is nothing but a physico-chemical mechanism.

However, the version of Behaviourism that I have just sketched is a very crude version, and its crudity lays it open to obvious objections. One obvious difficulty is that it is our common experience that there can be mental processes going on although there is no behaviour occurring that could possibly be treated as expressions of those processes. A man may be angry, but give no bodily sign; he may think, but say or do nothing at all.

In my view, the most plausible attempt to refine Behaviourism with a view to meeting this objection was made by introducing the notion of *a disposition to behave.* (Dispositions to behave play a particularly important part in Ryle's account of the mind.) Let us consider the general notion of disposition first. Brittleness is a disposition, a disposition possessed by materials like glass. Brittle materials are those that, when subjected to relatively small forces, break or shatter easily. A piece of glass may never shatter or break throughout its whole history, but it is still the case that it is brittle: it is liable to shatter or break if dropped quite a small way or hit quite lightly. Now a disposition to *behave* is simply a tendency or liability of a person to behave in a certain way under certain circumstances. The brittleness of

---

[3]The view of science presented here has been challenged in recent years by new Irrationalist philosophies of science. See, in particular, Thomas Kuhn [*The Structure of Scientific Revolutions*] (1962) and Paul Feyerabend [*Against Method*] (1975). A complete treatment of the problem would involve answering their contentions.

[4]See Reading 2.

glass is a disposition that the glass retains throughout its history, but clearly there also could be dispositions that come and go. The dispositions to behave that are of interest to the Behaviourist are, for the most part, of this temporary character.

Now how did Ryle and others use the notion of a disposition to behave to meet the obvious objection to Behaviourism that there can be mental processes going on although the subject is engaging in no relevant behaviour? Their strategy was to argue that in such cases, although the subject was not behaving in any relevant way, he or she was *disposed* to behave in some relevant way. The glass does not shatter, but it is still brittle. The man does not behave, but he does have a disposition to behave. We can say he thinks although he does not speak or act because at that time he was disposed to speak or act in a certain way. *If* he had been asked, perhaps, he would have spoken or acted. We can say he is angry although he does not behave angrily, because he is disposed so to behave. *If* only one more word had been addressed to him, he would have burst out. And so on. In this way it was hoped that Behaviourism could be squared with the obvious facts.

It is very important to see just how these thinkers conceived of dispositions. I quote from Ryle:

> To possess a dispositional property *is not to be in a particular state, or to undergo a particular change;* it is to be bound or liable to be in a particular state, or to undergo a particular change, when a particular condition is realized.[5]

So to explain the breaking of a lightly struck glass on a particular occasion by saying it was brittle is, on this view of dispositions, simply to say that the glass broke because it is the sort of thing that regularly breaks when quite lightly struck. The breaking was the normal behaviour, or not abnormal behaviour, of such a thing. The brittleness is not to be conceived of as a *cause* for the breakage, or even, more vaguely, a *factor* in bringing about the breaking. Brittleness is just the fact that things of that sort break easily.

But although in this way the Behaviourists did something to deal with the objection that mental processes can occur in the absence of behaviour, it

seems clear, now that the shouting and the dust have died, that they did not do enough. When I think, but my thoughts do not issue in any action, it seems as obvious as anything is obvious that there is something actually going on in me that constitutes my thought. It is not simply that I would speak or act if some conditions that are unfulfilled were to be fulfilled. Something is currently going on, in the strongest and most literal sense of "going on", and this something is my thought. Rylean Behaviourism denies this, and so it is unsatisfactory as a theory of mind.[6] Yet I know of no version of Behaviourism that is more satisfactory. The moral for those of us who wish to take a purely physicalistic view of man is that we must look for some other account of the nature of mind and of mental processes.

But perhaps we need not grieve too deeply about the failure of Behaviourism to produce a satisfactory theory of mind. Behaviourism is a profoundly unnatural account of mental processes. If somebody speaks and acts in certain ways, it is natural to speak of this speech and action as the *expression* of his thought. It is not at all natural to speak of his speech and action as identical with his thought. We naturally think of the thought as something quite distinct from the speech and action that, under suitable circumstances, brings the speech and action about. Thoughts are not to be identified with behaviour, we think; they lie behind behaviour. A man's behaviour constitutes the *reason* we have for attributing certain mental processes to him, but the behaviour cannot be identified with the mental processes.

This suggests a very interesting line of thought about the mind. Behaviourism is certainly wrong, but perhaps it is not altogether wrong. Perhaps the Behaviourists are wrong in identifying the mind and mental occurrences with behaviour, but perhaps they are right in thinking that our notion of a mind and of individual mental states is *logically tied to behaviour.* For perhaps what we mean by a mental state is some state of the person that, under suitable

---

[5]Ryle, 1949: 43; emphasis added.

[6]Armstrong is claiming here that Rylean behaviorism did not do well in the very territory that it staked out for itself—ordinary language about the mind. He is saying that Ryle's analysis of this language, by ruling out reference to internal processes or states, fails to notice what we clearly intend to say when we speak about mental items such as feelings, sensations, and even beliefs. ED.

circumstances, *brings about* a certain range of behaviour. Perhaps mind can be defined not as behaviour, but rather as the inner *cause* of certain behaviour. Thought is not speech under suitable circumstances, rather it is something within the person that, in suitable circumstances, brings about speech. And, in fact, I believe that this is the true account, or, at any rate, a true first account, of what we mean by a mental state.

How does this line of thought link up with a purely Physicalist view of man? The position is that while it does not make such a Physicalist view inevitable, it does make it *possible*. It does not entail, but it is compatible with, a purely Physicalist view of man. For if our notion of the mind and of mental states is nothing but that of a cause within the person of certain ranges of behaviour, then it becomes a scientific question, and not a question of logical analysis, what in fact the intrinsic nature of that cause is. The cause might be, as Descartes thought it was, a spiritual substance working through the pineal gland to produce the complex bodily behaviour of which men are capable. It might be breath, or specially smooth and mobile atoms dispersed throughout the body; it might be many other things.[7] But in fact the verdict of modern science seems to be that the sole cause of mind-betokening behaviour in man and the higher animals is the physico-chemical workings of the central nervous system. And so, assuming we have correctly characterized our concept of a mental state as nothing but the cause of certain sorts of behaviour, then we can identify these mental states with purely physical states of the central nervous system.[8]

At this point we may stop and go back to the Behaviourist's dispositions. We saw that, according to him, the brittleness of glass or, to take another example, the elasticity of rubber, is not a state of the glass or the rubber, but is simply the fact that things of that sort behave in the way they do. But now let us consider how a scientist would think about brittleness or elasticity. Faced with the phenomenon of breakage under relatively small impacts, or the phenomenon of stretching when a force is applied followed by contraction when the force is removed, he will assume that there is some current *state* of the glass or the rubber that is responsible for the characteristic behaviour of samples of these two materials. At the beginning, he will not know what this state is, but he will endeavour to find out, and he may succeed in finding out. And when he has found out, he will very likely make remarks of this sort: "We have discovered that the brittleness of glass is in fact a certain sort of pattern in the molecules of the glass." That is to say, he will *identify* brittleness with the state of the glass that is responsible for the liability of the glass to break. For him, a disposition of an object is a state of the object. What makes the state a state of brittleness is the fact that it gives rise to the characteristic manifestations of brittleness. But the disposition itself is distinct from its manifestations: it is the state of the glass that gives rise to these manifestations in suitable circumstances.

This way of looking at dispositions is very different from that of Ryle and the Behaviourists. The great difference is this: If we treat dispositions as actual states, as I have suggested that scientists do, even if states the intrinsic nature of which may yet have to be discovered, then we can say that dispositions are actual *causes*, or causal factors, which, in suitable circumstances, actually being about those happenings that are the manifestations of the disposition. A certain molecular constitution of glass that constitutes its brittleness is actually *responsible* for the fact that, when the glass is struck, it breaks.

Now I cannot argue the matter here, because the detail of the argument is technical and difficult, but I believe that the view of dispositions as states, which is the view that is natural to science, is the correct one.[9] I believe it can be shown quite strictly that, to the extent that we admit the notion of dispositions at all, we are committed to the view that they are actual *states* of the object that has the dis-

---

[7] This is where Armstrong begins to explicitly foreshadow the position that came to be known as *functionalism*: There may be many physically different systems that can affect, and be affected by, their environments in the same ways that the brains of animals do. The *concept* of mind does not limit minds to brains. In other words, physically different systems may be the functional equivalents of brains. ED.

[8] This is an important transition in Armstrong's two-stage argument. The first stage proposes a topic-neutral analysis of mental language as referring to inner causes (physical or not) of the kind of behavior we associate with mind. This analysis is often referred to as the Causal Theory. The second stage asserts that neuroscience provides sufficient evidence for identifying the inner causes as brain events or states. This claim is often called Central State Materialism. ED.

[9] I develop the argument in *Belief, Truth and Knowledge* (1973), ch. 2, sect. 2.

position. I may add that I think that the same holds for the closely connected notions of capacities and powers. Here I will simply have to assume this step in my argument.

But perhaps it will be seen that the rejection of the idea that mind is simply a certain range of man's behaviour in favour of the view that mind is rather the inner *cause* of that range of man's behaviour, is bound up with the rejection of the Rylean view of dispositions in favour of one that treats dispositions as states of objects and so as having actual causal power. The Behaviourists were wrong to identify the mind with behavior. They were not so far off the mark when they tried to deal with cases where mental happenings occur in the absence of behaviour by saying that these are dispositions to behave. But in order to reach a correct view, I am suggesting, they would have to conceive of these dispositions as actual *states* of the person who has the disposition, states that have actual causal power to bring about behaviour in suitable circumstances. But to do this is to abandon the central inspiration of Behaviourism: that in talking about the mind we do not have to go behind outward behaviour to inner states.

And so two separate but interlocking lines of thought have pushed me in the same direction. The first line of thought is that it goes profoundly against the grain to think of the mind as behaviour. The mind is, rather, that which stands behind and brings about our complex behaviour. The second line of thought is that the Behaviourist's dispositions, properly conceived, are really states that underlie behaviour and, under suitable circumstances, bring about behaviour. Putting these two together, we reach the conception of a mental state as *a state of the person apt for producing certain ranges of behaviour.* This formula: a mental state is a state of the person apt for producing certain ranges of behaviour, I believe to be a very illuminating way of looking at the concept of a mental state. I have found it fruitful in the search for detailed logical analyses of the individual mental concepts.

I do not think that Hegel's Dialectic has much to tell us about the nature of reality.[10] But I think that human thought often moves in a dialectical way, from thesis to antithesis and then to the synthesis. Perhaps thought about the mind is a case in point. I have already said that classical philosophy has tended to think of the mind as an inner arena of some sort. This we may call the Thesis. Behaviourism moves to the opposite extreme: the mind is seen as outward behaviour. This is the Antithesis. My proposed Synthesis is that the mind is properly conceived as an inner principle, but a principle that is identified in terms of the outward behaviour it is apt for bringing about. This way of looking at the mind and mental states does not itself entail a Materialist or Physicalist view of man, for nothing is said in this analysis about the intrinsic nature of these mental states. But if we have, as I have argued that we do have, general scientific grounds for thinking that man is nothing but a physical mechanism, we can go on to argue that the mental states are in fact nothing but physical states of the central nervous system.

THE PROBLEM OF CONSCIOUSNESS

Along these lines, then, I would look for an account of the mind that is compatible with a purely Materialist theory of man. There are, as may be imagined, all sorts of powerful objections that can be made to my view. But in the rest of this paper, I propose to do only one thing: I will develop one very important objection to my view of the mind—an objection felt by many philosophers—and then try to show how the objection should be met.

The view that our notion of mind is nothing but that of an inner principle apt for bringing about certain sorts of behaviour may be thought to share a certain weakness with Behaviourism. Modern philosophers have put the point about Behaviourism by saying that, although Behaviourism may

---

[10] Georg Wilhelm Friedrich Hegel (1770–1831) is one of the most influential of all philosophers, belonging in the ranks of Plato, Aristotle, and Kant, for his originality and scope. He interpreted the history not only of humankind but of the cosmos, as the progressive actualization of the self-awareness of infinite Spirit (of which we are each fragmentary manifestations). This progressive actualization typically has a *dialectical* structure of a kind that is exemplified when two people begin a discussion with sharply opposed viewpoints, come to see that each view is limited or partial, and overcome these limitations to achieve a higher, consensual viewpoint which preserves what was true in the previously opposed views. Commentators often describe this progression as one of *thesis* (assertion), *antithesis* (negation), and *synthesis,* but this terminology is not Hegelian. Another way to think of the dialectical progression is as a movement from a strict *either/or* to a *both/and* in which some of each disjunct is preserved. Ed.

be a satisfactory account of the mind from *an other-person point of view,* it will not do as a *first-person* account. To explain. In my encounters with other people, all I ever observe is their behaviour: their actions, their speech, and so on. And so, if we simply consider other people, Behaviourism might seem to do full justice to the facts. But the trouble about Behaviourism is that it seems so unsatisfactory as applied to our *own* case. In our own case, we seem to be aware of so much more than mere behaviour.

Suppose that now we conceive of the mind as an inner principle apt for bringing about certain sorts of behaviour. This again fits the other-person cases very well. Bodily behaviour of a very sophisticated sort is observed, quite different from the behaviour that ordinary physical objects display. It is inferred that this behaviour must spring from a very special sort of inner cause in the object that exhibits this behaviour. This inner cause is christened "the mind," and those who take a Physicalist view of man argue that it is simply the central nervous system of the body observed. Compare this with the case of glass. Certain characteristic behaviour is observed: the breaking and shattering of the material when acted upon by relatively small forces. A special inner state of the glass is postulated to explain this behaviour. Those who take a purely Physicalist view of glass then argue that this state is a *material* state of the glass. It is, perhaps, an arrangement of its molecules and not, say, the peculiarly malevolent disposition of the demons that dwell in glass.

But when we turn to our own case, the position may seem less plausible. We are conscious, we have experiences. Now can we say that to be conscious, to have experiences, is simply for something to go on within us apt for the causing of certain sorts of behaviour? Such an account does not seem to do any justice to the phenomena. And so it seems that our account of the mind, like Behaviourism, will fail to do justice to the first-person case.

In order to understand the objection better, it may be helpful to consider a particular case. If you have driven for a very long distance without a break, you may have had experience of a curious state of automatism, which can occur in these conditions. One can suddenly "come to" and realize that one has driven for long distances without being aware of what one was doing, or, indeed, without being aware of anything. One has kept the car on the road, used the brake and the clutch perhaps, yet all without any awareness of what one was doing.

Now if we consider this case, it is obvious that *in some sense* mental processes are still going on when one is in such an automatic state. Unless one's will was still operating in some way, and unless one was still perceiving in some way, the car would not still be on the road. Yet, of course, *something* mental is lacking. Now, I think, when it is alleged that an account of mind as an inner principle apt for the production of certain sorts of behaviour leaves out consciousness or experience, what is alleged to have been left out is just whatever is missing in the automatic driving case. It is conceded that an account of mental processes as states of the person apt for the production of certain sorts of behaviour very possibly may be adequate to deal with such cases as that of automatic driving. It may be adequate to deal with most of the mental processes of animals, which perhaps spend most of their lives in this state of automatism. But, it is contended, it cannot deal with the consciousness that we normally enjoy.

I will now try to sketch an answer to this important and powerful objection. Let us begin in an apparently unlikely place and consider the way that an account of mental processes of the sort I am giving would deal with *sense-perception.*

Now psychologists, in particular, have long realized that there is a very close logical tie between sense-perception and *selective behaviour.* Suppose we want to decide whether an animal can perceive the difference between red and green. We might give the animal a choice between two pathways, over one of which a red light shines and over the other of which a green light shines. If the animal happens by chance to choose the green pathway, we reward it; if it happens to choose the other pathway, we do not reward it. If, after some trials, the animal systematically takes the green-lighted pathway, and if we become assured that the only relevant differences in the two pathways are the differences in the colour of the lights, we are entitled to say that the animal can see this colour difference. Using its eyes, it selects between red-lighted and green-lighted pathways. So we say it can see the difference between red and green.

Now a Behaviourist would be tempted to say that the animal's regular selection of the green-lighted pathway *was* its perception of the colour difference. But this is unsatisfactory, because we all want to say that perception is something that goes on within the person or animal—within its mind—although, of course, this mental event is normally *caused* by the operation of the environment upon the organism. Suppose, however, that we speak instead of *capacities* for selective behaviour towards the current environment, and suppose we think of these capacities, like dispositions, as actual inner states of the organism. We can then think of the animal's perception as a state within the animal apt, if the animal is so impelled, for selective behaviour between the red- and green-lighted pathways.

In general, we can think of perceptions as inner states or events apt for the production of certain sorts of selective behaviour towards our environment. To perceive is like acquiring a key to a door. You do not have to use the key: you can put it in your pocket and never bother about the door. But if you do want to open the door, the key may be essential. The blind man is a man who does not acquire certain keys and, as a result, is not able to operate in his environment in the way that somebody who has his sight can operate. It seems, then, a very promising view to take of perceptions that they are inner states defined by the sorts of selective behaviour that they enable the perceiver to exhibit, if so impelled.

Now how is this discussion of perception related to the question of consciousness or experience, the sort of thing that the driver who is in a state of automatism has not got, but which we normally do have? Simply this. My proposal is that consciousness, in this sense of the word, is nothing but *perception or awareness of the state of our own mind.* The driver in a state of automatism perceives, or is aware of, the road. If he [was] not, the car would be in a ditch. But he is not currently aware of his awareness of the road. He perceives the road, but he does not perceive his perceiving, or anything else that is going on in his mind. He is not, as we normally are, conscious of what is going on in his mind.

And so I conceive of consciousness or experience, in this sense of the words, in the way that

Locke and Kant[11] conceived it, as like perception. Kant, in a striking phrase, spoke of "inner sense". We cannot directly observe the minds of others, but each of us has the power to observe directly our own minds, and "perceive" what is going on there. The driver in the automatic state is one whose "inner eye" is shut: who is not currently aware of what is going on in his own mind.

Now if this account is along the right lines, why should we not give an account of this inner observation along the same lines as we have already given of perception? Why should we not conceive of it as an inner state, a state in this case directed towards other inner states and not to the environment, which enables us, if we are so impelled, to behave in a selective way *towards our own states of mind?* One who is aware, or conscious, of his thoughts or his emotions is one who has the capacity to make discriminations between his different mental states. His capacity might be exhibited in words. He might say that he was in an angry state of mind, when, and only when, he *was* in an angry state of mind. But such verbal behaviour would be the mere *expression* or *result* of the awareness. The awareness itself would be an inner state: the sort of inner state that gave the man a capacity for such behavioural expressions.

So I have argued that consciousness of our own mental state may be assimilated to *perception* of our own mental state, and that, like other perceptions, it may then be conceived of as an inner state or event giving a capacity for selective behaviour, in this case selective behaviour towards our own mental state. All this is meant to be simply a logical analysis of consciousness, and none of it entails, although it does not rule out, a purely Physicalist account of what these inner states are. But if we are convinced, on general scientific grounds, that a purely physical account of man is likely to be the true one, then there seems to be no bar to our identifying these inner states with purely physical states of the central nervous system. And so consciousness of our own mental state becomes simply the scanning of one part of our central nervous system by another. Consciousness is a self-scanning mechanism in the central nervous system.

---

[11]Immanuel Kant (1724–1804), like his later compatriot Hegel, was one of the philosophical "greats." Kant's most famous work is *A Critique of Pure Reason* (1781, 1787).

As I have emphasized before, I have done no more than sketch a programme for a philosophy of mind. There are all sorts of expansions and elucidations to be made, and all sorts of doubts and difficulties to be stated and overcome. But I hope I have done enough to show that a purely Physicalist theory of the mind is an exciting and plausible intellectual option.

At the end of the section of his essay titled "The Authority of Science," Armstrong admits that there may be questions to which science cannot provide answers:

> But if science cannot assist us, what can? I conclude that it is the scientific vision of man, and not the philosophical or religious or artistic or moral vision of man, that is the best clue we can have to the nature of man. And it is rational to argue from the best evidence we have.

This is scientism in a very pure form. It is striking to read a philosopher dividing our intellectual pursuits between science's "raft of truths" and "the sea of our disputatious ignorance." Armstrong reveres science because it has achieved a consensus on so much that we have come to understand about the world, and because it can agree on how to resolve disputed questions. We certainly should admire the brilliance and dedication of those who have won these scientific truths for us, but we should not be surprised that science can achieve consensus. If you and I differ on how high or heavy something is, we nevertheless agree on how to resolve our dispute by using an appropriate measuring device. Properly formulated scientific hypotheses predict with precision publicly observable events, including the results of measurements. Discovering whether a predicted and measurable event occurs is a straightforward matter. Any discipline that limits itself to what is measurable is bound to achieve far more consensus than an intellectual pursuit that is not so limited. The fact that this limitation promotes consensus is not a conclusive argument for the claim that only what is measurable (in humans and in the world at large) is real or intelligible.

We are accustomed to the spectacle of expert scientific testimony on both or all sides of most important public policy issues. Whether it is safe and worthwhile to expand our use of nuclear power, whether we should trade away more wilderness for economic development, what economic and social policies will be good for our society, and whether we should invest heavily in space exploration—these and numerous other momentous social issues call upon us to formulate a vision of what is good for human beings and their communities, a vision which requires choosing among competing descriptions of what we are and what we need. We want to know all that science can tell us about these issues, but the divisions among scientists over these issues reflects the divisions among people in general, which suggests that science alone is not enough for their solution. If truth is accessible only in science, can we achieve consensus about the most important matters only through irrational means such as social pressure, propaganda, or violence?

As Armstrong himself says at the end of his essay, he has done no more than "sketch a programme" for the philosophy of mind. As he points out elsewhere (1980), the causal role of a mental state is usually quite complex. For instance, the visual perception of a piece of chocolate cake on the table must combine with a feeling of hunger or craving and other beliefs about the current environment before it brings about taking and eating behavior. Insofar as the causal theory characterizes mind in terms of what it *does,* i.e., in terms of its function, it points toward **functionalism,** a type of theory that is currently still in vogue and which we will examine in the next chapter.

REVIEW QUESTIONS

1. At the end of his essay, Armstrong claims that for a physicalist account of mind, "consciousness of our own mental state becomes simply the scanning of one part of our central nervous system by another. Consciousness is a self-scanning mechanism in the central nervous system." He is not saying that consciousness is a mechanism that scans *itself,* but rather that it scans what other mechanisms are doing, detects such things as inconsistencies between them, and has the capacity to generate reports or queries about them (e.g., "Why am I driving this way?"). What would Armstrong say about hyphenation, grammar- and spell-check programs that scan the text which the word-processing program is generating in response to input from the keyboard? Would that too satisfy his definition of "consciousness"? Is there any problem here?

2. If Armstrong is to succeed in his topic-neutral claim that *mental* states are by definition "apt for producing certain ranges of behaviour" (i.e., ranges of external behavior or bodily movement such as speech or carpentry), that definition must (1) not leave out anything essential to a process being *mental,* and it must (2) be neutral between dualism and materialism. Is his definition neutral with respect to Cartesian dualism (or, would Descartes accept this definition)? Explain.

11

Materialism

Jerry A. Fodor

Jerry Fodor is an American philosopher who teaches at Rutgers University. Among his many publications in philosophy of mind and language are *The Language of Thought* (1975) and *Psychosemantics* (1987).

Fodor's essay can be understood as picking up where Armstrong left off in Reading 10. Armstrong argued that mental states should be understood as essentially causal states—inner states (of human and other animals) understood solely in terms of the behavior they bring about. If you accept his thesis, says Armstrong, it becomes "a scientific question, and not a question of logical analysis, what in fact the intrinsic nature of that cause is." Given what we have been learning from neuroscience, he is confident that "we can identify these mental states with purely physical states of the central nervous system" (p. 140). However, as far as the Causal theory is concerned, mental states might belong to an immaterial Cartesian mind: What makes a mental state *mental* is its *causal* role, and not its physical or nonphysical constitution. Even if it so happens that a particular kind of mental state "is" a certain kind of brain state, *anything* playing the same causal role as one of those brain states will also be an instance of the same sort of mental state. Therefore, it would seem that Place and Smart were incorrect in as- similating the identity of mental and brain events with theoretical identities in physical science such as "Water is H_2O." No matter what causal role water plays that could also be served by something else, that something else can never be water because water must be composed of H_2O molecules (Kripke makes a similar point in Reading 7).

Where Armstrong speaks of mental states as "causal," Fodor characterizes them as "func- tional." These terms are closely related. The term "functional" adds to the meaning of "causal" a normative ingredient, a relation to a purpose or goal. A congested heart is no less a cause than a healthy heart, but a congested heart is *dys*functional because it is failing to do what a heart is supposed to do or what a functioning heart does. Every state that is functional is causal, but not every causal state is functional. The doctrine that mental states are essentially functional states or that psychological explanation is functional explanation is usually called *functionalism*.

It is frequently suggested in philosophical discus- sions of the mind-body problem that it might be reasonable to regard mind states and brain states as contingently identical.[1] How plausible one con- siders this suggestion to be depends on one's view of an extremely complicated tangle of philosophi- cal problems to which the materialist doctrine is

From: Jerry A. Fodor, *Psychological Explanation* (New York: Random House, Inc., 1968), pp. 90−91, 107−120. © Copyright 1968 by McGraw Hill, Inc.

[1]See Reading 5 (Place), especially sections 1−3; and the Replies to Objections 1 and 2 in Reading 6. Ed.

closely connected. Among these are problems that must clearly be faced during the course of providing an account of explanation in psychology.

For example, determining whether or not materialism can be true is part of understanding the relation between theories in psychology and theories in neurology—a relation that many philosophers believe poses a stumbling block for the doctrine of the unity of science.[2] In particular, it is sometimes maintained that the unity of science requires that it prove possible to "reduce" psychological theories to neurological theories, the model of reduction being provided by the relation between constructs in chemistry and those in physics. This is usually taken to mean that, for each theoretical term that appears in psychology, there must be a true statement that articulates a psychophysical identity[3] and that such statements are to be understood on the analogy of statements that identify hydrogen atoms with certain configurations of subatomic particles. On this view, neurological entities are the denotata[4] of psychological terms, just as physical entities are the denotata of chemical terms.[5]

This sort of issue suggests that rather more is at stake when the question of materialism is raised than may initially meet the eye. In this chapter, I shall therefore attempt to bring out some of the logical links between the controversy about materialism and some other problems in philosophical psychology, as well as to survey a number of arguments in which the truth of materialism is directly involved.

MATERIALISM AND THE RELATION BETWEEN PSYCHOLOGY AND NEUROLOGY

For purposes of the present investigation, we are primarily interested in materialism as it bears upon problems about psychological explanation. We need, therefore, to clarify the implications of the materialist view for an account of the relations between psychological and neurological theories. I shall argue that while it is by no means evident that materialism must be regarded as conceptually incoherent, it is equally unclear that the truth of materialism would entail the views of the relation between psychology and neurology that have often been held in conjunction with it. In particular, to claim that mind states and brain states are contingently identical need not be to hold that psychological theories are reducible to neurological theories. Nor would the truth of materialism entail that the relevant relation between psychological and neurological constructs is that the latter provide "microanalyses" of the former. It is to these issues that we now proceed.

Let us commence by trying to form some picture of how the problem of the relation between psychology and neurology emerges during the course of attempts to provide systematic scientific explanations of behavior.

Such attempts have characteristically exhibited two phases that, although they may be simultaneous in point of history, are nevertheless distinguishable in point of logic. In the first phase, the psychologist attempts to arrive at theories that provide what are often referred to as "functional" characterizations of the mechanisms responsible for the production of behavior. To say that the psychologist is seeking functional characterizations of psychological constructs is at least to say that, in this phase of explanation, the criteria employed for individuating[6] such constructs are based primarily upon hypotheses

---

[2] The term "unity of science" refers to the theoretical goal or ideal of a basic theory in some future physical science which would explain everything in the different subject matters of the various sciences. The ideal is reductionist in the sense that any sciences dealing with higher-level phenomena would be "reduced" to the science that deals with the next lower level, as in the reduction of chemistry to physics, and biology to chemistry. This intertheoretic reduction envisioned type identities between kinds of items in the domain of the reduced science and kinds of items in the reducing science. Thus, in reducing psychology to biology, types of mental events would be identified with types of neural events, so that the laws governing the lower-level domain of biology would, by substitution of mental for biological types, serve as laws for psychological events. ED.

[3] A psychophysical identity would obtain between types of psychological events such as visual experience, or perhaps the visual experience of a type of object, and a type of brain process or set of processes. ED.

[4] The denotata of a term are the objects referred to by that term. ED.

[5] Cf. Paul Oppenheim and Hilary Putnam, "Unity of Science as a Working Hypothesis," in *Minnesota Studies in the Philosophy of Science, Volume II: Concepts, Theories, and the Mind-Body Problem,* ed. Herbert Feigl, Michael Scriven and Grover Maxwell (Minneapolis: University of Minnesota Press, 1985), 3–36.

[6] "Individuating" is used here in the sense of "specifying" or "concretizing." ED.

about the role they play in the etiology of behavior. Such hypotheses are constrained by two general considerations. On the one hand, by the principle that the psychological states, processes, and so on hypothesized to be responsible for the production of behavior must be supposed to be sufficiently complex to account for whatever behavioral capacities the organism can be demonstrated to possess; on the other, by the principle that specific aspects of the character of the organism's behavior must be explicable by reference to specific features of the hypothesized underlying states and processes or of their interactions.

Thus, for example, a psychologist might seek to explain failures of memory by reference to the decay of a hypothetical memory "trace," an attempt being made to attribute to the trace properties that will account for such observed features of memory as selectivity, stereotyping, and so forth. As more is discovered about memory—for example, about the effects of pathology upon memory, or about differences between "short-" and "long-term" memory—the properties attributed to the trace, and to whatever other psychological systems are supposed to interact with it, must be correspondingly elaborated. It is, of course, the theorist's expectation that, at some point, speculations about the character of the trace will lead to confirmable experimental predictions about previously unnoticed aspects of memory, thus providing independent evidence for the claim that the trace does in fact have the properties it is alleged to have.

To say that, in the first phase of psychological explanation, the primary concern is with determining the functional character of the states and processes involved in the etiology of behavior is thus to say that, at that stage, the hypothesized psychological constructs are individuated primarily or solely by reference to their alleged causal consequences. What one knows (or claims to know) about such constructs is the effects their activity has upon behavior.[7] It follows that phase-one psychological theories postulate functionally equivalent mechanisms when and only when they postulate con-

structs of which the behavioral consequences are, in theoretically relevant respects, identical.

This sort of point has sometimes been made by comparing first-phase psychological theories with descriptions of a "machine table"[8]—that is, of the sets of directions for performing computations—of a digital computer. Neurological theories, correspondingly, are likened to descriptions of the "hardware"; that is, of the physical machinery into which such tables are programmed.[9] Since two physical realizations of the same table—that is, two computers capable of performing the mathematically identical set of computations in mathematically identical ways—may differ arbitrarily in their physical structure, mathematical equivalence is independent of physical similarity: two machines may, in this sense, share functionally equivalent "psychological" mechanisms even though they have neither parts nor configurations of parts in common.[10]

The second phase of psychological explanation has to do with the specification of those biochemical systems that do, in fact, exhibit the functional characteristics enumerated by phase-one theories. The image that suggests itself to many psychologists is that of opening a "black box": having arrived at a phase-one theory of the kinds of operations performed by the mechanisms that are causally responsible for behavior, one then "looks inside" to see whether or not the nervous system does in fact contain parts capable of performing the alleged functions. The situation is more complicated, however, than this image suggests since the notion of a "part," when applied to the nervous systems of organisms, is less than clear. The physiological psychologist's task of determining what, if any, organization into subsystems the nervous system of an organism exhibits is precisely the problem of determining whether the nervous system has subsystems

---

[7] This echoes Armstrong's thesis in Reading 10 (pp. 139–140 above) that "what we mean by a mental state is some state of the person that, under suitable circumstances, *brings about* a certain range of behaviour." ED.

[8] For an example and explanation of a machine table, see Reading 15. Fodor is referring to the kind of theory put forward by Putnam in Reading 16. ED.

[9] Cf. Putnam, op. cit.

[10] The earliest adding machines didn't even use electricity. Their hardware was grossly different from that of today's calculators: different materials, differently structured parts, different configurations, and enormous differences in the magnitudes of the parts and of the energies that drove them. Yet these early machines were (for many operations) their *functional equivalents*. ED.

whose functional characteristics correspond with those required by antecedently plausible psychological theories.[11]

The two phases of psychological explanation thus condition one another.[12] On the one hand, it is clear that a psychological theory that attributes to an organism a state or process that the organism has no physiological mechanisms capable of realizing is ipso facto incorrect. If memory is a matter of forming traces, then there must be subsystems of the nervous system that are capable of going from one steady state to another and that are capable of remaining in the relevant states for periods that are at least comparable to known retention periods. If no such mechanisms exist, then the trace is the wrong model for the functional organization of memory.

On the other hand, the relevant notion of a neurological subsystem is that of a biochemical mechanism whose operation can correspond to some state or process that is postulated by a satisfactory psychological theory. To say that the goals of physiological psychology are set by the attempt to find mechanisms that correspond to certain functions is to say that it is the psychological theory that articulates these functions that determines the principle of individuation for neurological mechanisms. Once again, analogies to the analysis of less complicated systems may be helpful. What makes a carbu-

retor part of an engine is not the spatial contiguity of its own parts (the parts of fuel injectors exhibit no such contiguity) nor is it the homogeneity of the materials of which it is composed. It is rather the fact that its operation corresponds to a function that is detailed in the theory of internal-combustion engines and that there is no sub- or superpart of the carburetor whose operation corresponds to that function.

The problem, then, is one of fit and mutual adjustment: on the one hand, there is a presumed psychological theory, which requires possibly quite specific, complex, and detailed operations on the part of the neurological mechanisms that underlie behavior; on the other hand, there is a putative articulation of the nervous system into subsystems that must be matched to these functional characteristics and that must also attempt to maximize anatomical, morphological, and biochemical plausibility. This extremely complex situation is sometimes abbreviated by materialist philosophers into the claim that identification between psychological and neurological states is established on the basis of constant correlation and simplicity.[13] We have seen that it is an open question whether the relevant relation is identification. Our present point is that the evidence required to justify postulating the relation is something considerably more complex than mere correlation. It is rather a nice adjustment of the psychological characterization of function to considerations of neurological plausibility, and vice versa.[14]

---

[11] The simplified drawing in figure 11.1 is a lateral view of the human cerebral cortex with numbers indicating different areas of the most commonly referenced cytoarchitectonic map of the cortex by the early twentieth-century neuroanatomist Brodmann. A cytoarchitectonic map demarcates groupings of structurally similar neurons. Some of the Brodmann areas have sharp boundaries with little or no overlap in neuron types, while other boundaries are fuzzier. There is an interesting degree of coincidence between this anatomical map and the functional map of the neocortex. For instance, the primary **somatosensory** area coincides with Brodmann 1, 2, and 3, and the primary visual area with Brodmann 17. But there are some areas that serve more than one function. Moreover, there is little agreement among neuroscientists on a full story of *how* these areas carry out their roles as members of their respective functional systems (visual, somatosensory, and so on). ED.

[12] The organization of Reading 4 ("Brain Events") reflects this two-stage process. The discussion begins with a functional description of an adaptive control system, and then looks at the various components of the nervous system that have the structure to carry out the different functions involved in adaptive control. ED.

Figure 11.1 Neocortex with Brodmann areas. Size of numeral is proportional to area.

[13] To find a "constant correlation" would be something like discovering that the effective decision to move one's arm always occurred concurrently with, and never without, a certain sequence of events in the motor cortex. The "simplicity" is that invoked by Occam's razor. ED.

[14] There can be many ways to analyze a complex functional system (e.g., vision) into subsystems. Our choice of alternatives will be affected by what we know of the neural hardware available to carry out the visual function. We should analyze a major functional system into *functional* subsystems whose work could plausibly be carried out by known *neuroanatomical* subsystems. For instance, since we know by microelectrode recordings that the preferred stimuli of neurons in the primary visual cortex is a line across a tiny portion of the visual field (see Reading 4, p. 70 above), we will want to divide the function of recognizing a shape among a large number of simultaneously acting line-detecting functional subsystems. Seeing what sorts of input-output relations these subsystems must have, we might then look for neuroanatomical pathways that we would not otherwise have found. It is this sort of interaction between functional and neuroscientific analysis that Fodor describes as "mutual adjustment" rather than as the mere correlation of preconceived psychological and neurological items. ED.

MICROANALYSIS AND FUNCTIONAL ANALYSIS

This discussion of the way in which psychological and neurological theories integrate during the course of the development of scientific explanations of behavior is, to be sure, no more than the barest sketch. But, insofar as the sketch is at all plausible, it suggests that the reductivist view of the relation between psychological and neurological theories is seriously misleading, even if one accepts a materialistic account of the relation between psychological and neurological constructs. The suggestion is that if materialism is true, a completed account of behavior would contain statements that identify certain neural mechanisms as having functions detailed during the course of phase-one theory construction and that some such statements would hold for each psychological construct. But such statements, clearly, are quite different in kind from those that articulate paradigmatic cases of reductive analysis.

This distinction seems to have been pretty widely missed by materialists, particularly in the literature that relates discussions of materialism to problems about the unity of science. Oppenheim and Putnam, for example, are explicit in referring to neurological theories, such as those of Hebb, as constituting "micro-reductions" of the corresponding psychological theories of memory, learning, motivation, and so on. On the Oppenheim-Putnam account, "the essential feature of micro-reduction is that the branch [of science] B_1 [which provides the micro-reduction of B_2] deals with the parts of the objects dealt with by B_2."[15]

Our present point is that it is difficult to understand how this could be the correct model for the relation between psychological and neurological theories. Psychological entities (sensations, for example) are not readily thought of as capable of being microanalyzed into *anything,* least of all neurons or states of neurons. Pains do not have parts, so brain cells are not parts of pains.

It is, in short, conceivable that there may be true psychophysical identity statements, but it seems inconceivable that such statements are properly analyzed as expressing what Place (1956)[16] has called identities of composition, that is, as expressing relations between wholes and their parts. It should be emphasized that not all statements of identities *are* identities of composition. Compare "Her hat is a bundle of straw" and "He is the boy I knew in Chicago."

It is worth pursuing at some length the difference between the present view of the relation between psychological and neurological constructs and the view typical of reductivist materialism. In reductive analysis (microanalysis), one asks: "what does X consist of?" and the answer has the form of a specification of the microstructure of Xs. Thus: "What does water consist of?" "Two atoms of hydrogen linked with one atom of oxygen." "What does lightning consist of?" "A stream of electrons." And so on. In typical cases of functional analysis, by contrast, one asks about a part of a mechanism *what role it plays* in the activities that are characteristic of the mechanism as a whole: "What does the camshaft do?" "It opens the valves, permitting the entry into the cylinder of fuel, which will then be detonated to drive the piston." Successful microanalysis is thus often contingent upon the development of powerful instruments of observation or precise methods of dissection. Successful functional analysis, on the other hand, requires an appreciation of the sorts of activity that are characteristic of a mechanism and of the contribution made by the functioning of each part of the mechanism to the economy of the whole.

Since microanalysis and functional analysis are very different ways of establishing relations between scientific theories, or between ordinary-language descriptions, conceptual difficulties may result when the vocabulary of one kind of analysis is confounded with the vocabulary of the other.

If I speak of a device as a "camshaft," I am implicitly identifying it by reference to its physical structure, and so I am committed to the view that it exhibits a characteristic and specifiable decomposition into physical parts.[17] But if I speak of the de-

---

[15] Cf. Oppenheim and Putnam, op. cit., p. 6. [The example Fodor gives at the beginning of his essay is the identification of the hydrogen atom, an entity in chemistry, with a configuration of sub-atomic particles (entities in nuclear physics). ED.]

[16] See Reading 5 pp. 78–79. ED.

[17] It's unclear why this mechanically complicated example is so regularly invoked in the literature, rather than something simple like a knife or a gate. A camshaft is a rotating shaft with disks (cams) at one end. It is designed to interact with the cylinder of an internal combustion en-

vice as a "valve lifter," I am identifying it by reference to its function and I therefore undertake no such commitment. There is, in particular, no sense to the question "What does a valve lifter consist of?" if this is understood as a request for microanalysis—that is, as analogous to such questions as "What does water consist of?" (There *is*, of course, sense to the question "What does *this* valve lifter consist of?" but the generic valve lifter must be *functionally* defined, and functions do not have parts.) One might put it that being a valve lifter is not reducible to (is not a matter of) being a collection of rods, springs, and atoms, in the sense in which being a camshaft is. The kinds of questions that it makes sense to ask about camshafts need not make sense, and are often impertinent, when asked about valve lifters.

It is, then, conceivable that serious confusions could be avoided if we interpreted statements that relate psychological and neurological constructs not as articulating microanalyses but as attributing certain psychological functions to corresponding neurological systems. For example, philosophers and psychologists who have complained that it is possible to trace an input from afferent to central neurological systems without once encountering motives, strategies, drives, needs, hopes, along with the rest of the paraphernalia of psychological theories, have been right in one sense but wrong in another, just as one would be if one argued that a complete mechanical account of the operation of an internal-combustion engine never encounters such a thing as a valve lifter. In both cases, the confusion occurs when a term that properly figures in functional accounts of mechanisms is confounded with terms that properly appear in mechanistic accounts, so that one is tempted to think of the function of a part as though it were itself one part among others.

From a functional point of view, a camshaft is a valve lifter and *this* valve lifter (i.e., this particular

mechanism for lifting valves) may be "nothing but" a camshaft. But a mechanistic account of the operations of internal-combustion engines does not seek to replace the concept of a valve lifter with the concept of a camshaft, nor does it seek to "reduce" the former to the latter. What it does do is to explain *how* the valves get lifted: that is, what mechanical transactions are involved when the camshaft lifts the valves. In the same way, presumably, neurological theories seek to explain what biochemical transactions are involved when drives are reduced, motives entertained, objects perceived, and so on.

In short, drives, motives, strategies, and such are, on the present view, internal states postulated in attempts to account for behavior, perception, memory, and other phenomena in the domain of psychological theories.[18] In completed accounts, they could presumably serve to characterize the functional aspects of neurological mechanisms; that is, they would figure in explanations of how such mechanisms operate to determine the molar[19] behavior of an organism, its perceptual capacities, and so on. But this does not entail that drives, motives, and strategies have microanalyses in terms of neurological systems any more than valve lifters can be microanalyzed into camshafts.

There are still further philosophically pertinent differences between the suggestion that psychophysical identity statements should be understood as articulating functional analyses and the suggestion that they should be analyzed as microreductions.

When, in paradigmatic cases, entities in one theory are reduced to entities in another, it is presupposed that both theories have available conceptual mechanisms for saying what the entities have in common. For example, given that water can be

---

gine. As the camshaft rotates, its disks cause the cyclical opening and closing of intake and exhaust valves at the end of the cylinder. The cycle begins with intake of fuel and air and ends with the exhausting of the spent intake after combustion. The cams on the shaft are arranged so that the rotation of the shaft causes them to open and close the intake and exhaust valves in exactly the right sequence for a single cycle of the cylinder with its enclosed piston. This effect on the cylinder is what Fodor is presumably describing when he refers to the camshaft as a "valve lifter." It could be objected that this expression is rather too abstract or generic since it doesn't characterize the system whose valves get lifted. ED.

[18] "Phenomena in the domain of psychological theories" are phenomena that are publicly observable—behavior of all sorts, including linguistic behavior such as reports of experiences and memories. These are contrasted with the *internal* unobserved states or events that directly or indirectly cause the behavior. These internal states start out in a "black box" and get characterized in the first stage of psychological theorizing only in a functional way as "drives" and so on. In the second stage they would be linked to neurological states. ED.

[19] "Molar" in this context refers to large units of behavior which are the usual starting points for functional analysis into smaller units. For instance, *seeing* is molar in relation to sub-items like orienting one's head, focusing one's eyes, recognizing (seeing something *as* such and such). ED.

"reduced" to H_2O, it is possible to say what all samples of water have in common either in the language of viscosity, specific gravity, and so on at the macrolevel, or in chemical language at the microlevel. It is patent that functional analysis need not share this property of reductive analysis. When we identify a certain mousetrap with a certain mechanism, we do not thereby commit ourselves to the possibility of saying in mechanistic terms what all members of the set of mousetraps have in common. Because it is (roughly) a sufficient condition for being a mousetrap that a mechanism be customarily *used* in a certain way, there is nothing in principle that requires that a pair of mousetraps *have* any shared mechanical properties. It is, indeed, because "mousetrap" is functionally rather than mechanically defined that "building a better mousetrap"—that is, building a mechanically novel mousetrap, which functions better than conventional mousetraps do—is a reasonable goal to set oneself.

It is a consequence of this consideration that the present interpretation of the relation between neurological and psychological constructs is compatible with very strong claims about the ineliminability of mental language from behavioral theories.[20] Let us suppose that there are true psychophysical statements that identify certain neurological mechanisms as the ones that possess certain psychologically relevant functional properties. It still remains quite conceivable that identical psychological functions could sometimes be ascribed to anatomically heterogeneous neural mechanisms.[21] In that case,

mental language will be required to state the conditions upon such ascriptions of functional equivalence. It is, in short, quite conceivable that a parsing of the nervous system by reference to anatomical or morphological similarities may often fail to correspond in any uniform way to its parsing in terms of psychological function. Whenever this occurs, explicit reference to the character of such functions will be required if we are to be able to say what we take the brain states that we classify together to have in common.

Every mousetrap can be identified with some mechanism, and being a mousetrap can therefore be identified with being a member of some (indefinite) set of possible mechanisms. But enumerating the set is not a way of dispensing with the notion of a mousetrap; that notion is required to say what all the members of the set have in common and, in particular, what credentials would be required to certify a putative new member as belonging to the set.

Such considerations may be extended to suggest not only that a *plausible* version of materialism will need to view psychological theories as articulating the functional characteristics of neural mechanisms, but also that that is the *only* version of materialism that is likely to prove coherent. Consider the following argument, which Sellars has offered as a refutation of materialism:

> Suppose I am experiencing a circular red raw feel. . . . (in certain cases) the most careful and sophisticated introspection will fail to refute the following statement: "There is a finite subregion ΔR of the raw feel patch ψr, and a finite time interval Δt, such that during Δt no property of ΔR changes."

The refutation may now proceed by appeal to Leibniz' Law. Suppose there is a brain state ϕr which is held to be identical with the psychological state ψr that one is in when one senses something red (i.e., with the "red raw feel"). Then substitution of ϕr for ψr permits the inference: there is a finite region ΔR of the brain state ϕr and a finite time interval Δt, such that during Δt no property of ΔR changes.

But this, as even pre-Utopian neurophysiology shows us, is factually false. . . . Thus, during, say, 500 milliseconds, the 5° region at the center of my phenomenal circle does not change in any property, whereas no region of the physical brain-event can be

---

[20] In Reading 20, Dennett also argues for the ineliminability of mental language, claiming that we must attribute intentional states to people and other objects in order to predict their behavior. ED.

[21] If sodium amytal, a fast-acting barbiturate, is injected into the right or left internal carotid artery, it will flow preferentially to the cerebral hemisphere on the side of the injection and briefly disable that hemisphere. This procedure has enabled researchers to test the correlations between hemispheric segregation or specialization of a function and whether a subject is left or right handed. They have discovered that 15% of left-handed people or ones with mixed handedness have control of speech in both hemispheres whereas 0% of right-handed people have this cerebral organization. It has also been discovered that if the sensory input from somatosensory receptors at a part of the skin surface is eliminated, the cortical area that normally receive this input will not "fall silent," but instead will begin to respond to stimulation from adjacent areas of the skin surface that normally project to correspondingly adjacent areas of the somatosensory map (see fn. 11 above) of the body surface [Kupferman (1991), 832]. These would be examples of what Fodor describes as "identical psychological functions . . . ascribed to anatomically heterogeneous neural mechanisms." ED.

taken small enough such that *none* of its properties change during a 500-millisecond period.[22]

The point of this argument is, I think, entirely independent of its appeal to such dubious psychological entities as "red raw feels." For it seems pretty clear that the principles we employ for individuating neurological states are in general different from, and logically independent of, those that we employ for individuating psychological states. Since what counts as one sensation, one wish, one desire, one drive, and so on is not specified by reference to the organism's neurophysiology, it seems hardly surprising that an organism may persist in a given psychological condition while undergoing neurological change.[23] If a materialist theory is so construed as to deny this, then materialism is certain to prove *contingently* false.

Nor does Sellars' argument depend solely upon the possibility of there being differences in "grain" between neurological and psychological variation. The problem is not just that slight changes in neurophysiology may be compatible with continuity of psychological state. It is rather that we have no right to assume a priori that the nervous system may not sometimes produce indistinguishable psychological effects by *radically* different physiological means. How much redundancy there may be in the nervous system is surely an open empirical question. It would be extraordinarily unwise if the claims for materialism or for the unity of science were to be formulated in such fashion as to require that for each distinguishable psychological state there must be one and only one corresponding brain state.

I see no way to accommodate such considerations that does not involve a wholesale employment of the notion of functional equivalence. For the point on which Sellars' argument turns is precisely that there may very well be sets of neurologically distinct brain states, whose members are nevertheless psychologically indistinguishable. In such cases, identification of the psychological state with any member of such a set produces problems with the substitutivity of identity.

It seems clear that a materialist can avoid these difficulties only at the price of assuming that the objects appropriate for identification with psychological states are sets of *functionally equivalent* neurological states. In particular, it must be true of any two members of such a set that an organism may alternate between them without thereby undergoing psychological change.

This is tantamount to saying that a materialist must recognize as scientifically relevant a taxonomy of neurological states according to their psychological functions. Such a taxonomy[24] defines a "natural kind"[25] (although very likely not the same natural kind as emerges from purely anatomical and biochemical considerations). Thus, a reasonable version of materialism might hold that psychological theories and neurological theories both involve taxonomies defined over the same objects (brain states), but according to different principles. What we require of the members of a set of anatomically similar brain states is *not* what we require of the members of a set of functionally equivalent brain states. Yet in neither case need the classification be arbitrary. The psychological consequences of being in one or another brain state are either distinguishable or they are not. If they are distinguishable, it is a question of fact whether or not the distinction is of the kind that psychological theories recognize as systematic and significant.

It is tempting to suppose that there must be only one principle of sorting (taxonomy by physical similarity), on pain of there otherwise being chaos, that either there is *one* kind of scientifically relevant similarity or there is *every* kind. It is, however, unnecessary to succumb to any such temptation. What justifies a taxonomy, what makes a kind

---

[22] Paul E. Meehl, "The Compleat Autocerebroscopist: A Thought-Experiment on Professor Feigl's Mind-Body Identity Thesis," in *Mind, Matter, and Method: Essays in Philosophy and Science in Honor of Herbert Feigl*, ed. Paul K. Feyerabend and Grover Maxwell (Minneapolis: University of Minnesota Press, 1966), 103–180, where the argument is attributed to Sellars. [See pages 167ff. in that volume.]

[23] The sequential, slightly differing neurological states correlated with the ongoing psychological state would be physically different but *functionally equivalent*. This is one example of what is called the "multiple realizability" of functional states. Just as one function, the control of language, can have different physical realizations at the same time in different individuals (control by one or other hemisphere or both), so one ongoing function can have multiple realizations over time as the brain process embodying the function changes in ways that are still consistent with that function. ED.

[24] "Taxonomy" is used by philosophers to signify a systematic classification scheme. ED.

[25] To say that gold and silver are natural kinds is to say that the distinctions by which they are set apart are not merely a function of human "taxonomical" or classification schemes. For instance, everything that is gold both has a different chemical composition than what is not gold and behaves differently from what is not gold. Although *gold* is a natural kind, the *gold-I-have-seen-thus-far* is not.

"natural," is the power and generality of the theories that we are enabled to formulate when we taxonomize in that way. Classifying together all the entities that are made up of the same kinds of parts is one way of taxonomizing fruitfully, but if we can find other principles for sorting brain states, principles that permit simple and powerful accounts of the etiology of behavior, then that is itself an adequate justification for sorting according to those principles.

It would seem, then, that both the traditional approach to materialism and the traditional approach to the unity of science are in need of liberalization. In the first case, if he is to accommodate the sort of problem that Sellars has raised, the materialist will have to settle for identifications of psychological states with sets of functionally equivalent brain states, and this means that the materialist thesis is at best no clearer than the notoriously unclear notion of functional equivalence. In the second case, it appears that if the doctrine of the unity of science is to be preserved, it will have to require something less (or other) than reducibility as the relation between constructs in neurology and those in psychology. It seems, then, that scientific theories can fit together in more than one way, perhaps in many ways. If this is correct, then reduction is only one kind of example of a relation between scientific theories that satisfies reasonable constraints on the unity of science. It would be interesting to know what other kinds of examples there are.

With Fodor's critique of the kind of Identity thesis put forward by Smart and Armstrong, we seem to have come full circle. The claim that mental events are brain events had seemed vulnerable to the objection that it is a category mistake—that a mental event is a kind of event that is essentially different from brain events (or any other sort of physical event) because it is private, or bound to phenomenal properties, or occurs in phenomenal space, or is intentional. To avoid this sort of objection, Smart and Armstrong provided topic-neutral translations of reports of mental events. Smart's translation made reports of sensations to be reports of some inner event-in-general that was so indeterminate that it could be without friction understood as a brain process. Armstrong's translation rendered *all* mental events or states as *inner* causes, a concept nearly as vague as *event,* and allowing brain science to identify the cause as neural. Fodor has argued that to assert an *identity* between a causally or functionally conceived mental state and a brain state is to make a category mistake. A causal/functional state is not the sort of entity that can be identical with something physical the way that water is with H_2O. Indefinitely many differently structured and composed objects can have the same function (e.g., being a prize or a barrier). But only H_2O molecules can be water.

Fodor concludes that the best a materialist can do is to assert an identity between a type of psychological state and a disjunctive set of the different sorts of brain states that can carry out that psychological function. Even this will not do, however, since the functional concept of a mental state does not specify embodiment in brain tissue or any other specific kind of stuff. So the set of functionally equivalent physical states or embodiments for a given type of psychological state becomes indefinitely vast. Does the concept of a functional system call for embodiment at all? Or could it be applied to a Cartesian mind? Does the notion of a functional state realized in a brain state do justice to the strong conviction of materialism that *there is nothing but the physical?*

REVIEW QUESTIONS

1. Fodor's argument depends on there being a sharp distinction between the functional and the physical characterization of a system, as in his example of a *valve lifter* and (its physical realization as) a *camshaft.* He says that identifying something as a camshaft does commit us to a kind of physical structure, and a configuration of parts. But he says there is "no such commitment" when I refer to a valve lifter. Discuss whether he is right in this claim.

2. Fodor says that those philosophers and psychologists who object against a neurological account of a psychological event "that it is possible to trace an input from afferent to central neurological systems without once encountering motives, strategies, drives, needs, hopes, along with the rest of the paraphernalia of psychological theories, have been right in one sense but wrong in another, just as one would be if one argued that a complete mechanical account of the operation of an internal-combustion engine never encounters such a thing as a valve lifter" (p. 151). Is this an accurate parallel? Is it really the case that the mechanical account of the engine does not "encounter" a valve-lifter in the same sense that a neurological account of brain events does not "encounter" a sensation or a thought?

12

Ontological Supervenience

John Haugeland

John Haugeland teaches philosophy at the University of Pittsburgh and has written frequently in the philosophy of mind and artificial intelligence. Among his publications are *Mind Design* (1981), an edited anthology, and *Artificial Intelligence: the Very Idea* (1985).

It really isn't easy to articulate the main thesis of materialism as an *ontology*—a doctrine of what sorts of things exist. One reason for this difficulty is that the clearest allegiance of materialist philosophers has been to a negative viewpoint: *anti-dualism,* with special emphasis on the interactionist kind of dualism represented by Descartes. By introducing a nonphysical cause into the domain of bodies, interactionism threatens the integrity of the scientific enterprise which materialists revere. Haugeland will argue that materialists should be satisfied with a version of supervenience that is strong enough to rule out interactionist dualism and that recognizes the primacy of the physical by making everything else depend on it. It is good, he argues, that materialism can do this without resorting to an identity theory, because identity theories don't work.

A couple of years ago I wrote and published a paper on supervenience. Unbeknownst to me, several of the important theses in that paper had been clearly stated a few years earlier in a pair of joint articles by Geoffrey Hellman and Frank Thompson.[1] Better late than never, I would now like to acknowledge their priority, and apologize for not having known of it sooner. Further (as if to compensate for the original omission, but really for substantive philosophical reasons), I also want to address directly certain further issues that they raise.

Hellman and Thompson (and I) seek to articulate the basic intuition of physicalist materialism in a way that does not imply too much; in particular, we all want to avoid any formulation that entails traditional reductionism.[2] They propose a conjunction of two distinct theses, which they call the principles of *physical determination,* and *physical exhaustion,* respectively. Physical determination is quite similar to what I (later) called "weak supervenience"; and, despite various differences, I am (not surprisingly) largely sympathetic.[3] The principle of physical exhaustion, on the other hand, has no ana-

---

[2] He doesn't want the formulation to state or imply that higher-level theories such as biology or psychology are reducible to lower-level theories such as chemistry. Such a reduction presupposes one can identify *types* of higher-level events with *types* of lower-level events (e.g., "Pain is (nothing but) the firing of a certain population of neurons at a certain frequency.") ED.

[3] Hellman and Thompson actually distinguish three variants of the determination principle; weak supervenience is similar to the one they call "determination of truth". That's the only version I will be concerned with here, and also, apparently, the one of which they are most confident.

From John Haugeland, "Ontological Supervenience," *The Southern Journal of Philosophy* XXII, Supplement (1983): 1–12. © 1984. Reprinted with permission of the Department of Philosophy, University of Memphis.

[1] "Physicalism: Ontology, Determinism, and Reduction," *Journal of Philosophy* LXXII (1975): 551–564; and "Physicalist Materialism," *Nous* 11 (1977), 309–345. My paper is "Weak Supervenience," *American Philosophical Quarterly,* 19 (1982), 93–103.

log in my paper; and, moreover, I am not very sympathetic. So that's what I want to talk about.

A little background first. Many recent authors have rejected so-called "type-type" identity (and the closely related reductionism), on the dual grounds that it is implausibly strong,[4] and that it is not necessary for materialism. All that's needed, they say, is a weaker "token-token" identity theory. The idea is this: even if psychological (or whatever) *types* (kinds, properties) cannot be identified (or **nomologically** correlated) with physical types, still individual psychological *tokens* (particular events, states, etc.), might be identifiable with individual physical tokens, on a one-by-one basis; and that would suffice for a materialist metaphysics.[5]

The question now is whether even token identity theory might be too strong, and unnecessary for materialism. I think it is, and that the determination/supervenience principle is sufficient by itself. That principle may be roughly paraphrased as follows:

> The world could not have been different in any respect, without having been different in some strictly physical respect— that is, in some respect describable in a canonical[6] language of physics.

The thing to notice is that this makes no mention of any particular individuals (other than the whole universe); hence, unlike earlier definitions,[7] it doesn't *explicitly* presuppose token identities. The main thrust of my paper was to argue that supervenience and identity theory are in fact independent, and that the latter is probably false. Hellman and Thompson agree about the independence,[8] and they are also dissatisfied with common versions of the identity thesis. But, rather than reject identities,

they propose a new and significantly more sophisticated theory.

Many philosophers, myself included, had been content to regard as physical any entity of which some "suitable" physical predicate is true—leaving it for another day to say just which predicates those are. Hellman and Thompson have a similar intuition, but a much better strategy. They begin only with "basic" physical predicates—like: 'X is a neutrino', 'X is an electromagnetic field', 'X is gravitationally attracting Y', and so on. They assume that positive instances of basic predicates are uncontroversially physical, and that collectively these constitute the whole physical universe. We are still not told just which predicates are "basic"; but they are clearly less problematic than "suitable" predicates in general. In fact, near as I understand it, the single predicate, 'X has non-zero mass', would suffice, according to contemporary physics.[9]

In any case, the essential innovation lies in what comes next: using the calculus of individuals (i.e., of parts and wholes) to *construct* all other physical entities out of positive instances of basic predicates. First, the physical universe is defined as the fusion (i.e., the sum, or spatio-temporal agglomeration) of all those instances; then all and only physical entities are parts (spatio-temporal portions) of that universe. The point of fusing and then repartitioning the universe is that there are no constraints on the "boundaries" of the new parts. They may be arbitrarily (perhaps infinitely) complex and bizarre; and they need not be definable, implicitly or explicitly, in any particular language.

These arbitrary parts of the physical universe are the physical "tokens" for Hellman and Thompson's identity theory. Since there are almost certainly more such tokens than there are predicates in any (finitistic) language, they provide not only a better specified physical basis than before, but also a large one. The principle of physical exhaustion, however, is not quite the same as the token identity

---

[4] Philosophers frequently use the terms "strong" and "weak" to characterize assertions and conclusions. Roughly speaking, a *strong* assertion says more, has more implications, than a *weak* one. For an assertion to be strong is both good and bad news: good insofar as it's true, because more truth is better than less; and bad insofar as the more you say, the more objections it is liable to. ED.

[5] The token identity thesis in its full generality would say something like this: Every token (single instance) of a higher-level type is identical with some token or other of a lower-level type (usually in the domain of physical science). ED.

[6] "Canonical" here means "official." ED.

[7] E.g., Davidson's and Kim's.

[8] See their remark about parallelism, ["Physicalism . . ."], p. 561.

[9] The attempt to find one or a small number of truly fundamental properties of the physical or material *as such* goes back to the very beginning of western philosophy and science, in the speculations of Greek thinkers of the sixth century B.C.E., some of whom thought that all matter was air or fire. Recall that Descartes thought that *extension* in three dimensions was the most fundamental property. Having non-zero mass doesn't seem to be this sort of property because something as physical as a photon doesn't have mass. ED.

thesis, for it also delimits abstract entities—namely, to what I will call "physically based" sets. These are just the sets appearing in a set-theoretic hierarchy, all of whose ur-elements (ultimate individuals) are physical tokens.[10] Thus, all that really exist, according to Hellman and Thompson, are physical tokens and physically based sets.[11]

This is manifestly a superior formulation of the identity thesis, both sharper and weaker than its antecedents; and it makes a tidy companion for the determination/supervenience principle. The question remains: does that principle *want* a companion? That is, in our effort to articulate our somewhat inchoate sense of materialism, is there reason to augment physical determination with physical exhaustion? I don't think so—though, I confess, it's not altogether clear to me how best to argue the point.

A plausible beginning is to ask why we want to be materialists in the first place. Then we could consider which (if either) candidate principle satisfies those original motivations. The common rationales for materialism, it turns out, are a surprisingly mixed bag; and that fact alone may make a modest catalog of them worthwhile. I have distinguished six loose categories, which I will list, and then briefly comment on.

1. *The call of the one.* Some folks take seriously a so-called "unity of science".[12] Now, if this unity is supposed to be a fact that needs explanation, then I simply don't see it. If, on the other hand, it's proposed as a desideratum or goal, then I wish its seekers all luck and happiness; but their fondest hopes are hardly a *reason* for adopting materialism. In fact, I think, only people who are

materialists already are inclined to hope for a "unification" of science; and all they really mean by it is that their materialism would be vindicated.[13]

A different unity issue, however, is more interesting. Without tarrying over details, we may roughly categorize entities three ways: (i) those which (almost) everyone agrees are physical; (ii) those which are disputed; and (iii) those which (almost) everyone agrees are not physical. The third category includes numbers, sets, Platonic forms, etc.—that is, *eternal* or even *necessary* entities, in the sense that means: not subject to generation, variation, or decay. By contrast, the first two categories comprise the *temporal* or *contingent*: i.e., entities that we might generically call "occurrences," subject to generation, variation, and decay. Now this temporal/atemporal contrast is quite significant, metaphysically; and it puts all the disputed cases on the same side as the clearly material.[14] To take a pertinent example, beliefs and feelings are like mountains and molecules (and unlike numbers and sets) in being temporal, contingent occurrences. The same could be said of institutions, moral actions, and what have you.

Now this, plausibly, *is* a fact to be explained; and materialism might be brought forward as the explanation. What is the principle of unity of the temporal/contingent? Matter! Cutely: if we ask, with Kant, why time is the form of *both* inner and outer sense, we can answer, contra Descartes (not to mention Kant), that time (not space) is

---

[10] This includes "pure" set theory (hence classical mathematics, as reconstructed therein), since the null set is a subset of the set of physical tokens.

[11] Such a hierarchy begins at the bottom with the set U of all physical tokens. This set is divided into subsets consisting of physical tokens, and then one constructs the set A whose members are all these subsets of physical tokens plus U. One can then perform the same sequence of operations on the member-sets of A that one performed on the members of U. This hierarchy of sets remains based on the same original totality of physical tokens—every *individual* included in the first set is still "there."

[12] This expression signifies a unity of methodology in all the sciences, or more ambitiously, a unity of their content as manifest in **intertheoretic reduction.**

[13] See, for instance, the last sentence of ["Physicalism . . ." (fn. 1, above)].

[14] Haugeland here is following the lead of Hellman and Thompson in *not* attempting to formulate a physicalist principle that would address the status of abstract entities, particularly mathematical items such as numbers, the part-whole relation, and sets (as they are studied in set theory in abstraction from the members of these sets). Plato was struck by what he interpreted as the *eternal truth* of mathematical theorems about these entities, for example, that $2 + 3 = 5$. He thought that they must be about *eternal objects* belonging to a different realm of being from that of bodies, a realm of what he called forms. He included in that realm such entities as *beauty* or *justice in itself,* about which philosophers supposedly were interested in discovering true and eternal definitions. When philosophers today talk about "Platonism," they frequently have in mind Plato's ontological dualism of the world of change perceived by the senses (what Haugeland refers to as the realm of the temporal/contingent), and the world of forms—eternal, unchanging objects to which the mind has access independently of the senses. Haugeland, like Hellman and Thompson, is not concerned with Platonic dualism, but rather with the Cartesian mind-body variety. ED.

the essence of matter—and everything (sensible) is material.[15]

2. *Seductive analogy.*   A novel, or even a drawing, can be filled with courage, conflict, pathos; it can break new artistic ground, while excitement and beauty leap from every page. Yet, in some sense, each copy is "nothing but" ink and paper; vaporize that paper, and you have eliminated that copy—snuffed it right out of being. Eliminate all the copies, and (in one way or another) you eliminate the work. Now, aren't people (and cultures and whatever else) just like that—vaporize their material embodiment and you snuff them out entirely? Sounds right to me.

3. *The way the wind blows (= History).*   Negatively: many opponents of materialism seem like die-hard stragglers, clinging desperately to some old system that's hit the metaphysical skids. More positively: science marches on. First they decided the stars are just (ordinary) matter,[16] then came the synthesis of urea, the theory of evolution, the double helix,[17] . . . and now the *avant garde* want to

talk to their computers. Again and again, it looks like matter in motion wins out—with nothing else needed. And, naturally, we'd all rather be winners than die-hard stragglers.

4. *Fear of darkness.*   Denizens of the mental, some say, are unclear, shadowy, elusive, and generally spooky—hence ontologically suspect. Not quibbling over the premise, we may inquire about the inference: *why* can't dark, slippery things be real? Well, it is a venerable (if peculiar and not always acknowledged) principle of metaphysics that: *To be is to be intelligible.*[18] It's hard to know what to make of that. It seems presumptuous on the face of it (in the absence of intelligent creation)[19]; but I'll still bet its root runs under lots of philosophical dirt.

Be that as it may, the argument from mere spooklessness to materialism can go several ways. One line has it that understanding is the product of explanation, and that the only really clear explanations we have are in the physical sciences. So, unless the other sciences start shaping up, their domains had better identify with the physical, on pain of gloomy non-being. A different tack maintains that intelligibility presupposes cognitive meaningfulness, which in turn always rests on objective observation. Then, supposing that only material objects (states, etc.) can be observed objectively,[20] only they can be intelligible, hence real.

5. *The Scrooge instinct.*   How many's the poor son gone to debt and ruin for frittering his metaphysical accounts? In theory, of course, Occam's famous razor, "Don't multiply entities beyond necessity," gets its edge from Beetle Bailey's more incisive "Don't do anything beyond necessity". But,

---

[15] The last sentence is a rather complicated historical aside that is not necessary for an understanding of Haugeland's point—which is that, given the general goal of the human mind to find unity in the apparent diversity of things, we seek a common, fundamental property which ties together not only the items generally acknowledged as within the domain of physical science, but everything else which is temporal and contingent, including mental processes. *Matter* is arguably not the best candidate for such a property since it is no more fundamental than energy in physics since Einstein's equation of matter and energy. ED.

[16] Plato, Aristotle and many thinkers up to the seventeenth century believed that heavenly bodies were composed of a special kind of matter with unearthly attributes such as being perfectly spherical, being capable of moving only in circular orbits, and being otherwise unchanging. Were this true, it would have been impossible to apply to these bodies the physical laws formulated by studying terrestrial phenomena. This belief kept physics earthbound until it was overthrown by observations of heavenly bodies made by telescope and by the successful extension to these bodies of laws of physical science such as gravitation. ED.

[17] *Urea* is one of the principal end products of the metabolic breakdown of proteins in mammals, and is excreted in urine. It was, in 1828, the first naturally occurring organic (carbon-based) compound to be artificially synthesized from inorganic compounds. This laboratory synthesis helped break down what was perceived as a great divide between processes (such as metabolism) that were believed to occur *only in living systems* and processes occurring in nonliving systems. The *theory of evolution* showed how animals (including humans) with mental functions could have arisen from lower-level organisms, and these in turn from nonliving systems; and the *double-helix* structure of DNA enabled us to understand in terms of chemical mechanisms such functions as **adaptive control** of

metabolism and the transmission of hereditary traits. These discoveries all tended to put under the wide umbrella of physical science what seemed to be irreducibly higher-level biological phenomena. ED.

[18] Not usually a biconditional—but maybe sometimes.

[19] For instance, when doing science we assume that every observable event occurs according to laws that can be formulated in the language of mathematics and that apply to either the observable aspects of the event or to lower-level ingredients. Why *should* nature be this way if we can't know that it was created by a rational being who causes it to be that way? ED.

[20] The contrast here is with such items as qualia that are not "objectively observable" because they are present only to the inner sense or introspection of each individual. ED.

in practical New England, the moral is keenly economical: "In all commitments, be as frugal as possible—nay even parsimonious. Buy a basic physics if you must, but avoid every frilly extravagance. And never, *never* squander your precious fluids in profligate hypostasis!"

I have occasionally wondered what makes ontology so expensive, or what limits our budget, or, indeed, what exactly we are spending. Having dwelt more summers in the Southwest than the Northeast, I feel no great longing for desert landscapes; and frankly, Occam's razor cuts little ice out there anyway. Perhaps, however, I can abide a prudent California compromise: We shall assume no entity before its time.

6. *Law and order.* Physics strives (and promises) to be *strict;* that is, to provide a closed, comprehensive system of exception-free laws.[21] In other words, setting aside any implications about other domains, physics takes care of its own very nicely, thank you. At the appropriate level of description, physical phenomena can be *fully* explained *physically.* This promise, in turn, fuels a standard criticism of interactionism: if physical phenomena are already fully explicable in their own terms, then how can anything non-physical (e.g., mental) make any difference to them? Only, it seems, by breaking the laws of physics. Moreover, the mental had better be able to affect the physical (e.g., in deliberate action), or it won't be much use. Unfortunately, the price tag on having mental entities both non-physical and effective is apparently the internal strictness of physics itself. That'll never sell in Boston.

***

That completes my little catalog of rationales for materialism; needless to say, some considerations impress me more than others. Now we can return to the problem of formulation: in particular, do these motivations support the identity theory, in addition to the principle of physical determination? It's easiest just to go through the list again in order.

1. *Call of the one.* Explaining the unity of the temporal/contingent is a tantalizing metaphysical prize, and a big plus for materialism. But what exactly in materialism promises us this prize? It seems to me that the principle of physical determination says it explicitly. For that principle addresses precisely whatever *could have been different:* i.e., essentially the temporal/contingent. And it is all and only this category that the principle ties down to the physical—thereby explicating the unity of the category, via the common supervenience on matter (as described in canonical physics).

I don't see that physical exhaustion would add anything to the foregoing; but it might offer an alternative account. For it entails that every entity is either a physical token or a set; and that division could plausibly be aligned with the temporal/atemporal distinction. Saying that temporal occurrences are all and only physical tokens would explain both the unity of the category, and also its connection with time (since physical tokens are spatio-temporal fragments of the universe). It's less obvious, however, how well this strategy accommodates temporal events, processes, and states. They would have to be identified with physical tokens (not sets), on pain of undermining the point; and that seems likely to cause problems.

In passing, I should warn against an attractive simplification. It's tempting to reformulate supervenience in terms of possible *changes:*

> The world could not change (become different) in any respect without changing in some (canonically describable) physical respect.[22]

Unfortunately, there are clear counterexamples. Thus, a person can change from married to single, or an item can change from your property to mine, at the stroke of midnight, when some prior legal decree takes effect—there being no physical change *at the time,* save, so to speak, the ticking of the clock. Of course, what the materialist wants to insist upon is physical changes back when the decree was promulgated (as well as many others during the evolution of matrimonial and proprietary institutions). Consequently, the general statement

---

[21] Davidson's phrases [see fn. 7 above. ED.]

[22] See my initial paraphrase of Davidson, ["Weak Supervenience"], p. 97; and compare Quine on "difference *in the world*" and change; in his "Facts of the Matter," *Southwestern Journal of Philosophy* (around 1978), p. 162. I am indebted to Joe Camp for a conversation during the course of which the point of this paragraph emerged.

of supervenience must be made "world-wide" through time as well as at each instant; hence, the looser formulation[23] in terms of how the world (*in toto*) could have been different.

2. *Seductive analogy.*   As everyone knows, the painting/story analogy is vulnerable to a dismissive ploy: there's no real pathos in the story—the story is just pathetic. By the same token, there are no real stories,[24] but only story-like inscriptions; and, according to some philosopher-like organisms, "real" mental entities can likewise be eliminated. I, however, find that all arch and boring.

So, suppose we take the analogy at face value: what does it really suggest? Well, basically, if you disintegrate enough material structures, you can wipe out lots of other entities as well. But *which* entities are liable to such extinction? Not, presumably, numbers, sets, and Platonic forms; in fact, potential victims seem limited exactly to the temporal/contingent—that is, to the very entities that supervenience binds to the physical. Indeed, the impossibility of any temporal realm at all without a physical realm is just a coarser way of expressing the intuition behind the principle of physical determination.

3. *How the wind blows.*   Marching with the winds of science won't help here until we have an independent argument about what scientific successes entail. Achievements like synthetic urea and statistical thermodynamics[25] are awkwardly strong,

if taken as a basis for induction—or they are *reductions,* and we've given up trying to generalize that. On the other hand, instances like the theory of evolution and functional psychology (if that counts as a success), are metaphysically ambiguous. At most they show that: It's only "because" matter got arranged as it did, that there exist life forms, minds, etc. In other words, if certain material structures vanished or fell apart, various lives and thoughts would go with them. But that doesn't imply that each particular mental (or biological) occurrence is identical with some particular material structure. Instead, the conclusion is simply that disintegrating enough material structures will wipe out lots of other entities—which is what we just discussed.

4. *Fear of darkness.*   Consider denizen of darkness, D, seeking materialist sanctuary from marauding scotophobes.[26] Now, classical type-reductions of D-kind would indeed flood them all with the prophylactic light of physics. But materialists no longer offer reduction *carte blanche;* some petitioners must settle for less. Is there safety in physical determination? Well, it forces D to hew the physical line rather closely; for D could not have been different, without the physical world having been different as well—and, this goes, of course, for each possible difference in D. That suffices, I think, to rule out demons, ghosts, disembodied spirits, magical auras and miscellaneous other sleazy shades—without necessarily eliminating thoughts, feelings, customs, institutions, and the like. On the other hand, it must be confessed that determination throws no particular *light* on the entities it spares; supervenience may thin the ranks of the immaterial, but it doesn't illuminate the remainder.

What about physical exhaustion? Being identical to some arbitrary fragment of the physical universe won't render D, *qua* D, a whit more intelligible either. And, remember, the exhaustion principle does not imply that D has any other identifying description than *qua* D; in particular, even

---

[23] The "looser formulation" is, of course, Haugeland's in the fourth paragraph of this reading. It says, in effect, no difference without a physical difference somewhere at some time. ED.

[24] There are only the physical inscriptions, or tellings, or enactments. There is no story entity apart from these physical tokens. Similarly, there are only the physical processes in various systems such as the brain; no mental entities over and above those tokens. These are the kinds of claims that "bore" Haugeland, presumably because they are needlessly strong, and their strength makes them needlessly hard to establish. ED.

[25] *Statistical thermodynamics* explains phenomena such as **entropy** in terms of the average behavior of the microconstituents of a macrosystem. Roughly speaking, the faster the constituent atoms and molecules in a substance move around, the higher its temperature. When you pour cold water into a container of hot water, the cold water doesn't stay together as a glob distinct from the hot. At the micro level, slower and faster moving particles bump each other, propagating their effects on each other's kinetic energy throughout the container. At the macro level, we observe that the cold and hot water mix evenly at an in-between temperature. Statistical thermodynamics explains the *irreversibility* of this equilibrium temperature in terms of the overwhelmingly greater statistical likelihood of a

distribution of faster and slower molecules consistent with the equilibrium temperature than one that would be consistent with distinct hot and cold parts of the water. In that sense, statistical thermodynamics provides a reductive explanation of the macro-phenomenon of entropy studied in classical thermodynamics (which had its beginnings before the atomic/molecular theory of matter was even established). ED.

[26] Scotophobes are folks with a pathological fear of darkness. ED.

if D is exhausted by the physical, it need not be describable in the language of physics. In other words, *neither* materialist clause (short of reductionism) [27] guarantees the intelligibility of all that is. And, in that case, identity theory fills no gap left open by supervenience.

5. *Scrooge*. Beetle Bailey's razor cuts both ways. To be sure, one corollary is: "Don't multiply entities beyond necessity". But another, just as sound and important, reads: "Don't multiply *principles* beyond necessity". The difficulty with each lies in deciding what's "beyond necessity": A spendthrift's need is a skinflint's poison. I have been urging that identity theory is not necessary for an intuitively satisfying materialism. And one of my claims is that mere parsimony in the entity account is, by itself, no reason at all to impose shotgun unions with the physical.

6. *Law and Order*. This argument must be handled carefully. To say that the motion of a certain molecule is "fully" explicable physically is to say that all the physical forces on it determine its motion completely: no other forces are needed or allowed. But that doesn't rule out other explanations. The very same molecule might be lodged in my thumbnail, and might rise three feet *because* I decide to raise my hand. The strictness of physics does not forbid such explanations; it only forbids that any decision contribute an additional *force* on any molecule. In other words, the psychological explanation is not allowed to interfere with or modify the physical one—but only to supplement it, by providing another point of view.

Consider, in a similar spirit, the punctuation mark printed at the end of this very sentence token. It's a little blob of ink; and the forces exerted on it by nearby paper fibers fully explain its present spatial location (in some reference frame). But one can also explain why that period is where it is by citing its terminal juxtaposition to a declarative inscription (which reflects my reasons for putting it there). Both of these explanations are perfectly correct; they are nowhere near equivalent; and they are *not*

competitors. Strict completeness means only that physics brooks no intrusions on its own turf; it does not mean that physics is the only explanatory game in town (or the only good one, or the only one we really need).

What does this tell us about the mental? If physics is complete in its own terms, then there could have been no difference in the mental (that made any difference to the physical), without there being concomitant differences in the physical itself (that sufficed to explain everything, at the level of particles, fields, forces, and whatnot). But this is just a special case of the principle of physical determination (by strict physics); physical exhaustion is beside the point.

One might, however, press a stronger interpretation. It's not just that there must be some "concomitant" physical difference or other; but rather, there must be some physical difference that makes the same difference—causes the same effects. Then add some hocus pocus about causal roles being nature's ownmost principle of individuation, and token identities spill right out. [28] But hold fire.

For *each* physical effect (each molecular motion, e.g.), precisely described in the language of physics, there must be a strict physical account, expressed in that same language. But a decision to act (e.g., to raise my hand) "involves" untold numbers of molecular motions in and around my body. The strictness of physics in no way requires that these can be *sorted* into:

i. the effective cause, as an integral unit (a complex physical token, identical to my decision);

ii. the relevant effect, as an integral unit (a complex physical token, identical to my act); and

iii. the innocent bystanders (such as my blood circulation, thermal vibrations in my thumbnail, protein synthesis in my cortex, and so on).

Yet, each of these distinctions is necessary to the token identity thesis: they are practically a statement of it, for the case at hand.

---

[27] The reductionism in question is one that would postulate type identities. The principle of exhaustion does not even require that there be a physical-science description of any token, only that the token be composed of instances of basic physical predicates. ED.

[28] In other words, if a certain configuration of neural activity has all of the same behavioral effects as the decision to move my arm, then that configuration just *is* the decision to move my arm. ED.

The point is not that the "boundaries" of decisions and actions are micro-physically fuzzy, indescribable, or even negotiable; rather, there are no such boundaries at all: decisions are not distinguishable (even in principle) as separate individuals *at the level of micro-physics*. Or, at any rate, the strictness of physics does not entail that they are. So, again I conclude that a familiar rationale for materialism supports the determination/supervenience principle, but not physical exhaustion.

* * *

There can, of course, be independent arguments for holding the identity thesis (over and above supervenience), even apart from the general reasons for materialism. I will consider two. First, one might suppose that the principle of physical exhaustion is needed to *explain why* the mental (etc.) is determined by the physical. But no such explanation is forthcoming: the two principles are, as Hellman and Thompson point out, quite independent. Supervenience is a relation between bodies of truths or facts; and, as such, it makes a strong claim on the expressive power of the "subvening" language—i.e., theoretical physics. Physical exhaustion, on the other hand, makes only a minimal claim on physics: a handful of "basic" predicates are required, but, beyond that, the relevant theory could be very weak and unexpressive.

In the meantime, it would be peculiar to ring in a whole new principle merely to explain an already established one. In other words, if there are further grounds for identity theory, well and good (let them do the work); but, if not, then, evidently, supervenience is all that's needed. It can perfectly well be a "principle" all by itself, exhaustion is no more fundamental, and would add no useful support.

The second argument is trickier. Physical determination (even conjoined with strict physics) seems quite compatible with parallelism, epiphenomenalism,[29] and similar ghosts of philosophy

past. Doesn't it take identity theory to stuff these back in their graves? Naturally, I doubt it. Let's consider a couple other hypotheses at the same time:

i. Once every few million millennia, the universe pauses—stops stock still—for about ten minutes, and then resumes motion exactly as it had been going; this last occurred just before William of Occam was born.

ii. Each sub-atomic particle actually has a rich and unique personality, which it expresses in deep, fervent conversations with its neighbors. Unfortunately, radical translation is hopeless, because quantum-mechanical behavior is never affected—except in statistical indeterminacies.

These hypotheses have much in common with parallelism and epiphenomenalism; in particular, they are theoretically unmotivated, magically undetectable and thoroughly bizarre. In my estimate, that's enough to damn them already. But, we can make a gesture of principled generalization, by articulating a *new corollary* (hitherto noticed, I think) to Bailey's razor: "Don't get weird beyond necessity". Needless to mention, this corollary (like Occam's before it) is essentially a dialectical foil, useful mainly for transferring burdens of proof to other people.

Identity theory looks, at first, like a happier, more positive answer. With it, parallelism and epiphenomenalism come out not merely peculiar and unproven: instead, they are contrary to the principle of physical exhaustion—a genuine no-no. But appearances are deceiving. For, suppose we change the example to a (roughly) Spinozistic[30] monism:

> There is really only one substance, God, but He has infinitely many attributes, all of which are complete, and correspond to one another perfectly; two of God's attributes are mind and matter.

---

[29] Epiphenomenalism is the doctrine that mental events are nonphysical effects of physical events, but that mental events have no causal power of their own. Parallelism is the view that mental events are nonphysical and that there is a regular correspondence between mental and physical events, but no causal relation between them in either direction. Arnold Geulincx (1625–1669) held this view, and compared the parallelism of the mental and bodily to the relationship between two precise clocks working in synchrony without affecting each other. Geulincx's version of parallelism is also called occasionalism, because he claimed that mental-physical correlations were brought about by God. For instance, my decision to move my arm is the sort of mental event that God has eternally willed to be accompanied by the relevant motion of my arm. Each time I decide to move my arm, this decision is an *occasion* for God to cause what I will (it doesn't *cause* God to do anything; God has freely decided to move my arm on such occasions). ED.

[30] Baruch Spinoza (1632–1677) developed Cartesian metaphysics into the doctrine that there is only one substance, God, and that everything else is an attribute or mode of the divine Substance. ED.

Thus, when we speak of physical tokens, we are speaking of God—specifically of His modes under the attribute matter. Likewise, when we speak of anything else, we are also speaking of God—the *very same* God. In other words, no matter what we talk about, it is *ontologically* the same thing as (identical to) what we talk about when we talk about physical tokens. Of course, unlike Hellman and Thompson's, Spinoza's system is symmetrical: it entails mental exhaustion as well.

The point is that brilliantly kooky metaphysics knows no bounds; if the seventeenth century doesn't persuade you, try the nineteenth. I don't think any definitive principle will ever suffice to rule out all and only those systems that are currently embarrassing. In other words, I expect that we will need our new corollary to handle arbitrarily many peculiar schemes that are compatible with supervenience, physical exhaustion, or what have you. And, if that's the case, then dismissing an odd fraction of them seems tenuous grounds for identity theory after all.

* * *

At this juncture, I would like to switch gears, and discuss the principle of physical exhaustion more directly.[31] It rests fundamentally on two "modes of composition": spatio-temporal fusion and set abstraction. These are both ways of getting new entities out of whatever ones you already have; thus, for many collections of things, you can form their sum, and/or the set containing them as members. Moreover, according to Hellman and Thompson, these are the *only* modes of composition that have *ontological* import. Any other purported "compound" either doesn't really exist, or is equivalent to one of these (i.e., a physical token or a set).[32]

One is entitled to wonder how fusion and set abstraction got such exclusive rights. I suspect it goes back to the Greek preference for permanence, and the resulting approach to the problem of change.[33] Forms (or essences) are top dog: eternal, hence incorruptible. The solution is to introduce another factor, matter, that fleshes out forms to constitute temporal entities. Matter as such is also permanent, in that it is conserved; but it has no intelligible features either to keep or lose. Rather, all change is localized in the way form and matter go together—which matter has which form is a function of time.[34]

The philosopher's weakness is to generalize. We know that, in addition to ordinary things, there

---

more compound physical tokens, such as the set of lakes existing in Canada for all of 1996, or the set of all hydrogen atoms existing in the first ten seconds of the universe. The difference between the *fusion* of water molecules in a lake, and the *set* of water molecules in that same lake during a specific time interval **t**, is that the fusion is itself a physical token capable of changing (e.g., as rain or evaporation alters the quantity of water molecules in the lake), whereas the set of water molecules in that lake during **t** is (like any set) a changeless entity. Compounding those molecules into a *set* lifts them out of the flux of events in the physical world, and gives them the eternal, incorruptible status of such entities as the set of all integers or the set of all sets of molecules. Thus we have a Platonic type of dualism in the materialism of Hellman and Thompson. ED.

[33] Parmenides (approx. 515–450 B.C.E.) had an enormous influence on Greek thought in this regard. He reasoned something like this: It is a fundamental law of thought and being that anything *is* what it is and *cannot not be* (something cannot both be and not be). What *is* coincides with what is intelligible or thinkable. One cannot think or understand nonbeing (= nothing). The world of changeable things is one in which everything which is whatever it is can also cease to be, in which there is an incessant and confusing oscillation between being and nonbeing. It is a world of semi-reality and semi-intelligibility. True being is eternal and changeless. ED.

[34] In simplified terms, the Aristotelian or hylomorphic analysis of change is like this: If a piece of Jell-O loses its cubic shape as it melts, something is gone and something remains. What remains is the subject of the melting process, in this case the Jell-O, which had and then lost a specific shape. Nothing has happened to the shape as such or as *form*— what-it-is-to-be-that-shape is something eternal and changeless, something that would be unaffected even if the entire world went shapeless like a big Jell-O. The Jell-O is *matter* in relation to the shape which is *form,* and in general bodies are combinations of matter and form because they are all subjects having in them for some interval a variety of forms such as a specific shape, size, and color which they typically cease to have under certain circumstances, acquiring other shapes, colors, and sizes instead. Since it is form that makes matter to be of one kind rather than another (not just being cubic or round, but also being wood or Jell-O in the first place), matter *in itself* is featureless. That is why, according to Aristotle, matter can't exist by itself; it's nothing in itself and must be combined with form to make a certain type of body. In itself matter is just the *potentiality for change* in the form/matter compound that is a body, enabling that body to take on a succession of forms. ED.

---

[31] In this final section of his paper, Haugeland is dealing with the metaphysical duality of matter and form, which is a development or transformation by Aristotle of the Platonic dualism described in fn. 14 above. Aristotle's Greek terms for matter and form were *hylē* and *morphē* respectively, from which comes the term *hylomorphism,* which names Aristotle's doctrine (and later theories inspired by it) that bodies or material **substances** are combinations of matter and form. Painting the history of philosophy with a very wide brush, Haugeland will compare the duality of matter and form with the duality of physical token and set in Hellman and Thompson. ED.

[32] In Hellman and Thompson's scheme objects such as water molecules certainly exist, and so do physical collections ("fusions") of them such as the water (molecules) in a lake, and also sets of these simpler or

can be unmaterialized forms (hippogriffs, e.g.); but, there is no uninformed matter. So . . . EVERYTHING is either a pure form, or some hunk of informed matter. Hellman and Thompson's principle of physical exhaustion is, I think, just this generalized hylomorphism in modern (mathematical) garb. Sets are the (more comprehensive and precise) replacement for timeless forms;[35] and arbitrary portions of space-time are the (more comprehensive and precise) replacement for hunks of informed matter. (Mass-energy may even do for "raw" matter.)

The fatal flaw in hylomorphism[36] is that it leaves too little room for distinctions: being concrete, individual, temporal (contingent), and material are all lumped together. That is, all and only material entities are particular, temporal concreta—everything else is an abstract, eternal kind. Moreover, there is only one possible relation between the two sides: inhesion (instantiation, set membership). And, finally, the modes of composition are asymmetrical: you can go horizontally or up, but not down. That is, you can take an arbitrary bunch of material individuals and fuse them into a new one; or, you can abstract away from all their matter,[37] to get a pure form (set); and, with modern apparatus, you can abstract a "higher" set from an arbitrary bunch of sets. What you can't do is go the other way, and make matter out of forms—once eternal, always eternal. The result is a rigid hierarchy, with all temporal individuals exactly on a par at the bottom.

Consider a story and its various "tokens". Written tokens are particular inscriptions—temporal individuals, plausibly identifiable with hunks of ink. (I will ignore oral tokens, recitations; they only make the case harder.) But what about the story itself, of which these are tokens? If we call it a "type," we still have to explain what that means. In *some* sense, a story-type is composed or "made up" of its tokens: it has its being in and through them—without them it wouldn't exist at all. Is it made up,

however, by either fusion or set abstraction? Not that I can see.

Try fusion. Then the story itself is just a larger and more scattered fraction of the physical universe—a bigger hunk of ink. It follows, presumably, that story types have mass and volume, which is startling, but perhaps not insufferable. More serious is collapsing the token/type relation into the part/whole relation: tokens (e.g., copies) of a story become, precisely, portions of it. That makes them comparable to, say, chapters, which (on this view) are also spatio-temporal portions of the whole. But, on the face of it, the chapter/story relation is completely different from the copy/story relation; they're not even similar. As if that weren't enough: in case there were only one copy of a story extant, the type and its token would be identical—which is surely unacceptable.

So, try set abstraction. That makes story-types like timeless kinds, which sounds congenial at first. But, on reflection, it seems to me incontestable that stories are *temporal, contingent individuals*. In the first place, they come into existence at some time, they evolve, they migrate, and sometimes they die out (possibly leaving progeny); this is not the habit of timeless kinds.

Second, stories are related as individuals, not as sub-varieties, to the obvious species and genera of literature. Thus, in the sequence, "Fido, spaniel, dog, mammal, . . . ," we recognize the first step as different from the others; Fido is not a narrower classification than spaniels, but an item classified. Likewise, in the sequence, "'The Sour Grapes', fable, allegory, fiction, . . . ", "The Sour Grapes" is not a narrower classification than the rest, but an item classified—that is, an individual. Hence, there seems as little hope for collapsing token/type into instance/kind or member/set as into part/whole. That's why I say there's too little room for distinctions.

Consider another homespun example. Take any dozen people from anywhere in history. There is a unique physical entity that is their fusion (or the fusion of their bodies, anyway); and there is a unique timeless entity that is the set containing exactly them. But suppose that a certain twelve people are friends with a common hobby, and they decide to form a club. Again, in *some sense,* a club is composed or "made up" of its members. But, I

---

[35] Just as nothing happens to the shape/form that the Jell-O loses, so nothing can happen to the *set* of all water molecules even though the lake dries up. ED.

[36] The remarks that follow apply more precisely to Hellman-Thompson "hylomorphism" than to Aristotle's. ED.

[37] In a hylomorphic context, abstracting from matter leaves out the potentiality for change, turning the object into something immutable. ED.

take it as obvious, without further argument, that club is identical neither to the set of its members, nor to the fusion of their bodies. Evidently, we need some other way(s) of composing new entities than the two allowed by the principle of physical exhaustion.

"Evidently," I hedge, because, as is well known, set theory is a boundless playground for those willing to invent astonishing interpretations for otherwise ordinary terms; indeed, the integers are a boundless playground for the truly open minded. Who knows what gawdawful set (or number) is identical (by somebody's lights) with "The Sour Grapes" or the Pittsburgh Quilters' Triangle? Who knows how predicates like 'is a temporal individual' might be construed so as to apply to them? And who cares? If preserving the principle of physical exhaustion is the primary motivation for such gymnastics, then I just don't feel the tug. Indeed, in such cases, I am sorely tempted to quote again our new corollary to Bailey: "Don't get weird beyond necessity!"

Haugeland's formulation of "Bailey's razor"—*Don't do anything beyond necessity*—is a mainstay of his argument. In general materialism should be satisfied with a weak supervenience principle because no more is necessary to slay the Cartesian dragon of interactionist dualism. Noninteractionist dualisms such as epiphenomenalism or parallelism are too "kooky" to be worth the trouble of a principled rejection. And, like Hellman and Thompson, he isn't especially worried about timeless objects such as numbers and sets coexisting with the domain of the temporal/contingent. As long as the temporal/contingent (including mental events) is unified by its dependence on the physical, materialism supposedly has all it needs and should mind Bailey's razor.

If we could forget the history of philosophy prior to Descartes, we might find it easier to share Haugeland's light-heartedness. But listen to what Plato had to say about eternal entities and our access to them: In the *Phaedo* Plato depicts Socrates in jail just before he must drink the poison prescribed by an Athenian court as a punishment for his alleged impiety and corrupting influence on young men. Appropriately enough, Socrates is discussing (with Cebes and Simmias) the prospect of the soul's survival after death. Socrates reminds these young men that he and they agree that the object of philosophical inquiry is an understanding of the forms— eternal entities such as *JUSTICE* and *BEAUTY*. What, asks Socrates, should we think of the soul since it longs for and can gain a vision of such objects?

> Consider then, Cebes, whether it follows from all that has been said that the soul is most like the divine, deathless, intelligible, uniform and indissoluble, always the same as itself, whereas the body is most like that which is human, mortal, multiform, unintelligible, soluble and never consistently the same. Have we anything else to say to show, my dear Cebes, that this is not the case?
>
> We have not.
>
> Well, then, that being so, is it not natural for the body to dissolve easily, and for the soul to be altogether indissoluble, or nearly so? (Tr. G. M. A. Grube, 1981, p.119)

The foregoing is hardly an airtight argument for soul(mind)-body dualism, but it does raise an important question: After all, Plato would say, ontologically speaking, there is a big difference between being temporal/contingent and being eternal/immutable. You physicalists or materialists, by definition, hold that there is nothing but the physical or the material, or, more weakly, you regard the material/physical as the most important or fundamental aspect of reality. At the very least, you should say more about forms or whatever you call your eternal objects these days. And how can your *minds,* with their affinity for eternal objects, be so entirely *dependent* on your all-too-perishable *brains?*

REVIEW QUESTION

Imagine this exchange between a neurobiologist and Haugeland:

H: Like the hypothesis that the universe just stops cold every few millennia for ten seconds and then resumes exactly as before, epiphenomenalism is theoretically unmotivated, magically undetectable, and thoroughly bizarre. That's why I don't think materialists need bother formulating their principle in such a way as to exclude epiphenomenalism. Hard cases make bad law and kooky cases make bad principles.

N: I didn't think philosophers tried to win arguments by calling people names. Let me tell you why I'm an epiphenomenalist, and you tell me how I'm being bizarre. I completely agree with materialists that interactionist dualism violates the integrity of neuroscience. After all, it has nonphysical—and therefore unobservable and unmeasurable—mental events causing brain events. To believe this is to believe that there are brain events that can never be scientifically explained, and I can't think that way. However, what you call the qualia in sensations and feelings seem all too real to me and I'm underwhelmed by philosophical attempts to make it intelligible that qualia *are* the brain events with which I'm so familiar. They're just an utterly different kind of reality from brain events. So I fall back on epiphenomenalism. It's not a pretty position, but it is an honest one, and I feel "theoretically motivated" to embrace it.

Continue this dialogue or just speak your mind directly on the issue.

13

The Mind-Body Problem:
Taking Stock after Forty Years

Jaegwon Kim

Jaegwon Kim teaches philosophy at Brown University. He has published extensively in the philosophy of mind. His most recent books are *Mind in a Physical World: An Essay on the Mind-Body Problem and Mental Causation* (1998), and *Philosophy of Mind* (1996).

In the previous reading, John Haugeland argued that what he called "weak supervenience" is sufficient to express the "basic intuition" of physicalist materialism. What Haugeland calls "weak" is more commonly known as *global* supervenience: "The world could not have been different in any respect, without having been different in some strictly physical respect—that is, in some respect describable in a canonical language of physics." This principle does not need to be supplemented by type identities of the sort presupposed by the usual account of theory reduction.[1] Nor does it need even token identities between instances of the mental and instances of the physical. He argued that it is good for materialism that it doesn't need identity claims, since these claims are unsuccessful. And, without identities, one cannot articulate a principle of ontological reduction—to the effect that the world consists of *nothing but* the physical.

Against this minimalist conception of the materialist intuition Kim will present a different, nonglobal formula for the supervenience relation as holding between higher- and lower-level properties. Using this formula, he will argue that a functional interpretation ("functionalization") of higher-level properties (1) makes intelligible the type identities required for theory reduction, and (2) makes sense of the ontologically reductive claim that for a system to have a mental property *M* is "nothing over and above" that system's having a physical property *P* that realizes *M*.

It has been just about forty years since J. J. C. Smart's "Sensations and Brain Processes"[2] and Herbert Feigl's "The 'Mental' and the 'Physical'"[3] appeared, both independently proposing an approach to the status of mind that has come to be variously called "the mind-body identity thesis", "central-state materialism", "type physicalism", and the "brain state theory". Although Smart, in particular, had been anticipated by U. T. Place's[4]

From: Jaegwon Kim, "The Mind-Body Problem: Taking Stock after Forty Years," *Philosophical Perspectives* 11: *Mind, Causation and the World*, ed. James Tomberlin (Boston: Blackwell Publishers, 1997): pp. 185–207.

[1] See fn. 12 of Reading 12. ED.

[2] Reading 6. ED.

[3] J. J. C. Smart, "Sensations and Brain Processes", *Philosophical Review* 68 (1958): 141–156. Herbert Feigl, "The 'Mental' and the 'Physical'",

Minnesota Studies in the Philosophy of Science, Vol. 2, ed. Herbert Feigl, Grover Maxwell, and Michael Scriven (Minneapolis: University of Minnesota Press, 1958).

[4] Reading 5. ED.

"Is Consciousness a Brain Process?",[5] published in 1956, it was arguably the two papers by Smart and Feigl that reintroduced the mind-body problem into mainstream metaphysics, and launched the vigorous debate that has continued to this day. True, Ryle's *The Concept of Mind* was out in 1948, and there were of course Wittgenstein's much discussed reflections on mentality and mental discourse, not to mention a much earlier and neglected classic, C. D. Broad's *The Mind and Its Place in Nature* (1925).[6] But it is fair to say that Ryle's and Wittgenstein's primary concerns were directed at the logic of psychological language rather than the metaphysical problem of explaining how our mentality is related to our physical nature, and that Broad's work, although robustly metaphysical, failed to connect with the mind-body debate in the second half of this century, especially in its critical early stages.

For many of us, the brain-state theory was our first encounter with the mind-body problem. The theory sounded refreshingly bold and tough-minded, and in tune with the optimistic scientific temper of the times. Why can't mentality just turn out to be brain processes just as light turned out to be electromagnetic radiation and the gene turned out to be the DNA molecule? As we all know, the brain-state theory was surprisingly short-lived—its precipitous decline began only several years after its initial promulgation. It is clear in retrospect, though, that in spite of its brief life, the theory made one crucial and fundamental contribution which has outlasted its reign as a theory of the mind. What I have in mind is the fact that the brain-state theory helped set the basic parameters for the debates that were to follow—the broadly physicalist assumptions and aspirations that still guide and constrain our thinking today. One indication of this is the fact that when the brain state theory began fading away in the late '60s and early '70s we didn't lapse back into Cartesianism or other serious forms of dualism. Almost all the participants in the debate stayed with a broadly physicalist framework, and even those who had a major hand in the demise of the Smart-Feigl materialism con-

tinued their allegiance to a physicalist world view. And this fact has played a central role in defining our *Problematik:* Through the '70s and '80s and down to the present, the mind-body problem—*our* mind-body problem—has been that of finding a place for the mind in a world that is fundamentally and essentially physical. If C. D. Broad were writing his 1925 book today, he might well have titled it "The Place of the Mind in the Physical World."

What made the demise of the mind-brain identity theory so quick and seemingly painless, causing few regrets among philosophers, was the fact that the principal objection that spelled its doom, the multiple realization argument advanced by Hilary Putnam,[7] contained within it seeds for an attractive alternative theory, namely functionalism. The core thesis of functionalism, that mental kinds are functional kinds, not physical kinds, was an appealing and eye-opening idea that seemed to help us make sense of "cognitive science", which was being launched about the same time. The functionalist approach to mentality seemed tailor-made for the new science of mentality and cognition, for it appeared to postulate a distinctive domain of mental/cognitive properties that could be scientifically investigated independently of their physical/biological implementations—an idea that promised both legitimacy and autonomy for psychology as a science. Functionalism made it possible for us to shed the restrictive constraints of physicalist **reductionism** without returning to the discredited dualisms of Descartes and others. Or so it seemed at the time. The functionalist conception of mentality still is "the official story" about the nature and foundation of cognitive science.[8]

But functionalists, by and large, were not metaphysicians, and few of them were self-consciously concerned about just what functionalism entailed about the mind-body problem.[9] The key term they

---

[5] U. T. Place, "Is Consciousness a Brain Process?", *British Journal of Psychology* 47, Part I (1956): 44–50.

[6] Gilbert Ryle, *The Concept of Mind* (London: Hutchinson and Company, Ltd., 1949), C. D. Broad, *The Mind and Its Place in Nature* (London: Routledge & Kegan Paul, 1925).

[7] In "Psychological Predicates" first published in 1968 and later reprinted under the title "The Nature of Mental States", in Hilary Putnam, *Collected Papers* II (Cambridge: Cambridge University Press, 1975). [Reading 16. ED.]

[8] See, e.g., Zenon Pylyshyn, *Computation and Cognition* (Cambridge: MIT Press, 1985).

[9] Two notable exceptions were David Armstrong and David Lewis. On the ambiguous metaphysical stance of functionalism concerning the mind-body problem, see Ned Block's "Introduction: What Is Functionalism?", in *Readings in Philosophy of Psychology*, Vol. 1, ed. Block (Cambridge: Harvard University Press, 1980).

used to describe the relation between mental properties (kinds, states, etc.) and physical properties was "realization" (or sometimes "implementation", "execution", etc.): mental properties are "realized" or "implemented" by (or in) physical properties, though not identical with, or reducible to, or definable in terms of them. But the term "realization" was introduced[10] and quickly gained wide currency, chiefly on the basis of computational analogies (in particular, Turing machines being realized in physical computers[11]), and few functionalists, especially in the early days of functionalism, made an explicit effort to explain what the realization relation consisted in—what this relation implied in terms of the traditional options on the mind-body problem.

I believe that the idea of "supervenience" came to the fore in the '70s and '80s, in part to fill this void. The doctrine that mental properties are supervenient on physical properties seemed perfectly to meet the needs of the post-reductionist physicalist in search of a metaphysics of mind; for it promised to give a clear and sturdy sense to the primacy of the physical domain and its laws, thereby vindicating the fundamental physicalist commitments of most functionalists, and do this without implying physical reductionism, thereby protecting the mental as a distinctive and autonomous domain. Further, by allowing multiple physical bases for supervenient mental properties, it was able to accommodate the multiple realizability of mental properties as well. Many philosophers, especially those who had been persuaded by the multiple realization argument to embrace antireductionism (and this included almost all the functionalists), sought in mind-body supervenience a satisfying metaphysical statement of **physicalism** without reductionism. By the mid-'70s, what Ned Block has aptly called "an antireductionist consensus"[12] was firmly in place. This position, standardly called "nonreductive physicalism", has been the most influential and widely shared view not only about the mind-body relation but, more importantly, about the relationship between "higher-level" properties and their underlying "lower-level" properties in other domains as well. Thus, the approach yielded as a bonus a general philosophical view about how the special sciences are related to basic physics.

One side effect of the entrenchment of the antireductionist consensus has been the return of emergentism—if not the full-fledged doctrine of classic emergentism of the 1920s and '30s, at least its characteristic vocabulary and slogans. When positivism and the idea of "unity of science"[13] ruled, emergentism was regarded with undisguised suspicion, as a mysterious and incoherent metaphysical doctrine. With reductionist physicalism out of favor, emergentism appears to be making a strong comeback,[14] and we now see an increasing and unapologetic use of terms like "emergence", "emergent characteristic", "emergent phenomenon", "emergent cause", and the like, seemingly in the sense intended by the classic emergentists,[15] not only in serious philosophical writings[16] but in primary scientific literature in many fields.[17]

To sum up, three ideas have been prominently on the scene in recent discussions of the mind-body relation: the idea that the mental is "realized" by the physical, the idea that the mental "supervenes" on the physical, and the idea that the mental is "emergent" from the physical. In this paper I want to explore the interplay of these three ideas, and the

---

[10] The first philosophical use of this term I know of in the current sense is in Hilary Putnam's "Minds and Machines", in *Dimensions of Mind,* ed. Sidney Hook (New York: New York University Press, 1960).

[11] Turing machines and their realizations are explained in Reading 15. ED.

[12] In his "Antireductionism Slaps Back", in *Philosophical Perspectives* 11 (1997), ed. J. Tomberlin, *Mind, Causation, and Word,* pp. 107–132.

[13] See fn. 12 of Reading 12. ED.

[14] I have argued elsewhere that classic emergentism is appropriately taken as the first articulation of nonreductive physicalism. See my "The Nonreductivist's Troubles with Mental Causation", in *Supervenience and Mind* (Cambridge: Cambridge University Press, 1993).

[15] In the paper to which he refers in note 14, Kim compares nonreductive physicalism to classic emergentism this way: "For both emergentism and nonreductive physicalism, then, the doctrine of irreducible higher-level properties is the centerpiece of their respective positions; and their proponents take it to be what makes their positions distinctive and important. As net additions to the world, the emergent higher-level properties cannot be reduced or explained away; and as irreducible new features of the world, they form an autonomous domain, and, as [Samuel] Alexander says [in *Space, Time, and Deity,* 1927], make 'an independent science of psychology' possible" (346–47). ED.

[16] See, e.g., John R. Searle, *The Rediscovery of the Mind* (Cambridge: The MIT Press, 1992). Another sign of new interest in emergence is the volume of essays on emergence, *Emergence or Reduction?,* ed. Ansgar Beckermann, Hans Flohr, and Jaegwon Kim (Berlin: De Gruyter, 1992).

[17] E.g., Francisco Varela, Evan Thompson, and Eleanor Rosch, *The Embodied Mind* (Cambridge: The MIT Press, 1993). See especially Part IV entitled "Varieties of Emergence".

roles they play, in the context of the mind-body problem, and, more generally, in the context of formulating and discussing some issues concerning the interlevel relationships of properties. My discussion will not be historical but reconstructive and philosophical—an old-fashioned "rational reconstruction" if you like.

I

Let us begin with supervenience. It is convenient to construe supervenience as a relation between two sets of properties, the supervenient properties and their base properties. As is by now well known, a variety of supervenience relations is available; for our purposes we can focus on what is called "strong supervenience". This relation is defined as follows:

> Set A of properties (*strongly*) *supervenes* on set B of properties just in case, necessarily, for any property F in A, if anything has F, there exists a property G in B such that the thing has G, and necessarily anything that has G has F.

Under certain plausible (but not uncontested) assumptions concerning property composition, supervenience defined this way (sometimes called "the modal operator definition") can be shown to be equivalent to the more familiar explanation of supervenience (sometimes called "the possible world" or "indiscernibility" definition) which goes like this:

> A-properties (*strongly*) *supervene* on B-properties just in case necessarily any two things (in the same or different possible worlds) indiscernible in B-properties are indiscernible in A-properties—more simply, B-indiscernibility entails A-indiscernibility.

I do not believe that for our purposes anything of philosophical significance hinges on whatever differences there might exist between these two formulations. We will therefore consider them equivalent, and use one or the other to suit the context.

If mental properties supervene, in the sense explained, on physical properties, then for any mental property M there is a physical "supervenience base", or "base property", P such that P is sufficient, as a matter of necessity, for M. That is, if anything instantiates M, it instantiates a certain physical property P such that necessarily anything that has P has M.[18] The modal force of "necessarily" here need not be specified in advance; different interpretations of necessity, whether it is metaphysical, logical, or nomological, will yield different supervenience theses.[19] In the case of mind-body supervenience it may even be that some mental properties supervene on their physical bases with logical/conceptual necessity, some may do so with metaphysical necessity, and perhaps others only with nomological necessity.

It has become customary to associate supervenience with the idea of *dependence* or *determination*: if the mental supervenes on the physical, the mental is dependent on the physical, or the physical determines the mental, roughly in the sense that the mentality of a thing is entirely fixed by its physical nature. Sometimes, this is put in terms of "worlds": the psychological character of a world is determined entirely by its physical character—as it is often put, worlds that are physically indiscernible are psychologically indiscernible (or indiscernible *tout*

---

[18] This is *not*, of course, the claim that there is a type identity between P and M. Any supervenience formula leaves open the possibility of multiple realizations—that M may have different kinds of physical bases. The formula merely claims that for any M there will be a P and any single occurrence of P will be an occurrence of M. It is *not* saying that any occurrence of M is an occurrence of P. Notice the comparative looseness in Haugeland's formula for supervenience: "The world could not have been different in any respect, without having been different in some strictly physical respect—that is, in some respect describable in a canonical language of physics." How does this formula differ from Kim's? ED.

[19] There are three possible senses of "necessity" in the supervenience claim that if a physical system has the property P, then it *necessarily* has M. If the necessity is *logical*, then the claim that any system with P will have M becomes what many philosophers call a *conceptual* truth, one that is known simply in virtue of the meanings of the term for P and the term for M. It would be inconceivable for an instance of P not to be an instance of M. Or one could say that the claim is true in all possible worlds, in any world that can be coherently described and in which a system with P is a member. *Metaphysical* necessity is of the sort that Kripke (Reading 7) attributes to scientific identity statements such as "Water is H_2O". This is not a conceptual truth; it is discovered a posteriori. But, if it is true, then it is necessarily true in all possible worlds. The claim would be *nomologically* (or *naturally*) necessary if any occurrence of P is an occurrence of M according to some law of nature. For example, there might be a law of nature to the effect that any neural configuration with the property N will also have V (it will be an occurrence of a visual experience). This natural necessity does not imply that an occurrence of N is inconceivable without V. ED.

court). The relation of dependence, or determination, is asymmetric: if *x* depends on, or is determined by, *y*, it cannot be that *y* in turn depends on or is determined by *x*. What does the determining must be taken to be, in some sense, ontologically prior to, or more basic than, what gets determined by it. But supervenience as defined above isn't asymmetric; the supervenience of *A* on *B* does not exclude the supervenience of *B* on *A*. The definition simply states a pattern of *covariance* between the two property sets, and such covariances can occur in the absence of a metaphysical dependence or determination relation. For example, two sets of properties may show the required covariance because each depends on a third, somewhat in the manner in which two collateral effects of the single cause exhibit a pattern of lawful correlation.[20] What needs to be added to property covariance to get dependence or determination, or whether dependence/determination must be taken as an independent primitive, are deep and difficult questions that need not be pursued here.[21] In this paper, we will follow the customary usage and understand supervenience to incorporate the component of dependence/determination. In fact, common expressions like "supervenience base" or "base property" already include a presumption of asymmetric dependence.

Suppose, then, that the mental supervenes on the physical. Do we have here a possible account of how our mentality is related to the physical nature of our being? That is, can we use supervenience itself to state a philosophical theory of the way minds are related to bodies? It has sometimes been thought that the answer is yes, that what might be called "supervenience physicalism" is a possible position to take on the mind-body problem. There is a long-standing controversy concerning whether supervenience, in the sense of strong supervenience, is consistent with the irreducibility of the superve-

nient properties to their subvenient bases. We may, however, bypass this issue, and focus on the question whether or not supervenience as such can be considered an account of the mind-body relation.[22]

Brief reflection shows that the answer is no, that mind-body supervenience by itself cannot constitute a theory of the mind-body relation. There are at least two reasons for this. First, mind-body supervenience is consistent with a host of classic positions on the mind-body problem; it is in fact a shared commitment of many mutually exclusionary mind-body theories. As we will shortly see, both emergentism and the view that the mental is exclusively physically realized—that is, there are no nonphysical realizations of mental properties (we can call this "physical realizationism")—imply mind-body supervenience. But emergentism is a form of dualism that takes mental properties to be nonphysical intrinsic causal powers, whereas physical realizationism, as I will argue, is a monistic physicalism. What is more obvious, mind-body supervenience is a trivial consequence of type physicalism, which reductively identifies mental properties with physical properties. Even epiphenomenalism is committed to supervenience: If two things differ in some mental respect, that must be because they are different in some physical respect—it must be because the physical cause of the mental respect involved is present in one and absent from the other. If mind-body supervenience is a commitment of each of these conflicting approaches to the mind-body problem,[23] it cannot itself be a position on this issue alongside these classic alternatives.[24]

What this shows is that the mere fact (assuming it is a fact) of mind-body supervenience leaves open the question of what *grounds* or *accounts for* it—that is, why the supervenience relation obtains

---

[20] The seventeenth-century doctrine of occasionalism discussed in fn. 29 of Reading 12 would prove an example of this. An occasionalist would hold that God has decreed that there will be a covariance in human beings of mental and physical states. This decree would make the psychophysical correlations law-like in our experience, without conferring any metaphysical priority of one type over the other. ED.

[21] I do not think there is a single answer to this question. What I will say later about *explaining* supervenience relations obviously has something to do with this "deep" question.

[22] One might object; if supervenience entails reduction, mind-body supervenience must be considered a theory of the mind-body relation, since mind-body reductionism clearly is one. My answer: when the question whether supervenience entails reduction is discussed, it is formulated in terms of what I now take to be an incorrect model of reduction. For further discussion, see below.

[23] Recall Haugeland's admission, in Reading 12, that his "weak supervenience" is consistent with such "brilliantly kooky" metaphysical views as parallelism and epiphenomenalism.

[24] Mind-body supervenience is not excluded even by Cartesian substance dualism. See my "Supervenience for Multiple Domains", reprinted in *Supervenience and Mind*.

between the mental and the physical.[25] To see the general issue involved here, consider normative supervenience, the widely accepted doctrine that normative or evaluative properties supervene on nonnormative, nonevaluative properties. Various metaethical[26] positions accept normative supervenience but offer differing accounts of its source. According to ethical naturalism, the supervenience holds because normative properties are definable in terms of nonnormative, naturalistic properties; that is, normative properties turn out to be naturalistic properties. Ethical intuitionists, like G. E. Moore, would see normative supervenience as a primitive synthetic a priori[27] fact not susceptible to further explanation; it is something we directly apprehend through our moral sense. R. M. Hare, a noncognitivist, would attempt to explain it as a form of a consistency condition essential to the regulative character of the language of commending and prescribing.[28] Still others may try to explain it as arising from the very concept of normative evaluation, maintaining that evaluative or normative properties must have nonnormative descriptive criteria.

_____

[25]On the need for explaining supervenience relations see Terence Horgan, "Supervenience and Cosmic Hermeneutics", *Southern Journal of Philosophy* 22 (1984), Supplement: 19–38, and Terence Horgan and Mark Timmons, "Troubles on Moral Twin Earth: Moral Queerness Revisited", *Synthese* 92 (1992): 221–260.

[26]*Metaethics* is a theory *about* ethics as a kind of discourse and about the kinds of arguments and evidence it uses. *Ethics* itself, as a philosophical discipline, seeks to draw conclusions about what is right and wrong. It is difficult to do ethics without also engaging in what could be classified as metaethical analysis. ED.

[27]If the claim one makes is supposed to be true independently of experience or verification by observation, then it is *a priori*. A claim is *analytic* if it is based on the meaning of the concepts involved, as in "Bachelors are unmarried." Otherwise, it is *synthetic*. According to Moore the normative property of an act—its goodness or badness—is intuited by a special moral sense. Since the connection between the normative property and the descriptive property of the act cannot be established by analysis of the descriptive property, a moral judgment is not analytic. Since the judgment cannot be verified by sensory perception, it is not a posteriori (its truth or falsehood is not based on experience). Therefore it must be synthetic a priori. ED.

[28]Hare is a noncognitivist in the sense that the goodness or badness of an act is not an addition to the list of properties we can come to know about the act. For Hare an important part of what makes an act good, or at least morally permissible, is its universalizability. He assimilates moral judgments to a special sort of command—a universal prescription. To say that lying is wrong, for instance, is to say that one *ought not* to lie. The ought(-not)-ness of an action *supervenes* on the descriptive property of the act, so that if a certain act ought not to be done because it is a case of lying, then any case of lying is a case of what ought not to be done. ED.

Similarly in the mind-body case we can think of different mind-body theories as offering competing explanations of mind-body supervenience: the explanation offered by type physicalism is parallel to the naturalistic explanation of normative supervenience—mind-body supervenience holds because mentality is physically reducible and mental properties turn out to be physical properties after all. Emergentism, like ethical intuitionism, takes mind-body supervenience as a brute fact not further explainable, something that should be accepted, as Samuel Alexander said, with "natural piety". In contrast, epiphenomenalism can invoke the causal relation (the "same cause, same effect" principle) to explain supervenience, and in physical realizationism, as we will see, mind-body supervenience is entailed by the view that mental properties are "second-order" properties defined over first-order physical properties. And so on.

We must conclude, then, that mind-body supervenience itself is not an *explanatory theory;* it merely states a pattern of property covariation between the mental and the physical, and points to the existence of a dependency relation between the two. Yet it is wholly silent on the nature of the dependence relation that might explain why the mental supervenes on the physical. Another way of putting the point would be this: Supervenience itself is not a *type* of dependence relation—it is not a relation that can be placed alongside causal dependence, mereological dependence,[29] dependence grounded in definability or entailment, and the like. It is not a metaphysically deep, explanatory relation, being only a phenomenological relation about patterns of property covariation. If this is right, mind-body supervenience *states* the mind-body problem—it is not a solution to it. Any putative solution to the problem must, at a minimum, specify a dependence relation that grounds mind-body supervenience. We expect mind-body theories to be explanatory theories.

These considerations, however, should not be taken to be entirely, or even significantly, deflationary about the utility of supervenience in philosophy of mind. Although they quash the hope

_____

[29]*Mereological* dependence is the kind that would obtain between part and whole. ED.

that supervenience itself might give us an account of the mind-body relation, there is also a positive message here: Mind-body supervenience captures a commitment common to all approaches to the nature of mentality that are basically physicalistic. For it represents the idea that mentality is at bottom physically based, an idea that can be shared by many diverse positions on the mind-body problem, from reductive type physicalism at one extreme to dualistic emergentism and epiphenomenalism at the other. In contrast, mind-body supervenience is inconsistent with radical forms of dualism, e.g., Descartes' dualism, which allow the mental world to float freely, unconstrained by the physical domain.[30] Thus, mind-body supervenience can serve as a useful dividing line: it defines *minimal physicalism*.

II

Cartesian substance dualism pictures the world as consisting of two independent spheres, the mental and the material, each with its own distinctive defining properties (consciousness and spatial extendedness respectively). There are causal interactions across the domains, but entities in each domain, being "substances", are ontologically independent of those of the other, and it is metaphysically possible for one domain to exist in the total absence of the other. What has replaced this picture of a dichotomized world is the familiar multi-layered model that views the world as stratified into different "levels", "orders", or "tiers", organized in a hierarchical structure. The bottom level is usually thought to consist of elementary particles, or whatever our best physics is going to tell us are the basic bits of matter out of which all material things are composed.[31] As we go up the

ladder, we find atoms, molecules, cells, larger living organisms, and so on. The ordering relation that generates the hierarchical structure is the mereological relation: entities belonging to a given level, except those at the very bottom, have an exhaustive decomposition, without remainder, into entities belonging to the lower levels. Entities at the bottom level have no physically significant proper parts.

What then of the *properties* of these entities? It is part of this layered model that at each level there are properties, activities, and functions that make their first appearance at that level (we may call them the "characteristic properties" of that level). Thus, among the characteristic properties of the molecular level are electrical conductivity, inflammability, density, viscosity, and the like; activities and functions like metabolism and reproduction are among the characteristic properties of the cellular and higher biological levels; consciousness and other mental properties make their appearance at the level of higher organisms. For much of this century, a layered picture of the world like this has formed an omnipresent, if only implicit, background for debates on the mind-body problem, emergence, reductionism, the status of the special sciences, and the like, and has exerted a powerful and pervasive influence on the way we formulate problems and discuss their solutions. Sometimes, the layered model is couched in terms of concepts and languages instead of entities in the world and their properties. Talk of levels of *descriptions,* of *analyses,* of *concepts,* of *explanations,* and the like is encountered everywhere—it has thoroughly pervaded primary scientific literature as well as philosophical writings about science.[32]

Now we come to a crucial question: How are the characteristic properties of a given level related to the properties at the adjacent levels—in particular, to those at the lower levels? How are biological ("vital") properties related to physico-

---

[30] There are forms of dualism, e.g., Spinozistic double-aspect theory and Leibniz's doctrine of preestablished harmony, that are consistent with supervenience as property covariation but not with full-fledged supervenience that includes asymmetric dependence. We may also note that although emergentism appears to be committed to mind-body supervenience it is by no means clear that another of its basic tenets, namely the doctrine of "downward causation", is consistent with the supervenience thesis. See my "Downward Causation" in Emergentism and Nonreductive Physicalism", in *Emergence or Reduction?*, ed. A. Beckermann, H. Flohr, and J. Kim (Berlin: De Gruyter, 1992).

[31] The layered model as such of course does not need to posit a bottom level; it is consistent with an infinitely descending series of levels.

[32] In his work on vision David Marr famously distinguishes three levels of analysis: the computational, the algorithmic, and the implementational. See his *Vision* (New York: Freeman Press, 1982). The emergentists, early in this century, appear to have been first to give an explicit formulation of the layered model; see, e.g., C. Lloyd Morgan, *Emergent Evolution* (London: Williams and Norgate, 1923). For a particularly clear and useful statement of the model, see Paul Oppenheim and Hilary Putnam, "Unity of Science as a Working Hypothesis", *Minnesota Studies in the Philosophy of Science,* Vol. 2 (1958).

chemical properties? How are consciousness and intentionality related to biological/physical properties? How are social phenomena, phenomena characteristic of social groups, related to phenomena involving individual members? As you will agree, these are among the fundamental questions of philosophy of science, metaphysics, and philosophy of mind. Possible answers to these questions define the classic philosophical options on the issues involved. Some of the well-known major alternatives include reductionism, antireductionism, methodological individualism,[33] functionalism, emergentism, neo-vitalism,[34] and the like. You may attempt to give a single uniform answer applicable to all pairs of adjacent levels, or you may take different positions regarding different levels. For example, you might argue that properties at every level (higher than the bottom level) are reducible, in some clear and substantial sense, to lower-level properties, or you might restrict the reductionist claim to certain selected levels (say, biological properties in relation to physicochemical properties) and defend an antireductionist stance concerning properties at other levels (say, mental properties). And it isn't even necessary to give a uniform answer in regard to all characteristic properties of a given level; concerning mental properties, for example, it is possible to hold that phenomenal or sensory properties, or qualia, are irreducible, while holding that intentional properties, including propositional attitudes, are reducible (say, functionally or biologically).

Let us now look at the layered model with supervenience in mind: when supervenience is superposed on the layered model, something like the following emerges as a general schema of supervenience claims about properties at a given level (other than the lowest one) in relation to properties at a lower level:

For any x and y, belonging to level L, if x and y are indiscernible in relation to properties at all levels lower than L (or, as we might say, x and y are *microindiscernible*), then x and y are indiscernible with respect to all properties at level L.

How do we explain the idea of microindiscernibility? The following seems pretty natural and straightforward:[35]

x and y are *microindiscernible* if for every decomposition D of x into proper parts there is an isomorphic decomposition C of y in the following sense: there is a one-one function I from D to C, and for any n-adic property or relation, P, $P(\mathbf{d}_n)$ IFF $P(I(\mathbf{d}_n))$, where $\mathbf{d}_n$ is any n-tuple of elements in D and $I(\mathbf{d}_n)$ is the image of $\mathbf{d}_n$ under I; and conversely for every decomposition of y into its proper parts there is an isomorphic decomposition of x.[36]

Unsurprisingly, therefore, supervenience claims, when applied to the layered model, turn into theses of *mereological supervenience,* to the effect that properties of wholes are determined by the properties and relations that characterize their parts. A general claim of supervenience, then, becomes the Democritean[37] doctrine that the world is the way it is because the microworld is the way it is.

Now, suppose that M is a characteristic property at a certain level for which the supervenience thesis

---

[33] *Individualism,* in the methodological sense, is the view that social facts are best understood from the point of view of individuals and their intentions and actions. The opposite view is often called *holism:* that it is the social group that makes intelligible the individual. ED.

[34] *Neo-vitalism* is the resurgence of the thesis of vitalism: that living systems have properties (including causal powers) that cannot be explained in physicochemical terms and which play a causal role in the functioning of a living system. ED.

[35] Although a bit too restrictive; see my "Supervenience for Multiple Domains", reprinted in *Supervenience and Mind*.

[36] When a whole at a higher level is decomposed or analyzed into a collection of parts at the same lower level, those parts stand in a certain relation to each other. The parts are "members" of the relation, and there are as many "places" (n) in the relation as there are members (n). The "n-adic property or relation" Kim refers to is the n-place relation the n parts have to each other as constituting the whole. To say that two decompositions are isomorphic is to say that there is a one-to-one mapping of places and members between the relation of the parts in one whole and the relation of parts in another whole at the same level. ED.

[37] Democritus (460–370 B.C.E.) was the co-founder of a doctrine called atomism. The atomists claimed that all bodies are composed of imperceptibly small and indivisible particles that differed only in size and shape (*atomos* is Greek for *indivisible*). All the properties of composite bodies were determined by the those of the constituent atoms. ED.

holds (so M is not a property of entities at the bottom level). We may assume that any object has a unique decomposition at the bottom level of basic physical particles; in fact, it makes sense to assume that every object has a unique decomposition at any *significant* lower-level, for example, at the levels of atoms, molecules, cells, and so on ("significant" here is intended to exclude unmotivated gerrymandered decompositions into arbitrary parts). In terms of the concepts introduced thus far, this means:

> If something x has M, then (1) x has a unique decomposition D into parts, $d_1 \ldots, d_n$ at the fundamental physical level, and there is a set $\mathbf{F}$ of lower-level properties and relations characterizing $d_1 \ldots, d_n$, and (2) necessarily any y which has a decomposition isomorphic to D preserving $\mathbf{F}$ has M.

Let us now consider mental properties and creatures with mentality: when applied to these, clauses (1) and (2) above yield the following two claims:

(I) [Ontological physicalism] Any creature (or system) with mentality is wholly constituted by physical parts—ultimately, basic physical particles. There are no nonphysical residues (e.g., Cartesian souls, entelechies, elan vital, and the like).

(II) [Mereological supervenience] Mental properties supervene on microstructures of the creatures that have them—that is, on the fact that these creatures are made up of such-and-such parts with such-and-such properties and configured in a structure defined by such-and-such relations.

There almost certainly are higher levels than the fundamental physical level (e.g., molecular and cellular levels) where indiscernibility at those levels entails mental indiscernibility. In any case, we should resist the temptation to read more into (II) than what's really there. As advertised, (II) tells us that mind-body supervenience is an instance of *mereological supervenience,* and this might tempt us into thinking that we might find here an informative explanation of mind-body supervenience, in

parallel with the way macrophysical properties are determined and hence explained by microphysical properties. But this would be an illusion. For one thing, the mind-body supervenience on offer here is consistent with the mental supervening on macrophysical properties. For it may be that mental properties are fixed by microphysical properties because microphysical properties fix macrophysical properties (as we expect) and the latter in turn fix mental properties. If this should be the case (I find this a plausible possibility), we would still have to explain why mental properties supervene on macrophysical properties and the mereological aspect of (II) would likely offer no help with this.

Moreover, even if mental properties should in some sense directly supervene on the microphysical, that would not automatically promise us an intelligible account of why the supervenience obtains. Given that mental property M is supervenient on a *micro*physical base P, the questions still remain: Is M reducible to P in some appropriate sense? Can we explain why something has M in terms of its having P? Are the P-M and other such supervenience relationships explainable (and what can "explanation" mean here?), or must they be taken as brute and fundamental? These questions are unaffected by the question whether P is micro or macro; if mereological considerations are going to help us here, it is by no means obvious just how that might happen.

But these remain legitimate questions that need to be addressed if we are seeking a full understanding of the interlevel property relationships. Let us now turn to the idea of "physical realization" as an approach to these questions.

III

Physical realizationism, as you may recall, is the claim that mental properties are physically realized—or more precisely, no mental properties can (at least as a matter of nomological necessity) have nonphysical realizations. The idea is closely related to—in fact, it is the heart of—the functionalist program on mentality. Functionalism views mental properties and kinds as functional properties, properties specified in terms of their roles as causal intermediaries between sensory inputs and behavioral outputs.[38] This is usually taken to be a conceptual truth arising from our notion of what it is to be a mental property; the further claim is that, as things are in this and other relevantly similar worlds (in particular, in regard to the basic categories of exist-ents and laws of nature), physical states and prop-erties are the only occupants, or realizers, of these causal roles definitive of mental properties. To use a stock example, for an organism to be in pain is for it to be in some internal state that is typically caused by tissue damage and which typically causes groans, winces, and other characteristic pain behavior. In this sense, being in pain is said to be a "second-order" property: for a system, *x,* to have this prop-erty is for *x* to have some "first-order" property, *P,* which satisfies a certain condition *D,* where in the present case *D* specifies *P*'s typical causes and typi-cal effects.

More generally, we can explain the idea of a second-order property in the following way.[39] Let **B** be a set of properties; these are our "first-order" (or "base") properties. They need not be "first-order" in any absolute sense; some, or all, of them may be second-order relative to another set of properties.[40] Since mental properties are to be gen-erated out of **B**, we take **B** to consist of nonmental properties (including physicochemical, biological, and behavioral properties). We then have this:

> *F* is a *second-order property* over set **B** of base properties IFF *F* is the property of having some property *P* in **B** such that *D(P)*, where *D* specifies a condition on members of **B**.

Second-order properties, therefore, are "second-order" in that they are generated by *quantifica-tion*[41]—existential quantification in the present case—over the base properties. We may call the base properties that satisfy condition *D* the "realiz-ers" of second-order property *F*. For example, if the base set **B** includes colors, then *the property of having a primary color* can be generated as a second-order property: having a property *P* in **B** such that *P* = red or *P* = blue or *P* = green. Thus, having red, having blue, and having green are the three re-alizers of having a primary color. If **B** is a set of minerals, being jade can be thought of as the sec-ond order property of being a mineral that is pale green or white in color and fit for use as gemstones or for carving. This second-order property has two known realizers, jadeite and nephrite.

A further parameter to be fixed is the vocabu-lary allowed for formulating condition *D;* for our present purposes we assume that the causal/nomo-logical relation[42] (holding for properties—or prop-erty instances, to be exact) is available, in addition to the usual logical expressions and appropriate de-scriptive terms (e.g., those referring to members of **B**). We may now define *functional properties* over **B** to be those second-order properties over **B** whose specification *D* involves the causal/nomic relation. That is, functional properties are second-order properties defined in terms of causal/nomic relations among first-order properties. An example of a functional property is *dormitivity:* a substance has this property just in case it has a chemical prop-erty that causes people to sleep. Both Valium and Seconal have this property, but in virtue of different first-order chemical realizers (diazepam and secor-barbital, respectively). Or consider *water-solubility:* something has this property in case it has some property or other *P* such that when it is immersed in water *P* causes it to dissolve. This conception of functional property accords well with the standard

---

[38] Standard versions of functionalism would also include mental states in the outputs; e.g., in the case of pain such mental states as a sense of dis-tress and a desire to be rid of it. For expository simplicity we ignore this complication here.

[39] Hilary Putnam is responsible for both the functionalist conception of mentality and the general idea of a second-order property. On the lat-ter see his "On Properties", in *Philosophical Papers,* Vol. I (Cambridge: Cambridge University Press, 1975). Ned Block has extensively used the notion of second-order property in discussions of functionalism. In "On Properties", however, Putnam did not explicitly relate the notion of re-alization to that of second-order property.

[40] Of course one might develop a sort of foundationalist argument to show that if there are second-order properties there must be properties that are first-order in some absolute sense.

[41] *Quantification* expresses the quantity of instances or realizations of a property. The two quantifiers (symbols of quantity) most commonly used in logic are "some" and "all" (usually symbolized as $\exists$ and $\forall$ respec-tively). ED.

[42] Two entities (events, situations, properties) are *causally* related when the existence of one "brings about" or necessitates the occurrence of the other. Insofar as nature is uniform, these causal relations can be stated in law-like (*nomic* or *nomological*) form. ED.

usage in the functionalist literature. On the functionalist conception, mental properties are specified by *causal roles,* that is, in terms of causal relations holding for first-order physical properties (including biological and behavioral properties). In this sense, mental properties turn out to be *extrinsic* or *relational* properties of individuals that have them. To be in a mental state is to be in a state with such-and-such as its typical causes and such-and-such as its typical effects. Whether or not a given property qualifies as an occupant of the specified role—that is, whether or not it is a realizer of a functional property—depends, definitionally and constitutively, on its causal/nomological relations to other properties, not on its intrinsic character. Intrinsic characters of course do matter, but only because of their capacity to get causally or nomologically hooked up with other properties. Clearly it is a metaphysically contingent fact about them that they have such capacities.[43]

It follows then that if mental properties are functional properties, they are not tied to the compositional/structural details of their realizers, since these are intrinsic features; any base properties with the right causal/nomological relations to other properties can serve as their realizers. And any mechanism that gets activated by the right input and that, when activated, triggers the right response serves as a realizer (in an extended sense) of a psychological capacity or function. It has long been a platitude in philosophy of mind/psychology that mental properties can have diverse and variable realizers in different species and systems, and that the formal/abstract character of mental properties, standardly taken to be a consequence of this fact, is just what makes cognitive science possible—a scientific investigation of cognitive properties *as such,* across the diverse biological species and perhaps nonbiological cognitive systems, independently of the particulars of their physical implementations. In fact, some have even speculated about the possibility of nonphysical realizations of psychologies; it is a seductive thought that there may be contingent empirical laws of cognition, or psychology, that

are valid for cognizers as such, whether they are protein-based biological organisms like us and other earthly creatures, electromechanical robots, noncarbon-based intelligent extraterrestrials, immaterial Cartesian souls, heavenly angels, and even the omniscient one itself! (This evidently stretches the idea of "rational psychology" to the breaking point.) Even when we bring in the materialist constraint of physical realizationism, the idea of universal laws of cognition and psychology, contingent and empirical, and applicable to all nomologically possible[44] physical systems with mentality, is heady stuff, indeed.

Whether a given physical property, P, is a realizer of a mental property, M, depends on the nature of the system in which P is embedded,[45] since in psychology the input-output behavior of the total system is what is at issue, and P's input/output causal functions will depend on the makeup of the system as a whole. Whether or not tissue damage will cause the nociceptive neurons to fire in a given organism obviously depends on the organism's neural organization, and what overt behavior will be triggered by the firing of these neural fibers again depends on the organism's neural and motor systems. So the same property P, when embedded in another system, may not realize M. Conversely, there may be "functional substitutes" in the following sense: If for some reason the normal mechanism for instantiating P in an organism turns dysfunctional, another mechanism with the right causal capacities, if available, may be recruited to supply another realizer of M for that organism.[46]

The status of P as a realizer of M varies along another dimension as well: Since P's credentials as M's realizer depend on its causal/nomic relations to other properties, if laws of nature should vary,

---

[43] For instance, many substances are poisonous to humans. They have that second-order property in virtue of their first-order chemical properties. But the destructive causal role of the chemical properties is *not intrinsic* to them; they are destructive only in relation to the susceptible chemical structure of humans and other organisms. ED.

[44] See fn. 19 above. ED.

[45] Unless we have in mind "total realizers" in something like Sydney Shoemaker's sense. See his helpful distinction between "core realization" and "total realization", in "Some Varieties of Functionalism", reprinted in *Identity, Cause, and Mind* (Cambridge: Cambridge University Press, 1984). See also Ronald Endicott, "Constructive Plasticity", *Philosophical Studies* 74 (1994): 51–75. The discussion here assumes that input and output specifications are held constant for all systems, which is a highly idealized (in fact, evidently false) assumption. Surely, what counts as pain input or pain output differ greatly for different species (say, humans and octopuses) from a purely physical-behavioral point of view, and is likely to show significant differences even among humans.

[46] A synthetic hip joint would be an example of a functional substitute or equivalent. ED.

thereby altering P's causal potential, that could affect P's status as a realizer of M. P realizes M in this world; however, in a world in which different laws prevail and hence different causal relations hold, P may fail to satisfy the functional specification that defines M. It may be that in such worlds, M may have realizers entirely different from its realizers in this world, or it may have no realizers at all.

Although the realization relation can shift in these ways, it is also important to note its constancy: Once the system's physical constitution and the prevailing laws of nature are fixed, that fixes whether or not P realizes M in that system. That is to say, if P realizes M in system s, then P will realize M in all systems that are subject to the same laws and that are relevantly similar to s—that is, in respect of all nomic properties. If, as most of us would accept, the microstructure of a system determines its causal/nomic properties, it follows that, with laws held constant, the realization relation remains invariant for systems with similar microstructures.

Consider a class S of systems sharing a relevantly similar microstructure. Biological conspecifics may constitute such a class. Suppose P realizes M in systems of kind S. From the definition of realization, it follows that P is sufficient for M—in fact, given the nomological constancy just noted of the realization relation, it follows that P is nomologically sufficient for M. Thus, if $(P_1, \ldots, P_n)$ is a realization of $(M_1, \ldots, M_n)$, in that each P_i is a realizer of M_i, it follows that the Ms are supervenient on the Ps, where the force of supervenience is that of nomological (rather that logical/metaphysical) necessity. This means that if there are no nonphysical realizations of the mental, mind-body supervenience holds. Physical realizationism, therefore, entails the supervenience thesis.[47]

Moreover, more importantly for us, this means that physical realizationism provides an *explanation* of mind-body supervenience. The mental supervenes on the physical because every mental property is a second-order functional property with physical realizers. And we have an explanation of mental-physical correlations: Why is it the case that whenever P is instantiated in a system, s, it also in-

stantiates mental property M? Because having M consists in having a property with causal specification D, and, in systems like s, P is the property (or one of the properties) meeting specification D. For systems like s, then, having M *consists in* having P. It isn't that when certain systems instantiate P, mental property M magically emerges or supervenes (in the dictionary sense of "supervene"), and that this psychophysical correlation must be taken as a brute unexplainable fact. It is rather that having M, for these systems, *is* having P, or P is one of the ways of having M. This must, by any reasonable standards, be sufficient to warrant the reductive claim that having M, for these systems, is "nothing over and above" having one of its physical realizers.[48]

This, I believe, accords well with the paradigm of reduction in science. To reduce a property, or phenomenon, we first construe it—or reconstrue it—functionally, in terms of its causal/nomic relations to other properties and phenomena. To reduce temperature, for example, we must first construe it, not as an intrinsic property, but as an extrinsic property characterized relationally, in terms of causal/nomic relations, perhaps something like this: it is that magnitude of an object that is caused to increase when the object is in contact with another with a higher degree of it; that, when high, causes a ball of wax in the vicinity to melt; that causes the sensation of warmth or cold in humans; that, when extremely low, can make steel brittle; that, when extremely high, can turn steel into a molten state—well, you get the idea. The gene is construed as the mechanism in a biological organism that is causally responsible for the transmission of heritable characteristics from parents to offsprings. To be transparent is to have the kind of molecular structure that causes light to pass through intact.[49] And so on. We then find properties or mechanisms, often at the microlevel, that satisfy these causal/nomic specifications—that is, fill the specified causal roles. Multiple realization and

---

[47] If the mental has both physical and nonphysical realizations, the supervenience of course fails. If the mental has only nonphysical realizations, mind-body supervenience can hold but only trivially.

[48] In other words, the occurrence of M in the system does not imply that there is any nonphysical entity or property in the system. ED.

[49] Even these informal examples show that the causal/nomic roles that define functional properties can vary widely in respect of complexity and determinateness. In the cases of the gene and transparency, the roles appear to have relatively simple and determinate characterizations, whereas temperature appears to be associated with a much more complex and less determinate set of roles. This reflects the familiar distinction between "single-track" and multi-track" dispositions.

nomic relativity hold in these cases as well. Temperature may be one thing in gases (the mean translational kinetic energy of molecules), but may be something else in solids, plasmas, and vacuums. The DNA molecule is the realizer of the gene, but in worlds with different laws of nature another kind of molecule may perform the causal function of the gene. Reductions, therefore, are doubly relative: first, in systems with different structures, the underlying mechanisms realizing the reduced property may vary, and, second, reductions remain valid only when the basic laws of nature are held constant—that is, only for nomologically possible worlds (relative to the reference world).[50]

What has just been described differs in some crucial ways from the standard model of theory reduction that has dominated the discussion of reduction, in particular, the possibility of mind-body reduction. This is Ernest Nagel's model of intertheoretic reduction whose principal focus is on the derivation of laws.[51] According to Nagel, reduction is basically a proof procedure, consisting in the logical-mathematical derivation of the laws of the target theory from those of the base theory, taken in conjunction with "bridge laws" connecting the predicates of the two theories. Standardly, these correlating bridge laws are taken to be biconditionals in form, providing each property in the domain of the theory to be reduced with a nomologically coextensive property in the reduction base. For mind-body reduction, then, Nagel's model requires that each mental property be provided with a nomologically coextensive physical property, across all species and structure types. This has made mind-body reductionism—in fact, all reductionisms—an easy target. The most influential antireductionist argument, one that had a decisive role in creating over two decades ago the antireductionist consensus that by and large is still holding, is based on the claim that, on account of their multiple realizability, mental properties fail to have coextensions in the physical domain, and that this makes mind-body bridge laws unavailable for Nagelian reduction. This argument was then generalized in defense of a general antireductionist position in regard to all special sciences.[52] This has made bridge laws the focal point of debates on reduction and reductionism: for three decades the battles over reductionisms have been fought on the question whether or not biconditional bridge laws are available for the domains involved.

But this is the wrong battlefield on which to contest the issue of reduction. What has gone largely unappreciated is the fact that the Nagel model of reduction is in effect the Hempelian D-N model of scientific explanation applied to intertheoretic contexts. Just as Hempelian explanation consists in the derivation of the statement describing the phenomenon to be explained from laws taken together with auxiliary premises describing relevant initial conditions, so Nagelian reduction is accomplished in the derivation of the target theory from the base theory taken in conjunction with bridge laws as auxiliary premises. It is, therefore, a surprising fact that while the D-N model of explanation has had few committed adherents for at least three decades, Nagelian derivational reduction via bridge laws still serves as the dominant standard in discussions of reductionism. I believe that Nagelian uniform reductions based on universal biconditional bridge laws are extremely rare (if there have been any) in the sciences—especially, in the case of microreductions, and that the kind of model adumbrated above, "the functionalization model", is not only more realistic but also, as we will see in the following section, more appropriate from a philosophical point of view. If this is right, the reducibility of a property depends on its functionalizability—whether or not it can be construed as a second-order functional property over properties in the base domain. We will return to this point in connection with the mind-body reduction.

We now turn to emergence as an approach to the problem of the interlevel relationships of properties.

---

[50] This, therefore, is in opposition to the claim principally associated with Saul Kripke that such reductive identities are metaphysically necessary; see his *Naming and Necessity* (Harvard: Cambridge University Press, 1980). The difference derives from the fact that I construe "temperature" and the like as nonrigid designators (in Kripke's sense). These terms are referentially stable only across nomologically possible worlds; we may call them "semi-rigid" or "nomologically rigid".

[51] See *The Structure of Science* (New York: Harcourt, Brace & World, 1961), chapter 11.

[52] See J. A. Fodor, "Special Sciences (or The Disunity of Science as a Working Hypothesis)", *Synthese* 28 (1974): 97–115.

IV

In a Nagel reduction, each property, M_i, of the theory to be reduced is correlated with a nomologically coextensive property, P_i, of the reducing theory:

$$(L)\ M_i \leftrightarrow P_i$$

As we saw, correlation laws of this form are used as additional premises of reductive derivations. One important reason that this account of reduction is unsatisfying is the fact that these bridge laws are assumed as unexplained primitives of the reduction. If we expect reduction to be an *explanatory* procedure, as we should, then it must be the principal explanatory task of microreduction to generate an explanation of macroproperties and macro-regularities in terms of microstructure and micro-regularities. This means that it is exactly these bridge laws that we need to have explained. So long as they are assumed as unexplained primitives of reductive derivations, the derivations alone cannot advance our understanding of just how macrophenomena and regularities arise out of the underlying microphenomena and their laws.[53]

When the emergentists claimed the irreducibility of emergent properties, explanatory reduction was evidently what they had in mind. They accepted both (I) and (II)—that is, a fundamental physicalist ontology and the supervenience of higher-level properties on the lower-level ones; and they were not concerned about the multiple realizability of the former in relation to the latter. The *availability* of biconditional correlation laws was the least of their concerns. The *intelligibility* of these laws was what agitated the emergentists. It is the phenomena of emergence, codified in our bridge laws, that they despaired of making intelligible: Why is it that pains emerge just when these physiological conditions obtain, and that itches emerge just when these other conditions obtain? Why isn't it the other way around? Why should *any* conscious phenomena emerge from biological processes? As far as the emergentists are concerned, we are welcome to help ourselves to as much Nagel reduction

of the mental as we please, but this would only be so much logical exercise—it would not advance by an iota our understanding of why, and how, mentality makes its appearance when certain propitious configurations of biological conditions occur. Attaining such an understanding is exactly the same task as explaining the likes of (L), that is, mind-body correlation laws.

So how might correlations of the form (L) be explained? In some cases, it may be possible to explain them by deriving them from other, perhaps more basic, correlations, connecting the properties of the two domains. But such derivations must always assume other cross-domain correlations as premises, and at some point we will need to find a way of explaining them directly, without recourse to further correlations. One familiar suggestion is that what we need to do is to upgrade property correlations to property identities:

$$(I)\ M_i = P_i$$

By identifying the correlated properties, we dissipate the need to provide a substantive explanation: the identity $M_i = P_i$ takes away the logical space in which to raise the question why it is that the two are correlated. The explanatory request makes sense only when different properties are involved. But how might such identities be motivated? What might justify the move from (L) to (I)? Our discussion in the preceding section suggests the following scenario: M_i is construed, or reconstrued, as a second-order functional property defined in terms of causal/nomic relations over a domain of "first-order" properties. We then show that P_i is precisely the first-order property filling the causal role that defines M_i.[54]

We must now confront the following question: if M_i is a second-order property and P_i a first-order property, or if M_i is a causal role and P_i is the occupant of that role, how could they be one and the same thing? Isn't it incoherent to think that a property could be both first-order and

---

[53] On this point see Robert Causey's persuasive arguments in his *Unity of Science* (Dordrecht: Reidel, 1977). See also Horgan, "Supervenience and Cosmic Hermeneutics".

[54] In most cases there will be more than one first-order property satisfying the functional specification—that is, there will be multiple occupiers of the causal role. This is the problem of multiple realization, which we cannot deal with here. See my "Multiple Realization and the Metaphysics of Reduction" and "Postscripts on Mental Causation", both in my *Supervenience and Mind* (Cambridge: Cambridge University Press, 1993).

second-order, both a role and its occupier? A good question![55]

So far we have been rather loose in our talk of properties, causal roles and their occupants, specifications of these things, and the like. It is time to tidy up things a bit. I will now sketch a way of doing this. We may begin by explicitly recognizing that by existential quantification over a given set of properties, we do not literally bring into being a new set of properties.[56] That would be sheer magic: by logical operations on our notations, like quantification, we cannot alter our ontology—we can neither diminish nor expand it. For something to have second-order property M is for it to have some first-order property or other meeting a certain specification. Say, there are three such first-order properties, P_1, P_2, and P_3. For something to have M, then, is for it to have P_1 or have P_2 or have P_3. Here there is a disjunctive proposition, or fact, that the object has one or another of the three first-order properties; that is exactly what the fact that it has M amounts to. There is no need here to think of M itself as a property in its own right—not even a disjunctive property with the Ps as disjuncts.[57] By quantifying over properties we cannot create new properties any more than by quantifying over individuals we can create new individuals.[58] Someone murdered Jones, and the murderer is either Smith or Jones or Wang. That "someone", who murdered Jones, is not a person in addition to Smith, Jones, and Wang, and it would be absurd to posit a disjunctive person, Smith-or-Jones-or-Wang, with whom to identify the murderer. The same goes for second-order properties and their realizers.

So it is less misleading to speak of second-order *descriptions* or *designators* of properties, or second-order *concepts,* than second-order properties. Second-order designators come in handy when we are not able or willing to name the properties we have in mind with first-order designators: so we say "having some property or other, P, such that . . .", instead of naming all the specific properties meeting the stated condition. The situation is analogous when we are dealing with individuals: we say, "I shook hands with a Democratic senator at the reception yesterday", instead of "I shook hands with Claiborne Pell, or Ted Kennedy, or Patrick Moynahan, or . . ." (pretty soon you run out of names, or you may not even know any). Of course, the second-order designators also carry information that is valuable, perhaps very important, in a given context, which is not conveyed by the canonical designators of the first-order realizers. We convey the information that we are talking about someone who is a Democratic senator, rather than, say, someone who owns a mansion in Newport or a family compound on Cape Cod. When we use the functional characterization of pain (that is, "pain" for the functionalist) we let others know that we are referring to a state with certain input-output properties; a neural characterization of its realizer, even if one is on hand, would in most ordinary contexts be useless and irrelevant. From the ordinary epistemic and practical point of view, the information carried by second-order designators can be indispensable and unavoidable, and these designators introduce a set of useful and practically indispensable concepts that group first-order properties in ways that are essential for communicative purposes. In building scientific theories we hope the concepts in our best theories pick out, or answer to, the real properties in the world. On the present view, the concepts introduced by second-order designators pick out first-order properties disjunctively. When I say, "x has property M", where "M" is a second-order designator (or property, if you insist), "the truth-maker" of this statement is the fact, or state of affairs, that x has P_1 or P_2 or P_3, where the Ps are the realizers of M. (The "or" here is sentence disjunction, not predicate disjunction; it does not introduce disjunctive predicates with disjunctive properties as their semantic values.) Suppose that in this particular case, x has M in virtue of having P_2, in which case the ultimate truth-maker of "x has M" is the fact that x has P_2. There is no further fact of the matter to the fact that x has M over and above the fact that x has P_2.

---

[55] As other writers have also noted, the huge and variegated functionalist literature is shot through with an ambiguity as to whether mental properties are to be identified with causal roles or with the occupants of these roles.

[56] Thus, we are working with what some have called the "sparse" conception of properties as opposed to the "abundant" conception. This is appropriate to the present context, but this is not a place to argue the point.

[57] Unless we accept a closure of properties under disjunction. But that would be an additional metaphysical (and widely disputed) step.

[58] You may recall the logical jokes in *Alice in Wonderland* based on such errors.

Let me briefly summarize the arguments of this section. A genuine explanatory reduction cannot be content with the likes of (L) assumed as unexplained premises of reductive derivations. These are exactly what need to be explained. One way of satisfying this further demand is to elevate correlations of the form (L) to identities, (I), and this can be done if the properties being reduced can be construed, or reconstrued, as causal/functional properties, second-order properties defined over the properties in the reduction base. And to allay some of the ontological worries this procedure raises, we may want to give up the talk of second-order properties altogether in favor of second-order designators of properties, or second-order concepts.[59]

V

I believe most cases of interlevel reduction conform to the model I have just sketched. The crucial step in the process of course is the *functionalization* of the properties to be reduced. The possibility of functionalization in our sense is a necessary condition of microreduction. For if both M_i and P_i are distinct intrinsic properties in their own right and the correlation, $M_i \leftrightarrow P_i$ is basic in the sense that it is not derivable from other laws, replacing "$\leftrightarrow$" with "$=$" is out of the question, and the correlation must be regarded as a brute fact that is not further explainable.

As noted earlier, that is the way the emergentists viewed the relationship between emergent properties and the lower-level properties from which they emerge. Their reason for thinking that the emergent relations are brute and unexplainable, or that emergents are irreducible to their "basal conditions", is often put in epistemic terms, namely that from a complete knowledge of the basal conditions, it is not possible to *predict* what properties will emerge at higher levels. For example, the emergentists early in this century argued that most chemical properties are emergent in this sense: From a complete knowledge of the hydrogen and the oxygen atoms in isolation, it is not possible to predict that they will bond in the ratio of 2 to 1 to

form water, or that the resulting substance will be transparent and dissolve sugar but not copper. However, the emergentists were wrong about these examples: solid-state physics has explained, or is in principle capable of predicting, these phenomena on the basis of microphysical facts.[60] I believe that the key to such explanation, or prediction, is the functional construal of the phenomenon, or property, to be explained. Consider the transparency of water, for example: it would seem that once this property has been functionalized, as the capacity of a substance to transmit light beams intact, there should be no in-principle obstacle to a microphysical explanation of why H_2O molecules have this capacity. The same strategy should allow microphysical explanations and predictions of biological phenomena as well, for it seems that most biological properties seem construable as second-order functional properties over physico-chemical properties.

So the central question for us, in considering the role of supervenience, emergence, and realization in the mind-body debate, is this: Is the mental amenable to the kind of functionalization required for reductive explanation, or does it in principle resist such functionalization? If the functionalist conception of the mental is correct—correct for all mental properties—then mind-body reduction is in principle possible, if not practically feasible. This is contrary to one piece of current philosophical wisdom, the claim that functionalism, as distinguished from classic type physicalism, is a form—in fact, the principal current form—of mind-body antireductionism. What I am urging here is the exact opposite—that the functionalist conception of mental properties is *required* for mind-body reduction.[61] In fact, it is necessary and sufficient for re-

---

[59] For further details and development, see my "Postscripts to Mental Causation" in *Supervenience and Mind,* and *Mind in a Physical World* (Cambridge: MIT Press, 1998).

[60] Brian McLaughlin makes this point in his "The Rise and Fall of British Emergentism", in *Emergence or Reduction?,* ed. A. Beckermann, H. Flohr, and J. Kim.

[61] On this point concerning reducibility and functionalization, what I am advocating here has a good deal in common with David Armstrong's argument for central-state materialism, although of course we differ on the functionalizability of phenomenal properties. See his *A Materialist Theory of the Mind* (London: Routledge Kegan Paul, 1968). See also the papers by Horgan and by Horgan and Timmons cited in note 25; Robert Van Gulick's "Nonreductive Materialism and the Nature of Intertheoretical Constraint", in *Emergence or Reduction?;* and Joseph Levine, "On Leaving Out What It Is Like", in *Consciousness,* ed. Martin Davies and Glyn W. Humphries (Oxford: Blackwell, 1993).

ducibility, although whether the reduction will actually be executed is an empirical, and in part pragmatic, question of science. If this is right, mind-body reductionism and the functionalist approach to mentality stand or fall together; they share the same metaphysical fate.

In assessing where we now are with the mind-body problem, therefore, we must know where we stand with the functional approach to the mental. It has been customary to distinguish between two broad categories of mental phenomena, the **intentional**[62] and the **phenomenal,** without excluding those that have aspects of both (e.g., emotions). Intentionality is particularly evident in **propositional attitudes**—states carrying content. There has been much skepticism about the viability of a functionalist account of intentionality; in particular, Hilary Putnam, who first formulated functionalism in the 1960s, has recently mounted sustained attacks on the causal/functionalist accounts of content and reference, and John Searle has also vigorously resisted the functionalization of intentionality.[63] However, I remain unconvinced by these arguments; I don't see insurmountable obstacles to a causal/functional account of intentionality. Let me just say here that it seems to me inconceivable that a possible world exists that is an exact physical duplicate of this world but lacking wholly in intentionality.[64]

The trouble comes from **qualia.**[65] For, unlike the case of intentional phenomena, we seem able, without difficulty, to conceive a physical duplicate of this world in which qualia are distributed differently or entirely absent (a "zombie world" as some call it). To get to the point without fuss, it seems to me that the felt, phenomenal qualities of experiences, or qualia, are intrinsic properties if anything is. To be sure, we commonly refer to them using extrinsic/causal descriptions; e.g., "the color of jade", "the smell of ammonia", "the taste of avocado", and so on. However, this is entirely consistent with the claim that what these descriptions pick out are intrinsic qualities, not something ex-

trinsic or relational. (Arguably it is because they are intrinsic and subjective that we need to resort to relational descriptions for intersubjective reference.) Compare our practice of ascribing intrinsic physical properties to material objects by the use of relational descriptions; e.g., "two kilograms", "32 degrees Fahrenheit", etc. To say that an object has a mass of 2 kilograms is to say that it will balance, on an equal arm balance, two objects each of which would balance the Prototype Kilogram (an object stored somewhere in France). That is the linguistic meaning, the "concept" if you prefer, of "2 kilograms"; however, the property it designates, having a mass of two kilograms, is an intrinsic property of material bodies.

Why should we think that the functionalization of qualia won't work? We obviously cannot open this much debated issue here,[66] and I have nothing new to offer—at least not here. My doubts about the functionalist accounts of qualia are by and large based on the well-known, and not uncontested, arguments from qualia inversions[67] and the familiar epistemic considerations.[68] In any case, it seems to me that if emergentism is correct about anything, it is more likely to be correct about qualia than about anything else.

VI

To sum up the arguments of this paper, then, the three concepts of supervenience, realization, and emergence have played a central role in our thinking about the interlevel property relationships in the layered model of reality that is part of the modern-day metaphysics of science. The concept of supervenience is useful in formulating a general thesis of micro-to-macro determination of properties. However, supervenience itself only describes patterns of property covariance, and does not offer

---

[62] See sec. 5 of the Introduction for a brief look at this notion. ED.

[63] See Putnam, *Representation and Reality* (Cambridge: MIT Press, 1988); John R. Searle, *The Rediscovery of the Mind.*

[64] I believe others (perhaps, Shoemaker and Block) have made a similar observation.

[65] See sec. 6 of the Introduction for a brief look at this notion. ED.

[66] For an interesting functional account of qualia, see Reading 26. ED.

[67] Many philosophers argue that it is perfectly conceivable that someone may exhibit the same color vocabulary, and make the same color discriminations, as another person, yet experience colors in a systematically different way such as having my yellow experience when seeing what I call blue, and vice versa. The claim is that this condition would make no functional difference, and therefore functional analysis fails to capture something about qualia. ED.

[68] These considerations are presented by Frank Jackson in Reading 25. ED.

us an explanatory account of the covariance in terms of some underlying dependency relation. This is where the idea of realization steps in: it opens the possibility of explaining the supervenience relation by construing the supervenient macroproperties as second-order functional properties with lower-order microproperties as their realizers. A successful execution of this program would amount to nothing less than a reductive account of macroproperties in terms of microproperties. Where such functionalization cannot be carried out, there appears to be no alternative but to accept the higher-level properties involved as emergent properties—intrinsic properties in their own right whose supervenience on their base microproperties must be taken as brute, unexplainable correlations.

Physicalists will in general accept the supervenience thesis. This leaves open the choice between physical realizationism (or physicalist functionalism) and emergentism (at least about a specified subset of mental properties). The former leads to reductionism, on the model of reduction I have urged here, and the latter to nonreductive dualism of properties. Whether or not the latter, property dualism, is a coherent view that squares with the basic metaphysics of physicalism is an open question. Also open is the question how the causal powers of mental properties, whether reduced or emergent, are to be explained in a way that is consistent with physicalism—in particular, the causal closure of the physical domain.[69] What I have tried to do in this paper is to set out a general framework within which we can coherently formulate these questions as well as other related ones and think about them in a systematic way.[70]

---

[69] "The causal closure of the physical domain" is the notion that all events in the physical domain have causes that are themselves in the physical domain. Interactionist dualism (as in Descartes) breaks this closure by claiming that nonphysical causes (such as the mental event of deciding) can cause physical events in the brain (the brain processes that result in motor impulses going to muscle tissue involved in executing the decision). ED.

[70] An earlier version of this paper was delivered as the Perspectives Lecture at University of Notre Dame in November, 1995. I am indebted to my fellow participants in the event, Marian David, Fred Dretske, and Terry Horgan, as well as members of the audience for helpful comments. An even earlier version was given at the Pittsburgh-Konstanz Colloquium in April, 1995. My thanks go to Paul Hoyningen-Huene, who was my commentator there.

Kim has tried to do for materialism what Haugeland claimed need not, and could not, be done: supply it with a principle of ontological reduction:

[Ontological physicalism] Any creature (or system) with mentality is wholly constituted by physical parts—ultimately, basic physical particles. There are no nonphysical residues (e.g., Cartesian souls, entelechies, elan vital, and the like). (p. 176)

Kim is unsure whether it is consistent with ontological physicalism to accept property dualism (which he calls "emergentism"): the existence of irreducible, higher-level "emergent properties—intrinsic properties in their own right whose supervenience on their base microproperties must be taken as brute, unexplainable correlations." It is clear that he thinks the preferable alternative for physicalism is what he calls "physical realizationism," the analysis of "supervenient macroproperties as second-order functional properties with lower-order microproperties as their realizers." To the extent that this analysis can be applied to all properties above the level of "basic physical particles," an ambitious program of intertheoretic reduction becomes possible (at least in principle). Everything depends on the possibility of "functionalizing" macroproperties. Whether the macroproperty is mental, biological or merely chemical, functionalization will reveal that the macroproperty is nothing but a way of interacting with other entities, and one can then explain this interaction in terms of the behavior or causal powers of entities at the microlevel (or, at least, at some lower level in between). The drama of Kim's argument is in his claim that functionalism, far from sounding the death knell for intertheoretic reduction (as Fodor would have it in Reading 11), actually calls for such reduction.

As he points out, many philosophers would argue that intentionality and qualia are aspects of the mental that resist functional analysis. If these philosophers are correct, then he would concede that at least some mental properties will have to be accepted as "brute, unexplainable" facts. He is confident that a functional analysis of intentionality will succeed, but he is skeptical about the prospects for qualia: "It seems to me that the felt, phenomenal qualities of experiences, or qualia, are intrinsic properties if anything is." The readings in Parts VI and VII will look closely at these very controversial issues.

There is a deep metaphysical issue lurking in Kim's physical realizationism. It arises in connection with his description of the multi-layered, hierarchical structure of the natural world. Beginning with the most basic physical particles, we ascend through levels such as the atomic, molecular, cellular, multicellular, vertebrate and human. There is even a rough correspondence between these tiers and various (groups of) sciences (e.g., from physical to life to social sciences). Each of these sciences is reducible to the extent that the properties it investigates can be functionalized. By analyzing these properties into causal interactions executed by causes at a lower level, functional analysis makes the upper-level properties *relational* rather than *intrinsic*. Kim tells us that once we perform this sort of analysis on macroproperties, they need not be called properties anymore. We could instead call them "second-order designators of properties, or second-order concepts." Properties could be regarded as intrinsic and first-order in relation to properties at a higher level, and second-order/relational in relation to those of a lower level. Kim admits in footnote 40 that such a scheme seems to call for an ontological foundation. Somewhere in the downward progression of intertheoretic reduction it seems there would need to be intrinsic, nonrelational predicates. Presumably these would be at the level of basic physical particles which "have no physically significant proper parts."

Kim seems to take for granted that basic physical predicates *are* intrinsic; that, for instance, "having a mass of two kilograms is an intrinsic property of material bodies." Physicalism would seem to depend on this being the case. After all, it is an **ontology**—it's supposed to tell us about what kinds of things exist. But the claim that physical predicates are intrinsic has been, and continues to be, debatable. Consider this passage from David Chalmers' *The Conscious Mind* (1996):

> *The intrinsic nature of the physical.* The strategy to which I am most drawn stems from the observation that physical theory only characterizes its basic entities *relationally,* in terms of their causal and other relations to entities. Basic particles, for instance, are largely characterized in terms of their propensity to interact with other particles. Their mass and charge is specified, to be sure, but all that a specification of mass ultimately comes to is a propensity to be accelerated in certain ways by forces, and so on. . . . Reference to the proton is fixed as the thing that causes interactions of a certain kind, that combines in certain ways with other entities, and so on; but what is the thing that is doing the causing and combining? As Russell (1927) [in *The Analysis of Matter*] notes, this is a matter about which physical theory is silent (153).

REVIEW QUESTIONS

1. Go to a dictionary of science or an encyclopedia and check out the definitions of some basic predicates of material bodies such as mass, charge, kinetic energy, velocity and so on. Are any of these "intrinsic" as Kim would have it, or is Chalmers right about them all being relational?

2. Haugeland and Kim disagree over what formula of supervenience is best for physicalism. Haugeland is content with global supervenience, whereas Kim opts for a formula in which higher-level properties supervene on specific lower-level ones. As Kim says about a mental property M and its physical realizer P_2: "The ultimate truthmaker of "x has M" is the fact that x has P_2. There is no further fact of the matter to the fact that x has M over and above the fact that x has P_2" (p. 182). According to Kim, unless we can analyze mental properties in this way, we are left with "brute, unexplainable" mental facts. What would Haugeland have to say about Kim's worry?

PART V

MINDS AND COMPUTERS

INTRODUCTION

The way that human beings understand and respond to the world around them is at present being transformed by the computer revolution, a successor to the scientific revolution of the sixteenth and seventeenth centuries and the industrial revolution that began in eighteenth-century England and is still making its way into undeveloped countries today. It's obvious that our computer technology is the product of centuries of scientific progress using the experimental method and quantitative analysis of natural phenomena inaugurated in the *scientific* revolution. Less obvious, but no less important, is the relation of the computer to the *industrial* revolution. It could be said that the computer revolution is bringing about the industrialization of thought.

Two ingredients of the industrial revolution are especially relevant here: (1) the factory system with its assembly-line division of labor, and (2) the invention of mechanical substitutes for human labor. Adam Smith began the first chapter of *The Wealth of Nations* (1776) by proclaiming that

> The greatest improvement in the productive powers of labor, and the greater part of the skill, dexterity, and judgment with which it is anywhere directed, or applied, seem to have been the effects of the division of labor. . . .

There is great unintended irony in Smith's claim. The division of labor practiced in the factory system had the effect of *minimizing* "skill, dexterity, and judgment" in individual workers even as it maximized worker productivity (the product or output per worker). Smith's example for the division of labor was "the trade of the pin-maker." The productivity of a single pin-maker performing all the operations that go into the making of a pin from raw material would be ten or twenty times less than that of each worker in a pin "manufactory." Each manufactory worker does only one or a very few of the pin-making operations (e.g., cutting and straightening the wire). Consequently, a worker can stay in one place, use only one tool, and become so adept at his repetitive and comparatively simple task that he can do it much faster and with fewer errors than would a worker who did all the different operations in succession.

The human cost of the factory system's gain in productivity was, of course, that it made little call on the mind and heart of the worker. When individual pin-makers used to make entire pins, they needed to think about and pay attention to what they were doing—they had to organize and execute a complex process, obtain raw materials, and perhaps handle the distribution and sale of their products. And their hearts could also be engaged: the product was theirs, made by them, and for them to sell—something that could arouse such feelings as pride and satisfaction. Performing the same simple task hundreds of times per day for the owner(s) of the factory posed little challenge to the mind and took away the experience of completing something of value. The worker's attention, energy and persistence now had to be coerced by the threat of being fired.

Transforming the individual work of an artisan or craftsman into a factory production process was a considerable analytical achievement. The designers of the first assembly lines had to reduce a succession of complex and skilled movements into a sequence of simple movements which an unskilled or less skilled worker could make.

This in turn made it easier to design mechanical functional equivalents for many of the simplified movements of the unskilled worker. The factory system, by reducing to a bare minimum the distinctively human elements—mental and physical—in the subdivisions of the production process, made it easier to abstract from these human elements and conceive of mechanical substitutes for the flesh, blood, and minds of workers. (I haven't meant to sound only negative about the outcome of the industrial revolution. The vastly increased efficiency of the factory system made available great quantities of goods at lower prices as well as products that could only be made by mechanized factories, and the mechanical substitutes for human labor were in many cases substitutes for what had always been stressful drudgery such as shoveling, chopping, or hauling.)

The computer revolution is doing for many mental processes what the factory system did to the work of the artisan or craftsman of the pre-industrial era. We can begin to see the parallel if we look at the process of addition. For most of its history, addition was a mental process, the conscious following of a set of rules for transforming an input such as "1.25 + 14.515" into an output such as "15.765." Two of these rules might be

1. line up the decimal points of the various numbers under each other;
2. align the other numerals in columns corresponding to their distance from the decimal point in each direction.

Of course, there would be many more rules to follow in the complete process of addition, but let's focus on these two steps. It isn't hard to imagine a machine that could do with physical tokens what these rules call for, because following each of the two rules has the kind of simplicity that readily suggest its mechanical equivalent (each step is just a case of placement of tokens). Whenever a complex behavior of a human can be analyzed into very simple components, it is always conceivable that you can build from the mechanical equivalents of these simple components a complex machine that will be the functional equivalent of the human. You have gone from thinking about an agent that perceives, understands, and applies rules, and voluntarily moves, to thinking about a physical system that you configure in such a way that its output is the equivalent of the output of a rule-following, conscious process.

It's easier to conceive of the mechanization of addition if we think of the various numbers as sets of units (e.g., $0 = 1$, $1 = 1\ 1$, $2 = 1\ 1\ 1$, etc.). The different arithmetical operations can then be reduced to simple repetitive motions such as removing one unit at a time from an input set, or adding one unit at a time to it (keeping in mind that a multiplication such as "7×3" can be reduced to adding 3 to itself six times, and that the output of "$21 \div 3$" is the number of times 3 can be subtracted from 21). The notion of a unit here is very abstract—it can be embodied in indefinitely many ways such as a standardized mark on a sheet of paper, the tooth-by-tooth rotation of a gear wheel, or the on/off flow of current for a fixed interval (as in an electronic device or a neuron).

Like the mechanization of labor in the industrial revolution, the mechanization of mental processes in the computer revolution would have been impossible without the development of new materials and energy sources. The mechanization of labor required substitutes for the muscle power of humans and other animals. For instance, at the beginning of the industrial revolution in eighteenth-century England a succession of refinements in the materials and design of the steam engine allowed thermal energy from the combustion of fossil fuels to be converted into mechanical energy that could drive vehicles and factory machinery. The internal combustion engine took over this function in the twentieth century. And the nineteenth century saw the development of machines for converting mechanical energy into electrical energy. The factory machinery powered in these ways had far more speed and strength than human or animal bodies. When integrated with the subdivided labor of factory workers, this machinery greatly enhanced worker productivity. In a sense, the less workers did, the more they did.

To get some idea of the hardware requirements for mechanizing mental processes, let's go back to imagining machines for implementing arithmetical operations over numerical inputs in the form of units or unitary notation. For a machine working with this sort of symbol to be useful, it would have to be much more accurate and faster than a human being because it would be carrying out a vastly greater number of discrete and repetitive steps in any arithmetical operation than a human would consciously execute. It should be small and light enough to be portable (since we want it as a substitute for our using our brains in all those situations in which we want to calculate arithmetically). To reduce the length of number strings in unary code, this machine uses a code or notation that is binary (e.g., 1, 0 in script, or on, off as states of a switch) and positional: In this notation, the value of the rightmost position is 1 or 0 multiplied by 2^0, the next position is 1 or 0 multiplied by 2^1, and so on. The value of the entire string is the sum of the values at each position. Thus $0000001 = 1$, and $0001010 = 10$. Addition of binary numbers follows a carry rule—that when a 1 is below a 1, write 0 and carry the 1 leftward by one column—as in $9 + 8$:

$$
\begin{array}{r}
1000 \ (8{+}0{+}0{+}0) \\
+\,1001 \ (8{+}0{+}0{+}1) \\
\hline
0001 \ (0{+}0{+}0{+}1) \\
\end{array}
$$

Carry $\underline{\quad 1 \qquad\qquad}$

$$10001 \ (16{+}0{+}0{+}0{+}1)$$

We can see in this example a reduction of an arithmetical operation to simple repetitive placements of 1s and 0s on a columnar grid, a degree of simplicity comparable to that for unitary notation.

Industrial machinery had to equal or exceed the energy output of human muscle. Computer machinery needs to compete in speed, complexity, miniaturization, and low energy utilization with the human brain and nervous system. A cubic millimeter of brain tissue may contain as many as 75,000 neurons, each of which functions as a switch that turns on or off a current in the form of a traveling action potential generated at the axon hillock (see section 3.1 of Reading 4). The neuron can "fire," or switch on and off, several hundred times per second. A square millimeter of silicon in a computer chip can hold as many as 100,000 transistors, electronic switches that can open and close a flow of electrons as many as 75 billion times per second. Thus we now have miniaturized, low-energy machines that, like the human brain, are composed of vast numbers of microcomponents that jointly perform, in indefinitely many spatial and temporal configurations, great numbers of simple, repetitive operations. To the extent that we can reduce mental processes to the level of simple steps that can be embodied in the operations of these machines, we can expect enormous increases in the productivity of our intellectual work, and intellectual products in science and engineering that are beyond the capacity of the unaided human brain.

Is this prospect all good? Should we fear eventually making ourselves, our humanity, obsolete? These are the sorts of questions that will be canvassed by the panel members in the next reading.

14

Our Machines, Ourselves

A *Harper's Magazine* Forum

This month, in a conference room in midtown Manhattan, some measure of our humanity will be put to trial when Garry Kasparov, the world chess champion, sits down for a rematch[1] with Deep Blue, IBM's chess-playing computer, which he narrowly defeated in a match last year. If the game indeed presents a test of our humanity, it is one that is part of a long and anxious tradition. From John Henry's fatal victory over a steam-powered mining machine[2] to the square-root showdowns between precocious mathematicians and first-generation calculators, the only instinct that has proved more consistently human than our drive to invent tools has been our need to demonstrate our superiority over them.

What, then, is at stake in the match? If Kasparov loses, are we all somehow diminished? Will humanity have been defeated by its own machines or, having had the wit to program a triumphant computer, will we once again declare the supremacy of our inventive genius and so give to the loss the name of victory?

In the hope of analyzing the anxiety that attends this contest, *Harper's Magazine* invited four humans to lunch—that very human invention—to discuss our machines, ourselves, and the post-Deep Blue future.

The following forum is based on a discussion held at Savoy, a restaurant in New York City. Jack Hitt served as moderator.

JACK HITT
is a contributing editor of Harper's Magazine.

JAMES BAILEY
is the author of After Thought: The Computer Challenge to Human Intelligence.
He is a former manager at Thinking Machines Corporation.

DAVID GELERNTER
is a professor of computer science at Yale University and an adjunct fellow at the Manhattan Institute. He is the author of The Muse in the Machine: Computerizing the Poetry of Human Thought *and* 1939: The Lost World of the Fair.
Drawing Life, *his memoir of surviving an attack by the Unabomber, will be published this summer.*

[1] The rematch took place May 3–11. Deep Blue won by 3.5 to 2.5. ED.

[2] John Henry is the hero of a Black folk ballad according to which he crushed more rock than a steam drill but died with a hammer in his hand. ED.

JARON LANIER
is a computer scientist, composer, visual artist, and author. He coined the term "virtual reality"
and founded the world's first virtual-reality company. He is currently a visiting artist at the
New York University Interactive Telecommunication Program.

CHARLES SIEBERT
is a poet and journalist whose essays have appeared in Harper's Magazine.
His book Wickerby: An Urban Pastoral *will be published next winter.*

I. ASSAULTS ON OUR SPECIALNESS

JACK HITT: In February 1996, in Philadelphia, the world chess champion, Garry Kasparov, played a six-game chess match against a computer named Deep Blue. Although Deep Blue won the first game, beating Kasparov in thirty-seven moves, Kasparov came back to win the match 4-2. The competition seemed to catch the public's imagination in unusual ways, to stir hopes and fears that were sometimes hard for us to articulate. Why do you think we were so obsessed with this match?

JAMES BAILEY: We've been taught for centuries that rational thought is the height of human achievement and that chess is the ultimate expression of rational thought. People playing chess are supposedly people at their mental best. So it makes sense that we'd be intrigued by the prospect of a machine beating a human at such a supposedly lofty pursuit.

DAVID GELERNTER: And chess itself is intrinsically fascinating. I'm not a good chess player, but I can't help noticing that it holds a certain allure. There are many writers and artists who have fallen under its sway, people like Marcel Duchamp and Vladimir Nabokov, who spent huge periods of their lives completely obsessed with the game.

HITT: Much of the reaction to the match in the press, and from people I spoke to, was one of anxiety. The fact that Deep Blue defeated Kasparov in the first game of the match and the prospect that a new and improved version of Deep Blue might win the rematch that's scheduled for this May— those are developments that many people have found personally threatening. Why is that?

CHARLES SIEBERT: There is a perception that our specialness—our humanness—has been taking it on the chin a lot lately. It seems that every day in the daily paper there's another assault on the essence of what a human being is. We find out chimps are 98 percent the same DNA as we are. A sheep is cloned, and people begin to think that this is all we are, an assemblage of biological juices— line them up the right way, and we can be reproduced. And so there's a tendency with this chess match to say, "Oh no, not this too!" It's part of our larger sense of an assault on our specialness.

JARON LANIER: People have an enormous amount of anxiety about what a person is. The better computers get at performing tasks that people find hard to do, the more that definition is threatened. It's the same question that drives all the fire around the abortion debate—the question of which things in the universe we consider to be enough like us to deserve our empathy, to deserve our moral support. I think ultimately it has to do with whether we define people in a sacred way or in a functional way.

SIEBERT: The hysteria over cloning is related to this very confusion. Is this all we are? Are we this reducible and finite? In fact, we are not, but people are having a tough time accommodating these incursions on our spirituality.

BAILEY: Of course the chess match isn't really an incursion on our spirituality at all. We as a species made a decision at some point to define human uniqueness around our intelligence, our ability to do mind tasks, but I would argue that that decision was a mistake. That purported strut of uniqueness is about to get kicked out from under us, by Deep Blue, among other things, and that's certainly going to force us to come to some different understandings of what is uniquely human. It's going to be a painful process, but if in that process we come to understand that we're not essentially analytical beings, that our essence is something higher, then that's a positive development.

SIEBERT: I felt a kind of claustrophobia when I read about this chess match. I didn't feel threatened by

Deep Blue's ability; I felt bothered by the idea that chess is a good measure of us. Chess is such a narrow prism through which to view our humanness that there's something almost offensive about it. It's just a game that we made up.

LANIER: And since computers are getting faster and faster, it's only a matter of time before a computer becomes world chess champion. Chess just happens to be a mental activity that people find very difficult. That's why we find it fascinating.

SIEBERT: There is something touching, though, in our reaction to this contest. To some extent, it is our way of embodying the otherness of the machine. In other words, this is an attempt on our part to anthropomorphize the computer. The chess match becomes *mano a mano,* even though it's really *mano a máchina.* We're assigning the computer almost human properties to help us embrace its otherness. And it's a difficult embrace.

BAILEY: One of the frustrations for me is that I don't think this is a story about *mano a silicio.* It's about a bunch of guys at IBM who by themselves had no chance of ever getting into an international chess tournament, and therefore chose to collaborate with a computer. The computer by itself also didn't have a chance of making it into an international chess game. But together they were able to go where neither of them could go alone. Now, the press is always going to see the story as Kasparov versus Deep Blue, but in reality it is Deep Blue *with* a team of us—a team of humans.

GELERNTER: It's true that the story does engender a certain amount of fear and hysteria, but there's a positive aspect to it too. There are a lot of people who get a kick out of seeing how smart we are. To be able to program a computer that is capable of doing what this computer does requires exceptionally clever guys.

BAILEY: I think it would be exciting if, in fact, the computer developed whole new ways of playing the game of chess. The machine would be interesting if it not only won but found new ways of winning. What makes chess so uninteresting is that it is dead. The chess pieces don't change their behavior, they don't adapt, they don't do anything differently because of where they are on the board. There are sixty-four squares and two players. Chess is a very small data problem. It's not

something we need help with. It's not, to my mind, an unsolved problem in the world. People aren't dying for the lack of good chess play. And so while it's eye-catching, it's not important. I think that the real fun is going to come when these machines are put seriously to work at things we're bad at.

HITT: What's an example, James? What kinds of things are we bad at?

BAILEY: Well, we're starting to get a lot of very useful information about the planet we live on and its creatures and their behavior—information that comes from places like satellites, some of it in trivial form coming from checkout scanners and things like that. And we're helpless to deal with it. Increasingly, we don't have the ability to make sense of the trillions of pieces of information we receive each day—economic data, ecological data, even weather data. Computers are very good at examining these huge databases and noticing patterns that we are oblivious to.

GELERNTER: There's another aspect to this chess match that we have to be aware of, and that is public relations. It would be good for people at large to know more about technology than they do, and the question is, How can you convey to them what the current state of the art is? If a computer produces a proof of the four-color theorem,[3] let's say, that runs on for 300 million pages, and not even 2 percent of the world's mathematicians understand it, so what? But if it beats a chess grand master—that's something people can grasp. It seems to me we do well as a society when we let research flow. Research is good for us. And the sort of thing that gets people's attention is a contest. When the Soviets put the first satellite in orbit in the late Fifties, that was wonderful, because we wanted to beat them. Money flowed into science. Science is starving now. The public doesn't owe us a living. The question is, Can we do something that makes them interested in what we're doing? This is the sort of thing that gets people's attention.

---

[3] In 1976 Kenneth Apel and Wolfgang Haken devised, with the help of a computer, a proof that was several hundred pages long. The theorem is a solution to the four-color map problem: to prove that four colors at most are needed on any planar map to differently color any two regions sharing a boundary. ED.

II. STUCK IN THE STATIC PRESENT

HITT: How do the anxieties that people feel about this chess competition compare with the feelings or anxieties that people have felt at other moments in history about the machines they live with? Is this a new anxiety or just a new form of an old anxiety?

SIEBERT: I think it's a new form of an old anxiety, perhaps best summed up by this story I read recently about people who are defecting from modern life to go live with the Amish because—is this the age-old complaint?—the world is going too fast these days. One of them said that first we had the horse and buggy and then it was the automobile and now the world is going at an electronic speed. He said, "We're finding that people can't live at that speed. We're being crushed by the way we live." And I thought, What does that mean? The world is going at the same speed it ever did. Human beings walk at the same speed they ever did. What people really mean when they say this is that our *things* are going a little faster than they used to, and the sadness is that we can't accompany them. I think it's a feeling of disappointment; we are left behind in the static present, a present that feels more static than it ever did because these computers go that much faster. In a way, it's the same complaint as the Victorians had about tool-and-die machines displacing a physical function, but computers seem more frightening to people because they perform an unseen work. Since the Industrial Revolution there's been a feeling of physical disappointment, one that has become inherent in the modern psyche. Now with the computer there comes a mental disappointment.

LANIER: But it's a disappointment that doesn't reflect reality. For people even to imagine that the human mind is slower than a computer reflects a profound misunderstanding of what minds are able to do. It's a misunderstanding that goes way back, and in order to understand it, you have to understand a bit about the history of artificial intelligence. The field of artificial intelligence has its roots in a paper written in 1950 by Alan Turing. He was a famous code breaker during World War II who worked with some of the earliest electronic computers. Turing figured that eventually we would reach a point where computers would become in-

telligent, and he reasoned that we would need a test to help us decide when that point is reached. What he ended up with was something called the Turing Test, in which a tester communicates with both a computer and a human via a screen and a keyboard. If the tester can't distinguish between them,[4] Turing says, then the computer is intelligent. Deep Blue is just the latest step in the project that Turing started. Now, Turing's interpretation of his own thought experiment was that if you can't tell the computer from the person, it must mean that the computer has become more human-like. But, of course, there is another interpretation, which is that the person has become more computer-like.

GELERNTER: That's absolutely right. Turing set us off on an extremely superficial, behaviorist view of intelligence. He was willing to attribute intelligence—the capacity to think and understand and have mental states—to an electronic box, as long as the box behaved in a certain way.

BAILEY: I'm not so concerned with being able to replicate the wonders of human intelligence. What I would be very intrigued to see are forms of intelligence that are distinctly nonhuman, that solve the same problems human intelligence solves but in a way we humans never thought of. If Deep Blue totally revolutionizes the game of chess, if it comes up with whole new openings and approaches that render the existing methods obsolete, then that's exciting.

LANIER: In the computer-science community, there's a perspective, which is difficult to communicate to the outside world, that things are going to continue to change in our field at such a rapid rate that at some point something very dramatic will change about the fundamental situation of people in the universe. I don't know if I share that belief, but it's a widespread belief. In the mythology of computer science, the limits for the speed and capacity of computers are so distant that they effectively don't exist. And it is believed that as we hurtle toward more and more powerful computers, eventually there'll be some sort of very dramatic Omega Point at which everything changes—not just in terms of our technology but

---

[4] The tester is even allowed to ask questions designed to bring out which respondent is the computer. ED.

in terms of our basic nature. This is something you run across again and again in the fantasy writings of computer scientists: this notion that we're about to zoom into a transformative moment of progress that we cannot even comprehend.

SIEBERT: Filippo Marinetti, the Italian futurist, said in the Twenties that in about a hundred years the Danube would be flowing in a straight line at two hundred miles an hour, this being the effect of speed on the physical world. It's a confusion born of this disjuncture between our plodding sameness and the speed of the machines we make. There's a great line at the beginning of *The Hunchback of Notre Dame*. The priest looks out across at the cathedral and right behind him is a printing press, and he says that cathedrals are the handwriting of the past, but with the printing press everything will change. The proliferation of the written word shifted the burden of telling stories away from sculpture and cathedrals. So yes, inventions do shape the imperative behind various forms in the realm of art. But the impulse to make that art is the same. For example, a lot of people say that poetry's dead. Well, no. Poetry's quite alive, but the imperative behind what you say in poetry and how you say it has changed, because now you have printers and word processors and high-speed copiers, and you don't need rhyme as much as you once did. Rhyme originally existed so that you could lock a thought on the air and keep it.

GELERNTER: What you say about rhyme is relevant in the sense that rhyme is unquestionably a good memorization device and so it has heuristic value, particularly if you can't write. Nowadays, however, if you write a poem and it rhymes—and by "nowadays" I mean for the last several centuries—you're doing it for its own sake, because of the music of it. By the same token, when computers carry out various analytic tasks that we thought were uniquely human but we now see are not, we are able to refine our idea of what humanity really is. Humans will play chess even when no human has a hope of being the best chess player in the world, just as we continue to rhyme even though rhyming no longer serves any practical purpose. We do it for the fun of it, because we enjoy it.

LANIER: The reason I never became a chess fanatic is that I realized the game had a formal framework that would make it difficult to turn it into a purely aesthetic experience. Since it's a game with a formal sense of what winning is, it has limited options for creative extrapolation. There's no such thing as freestyle chess, in which making elegant moves is valued more highly than capturing your opponent's king—though that could be a serendipitous result of Deep Blue's success. In the old days, there was an idea that when you got good at chess, you knew you were at the outer reaches of a certain type of thought. There was an Olympian quality to it. After Deep Blue, you can no longer quite feel that way. Chess after Deep Blue becomes something like fencing—an aesthetic activity that can be enjoyed in a nostalgic way and as something that is good for the spirit, but one that no longer feels like exploring the outer edge of human ability. Chess becomes like karate after the nuclear bomb.

HITT: Does everything eventually lose its usefulness and become aesthetic?[5]

LANIER: That's a wonderful thing. That should be considered a goal of life.

SIEBERT: I agree. This reminds me of the Industrial Revolution, when Carlyle and Schiller and the Romantics were all voicing their complaints about how these machines reduce us and how man will lose his soul standing before this repeated mechanization. Carlyle would invoke Greek culture all the time as his paradigm of a culture that had this moral imperative, in which art reached its peak. And the great response to Carlyle came from a Cincinnati-based lawyer, Timothy Walker. He said: That's preposterous. The reason why the Greeks reached the heights they did is because they dispatched all their physical work to slaves and they had time to sit around and think and achieve this higher aspect of themselves. And his argument was, the more we unshoulder these burdens to our machinery, the more we become our essence.

LANIER: But we're doing the reverse of what the Greeks did. It's as if they had compelled their slaves to enjoy their philosophical whimsies and have their fun. We're assigning our philosophical

---

[5] Consider all the kinds of products and services that we are willing to pay extra for when they are done the old-fashioned or handcrafted (i.e., inefficient) way. ED.

thinking to the computers. When we talk about using artificial intelligences to choose what book we might want to read, then what we're doing is placing the burden of ourselves as philosophers onto these so-called intelligent agents.

HITT: We already do that. They're called magazine editors. You subscribe to a magazine because you like the intelligent agent who is editing the magazine and making choices for you.

GELERNTER: The term "intelligent agent" can legitimately be applied to an editor, but there is no machine or computer program to which the term can legitimately be applied. I mean, there's an important distinction between following some*body's* advice and following some*thing's* advice. Following a thing's advice is a lot lazier than following a person's advice.

BAILEY: I don't understand. Isn't there only the difference between following good advice and following bad advice?

LANIER: This gets us into very mysterious territory: trying to understand how communication can be possible in the first place. If you believe that a conversation between two people consists of objectifiable bits of information that are transmitted from one to the other and decoded by **algorithms,** then certainly what you said, James, is correct, and there's no difference. If you believe that meaning is something more mysterious than that, something that no one has yet been able to find a method of reducing, then you would not agree with your statement. I'm in the latter category. I think that the fundamental process of conversation is one of the great miracles of nature, that two people communicating with each other is an extraordinary phenomenon that has so far defied all attempts to capture it. There have been attempts made in many different disciplines—in cognitive science, in linguistics, in social theory—and no one has really made much progress. Communicating with another person remains an essentially mystical act.

III. SEVENTY-SEVEN NOSES UNDER THE TENT

HITT: When I think about the prospect of Deep Blue actually defeating Kasparov, for some reason I feel like we as a species would lose something.

Somehow I feel like it would be a sad thing for us. Am I wrong?

LANIER: It is not a coincidence that at the same time science is improving its ability to simulate some tasks that we used to think of as being in the domain of the brain—like chess—we are also seeing a rise in religious fundamentalism around the world, a quest for an anchor of meaning and an anchor of identity. I think that those two events are linked. There is a fear of losing one's own grounding, one's own identity, as technologies become able to either simulate or perhaps take on human identity. Because if technology's capable of making you, of making a person or making a mind, then technology's also capable of making variants of you and betters of you. It becomes profoundly threatening.

GELERNTER: Anybody who looks at modern society and compares us to, let's say, America in the Forties realizes that our technology is vastly more powerful, that we live a lot longer, we're a lot healthier, we're vastly richer, that our laws are better, that we've done all sorts of good things—but life has gotten worse. It's absolutely clear that the texture of society has tended to unravel in recent decades. It's not technology that's caused the unraveling, but people are worried that the unravelers keep winning.

HITT: Isn't that the fear that I'm talking about?

GELERNTER: Absolutely. People are afraid when they see software do incredibly powerful new things, because they say that this world that software built stinks. It's great in all sorts of material ways, but it's a spiritual and moral wasteland. It may not be a cultural wasteland, but certainly it's culturally inferior to what this country was fifty years ago.

BAILEY: If we are, in fact, going through a cultural transition of many-century scale, if, in fact, we are leaving a machine age and an industrial age and moving into an information age, then there's a lot of unraveling to be done. There are going to be a lot of raw nerves. But I think it's a positive development that a lot of old assumptions tied to the industrial age are loosening. Life is no longer as hierarchical as it has been for thousands of years. It's more democratic. It's more parallel. That's progress.

GELERNTER: But people are aware of the fact that they're losing something. It's not the fault of technologists that they're losing it, but they certainly associate it with technology.

HITT: How are those two things connected, our advances in technology and our increasing disappointment?

GELERNTER: Technologists do their job when they build the best machines they can and make them available to us. That's what they're supposed to do and that's what they in fact do. They don't make choices for us about how we should use the machines they've built. Ruskin made famous statements in the nineteenth century about the railroad. He said, Everybody's streaking here and there on the railroad, but there was always more in the world than men could see, walk they ever so fast. And what the hell are they going to gain by going faster? Now, the existence of the railroad doesn't mean that Ruskin can't take a walk in his backyard; he can. The technologists have accomplished something useful—they've made people richer, they've made people happier in a lot of ways—but people don't feel the spiritual strength to turn down technology in the cases where it diminishes rather than makes better the texture of their lives. Technology is a constant temptation to them. People don't like to live being constantly tempted. They don't like to be given these tough choices all the time. And technology never lets up. It's one tough choice after another.

SIEBERT: So would you rather live in a world without technology?

GELERNTER: Absolutely not. I'm not against technology. I'm explaining why I think it upsets people, makes them melancholy, depresses them. If I had a vote I'd vote for this world over a nontechnology world, but I can understand why it's an upsetting world to live in.

BAILEY: I think the reason that Deep Blue's success is so troubling to us is the fact that we're all carrying around a backlog of evidence that a new information world is aborning and an old industrial world is dying, and it's evidence that we're having trouble coming to terms with. Eventually a camel's nose is going to get under the tent that causes us not just to recognize that *that* nose is there but to go back and relook at the other seventy-seven noses that are also poking into the tent. Deep Blue really has the potential to break this conceptual logjam, to force each of us to ac-

knowledge not just that chess has changed but that many other things have changed as well.

IV. A NEW *WUTHERING HEIGHTS* EVERY WEEK

HITT: I think what's truly, profoundly disturbing about the Deep Blue contest is that for most of this last aeon, we have thought that where our individuality, where our humanness resided was precisely where Deep Blue is now moving in.

BAILEY: One of the things that make people unique is the profound desire to *believe* that we're unique. We're always hanging our sense of our uniqueness on something, and over the past couple of centuries a lot of people have hung it on rational thought. Bad place to hang it, but that's where they hung it.

GELERNTER: But is it clear that rational thought is reducible to chess playing? I think that most people, if they thought about it carefully, would not believe that what's going on in the computer is anything like what goes on in their head, whether it wins the chess match or not.

SIEBERT: What goes on in a human head is not, in the end, entirely knowable; we make stabs at expressing it, in art and novels and poems, but it's not replicable. I'll use Nabokov's account of his own work. He talks about what an epiphany is: He's walking down the street, the sun hits a leaf on a tree above him in a certain way at the same time that he remembers his mother, and then a carriage goes by—it's a compacted moment, the meaning of which is not readily apparent to the person who had the moment. He describes the art process as a dismantling and reassembling of the moment with such suppleness and simultaneity that the reader gets some approximation of the very experience that moved the artist. If one day a computer could do that kind of decoding of the simultaneity of inspiration and perception, *then* I would feel melancholy.

GELERNTER: But even if it could do that, you still wouldn't necessarily want to attribute thought to it, would you? You wouldn't think that it had any beliefs or any desires or any feelings or any of the content that your own internal mental landscape does. I mean, would any kind of behavior that a machine showed convince you that it had mental states in the sense that you do?

SIEBERT: No, because all you could do to get a computer to do that is give it the information with which to spit it back. And then you would have a simulacrum of the thing, and it's a pale, lifeless, bloodless imitation.

GELERNTER: Right, even if it were a *great* imitation. If you were to get a computer to write beautiful novels and everybody loved them, that might be good. We don't have that much of a novelist shortage, but let's say we did—that still wouldn't necessarily convince you that what the computer was doing was comparable to what a human being does.

BAILEY: But if they're beautiful novels, who cares?

GELERNTER: It's strictly an emotional issue. It has no pragmatic significance. If the computer can write a better novel than I can, fine, read the computer's novel. It's an emotional issue of where does humanness lie, and do we think this object is like us or do we just think it's a tremendously valuable machine.

HITT: Would the fact that a computer was writing beautiful novels affect you?

GELERNTER: Absolutely. I'm sure it would change my feeling about the culture. It wouldn't change my feeling about the essence of humanness or the capabilities of software. But on a pragmatic level, we build machines to do things that are useful. And writing novels is one useful thing. People get pleasure and satisfaction from reading novels. Most novels are no good, so if the average quality of novels got better and I knew that I could go into any newspaper store and pick up a novel that was as good as my favorite novel, that was the artistic equivalent of *Wuthering Heights*, let's say, then that's great, because then instead of just one *Wuthering Heights* I can get a new *Wuthering Heights* every week.

LANIER: Wait, wait, wait. Are you speaking sarcastically or seriously when you say that?

GELERNTER: It's a thought experiment. I don't think it's a likely outcome.

LANIER: To me your statement is like a *reductio ad absurdum* of positivism, of this idea that humanity is reducible. If there were in fact a different *Wuthering Heights* every week, *Wuthering Heights* would lose meaning.

GELERNTER: I'm not willing to rule out on logical grounds that software could be made to write novels that I would enjoy as much or that would move me or interest me or grip me as much as *Wuthering Heights*. I think it's extremely unlikely, I would bet against it, but I don't rule it out logically. Even if it were to be accomplished, though, I wouldn't wind up attributing thought to the computer that did it and it wouldn't wind up changing my estimation of what humanity and humanness are.

SIEBERT: I would think of it as a kind of game. It wouldn't threaten my humanity. I would think, Why do we need it?

GELERNTER: Even if a novel were, in some objective sense, plotted so well, written so tightly, that there was nothing objective to distinguish between it and *Wuthering Heights*, I could also say that ultimately I read a novel for human communication. I want to hear from another human being. And no matter how brilliant the language is, no matter what kind of proof you can give me that it's a great novel, if I know that it's not a human being who's communicating with me I shrug it off.

HITT: Would it be a fulfilling moment or not, going into that store and buying this brand-new *Wuthering Heights*? If a computer gives you a great novel every week, a novel that you really want to read, wouldn't that make you happy?

GELERNTER: It wouldn't give you a great novel.

HITT: Well, what if it could?

GELERNTER: I don't really think it is conceivable except technically. It could be achieved in a technical way but not in a way that has any meaning in human terms.

LANIER: The moment you start believing that automatically generated media has as much meaning as human-generated media is the moment that you enter a Zen monastery for a couple of years to get in touch with your humanity again. This gets us back to the Turing Test's fatal flaw; if you accept computer-written novels, has the computer been elevated or has your humanity been reduced?

HITT: What is the distinction between writing novels and playing chess? Why do we believe that

Deep Blue is going to beat Kasparov sometime in the next year or five years but don't believe that any computer is ever going to be able to write convincing novels?

LANIER: I don't think anybody said that. It might very well write convincing novels. But we'll never be able to say that for certain, so the question is not a productive one. You can say for sure that a computer has won a chess game, but you can't say for sure that a computer has written a good novel. Aesthetic judgments rely on the preferences of human beings, who can be supremely flexible and accommodating.

GELERNTER: This thing could beat Kasparov, and I could look at its winning game and say, This doesn't move me, I'm not able to consider this beautiful the way I consider Kasparov's game beautiful. I mean, chess doesn't speak to me, I don't consider it a form of communication, because I don't know it well enough, but I could imagine that if a grand master looked at a chess game as the manifestation of a particular style, of a particular personality, of a particular way of attack, then he would feel a certain emptiness when he looked at the brilliant winning games of Deep Blue. It really depends on how you evaluate the objects that you deal with. Some of them you evaluate simply as objects, and some of them you value because they're forms of human communication and people like to communicate with each other. If there's no person at the other end, ultimately the object is meaningless. With a synthetic novel, you could read the whole thing thinking that a human being wrote it and enjoy it, and when you found out that a human being didn't write it, you would feel betrayed and no longer able to think of it as a thing of beauty in any sense.

BAILEY: I don't think I would feel betrayed. I think I would feel intrigued. There is a separate ecology, if you will, of these machines that is different from ours. Computers talk to each other in ways that are different from the ways we talk to each other. We can ascribe meaning to our communications and no meaning to their communications—that's fine. But I think as their separate ecology grows into something quite formidable and quite productive, particularly as it begins to do things that we wish we could do but can't, simply because

we're wired differently, then that is both valuable and intriguing. Blotches of color that are placed on a canvas by a set of electronic circuits are different from blotches of color that are placed on a canvas by a human being, but they're both intriguing.

V. A VERY LONELY ENTITY

HITT: From what I seem to hear, what you all would define as special about human beings is our ability to communicate. In other words, it doesn't seem to trouble you that a computer might be able to replicate almost any human thought process, including writing a novel. You can say that playing chess is the highest human act, or that writing a novel is, or creating art, but if you agree that all of those acts could be simulated in some way so that we would be confused by the end product, then is the only source of human specialness the fact that we can communicate among ourselves?

LANIER: I would define human specialness as follows: What's special about people is that we're conscious, and we have faith in the possibility that we might be able to contact other consciousnesses.

HITT: What do you mean by conscious?

LANIER: That's an interesting question. Consciousness is the slipperiest subject imaginable. It's the hardest thing to talk about. Consciousness is the experience of experience itself. It's not empirically verifiable. It's the only thing that can be shared that can't be shared objectively. One could have a device that looks at the neurons in my brain that are doing the activity of treasuring my consciousness and re-creates the activity of those neurons in a computer so that the computer could be said to be treasuring my consciousness, but consciousness still wouldn't be there. You can simulate every damn thing about the interior of the brain except for consciousness itself.

SIEBERT: Maybe we keep trying to assign human qualities to these machines because we feel so lonely. Consciousness is a very lonely entity. Why did our DNA tipple over into an ability to comment on our own DNA? I mean, let's just take the Garden of Eden. Adam and Eve took of the forbidden fruit. Well, we *had* the forbidden fruit to begin with: it's self-knowledge. It's as if we have to keep making up stories about why the other DNA assemblages on this planet don't sit around and argue with themselves, don't have this isolating, lonely capacity to think in this way. Maybe what we're doing with computers is trying to give this loneliness to something else.

LANIER: So we'll be satisfied when we see some computers sitting miserable in a French café bemoaning their sorry fate.

SIEBERT: Exactly!

BAILEY: To me what makes us unique is our humanity. And if people choose to isolate that in something they call logical thought or consciousness, they can go ahead, but things like Deep Blue seem to be undercutting that idea. It's hard for me to understand how qualitatively the argument for tying humanity to consciousness is stronger than the old argument of tying humanity to rational thought, or the one before that of tying humanity to being at the center of the universe. So I'm stuck there: I know we're unique because of our humanity. I can't subdivide it.

HITT: There is a sense of despair, though, in watching technology gobble up what we do. People feel bewildered by the fact that machines not only can do so much of what humans can do but also can perform these almost magical tasks, repairing broken organs and so on. It does reduce us to a sense of medieval magic, a sense that we're inhabiting this world run by either somebody or something else. I think that's the source of a lot of people's anxiety about the encroaching ideal of the computer.

SIEBERT: Because my father was a tool-and-die man, I had a real personal involvement in this myth of our remaking. He was very enthusiastic about progress, and I used to think about the pathos behind a man being enthusiastic about the machines that make the machines that will eventually make obsolete his own job. But he taught me early on that this is what we humans do. I remember the first time I went behind the TV set for something that had fallen there and looking at that little cityscape of tubes and smelling that warm acrid electricity that comes out. It was this numinous world, and it was quite incredible. It was a seminal moment for me in my childhood. But as I've

looked back at that moment, I've realized that the inherent sadness in it was that my father spent his whole life selling two or three of the parts in that television set. I went to the tool-and-die convention last year in Chicago. I wanted to see the evolution of the myth of our remaking. Die machines used to look like mechanical men, but now all the armature's gone and it's just a box with a window lit from within. All you saw in booth after booth was a man in a smock pushing a button. The work happened inside, and through the window you could see it being washed down and cooled off, and the water spraying up. It was like a TV screen. And I went to another booth and it was just robot arc welders that looked like little gooseheads coming up, talking to each other briefly, coming back down. And at one point these three human arc welders came up—they had their union hats on—and they watched the part get dropped off in the bin, and they picked it up and they said, "Pretty damn good." And they walked off. What do these guys do? They've been displaced, and there's a kind of sadness in that, but, hey, this is evolution.

HITT: If people feel anxiety when they think about this chess match, is there another way for us to suggest that they think about it, another paradigm, another myth that is either a more positive or a more realistic one?

LANIER: A number of ideas have been presented in the conversation already. One of them is to say, Isn't it great how these clever people who themselves couldn't beat Kasparov could think of a way to write a program that could. Another way is to say, Isn't it magical how humanity persists even as we try to isolate what we thought made it up.

BAILEY: That's a very powerful statement: the more you think you chip away at our humanity, the more it's there. That's a very positive and very nourishing idea: Humanity is not at stake in this. Old ideas, old oversimplified ideas, are at stake, but that's good. Humans and computers are going to make a good team.

SIEBERT: We argue with our biology, and the result of that argument is civilization. That is what is unique about what we do. Sometimes the result is a Bach fugue, sometimes it's a glorious building. That's it, that's us, and it's amazing.

REVIEW QUESTIONS

1. On pp. 197–198, Lanier and Siebert discuss the analogy between the computer and industrial revolutions. Siebert points out that romantic thinkers of the nineteenth century worried that industrial mechanization of human labor would alienate humans by letting machinery supplant them. In response to this worry, he endorses the view that mechanization increasingly *liberated* humans from kinds of labor that were less fulfilling, and created leisure for culture and reflection, much as the institution of slavery did for male citizens of Athens in its golden classical age. Mechanization is, of course, a better form of liberation, because it does not subordinate one class of humans to another. Instead, it exploits machines. And so it is with the mechanization of human intellectual labor in the computer revolution.

Lanier suggests that the computer revolution may be doing the very opposite of what the Greeks did with slavery: We humans are increasingly turning over our *distinctively human activities* to machines. After all, the goal of research in artificial intelligence is to move computer technology *beyond* the level of mathematical calculations, pattern recognition, and other limited cognitive tasks, *toward* capabilities for speech, theorizing, decision-making and other high-level analytical tasks. Perhaps we will get to the stage where human intellectual activity is valued only for the pleasure it gives humans who engage in it, and not for any understanding or practical value it may produce. What do you think?

2. Imagine that we reach the stage where computational systems are capable of writing novels that compare favorably with the works of human authors as literary art and/or entertainment. Or they can generate paintings of a quality comparable to that of famous human artists. Would this lessen the value of the human artists? Would it seem "weird" to be reading what a machine wrote? Would it be like listening to what a machine has to say to you? And what would that be like, anyway? Would we feel alone because there's no real author behind the writing, or no self behind the speaking? Or would it be an experience of what we ourselves are: computational systems with cellular hardware having input/output relations with each other?

15

Some Basic Concepts of
Computability Theory

Richard B. White

Richard B. White teaches philosophy at Centre College and is the author of numerous papers in logic.

In the reading that follows, Richard B. White will introduce us to the mathematical theory of computability, which deals with simple, repeatable, step-by-step operations at a level of abstraction where a mathematical function is also referred to as a machine. This reading will help us to understand some of the general principles and ideas underlying the operation of computers.

Recent literature in the philosophy of mind, especially work concerned with "functionalism" and artificial intelligence, often refers to subjects from the branches of mathematics and theoretical computer science known as recursion theory and automata theory. The purpose of this expository essay is to acquaint the reader with a few basic ideas from those fields, with emphasis on concepts and terminology necessary for reading comfortably the selections in this anthology by Hilary Putnam and John Searle.

The exposition is divided into seven sections and an appendix. The first section reviews the fundamental concept of a function (in the mathematical sense) as a special kind of relation, and gives some notation needed for describing particular functions succinctly. The second section presents the simplest abstract computing devices, the finite automata. Section three is an introduction to Turing

machines, which are essentially highly idealized digital[1] computers in the modern sense—a Turing machine may be thought of as a digital computer with an unlimited storage capacity. An especially important Turing machine program, the "universal Turing machine," is the subject of section five. The fourth section deals with "Church's thesis" to which Searle's essay refers as "the Church-Turing thesis." The final two sections very briefly describe a variety of abstract machines and introduce the concept of "multiple realizability" which figures in Searle's work and in discussions of functionalism.

An especially interesting limitative theorem of recursion theory is Turing's result that no Turing machine program can decide the "halting problem" for Turing machine programs. Because this subject is somewhat more technical than the others, requiring the sketch of a rather abstract argument, it has been put in an appendix.

1st line of a 2-line credit to come — per msp 250
2nd line of credit

---

[1] A *digital* computer operates over input that consists of digits or numbers or discrete units rather than continuously varying magnitudes. ED.

1. FUNCTIONS

In ordinary language "function" commonly means an activity or action characteristic of a thing, as when one says that the function of an automobile radiator is to cool the engine, but in mathematics and logic a function is something quite different. Examples of mathematical functions are familiar from high school, where one encounters trigonometric functions such as the sine function or algebraic functions such as $f(x) = x^2 + 2$ whose graph is a parabola. Functions are special kinds of *relations,* and a relation from an abstract point of view is a set of *ordered pairs.* For example, the relation $<$ ("less than") between numbers may be identified with the set of all ordered pairs (m,n) in which the first member m of the pair is less than the second member n, so that for instance the pair $(3,5)$ belongs to the relation $<$ but the pairs $(5,3)$ and $(5,5)$ do not. (Instead of writing "(m,n) is in the relation $<$" it is customary to write "$m < n$.")

What makes a relation f a *function* is that f never contains two or more distinct ordered pairs with the same first member; in other words, if f is a function and (a,b) is any pair in f then b is the *unique* y such that (a,y) is in f. This justifies writing $b = f(a)$ and saying "b is f of a," meaning "b is *the* f of a." For example, the kinship relation "x is an offspring of y" is not a function, because a person has two biological parents; on the other hand, "x was born of y" is a function, because each person has a unique birth mother, and therefore one could write $y = m(x)$ to mean that y is *the* mother of x.

Every relation **R,** and so every function, has a *domain* which is the set of all first members a of the pairs (a,b) in **R,** and a *range* which is the set of all second members b of the pairs (a,b) in **R.** In the case of a relation which is a function f, when (a,b) is in f one may write $b = f(a)$ and say that b is the *value* of f at a, or b is the *output* of f for the *input* a. The members of a function's domain are said to be *arguments* of the function. This is rather unfortunate terminology because "argument" in this sense has nothing to do with the usual meaning of "argument" in logic, where an argument is the inference of a conclusion from premises, but the function-argument terminology is historically entrenched. (For "argument" in this context one may prefer "input", just as "output" may be used for

"value.")[2] A function may have one, two, or more than two arguments. For instance, the numerical function $f(x,y) = x + y$ is a function of two arguments. The function $g(x,y,z) = (x + y) - z$ is a function of three arguments. The domain of a function with two arguments may be regarded as a set of ordered pairs. The domain of a function with three arguments is a set of ordered triples, and so on.

Some abbreviating notation is very handy in talking about functions, and we shall use the following. The set of all ordered pairs (a,b) with a in a set A and b in a set B is $A \times B$. A and B need not be different. For example, if N is the set of all nonnegative integers $\{0, 1, 2, \dots\}$ then $N \times N$ is the set of all ordered pairs (m,n) in which m and n are both nonnegative integers. The notation $f: A \to B$ means that f is a function whose domain is the set A and whose range is included in the set B, i.e., that f is a function such that for every x in A the value $f(x)$ of the function is in B. Thus $f:(A \times B) \to C$ means that f is a function of two inputs such that for every a in A and b in B, $f(a,b)$ is in C. For some set A, one may wish to consider functions whose domains are various subsets of A as well as those whose domains are all of A. In this case the functions whose domains are subsets of A are said to be *partial* functions on A, and the functions whose domains are A are said to be *total* on A. If m is in the domain of a function f then $f(m)$ is said to be *defined* and f is said to be *defined at m.* If m is not in the domain of f then $f(m)$ is *undefined* and f is *undefined at m.*

---

[2] Although, as White said at the beginning of this section, the meaning of "function" is different in mathematics from its meaning in the philosophical theory called functionalism, the terms "input" and "output" suggest that the two meanings overlap. A mathematical function is not only a kind of relation between two members of a pair; it is also an *operation* to be performed on the input so as to yield the unique output or product for that input. Let's compare the meanings of "function" in "$f(x,y) = x + y$ is the addition function" and "The function of this calculator is addition." An important difference between the two cases is that the function of the calculator is *embodied* in a physical structure that is subject to breakdown, whereas breakdown is not a relevant notion for the mathematical function because it is not embodied or, at least, not treated as such. A mathematical function can only be what it is or do what it does to its input, but if the machine embodying the addition function breaks down, its output may not be the unique product of the summing of its input. It may show 5 for the sum of 2 and 2. Because embodiments of functions can become *dys*functional and operate differently than what their function calls for, the second, embodied sense of "function" includes the further element of *purpose,* because it includes only a subset of all the physically possible outputs of the calculator, the subset of correct or desired outputs, the outputs that the machine was made *for.* ED.

2. FINITE AUTOMATA

The simplest abstract machines currently relevant to the philosophy of mind are the *finite deterministic automata,* also known as *finite-state machines, sequential machines,* or *finite transducers.* A finite automaton m may be visualized as a device capable of receiving *input tapes* which are just finite sequences $i_0 \ldots i_n$ (for any n, n ≥ 0) in which each i_k is a symbol from a finite *input alphabet.* m can assume any one of a finite number of *internal states* $q_0, \ldots, q_m$ (m ≥ 0) . When m is started in its *initial state* q_0 and given an input tape, it "reads" the tape, say from left to right, in discrete steps, at each step changing state in accordance with its *transition function* and giving an output in accordance with its *output function.*[3] (Caution: don't confuse this special *machine output function* with the "outputs", i.e., values, of it or other functions such as the transition function.) When m has read through its input tape it halts, having produced a sequence of outputs which may be regarded as an *output tape.* Formally then, a finite automaton m consists of:

(i)   A finite set I whose members are the *input alphabet* of M.

(ii) A finite set O whose members are the *output alphabet* of M.

(iii) A finite set S whose members are the *states* of M. One of these states, q_0, is the *initial state* of M.

(iv) A *next-state* or *transition function* α: (S × I) → S. (That is, recalling our shorthand, α is a function of two arguments such that for each q in S and I in I, $\alpha(q,i)$ is in S.)

(v)   An *output function* β: S → O. (That is, for each state q in S, $\beta(q)$ is in O.)

An automaton m therefore operates as follows. When given an input tape $i_0\, i_1 \ldots i_n$ and started in state q_0, m reads input i_0, and goes to state $\alpha(q_0,i_0)$ which is some q_k, say q_1. Then m prints output $\beta(q_1)$, reads i_1, and goes to state $\alpha(q_1,i_1)$. m contin-

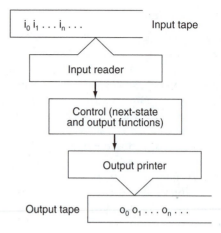

Figure 15.1 A schematic finite automaton

ues in this way, changing state as determined by its transition function applied to state and input and giving outputs in accordance with its output function applied to states, until it has read through its whole input tape and halts.

Examples of finite automata are easy to come by. Switching circuits may be regarded as automata; a switching circuit has a finite number of switches (often called "logic gates" such as "and", "or", and "not gates"),[4] each of which at a given time is either on or off. Therefore a circuit with n switches is naturally regarded as having 2^n states, a state consisting of a description of each of the n gates as either on or off. Many common devices, such as the controls of automatic elevators and vending machines, are automata.

As an example of a finite deterministic automaton, consider a simple automaton m with input alphabet {a,b} and output set {yes-no}. m is designed to say "yes" as soon as it has read two a's on its input tape and to say "no" until it has read two a's; therefore if the machine halts with a "yes" it has "recognized" an input with at least two a's.

---

[3]Many authors in defining "finite automaton" omit an output function and instead stipulate a set of "designated" states as a subset of the set of states. Then an automaton is said to "accept" an input string if it halts in a designated state after going through the string. What is here called a finite deterministic automaton is sometimes called a "Moore machine."

[4]The diagram on the right represents the simplest logic circuit, one that functions as a "not gate": "1" represents current on, and "0" represents current off, the only two possibilities for the switch. These symbols can therefore be used for the two possible truth values (T and F respectively) of a proposition P. It might be a helpful exercise for you to construct for yourself circuits that simulate other logical operators such as "or" and "and." ED.

M's transition function and output functions are given in tabular form as follows, where, for example, the "q_0,no" at the intersection of the first row and the second column shows that $\alpha(q_0,b) = q_0$ and $\beta(q_0) = $ no. The output function for m is therefore $\beta(q_0) = \beta(q_1) = $ no and $\beta(q_2) = $ yes.

	a	b
q_0	q_1, no	q_0, no
q_1	q_2, yes	q_1, no
q_2	q_2, yes	q_2, yes

(A table such as this is what Putnam and other authors have in mind when they mention "machine tables.") The reader may easily verify that, for instance, m halts with output "yes" when given the input babbaabb and with "no" when given babb.

Finite automata are deterministic because the state q and the input I give a unique result $\alpha(q,i)$ as the next state determined by the transition function α. However, actual sequential switching circuits, vending machines, elevators, and the like can undergo random malfunctions causing them to go into unintended states. A plausible generalization therefore of the concept of a deterministic automaton is that of a *probabilistic finite automaton*.[5] These are the automata to which Putnam refers in his "The Nature of Mental States."

The only difference between a probabilistic automaton and a deterministic one is in the transition function α. In a probabilistic machine with n states α assigns to each state-input pair (q,i) an n-tuple $(p_1, \ldots, p_n)$ in which each p_k gives the probability that at the next step the machine will be in state q_k. Since the p_k's are probabilities, it is required that each p be a real number no less than 0 and no greater than 1 and that their sum be 1. For example, if an automaton m has three states then $\alpha(q_1,I) = (.1,.3,.6)$ says that if m is in state q_1 receiving input I the probability that its next states will be q_0 is .1, that it will be q_1 is .3, and that it will be q_2 is .6. (The definition of the transition function for finite *sequences* of members of I is somewhat complex for a probabilistic automaton, involving products of "stochastic matrices" [Rabin, 102], and need not concern us here.)

3. TURING MACHINES

The finite deterministic automata are mathematical models of simple input-output systems with only the limited "memory" available through their internal states: the state of an automaton at any step in its operation gives all the information concerning previous inputs necessary to determine the outputs of the system at all subsequent inputs.[6] Far more powerful are the abstract computers which historically came first in the development of automata theory, the idealized digital computers described by A. M. Turing (and independently by E. L. Post) in 1936. There is a great deal of evidence that a suitably programmed Turing or Post machine is able to compute *any* function which is calculable by a routine clerical procedure—any function which is "effectively computable" or "algorithmic". (That Turing machines have this capability is a consequence of "Church's Thesis", of which more below.)

A Turing machine may be regarded as the control[7] of a finite deterministic automaton coupled to an *unbounded* external memory in the form of a single tape, divided into squares like the input tapes of sequential machines. However, unlike the finite-state machine which merely reads its inputs one after the other until it has exhausted the input tape, a Turing machine can move back and forth on its tape and print or erase symbols on the tape squares. Thus the tape of a Turing machine serves not only

---

[5] Probabilistic automata must not be confused with *nondeterministic automata*, in which the transition function is from states to subsets of the set of states.

[6] The term *memory* in this context refers to the capacity of a system to be influenced by previous input (prior to the current input) and past behavior or output. If a machine can move only to the right along its tape, its future output is less specifically influenced by previous input than if (like the Turing machine discussed next) it can move in both directions. In the latter case, it can go back to a previous input (which may also be an output, because the Turing machine also has the capacity to erase and replace an input). Ed.

[7] The term *control* in this context is used in a way that is similar to its use in the phrase *control system*—as explained in sec. 2 ("The Nervous System") of Reading 4. The Turing machine as control especially resembles the *modulator* of a control system: one "reads" input, the other "detects" it; one is a transition function determining an output directly or indirectly, the other "selects" a response. Ed.

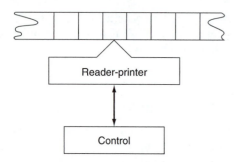

Figure 15.2 A schematic Turing machine. The tape is unbounded in both directions, and as directed by the control (the machine's transition function) the reader-printer can move to the left or right one square at a time.

to supply the machine with input, but also as a memory space on which the device can store intermediate results in the course of a computation and on which it can finally display its output, *if* it yields an output value for a given input. (A Turing machine, unlike a finite automaton, may in some cases never halt. This happens if the machine is programmed to compute a partial function f which is undefined at the input given to the machine.)

Turing machines can be made to process symbols from any alphabet of discrete signs, but it is sufficient to consider machines which compute numerical functions. (The reason this is not a restriction is that any alphabet can be encoded numerically.) A convenient representation of the numbers (nonnegative integers) is the unary system, in which zero is represented as 1, one as 1 1, two as 1 1 1, and so on, the number n being represented by a string of n + 1 1's or "tallies". Then numbers can be represented on a Turing machine tape as blocks of tallies, with empty squares used as separators. For example, the tape

	1	1	1	1		1	1	1	1	1	1	

with all squares blank except for those shown occupied by tallies, represents the number pair (3,5). The empty squares on a tape may be considered occupied by the symbol "B" meaning "blank". Then the above tape is conveniently typewritten as B1111B 111111B, with the understanding that all

the tape squares not shown are empty (i.e., contain B).

Like a finite automaton, a Turing machine has a finite number of internal states and always begins a computation in a designated initial state q_0. The machine scans its tape one square at a time and, depending on its state and input (i.e., the contents of the scanned square), may perform any operation of one of the following four kinds, abbreviated as shown in parentheses:[8]

> Move one square to the right and enter state q_k. (R,q_k)
> Move one square to the left and enter state q_k. (L,q_k)
> Print a B in the scanned square and enter state q_k. (PB,q_k)
> Print a 1 in the scanned square and enter state q_k. (P1,q_k)
> Halt. (H)

It is understood that the printing operations are executed by printing over (i.e., replacing) the symbol already on the scanned square. For example, if a machine is in state q_1 and scanning a square occupied by a 1, then it performs the operation PB,q_6 by erasing the 1 (replacing it with the blank B) and going into state q_6. It performs R,q_1 by moving to the square one to the right of the scanned square while remaining in state q_1.

Formally a Turing machine is essentially just a transition function α: SxI → O × S, where S is the set of states, I is the alphabet {1,B}, and O is the set of operations {PB, P1, L, R, H}. Since all the sets involved are finite a Turing machine may, like an automaton, be represented by a table which displays the transition function. (Recall the table for the automaton m above.)

A Turing machine program *computes* a function f (of one variable) if whenever f(m) is defined and the machine is started in state q_0 with the reader-printer reading the leftmost 1 in a block of m + 1 consecutive tallies on the tape, all other cells of the tape being empty, the machine sooner or later halts with f(m) + 1 tallies on the tape. If f(m) is undefined

---

and the machine is started as above, then the machine never stops. Computation for functions of two or more arguments is described similarly, with the machine started on a tape having two or more blocks of 1's (the input numbers) separated by B's.

As an example of a Turing machine, here is one that computes a predecessor function p(x) which is x − 1 if x ≥ 1 and is undefined if x = 0: $\alpha(q_0,B) = H\alpha(q_0,1) = PB,q_1\alpha(q_1,B) = R,q_1(q_1,1) = H$. In tabular form:

	B	1
q_0	H	PB, q_1
q_1	R, q_1	H

If this program is started in state q_0 with input one (i.e., B11B) and reading the leftmost 1, which we may indicate by $Bq_0$11B, it will proceed as follows: $Bq_0$11B, Bq_1B1B, $BBq_1$1B. (It must halt in state q_1 when reading a 1.) Therefore the program has computed p(1) = 0, as it should. If the program is started with input 0 the machine will move forever to the right: $Bq_0$1B, Bq_1BB, Bbq_1B, $BBBq_1$B, ... Therefore the machine never halts when given the input 0 at which the function p is undefined. (This particular p is a partial function, with 0 not in its domain, and to be a faithful mechanization of *this* predecessor function the Turing machine must not stop with *any* result as an output for the input 0.)

Turing machines can be generalized in various natural ways. For example, one can consider machines with more than one reader-printer under the command of the control; such machines are called "polycephalic" (many-headed).

It can be shown that any function computable by a polycephalic machine is computable by an ordinary Turing machine, but that a polycephalic machine may compute a function f *much faster* (i.e., in fewer computational steps) than its one-headed equivalent.

4. ALGORITHMS, RECURSIVE FUNCTIONS AND CHURCH'S THESIS

Intuitively, a function f is effectively computable if there is an *algorithm* which will yield the value f(m) for any input m at which f is defined and will give no result for f(m) if f is not defined at m. But what does "algorithm" mean? In its most general sense it applies to any well-defined process of calculation, including methods involving analog[9] or probabilistic procedures, but usually in mathematics (and always in recursion theory) the word has a narrower meaning, connoting a completely deterministic, step-by-step method of computation. In this sense an algorithm, also called an "effective procedure" or a "finite combinatorial procedure," is a finite set of instructions giving a mechanical routine method for solving any instance of a general problem. The method must be a "recipe" that could be followed by an automatic machine or by an unerring, tireless human clerk. Examples of algorithms are familiar from secondary-school mathematics. For instance, the construction for bisecting an arbitrary angle with ruler and compass in plane geometry and the formula which can be applied to find the roots of any quadratic equation in algebra give algorithms. In this strict sense of "algorithm" the algorithmic routine must consist of discrete, completely determined steps. Analog or randomizing methods are not permitted.

A standard textbook on recursive function theory gives the following informal characterization of the concept:

1. *An algorithm is given as a set of instructions of finite size.* (Any classical mathematical algorithm, for example, can be described in a finite number of English words.)

---

[9] Analog methods use a continuously varying quantity rather than discrete units or numbers. For instance, I can add two lengths either by adding the two numbers that sum the units of length (e.g., feet and inches) in each length, or I can use a tape measure, marking the end of one length on the tape, and using that mark to state my measure of the second length. *Analog* in this sense is usually contrasted with *digital* (see fn. 1 above).

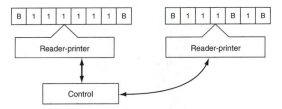

Figure 15.3 A two-headed Turing machine.

2. *There is a computing agent . . . which can react to the instructions and carry out the computations.*

3. *There are facilities for making, storing, and retrieving steps in a computation.*

4. *Let P be the set of instructions as in 1 and L be the computing agent as in 2. Then L reacts to P in such a way that, for any given input, the computation is carried out in a discrete stepwise fashion, without any use of continuous methods or analogue devices.*

5. *L reacts to P in such a way that, for any input, a computation is carried forward deterministically, without resort to random methods or devices, e.g., dice.*

Virtually all mathematicians would agree that features 1 to 5, although inexactly stated, are inherent in the idea of algorithm. [Rogers, 2]

We note that implicit in these requirements for an algorithm is the *repeatability* of the procedure: it must be possible to apply an algorithm any number of times, always with the *same* result when started with the same input. This is one reason for disallowing random methods. For example, the following instruction for computing a numerical function $f(m)$ is not considered algorithmic: given m, spin a fair roulette wheel m times, at each spin making a digit of $f(m)$ equal to 1 if the ball lands on red, to 2 if it lands on black. This procedure might make $f(5) = 12,221$ on one application and $f(5) = 11,122$ on the next. The algorithms incorporated in portable calculators have the requisite feature of exact duplicability; one can always push "clear" on the calculator and repeat a calculation to get the same result, as in adding up a column of figures twice. The requirement of exact repeatability seems to be neglected by philosophers who speak of arbitrarily chosen objects, such as walls or fountain pens, as "implementing" computer programs (i.e., formalized algorithms).[10] How does one *reset* a wall to run through the same algorithm it just executed five minutes ago?

It is also important to remember that a perfectly good algorithm may sometimes not terminate when given certain inputs. (This is why Turing machines must not be required to halt for every input.)

We saw an example above in the Turing machine program to compute a predecessor function. Another simple example is a subtraction algorithm to calculate $x - y$ for arbitrary natural numbers x and y. If $y \leq x$ then the algorithm must yield the difference between x and y, but if $y > x$ then a subtraction algorithm may run on forever without giving an answer. The fact that an algorithm must be "partial" when it corresponds to a partial function is crucial for a consistent and adequate mathematical theory of computable functions, because among those functions are partial as well as total ones.

Historically mathematicians and logicians have been interested in showing that certain problems *cannot* be solved algorithmically. In order to do this, one must have a precise, formal analysis of the informal concept of an algorithm, and this is what Turing provided with his ideal, unbounded computing machines. These machines put a theoretical upper limit on computability: if a function is not computable by a Turing machine, which can have any finite number of states and which never exhausts its memory space, then surely it cannot be computed by any actual digital computer, no matter how powerful. For instance, Turing proved that no Turing machine could compute a "halting" function for Turing machines.[11] (See the Appendix.)

The exact definition of computability via Turing machines is only one among many ways of precisely defining "algorithmically computable." Other definitions have been given in terms of representability in various formal logical systems and computability by idealized machines (e.g., "register machines") significantly different from Turing machines. However, quite remarkably, all of these different approaches have been proved equivalent: they all classify exactly the same functions as computable. Moreover, no one has succeeded in producing a function which is in the informal, intuitive sense computable by an algorithm but which is not computable by a Turing machine. The functions which are Turing-machine computable, and so computable under any precise analysis of computability so far proposed, are known as the *partial recursive functions,* or nowadays, for short, the *recur-*

---

[10] White's remark applies to Searle on p. 258 below. ED.

[11] A halting function would decide, given any computable function f and number m, whether or not f halts when given input m. ED.

sive functions. The hypothesis that every function which is algorithmic in the informal sense is also recursive is known as "Church's thesis."[12] Church stated his thesis as a "definition":

> We now define the notion, already discussed, of an *effectively calculable* function of positive integers by identifying it with the notion of a recursive function of positive integers. . . . This definition is thought to be justified by the considerations which follow, so far as positive justification can ever be obtained for the selection of a formal definition to correspond to an intuitive notion. [Church, 100]

The evidence for Church's thesis consists in the fact (i) that so far all proposed formal analyses of the informal notion of computable function, most of them made independently of one another, have turned out to be equivalent; (ii) that no intuitively computable function has yet been proposed which is not also recursive; and (iii) that the set of recursive functions has been proved to be closed[13] under very powerful methods for defining new computable functions from given ones.[14] Under (iii), for example, Kleene's "recursion theorem" implies that for every recursive function g (of two arguments) there is a recursive function f (of one argument) such that $f(x) = g(e,x)$ for all x, where e is a number that in a certain sense describes or "encodes" a program for computing f *itself*. This means that a remarkable amount of self-reference can be allowed consistently in generating recursive functions. Since formal programs can be given numerical descriptions and recursive functions operate on numbers, recursive functions can operate on recursive functions; i.e., in the machine analysis of recursive functions, Turing machines can operate on Turing machines. An important consequence of this is the existence of "universal" functions or Turing machines.

5. THE UNIVERSAL TURING MACHINE

The Turing machine programs are transition functions which can be regarded as finite sequences of instructions. These finite sequences can be encoded as numbers.[15] Consequently one can speak of the computable (i.e., recursive) function f_e, meaning the function computed by program number e. A program for computing the function can then effectively be found by a machine which decodes the number e.

One of the early profound results in recursion theory was Turing's proof that there is a single Turing machine program, a "universal" program, which can simulate any Turing machine program. In the case of functions of one argument this can be put as follows: there is a computable function u of two arguments such that for *any* computable function f_e of one argument $u(e,x) = f_e(x)$ for all x (i.e., for all x for which the two sides of this equation are defined). In other words, if the universal function u is given a code number e for any function f_e, together with any input x, it will follow the instructions encoded by e to perform on x the same computation which f_e would perform on x. One may picture a Turing machine for u as a device with two input "hoppers." Into one hopper e is dropped, and then when any x is dropped into the other hopper the device acts just as a one-hopper machine for f_e would act (Figure 15.4).

A more concrete representation of the action of the universal machine is shown in Figure 15.5.

When the disc for a special program e is inserted into a modern all-purpose ("stored program") digital computer, the universal "executive" program u stored in the machine then works on any input x in the same way that a special-purpose machine built to execute only e would work on x. ("Program e" here of course means "the program represented in numerical form by the number e.") Thus, as Figure 15.4 and 15.5 illustrate, the universal Turing machine is not only of theoretical

---

[12] To give credit to A. M. Turing who independently stated a thesis very similar to Church's, many writers now refer to "the Church-Turing thesis" rather than just "Church's thesis."

[13] A *set* is said to be *closed* when an operation performed on its members produces only members of the same set. For instance, the set of whole numbers is closed with respect to addition and multiplication. And, White goes on to say, when various operations that generate one computable function from another are performed on members of the set of recursive functions, the products are also recursive functions (i.e., the set of recursive functions is closed with respect to these operations).

[14] A set S is *closed* under an m-place operation O if whenever $f_1, \ldots, f_m$ are in S then so is $O(f_1, \ldots, f_m)$.

[15] There are indefinitely many operations by which a single number as input can be read as a sequence of numbers. For example, if the number is binary, a particular sequence of 1s and 0s within an enclosing string of these symbols could be read by a program as a "separator" marking off one number from another. Each separate number would encode an instruction, and the order of the instructions would be coded by the order in which the numbers occurred between separators.

Figure 15.4 Supplied with the code **e** for a function f_e, the universal machine **u** becomes equivalent to a machine designed just to compute the values of f_e.

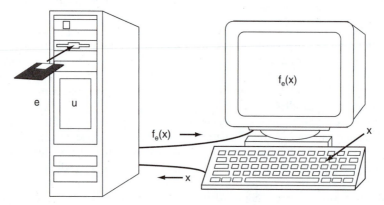

Figure 15.5 A universal machine in the familiar guise of a "PC".

interest. The idea directly inspired work on practical all-purpose computers and, as Searle points out, it also thereby stimulated the field of artificial intelligence. A recent excellent exposition of recursion theory emphasizes the practical importance of Turing's universal program:

> The interest of the notion is that *a universal Turing machine is a computer in the modern sense of the word, and it works as an interpreter,* decoding the program e given to it as data (in the same form as the other inputs) and simulating it. In other words, a universal Turing machine is not a special purpose machine: it is programmable in essence, and thus all-purpose. . . . Conversely, *any of the present-day automatic computers (if abstracted from physical malfunctioning) is equivalent to a universal Turing machine, if it is given the possibility of having a potentially infinite memory.* . . . [Odifretti, 133]

Of course, there are two very big "if's" in Odifretti's observation (because every actual computer has a bounded memory and sometimes malfunctions), and therefore automata theory abounds with mathematical models of computers which are less powerful but more realistic than Turing machines, as well as with powerful machines that (by Church's thesis) cannot compute any function not already computable by a Turing machine, but which may be much faster and more efficient than Turing machines.

6. A SPECTRUM OF ABSTRACT COMPUTERS

In the literature of automata theory there is a wide range of abstract computing machines. The models at the low end of this spectrum are no doubt exemplified in nature as well as in artifacts, but the ones at the upper end, the Turing machines and other devices capable of computing any recursive function, can only be approximated by actual physical systems. This is because there are bounds on the storage capacity of any actual computer, whereas a Turing machine has an unlimited tape. (Any all-purpose digital computer as in figure 15.5 is really an approximation of a universal Turing machine.) Therefore it would seem that philosophers who discuss the "realizability" of mathematical computer models should specify precisely the kinds of machines at issue; sometimes terms like "Turing machine" or "finite automaton" occur almost vacuously in philosophical discussion, in that nothing would change if, for example, "finite automaton" were replaced with "pushdown automaton" or even "Turing machine." (This seems to be the case with Putnam's use of "probabilistic finite automaton" in his "Mental States.")

Here is a partial view of the automaton spectrum, in order of increasing capabilities:

1. Finite deterministic and nondeterministic automata.

2. Finite probabilistic automata.[16]

3. Pushdown automata (finite automata which control both an input tape and a "first-in-last-out" or "pushdown" memory).

4. Auxiliary pushdown automata (pushdown automata with the additional storage provided by a bounded Turing-style tape).

5. Turing machines, register machines, and other sequential computers that can compute any recursive function.

6. Cellular automata, which are configurations of indefinitely many finite automata, with each automaton occupying a "cell" and having its next state determined at each step by the states of automata in neighboring cells.

The cellular automata are exemplified by Conway's "Game of Life" automaton, which may be envisioned as an infinite checkerboard each of whose squares is occupied by a finite automaton C with two states, "on" and "off" [Poundstone, 24–26]. Each C receives as input the number of "on" C's occupying the eight squares immediately neighboring its square, and has the transition or "next-state" table shown below.

C C C
C Ⓒ C   The indicated C has 8 neighbors.
C C C

Transition table:

| | Input (number of neighbor automata that are "on") | | | | | | | | |
	0	1	2	3	4	5	6	7	8
State on	off	off	on	on	off	off	off	off	off
off	off	off	off	on	off	off	off	off	off

As the transition table shows, if the finite automaton C in any cell is "off" but bordered by three "on" C's then it changes in its next state to "on." If it is "on" and is bordered by two or three "on" C's, it stays in state "on"; otherwise its next state is "off."

The simple description of the Life cellular automaton belies the complexity of the patterns which can be generated from an initial configuration (i.e., a finite number of "on" cells). Some of these patterns are even "self-reproducing" arrangements, and in fact Life is a dramatic illustration of the possibility, sometimes denied by philosophers, that there could be growth and at least apparent novelty in a completely deterministic universe.[17] Cellular automata can be designed to compute the values of numerical functions. By Church's thesis any such computable function must be recursive, and so computable by some Turing machine; however, cellular automata are among the abstract machines capable of the *parallel*[18] computation mentioned by Searle, and are far faster than their equivalent Turing machines.

7. MULTIPLE REALIZABILITY OF ABSTRACT AUTOMATA

Here is a typical Turing machine program in tabular form:

---

[16] For an explanation of the difference between nondeterministic and probabilistic automata, see note 5. ED.

[17] For example, the game of Life would seem to refute C. S. Peirce's well known contention that in a completely deterministic universe there could be no growth or novelty.

[18] Machines capable of *parallel processing* can do two or more calculations independently and simultaneously. Insofar as the human brain can be understood as a computer, it appears to do a great deal of parallel processing. For instance, input from the different "patches" on the retina is independently received and operated on by corresponding "patches" of the visual cortex. Moreover, within the visual, auditory, and somatosensory cortices, there appears to be simultaneous processing of concurrent sensory inputs to multiple neocortical maps of the same receptor surfaces. (See Reading 4, sec. 4—"The Neocortex".) ED.

	B	1
q_0	R, q_1	PB, q_0
q_1	P1, q_2	R, q_1
q_2	L, q_3	R, q_2
q_3	H	PB, q_3

(This program computes the addition function $x + y$, as is easily verified.[19]) One could say that this table implicitly defines the state q_2, for example, by showing the role that state plays in relation to the tape symbols b and 1 and the states q_1 and q_3. If this machine table were implemented by some electronic device, then q_2 might be realized by a switch whose on-off status is affected by the positions of two other switches; if it were implemented by some clockwork mechanism then q_2 might be represented by the position of a gear in contact with other gears, and so on. However, all that is essential to q_2 as a state in the *program* is the role that it plays in achieving transitions among the tape symbols and the other program states.

The kind of functionalist theory of mind presented by Putnam in the next reading draws a close analogy between Turing machine states and mental states. For the functionalist, a [type of] mental state is defined by that state's causal role in relation to environmental inputs, behavioral outputs, and other mental states. What is essential to a mental state's being, for example, a pain state is not the particular physical realization of that state but rather the causal role the state plays in any physical realization of it and its attendant states.

In relating automata theory to the philosophy of mind, care is required to avoid equivocating on some key terms. In particular, "machine" and "state" are ambiguous. In one sense a Turing machine is a *program;* in this sense one speaks of a Turing machine which computes the function $x + y$, or of a universal Turing machine. In another sense a Turing machine is an imagined *device,* with a tape, a reader-printer, and a control. In this sense one

might say that the magnetic disc of an electronic digital computer approximates the tape of a Turing machine. Similarly "state" has at least two meanings. States as they figure in programs may be regarded simply as instruction locators or markers. Thus the Turing machine table above could be written as follows, where the states have just become instruction numbers, and change of state is passage from one instruction to another:

0. If reading a B, move right and follow instruction #1; if reading a 1, replace it with a B and follow instruction #0.

1. If reading a B, replace it with a 1 and follow instruction #2; if reading a 1, move right and follow instruction #1.

2. If reading a B, move left and follow instruction #3; if reading a 1, move right and follow instruction #2.

3. If reading a B, halt; if reading a 1, replace it with a B and follow instruction #3.

In another sense of "state," a state is a *physical* state, for instance a state of some organism or piece of hardware. Thus a three-state (three-instruction) program might be executed on a switching network with six on-off switches and therefore at least sixty-four naturally distinguishable physical states.

A program, in the mathematical or formal sense now being discussed, determines little in the way of necessary or sufficient conditions on the physical systems which may implement the program.[20] In fact, in considering the formal definition of "Turing machine", "recursive function", or "finite automaton" one can be struck by the absence of any reference to time,[21] even in the form of an abstract set of "instants." For example, a finite deterministic automaton as defined above is deterministic because the values which the transition function as-

---

[19] Do this for yourself, using the following input: B11B111B [which is the pair (1,2), which calls for B1111B (3) as output (what's left on the tape after the program operates on the input)]. Remember that the program begins in q_0 reading the leftmost 1 and that it continues to read a square after altering it. ED.

[20] As White indicated earlier, the notion of a program *does* impose this constraint at least: that the system permit re-setting, that it be able to perform repeatedly the same operation or set of operations on the same sort of input. ED.

[21] In his earlier description of a Turing machine White refers to its "memory," which is the capability of a machine to be influenced by behavior and input that preceded its current input. If he is correct about the intelligibility of an a-temporal description of a Turing machine, memory would have to be described very differently and probably called something else. He and I have agreed to disagree over the very interesting issue of whether the concept of automata can be rendered intelligible apart from spatiotemporal and very general physical content. ED.

signs to the pairs $<q,i>$, for states q and input alphabet symbols I, completely determine the value which is assigned to $<q,i_0 i_1 \ldots i_n>$, where q is any state and $i_0 i_1 \ldots i_n$ any *string* of input symbols. However, the meaning of "determines" here is purely logical, not temporal or causal.

But even with the natural constraint that a physical executor of a program must perform steps in some temporal order, there is an almost unlimited variety of possible physical realizations. Computers can be made of wires and pulleys, of gears and levers, of hydraulic piping and valves, and even of TinkerToys. As one moves up the automaton scale, however, from simple finite-state machines to powerful parallel machines such as cellular automata, the possibilities for real physical implementation are greatly narrowed. Realistic high-speed, large-memory digital computers with the capabilities of even today's home "PC's" simply could not be built from bronze gears. Still, it is true that a formalized algorithm can in principle be run on all sorts of hardware or living-ware, and this multiple realizability of programs has strongly reinforced functionalism in the philosophy of mind.

There is a kind of converse to the multiple realizability of programs, which may be called the universal realizability thesis. Searle puts it this way:

> 1. For any object there is some description of that object such that under that description the object is a digital computer.
>
> 2. For any program there is some sufficiently complex object such that there is a description of the object under which it is implementing the program. Thus for example the wall behind my back is right now implementing the Wordstar program, because there is some pattern of molecular movements which is isomorphic with the formal structure of Wordstar. But if the wall is implementing Wordstar then if it is a big enough wall then it is implementing any program, including any program implemented by my brain. [Reading 18, pp. 258–259]

This is very difficult to understand. For one thing, it is not at all clear what Searle means by "isomorphic with the formal structure of Wordstar." The standard meaning of "isomorphism" is that there is a one-to-one relation-preserving map of one relational structure onto another. If that is what Searle has in mind here, what does he mean by "the for-

mal structure of Wordstar?" Does he mean the program as a set of instructions, or a particular "run" of the program in application to specific inputs, or what? In general, the universal realizability thesis at present seems too vague to evaluate.

APPENDIX: THE UNSOLVABILITY OF THE HALTING PROBLEM

The existence of a universal computable function u may strike one as paradoxical, for the following reason. The universal function applied to any m and n gives the value of the one-argument function number m for input n: $u(m,n) = f_m(n)$. But if u is computable then surely also computable is the function of one argument $d(x) = u(x,x)$, and if d is computable then so is $g(x) = d(x) + 1$. But this is impossible! For if g is the computable function f_e then $g(e) = d(e) + 1 = u(e,e) + 1 = f_e(e) + 1 = g(e) + 1$, and $g(e) = g(e) + 1$ is impossible for any number $g(e)$. However, there is an easy solution to this paradox, which is simply to recall that "computable function" means "*partial* recursive function", and for a partial function g the equation $g(e) = g(e) + 1$ must be read, "either $g(e)$ and $g(e) + 1$ are both defined and equal, or else they are both undefined." (In this case they are both undefined.) Therefore g must be a *partial* function whose domain is a proper subset of N, and the above argument is just a proof that g is undefined at e.

By reasoning closely related to the above, Turing proved that there cannot be a Turing machine which decides the question "does the Turing machine program number m when given the input n ever halt or not?" That is, Turing showed that there cannot be a *total* recursive function h such that

$$h(x,y) = 1 \text{ ("yes") if } f_x(y) \text{ is defined.}$$

$$H(x,y) = 0 \text{ ("no") if } f_x(y) \text{ is undefined.}$$

To prove this, assume, for a *reductio ad absurdum,* that there is such a total h. Given that h is total, let another function g be defined by

$$g(x) = 1 \text{ if } h(x,x) = 0.$$

$$g(x) \text{ is undefined if } h(x,x) = 1.$$

Since h is Turing-machine computable, g must be also. (If H is a program for computing h, let a program G for computing g(m) first compute h(m,n) just as H does and then if H's output is B1B, i.e., the tape representation of 0, simply change that output to B11B and halt, or else, if H's output is B11B, move forever to the right on the tape.)

But g cannot be computable. For if g is the computable function f_e then g(e) cannot be either defined or undefined, a contradiction:

If g(e) is defined then $f_e(e)$ is defined and h(e,e) = 1, so g(e) is undefined.

If g(e) is undefined then $f_e(e)$ is undefined, so h(e,e) = 0 and g(e) = 1, which makes g(e) defined (it has the value 1).

Therefore since g cannot be computable, the total computable "halting" function h from which g was constructed cannot exist.

We can adapt the description of the "Game of Life" automaton to something more like a network of neurons (or neural net) that works as a **modulator:** Imagine a finite, rectangular, three-dimensional sheet or "tissue" made up of cells each having connections to, for example, five to ten other cells (neurons have thousands of such connections, but that's not easy to imagine, so let's simplify). In neurons, the magnitude of the postsynaptic potential degrades with time and distance as the **ionic** current propagates from the site of the synapse toward the axon hillock where the neuron's all-or-nothing output (action potential) is initiated (see sec. 3.1 of Reading 4). We can imitate this variation in the strengths of neural inputs as they affect the hillock by assigning to our artificial neuron a threshold for turning **on**, and different strengths to its individual input and output connections with other cells. Furthermore, a real neuron's postsynaptic potentials are either excitatory or inhibitory, so the different strengths of connections among our artificial cells will have either positive or negative values. For example, if we assign a threshold of **10** to each cell, then the connection strengths could be in the **±1 − 10** range. Since the neural net must function as a modulator unit, let's designate one side of the sheet as the input or receptor surface and the opposite side as the output or effector surface. The modulator unit will then consist of three distinct groupings of cells: *input, inter* and *output,* as in figure 15.6 below.

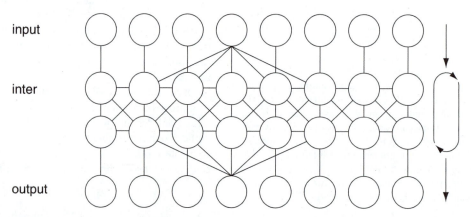

Figure 15.6 Schematic drawing of a portion of a neural net. Each input and output cell connects with five cells in the adjacent inter layer. Each inter cell also connects with five other inter cells. Connections can be either excitatory or inhibitory, and thresholds as well as connection strengths can be adjusted up or down. This scheme does not reflect any specific device used in actual experiments; it serves only to illustrate in a general way the kind of structure that is a neural net. As a rule, the numbers of cells in the input, inter and output layers are not equal.

The input and output surfaces are the interfaces between the net system and its environment. They are analogous to the keyboard and video display of a computer. The "computation" goes on within the inter layers, which are composed of interconnected automata working in parallel according to transition tables like the cellular automata in the Game of Life. Input cells turn on or off in response to external energy inputs (e.g., from an experimenter's clamp or switch). Each output cell turns on or off depending on whether the sum of the weighted inputs from its five inter cells reaches threshold level or not. Any particular pattern of input initiates a very complex set of interactions within the inter layers until they reach an equilibrium distribution of **on** and **off** cells which is reflected in a stable output pattern.

Jack Copeland, in his excellent introductory book *Artificial Intelligence* (1993), presents a simple example of the capabilities of such a system: Suppose you want the output pattern to be the inverse of the input pattern (e.g., an input sequence of two **on**'s followed by three **off**'s would be reversed in the output: three **off**'s followed by two **on**'s). You start out with no idea what set of connection strengths and threshold levels will generate the desired result for a particular input pattern, so you begin with arbitrary settings and see what happens. Then you check each output cell to see whether its matches the **on/off** state of its correlate in the input surface. If it doesn't, you alter the strengths or thresholds of the cells affecting it until it goes into the appropriate state. This same "training" procedure goes on for a representative number of other input patterns. The more patterns involved, the less adjustment is needed for each new pattern, until finally the system is trained so well that it very rarely, if ever, makes an error. Even for a simple system such as the one depicted in figure 15.6 the number of potential adjustments within the inter layers is vast, and experimenters will usually call on the tireless patience of a computer using a training algorithm.

The above example brings out some important properties of neural nets. Unlike the digital computers discussed by Bruce White, this system is not following a program in the usual sense. It would be easy to formulate rules for inverting input sequences. But the system has not been given strings of symbolic input that "tell" it what to do with other input. The experimenter knows what the output should be for a specific input, but (unlike a programmer) doesn't know *how* the system should arrive at it. Instead, the experimenter, by a moronically repetitive and simple algorithm, causes the system to become configured (in connection strengths and thresholds) so that it reliably executes a function. D. E. Rumelhart and J. L. McClelland, in an article describing a system that produced the past tense of an English verb when given the root form of that verb, mention a good analogy for this feature of neural nets:

> We suggest that the mechanisms that process language and make judgments of grammaticality are constructed in such a way that their performance is characterizable by rules, but that the rules themselves are not written in explicit form anywhere in the mechanism. An illustration of this view . . . is provided by the honeycomb. The regular structure of the honeycomb arises from the interaction of forces that wax balls exert on each other when compressed. The honeycomb can be described by a rule, but the mechanism which produces it does not contain any statement of this rule. (1986, 217)

Once a neural net is trained into a task, it has the functional equivalent of *knowing how* to do the task. However, this "knowledge" is not stored in a particular location within the system the way that the symbols in program instructions are stored in a physically distinct register within your computer. Instead, this knowledge is nothing but the pattern of connection and threshold settings *distributed throughout* the system. For this reason, what is going on when all the constituent automata within the neural net are more or less simultaneously computing their respective inputs is often called *parallel distributed processing (PDP)*. The use of PDP systems as a strategy for investigation and simulation of cognitive processes is often called *connectionism* (reflecting the focus on adjusting connections in such systems).

There are many reasons for adopting a connectionist approach to human cognitive processes. The components and interactions within PDP systems are much more brainlike than those of standard digital computers. Like PDP systems, the brain exhibits a great deal of parallel processing, not only in the large numbers of its neurons working simultaneously, but also in the discreteness of cortical patches corresponding to **cortical fields** and the multiplicity of cortical maps of overlapping receptor surfaces (see sec. 4 of Reading 4). As with the brain's wetware, physical failure or destruction of some of the cells or other hardware in a PDP system often doesn't cause the system to "crash." Instead there is a graded or proportional decay such as an increase in frequency of errors for all or some tasks. Furthermore, PDP systems do much better at various classification tasks that are routine for the human brain but are extremely difficult for programmable computers. PDP systems have been trained to do such things as recognize faces despite changes in their expression and angle of presentation, and recognize the same letter in a wide variety of fonts and scripts. The task of devising algorithms for such functions is formidable, and is one of the most serious obstacles faced by researchers trying to program computers to simulate cognitive processes.

Despite its promise, the successes of connectionism thus far are limited. There is a great deal of discussion and disagreement among researchers in cognitive science and artificial intelligence over the prospects of PDP and the extent to which it points in a fundamentally different direction than mainstream work with digital computers. It is interesting to note that most connectionist research is done with digital computers that simulate the operation of PDP systems. If what is going on in a connectionist system were so fundamentally different, how could it be simulated in this way? And if we accept the functionalist thesis presented by Fodor in Reading 11—that mental states are *functional* states—then functionally equivalent mental processes (ones having the same input/output relations with their environments) are instances of the *same* mental process. In that case, what *philosophical* or *psychological* importance is there to the internal differences between connectionist and standard computational systems? These are difficult and interesting questions.

WORKS CITED

Church, Alonzo. "An Unsolvable Problem of Elementary Number Theory," *The American Journal of Mathematics* 58 (1936): 345–363. Rpt. In *The Undecidable*. Ed. Martin Davis. Hewlett, New York: Raven Press, 1965. 88–107.

Odifretti, Piergiorgio. *Classical Recursion Theory*. Amsterdam: North-Holland Publishing Co., 1989.

Poundstone, William. *The Recursive Universe*. New York: William Morrow and Co., 1985.

Rabin, Michael O. "Probabilistic Automata." *Sequential Machines, Selected Papers*. Ed. E. F. Moore. Palo Alto: Addison-Wesley, 1964.

Rogers, Jr., Hartley. *Theory of Recursive Functions and Effective Computability*. New York: McGraw-Hill, 1967.

Rumelhart, David E., and James L. McClelland. "On Learning the Past Tenses of English Verbs." In *Parallel Distributed Processing: Explorations in the Microstructure of Cognition*. Vol. 2, *Psychological and Biological Models*. Cambridge, MA: MIT Press, 1986.

Searle, John R. "Is the Brain a Digital Computer?" *American Philosophical Association Proceedings* 64.3 (1990): 21–37.

16

The Nature of Mental States

Hilary Putnam

It is on computer modeling [of the mind], rather than on direct physical or chemical explanation, that thinkers of a reductionist bent, like
my former self, now pin their hopes.—Hilary Putnam (1992)

Hilary Putnam is a professor of philosophy at Harvard University. He has published numerous
books and articles in theory of knowledge, philosophy of language, logic, philosophy of mind
and many other areas. Among his most recent books are *Representation and Reality* (1988) in
which he argues against functionalism in the philosophy of mind, including the theory his "former self" put forward in the reading below, and *Renewing Philosophy* (1992), from which
comes the quotation above.

In this reading (a very influential paper first published in 1967), Putnam presents the "hypothesis" that mental states such as pain are best understood as functional states of an organism that embodies a Turing machine variation called a Probabilistic Automaton (explained by
Bruce White in section 2 of the previous reading). In addition he gives reasons for preferring
functionalism to either logical behaviorism or the mind-brain identity theory.

The typical concerns of the Philosopher of Mind
might be represented by three questions: (1) How
do we know that other people have pains? (2) Are
pains brain states? (3) What is the analysis of the
concept *pain?*[1] I do not wish to discuss questions
(1) and (3) in this paper. I shall say something about
question (2).[2]

I. IDENTITY QUESTIONS

"Is pain a brain state?" (Or, "Is the property of
having a pain at time *t* a brain state?")[3] It is impossible to discuss this question sensibly without saying something about the peculiar rules which, far
from leading to an end to all conceptual confusions,
themselves represent considerable conceptual confusion. These rules—which are, of course, implicit
rather than explicit in the practice of most analytical philosophers—are (1) that a statement of the
form "being A is being B" (e.g., "being in pain is

Originally published as "Psychological Predicates," by Hilary Putnam, in
Art, Mind, and Religion, W. H. Capitan and D. D. Merrill, eds. © 1967
by the University of Pittsburgh Press. Reprinted by permission of the
publisher.

[1] The third question addresses the concept of *pain* as opposed to, let's
say, the concept of *anger*. The second question deals with pain as a representative mental state having some relation to a brain state, whereas the
first is the criterial question discussed by Malcolm in Reading 3 and
Rorty in Reading 8. ED.

[2] I have discussed these and related topics in the following papers:
"Minds and Machines," in *Dimensions of Mind,* ed. Sidney Hook, New
York, 1960, pp. 148–179; "Brains and Behavior," in *Analytical Philosophy,
second series,* ed. Ronald Butler, Oxford, 1965, pp. 1–20; and "The Men-

tal Life of Some Machines," in *Intentionality, Minds, and Perception,* ed.
Hector-Neri Castañeda, Detroit, 1966, pp. 177–200.

[3] In this paper I wish to avoid the vexed question of the relation between *pains* and *pain states.* I only remark in passing that one common argument *against* identification of these two—viz., that a pain can be in
one's arm but a state (of the organism) cannot be in one's arm—is easily
seen to be fallacious.

being in a certain brain state") can be *correct* only if it follows, in some sense, from the meaning of the terms A and B; and (2) that a statement of the form "being A is being B" can be philosophically *informative* only if it is in some sense reductive[4] (e.g., "being in pain is having a certain unpleasant sensation" is not philosophically informative; "being in pain is having a certain behavior disposition" is, if true, philosophically informative). These rules are excellent rules if we still believe that the program of reductive analysis (in the style of the 1930's) can be carried out;[5] if we don't, then they turn analytical philosophy into a mug's game, at least so far as "is"questions are concerned.

In this paper I shall use the term 'property' as a blanket term for such things as being in pain, being in a particular brain state, having a particular behavior disposition, and also for magnitudes such as temperature, etc.—i.e., for things which can naturally be represented by one-or-more-place predicates or functors. I shall use the term 'concept' for things which can be identified with synonymy-classes of expressions. Thus the concept *temperature* can be identified (I maintain) with the synonymy-class[6] of the word 'temperature.'[7] (This is like saying that the number 2 can be identified with the class of all pairs. This is quite a different statement from the peculiar statement that 2 *is* the class of all pairs. I do not maintain that concepts *are* synonymy-classes, whatever that might mean, but that they can be identified with synonymy-classes, for the purpose of formalization of the relevant discourse.)

The question "What is the concept *temperature?*" is a very "funny" one. One might take it to mean "What is temperature? Please take my question as a conceptual one." In that case an answer might be (pretend for a moment 'heat' and 'temperature' are synonyms) "temperature is heat," or even "the concept of temperature is the same concept as the concept of heat." Or one might take it to mean "What are *concepts,* really? For example, what is 'the concept of temperature?'" In that case heaven knows what an "answer" would be. (Perhaps it would be the statement that concepts *can be identified with* synonymy-classes.)

Of course, the question "What is the property temperature?" is also "funny." And one way of interpreting it is to take it as a question about the concept of temperature. But this is not the way a physicist would take it.

The effect of saying that the property P_1 can be identical with the property P_2 only if the terms P_1, P_2 are in some suitable sense "synonyms" is, to all intents and purposes, to collapse the two notions of "property" and "concept" into a single notion. The view that concepts (intensions[8]) *are* the same as properties has been explicitly advocated by Carnap (e.g., in *Meaning and Necessity*). This seems an unfortunate view, since "temperature is mean molecular kinetic energy" appears to be a perfectly good example of a true statement of identity of properties, whereas "the concept of temperature is the same concept as the concept of mean molecular kinetic energy" is simply false.

Many philosophers[9] believe that the statement "pain is a brain state" violates some rules or norms

---

[4] In general, a *reductive* analysis of a term or phenomenon claims that X means or is "nothing but" Y, where Y is something other than what X seems to mean or be. Reductions or reductive analyses in science typically render the macro in terms of the micro, as in "Lightning is a motion of electric charges. . . ." Putnam will refer (six paragraphs below) to such scientific claims as "*empirical* reductions" because they occur in the context of theories based on scientific observations. By contrast, the reductions of mental terms in Rylean behaviorism are supposedly based on analyses of concepts rather than on observation. In that sense, the reductions are not empirical, but *a priori* (their truth or falsehood is *not* dependent on observation, including the kind that supports scientific theory). ED.

[5] This description of "analytical philosophy" fits Ryle's logical behaviorism very well (see my concluding remarks after Reading 2). ED.

[6] The synonymy-class of the word "temperature" consists of all expressions in whatever language that have the same meaning as "temperature." ED.

[7] There are some well-known remarks by Alonzo Church on this topic. Those remarks do not bear (as might at first be supposed) on the identification of concepts with synonymy-classes as such, but rather support the view that (in formal semantics) it is necessary to retain Frege's distinction between the normal and the "oblique" use of expressions. That is, even if we say that the concept of temperature *is* the synonymy-class of the word 'temperature,' we must not thereby be led into the error of supposing that 'the concept of temperature' is synonymous with 'the synonymy-class of the word "temperature"'—for then 'the concept of temperature' and 'der Begriff der Temperatur' would not be synonymous, which they are. Rather, we must say that 'the concept of temperature' *refers to* the synonymy-class of the word 'temperature' (on this particular reconstruction); but that class is *identified* not as "the synonymy class to which such-and-such a word belongs," but in another way (e.g., as the synonymy-class whose members have such-and-such a characteristic use).

[8] The *intension* of a term or concept is its definition, its internal content, and is usually opposed to the concept or term's *extension* (the range of items to which the concept or term applies). ED.

[9] This would include Ryle and other "ordinary language" philosophers. ED.

of English. But the arguments offered are hardly convincing. For example, if the fact that I can know that I am in pain without knowing that I am in brain state S shows that pain cannot be brain state S, then, by exactly the same argument, the fact that I can know that the stove is hot without knowing that the mean molecular kinetic energy is high (or even that molecules exist) shows that it is *false* that temperature is mean molecular kinetic energy, physics to the contrary. In fact, all that immediately follows from the fact that I can know that I am in pain without knowing that I am in brain state S is that the concept of pain is not the same concept as the concept of being in brain state S. But either pain, or the state of being in pain, or some pain, or some pain state, might still be brain state S. After all, the concept of temperature is not the same concept as the concept of mean molecular kinetic energy. But temperature is mean molecular kinetic energy.

Some philosophers maintain that both 'pain is a brain state' and 'pain states are brain states' are unintelligible. The answer is to explain to these philosophers, as well as we can, given the vagueness of all scientific methodology, what sorts of considerations lead one to make an empirical reduction (i.e., to say such things as "water is H_2O," "light is electro-magnetic radiation," "temperature is mean molecular kinetic energy").[10] If, without giving reasons, he still maintains in the face of such examples that one cannot imagine parallel circumstances for the use of 'pains are brain states' (or, perhaps, 'pain states are brain states') one has grounds to regard him as perverse.

Some philosophers maintain that "P_1 is P_2" is something that can be true, when the 'is' involved is the 'is' of empirical reduction, only when the properties P_1 and P_2 are (a) associated with a spatiotemporal region; and (b) the region is one and the same in both cases. Thus "temperature is mean molecular kinetic energy" is an admissible empirical reduction, since the temperature and the molecular energy are associated with the same spacetime region, but "having a pain in my arm is being in a brain state" is not, since the spatial regions involved are different.

This argument does not appear very strong. Surely no one is going to be deterred from saying that mirror images are light reflected from an object and then from the surface of a mirror by the fact that an image can be "located" three feet *behind* the mirror! (Moreover, one can always find *some* common property of the reductions one is willing to allow—e.g., temperature is mean molecular kinetic energy—which is not a property of some one identification one wishes to disallow. This is not very impressive unless one has an argument to show that the very purposes of such identification depend upon the common property in question.)

Again, other philosophers have contended that all the predictions that can be derived from the conjunction of neurophysiological laws with such statements as "pain states are such-and-such brain states" can equally well be derived from the conjunction of the same neurophysiological laws with "being in pain is correlated with such-and-such brain states," and hence (sic!) there can be no methodological grounds for saying that pains (or pain states) *are* brain states, as opposed to saying that they are *correlated* (invariantly) with brain states. This argument, too, would show that light is only correlated with electromagnetic radiation. The mistake is in ignoring the fact that, although the theories in question may indeed lead to the same predictions, they open and exclude different *questions*. "Light is invariantly correlated with electromagnetic radiation" would leave open the questions "What is the light then, if it isn't the same as the electromagnetic radiation?" and "What makes the light accompany the electromagnetic radiation?"—questions which are excluded by saying that the light *is* the electromagnetic radiation. Similarly, the purpose of saying that pains are brain states is precisely to exclude from empirical meaningfulness the questions "What is the pain, then, if it isn't the same as the brain state?" and "What makes the pain accompany the brain state?" If there are grounds to suggest that these questions represent, so to speak, the wrong way to look at the matter, then those grounds are grounds for a theoretical identification of pains with brain states.

If all arguments to the contrary are unconvincing, shall we then conclude that it is meaningful (and perhaps true) to say either that pains are brain states or that pain states are brain states?

---

[10] Place, in Reading 5, and Smart, in Reading 6, advance explanations of this sort. Ed.

(1) It is perfectly meaningful (violates no "rule of English," involves no "extension of usage") to say "pains are brain states."

(2) It is not meaningful (involves a "changing of meaning" or "an extension of usage," etc.) to say "pains are brain states."

My own position is not expressed by either (1) or (2). It seems to me that the notions "change of meaning" and "extension of usage" are simply so ill-defined that one cannot in fact say *either* (1) or (2). I see no reason to believe that either the linguist, or the man-on-the-street, or the philosopher possesses today a notion of "change of meaning" applicable to such cases as the one we have been discussing. The *job* for which the notion of change of meaning was developed in the history of the language was just a *much* cruder job than this one.

But, if we don't assert either (1) or (2)—in other words, if we regard the "change of meaning" issue as a pseudo-issue in this case—then how are we to discuss the question with which we started? "Is pain a brain state?"

The answer is to allow statements of the form "pain is A," where 'pain' and 'A' are in no sense synonyms, and to see whether any such statement can be found which might be acceptable on empirical and methodological grounds. This is what we shall now proceed to do.

II. IS PAIN A BRAIN STATE?

We shall discuss "Is pain a brain state?," then. And we have agreed to waive the "change of meaning" issue.

Since I am discussing not what the concept of pain comes to, but what pain is, in a sense of 'is' which requires empirical theory-construction (or, at least, empirical speculation), I shall not apologize for advancing an empirical hypothesis. Indeed, my strategy will be to argue that pain is *not* a brain state, not on *a priori* grounds, but on the grounds that another hypothesis is more plausible. The detailed development and verification of my hypothesis would be just as Utopian a task as the detailed development and verification of the brain-state hypothesis. But the putting-forward, not of detailed and scientifically "finished" hypotheses, but of schemata for hypotheses, has long been a function of philosophy. I shall, in short, argue that pain is not a brain state, in the sense of a physical-chemical state of the brain (or even the whole nervous system), but another *kind* of state entirely. I propose the hypothesis that pain, or the state of being in pain, is a functional state of a whole organism.

To explain this it is necessary to introduce some technical notions. In previous papers I have explained the notion of a Turing Machine and discussed the use of this notion as a model for an organism. The notion of a Probabilistic Automaton[11] is defined similarly to a Turing Machine, except that the transitions between "states" are allowed to be with various probabilities rather than being "deterministic." (Of course, a Turing Machine is simply a special kind of Probabilistic Automaton, one with transition probabilities 0, 1.) I shall assume the notion of a Probabilistic Automaton has been generalized to allow for "sensory inputs" and "motor outputs"—that is, the Machine Table specifies, for every possible combination of a "state" and a complete set of "sensory inputs," an "instruction" which determines the probability of the next "state," and also the probabilities of the "motor outputs." (This replaces the idea of the Machine as printing on a tape.)[12] I shall also assume that the physical realization of the sense organs responsible for the various inputs, and of the motor organs, is specified, but that the "states" and the "inputs" themselves are, as usual, specified only "implicitly"—i.e., by the set of transition probabilities given by the Machine Table.

Since an empirically given system can simultaneously be a "physical realization" of many different Probabilistic Automata, I introduce the notion of a *Description* of a system. A Description of S where S is a system, is any true statement to the effect that S possesses distinct states $S_1, S_2, \ldots, S_n$ which are related to one another and to the motor outputs and sensory inputs by the transition probabilities given in such-and-such a Machine Table.[13]

---

[11] See section 2 of Reading 15. Ed.

[12] Instead of reading a tape, the automaton senses or detects events (see the discussion of a control system in section 2 of Reading 4). Presumably, the interactions between the environment and the automaton's receptors are **transduced** into binary form. Similarly, instead of printing its output on a tape, the automaton will generate output in binary form that will be transduced into forms of energy that direct the behavior of the body parts associated with the automaton. Ed.

[13] See section 2 of Reading 15. Ed.

The Machine Table mentioned in the Description will then be called the Functional Organization of S relative to that Description, and the S_i such that S is in state S_i at a given time will be called the Total State of S (at that time) relative to that Description. It should be noted that knowing the Total State of a system relative to a Description involves knowing a good deal about how the system is likely to "behave," given various combinations of sensory inputs, but does *not* involve knowing the physical realization of the S_i as, e.g., physical-chemical states of the brain. The S_i, to repeat, are specified only *implicitly* by the Description—i.e., specified *only* by the set of transition probabilities given in the Machine Table.

The hypothesis that "being in pain is a functional state of the organism" may now be spelled out more exactly as follows:

(1) All organisms capable of feeling pain are Probabilistic Automata.

(2) Every organism capable of feeling pain possesses at least one Description of a certain kind (i.e., being capable of feeling pain *is* possessing an appropriate kind of Functional Organization).

(3) No organism capable of feeling pain possesses a decomposition into parts which separately possess Descriptions of the kind referred to in (2).

(4) For every Description of the kind referred to in (2), there exists a subset of the sensory inputs such that an organism with that Description is in pain when and only when some of its sensory inputs are in that subset.

This hypothesis is admittedly vague, though surely no vaguer than the brain-state hypothesis in its present form. For example, one would like to know more about the kind of Functional Organization that an organism must have to be capable of feeling pain, and more about the marks that distinguish the subset of the sensory inputs referred to in (4). With respect to the first question, one can probably say that the Functional Organization must include something that resembles a "preference function," or at least a preference partial ordering, and something that resembles an "inductive logic"

(i.e., the Machine must be able to "learn from experience"). (The meaning of these conditions, for Automata models, is discussed in my paper "The Mental Life of Some Machines.") In addition, it seems natural to require that the Machine possess "pain sensors," i.e., sensory organs which normally signal damage to the Machine's body, or dangerous temperatures, pressures, etc., which transmit a special subset of the inputs, the subset referred to in (4). Finally, and with respect to the second question, we would want to require at least that the inputs in the distinguished subset have a high disvalue on the Machine's preference function or ordering (further conditions are discussed in "The Mental Life of Some Machines"). The purpose of condition (3) is to rule out such "organisms" (if they can count as such) as swarms of bees as single pain-feelers. The condition (1) is, obviously, redundant, and is only introduced for expository reasons. (It is, in fact, empty, since everything is a Probabilistic Automaton under *some* Description.) [14]

I contend, in passing, that this hypothesis, in spite of its admitted vagueness, is far *less* vague than the "physical-chemical state" hypothesis is today, and far more susceptible to investigation of both a mathematical and an empirical kind. Indeed, to investigate this hypothesis is just to attempt to produce "mechanical" models of organisms—and isn't this, in a sense, just what psychology is about? The difficult step, of course, will be to pass from models of *specific* organisms to a *normal form* for the psychological description of organisms [15]—for this is what is required to make (2) and (4) precise. But this too seems to be an inevitable part of the program of psychology.

I shall now compare the hypothesis just advanced with (a) the hypothesis that pain is a brain state, and (b) the hypothesis that pain is a behavior disposition.

---

[14] See Bruce White's caution about the "universal realizability thesis" toward the end of section 7 in Reading 15. ED.

[15] This "normal form" would have to be very abstract indeed. It should apply to all *organisms*, whether carbon-based like those on earth or not, of whatever body form with whatever functional equivalent of a brain and nervous system. An organism in pain would have to be described without resort to introspection of what it is like to be in pain, without resort to physically specified body parts and materials and to the kinds of behavior that are strongly linked to them (e.g., groaning or crying out). ED.

III. FUNCTIONAL STATE VERSUS BRAIN STATE

It may, perhaps, be asked if I am not somewhat unfair in taking the brain-state theorist to be talking about *physical-chemical* states of the brain. But (a) these are the only sorts of states ever mentioned by brain-state theorists. (b) The brain-state theorist usually mentions (with a certain pride, slightly reminiscent of the Village Atheist) the incompatibility of his hypothesis with all forms of dualism and mentalism. This is natural if physical-chemical states of the brain are what is at issue. However, functional states of whole systems are something quite different. In particular, the functional-state hypothesis is *not* incompatible with dualism! Although it goes without saying that the hypothesis is "mechanistic" in its inspiration, it is a slightly remarkable fact that a system consisting of a body and a "soul," if such things there be, can perfectly well be a Probabilistic Automaton.[16] (c) One argument advanced by Smart is that the brain-state theory assumes only "physical" properties, and Smart finds "non-physical" properties unintelligible. The Total States and the "inputs" defined above are, of course, neither mental nor physical *per se,* and I cannot imagine a functionalist advancing this argument. (d) If the brain-state theorist does mean (or at least allow) states other than physical-chemical states, then his hypothesis is completely empty, at least until he specifies *what* sort of "states" he *does* mean.

Taking the brain-state hypothesis in this way, then, what reasons are there to prefer the functional-state hypothesis over the brain-state hypothesis? Consider what the brain-state theorist has to do to make good his claims. He has to specify a physical-chemical state such that *any* organism (not just a mammal) is in pain if and only if (a) it possesses a brain of a suitable physical-chemical structure; and (b) its brain is in that physical-chemical state. This means that the physical-chemical state in question must be a possible state of a mammalian brain, a reptilian brain, a mollusc's brain (octopuses are mollusca, and certainly feel pain), etc. At the same time, it must *not* be a possible (physically possible) state of the brain of any physically possible creature that cannot feel pain. Even if such a state can be found, it must be nomologically certain that it will also be a state of the brain of any extra-terrestrial life that may be found that will be capable of feeling pain before we can even entertain the supposition that it may *be* pain.

It is not altogether impossible that such a state will be found. Even though octopus and mammal are examples of parallel (rather than sequential) evolution, for example, virtually identical structures (physically speaking) have evolved in the eye of the octopus and in the eye of the mammal, notwithstanding the fact that this organ has evolved from different kinds of cells in the two cases. Thus it is at least possible that parallel evolution, all over the universe, might *always* lead to *one and the same* physical "correlate" of pain. But this is certainly an ambitious hypothesis.

Finally, the hypothesis becomes still more ambitious when we realize that the brain state theorist is not just saying that *pain* is a brain state; he is, of course, concerned to maintain that *every* psychological state is a brain state. Thus if we can find even one psychological predicate which can clearly be applied to both a mammal and an octopus (say "hungry"), but whose physical-chemical "correlate" is different in the two cases, the brain-state theory has collapsed. It seems to me overwhelmingly probable that we can do this. Granted, in such a case the brain-state theorist can save himself by *ad hoc* assumptions (e.g., defining the disjunction of two states to be a single "physical-chemical state"), but this does not have to be taken seriously.[17]

Turning now to the considerations *for* the functional-state theory, let us begin with the fact that we identify organisms as in pain, or hungry, or angry, or in heat, etc., on the basis of their *behavior.* But it is a truism that similarities in the behavior of two systems are at least a reason to suspect similarities in the functional organization of the two systems, and a much *weaker* reason to suspect similarities in the actual physical details. Moreover, we expect the various psychological states—at least the basic ones, such as hunger, thirst, aggression, etc.—

---

[16] This claim is not immune to objection. For further discussion of the issue of constraints on the realizability of automata, see section 7 (esp. footnotes 11 and 13) of Reading 15. ED.

[17] If we were to claim that a certain kind of mental state, such as pain, is (nothing but) a certain kind of physical state in one sort of organism, and another in another, we are not analyzing what is *mental* about the different physical states. The claim would risk being vacuous. ED.

to have more or less similar "transition probabilities" (within wide and ill-defined limits, to be sure) with each other and with behavior in the case of different species, because this is an artifact of the way in which we identify these states. Thus, we would not count an animal as *thirsty* if its "unsatiated" behavior did not seem to be directed toward drinking and was not followed by "satiation for liquid." Thus any animal that we count as capable of these various states will at least *seem* to have a certain rough kind of functional organization. And, as already remarked, if the program of finding psychological laws that are not species-specific—i.e., of finding a normal form for psychological theories of different species—ever succeeds, then it will bring in its wake a delineation of the kind of functional organization that is necessary and sufficient for a given psychological state, as well as a precise definition of the notion "psychological state." In contrast, the brain-state theorist has to hope for the eventual development of neurophysiological laws that are species-independent, which seems much less reasonable than the hope that psychological laws (of a sufficiently general kind) may be species-independent, or, still weaker, that a species-independent *form* can be found in which psychological laws can be written.

IV. FUNCTIONAL STATE VERSUS BEHAVIOR-DISPOSITION

The theory that being in pain is neither a brain state nor a functional state but a behavior disposition has one apparent advantage: it appears to agree with the way in which we verify that organisms are in pain. We do not in practice know anything about the brain state of an animal when we say that it is in pain; and we possess little if any knowledge of its functional organization, except in a crude intuitive way. In fact, however, this "advantage" is no advantage at all: for, although statements about how we verify that *x* is *A* may have a good deal to do with what the concept of being *A* comes to, they have precious little to do with what the property *A* is. To argue on the ground just mentioned that pain is neither a brain state nor a functional state is like arguing that heat is not mean molecular kinetic energy from the fact that ordinary people do not (they think) ascertain the mean molecular kinetic energy

of something when they verify that it is hot or cold. It is not necessary that they should; what is necessary is that the marks that they take as indications of heat should in fact be explained by the mean molecular kinetic energy. And, similarly, it is necessary to our hypothesis that the marks that are taken as behavioral indications of pain should be explained by the fact that the organism is in a functional state of the appropriate kind, but not that speakers should *know* that this is so.

The difficulties with "behavior disposition" accounts are so well known that I shall do little more than recall them here. The difficulty—it appears to be more than "difficulty," in fact—of specifying the required behavior disposition except as "the disposition of X to behave as if X were in *pain*," is the chief one, of course.[18] In contrast, we *can* specify the functional state with which we propose to identify pain, at least roughly, without using the notion of pain. Namely, the functional state we have in mind is the state of receiving sensory inputs which play a certain role in the Functional Organization of the organism. This role is characterized, at least partially, by the fact that the sense organs responsible for the inputs in question are organs whose function is to detect damage to the body, or dangerous extremes of temperature, pressure, etc., and by the fact that the "inputs" themselves, whatever their physical realization, represent a condition that the organism assigns a high disvalue to. As I stressed in "The Mental Life of Some Machines," this does *not* mean that the Machine will always *avoid* being in the condition in question ("pain"); it only means that the condition will be avoided unless not avoiding it is necessary to the attainment of some more highly valued goal. Since the behavior of the Machine (in this case, an organism) will depend not merely on the sensory inputs, but also on the Total State (i.e., on other values, beliefs, etc.), it seems hopeless to make any general statement about how an organism in such a condition *must* behave;[19] but this does not mean that we must

---

[18] Think of all the different ways that one could behave when in pain—ways too many and too various to be included or characterized in a useful definition. ED.

[19] And yet it is just such a general statement that logical behaviorism is committed to making, because it insists that mental states such as pain, thirst, or anger consist entirely in being dispositions to behavior of one kind or another. ED.

abandon hope of characterizing the condition. Indeed, we have just characterized it.[20]

Not only does the behavior-disposition theory seem hopelessly vague; if the "behavior" referred to is peripheral behavior, and the relevant stimuli are peripheral stimuli (e.g., we do not say anything about what the organism will do if its brain is operated upon), then the theory seems clearly false. For example, two animals with all motor nerves cut will have the same actual and potential "behavior" (viz., none to speak of); but if one has cut pain fibers and the other has uncut pain fibers, then one will feel pain and the other won't. Again, if one person has cut pain fibers, and another suppresses all pain responses deliberately due to some strong compulsion, then the actual and potential peripheral behavior may be the same, but one will feel pain and the other one won't.[21] (Some philosophers maintain that this last case is conceptually impossible, but the only evidence for this appears to be that *they* can't, or don't want to, conceive of it.)[22] If, instead of pain, we take some sensation the "bodily expression" of which is easier to suppress—say, a slight coolness in one's left little finger—the case becomes even clearer.

Finally, even if there *were* some behavior disposition invariantly correlated with pain (species-independently!), and specifiable without using the term 'pain,' it would still be more plausible to identify being in pain with some state whose presence *explains* this behavior disposition—the brain state or functional state—than with the behavior disposition itself. Such considerations of plausibility may be somewhat subjective; but if other things *were* equal (of course, they aren't) why shouldn't we allow considerations of plausibility to play the deciding role?

V. METHODOLOGICAL CONSIDERATIONS

So far we have considered only what might be called the "empirical" reasons for saying that being in pain is a functional state, rather than a brain state or behavior disposition; viz., that it seems more likely that the functional state we described is invariantly "correlated" with pain, species-independently, than that there is either a physical-chemical state of the brain (must an organism have a *brain* to feel pain? perhaps some ganglia will do) or a behavior disposition so correlated. If this is correct, then it follows that the identification we proposed is at least a candidate for consideration. What of methodological considerations?

The methodological considerations are roughly similar in all cases of reduction, so no surprises need be expected here. First, identification of psychological states with functional states means that the laws of psychology can be derived from statements of the form "such-and-such organisms have such-and-such Descriptions" together with the identification statements ("being in pain is such-and-such a functional state," etc.).[23] Secondly, the presence of the functional state (i.e., of inputs which play the role we have described in the Functional Organization of the organism) is not merely "correlated with" but actually explains the pain behavior on the part of the organism. Thirdly, the identification serves to exclude questions which (if a naturalistic view is correct) represent an altogether wrong way of looking at the matter, e.g., "What *is* pain if it isn't either the brain state or the functional state?" and "What causes the pain to be always accompanied by this sort of functional state?" In short, the identification is to be tentatively accepted as a theory which leads to both fruitful predictions and to fruitful *questions,* and which serves to discourage fruitless and empirically senseless questions, where by 'empirically senseless' I mean "senseless" not merely from the standpoint of verification, but from the standpoint of what there in fact *is.*

---

[20] In "The Mental Life of Some Machines" a further, and somewhat independent, characteristic of the pain inputs is discussed in terms of Automata models—namely the spontaneity of the inclination to withdraw the injured part, etc. This raises the question, which is discussed in that paper, of giving a functional analysis of the notion of a spontaneous inclination. Of course, still further characteristics come readily to mind—for example, that feelings of pain are (or seem to be) *located* in the parts of the body.

[21] If you still sympathize with the logical behaviorist notion that pain is not an internal state, but merely a disposition (= likelihood) of behaving a certain way, ask yourself if you would be willing to be "anesthetized," prior to what would otherwise be painful surgery, with only curare—a substance that would remove all likelihood of engaging in pain behavior by paralyzing all your muscles. ED.

[22] Cf. the discussion of "super-spartans" in "Brains and Behavior."

[23] A psychological law would be something like "Whenever an organism is in pain, and in such and such circumstances, then it will. . . ." The term "pain" specifies certain kinds of sensory input, and the machine table "Description" enables a prediction of behavior given the specification of other sensory input to specify the content of "such and such circumstances." ED.

In "Philosophy and our Mental Life" (1975), a paper given six years after the first publication of "The Nature of Mental States," Putnam rejected as simplistic and inadequate his hypothesis that a human organism as a whole is a Turing machine and that psychological states such as pain could be identified with single Turing machine states or disjunctive sets of such states. It's not hard to see the problem. A pain, by itself, could never constitute the entire psychological state that a human organism is in, the state that would determine its full response to the entire range of its current sensory input at the time that it is experiencing pain. The complete psychological state will include other perceptions, beliefs, memories, intentions, and so on. Since pain can't be the entire psychological state, it can't be the machine state of a human Turing machine.

Moreover, Turing machine states are intrinsically independent of each other. A current state may have been actualized by the combination of a preceding state and an input, but the current state is what it is regardless of the prior history of the machine. Psychological states are quite otherwise. The reason why I don't just get up and leave the dentist chair when the anesthetizing needle hurts my gum is that my prior psychological states included a toothache and the intention of going to the dentist, and these prior states determine the content of my current state and thereby condition my behavior. So again it just doesn't seem that a psychological state can be understood as a Turing machine state.

These objections against Putnam's 1967 hypothesis do not immediately refute the general thesis that human mental processes are best understood in terms of the operations of a digital computer. Let's refer to this more general view as the *computational model* of the human mind. A defender of this model could point out that it doesn't require us to think of the entire human organism as a single Turing machine or automaton. Instead, a human being could be a system with a computational *sub*system (such as an adaptive control system) composed of any number of automata working in parallel and perhaps even as part of a neural net. John R. Searle, in Reading 18, will put forward more sweeping objections against the very idea of assimilating human mentality to the workings of an automaton.

REVIEW QUESTION

Look again at what Putnam has to say in section II about the organism–machine's "preference function" as an important functional characteristic of pain. Some critics (such as Campbell in Reading 24) have argued that this sort of analysis fails to capture the clearly felt difference between two equally intense but qualitatively different pains such as a muscle pain and a toothache. From a functional point of view, each could do the *job* of the other, and thus the functional account is inadequate. What do you think?

17

Methodological Solipsism Considered as a Research Strategy in Cognitive Psychology[1]

J. A. Fodor

. . . to form the idea of an object and to form an idea simply is the same thing; the reference of the idea to an object being an extraneous denomination, of which in itself it bears no mark or character. Hume's *Treatise,* Book I

(For information on Fodor, see Reading 11)

The theory of mental processes that Fodor outlines in this reading is a variant of representationalism (or the representational theory of mind). According to this theory, minds are not directly related to objects in the world; instead, the perceiving or knowing subject is directly related to or aware of some intermediate intramental entity. Descartes, Locke, and many other philosophers of the seventeenth and eighteenth centuries called these entities "ideas." Ideas were supposed to be the immediate objects of perception, and thinking processes related ideas to one another. Ideas stood in some hard-to-define relation to objects in the world—for instance, they were supposed to resemble them to some degree, more so in the case of mathematical ideas of the *primary qualities* of things, and less so in the case of the more sensuous ideas of *secondary qualities.* Although something like this theory is hard to avoid in thinking of the mind's relation to the world, it was susceptible to the serious objection raised by Berkeley and others that if awareness was only of ideas, then the relation between ideas and objects in the world becomes unintelligible, and we are left with nothing but ideas.

Fodor's version of representationalism substitutes "symbols" for ideas. The entities he calls symbols are comparable to the sequences of bits and bytes embodied in states of computer circuits. As it is with computers, the notion of a symbol here is clearly a functional one. Something

[1] I've had a lot of help with this one. I'm particularly indebted to: Professors Ned Block, Sylvain Bromberger, Janet Dean Fodor, Keith Gundersen, Roben Richardson, Judith Thomson; and to Mr. Israel Krakowski.

is a symbol not because of its physical nature, but solely in virtue of the role it plays within a certain sort of system. Instead of the quasi-pictorial relation of seventeenth-century ideas to objects, we have "propositional contents," "meanings," or "interpretations" that somehow get assigned to symbol sequences from outside the symbol-processing system. Just as seventeenth-century representationalists understood thinking processes as relating *ideas* to *ideas,* so Fodor's computational model of mental processes limits the mind to relating *symbols* (or sequences thereof) to each other. Just as for Descartes or Locke, the mind can compare a branch to a tree only in virtue of the relations that the relevant *ideas* have to one another, so in Fodor's theory the mind's comparison of branch to tree is limited to the relations that the relevant *symbol sequences* have to one another, specifically their *syntactical* relations (e.g., the way symbols combine into well-formed formulae and one formula follows another in inferential sequences).

Just as, in Descartes or Locke, the mind is directly aware of only itself and its ideas, so in Fodor's theory, psychological states as such cannot include any relation to the world of *objects* symbolically represented in these states. In both forms of representationalism, the mind is, as it were, *alone with its contents,* a situation philosophers call *solipsism.* Because his solipsism is limited to psychological theory, and is not a metaphysical statement about what (else) exists, Fodor calls his theory *methodological solipsism.*

Your standard contemporary cognitive psychologist—your thoroughly modern mentalist[2]—is disposed to reason as follows. To think (e.g.) that Marvin is melancholy is to represent Marvin in a certain way; viz., as being melancholy (and not, for example, as being maudlin, morose, moody, or merely moping and dyspeptic). But surely we cannot represent Marvin as being melancholy except as we are in some or other relation to a representation of Marvin; and not just to *any* representation of Marvin, but, in particular, to a representation the content of which is *that* Marvin is melancholy; a representation which, as it were, expresses the proposition that Marvin is melancholy. So, a fortiori, at least some mental states/processes are or involve at least some relations to at least some representations. Perhaps, then, this is the *typical* feature of such mental states/processes as cognitive psychology studies; perhaps all such states can be viewed as relations to representations and all such processes as operations defined on representations.

This is, prima facie, an appealing proposal since it gives the psychologist two degrees of freedom to play with and they seem, intuitively, to be the right two. On the one hand, mental states are distinguished by the *content* of the associated representations, so we can allow for the difference between thinking that Marvin is melancholy and thinking that Sam is (or that Albert isn't, or that it sometimes snows in Cincinnati); and, on the other hand, mental states are distinguished by the *relation* that the subject bears to the associated representation (so we can allow for the difference between thinking, hoping, supposing, doubting and pretending that Marvin is melancholy). It's hard to believe that a serious psychology could make do with fewer (or less refined) distinctions than these, and it's hard to believe that a psychology that makes these distinctions could avoid taking the notion of mental representation seriously. Moreover, the burden of argument is clearly upon anyone who claims that we need *more* degrees of freedom than just these two: the least hypothesis that is remotely plausible is that a mental state is (type) individuated by specifying a relation and a representation such that the subject bears the one to the other.[3]

From: Jerry A. Fodor, "Methodological Solipsism Considered as a Research Strategy in Cognitive Psychology," in *The Behavioral and Brain Sciences* III, 1 (March, 1980): 63–72. Copyright © 1980 by Cambridge University Press. Reprinted with the permission of Cambridge University Press.

[2]A psychological theory is *mentalist* insofar as it uses explicitly mental or intentional states or processes as explanatory entities. What Fodor calls a "thoroughly modern" mentalist would seem to be someone who is a materialist rather than a dualist, who has adopted the research strategy of computational modeling of mental states, and understands mental states as cognitive—as having propositional content to which the subject has a propositional attitude such as belief or doubt. ED.

[3]I shall speak of "type identity" (distinctness) of mental states to pick out the sense of "same mental state" in which, for example, John and Mary are in the same mental state if both believe that water flows. Correspondingly, I shall use the notion of "token identity" (distinctness) of mental state to pick out the sense of "same mental state" in which it's necessary that if x and y are in the same mental state, then x = y.

I'll say that any psychology that takes this line is a version of the REPRESENTATIONAL THEORY OF THE MIND. I think that it's reasonable to adopt some such theory as a sort of working hypothesis, if only because there aren't any alternatives which seem to be even remotely plausible and because empirical research carried out within this framework has, thus far, proved interesting and fruitful.[4] However, my present concern is neither to attack nor to defend this view, but rather to distinguish it from something other—and stronger—that modern cognitive psychologists also hold. I shall put this stronger doctrine as the view that mental states and process are COMPUTATIONAL. Much of what is characteristic of cognitive psychology is a consequence of adherence to this stronger view. What I want to do in this paper is to say something about what this stronger view is, something about why I think it's plausible, and, most of all, something about the ways in which it shapes the cognitive psychology we have.

I take it that computational processes are both *symbolic*[5] and *formal*[6]. They are symbolic because they are defined over representations, and they are formal because they apply to representations, in virtue of (roughly) the *syntax* of the representations. It's the second of these conditions that makes the claim that mental processes are computational stronger than the representational theory of the mind. Most of this paper will be a meditation upon the consequences of assuming that mental processes are formal processes.

I'd better cash the parenthetical "roughly." To say that an operation is formal isn't the same as saying that it is syntactic since we could have formal processes defined over representations which don't, in any obvious sense, *have* a syntax. Rotating an image would be a timely example. What makes syntactic operations a species of formal operations is that being syntactic is a way of *not* being semantic.

Formal operations are the ones that are specified without reference to such semantic properties of representations as, for example, truth, reference and meaning. Since we don't know how to complete this list (since, that is, we don't know what semantic properties there are), I see no responsible way of saying what, in general, formality amounts to. The notion of formality will thus have to remain intuitive and metaphoric, at least for present purposes: formal operations apply in terms of the, as it were, "shapes" of the objects in their domains.[7]

To require that mental processes be computational (viz., formal-syntactic) is thus to require something not very clear. Still, the requirement has some clear consequences, and they are striking and tendentious. Consider that we started by assuming that the *content* of representations is a (type) individuating feature of mental states.[8] So far as the *representational* theory of the mind is concerned, it's possibly the *only* thing that distinguishes Peter's thought that Sam is silly from his thought that Sally is depressed. But, now, if the *computational* theory of the mind is true (and if, as we may assume, content is a semantic notion par excellence) it follows that content alone cannot distinguish thoughts. More exactly, the computational theory of the mind requires that two thoughts can be distinct in content only if they can be identified with relations to formally distinct representations. More generally: fix the subject and the relation, and then mental states can be (type) distinct only if the representations which constitute their objects are formally distinct.[9]

Again, consider that accepting a formality condition upon mental states implies a drastic narrowing of the ordinary ontology of the mental; all sorts of states which look, prima facie, to be mental states in good standing are going to turn out to be none of the psychologist's business if the formality condition is endorsed. This point is one that philosophers

---

[4] For extensive discussion, see Fodor (1975).

[5] The term "symbol" is often used, as in this case, without definition. In general, a symbol is something that "stands for" or "signifies" or is a sign for something else. However, each of these terms is equally in need of analysis. As Fodor is using the term, it seems to mean the same as "representation." ED.

[6] To say that computational processes are *formal* is to say that they relate not to the content or interpretation of symbols, but instead to characteristics such as their syntax (the ways in which they are combined in strings, sentences or formulae) or shape. ED.

[7] This is not, notice, the same as saying "formal operations are the ones that apply mechanically"; in this latter sense, *formality* means something like *explicitness*. There's no particular reason for using "formal" to mean both "syntactic" and "explicit," though the ambiguity abounds in the literature.

[8] The *type* might be as specific as the belief that John is in the room. Even such a highly specific state might be instantiated in indefinitely many people who are acquainted with John. ED.

[9] If mental processes are computational, they can work only with *formal* differences between representations. So unless the (semantic) differences in content is reflected in formal (typically syntactic) differences, the mental system cannot recognize the differences in content. ED.

have made in a number of contexts, and usually in a deprecating tone of voice. Take, for example, knowing that such-and-such, and assume that you can't know what's not the case. Since, on that assumption, knowledge is involved with truth, and since truth is a semantic notion, it's going to follow that there can't be a psychology of *knowledge* (even if it is consonant with the formality condition to hope for a psychology of *belief*). Similarly, it's a way of making a point of Ryle's to say that, strictly speaking, there can't be a psychology of perception if the formality condition is to be complied with. Seeing is an achievement; you can't see what's not there. From the point of view of the representational theory of the mind, this means that seeing involves relations between mental representations *and their referents;* hence, semantic relations within the meaning of the act.[10]

I hope that such examples suggest (what, in fact, I think is true) that even if the formality condition isn't very clear, it is quite certainly very strong. In fact, I think it's not all *that* anachronistic to see it as the central issue which divides the two main traditions in the history of psychology: "Rational psychology" on the one hand, and "Naturalism" on the other. Since this is a mildly eccentric way of cutting the pie, I'm going to permit myself a semi-historical excursus before returning to the main business of the paper.

Descartes argued that there is an important sense in which how the world is makes no difference to one's mental states. Here is a well-known passage from the *Meditations:*

> At this moment it does indeed seem to me that it is with eyes awake that I am looking at this paper, that this head which I move is not asleep, that it is deliberately and of set purpose that I extend my hand and perceive it. . . . But in thinking over this I remind myself that on many occasions I have been deceived by similar illusions, and in dwelling on this reflection I see so manifestly that there are no certain indications by which we may clearly distinguish wakefulness from sleep that I am lost in astonishment. And my astonishment is such that it is almost capable of persuading me that I now dream. (Descartes 1931)

At least three sorts of reactions to this kind of argument are distinguishable in the philosophical literature. First, there's a long tradition, including both **Rationalists** and **Empiricists**, which takes it as axiomatic that one's experiences (and, a fortiori, one's beliefs) might have been just as they are even if the world had been quite different from the way that it is. See, for example, the passage from Hume which serves as an epigraph to this paper. Second, there's a vaguely Wittgensteinian mood in which one argues that it's just *false* that one's mental states might have been what they are had the world been relevantly different. For example, if there had been a dagger there, Macbeth would have been *seeing* not just hallucinating. And what could be more different than that? If the Cartesian feels that this reply misses the point, he is at least under an obligation to say precisely which point it misses; in precisely *which* respects the way the world is is irrelevant to the character of one's beliefs, experiences, etc. Finally there's a tradition which argues that—epistemology to one side—it is at best a strategic mistake to attempt to develop a psychology which individuates mental states without reference to their environmental causes and effects (e.g., which counts the state that Macbeth was in as type-identical to the state he would have been in had the dagger been supplied). I have in mind the tradition which includes the American Naturalists (notably Peirce and Dewey), all the learning theorists, and such contemporary representatives as Quine in philosophy and Gibson in psychology. The recurrent theme here is that psychology is a branch of biology, hence that one must view the organism as embedded in a physical environment. The psychologist's job is to trace those organism/environment interactions which constitute its behavior. A passage from William James (1890, p. 6) will serve to give the feel of the thing:

> On the whole, few recent formulas have done more service of a rough sort in psychology than the Spencerian one that the essence of mental life and of bodily life are one, namely, 'the adjustment of inner to outer relations.' Such a formula is vagueness incarnate; but because it takes into account the fact that minds inhabit environments which act on them and on which they in turn react; because; in short, it takes mind in the midst of all its concrete relations, it is immensely more fertile than the old-fashioned 'rational psychology' which treated the soul as a

---

[10] A psychology of perception would encompass relations between representations and their referents. The latter are outside the mind's internal symbol system, and thus cannot have the kinds of formal syntactic properties over which mental processes operate. ED.

detached existent, sufficient unto itself, and assumed to consider only its nature and its properties.

A number of adventitious intrusions have served to muddy the issues in this long-standing dispute. On the one hand, it may well be that Descartes was relying on a specifically introspectionist construal of the claim that the individuation of mental states is independent of their environmental causes. That is, Descartes' point may have been that (a) mental states are (type) identical if and only if (iff) they are introspectively indistinguishable, and (b) introspection cannot distinguish (e.g.) perception from hallucination, or knowledge from belief. On the other hand, the naturalist, in point of historical fact, is often a behaviorist as well. He wants to argue not only that mental states are individuated by reference to organism/environment relations, but also that such relations constitute the mental. In the context of the present discussion, he is arguing for the abandonment not just of the formality condition, but of the notion of mental representation as well.

If, however, we take the computational theory of the mind as what's central to the issue, we can reconstruct the debate between rational psychologists and naturalists in a way that does justice to both their points; in particular, in a way that frees the discussion from involvement with introspectionism on the one side and behaviorism on the other.

Insofar as we think of mental processes as computational (hence as formal operations defined on representations) it will be natural to take the mind to be, inter alia, a kind of computer. That is, we will think of the mind as carrying out whatever symbol manipulations are constitutive of the hypothesized computational processes. To a first approximation, we may thus construe mental operations as pretty directly analogous to those of a Turing machine.[11] There is, for example, a working memory (corresponding to a tape) and there are capacities for scanning and altering the contents of the memory (corresponding to the operations of reading and writing on the tape). If we want to extend the computational metaphor by providing access to information about the environment, we can think of the computer as having access to "oracles" which serve, on occasion, to enter information in the memory. On the intended interpretation of this model, these oracles are analogs to the senses. In particular, they are assumed to be transducers, in that what they write on the tape is determined solely by the ambient environmental energies that impinge upon them. (For elaboration of this sort of account, see Putnam [1960]; it is, of course, widely familiar from discussions in the field of artificial intelligence.)

I'm not endorsing this model, but simply presenting it as a natural extension of the computational picture of the mind. Its present interest is that we can use it to see how the formality condition connects with the Cartesian claim that the character of mental processes is somehow independent of their environmental causes and effects. The point is that, so long as we are thinking of mental processes as purely computational, the bearing of environmental information upon such processes is exhausted by the formal character of whatever the oracles write on the tape. In particular, it doesn't matter to such processes whether what the oracles write is *true;* whether, for example, they really are transducers faithfully mirroring the state of the environment, or merely the output end of a typewriter manipulated by a Cartesian demon bent on deceiving the machine. I'm saying, in effect, that the formality condition, viewed in this context, is tantamount to a sort of methodological solipsism.[12] If mental processes are formal, then they have access only to the formal properties of such representations of the environment as the senses provide. Hence, they have no access to the *semantic* properties of such representations, including the property of being true, of having referents, or, indeed, the property of being representations *of the environment*.

That some such methodological solipsism really is implicated in much current psychological practice is best seen by examining what researchers actually do. Consider, for example, the well known work of Professor Terry Winograd. Winograd was primarily interested in the computer simulation of certain processes involved in the handling of verbal information; asking and answering questions, drawing inferences, following instructions and the like. The form of his theory was a program for a com-

---

[11] See Bruce White's explanation of Turing machines in section 3 of Reading 15. ED.

[12] As far as the *method* of cognitive psychology would be concerned, it would be as if there *is nothing else* but the symbols internal to the mental system since they constitute the only domain over which mental processes can operate. ED.

puter which "lives in" and operates upon a simple world of block like geometric objects (see Winograd 1972). Many of the capacities that the device exercises vis-a-vis its environment seem impressively intelligent. It can arrange the blocks to order, it can issue "perceptual" reports of the present state of its environment and "memory" reports of its past states, it can devise simple plans for achieving desired environmental configurations, and it can discuss its undertakings (more or less in English) with whoever is running the program.

The interesting point for our purposes, however, is that the machine environment which is the nominal object of these actions and conversations actually isn't there. What actually happens is that the programmer so arranges the memory states of the machine that the available data are whatever they would be *if* there were objects for the machine to perceive and manipulate for it to operate upon. In effect, the machine lives in an entirely notional world; all its beliefs are false. Of course, it doesn't matter to the machine that its beliefs are false since falsity is a semantic property and, qua computer, the device satisfies the formality condition; viz., it has access only to formal (nonsemantic) properties of the representations that it manipulates. In effect the device is in precisely the situation that Descartes dreads; it's a mere computer which dreams that it's a robot.

I hope that this discussion suggests how acceptance of the computational theory of the mind leads to a sort of methodological solipsism as a part of the research strategy of contemporary cognitive psychology. In particular, I hope it's clear how you get that consequence from the formality condition alone, without so much as raising the introspection issue. I stress this point because it seems to me that there has been considerable confusion about it among the psychologists themselves. People who do machine simulation, in particular, very often advertise themselves as working on the question how thought (or language) is related to the world. My present point is that, whatever else they're doing, they certainly aren't doing *that*. The very assumption that defines their field—viz., that they study mental processes qua formal operations on symbols—guarantees that their studies won't answer the question how the symbols so manipulated are semantically interpreted. You can, for example,

build a machine that answers baseball questions in the sense that (e.g.) if you type in "Who had the most wins by a National League pitcher since Dizzy Dean?" it will type out "Robin Roberts, who won 28." But you delude yourself if you think that a machine which in this sense answers baseball questions, is thereby answering questions *about* baseball (or that the machine has somehow referred to Robin Roberts). If the *programmer* chooses to interpret the machine inscription "Robin Roberts won 28" as a statement about Robin Roberts (e.g., as the statement that he won 28), that's all well and good, but it's no business of the machine's. The machine has no access to that interpretation, and its computations are in no way affected by it. The machine doesn't know what it's talking about, it doesn't care; *about* is a semantic relation.[13]

This brings us to a point where, having done some sort of justice to the Cartesian's insight, we can also do some sort of justice to the naturalist's. For, after all, mental processes are supposed to be operations on representations, and it is in the nature of representations to represent. We have seen that a psychology which embraces the formality condition is thereby debarred from raising questions about the semantic properties of mental representations; yet surely such questions ought *somewhere* to be raised. The computer which prints out "RR won 28" is not thereby referring to RR. But, surely, when I think: *RR won 28*, I *am* thinking about RR, and if not in virtue of having performed some formal operations on some representations, then presumably in virtue of something else. It's perhaps borrowing the least tendentious fragment of causal theories of reference[14] to assume that what fixes the interpretation of my mental representations of RR is something about the way that he and I are embedded in the world; perhaps not a causal chain stretching between us, but anyhow *some* facts about how he and I are causally situated; *Dasein,*[15]

---

[13] Some fairly deep methodological issues in Artificial Intelligence are involved here. See Fodor (1978) where this surface is lightly scratched.

[14] These are accounts which assert that words are linked to objects in the world by some sort of causal connection or chain of causal connections. ED.

[15] This German word signifies "to exist" or "to be there." It is a major technical term in the philosophy of Martin Heidegger (1889–1976), where it denotes *human* existence, and especially its concrete interrelatedness with others and with the world (a very different perspective from the abstractedness of the Cartesian thinking thing). ED.

as you might say. Only a **naturalistic** psychology will do to specify these facts, because here we are explicitly in the realm of organism/environment transactions.

We are on the verge of a bland and ecumenical conclusion: that there is room both for a computational psychology—viewed as a theory of formal processes defined over mental representations—and a naturalistic psychology, viewed as a theory of the (presumably causal) relations between representations and the world which fix the semantic interpretations of the former. I think that, in principle, this is the right way to look at things. In practice, however, I think that it's misleading. So far as I can see, it's overwhelmingly likely that computational psychology is the only one that we are going to get. I want to argue for this conclusion in two steps. First, I'll argue for what I've till now only assumed: that we must at least have a psychology which accepts the formality condition. Then I'll argue that there's good reason to suppose that that's the most that we can have; that a naturalistic psychology isn't a practical possibility and isn't likely to become one.

The first move, then, is to give reasons for believing that at least *some* part of psychology should honor the formality condition. Here too the argument proceeds in two steps. I'll argue first that it is typically under an *opaque*[16] construal that attributions of propositional attitudes to organisms enter into explanations of their behavior, and second that the formality condition is intimately involved with the explanation of propositional attitudes so construed: roughly, that it's reasonable to believe that we can get such explanations only within computational theories. *Caveat emptor*: the arguments under review are, in large part, nondemonstrative. In particular, they will assume the perfectibility in principle of the kinds of psychological theories now

being developed, and it is entirely possible that this is an assumption contrary to fact.

Thesis: when we articulate the generalizations in virtue of which behavior is contingent upon mental states, it is typically an opaque construal of the mental state attributions that does the work; for example, it's a construal under which believing that *a is F* is logically independent from believing that *b is F*, even in the case where a = b. It will be convenient to speak not only of opaque construals of propositional attitude ascriptions, but also of *opaque taxonomies* of mental state types; e.g., of taxonomies which, inter alia, count the belief that the Morning Star rises in the east as type distinct from the belief that the Evening Star does.[17] (Correspondingly, *transparent* taxonomies are such as, inter alia, would count these beliefs as type-identical). So, the claim is that mental states are typically opaquely taxonomized for purposes of psychological theory.[18]

The point doesn't depend upon the examples, so I'll stick to the most informal sorts of cases. Suppose I know that John wants to meet the girl who lives next door, and suppose I know that this is true when "wants to" is construed opaquely. Then, given even rough-and-ready generalizations about how people's behaviors are contingent upon their utilities, I can make some reasonable predictions (guesses) about what John is likely to do: he's likely to say (viz., utter), "I want to meet the girl who lives next door." He's likely to call upon his neighbor. He's likely (at a minimum, and all things being equal) to exhibit next-door-directed behavior. None of this is frightfully exciting, but it's all I need for present purposes, and what more would you expect from folk psychology?

On the other hand, suppose that all I know is that John wants to meet the girl next door where

---

[16] Terms refer either *opaquely* or *transparently*. If one can substitute for a particular term *a* in an expression any other terms referring to the same thing without affecting the truth of the sentence including the expression, then the expression provides a *transparent context* for that term. If that is not the case, then the term refers opaquely, or the expression is an *opaque context* for that term. Take "water" for instance: since water = H_2O, if water is a liquid, then H_2O is a liquid, and vice versa. "Water" refers *transparently* in this case. However, even if water = H_2O, it is not the case that anyone who *believes* water is a liquid *also believes* that H_2O is a liquid. The person may not know that water = H_2O. The reference of "water" after "believes" is *opaque*. Expressions that state *propositional attitudes* such as belief, hope, or doubt typically create opaque contexts. ED.

[17] The two beliefs would be type-distinct even though "morning star" and "evening star" have the same referent and thus refer to the same fact about the world. ED.

[18] I'm told by some of my friends that this paragraph could be read as suggesting that there are two kinds of beliefs: opaque ones and transparent ones. That is not, of course, the way that it is intended to be read. The idea is rather that there are two kinds of conditions that we can place on determinations that a pair of belief tokens count as tokens of the same belief type. According to one set of conditions (corresponding to transparent taxonomy) a belief that the Morning Star is such and such counts as the same belief as a belief that the Evening Star is such and such; whereas, according to the other set of conditions (corresponding to opaque taxonomy), it does not.

"wants to" is construed transparently; i.e., all I know is that it's true of the girl next door that John wants to meet her. Then there is little or nothing that I can predict[19] about how John is likely to proceed. And this is *not* just because rough and ready psychological generalizations want *ceteris paribus* clauses[20] to fill them in; it's also for the deeper reason that I can't infer from what I know about John to any relevant description of the mental causes of his behavior. For example, I have no reason to predict that John will say such things as "I want to meet the girl who lives next door" since, let John be as cooperative and as truthful as you like, and let him be utterly a native speaker, still, he *may* believe that the girl he wants to meet languishes in Latvia. In which case, "I want to meet the girl who lives next door" is the last thing it will occur to him to say. (The contestant wants to say "suspender," for "suspender" is the magic word. Consider what we can predict about his probable verbal behavior if we take this (a) opaquely and (b) transparently. And, of course, the same sorts of points apply, mutatis mutandis, to the prediction of nonverbal behavior.)

Ontologically, transparent readings are stronger than opaque ones; for example, the former license existential inferences which the latter do not.[21] But psychologically opaque readings are stronger than transparent ones; they tell us more about the character of the mental causes of behavior. The representational theory of mind offers an explanation of this anomaly. Opaque ascriptions are true in virtue of the way that the agent represents the objects of his wants (intentions, beliefs, etc.) *to himself*. And, by assumption, such representations function in the causation of the behaviors that the agent produces. So, for example, to say that it's true *opaquely* that Oedipus did such-and-such because he wanted to marry Jocasta, is to say something like (though not, perhaps, *very* like): "Oedipus said to himself, 'I want to marry Jocasta,' and his so saying was among the causes of his behavior." Whereas to say (only)

that it's true transparently that O. wanted to marry J. is to say no more than that among the causes of his behavior was O.'s saying to himself "I want to marry . . . " where the blank was filled by *some* expression that denotes J.[22] But now, what O. *does,* how he in the proprietary sense behaves, will depend on which description he (literally) had in mind.[23] If it's "Jocasta," courtship behavior follows *ceteris paribus.* Whereas, if it's "my Mum," we have the situation towards the end of the play and Oedipus at Colonus eventually ensues.

I dearly wish that I could leave this topic here, because it would be very convenient to be able to say, without qualification, what I strongly implied above: the opaque readings of propositional attitude ascriptions tell us how people represent the objects of their propositional attitudes. What one would like to say, in particular, is that if two people are identically related to formally identical mental representations, then they are in opaquely type-identical mental states. This would be convenient because it yields a succinct and gratifying characterization of what a computational cognitive psychology is about: such a psychology studies propositional attitudes opaquely taxonomized.

I think, in fact, that this is *roughly* the right thing to say since what I think is *exactly* right is that

---

[22] I'm leaving it open that it may be to say still less than this (e.g., because of problems about reference under false descriptions). For purposes of the present discussion, I don't need to run a line of the truth conditions for transparent propositional attitude ascriptions. Thank Heaven, since I do not have one.

[23] It's worth emphasizing that the sense of "behavior" is proprietary, and that that's pretty much what you would expect. Not every true description of an act can be such that a theory of the mental causation of behavior will explain the act under that description. (In being rude to Darcy, Elizabeth is insulting the man whom she will eventually marry. A theory of the mental causation of her behavior might have access to the former description, but not, surely, to the latter.)

Many philosophers—especially since Wittgenstein—have emphasized the ways in which the description of behavior may depend upon its context, and it is a frequent charge against modern versions of Rational psychology that they typically ignore such characterizations. So they do, but so what? You can't have explanations of everything under every description, and it's a question for empirical determination which descriptions of behavior reveal its systematicity vis-a-vis its causes. The Rational psychologist is prepared to bet that—to put it very approximately—behavior will prove to be systematic under some of the descriptions under which it is intentional.

At a minimum, the present claim goes like this: there is a way of taxonomizing behaviors and a way of taxonomizing mental states such that, given these taxonomies, theories of the mental causation of behavior will be forthcoming. And that way of taxonomizing mental states construes them nontransparently.

---

[19] We don't know, on the transparent construal, whether John even knows that the woman he wants to meet happens to live next door, and thus can't know whether the mental process of wanting to meet the woman next door would ever occur in him. ED.

[20] In the opaque construal we assume many things about John by regarding him as a typical case—that he is not agoraphobic or hopelessly shy, that he is not a fugitive, and so on. ED.

[21] For instance, it follows from the transparent construal that there is indeed a woman next door to John. ED.

the construal of propositional attitudes which such a psychology renders is nontransparent. (It's nontransparency that's crucial in all the examples we have been considering.) The trouble is that nontransparency isn't quite the same notion as opacity, as we shall now see.

The question before us is: "What are the relations between the pretheoretic notion of type identity of mental states opaquely construed and the notion of type identity of mental states that you get from a theory which strictly honors the formality condition?" And the answer is: complicated. For one thing, it's not clear that we have a pretheoretic notion of the opaque reading of a propositional attitude ascription: I doubt that the two standard tests for opacity (failure of existential generalization[24] and failure of substitutivity of identicals) even pick out the same class of cases. But what's more important are the following considerations. While it's notorious that extensionally identical thoughts may be opaquely type-distinct (e.g., thoughts about the Morning Star and thoughts about the Evening Star) there are nevertheless some semantic conditions on opaque type identification. In particular:

(a) there are some cases of formally distinct but coextensive token thoughts which count as tokens of the same (opaque) type (and hence as identical in content at least on one way of individuating contents); and

(b) *non*coextensive thoughts are ipso facto type-distinct (and differ in content, at least on one way of individuating contents).

Cases of type (a): 1. I think I'm sick and you think I'm sick. What's running through my head is "I'm sick"; what's running through your head is "he's sick." But we are both having thoughts of the same (opaque) type (and hence of the same content).

2. You think: "that one looks edible"; I think: "this one looks edible." Our thoughts are

opaquely type-identical if we are thinking about the same one.

It connects with the existence of such cases that pronouns and demonstratives are typically (perhaps invariably) construed as referring, even when they occur in what are otherwise opaque constructions. So, for example, it seems to me that I can't report Macbeth's hallucination by saying: "Macbeth thinks that's a dagger" if Macbeth is staring at nothing at all. Which is to say that "that's a dagger" doesn't report Macbeth's mental state even though "that's a dagger" may be precisely what is running through Macbeth's head (precisely the representation his relation to which is constitutive of his belief).

Cases of type (b): 1. Suppose that Sam feels faint and Misha knows he does. Then what's running through Misha's head may be "he feels faint." Suppose too that Misha feels faint and Alfred knows he does. Then what's running through Alfred's head, too, may be "he feels faint." I have no, or rather no univocal, inclination to say, in this case, that Alfred and Misha are having type-identical thoughts even though the principle of type individuation is, by assumption, opaque and even though Alfred and Misha have the same things running through their heads. But if this is right, then formal identity of mental representations cannot be sufficient for type identity of opaquely taxonomized mental states.[25] (There is an interesting discussion of this sort of case in Geach [1957] . Geach says that Aquinas says that there is no "intelligible difference" between Alfred's thought and Misha's. I don't know whether this means that they are having the same thought or that they aren't.)

2. Suppose that there are two Lake Eries (two bodies of water so-called). Consider two tokens of the thought "Lake Erie is wet," one of which is, intuitively speaking about the Lake Erie in North

---

[24] *Existential generalization* is the inference rule that allows one to conclude from "Socrates was a philosopher" to the (existentially quantified) statement that "There existed at least one philosopher." Opaque contexts constituted by the ascription of propositional attitudes resist existential generalization. For instance, it does not follow from "He is thinking about the present king of Greece" that "There is a king of Greece at present, about which he is thinking." ED.

[25] One might try eying: what counts for opaque type individuation is what's in your head, not just what's running through it. So, for example, though Alfred and Misha are both thinking "he feels faint," nevertheless different counterfactuals are true of them: Misha would cash his pronoun as: "he, Sam" whereas Alfred would cash his pronoun as: "he, Misha." The problem would then be to decide which such counterfactuals are relevant since, if we count all of them, it's going to turn out that there are few, if any, cases of distinct organisms having type-identical thoughts.

I won't, in any event, pursue this proposal since it seems clear that it won't, in principle, cope with all the relevant cases. Two people would be having different thoughts when each is thinking "I'm ill" even if everything in their heads were the same.

America and one of which is about the other one. Here again, I'm inclined to say that the aboriginal, uncorrupted pretheoretical notion of type-wise same thought wants these to be tokens of *different* thoughts and takes these thoughts to differ in content. (Though in this case, as in the others, I think there's also a countervailing inclination to say that they count as type-identical—and as identical in content—for some relevant purposes and in some relevant respects. How like aboriginal, uncorrupted, pretheoretical intuition!)

I think, in short, that the intuitive opaque taxonomy is actually what you might call "semitransparent." On the one hand, certain conditions on coreference are in force (Misha's belief that he's ill is type-distinct from Sam's belief that he's ill and my thought *this is edible* may be type-identical to your thought *that is edible*.) On the other hand, you don't get free substitution of coreferring expressions (beliefs about the Morning Star are type-distinct from beliefs about the Evening Star) and existential generalization doesn't go through for beliefs about Santa Claus.

Apparently, then, the notion of same mental state that we get from a theory which honors the formality condition is related to, but not identical to, the notion of same mental state that unreconstructed intuition provides for opaque construals. And it would certainly be reasonable to ask whether we actually need both. I think the answer is probably: yes, if we want to capture all the intuitions. For if we restrict ourselves to either one of the taxonomies, we get consequences that we don't like. On the one hand, if we taxonomize *purely* formally, we get identity of belief compatible with difference of truth value. (Misha's belief that he's ill will be type-identical to Sam's belief that *he's* ill, but one may be true while the other is false.) On the other hand, if we taxonomize solely according to the pretheoretic criteria, we get trouble with the idea that people act out of their beliefs and desires. We need, in particular, some taxonomy according to which Sam and Misha have the same belief in order to explain why it is that they exhibit the same behaviors.[26] It is, after all, *part* of the pretheoretic notion of belief that difference in belief ought *cete-*

ris paribus to show up in behavior somewhere; ("ceteris paribus" means "given relevant identities among other mental states"). Whereas, it's possible to construct cases where differences like the one between Misha's belief and Sam's can't show up in behavior even in principle (see note 25). What we have, in short, is a tension between a partially semantic taxonomy and an entirely functional one, and the recommended solution is to use both.

Having said all this, I now propose largely to ignore it and use the term "opaque taxonomy" for principles of type individuation according to which Misha and Sam are in the same mental state when each believes himself to be ill. When I need to distinguish this sense of opaque taxonomy from the pretheoretic one, I'll talk about *full* opacity and fully opaque type identification.[27]

My claim has been that, in doing our psychology, we want to attribute mental states fully opaquely because it's the fully opaque reading which tells us what the agent has in mind, and it's what the agent has in mind that causes his behavior. I now need to say something about how, precisely, all this is supposed to constitute an argument for the formality condition.

Point one: it's just as well that it's the fully opaque construal of mental states that we need since, patently, that's the only one that the formality condition permits us. This is because the formality condition prohibits taxonomizing psychological states by reference to the semantic properties of mental representations and, at bottom, transparency is a semantic (viz., nonformal; viz., nonsyntactic) notion. The point is sufficiently obvious: if we count the belief that the Evening Star is F as (type) identical to the belief that the Morning Star is F, that must be because of the coreference of such expressions as "the Morning Star" and "the Evening Star." But coreference is a semantic property, and not one which could conceivably have a formal doppelganger; it's inconceivable, in particular, that there should be a system of mental representations such that, in the general case, coreferring expressions are formally identical in that system. (This might be true for God's mind, but not, surely, for

---

[26] The behaviors may be of the same general type, but they would, of course, be directed at different persons. ED.

[27] As Fodor has just explained, the pretheoretic opacity is not fully opaque; instead, it is "semitransparent": it has a degree of referential constraint. ED.

anybody else's [and not for God's either unless he is an Extensionalist [28]; which I doubt.]) So if we want transparent taxonomies of mental states, we will have to give up the formality condition. So it's a good thing for the computational theory of the mind that it's not transparent taxonomies that we want.

What's harder to argue for (but might, nevertheless, be true) is point two: that the formality condition *can* be honored by a theory which taxonomizes mental states according to their content. For, barring caveats previously reviewed, it may be that mental states are distinct in content only if they are relations to formally distinct mental representations; in effect, that aspects of content can be reconstructed as aspects of form, at least insofar as appeals to content figure in accounts of the mental causation of behavior. The main thing to be said in favor of this speculation is that it allows us to explain, within the context of the representational theory of mind, how beliefs of different content can have different behavioral effects, even when the beliefs are transparently type-identical. The form of explanation goes: it's because different content implies formally distinct internal representations (via the formality condition) and formally distinct internal representations can be functionally different; can differ in their causal role. Whereas, to put it mildly, it's hard to see how internal representations could differ in causal role *unless* they differed in form.

To summarize: transparent taxonomy is patently incompatible with the formality condition whereas taxonomy in respect of content *may* be compatible with the formality condition, plus or minus a bit. That taxonomy in respect of content is compatible with the formality condition, plus or minus a bit, is perhaps *the* basic idea of modern cognitive theory. The representational theory of mind and the computational theory of mind merge here for, on the one hand, it's claimed that psychological states differ in content only if they are relations to type-distinct mental representations; and, on the other, it's claimed that only formal properties of mental representations contribute to their type individuation for the purposes of theories of mind/body interaction. Or, to put it the other way 'round, it's allowed that mental representations affect behavior in virtue of their content, but it's maintained that mental representations are distinct in content only if they are also distinct in form. The first clause is required to make it plausible that mental states are relations to mental representations and the second is required to make it plausible that mental processes are computations. (Computations just *are* processes in which representations have their causal consequences in virtue of their form.) By thus exploiting the notions of content and computation *together,* a cognitive theory seeks to connect the *intensional* properties [29] of mental states with their *causal* properties vis-a-vis behavior. Which is, of course, exactly what a theory of the mind ought to do.

As must be evident from the preceding, I'm partial to programmatic arguments: ones that seek to infer the probity of a conceptual apparatus from the fact that it plays a role in some prima facie plausible research enterprise. So, in particular, I've argued that a taxonomy of mental states which honors the formality condition seems to be required by theories of the mental causation of behavior, and that that's a reason for taking such taxonomies very seriously.

But there lurks, within the general tradition of representational theories of mind, a deeper intuition: that it is not only *advisable* but actually *mandatory* to assume that mental processes have access only to formal (nonsemantic) properties of mental representations; that the contrary view is not only empirically fruitless but also conceptually unsound. I find myself in sympathy with this intuition, though I'm uncertain precisely how the arguments ought to go. What follows is just a sketch.

I'll begin with a version that I *don't* like, an epistemological version:

---

[28] Extensionalism is the ontological doctrine that the domain of a theory must be restricted to existent entities. Thus, an extensionalist theory of reference cannot admit (must analyze away) the apparent occurrences of references to nonexistent entities (such as to minotaurs or the present king of France). In such a theory the meaning or content of an expression is the existing object or set of objects the expression denotes. Coreferring expressions could not have different meanings and the mental correlates of these expressions could not differ formally. Fodor's joke appears to be that perhaps *God* could understand how there could be formal identity for coreferring expressions if God were an extensionalist; but it is unlikely that God would hold such a theory. ED.

[29] In this context *intensional* properties of mental states are the properties these states have as bearers of content or meaning. ED.

Look, it makes no *sense* to suppose that mental operations could apply to mental representations in virtue of (e.g.) the truth or falsity of the latter. For, consider: truth value is a matter of correspondence to the way the world is. To determine the truth value of a belief would therefore involve what I'll call 'directly comparing' the belief with the world; i.e., comparing it with the way the world *is,* not just with the way the world is represented as being. And the representational theory of mind says that we have access to the world only via the ways in which we represent it. There is, as it were, nothing that corresponds to looking around (behind? through? what's the right metaphor?) one's beliefs to catch a glimpse of the things they represent. Mental processes can, in short, compare representations, but they can't compare representations with what they're representations of. Hence mental processes can't have access to the truth value of representations or, mutatis mutandis, to whether they denote. Hence the formality condition.

This line of argument could, certainly, be made a good deal more precise. It has been in, for example, some of the recent work of Nelson Goodman (see especially Goodman, 1978). For present purposes, however, I'm content to leave it *im*precise so long as it sounds familiar. For I suspect that all versions of the argument suffer from a common deficiency: they assume that you can't run a *correspondence* theory of truth together with a coherence theory[30] of evidence. Whereas I see nothing compelling in the inference from "truth is a matter of the correspondence of a belief with the way the world is" to "*ascertaining* truth is a matter of 'directly comparing' a belief with the way the world is." Perhaps we ascertain the truth of our beliefs by comparing them with one another, appealing to inference to the best explanation whenever we need to do so.

Anyhow, it would be nice to have a *non*epistemological defence of the formality condition; one

which saves the intuition that there's something conceptually wrong with its denial but doesn't acquire the skeptical/relativistic commitments with which the traditional epistemic versions of the argument have been encumbered. Here goes:

Suppose, just for convenience, that mental processes are algorithms. So, we have rules for the transformation of mental representations, and we have the mental representations that constitute their ranges and domains.[31] Think of the rules as being like hypothetical imperatives; they have antecedents which specify conditions on mental representations, and they have consequents which specify what is to happen if the antecedents are satisfied. And now consider rules (a) and (b):

(a) Iff it's the case that P, do such and such.

(b) Iff you believe it's the case that P, do such and such.

Notice, to begin with, that the compliance conditions on these injunctions are quite different. In particular, in the case where P is *false but believed true,* compliance with (b) consists in doing such and such, whereas compliance with (a) consists in not doing it. But despite this difference in compliance conditions, there's something very peculiar (perhaps *pragmatically* peculiar, whatever precisely that may mean) about supposing that an organism might have different ways of going about attempting to comply with (a) and (b). The peculiarity is patent in (c). To borrow a joke from Professor Robert Jagger, (c) is a little like the advice: "buy low, sell high." One knows just what it would be *like* to comply with either, but somehow knowing that doesn't help much.

(c) Do such and such iff it's the case that P, *whether or not* you believe that it's the case that P.[32]

The idea is this: when one has done what one can to establish that the belief that P is warranted, one has done what one can to establish that the antecedent of (a) is satisfied. And, conversely, when

---

[30] The *correspondence theory of truth* has traditionally done battle with the *coherence theory of truth* over what it is that makes propositions true. The former theory anchors truth in a relation of correspondence between propositions and the reality they represent. Coherence theorists argue that we cannot step outside the system of our beliefs in order to compare a belief with some fact that is independent of our beliefs. Truth consists instead in a proposition belonging to a set of propositions with certain attributes such as consistency and completeness with respect to a given domain. Fodor is claiming that one can combine a correspondence theory of *truth* with a coherence theory of *evidence* (of what commands our assent to the truth of a proposition). ED.

[31] The terms *domain* and *range* are explained in section 1 of Reading 15, and what it means for a function to be an *algorithm* is explained in section 3. ED.

[32] I'm assuming, for convenience that all the Ps are such that either they or their denials are believed. This saves having to relativize to time (e.g., having (b) and (c) read ". . . you believe or come to believe . . .").

one has done what one can do to establish that the antecedent of (a) is satisfied, one has done what one can to establish the warrant of the belief that P. Now, I suppose that the following is at least *close* to being true: to have the belief that P is to have the belief that the belief that P is warranted; and conversely, to have the belief that the belief that P is warranted is to have the belief that P. And the upshot of *this* is just the formality condition all over again. Given that mental operations have access to the fact that P is believed (and hence that the belief that P is believed to be warranted, and hence that the belief that the belief that P is warranted is believed to be warranted, . . . etc.) there's nothing further left to do; there is nothing that corresponds to the notion of a mental operation which one undertakes to perform just in case one's belief that P is *true*.

This isn't, by the way, any form of skepticism, as can be seen from the following: there's nothing wrong with Jones having one mental operation which he undertakes to perform iff it's the case that P and another *quite different* mental operation which he undertakes to perform iff *Smith* (≠ Jones) believes that it's the case that P. (Cf. "I promise . . . though I don't intend to . . ." vs. "I promise . . . though Smith doesn't intend to . . .") There's a first person/third person asymmetry here, but it doesn't impugn the semantic distinction between "P is true" and "P is believed true."[33] The suggestion is that it's the tacit recognition of this pragmatic asymmetry that accounts for the traditional hunch that you can't both identify mental operations with transformations on mental representations and at the same time flout the formality condition; that the representational theory of mind and the computational theory of mind are somehow conjoint options.

---

[33] This paragraph isn't easy to read. Fodor seems to be saying this much at least: His conclusion in the previous paragraph that "to have the belief that P is to have the belief that the belief that P is warranted" is not a concession that one can't know whether one's beliefs are true, or that there is nothing more that I can do to verify a belief than to certify that I actually have it. There's a big difference in credibility about P between *my* believing that P and my believing that someone *else* believes that P. The coherence theory of *evidence* embraced by Fodor assigns a large *functional/computational* difference between these two beliefs, one that is independent of the *semantic* difference between "P is true" and "P is believed." Ed.

So much, then, for the formality condition and the psychological tradition[34] which accepts it. What about Naturalism? The first point is that none of the arguments *for* a rational psychology is, in and of itself, an argument *against* a Naturalistic psychology. As I remarked above, to deny that mental operations have access to the semantic properties of mental representations is *not* to deny that mental representations *have* semantic properties. On the contrary, beliefs are *just* the kinds of things which exhibit truth and denotation, and the Naturalist proposes to make science out of the organism/environment relations which (presumably) fix these properties. Why, indeed, should he not?

This all *seems* very reasonable. Nevertheless, I now wish to argue that a computational psychology is the only one that we are likely to get; that qua research strategy, the attempt to construct a *naturalistic* psychology is very likely to prove fruitless. I think that the basis for such an argument is already to be found in the literature, where it takes the form of a (possibly inadvertent) **reductio ad absurdum** of the contrary view.

Consider, to begin with, a distinction that Professor Hilary Putnam introduces in "The Meaning of Meaning" (1975) between what he calls "psychological states in the wide sense" and "psychological states in the *narrow* sense." A psychological state in the narrow sense is one the ascription of which does not "(presuppose) the existence of any individual other than the subject to whom that state is ascribed" (p. 10). All others are psychological states in the wide sense. So, for example, *x's jealousy of y* is a schema for expressions which denote psychological states in the wide sense since such expressions presuppose the existence, not only of the *x*s who are in the states, but also of the *y*s who are its objects. Putnam remarks that methodological solipsism (the phrase, by the way, is his) can be viewed as the requirement that only psychological states in the narrow sense are allowed as constructs in psychological theories.

Whereas, it's perhaps Putnam's main point that there are at least *some* scientific purposes (e.g., semantics and accounts of intertheoretical reference) which demand the wide construal. Here, rephrased

---

[34] I.e., representationalism. Ed.

slightly, is the sort of example that Putnam finds persuasive.

There is a planet (call it "Yon") where things are very much like here. In particular, by a cosmic accident, some of the people on Yon speak a dialect indistinguishable from English and live in an urban conglomerate indistinguishable from the Greater Boston Area. Still more, for every one of our Greater Bostonians, there is a doppelganger on Yon who has precisely the same neurological structure down to and including microparticles. We can assume that, so long as we're construing "psychological state" narrowly, this latter condition guarantees type identity of our psychological states with theirs.

However, Putnam argues, it doesn't guarantee that there is a corresponding identity of psychological states, hither and Yon, if we construe "psychological state" *widely*. Suppose that there is this difference between Yon and Earth; whereas, over here, the stuff we call "water" has the atomic structure H_2O, it turns out that the stuff that they call "water" over there has the atomic structure XYZ ($\neq H_2O$). And now, consider the mental state *thinking about water*. The idea is that, so long as we construe that state widely, it's one that we, but not our doppelgangers, can reasonably aspire to. For, construed widely, one is thinking about water only if it is water that one is thinking about. But it's water that one's thinking about only if it is H_2O that one's thinking about; water is H_2O. But since, by assumption, they never think about H_2O over Yon, it follows that there's at least one wide psychological state that we're often in and they never are, however neurophysiologically like us they are, and however much our narrow psychological states converge with theirs.

Moreover, if we try to say what they speak about, refer to, mention, etc.; if, in short, we try to supply a semantics for their dialect, we will have to mention XYZ, not H_2O. Hence it would be wrong, at least on Putnam's intuitions, to say that they have a word for water. A fortiori, the chemists who work in what they call "M.I.T." don't have theories about *water,* even though what runs through their heads when they talk about XYZ may be identical to what runs through our heads when we talk about H_2O. The situation is analo-

gous to the one that arises for demonstratives and token reflexives,[35] as Putnam insightfully points out.

Well, what are we to make of this? Is it an argument against methodological solipsism? And, if so, it is a *good* argument against methodological solipsism?

To begin with, Putnam's distinction between psychological states in the narrow and wide sense looks to be very intimately related to the traditional distinction between psychological state ascriptions opaquely and transparently construed. I'm a bit wary about this[36] since what Putnam says about wide ascriptions is only that they "presuppose the existence" of objects other than the ascribee; and, of course *a believes Fb and b exists* does not entail *b is such that a believes F of him,* or even $\exists x$ *(a believes Fx)*. Moreover, the failure of such entailments is notoriously important in discussions of quantifying in[37]. For all that, however, I don't think that it's Putnam's intention to exploit the difference between the existential generalization test for transparency and the presupposition of existence test for wideness. On the contrary, the burden of Putnam's argument seems to be precisely that "John believes (widely) that water is F" is true only if water (viz., H_2O) is such that John believes it's F. It's thus unclear to me why Putnam gives the weaker condition[38] on wideness when it appears to be the stronger one that does the work.[39]

But whatever the case may be with the wide sense of belief, it's pretty clear that the narrow sense must be (what I've been calling) fully opaque. (This is because only full opacity allows type identity of

---

[35] *Demonstratives* are words such as "this" and "that." *Token reflexives* are expressions that refer to themselves, such as "this sentence." Both belong to the class of *indexical*, terms for which the reference is determined by the context of utterance. For example, "I spoke" has a different reference depending on who the speaker is. Thus indexicals are similar to the case of "water" discussed by Putnam. ED.

[36] I.e., about interpreting Putnam this way. ED.

[37] To *quantify in* is to use an existential quantifier ($\exists$) outside an opaque expression to bind a variable within it (e.g., to reformulate "P believes J is angry" as "There exists someone whom P believes to be angry" [($\exists x$)(P believes that x is angry)]. The problem, of course, is that the person P actually (opaquely) believes is angry may not even exist. ED.

[38] I.e., the condition of presupposing the existence of something other than the ascribee. The stronger condition for wideness would be transparency. ED.

[39] I blush to admit that I had missed some of these complexities until Sylvain Bromberger kindly rubbed my nose in them.

beliefs that have different truth conditions [Sam's belief that he's ill with Misha's belief that *he* is; Yon beliefs about XYZ with hither beliefs about H_2O.]) I want to emphasize this correspondence between narrowness and full opacity and not just in aid of terminological parsimony. Putnam sometimes writes as though he takes the methodological commitment to a psychology of narrow mental states to be a sort of vulgar prejudice: "Making this assumption is, of course, adopting a *restrictive program*—a program which deliberately limits the scope and nature of psychology to fit certain mentalistic preconceptions or, in some cases, to fit an **idealistic** reconstruction of knowledge and the world" (p. 137). But, in light of what we've said so far, it should be clear that this is a methodology with malice aforethought. Narrow psychological states are those individuated in light of the formality condition; viz., without reference to such semantic properties as truth and reference. And honoring the formality condition is part and parcel of the attempt to provide a theory which explains (a) how the belief that the Morning Star is F could be different from the belief that the Evening Star is F despite the well-known astronomical facts; and (b) how the behavioral effects of believing that the Morning Star is F could be different from those of believing that the Evening Star is F, astronomy once again apparently to the contrary notwithstanding. Putnam is, of course, dubious about this whole project: ". . . The three centuries of failure of mentalistic psychology is tremendous evidence against this procedure, in my opinion" (p. 137). I suppose this is intended to include everybody from Locke and Kant to Freud and Chomsky. I should have such failures.

So much for background. I now need an argument to show that a naturalistic psychology (a psychology of mental states transparently individuated; hence, presumably, a psychology of mental states in the wide sense) is, for practical purposes, out of the question. So far as I can see, however, Putnam has given that argument. For, consider: a naturalistic psychology is a theory of organism/environment transactions. So, to stick to Putnam's example, a naturalistic psychology would have to find some stuff S and some relation R, such that one's narrow thought that water is wet is a thought about S in virtue of the fact that one bears R to S. Well, *which* stuff? The natural thing to say would be: "Water, of

course." Notice, however, that if Putnam is right, it may not even be *true* that the narrow thought that water is wet is a thought about water, it *won't* be true of tokens of that thought which occur on Yon. Whether the narrow thought that water is wet is about water depends, on whether it's about H_2O; and whether it's about H_2O depends on "how science turns out"—viz., on what chemistry is true. (Similarly, mutatis mutandis, "water" refers to water is *not,* on this view, a truth of any branch of linguistics; it's chemists who tell us what it is that "water" refers to.) Surely, however, characterizing the objects of thought is methodologically prior to characterizing the causal chains that link thoughts to their objects. But the theory which characterizes the objects of thought is the theory of *everything;* it's all of science. Hence, the methodological moral of Putnam's analysis seems to be: the naturalistic psychologists will inherit the Earth, but only after everybody else is finished with it. No doubt it's alright to have a research strategy that says "wait awhile." But who wants to wait *forever?*

This sort of argument isn't novel. Indeed, it was anticipated by Bloomfield (1933). Bloomfield argues that, for all practical purposes, you can't do semantics. The reason that you can't is that to do semantics you have to be able to say, for example, what "salt" refers to. But what "salt" refers to is NaCl, and that's a bit of chemistry, not linguistics:

> The situations which prompt people to utter speech include every object and happening in their universe. In order to give a scientifically accurate definition of meaning for every form of a language, we would have to have a scientifically accurate knowledge of everything in the speaker's world. The actual extent of human knowledge is very small compared to this. We can define the meaning of a speech-form accurately when this meaning has to do with some matter of which we possess scientific knowledge. We can define the names of minerals, as when we say that the ordinary meaning of the English word salt is 'sodium chloride (NaCl),' and we can define the names of plants or animals by means of the technical terms of botany or zoology, but we have no precise way of defining words like love or hate, which concern situations that have not been accurately classified. . . . The statement of meanings is therefore the weak point in language-study, and will remain so until knowledge advances very far beyond its present state. (pp. 139–140)

It seems to me as though Putnam ought to endorse all of this *including the moral:* the distinction between wanting a naturalistic semantics (psychology) and not wanting any is real but academic.[40]

The argument just given depends, however, on accepting Putnam's analysis of his example. But suppose that one's intuitions run the other way. Then one is at liberty to argue like this:

1. They do too have water over Yon; all Putnam's example shows is that there could be two kinds of water, our kind (= H_2O) and their kind (= XYZ).

2. Hence, Yon tokens of the thought that water is wet are thoughts about water after all.

3. Hence, the way chemistry turns out is irrelevant to whether thoughts about water are about water.

4. Hence, the naturalistic psychology of thought need not wait upon the sciences of the objects of thought.

5. Hence, a naturalistic psychology may be in the cards after all.

Since the premises of this sort of reply may be tempting (since, indeed, they may be *true*) it's worth presenting a version of the argument which doesn't depend on intuitions about what XYZ is.

A naturalistic psychology would specify the relations that hold between an organism and an object in its environment when the one is thinking about the other. Now, think how such a theory would have to go. Since it would have to define its generalizations over mental states on the one hand and environmental entities on the other, it will need, in particular, some canonical way of referring to the latter. Well, *which* way? If one assumes that what makes my thought *about Robin Roberts* a thought about Robin Roberts is some causal con-

nection between the two of us, then we'll need a description of RR such that the causal connection obtains in virtue of his satisfying that description. And *that* means, presumably, that we'll need a description under which the relation between him and me instantiates a law.

Generally, then, a naturalistic psychology would attempt to specify environmental objects in a vocabulary such that environment/organism relations are law-instantiating when so described. But here's the depressing consequence again: we have no access to such a vocabulary prior to the elaboration (completion?) of the nonpsychological sciences. "What Granny likes with her herring" isn't, for example, a description under which salt is law-instantiating; nor, presumably, is "salt." What we need is something like "NaCl," and descriptions like "NaCl" are available only *after* we've done our chemistry. What this comes down to is that, at a minimum, "x's being F causally explains . . ." can be true only when "F" expresses nomologically necessary properties of the xs. Heaven knows it's hard to say what *that* means, but it presumably rules out both "Salt's being what Granny likes with herring . . ." and "Salt's being salt . . ."; the former for want of being necessary, and the latter for want of being nomological. I take it, moreover, that Bloomfield is right when he says (a) that we don't know relevant nomologically necessary properties of most of the things we can refer to (think about) and (b) that it isn't the linguist's (psychologist's) job to find them out.

Here's still another way to put this sort of argument. The way Bloomfield states his case invites the question: "Why *should* a semanticist want a definition of 'salt' that's 'scientifically accurate' in your sense? Why wouldn't a 'nominal' definition[41] do?" There is, I think, some point to such a query. For example, as Hartry Field has pointed out (1972), it wouldn't make much difference to the way that truth-conditional semantics[42] goes if we

---

[40] It may be that Putnam does accept this moral. For example, the upshot of the discussion around p. 153 of his article appears to be that a Greek semanticist prior to Archimedes could not (in practice) have given a correct account of what (the Greek equivalent of) "gold" means; viz., because the theory needed to specify the extension of the term was simply not available. Presumably we are in that situation vis-a-vis the objects of many of our thoughts and the meanings of many of our terms; and, presumably, we will continue to do so into the indefinite future. But, then, what's the point of defining psychology (semantics) so that there can't be any?

[41] A *nominal* definition would list enough of a thing's properties to distinguish it from other types of things, without expressing its "underlying" structure or "essence." Nominal definitions are, in this sense, often contrasted with *real* definitions. ED.

[42] A *truth-conditional semantics* has the meaning of a proposition consistent in its truth conditions—i.e., what facts or states of affairs must obtain for the proposition to be true. E.g., "All swans are white" is true only if all swans are white. ED.

were to say only "'salt' refers to whatever it refers to." All we need for this sort of semantics is some way or other of referring to the extension of "salt"; we don't, in particular, need a "scientifically accurate" way.[43] It's therefore pertinent to do what Bloomfield notably does not: distinguish between the goals of *semantics* and those of a naturalistic psychology of language. The latter, by assumption, purports to explicate the organism/environment transactions in virtue of which relations like reference hold. It therefore requires, at a minimum, lawlike generalizations of the (approximate) form: *X's utterance of 'salt' refers to salt iff X bears relation R to* _____. Since this whole thing is supposed to be lawlike, what goes in for "   " must be a projectible characterization of the extension of "salt." But, in general, we discover which descriptions are projectible only *a posteriori;* in light of how the sciences (including the nonpsychological sciences) turn out. We are back where we started. Looked at this way, the moral is that we can do (certain kinds of) semantics if we have a way of referring to the extension of "salt." But we can't do the naturalistic psychology of reference unless we have some way of saying what salt is; which of its properties determine its causal relations.

It's important to emphasize that these sorts of arguments do *not* apply against the research program embodied in "Rational psychology"; viz., to the program which envisions a psychology that honors the formality condition. The problem we've been facing is: under what description does the object of thought enter into scientific generalizations about the relations between thoughts and their objects? It looks as though the naturalist is going to have to say: under a description that's law-instantiating; e.g., under physical description. Whereas the rational psychologist has a quite different answer. What *he* wants is *whatever description the organism has in mind* when it thinks about the object of thought, construing "thinks about" fully opaquely. So, for a theory of psychological states narrowly construed, we want such descriptions of Venus as, e.g., "the Morning Star," "the Evening Star," "Venus," etc., for it's these sorts of descrip-

tions which we presumably entertain when we think that the Morning Star is *F.* In particular, it's our relation to these sorts of descriptions that determines what psychological state type we're in insofar as the goal in taxonomizing psychological states is explaining how they affect behavior.

A final point under the general head: the hopelessness of naturalistic psychology. Practicing naturalistic psychologists have been at least dimly aware all along of the sort of bind that they're in. So, for example, the "physical specification of the stimulus" is just about invariably announced as a requirement upon adequate formulations of S-R generalizations. We can now see why. Suppose, wildly contrary to fact, that there exists a human population (e.g., English speakers) in which pencils are, in the technical sense of the notion, discriminative stimuli[44] controlling the verbal response "pencil." The point is that, even if some such generalization were true, it wouldn't be among those enunciated by a naturalistic psychology; the generalizations of naturalistic psychology are presumably supposed to be nomological, and there aren't any laws about pencils *qua* pencils. That is: expressions like "pencil" presumably occur in no true, lawlike sentences. Of course, there presumably is some description in virtue of which pencils fall under the organism/environment laws of a naturalistic psychology, and everybody (except, possibly, Gibson) has always assumed that those descriptions are, approximately, physical descriptions. Hence, the naturalist's demand, perfectly warranted by his lights, that the stimulus should be physically specified.

But though their theory has been consistent, their practice has uniformly not. In practice, and barring the elaborately circumscribed cases that psychophysics studies, the requirement that the stimulus be physically specified has been ignored by just about *all* practitioners. And, indeed, they were well advised to ignore it; how else could they get on

---

[43] I.e., we don't need a "real" definition. That can wait until the fullness of the relevant science. Ed.

[44] The *discriminative stimulus* is the *specific aspect* of the total situation which elicits the behavior. For instance, it may be the flashing of a green light that elicits the seeking behavior of a white rat, no matter what the color of the background against which it flashes (as long as there is sufficient contrast for detection). The flashing green light is then the discriminative stimulus. Fodor will go on to point out that it is hard to get beyond such rough-and-ready characterizations of the discriminative stimulus to a scientifically precise (lawlike) characterization of the causal relation. Ed.

with their job? If they really had to wait for the physicists to determine the description(s) under which pencils are law-instantiators,[45] how would the psychology of pencils get off the ground?

So far as I can see, there are really only two ways out of this dilemma:

1. We can fudge, the way that learning theorists usually do. That is, we can "read" the description of the stimulus from the character of the organism's response. In point of historical fact, this has led to a kind of naturalistic psychology which is merely a solemn paraphrase of what everybody's grandmother knows: e.g., to saying "pencils are discriminative stimuli for the utterance of 'pencil'" where Granny would have said "pencil" refers to pencils. I take it that Chomsky's review of *Verbal Behavior* (1959) demonstrated, once and for all, the fatuity of this course. What *would* be interesting—what would have surprised Grandmother—is a generalization of the form Δ *is the discriminative stimulus for utterances of "pencil"* where Δ is a description which picks out pencils in some projectible vocabulary (e.g., in the vocabulary of physics). Does anybody suppose that such descriptions are likely to be forthcoming in, say, the *next* three hundred years?

2. The other choice is to try for a computational psychology; which is, of course, the burden of my plaint. On this view, what we can reasonably hope for is a theory of mental states fully opaquely type-individuated. We can try to say what the mental representation is, and what the relation to a mental representation is, such that one believes that the Morning Star is F in virtue of bearing the latter to the former. And we can try to say how that representation, or that relation, or both, differ from the representation and the relation constitutive of believing that the Evening Star is F. A naturalistic psychology, by contrast, remains a sort of ideal of pure reason; there must *be* such a psychology since, presumably, we do sometimes think of Venus and, presumably, we do so in virtue of a causal relation between it and us. But there's no practical hope of making science out of this relation. And, of course, for methodology, practical hope is *everything*.

One final point, and then I'm through. Methodological solipsism isn't, of course, solipsism *tout court*. It's not part of the enterprise to assert, or even suggest, that you and I are actually in the situation of Winograd's computer. Heaven only knows what relation between me and Robin Roberts makes it possible for me to think of him (refer to him, etc.), and I've been doubting the practical possibility of a science whose generalizations that relation instantiates. But I *don't* doubt that there is such a relation or that I do sometimes think of him. Still more: I have reasons not to doubt it; precisely the sorts of reasons I'd supply if I were asked to justify my knowledge claims about his pitching record. In short: it's true that Roberts won twenty-eight, and it's true that I know that he did, and nothing in the preceding tends to impugn these truths. (Or, contrariwise, if he didn't and I'm mistaken, then the reasons for my mistake are philosophically boring; they're biographical, not epistemological or ontological). My point, then, is *of course* not that solipsism is true; it's just that truth, reference and the rest of the semantic notions aren't psychological categories. What they are is: they're modes of *Dasein*. I don't know what *Dasein* is, but I'm sure that there's lots of it around, and I'm sure that you and I and Cincinnati have all got it. What more do you want?

REFERENCES

Bloomfield, Leonard. (1938) *Language*. New York: H. Holt & Co.

Chomsky, N. (1959) Review of Skinner's *Verbal Behavior. Language* 35:26–58.

Davidson, D. (1975) Thought and talk. In: Guttenplan, S. (ed.), *Mind and language*. Oxford: Oxford University Press.

Dennett, D. C. (1969) *Content and consciousness*. London: Routledge and Kegan Paul.

Descartes, R. (1931) *Meditations on first philosophy*, trans. E. S. Haldane and G. R. T. Ross. Cambridge: Cambridge University Press.

Field, H. (1972) Tarski's theory of truth. *Journal of Philosophy* 69:347–375.

Fodor, J. A. (1975) *The language of thought*. New York: Thomas Y. Crowell.

---

[45] I.e., exactly under what physical aspect(s) in general pencils cause the utterance of 'pencil.' ED.

——— (1978) Tom Swift and his procedural grand-mother. *Cognition* 6:229–247.

——— (1978) Propositional attitudes. *The Monist* 61:4.

Geach, P. (1957) *Mental acts.* London: Routledge & Kegan Paul.

Goodman, N. (1978) *Ways of world making.* Indianapolis: Hackett.

James, W. (1890) *Principles of psychology,* vol. I. (repr., New York: Dover, 1950) New York: Henry Holt.

Putnam, H. (1960) Minds and machines. In: Hook, S. (ed.), *Dimensions of the mind.* New York: New York University Press.

——— (1975) The meaning of meaning. In: Gunderson, K. (ed.), *Minnesota studies in the philosophy of science* 7: Language, mind, and knowledge. Minneapolis: University of Minnesota Press.

Quine, W. V. O. (1960) *Word and object.* Cambridge, Mass.: MIT Press.

Stich, S. P. (1978) Autonomous psychology and the belief-desire thesis. *The Monist* 61:4.

——— (1979) Do animals have beliefs? *Australasian Journal of Philosophy* 57:1.

——— (forthcoming) On the ascription of content. In: Woodfield, A. (ed.), *Mental representation and intentional content.*

Winograd, T. (1972) *Understanding natural language.* New York: Academic Press.

Fodor is right to say that his "computational" theory of mental states "has some clear consequences, and they are striking and tendentious" (p. 230). Let's focus on these consequences, especially as they are the ground for Searle's attack on the computational model in the next reading.

There is a strongly paradoxical aspect to Fodor's initial presentation of the computational theory as a strong version of representationalism. At the heart of the latter, he insists, is the notion that mental states are relations to, and mental processes are operations over, representations. What makes something a representation is that it has content, and what distinguishes one representation from another is difference in content. Yet "content is a semantic notion par excellence"—it involves such features as reference and meaning (p. 230). Yet Fodor's computational theory includes what he calls the "formality condition": Representations differ from one another, or are type distinct, only by their forms (= syntactical properties), and specifically not by their semantic properties. The bridge over this apparent abyss between a representational and a computational theory is the supposition that differences in content will be correlated with formal differences.

Such correlations would presumably be the result of natural selection. Those organisms whose sensory systems achieved optimal correlation between formal differences in representations and biologically important events in the environment would be more likely to survive and reproduce. Evolutionary pressures would play the same role here that Descartes' God played: bringing about a relation between representation and object, a relation to which the subject has no direct access.

A conversation between a seventeenth-century representationalist (R) and a proponent of the computational theory (C) might go like this:

C: The computational model is an improvement over your quasi pictorial "ideas". As Berkeley pointed out, since the mind has no access to the originals for its idea-pictures, the pictorial or resemblance relation between idea and object-in-the-world is unintelligible. All the mind can do is compare one idea with another. You and Descartes tried to have your cake and eat it. You admitted that the mind has no access to the external object, but then you introduced a paler version of the pictorial relation inside the mental process, a mental content that served as a proxy for the real object.

R: Without this intramental content you're criticizing, what makes those entities in your mind or head representations? Sure, they intervene causally between sensory stimuli and behavioral responses. But so do hormonal secretions, blood flows, and muscle contractions.

What makes a certain class of physiological events (a subset of neural events) different enough that we call them mental or psychological? The trouble with what you call "representations" is that they don't represent.

REVIEW QUESTION

What do you think? Join the conversation between C and R.

18

Do Minds Compute?

John R. Searle

John R. Searle teaches philosophy at the University of California, Berkeley. He has written extensively in the philosophy of mind and language. Among his most recent publications are *The Rediscovery of the Mind* (1992) and *The Construction of Social Reality* (1995). The argument in the first essay below has been one of the most discussed and criticized in the philosophy of mind since it first appeared in 1980. The second part of the reading is an address given by Searle on the same topic ten years later.

One of the central points in both selections is the significance for the philosophy of mind of the capacity of computers to *simulate* the operations of other systems, and especially the mental or cognitive processes carried out by the human brain or mind. Copeland (1993) provides a useful definition of "simulation" as it is used here by Searle: "To say that a computer can simulate another system is simply to say that the computer can be programmed so that it will generate correct symbolic descriptions of the system's outputs from descriptions of inputs into the system, for all possible outputs" (231). Take, for instance, the addition function of a calculator. The specific numerals and '+' sign we input to the calculator is automatically translated into the appropriate binary symbols, and the output string of binary symbols is automatically translated into a string of numerical symbols representing the sum. To say that the calculator *simulates* what we do when *we* add is to say that whenever we correctly input on the keypad the formula for the addition of a specific set of numbers, the output on the paper tape or video display will correctly symbolize what would have been the output if *we* ourselves had performed the addition (correctly). To make the calculator more like what we call a computer, suppose that it is programmable: With the same keypad I can temporarily store in the calculator a sequence of arithmetic operations I want it to perform on a set of inputs. Storing this program causes the internal behavior and the output of the machine to be different than they would be for the same input without the program. In the sense defined above, the calculator running this program of mine *simulates* what I would have done (though it operates much faster).

What goes on within the calculator/computer is all very algorithmic and "moronic,"[1] strictly digital and binary (currents turning on and off at unimaginably high frequencies, in sequences and configurations that we think of as corresponding to strings of *1*s and *0*s). Whether a computer is doing something as simple as addition or as complex as analyzing statistics or searching the Internet, it's all just more of the same. Functionalists such as Fodor and the early Putnam argue that mental states are nothing but functional states, so that functionally equivalent mental states will be the same mental state (no matter how different their physical embodiments may be). Should we then conclude that computer simulations of human cognitive processes, to the extent that they generate the same output for the same input, are functional equivalents of the

---

[1] See White's discussion of algorithms in section 4 of Reading 15. ED.

human mental processes being simulated, and are therefore the *same* mental or cognitive processes? If what the computer does is called "thinking" or "reasoning" when it goes on in us, shouldn't we say that the computer itself *thinks* and *reasons?* In the reading below, Searle asks this sort of question about a fanciful computer simulation of speaking Chinese. The relevance of Searle's argument to the previous reading will be obvious.

Minds, Brains, and Programs

What psychological and philosophical significance should we attach to recent efforts at computer simulations of human cognitive capacities? In answering this question, I find it useful to distinguish what I will call "strong" AI from "weak" or "cautious" AI (Artificial Intelligence). According to weak AI, the principal value of the computer in the study of the mind is that it gives us a very powerful tool. For example, it enables us to formulate and test hypotheses in a more rigorous and precise fashion.[2] But according to strong AI, the computer is not merely a tool in the study of the mind; rather, the appropriately programmed computer really is a mind, in the sense that computers given the right programs can be literally said to understand and have other cognitive states. In strong AI, because the programmed computer has cognitive states, the programs are not mere tools that enable us to test psychological explanations; rather, the programs are themselves the explanations.

I have no objection to the claims of weak AI, at least as far as this article is concerned. My discussion

here will be directed at the claims I have defined as those of strong AI, specifically the claim that the appropriately programmed computer literally has cognitive states and that the programs thereby explain human cognition. When I hereafter refer to AI, I have in mind the strong version, as expressed by these two claims.

I will consider the work Roger Schank and his colleagues at Yale (Schank & Abelson 1977), because I am more familiar with it than I am with any other similar claims, and because it provides a very clear example of the sort of work I wish to examine. But nothing that follows depends upon the details of Schank's programs. The same arguments would apply to Winograd's SHRDLU (Winograd 1973), Weizenbaum's ELIZA (Weizenbaum 1965), and indeed any Turing machine simulation of human mental phenomena.

Very briefly, and leaving out the various details, one can describe Schank's program as follows: the aim of the program is to simulate the human ability to understand stories. It is characteristic of human beings' story-understanding capacity that they can answer questions about the story even though the information that they give was never explicitly stated in the story. Thus, for example, suppose you are given the following story: "A man went into a restaurant and ordered a hamburger. When the hamburger arrived it was burned to a crisp, and the man stormed out of the restaurant angrily, without paying for the hamburger or leaving a tip." Now, if you are asked "Did the man eat the hamburger?" you will presumably answer, "No, he did not." Similarly, if you are given the following story: "A man went into a restaurant and ordered a hamburger; when the hamburger came he was very pleased with it; and as he left the restaurant he gave the waitress a large tip before paying his bill," and you are asked the question, "Did the man eat the

From John R. Searle, "Minds, Brains, and Programs," *The Behavioral and Brain Sciences* 3 (1980): 417–419. Copyright © 1980 by Cambridge University Press. Reprinted with the permission of the Cambridge University Press.

[2]Suppose we are investigating human depth perception. Many kinds of sensory input vary with depth, such as color brightness, linear convergence, relative size, and muscle sensations generated by eye muscles involved in focusing. There are many conceivable ways in which these different types of input could be combined and weighed to generate depth awareness. We are talking here about an unconscious process, one that is ongoing even as we are reading this text, and therefore one which we can't analyze merely by observing or introspecting it. Knowing what kinds of sensory input are available to humans, and what depth perceptions these inputs generate, we can program a computer to combine and weigh these sensory inputs in various ways until its output matches human performance in both its strengths and limitations. We would then have a successful *simulation* of human depth perception and a good hypothesis about the functional structure of depth perception. "Weak" or "cautious" AI, to which Searle has no objection, uses computers as research tools in this way, without identifying what the computer does with what we do. Ed.

hamburger?", you will presumably answer, "Yes, he ate the hamburger." Now Schank's machines can similarly answer questions about restaurants in this fashion. To do this, they have a "representation" of the sort of information that human beings have about restaurants, which enables them to answer such questions as those above, given these sorts of stories. When the machine is given the story and then asked the question, the machine will print out answers of the sort that we would expect human beings to give if told similar stories. Partisans of strong AI claim that in this question and answer sequence the machine is not only simulating a human ability but also

1. That the machine can literally be said to understand the story and provide the answers to questions, and
2. That what the machine and its program do explains the human ability to understand the story and answer questions about it.

Both claims seem to me to be totally unsupported by Schank's[3] work, as I will attempt to show in what follows.

One way to test any theory of the mind is to ask oneself what it would be like if my mind actually worked on the principles that the theory says all minds work on. Let us apply this test to the Schank program with the following Gedanken experiment[4]. Suppose that I'm locked in a room and given a large batch of Chinese writing. Suppose furthermore (as is indeed the case) that I know no Chinese, either written or spoken, and that I'm not even confident that I could recognize Chinese writing as Chinese writing distinct from, say, Japanese writing or meaningless squiggles. To me, Chinese writing is just so many meaningless squiggles. Now suppose further that after this first batch of Chinese writing I am given a second batch of Chinese script together with a set of rules for correlating the second batch with the first batch. The rules are in English, and I understand these rules as well as any other native speaker of English. They enable me to correlate one set of formal symbols with an-

other set of formal symbols, and all that "formal" means here is that I can identify the symbols entirely by their shapes. Now suppose also that I am given a third batch of Chinese symbols together with some instructions, again in English, that enable me to correlate elements of this batch with the first two batches, and these rules instruct me how to give back certain Chinese symbols with certain sorts of shapes in response to certain sorts of shapes given me in the third batch. Unknown to me, the people who are giving me all of these symbols call the first batch "a script,"[5] they call the second batch a "story," and they call the third batch "questions." Furthermore, they call the symbols I give them back in response to the third batch "answers to the questions," and the set of rules in English that they gave me, they call "the program." Now just to complicate the story a little, imagine that these people also give me stories in English, which I understand, and they then ask me questions in English about these stories, and I give them back answers in English. Suppose also that after a while I get so good at following the instructions for manipulating the Chinese symbols and the programmers get so good at writing the programs that from the external point of view—that is, from the point of view of somebody outside the room in which I am locked—my answers to the questions are absolutely indistinguishable from those of native Chinese speakers. Nobody just looking at my answers can tell that I don't speak a word of Chinese. Let us also suppose that my answers to the English questions are, as they no doubt would be, indistinguishable from those of other native English speakers, for the simple reason that I am a native English speaker. From the external point of view—from the point of view of someone reading my "answers"—the answers to the Chinese questions and the English questions are equally good. But in the Chinese case, unlike the English case, I produce the answers by manipulating uninterpreted formal symbols. As far as the Chinese is concerned, I simply behave like a computer; I perform computational operations on formally specified elements.[6] For the purposes of

---

[3] I am not, of course, saying that Schank himself is committed to these claims.

[4] A *Gedankenexperiment* is an experiment carried out in imagination and thought only. ED.

[5] "Script" here would seem to correspond to the background information provided to Schank's computer. ED.

[6] In other words, Searle the computer is performing purely *syntactical* operations on Chinese symbols which have no meaning for him. *Syntax* comprises the (study of the) relations of signs or symbols to each other,

the Chinese, I am simply an instantiation of the computer program.[7]

Now the claims made by strong AI are that the programmed computer understands the stories and that the program in some sense explains human understanding. But we are now in a position to examine these claims in light of our thought experiment.

1. As regards the first claim, it seems to me quite obvious in the example that I do not understand a word of the Chinese stories. I have inputs and outputs that are indistinguishable from those of the native Chinese speaker, and I can have any formal program you like, but I still understand nothing. For the same reasons, Schank's computer understands nothing of any stories, whether in Chinese, English, or whatever, since in the Chinese case the computer is me, and in cases where the computer is not me, the computer has nothing more than I have in the case where I understand nothing.

2. As regards the second claim, that the program explains human understanding, we can see that the computer and its program do not provide **sufficient conditions** of understanding since the computer and the program are functioning, and there is no understanding. But does it even provide a **necessary condition** or a significant contribution to understanding? One of the claims made by the supporters of strong AI is that when I understand a story in English, what I am doing is exactly the same—or perhaps more of the same—as what I was doing in manipulating the Chinese symbols. It is simply more formal symbol manipulation that distinguishes the case in English, where I do understand, from the case in Chinese, where I don't. I have not demonstrated that this claim is false, but it would certainly appear an incredible claim in the

example. Such plausibility as the claim has derives from the supposition that we can construct a program that will have the same inputs and outputs as native speakers, and in addition we assume that speakers have some level of description where they are also instantiations of a program. On the basis of these two assumptions we assume that even if Schank's program isn't the whole story about understanding, it may be part of the story. Well, I suppose that is an empirical possibility, but not the slightest reason has so far been given to believe that it is true, since what is suggested—though certainly not demonstrated—by the example is that the computer program is simply irrelevant to my understanding of the story. In the Chinese case I have everything that artificial intelligence can put into me by way of a program, and I understand nothing; in the English case everything, and there is so far no reason at all to suppose that my understanding has anything to do with computer programs, that is, with computational operations on purely formally specified elements. As long as the program is defined in terms of computational operations on purely formally defined elements, what the example suggests is that these by themselves have no interesting connection with understanding. They are certainly not sufficient conditions, and not the slightest reason has been given to suppose that they are necessary conditions or even that they make a significant contribution to understanding. Notice that the force of the argument is not simply that different machines can have the same input and output while operating on different formal principles—that is not the point at all. Rather, whatever purely formal principles you put into the computer, they will not be sufficient for understanding, since a human will be able to follow the formal principles without understanding anything. No reason whatever has been offered to suppose that such principles are necessary or even contributory, since no reason has been given to suppose that when I understand English I am operating with any formal program at all.

Well, then, what is it that I have in the case of the English sentences that I do not have in the case of the Chinese sentences? The obvious answer is that I know what the former mean, while I haven't the faintest idea what the latter mean. But in what

---

and the ways in which they combine to form new signs or symbols. By contrast, *semantics* comprises the (study of the) relation between a sign or symbol and what it stands for. It includes such notions as the *meaning* and *reference* of terms. Searle is saying that knowing how to perform the computational/syntactical operations that produce correct answers in Chinese does *not* amount to *understanding* Chinese. The semantic dimension of the language is absent; its symbols are meaningless to him, and therefore meaningless to any machine following the same syntactical rules. Ed.

[7] "Instantiation" here means roughly the same as "instance" or "actualization." He is saying that his conscious following of the English-language instructions for manipulating Chinese symbols is equivalent to the running of the corresponding program in a computer. Ed.

does this consist and why couldn't we give it to a machine, whatever it is? I will return to this question later, but first I want to continue with the example.

I have had the occasions to present this example to several workers in artificial intelligence, and, interestingly, they do not seem to agree on what the proper reply to it is. I get a surprising variety of replies, and in what follows I will consider the most common of these (specified along with their geographic origins).

But first I want to block some common misunderstandings about "understanding": in many of these discussions one finds a lot of fancy footwork about the word "understanding." My critics point out that there are many different degrees of understanding; that "understanding" is not a simple two-place predicate; that there are even different kinds and levels of understanding, and often the law of excluded middle[8] doesn't even apply in a straightforward way to statements of the form "x understands y"; that in many cases it is a matter for decision and not a simple matter of fact whether x understands y; and so on. To all of these points I want to say: of course, of course. But they have nothing to do with the points at issue. There are clear cases in which "understanding" literally applies and clear cases where it does not apply; and these two sorts of cases are all I need for this argument.[9] I understand stories in English; to a lesser degree, stories in German; and in Chinese, not at all. My car and my adding machine, on the other hand, understand nothing: they are not in that line of business. We often attribute "understanding" and other cognitive predicates by metaphor and analogy to cars, adding machines, and other artifacts, but nothing is proved by such attributions. We say, "The door knows when to open because of its photoelectric cell," "The adding machine knows how (understands how, is able) to do addition and subtraction but not division," and "The thermostat perceives changes in the temperature." The reason we make these attributions is quite interesting, and it has to do with the fact that in artifacts we extend our own intentionality;[10] our tools are extensions of our purposes, and so we find it natural to make metaphorical attributions of intentionality to them; but I take it no philosophical ice is cut by such examples. The sense in which an automatic door "understands instructions" from its photoelectric cell is not at all the sense in which I understand English. If the sense in which Schank's programmed computers understand stories is supposed to be the metaphorical sense in which the door understands, and not the sense in which I understand English, the issue would not be worth discussing. But Newell and Simon (1963) write that the kind of cognition they claim for computers is exactly the same as for human beings. I like the straightforwardness of this claim, and it is the sort of claim I will be considering. I will argue that in the literal sense the programmed computer understands what the car and the adding machine understand, namely, exactly nothing. The computer understanding is not just (like my understanding of German) partial or incomplete; it is zero.

---

[8] If p stands for a proposition, then the law of the excluded middle states that "Either p is true or p is false—there is no third possibility." ED.

[9] Also, "understanding" implies both the possession of mental (intentional) states and the truth (validity, success) of these states. For the purposes of this discussion we are concerned only with the possession of the states.

[10] Intentionality is by definition that feature of certain mental states by which they are directed at or about objects and states of affairs in the world. Thus, beliefs, desires, and intentions are intentional states; undirected forms of anxiety and depression are not. For further discussion see Searle (1979c).

A supporter of "strong AI" could make the following objection: Searle is blurring crucial differences between a computational account of a person speaking English in the ordinary sense and the account of the person engaged in the artificially isolated activity of answering questions in Chinese from inside the Chinese room. To see this let's use the computational model to describe Campbell's Imitation Man in Reading 24. In body, sensory organs, and behavior, the Imitation Man has a very close external resemblance to a biological human. The account of his language comprehension and production would be nested within a computational model of his mind that would include the translation or transduction of sensory input into binary code, and of binary motor signals into the motions of body parts, including those involved in the production of speech. Unlike the forlorn user of alien symbols inside the Chinese room, the Imitation Man did not learn his language (English) by being confined within a room and given rules for combining such items as letters and morphemes. No, he was programmed to learn and use his English within a rich context of perception and of interaction with a community of English speakers. As a result, the English subsystem within his mind-system has complex relationships with other subsystems serving perceptual memory, social behavior, and other aspects of a complete human existence. It is these relationships that give *meaning* to the symbols of a language. So we should not be surprised that the denizen of the Chinese room seems to have a severe deficit in what we would recognize as language comprehension.

The gist of Searle's objection is better seen when it is applied to the Imitation Man in his full behavioral splendor. Imagine yourself inside his imitation head. There you have many sets of instructions for processing incoming strings of binary symbols from various points of entry into the cranial cavity, and other instructions for emitting strings through various output openings. These strings of symbols have absolutely no meaning for you. You categorize and process them solely on the basis of features such as point of entry and order of 1s and 0s. Of course there is no conceivable way you could do all this with enough speed and accuracy to generate the appropriate responses of the Imitation Man to the flux of his sensory input. But the perceptual and motor requirements of the person in the Chinese Room are also impossible, as Searle admits. To make your intracranial computation task slightly easier, suppose that you have numerous assistants carrying out various subroutines under your supervision. Presumably, Searle would say that neither they nor you nor the entire system composed of you, your assistants, and the enclosing structure of the Imitation Man have any understanding of the words spoken by the Imitation Man or indeed any understanding of anything that the Imitation Man may seem to be consciously doing. Processing uninterpreted symbols, Searle would say, is not a sufficient condition for having a mental life. In fact, it has so little apparent relationship to mental life that we have no good reason to regard it as being a necessary condition or a contribution to mental life.

REVIEW QUESTION

Searle is emphatic in his rejection of dualism. He considers consciousness and thought to be as natural, as *biological,* an activity for the brain with its specific biochemical make-up as is the digestion of food for the stomach and intestines. You saw in Reading 4 a description of the sorts of processes taking place in the human brain when there is ongoing consciousness and thought. In fact we have a much better description of what's going on in the brain than what Searle or anyone else today could provide of the kinds of digital computation that would enable speech at the human level. Do brain processes as currently understood seem to have any greater promise of explaining thought or consciousness than computational processes as currently understood? (This question, like Searle's argument, is an appeal to your intuition.)

Is the Brain a Digital Computer?

In the previous selection Searle attacked the computational model of the mind by arguing that purely syntactical (computational) operations within a system will not be sufficient for us to attribute to that system an understanding of language, even if the system were, in its input and output, the functional equivalent of a human speaker of a language. In this next selection

Searle continues his attack on the computational model by arguing that there can be no fact of the matter as to whether a brain *is* a digital computer. A physical system is a computer only in relation to a conscious agent, and insofar as the system's structure allows it to be used by that agent for the purpose of computation. Therefore being a computer cannot be an intrinsic feature of the brain, and its being a computer of some sort cannot be what makes human cognitive processes possible.

I. INTRODUCTION, STRONG AI, WEAK AI AND COGNITIVISM

There are different ways to present a Presidential Address to the APA; the one I have chosen is simply to report on work that I am doing right now, on work in progress. I am going to present some of my further explorations into the computational model of the mind.[11]

The basic idea of the computer model of the mind is that the mind is the program and the brain the hardware of a computational system. A slogan one often sees is "the mind is to the brain as the program is to the hardware."[12]

Let us begin our investigation of this claim by distinguishing three questions:

1. Is the brain a digital computer?
2. Is the mind a computer program?
3. Can the operations of the brain be simulated on a digital computer?

I will be addressing 1 and not 2 or 3. I think 2 can be decisively answered in the negative. Since programs are defined purely formally or syntactically and since minds have an intrinsic mental content, it follows immediately that the program by itself cannot constitute the mind. The formal syntax of the program does not by itself guarantee the presence of mental contents. I showed this a decade ago in the Chinese Room Argument (Searle, 1980). A computer, me for example, could run the steps of the program for some mental capacity, such as understanding Chinese, without understanding a word of Chinese. The argument rests on the simple logical truth that syntax is not the same as, nor is it by itself sufficient for, semantics. So the answer to the second question is obviously "No".

The answer to 3 seems to me equally obviously "Yes", at least on a natural interpretation. That is, naturally interpreted, the question means: Is there some description of the brain such that under that description you could do a computational simulation of the operations of the brain. But since according to Church's thesis,[13] anything that can be given a precise enough characterization as a set of steps can be simulated on a digital computer, it follows trivially that the question has an affirmative answer. The operations of the brain can be **simulated** on a digital computer in the same sense in which weather systems, the behavior of the New York stock market or the pattern of airline flights over Latin America can. So our question is not, "Is the mind a program?" The answer to that is, "No". Nor is it, "Can the brain be simulated?" The answer to that is, "Yes". The question is, "Is the brain a digital computer?" And for purposes of this discussion I am taking that question as equivalent to: "Are brain processes computational?"

One might think that this question would lose much of its interest if question 2 receives a negative answer. That is, one might suppose that unless the mind is a program, there is no interest to the question whether the brain is a computer. But that is not really the case. Even for those who agree that programs by themselves are not constitutive of mental phenomena, there is still an important question: Granted that there is more to the mind than the syntactical operations of the digital computer; nonetheless, it might be the case that mental states are at least computational states and mental processes are computational processes operating over

From John R. Searle, "Is the Brain a Digital Computer?", *Proceedings and Addresses of the American Philosophical Association* 64 (November, 1990): 21–37. Reprinted with permission of the American Philosophical Association.

[11] For earlier explorations see Searle (1980) and Searle (1984).

[12] This view is announced and defended in a large number of books and articles many of which appear to have more or less the same title, e.g., *Computers and Thought* (Feigenbaum and Feldman, eds., 1963), *Computers and Thought* (Sharples et al., 1988), *The Computer and the Mind* (Johnson-Laird, 1988), *Computation and Cognition* (Pylyshyn, 1985), "The Computer Model of the Mind" (Block, 1990, forthcoming), and of course, "Computing Machinery and Intelligence" (Turing, 1950).

[13] See Reading 15, section 4. ED.

the formal structure of these mental states. This, in fact, seems to me the position taken by a fairly large number of people.

I am not saying that the view is fully clear, but the idea is something like this: At some level of description brain processes are syntactical; there are so to speak, "sentences in the head". These need not be sentences in English or Chinese, but perhaps in the "Language of Thought" (Fodor, 1975). Now, like any sentences, they have a syntactical structure and a semantics or meaning, and the problem of syntax can be separated from the problem of semantics. The problem of semantics is: How do these sentences in the head get their meanings? But that question can be discussed independently of the question: How does the brain work in processing these sentences? A typical answer to that latter question is: The brain works as a digital computer performing computational operations over the syntactical structure of sentences in the head.

Just to keep the terminology straight, I call the view that all there is to having a mind is having a program, Strong AI, the view that brain processes (and mental processes) can be simulated computationally, Weak AI, and the view that the brain is a digital computer, Cognitivism.

This paper is about Cognitivism, and I had better say at the beginning what motivates it. If you read books about the brain (say Shepherd [1983] or Kuffler and Nicholls [1976]) you get a certain picture of what is going on in the brain. If you then turn to books about computation (say Boolos and Jeffrey, 1989) you get a picture of the logical structure of the theory of computation. If you then turn to books about cognitive science (say Pylyshyn, 1985) they tell you that what the brain books describe is really the same as what the computability books were describing. Philosophically speaking, this does not smell right to me and I have learned, at least at the beginning of an investigation, to follow my sense of smell.

II. THE PRIMAL STORY

I want to begin the discussion by trying to state as strongly as I can why Cognitivism has seemed intuitively appealing. There is a story about the relation of human intelligence to computation that goes back at least to Turing's classic paper (1950),

and I believe it is the foundation of the Cognitivist view. I will call it the Primal Story:

> We begin with two results in mathematical logic, the Church-Turing thesis (sometimes called Church's thesis) and Turing's theorem. For our purposes, the Church-Turing thesis states that for any algorithm there is some Turing machine that can implement that algorithm. Turing's theorem says that there is a Universal Turing Machine which can simulate any Turing Machine. Now if we put these two together we have the result that a Universal Turing Machine can implement any algorithm whatever.

But now, what made this result so exciting? What made it send shivers up and down the spines of a whole generation of young workers in artificial intelligence is the following thought: Suppose the brain is a Universal Turing Machine.

Well, are there any good reasons for supposing the brain might be a Universal Turing Machine? Let us continue with the Primal Story.

> It is clear that at least some human mental abilities are algorithmic. For example, I can consciously do long division by going through the steps of an algorithm for solving long division problems. It is furthermore a consequence of the Church-Turing thesis and Turing's theorem that anything a human can do algorithmically can be done on a Universal Turing Machine. I can implement, for example, the very same algorithm that I use for long division on a digital computer. In such a case, as described by Turing (1950), both I, the human computer, and the mechanical computer are implementing the same algorithm; I am doing it consciously, the mechanical computer nonconsciously. Now it seems reasonable to suppose there might also be a whole lot of mental processes going on in my brain nonconsciously which are also computational. And if so, we could find out how the brain works by simulating these very processes on a digital computer. Just as we got a computer simulation of the processes for doing long division, so could get a computer simulation of the processes for understanding language, visual perception, categorization, etc.

"But what about semantics? After all, programs are purely syntactical." Here another set of logico-mathematical results comes into play in the Primal Story.

> The development of proof theory showed that within certain well known limits the semantic relations

between propositions can be entirely mirrored by the syntactic relations between the sentences that express those propositions. Now suppose that mental contents in the head are expressed syntactically in the head, then all we would need to account for mental processes would be computational processes between the syntactical elements in the head. If we get the proof theory right the semantics will take care of itself; and that is what computers do: they implement the proof theory.[14]

We thus have a well defined research program. We try to discover the programs being implemented in the brain by programming computers to implement the same programs. We do this in turn by getting the mechanical computer to match the performance of the human computer (i.e., to pass the Turing Test)[15] and then getting the psychologists to look for evidence that the internal processes are the same in the two types of computer.

Now in what follows I would like the reader to keep this Primal Story in mind—notice especially Turing's contrast between the conscious implementation of the program by the human computer and the nonconscious implementation of programs,

whether by the brain or by the mechanical computer; notice furthermore the idea that we might just discover programs running in nature, the very same programs that we put into our mechanical computers.

If one looks at the books and articles supporting Cognitivism one finds certain common assumptions, often unstated, but nonetheless pervasive. First, it is often assumed that the only alternative to the view that the brain is a digital computer is some form of dualism. The idea is that unless you believe in the existence of immortal Cartesian souls, you must believe that the brain is a computer. Indeed, it often seems to be assumed that the question whether the brain is a physical mechanism determining our mental states and whether the brain is a digital computer are the same question. Rhetorically speaking, the idea is to bully the reader into thinking that unless he accepts the idea that the brain is some kind of computer, he is committed to some weird antiscientific views. Recently the field has opened up a bit to allow that the brain might not be an old fashioned von Neumann style digital computer, but rather a more sophisticated kind of parallel processing computational equipment. Still, to deny that the brain is computational is to risk losing your membership in the scientific community.

Second, it is also assumed that the question whether brain processes are computational is just a plain empirical question. It is to be settled by factual investigation in the same way that such questions as whether the heart is a pump or whether green leaves do photosynthesis were settled as matters of fact. There is no room for logic chopping or conceptual analysis, since we are talking about matters of hard scientific fact. Indeed I think many people who work in this field would doubt that the title of this paper poses an appropriate philosophic question at all. "Is the brain really a digital computer?" is no more a philosophical question than "Is the neurotransmitter at neuro-muscular junctions really acetylcholene?"

Even people who are unsympathetic to Cognitivism, such as Penrose and Dreyfus[16], seem to treat

---

[14] This is a difficult passage. "Proof theory" is just what the words in the phrase suggest: a theory in mathematics or logic about the properties of proofs. A "proof" in proof theory is a sequence of formulae (sequences of uninterpreted symbols) of which each member is either an axiom (a formula which is an *un*derived starting point for derivations of other formulas) or a formula derived by syntactical rules from an axiom (derived formulas are called *theorems*) or a formula derived from a theorem; and terminating with the derivation of a theorem. As you can see from this definition, derivation and proof are purely syntactical, dealing only with the relationships among sequences of uninterpreted symbols. To understand Searle's point, we also need the notion of a *logical consequence*. A proposition C is a logical consequence of, or follows from, a set of propositions P, if whenever each proposition in P is true, then C is true. Logical consequence is what Searle would call a "semantic relation" since it obtains between *propositions* or *interpreted* formulae. What proof theory tells us is that, in most cases, if C is a logical consequence of P, then there is a derivation of C from P according to purely syntactical rules. In that sense the "semantic relations between propositions can be entirely mirrored by the syntactic relations between the sentences [formulas] that express those propositions." According to the cognitivist, as interpreted by Searle, we can just "bracket" the semantic dimension of the sentences, knowing that purely syntactic operations can preserve truth in the derivations of one sentence from another. ED.

[15] This test was devised by mathematician Alan Turing (inventor of the Turing machine and pioneer of computer theory) in 1950 as a criterion by which we could judge at what point computers had developed sufficiently to be said to "think" in the sense that humans are said to think. The test would go as follows: A human interrogator would ask questions via a computer to a human and to a computer. The human was allowed to lie. If the interrogator was unable to tell, after an appropriate interval, which respondent was the computer, then, according to Turing, the computer was indeed thinking. ED.

[16] Physicist Roger Penrose, in his *The Emperor's New Mind: Concerning Computers, Minds, and the Laws of Physics* (1989), and philosopher Hubert L. Dreyfus, in *What Computers Can't Do: A Critique of Artificial Reason* (1972), argue against the adequacy of the computational model of mind. ED.

it as a straightforward factual issue. They do not seem to be worried about the question what sort of claim it might be that they are doubting. But I am puzzled by the question: What sort of fact about the brain could constitute its being a computer?

Third, another stylistic feature of this literature is the haste and sometimes even carelessness with which the foundational questions are glossed over. What exactly are the anatomical and physiological features of brains that are being discussed? What exactly is a digital computer? And how are the answers to these two questions supposed to connect? The usual procedure in these books and articles is to make a few remarks about 0's and 1's, give a popular summary of the Church-Turing thesis, and then get on with the more exciting things such as computer achievements and failures. To my surprise in reading this literature I have found that there seems to be a peculiar philosophical hiatus. On the one hand, we have a very elegant set of mathematical results ranging from Turing's theorem to Church's thesis to recursive function theory. On the other hand, we have an impressive set of electronic devices which we use every day. Since we have such advanced mathematics and such good electronics, we assume that somehow somebody must have done the basic philosophical work of connecting the mathematics to the electronics. But as far as I can tell that is not the case. On the contrary, we are in a peculiar situation where there is little theoretical agreement among the practitioners on such absolutely fundamental questions as, What exactly is a digital computer? What exactly is a symbol? What exactly is a computational process? Under what physical conditions exactly are two systems implementing the same program?

III. THE DEFINITION OF COMPUTATION

Since there is no universal agreement on the fundamental questions, I believe it is best to go back to the sources, back to the original definitions given by Alan Turing.

According to Turing, a Turing machine[17] can carry out certain elementary operations: It can rewrite a 0 on its tape as a 1, it can rewrite a 1 on

its tape as a 0, it can shift the tape [one] square to the left, or it can shift the tape [one] square to the right. It is controlled by a program of instruction and each instruction specifies a condition and an action to be carried out if the condition is satisfied.

That is the standard definition of computation, but, taken literally, it is at least a bit misleading. If you open up your home computer you are most unlikely to find any 0's and 1's or even a tape. But this does not really matter for the definition. To find out if an object is really a digital computer, it turns out that we do not actually have to look for 0's and 1's, etc.; rather we just have to look for something that we could treat as or count as or could be used to function as 0's and 1's. Furthermore, to make the matter more puzzling, it turns out that this machine could be made out of just about anything. As Johnson-Laird says, "It could be made out of cogs and levers like an old fashioned mechanical calculator; it could be made out of a hydraulic system through which water flows; it could be made out of transistors etched into a silicon chip through which an electrical current flows. It could even be carried out by the brain. Each of these machines uses a different medium to represent binary symbols—the positions of cogs, the presence or absence of water, the level of the voltage and perhaps nerve impulses" (Johnson-Laird, 1988, p. 39).

Similar remarks are made by most of the people who write on this topic. For example, Ned Block (Block, 1990), shows how we can have electrical gates where the 1's and 0's are assigned to voltage levels of 4 volts and 7 volts respectively. So we might think that we should go and look for voltage levels. But Block tells us that 1 is only "conventionally" assigned to a certain level. The situation grows more puzzling when he informs us further that we did not need to use electricity at all but we could have used an elaborate system of cats and mice and cheese and make our gates in such a way that the cat will strain at the leash and pull open a gate which we can also treat as if it were an 0 or 1. The point, as Block is anxious to insist, is "the irrelevance of hardware realization to computational description. These gates work in different ways but they are nonetheless computationally equivalent" (p. 260). In the same vein, Pylyshyn says that a computational sequence could be realized by "a group of pigeons trained to peck as a Turing machine!" (Pylyshyn, 1985, p. 57)

---

[17]For an explanation of Turing machines, see Reading 15, sections 3–5. ED.

But now if we are trying to take seriously the idea that the brain is a digital computer, we get the uncomfortable result that we could make a system that does just what the brain does out of pretty much anything. Computationally speaking, on this view, you can make a "brain" that functions just like yours and mine out of cats and mice and cheese or levers "computationally equivalent". You would just need an awful lot of cats, or pigeons or water pipes, or whatever it might be. The proponents of Cognitivism report this result with sheer and unconcealed delight. But I think they ought to be worried about it, and I am going to try to show that it is just the tip of a whole iceberg of problems.

IV. FIRST DIFFICULTY: SYNTAX IS NOT INTRINSIC TO PHYSICS

Why are the defenders of computationalism not worried by the implications of multiple realizability? The answer is that they think it is typical of functional accounts that the same function admits of multiple realizations. In this respect, computers are just like carburetors and thermostats. Just as carburetors can be made of brass or steel, so computers can be made of an indefinite range of hardware materials.

But there is a difference: The classes of carburetors and thermostats are defined in terms of the production of certain physical effects. That is why, for example, nobody says you can make carburetors out of pigeons.[18] But the class of computers is defined syntactically in terms of the assignment of 0's and 1's. The multiple realizability is a consequence not of the fact that the same physical effect can be achieved in different physical substances, but that the relevant properties are purely syntactical. The physics is irrelevant except insofar as it admits of the assignments of 0's and 1's and of state transitions between them.

But this has two consequences which might be disastrous:

1. The same principle that implies multiple realizability would seem to imply universal realizability.[19] If computation is defined in terms of the assignment of syntax then everything would be a digital computer, because any object whatever could have syntactical ascriptions made to it. You could describe anything in terms of 0's and 1's.

2. Worse yet, syntax is not intrinsic to physics. The ascription of syntactical properties is always relative to an agent or observer who treats certain physical phenomena as syntactical.

Now why exactly would these consequences be disastrous?

Well, we wanted to know how the brain works, specifically how it produces mental phenomena. And it would not answer that question to be told that the brain is a digital computer in the sense in which stomach, liver, heart, solar system, and the state of Kansas are all digital computers. The model we had was that we might discover some fact about the operation of the brain which would show that it is a computer. We wanted to know if there was not some sense in which brains were intrinsically digital computers in a way that green leaves intrinsically perform photosynthesis or hearts intrinsically pump blood. It is not a matter of us arbitrarily or "conventionally" assigning the word "pump" to hearts or "photosynthesis" to leaves. There is an actual fact of the matter. And what we were asking is, "Is there in that way a fact of the matter about brains that would make them digital computers?" It does not answer that question to be told, yes, brains are digital computers because everything is a digital computer.

On the standard textbook definition of computation,

1. For any object there is some description of that object such that under that description the object is a digital computer.

2. For any program there is some sufficiently complex object such that there is some description of the object under which it is implementing the program.[20] Thus for

---

[18] For instance, the function of a carburetor is to mix air and gas in an internal combustion engine. Pigeons don't seem up to this task. ED.

[19] For instance, Putnam in section II of Reading 16 says that "everything is a Probabilistic Automaton under some description." This claim is, of course, very debatable. ED.

[20] See White's discussion of this passage in Reading 15 at the end of section 7. It's hard to know what "implementing" means here. If it means what it means for computers running a word processing program, then it should be possible to input text and the program should respond in the same ways to the same input text and commands every time. It's difficult to understand how a wall could be described as doing such things. ED.

example the wall behind my back is right now implementing the Wordstar program, because there is some pattern of molecule movements which is isomorphic with the formal structure of Wordstar. But if the wall is implementing Wordstar then if it is a big enough wall it is implementing any program, including any program implemented in the brain.

I think the main reason that the proponents do not see that multiple or universal realizability is a problem is that they do not see it as a consequence of a much deeper point, namely that the "syntax" is not the name of a physical feature, like mass or gravity. On the contrary they talk of "syntactical engines" and even "semantic engines"[21] as if such talk were like that of gasoline engines or diesel engines, as if it could be just a plain matter of fact that the brain or anything else is a syntactical engine.

I think it is probably possible to block the result of universal realizability by tightening up our definition of computation. Certainly we ought to respect the fact that programmers and engineers regard it as a quirk of Turing's original definitions and not as a real feature of computation. Unpublished works by Brian Smith, Vinod Goel, and John Batali all suggest that a more realistic definition of computation will emphasize such features as the causal relations among program states, programmability and controllability of the mechanism, and situatedness in the real world. But these further restrictions on the definition of computation are no help in the present discussion because the really deep problem is that syntax is essentially an observer relative notion. The multiple realizability of computationally equivalent processes in different physical media was not just a sign that the processes were abstract, but that they were not intrinsic to the system at all. They depended on an interpretation from outside. We are looking for some facts of the matter which make brain processes computational; but given the way we have defined computation, there never could be any such facts of the matter. We can't, on the one hand, say that anything is a digital computer if we can assign a syntax to it and then suppose there is a factual question intrinsic to its physi-

cal operation whether or not a natural system such as the brain is a digital computer.

And if the word "syntax" seems puzzling, the same point can be stated without it. That is, someone might claim that the notions of "syntax" and "symbols" are just a manner of speaking and that what we are really interested in is the existence of systems with discrete physical phenomena and state transitions between them.[22] On this view we don't really need 0's and 1's; they are just a convenient shorthand. But, I believe, this move is no help. A physical state of a system is a computational state only relative to the assignment to that state of some computational role, function, or interpretation. The same problem arises without 0's and 1's because notions such as computation, algorithm and program do not name intrinsic physical features of systems. Computational states are not discovered within the physics, they are assigned to the physics.

This is a different argument from the Chinese Room Argument and I should have seen it ten years ago but I did not. The Chinese Room Argument showed that semantics is not intrinsic to syntax. I am now making the separate and different point that syntax is not intrinsic to physics. For the purposes of the original argument I was simply assuming that the syntactical characterization of the computer was unproblematic. But that is a mistake. There is no way you could discover that something is intrinsically a digital computer because the characterization of it as a digital computer is always relative to an observer who assigns a syntactical interpretation to the purely physical features of the system. As applied to the Language Of Thought hypothesis,[23] this has the consequence that the

---

[21] These "engines" would be systems of rules for generating the sentences and propositions of a language. ED.

[22] In other words, we need a system which goes in a regular and specifiable manner from one measurable state to another, without a continuous transition between them, e.g., a current flowing or not, without continuous variation in the voltage of the current. ED.

[23] This hypothesis was first put forward by Jerry Fodor in *The Language of Thought* (1975). It asserts that there is a language or symbol system (often referred to as "mentalese") innate to the human brain. All human thinking consists in the unconscious computation of the symbols and formulae or sentences of this language. It is thus a universal language independent of any particular natural language such as English or Japanese. It is the bearer of the common human stock of possible *meanings*, subsets of which get expressed in particular languages, both natural and artificial. This language is the basis for communication across natural languages—expressing the same *thought* in different languages—and for there being such things as a French-English dictionary. This *unlearned* language is the basis for children coming to learn the meanings of words and expressions in the language in which they learn to speak. For a child to learn these meanings, it is not enough that words in English, for instance, come to be

thesis is incoherent. There is no way you could discover that there are, intrinsically, unknown sentences in your head because something is a sentence only relative to some agent or user who uses it as a sentence. As applied to the computational model generally, the characterization of a process as computational is a characterization of a physical system from outside; and the identification of the process as computational does not identify an intrinsic feature of the physics, it is essentially an observer relative characterization.

This point has to be understood precisely. I am not saying there are a priori limits on the patterns we could discover in nature. We could no doubt discover a pattern of events in my brain that was isomorphic to the implementation of the vi program on this computer. But to say that something is functioning as a computational process is to say something more than that a pattern of physical events is occurring. It requires the assignment of a computational interpretation by some agent. Analogously, we might discover in nature objects which had the same sort of shape as chairs and which could therefore be used as chairs; but we could not discover objects in nature which were functioning as chairs, except relative to some agents who regarded them or used them as chairs.

V. SECOND DIFFICULTY: THE HOMUNCULUS FALLACY IS ENDEMIC TO COGNITIVISM

So far, we seem to have arrived at a problem. Syntax is not part of physics. This has the consequence that if computation is defined syntactically then nothing is intrinsically a digital computer solely in virtue of its physical properties. Is there any way out of this problem? Yes, there is, and it is a way standardly taken in cognitive science, but it is out of the frying pan and into the fire. Most of the works I have seen in the computational theory of the mind commit some variation on the homunculus[24] fallacy. The idea always is to treat the brain as if there were some agent inside it using it to compute with. A typical case is David Marr (1982) who describes the task of vision as proceeding from a two-dimensional visual array on the retina to a three-dimensional description of the external world as output of the visual system. The difficulty is: Who is reading the description? Indeed, it looks throughout Marr's book, and in other standard works on the subject, as if we have to invoke a homunculus inside the system in order to treat its operations as genuinely computational.

Many writers feel that the homunculus fallacy is not really a problem, because, with Dennett (1978), they feel that the homunculus can be "discharged". The idea is this: Since the computational operations of the computer can be analyzed into progressively simpler units, until eventually we reach simple flip-flop, "yes-no", "1-0" patterns, it seems that the higher-level homunculi can be discharged with progressively stupider homunculi, until finally we reach the bottom level of a simple flip-flop that involves no real homunculus at all. The idea, in short, is that recursive decomposition will eliminate the homunculi.

It took me a long time to figure out what these people were driving at, so in case someone else is similarly puzzled I will explain an example in detail: Suppose that we have a computer that multiplies six times eight to get forty-eight. Now we ask "How does it do it?" Well, the answer might be that it adds six to itself seven times.[25] But if you ask "How does it add six to itself seven times?", the answer might be that, first, it converts all of the numerals into binary notation, and second, it applies a simple algorithm for operating on binary notation until finally we reach the bottom level at which the only instructions are of the form, "Print a zero, erase a one." So, for example, at the top level our intelligent homunculus says "I know how to multiply six times eight to get forty-eight". But at the next lower-level he is replaced by a stupider homunculus who says "I do not actually know how to do multiplication, but I can do addition." Below him are some stupider ones who say "We do not actually know how to do addition or multiplication, but we know how to convert decimal to binary."

---

associated with objects or situations they perceive. The child must learn *how to think* of these associated objects and situations or, in other words, what is *meant* by the associated expressions. ED.

[24] *Homunculus* is a Latin term for "little man." ED.

[25] People sometimes say that it would have to add six to itself *eight* times. But that is bad arithmetic. Six added to itself eight times is fifty-four, because six added to itself zero times is still six. It is amazing how often this mistake is made.

Below these are stupider ones who say "We do not know anything about any of this stuff, but we know how to operate on binary symbols." At the bottom level are a whole bunch of homunculi who just say "Zero one, zero one". All of the higher levels reduce to this bottom level. Only the bottom level really exists; the top levels are all just as-if.[26]

Various authors (e.g. Haugeland [1981], Block [1990]) describe this feature when they say that the system is a syntactical engine driving a semantic engine.[27] But we still must face the question we had before: What facts intrinsic to the system make it syntactical? What facts about the bottom level or any other level make these operations into zeros and ones? Without a homunculus that stands outside the recursive decomposition, we do not even have a syntax to operate with.[28] The attempt to eliminate the homunculus fallacy through recursive decomposition fails, because the only way to get the syntax intrinsic to the physics is to put a homunculus in the physics.

There is a fascinating feature to all of this. Cognitivists cheerfully concede that the higher levels of computation, e.g. "multiply 6 times 8," are observer relative; there is nothing really there that corresponds directly to multiplication; it is all in the eye of the homunculus/beholder. But they want to stop this concession at the lower levels. The electronic circuit, they admit, does not really multiply 6 × 8 as such, but it really does manipulate 0's and 1's and these manipulations, so to speak, add up to multiplication. But to concede that the higher levels of computation are not intrinsic to the physics is

already to concede that the lower levels are not intrinsic either. So the homunculus fallacy is still with us.

For real computers of the kind you buy in the store, there is no homunculus problem, each user is the homunculus in question. But if we are to suppose that the brain is a digital computer, we are still faced with the question "And who is the user?" Typical homunculus questions in cognitive science are such as the following: "How does the visual system compute shape from shading; how does it compute object distance from size of retinal image?" A parallel question would be, "How do nails compute the distance they are to travel in the board from the impact of the hammer and the density of the wood?" And the answer is the same in both sorts of case: If we are talking about how the system works intrinsically neither nails nor visual systems compute anything. We as outside homunculi might describe them computationally, and it is often useful to do so. But you do not understand hammering by supposing that nails are somehow intrinsically implementing hammering algorithms and you do not understand vision by supposing the system is implementing, e.g., the shape from shading algorithm.

VI. THIRD DIFFICULTY: SYNTAX HAS NO CAUSAL POWERS

Certain sorts of explanations in the natural sciences specify mechanisms which function causally in the production of the phenomena to be explained. This is especially common in the biological sciences. Think of the germ theory of disease, the account of photosynthesis, the DNA theory of inherited traits, and even the Darwinian theory of natural selection. In each case a causal mechanism is specified, and in each case the specification gives an explanation of the output of the mechanism. Now if you go back and look at the Primal Story it seems clear that this is the sort of explanation promised by Cognitivism. The mechanisms by which brain processes produce cognition are supposed to be computational, and by specifying the programs we will have specified the causes of cognition. One beauty of this research program, often remarked, is that we don't need to know the details of brain functioning in order to explain cognition. Brain processes provide only the

---

[26] This progression is typical of *reductive* analyses in science and elsewhere: A macro or molar phenomenon is understood as "nothing but" a configuration of quantitatively and/or functionally lower-level entities. ED.

[27] As the Chinese Room tends to show, purely syntactical operations on meaningless symbols are deficient in understanding (i.e., "stupid") compared to mental operations using symbols with meaning. If propositions or sentences with meaning can be generated by purely syntactical devices, then a cognitively higher-level function is reduced to a lower-level one. ED.

[28] There is a very important set of issues hovering in the background of Searle's argument against the homuncular fallacy: How are *consciousness* or *intentionality* to be defined for the purposes of this discussion? What exactly is it about them that constitutes a *necessary condition* of a system having syntactical or semantic properties? It was clear to Descartes that *thinking* was an essentially conscious, implicitly self-aware activity. In his dualistic scheme, *unconscious* activity belonged to the realm of bodily mechanisms. It could not be mental. But Searle is not a dualist. ED.

hardware implementation of the cognitive programs, but the program level is where the real cognitive explanations are given. On the standard account, as stated by Newell for example, there are three levels of explanation, hardware, program, and intentionality (Newell calls this last level, the knowledge level), and the special contribution of cognitive science is made at the program level.

But if what I have said so far is correct, then there is something fishy about this whole project. I used to believe that as a causal account the cognitivist's theory was at least false; but I now am having difficulty formulating a version of it that is coherent even to the point where it could be an empirical thesis at all. The thesis is that there is a whole lot of symbols being manipulated in the brain, 0's and 1's flashing through the brain at lightning speed and invisible not only to the naked eye but even to the most powerful electron microscope, and it is these which cause cognition. But the difficulty is that the 0's and 1's as such have no causal powers at all because they do not even exist except in the eyes of the beholder. The implemented program has no causal powers other than those of the implementing medium because the program has no real existence, no ontology, beyond that of the implementing medium. Physically speaking there is no such thing as a separate "program level".

You can see this if you go back to the Primal Story and remind yourself of the difference between the mechanical computer and Turing's human computer. In Turing's human computer there really is a program level intrinsic to the system and it is functioning causally at that level to convert input to output. This is because the human is consciously following the rules for doing a certain computation, and this causally explains his performance. But when we program the mechanical computer to perform the same computation, the assignment of a computational interpretation is now relative to us, the outside homunculi. And there is no longer a level of intentional causation[29]

intrinsic to the system. The human computer is consciously following rules, and this fact explains his behavior, but the mechanical computer is not literally following any rules at all. It is designed to behave exactly as if it were following rules, and so for practical, commercial purposes it does not matter. Now Cognitivism tells us that the brain functions like the commercial computer and this causes cognition. But without a homunculus, both commercial computer and brain have only patterns and the patterns have no causal powers in addition to those of the implementing media. So it seems there is no way Cognitivism could give a causal account of cognition.

However there is a puzzle for my view. Anyone who works with computers even casually knows that we often do in fact give causal explanations that appeal to the program. For example, we can say that when I hit this key I got such and such results because the machine is implementing the vi program and not the emacs program; and this looks like an ordinary causal explanation. So the puzzle is, how do we reconcile the fact that syntax, as such, has no causal powers with the fact that we do give causal explanations that appeal to programs? And, more pressingly, would these sorts of explanations provide an appropriate model of Cognitivism, will they rescue Cognitivism? Could we for example rescue the analogy with thermostats by pointing out that just as the notion "thermostat" figures in causal explanations independently of any reference to the physics of its implementation, so the notion

---

[29]When Searle talks about "intentional causation" and how the *conscious* following of rules "causally explains" a performance, he is invoking a special sense of causality that philosophers often call *agent causation* in contrast to *event causation*. As an example of event causation consider what will happen when I release my grip on the can of soda I'm holding in my hand. In conjunction with the gravitational attraction of the earth on the can, which is expressed in Newton's law, the event that is my releasing my

grip will cause the can to fall. In general, one *event* or set of events is said to *cause* another (the effect) when the effect follows the prior event(s) according to a law of nature.

Let's turn our attention to the event of releasing the grip. Like the falling of the can, it too is an effect of a cause. What sort of cause—event or agent? Suppose that I inadvertently released my grip, or the release was due to a muscle spasm in my hand. In both cases, the release is an effect of some event inside me. But it was not something that *I did*. It just *happened*, though perhaps I should have taken care that it wouldn't. For the release to be something *I do*, for there to be *intentional causality*, it's not enough that the cause of the event be in me the way a sensation or a mood is in me. I can be just as passive toward such internal events as I am toward external events that are not my doing. (Hume, in Reading 31, reduces the self to a passive spectator of the comings and goings of impressions and ideas.) For the release to be what *I did*, it must come *from me*; I must originate it. My agency, my acting, is somehow not part of the sequence of events following each other according to the laws of nature that science is concerned to discover. We do think of ourselves as agents in this sense. But it is a large philosophical task to understand how this sort of causality can belong to a world of events governed by scientific laws. ED.

"program" might be explanatory while equally in-dependent of the physics?

To explore this puzzle let us try to make the case for Cognitivism by extending the Primal Story to show how the Cognitivist investigative procedures work in actual research practice. The idea, typically, is to program a commercial computer so that it simulates some cognitive capacity, such as vision or language. Then, if we get a good simulation, one that gives us at least Turing equivalence, we hypothesize that the brain computer is running the same program as the commercial computer, and to test the hypothesis we look for indirect psychological evidence, such as reaction times.[30] So it seems that we can causally explain the behavior of the brain computer by citing the program in exactly the same sense in which we can explain the behavior of the commercial computer. Now what is wrong with that? Doesn't it sound like a perfectly legitimate scientific research program? We know that the commercial computer's conversion of input to output is explained by a program, and in the brain we discover the same program, hence we have a causal explanation.

Two things ought to worry us immediately about this project. First, we would never accept this mode of explanation for any function of the brain where we actually understood how it worked at the neurobiological level. Second, we would not accept it for other sorts of systems that we can simulate computationally. To illustrate the first point, consider for example, the famous account of "What the Frog's Eye Tells the Frog's Brain" (Lettvin, et al., 1959 in McCulloch, 1965). The account is given entirely in terms of the anatomy and physiology of the frog's nervous system. A typical passage, chosen at random, goes like this:

1. Sustained Contrast Detectors

An unmyelinated axon of this group does not respond when the general illumination is turned on or off. If the sharp edge of an object either lighter or darker than the background moves into its field and stops, it discharges promptly and continues discharg-

ing, no matter what the shape of the edge or whether the object is smaller or larger than the receptive field. (p. 239)

I have never heard anyone say that all this is just the hardware implementation, and that they should have figured out which program the frog was implementing. I do not doubt that you could do a computer simulation of the frog's "bug detectors". Perhaps someone has done it. But we all know that once you understand how the frog's visual system actually works, the "computational level" is just irrelevant.

To illustrate the second point, consider simulations of other sorts of systems. I am, for example, typing these words on a machine that simulates the behavior of an old fashioned mechanical typewriter.[31] As simulations go, the word processing program simulates a typewriter better than any AI program I know of simulates the brain. But no sane person thinks: "At long last we understand how typewriters work, they are implementations of word processing programs." It is simply not the case in general that computational simulations provide causal explanations of the phenomena simulated.

So what is going on? We do not in general suppose that computational simulations of brain processes give us any explanations in place of or in addition to neurobiological accounts of how the brain actually works. And we do not in general take "X is a computational simulation of Y" to name a symmetrical relation. That is, we do not suppose that because the computer simulates a typewriter that therefore the typewriter simulates a computer. We do not suppose that because a weather program simulates a hurricane, that the causal explanation of the behavior of the hurricane is provided by the program. So why should we make an exception to these principles where unknown brain processes are concerned? Are there any good grounds for making the exception? And what kind of a causal explanation is an explanation that cites a formal program?

Here, I believe, is the solution to our puzzle. Once you remove the homunculus from the system, you are left only with a pattern of events to which someone from the outside could attach a computational interpretation. Now the only sense in which the specification of the pattern by itself

---

[30] In other words, we infer from the hypothesis that the brain is implementing a certain program that human subjects should be, for instance, slower or faster in responding to certain stimuli in experimental situations. If tests of humans give us the predicted results, the program hypothesis is further confirmed. ED.

[31] The example was suggested by John Batali.

provides a causal explanation is that if you know that a certain pattern exists in a system you know that some cause or other is responsible for the pattern. So you can, for example, predict later stages from earlier stages. Furthermore, if you already know that the system has been programmed by an outside homunculus, you can give explanations that make reference to the intentionality of the homunculus. You can say, e.g., this machine behaves the way it does because it is running vi. That is like explaining that this book begins with a bit about happy families and does not contain any long passages about a bunch of brothers, because it is Tolstoy's *Anna Karenina* and not Dostoevsky's *The Brothers Karamazov*. But you cannot explain a physical system such as a typewriter or a brain by identifying a pattern which it shares with its computational simulation, because the existence of the pattern does not explain how the system actually works as a physical system. In the case of cognition the pattern is at much too high a level of abstraction to explain such concrete mental (and therefore physical) events as the occurrence of a visual perception or the understanding of a sentence.

Now, I think it is obvious that we cannot explain how typewriters and hurricanes work by pointing to formal patterns they share with their computational simulations. Why is it not obvious in the case of the brain?

Here we come to the second part of our solution to the puzzle. In making the case for Cognitivism we were tacitly supposing that the brain might be implementing algorithms for cognition, in the same sense that Turing's human computer and his mechanical computer implement algorithms. But it is precisely that assumption which we have seen to be mistaken. To see this, ask yourself what happens when a system implements an algorithm. In the human computer the system consciously goes through the steps of the algorithm, so the process is both causal and logical; logical, because the algorithm provides a set of rules for deriving the output symbols from the input symbols; causal, because the agent is making a conscious effort to go through the steps. Similarly in the case of the mechanical computer, the whole system includes an outside homunculus, and with the homunculus the system is both causal and logical; logical, because the homunculus provides an interpretation to the processes of the machine; and

causal, because the hardware of the machine causes it to go through the processes. But these conditions cannot be met by the brute, blind nonconscious neurophysiological operations of the brain. In the brain computer there is no conscious intentional implementation of the algorithm as there is in the mechanical computer either, because that requires an outside homunculus to attach a human computer, but there can't be any nonconscious implementation as there is in the computational interpretation to the physical events. The most we could find in the brain is a pattern of events which is formally similar to the implemented program in the mechanical computer, but that pattern, as such, has no causal powers to call its own and hence explains nothing.

In sum, the fact that the attribution of syntax identifies no further causal powers is fatal to the claim that programs provide causal explanations of cognition. To explore the consequences of this, let us remind ourselves of what Cognitivist explanations actually look like. Explanations such as Chomsky's account of the syntax of natural languages or Marr's account of vision proceed by stating a set of rules according to which a symbolic input symbol, S, is converted into any one of a potentially infinite number of sentences by the repeated application of a set of syntactical rules. In Marr's case, representations of a two dimensional visual array are converted into three dimensional "descriptions" of the world in accordance with certain algorithms. Marr's tripartite distinctions between the computational task, the algorithmic solution of the task and the hardware implementation of the algorithm has (like Newell's distinctions) become famous as a statement of the general pattern of the explanation.

If you take these explanations naively, as I do, it is best to think of them as saying that it is just as if a man alone in a room were going through a set of steps of following rules to generate English sentences or 3D descriptions, as the case might be. But now, let us ask what facts in the real world are supposed to correspond to these explanations as applied to the brain. In Chomsky's case, for example, we are not supposed to think that the agent consciously goes through a set of repeated applications of rules; nor are we supposed to think that he is unconsciously thinking his way through the set of rules. Rather the rules are "computational" and the brain is carrying out the computations. But what does that mean? Well, we are supposed to think that it is just like a commercial computer. The sort of thing that corresponds to the ascription of those rules to a commercial computer is supposed to correspond to the ascription of those rules to the brain. But we have seen that in the commercial computer the ascription is always observer relative, the ascription is made relative to a homunculus who assigns computational interpretations to the hardware states. Without the homunculus there is no computation, just an electronic circuit. So how do we get computation into the brain without a homunculus? As far as I know, neither Chomsky nor Marr ever addressed the question or even thought there was such a question. But without a homunculus there is no explanatory power to the postulation of the program states. There is just a physical mechanism, the brain, with its various real physical and physical/mental causal levels of description.

VII. FOURTH DIFFICULTY: THE BRAIN DOES NOT DO INFORMATION PROCESSING

In this section I turn finally to what I think is, in some ways, the central issue in all of this, the issue of information processing. Many people in the "cognitive science" scientific paradigm will feel that much of my discussion is simply irrelevant and they will argue against it as follows:

> There is a difference between the brain and all of these other systems you have been describing, and this difference explains why a computational simulation in the case of the other systems is a mere simulation, whereas in the case of the brain a computational simulation is actually duplicating and not merely modeling the functional properties of the brain. The reason is that the brain, unlike these other systems, is an information processing system.[32] And this fact about the brain is, in your words, "in-

trinsic". It is just a fact about biology that the brain functions to process information, and since we can also process the same information computationally, computational models of brain processes have a different role altogether from computational models of, for example, the weather. So there is a well defined research question: "Are the computational procedures by which the brain processes information the same as the procedures by which computers process the same information?"

What I just imagined an opponent saying embodies one of the worst mistakes in cognitive science. The mistake is to suppose that in the sense in which computers are used to process information, brains also process information. To see that that is a mistake, contrast what goes on in the computer with what goes in the brain. In the case of the computer, an outside agent encodes some information in a form that can be processed by the circuitry of the computer. That is, he or she provides a syntactical realization of the information that the computer can implement in, for example, different voltage levels. The computer then goes through a series of electrical stages that the outside agent can interpret both syntactically and semantically even though, of course, the hardware has no intrinsic syntax or semantics: It is all in the eye of the beholder. And the physics does not matter provided only that you can get it to implement the algorithm. Finally, an output is produced in the form of physical phenomena which an observer can interpret as symbols with a syntax and a semantics.

But now contrast that with the brain. In the case of the brain, none of the relevant neurobiological processes are observer relative (though of course, like anything, they can be described from an observer relative point of view) and the specificity of the neurophysiology matters desperately. To make this difference clear, let us go through an example. Suppose I see a car coming toward me. A standard computational model of vision will take in information about the visual array on my retina and eventually print out the sentence, "There is a car coming toward me". But that is not what happens in the actual biology. In the biology a concrete and

---

[32] As Searle is using this expression, it seems to mean roughly the same as "symbol processing system." ED.

specific series of electro-chemical reactions are set up by the assault of the photons on the photo receptor cells of my retina, and this entire process eventually results in a concrete visual experience. The biological reality is not that of a bunch of words or symbols being produced by the visual system, rather it is a matter of a concrete specific conscious visual event; this very visual experience. Now, that concrete visual event is as specific and as concrete as a hurricane or the digestion of a meal. We can, with the computer, do an information processing model of the weather, digestion or any other phenomenon, but the phenomena themselves are not thereby information processing systems.

In short, the sense of information processing that is used in cognitive science is at much too high a level of abstraction to capture the concrete biological reality of intrinsic intentionality. The "information" in the brain is always specific to some modality or other. It is specific to thought, or vision, or hearing, or touch, for example.[33] The level of information processing which is described in the cognitive science computational models of cognition, on the other hand, is simply a matter of getting a set of symbols as output in response to a set of symbols as input.

We are blinded to this difference by the fact that the same sentence, "I see a car coming toward me", can be used to record both the visual intentionality and the output of the computational model of vision. But this should not obscure from us the fact that the visual experience is a concrete event and is produced in the brain by specific electrochemical biological processes. To confuse these events and processes with formal symbol manipulation is to confuse the reality with the model. The upshot of this part of the discussion is that in the sense of "information" used in cognitive science, it is simply false to say that the brain is an information processing device.

VIII. SUMMARY OF THE ARGUMENT

This brief argument has a simple logical structure and I will lay it out.

1. On the standard textbook definition, computation is defined syntactically in terms of symbol manipulation.

2. But syntax and symbols are not defined in terms of physics. Though symbol tokens are always physical tokens, "symbol " and "same symbol" are not defined in terms of physical features. Syntax, in short, is not intrinsic to physics.

3. This has the consequence that computation is not discovered in the physics, it is assigned to it. Certain physical phenomena are assigned or used or programmed or interpreted syntactically. Syntax and symbols are observer relative.

4. It follows that you could not discover that the brain or anything else was intrinsically a digital computer, although you could assign a computational interpretation to it as you could to anything else. The point is not that the claim "The brain is a digital computer" is false. Rather it does not get up to the level of falsehood. It does not have a clear sense. You will have misunderstood my account if you think that I am arguing that it is simply false that the brain is a digital computer. The question "Is the brain a digital computer?" is as ill defined as the questions "Is it an abacus?", "Is it a book?", "Is it a set of mathematical formulae?"

5. Some physical systems facilitate the computational use much better than others. That is why we build, program, and use them. In such cases we are the homunculus in the system interpreting the physics in both syntactic and semantic terms.

6. But the causal explanations we then give do not cite causal properties different from the physics of the implementation and the intentionality of the homunculus.

---

[33]A proponent of "strong AI" would have a different perspective here. As I pointed out in section 4 of Reading 4, the neuronal events in one modality-specific area of the neocortex strongly resemble those in other such areas as well as in nonspecific "association" cortices. It is hard to understand how the brain and nervous system could carry out their essential function of integrating sensory input from many different receptor surfaces unless the physically different stimulus events in receptors such as the retina and the skin surface were transduced into a standardized signal of a sort that goes everywhere in the nervous system. The binary all-or-nothing impulse that is coin of the neural realm is at least to some extent comparable to the binary signals of computers. ED.

7. The standard, though tacit, way out of this is to commit the homunculus fallacy. The homunculus fallacy is endemic to computational models of cognition and cannot be removed by the standard recursive decomposition arguments. They are addressed to a different question.

8. We cannot avoid the foregoing results by supposing that the brain is doing "information processing". The brain, as far as its intrinsic operations are concerned, does no information processing. It is a specific biological organ and its specific neurobiological processes cause specific forms of intentionality. In the brain, intrinsically, there are neurobiological processes and sometimes they cause consciousness. But that is the end of the story.[34]

REFERENCES

Block, Ned (1990), "The Computer Model of the Mind". In D. Osherson and E. E. Smith (eds.), *An Invitation to Cognitive Science,* 3 (pp. 247–89) Cambridge, Mass.: MIT Press.

Boolos, George S. and Jefferey, Richard C. (1989). *Computability and Logic.* Cambridge: Cambridge University Press.

Dennett, Daniel C. (1978). *Brainstorms: Philosophical Essays on Mind and Psychology.* Cambridge, Mass.: MIT Press.

Feigenbaum, E. A. and Feldman, J., eds. (1963). *Computers and Thought.* New York and San Francisco: McGraw-Hill.

Fodor, J. (1975). *The Language of Thought.* New York: Thomas Y. Cromwell.

Haugeland, John, ed. (1981). *Mind Design.* Cambridge, Mass.: MIT Press.

Johnson-Laird, P.N. (1988). *The Computer and the Mind.* Cambridge, Mass.: Harvard University Press.

Kuffler, Stephen W. and Nicholls, John G. (1976). *From Neuron to Brain.* Sunderland, Mass.: Sinauer Associates.

Lettvin, J. Y., Maturana, H. R., McCulloch, W. S., and Pitts, W. H. (1959). "What the Frog's Eye Tells the Frog's Brain". *Proceedings of the Institute of Radio Engineers* 47, 1940–1951, reprinted in McCulloch, 1965, pp. 230–255.

Marr, David (1982). *Vision.* San Francisco: W. H. Freeman and Company.

McCulloch, Warren S. (1965). *The Embodiments of Mind.* Cambridge Mass.: MIT Press.

Pylyshyn, Z. (1985). *Computation and Cognition.* Cambridge, Mass.: MIT Press.

Schank, R. C. & Abelson, R. P. (1977) *Scripts, plans, goals, and understanding.* Hillsdale, N.J.: Lawrence Erlbaum Press.

Searle, John R. (1980). "Minds, Brains and Programs", *The Behavioral and Brain Sciences* 3, pp. 417–424.

Searle, John R. (1984). *Minds, Brains and Science.* Cambridge Mass.: Harvard University Press.

Sharples, M., Hogg, D., Hutchinson, C., Torrance, S., and Young D. (1988). *Computers and Thought.* Cambridge, Mass., and London: MIT Press.

Shepherd, Gordon M. (1983). *Neurobiology.* New York and Oxford: Oxford University Press.

Turing, Alan (1950). "Computing Machinery and Intelligence." *Mind,* 59, 433–460.

Weizenbaum, J. (1965) Eliza—a computer program for the study of natural language communication between man and machine. *Communication of the Association for Computing Machinery* 9:36–45.

Winograd, T. (1973) A procedural model of language understanding. In: *Computer models of thought and language,* ed. R. Schank & K. Colby. San Francisco: W. H. Freeman.

---

[34] I am indebted to a remarkably large number of people for discussions of the issues in this paper. I cannot thank them all, but special thanks are due to John Batali, Vinod Goel, Ivan Havel, Kirk Ludwig, Dagmar Searle and Klaus Strelau.

Despite Searle's characterization of his argument, at the beginning of section VIII, as "brief" and having "a simple logical structure," as addresses go, his is a long one with a lot going on. Let's visit again a couple of its main points as they are reflected in the following passage:

> We wanted to know if there was not some sense in which brains were intrinsically digital computers in a way that green leaves intrinsically perform photosynthesis or hearts intrinsically pump blood. It is not a matter of us arbitrarily or "conventionally" assigning the word "pump" to hearts or "photosynthesis" to leaves. There is an actual fact of the matter. And what we were asking is, "Is there in that way a fact of the matter about brains that would make them digital computers?"

It does not answer that question to be told, yes, brains are digital computers because everything is a digital computer. (p. 258)

1. In the final two sentences of the above passage Searle uses the *universal realizability* thesis asserted by the early Putnam and others to argue that being a computer tells us nothing about the brain. If *everything* is, under some description, a computer, then saying that the brain is a computer tells us nothing distinctive or informative about the brain.

However, the universal realizability thesis is hard to defend or even make intelligible. Searle himself admits that the "implication" of universal realizability may be simply a quirk of Turing's very abstract definition of computation, and that a fuller definition may block the inference (see p. 259). Even so, argues Searle, even if there is only *multiple* realizability for the concept of a computer (as there is for functional concepts in general), saying that the brain is a computer tells us nothing about the brain itself. His principal reason for arguing this way is the second point I want to discuss here.

2. Searle argues that there is no "fact of the matter about brains that would make them digital computers." And in the above passage he seems to equate this thesis with the claim that neither the brain nor anything else can be "*intrinsically*" a computer in the sense in which leaves "intrinsically perform photosynthesis or hearts intrinsically pump blood." If a property or process is intrinsic to a system, its being in that system is a "fact of the matter" rather than a merely "arbitrary" or "conventional" attribution.

Let's look at photosynthesis in leaves and the heart's pumping action, the two examples of intrinsic and factual attributes that Searle gives in the passage. The input for leaves as photosynthetic systems includes the energy of sunlight, and simple ingredients such as water and carbon dioxide; their output consists of complex organic molecules such as carbohydrates. Conceptualized in this way, photosynthesis is a *functional* concept of a process internal to leaves but characterized only in terms of input and output in relation to the internal and external environments of the tree or plant. From the vena cava the input to the heart consists of blood depleted of oxygen. Its output to the aorta consists of oxygenated blood. Being a pump is also clearly a functional attribute of the heart. Temporary artificial hearts have been implanted in patients awaiting transplants from human donors. So far medical engineers have not invented a true functional equivalent of the heart, but they are trying. Two other examples Searle gives of functional attributes that are intrinsic and factual are *carburetor* (which mixes air and gas in an internal combustion engine) and *thermostat* (the function of which is to detect and regulate temperature). However, Searle denies that the functional attributes of being a computer or a computational process are intrinsic or factual. Why? Why carburetion and not computation?

Searle answers that "There is a difference: The classes of carburetors and thermostats are defined in terms of the production of certain physical effects" (p. 258). The functions he admits as intrinsic all have specific physical input and output such as oxygenated blood or heated air. It is this physical specificity which anchors the attribution of these functions in the world of facts—hard, measurable, scientific facts. By contrast, the input and output of computers consists of nothing but syntactically ordered symbols, and computation as a process within the computer is nothing but the implementing of syntactical rules for the ordering of symbols. There is no physical specificity here at all. What counts as a symbol is as purely conventional as what the symbol stands for. As Searle says in no. 2 of his "*Summary of the Argument*":

> Syntax and symbols are not defined in terms of physics. Though symbol tokens [the instances of symbol types such as "1" and "0"] are always physical tokens, "symbol" and "same symbol" are not defined in terms of physical features. Syntax, in short, is not intrinsic to physics.

Calling the brain a computer doesn't pick out any physical features of the brain. Therefore, whether or not the brain is a computer is not a scientific fact waiting for brain scientists or cognitive scientists to discover.

A "cognitivist" might say to a Searlean at this point: "Hold on! From the way Searle has been arguing, it follows (as he himself says in no. 4 of his summary) that there can be no fact of the matter about *any* system being a computer or any process being computational. But surely you have no doubt that your laptop or desktop system is in fact a computer!"

Searlean: "Of course I don't! As Searle said in no. 5 of his summary, what we call computers are physical systems whose input, output, and inner workings are especially suitable to being interpreted and used as symbol processors. By integrating our intentions and behavior with these systems, we create a *fact,* a reality that is missing from the computer by itself. Computation is intrinsic to the system created by the conjunction of the hardware, software, and user. But you can't say the same about the brain. There's no user inside your head, there's nothing more than the brain doing what it does as a biological system. No user/interpreter, no computer."

Cognitivist: "Human brains are not stand-alone machines with isolated interpreter/users. They are more like computers in a network, or even that network of networks that we call the Internet. We communicate with each other all the time, programming each other with shared ideas, instructions, gossip and so on. And we give to each other's output, as we do to the output of computers, syntactical and semantic interpretations. Sometimes we even talk to ourselves the way we do to others, cheering ourselves or trying to figure out why we believe and act as we do. Over the past few decades we have invented machines that can interact with us at a cognitive, symbol-system level, and now cognitive scientists are investigating how the workings of these artificial computers can help us understand the biological computers in us."

REVIEW QUESTION

Join this discussion between the Searlean and the Cognitivist. Can you take one side or the other?

PART VI

INTENTIONALITY

INTRODUCTION

The soul is [potentially] in a way all existing things; for existing things are either sensible or thinkable, and knowledge is in a way what is knowable, and sensation is in a way what is sensible; in *what* way we must inquire. . . . They [knowledge and sensation] must be either the things themselves or their forms. The former alternative is of course impossible: it is not the stone which is present in the soul but its form. [Aristotle (384 B.C.E.–322 B.C.E.), *On the Soul*][1]

Beings without knowledge have *only their own form:* but a knower is by nature suited to have *also the form of another thing:* for the representation [Latin: *species*] of the object known is in the knower. . . ." [Thomas Aquinas (1224–1274), *Summa Theologica*, 1, 14, 1][2]

I notice there that Divine Thomas [Aquinas] did not say that knowers could have *another form,* but *the form of another thing.* . . . Beings capable of knowledge are superior to those without it in that they can receive into themselves *that which is other, as other.* . . . [John of Saint Thomas (1589–1644), commentary on the preceding passage from Aquinas].[3]

Every mental phenomenon is characterized by what the scholastics of the Middle Ages called the intentional . . . inexistence (*Inexistenz*) of an object (*Gegenstand*).

Aristotle has already spoken of this mental inherence. In his books on the soul, he says that what is experienced, insofar as it is experienced, is in the one experiencing it, that sense contains what is experienced without its matter, that what is thought is in the thinking intellect. [Franz Brentano (1874)][4]

Nothing we know about the brain, including its relations to the world, seems capable of rendering unmysterious the capacity of conscious states to 'encompass' external states of affairs. . . . I think this is a very primitive notion, by which I suspect many of us have been struck at some point in our philosophical lives. How *can* our minds reach out to the objects of experience? What is it about our brains, and their location in the world, that could possibly explain the way consciousness *arcs out* into the world? . . . We flounder in similes. [Colin McGinn (1991), 40]

---

[1] McKeon, ed. (1941), 595.

[2] My translation of "Non cognoscentia nihil habent nisi *formam suam tantum:* sed cognoscens natum est habere *formam etian rei alterius:* nam species cogniti est in cognoscente", quoted in Maréchal (1949), 118.

[3] My translation of "Ubi adverto non dixisse D. Thomam quod cognoscentia possunt habere *formam alteran,* sed *formam rei alterius.* . . . Cognoscentia autem in hoc elevantur super non cognoscentia, quia *id quod est alterius, ut alterius* . . . possunt in se recipere", quoted in Maréchal (1949) 123.

[4] The first part of this quotation is from the passage quoted by Chisholm in Reading 19. The second part is from one of Brentano's footnotes to this passage.

From the readings in Part IV it would be easy to gain the impression that the only serious obstacle in the way of materialists happily proclaiming that there is nothing but physical reality is the problem of phenomenal properties of which we supposedly have an essentially subjective sort of awareness. We will re-visit this issue at length in Part VII. However, there is another closely related feature of consciousness that also poses a problem for materialism. It is the topic of each of the five passages quoted above, dating from the fourth century B.C.E. to just a few years ago. This complex feature is now usually referred to as *intentionality*. It designates a global and pervasive feature of human experience, one that seems familiar enough at first glance but is difficult to analyze. The word "intentionality" has been used by many past and present philosophers in different but related senses, often capturing only some of the real-life complexity of what it designates.

Let's go back to what Smart, in Reading 6, says in reply to Objection 4:

> I am not arguing that the after-image is a brain process, but that the experience of having an after-image is a brain process. . . .There is, in a sense, no such thing as an after-image or a sense-datum, though there is such a thing as the experience of having an image. . . .

One wonders about the phrase "in a sense" which Smart uses when he tells us that "there is, in a sense, no such thing as an after-image." Is there *another* sense of "is" in which there *is* such a thing as an after-image? If so, does this other sense imply that the image is *real* in some way or to some degree? If it does, then would that contradict the materialist thesis that there is nothing but the physical? Or is the after-image a nonentity, a nothing? How would the experience of nothing be different from *no* experience or *un*consciousness? He tells us that the experience really occurs, and that it is a brain process. But if the experience *really* occurs, then it *really* is *of* something; there is within this real experience a real relation expressed in the preposition "of." And a real relation would seem to require real relata (you can't even stand next to nothing, let alone lean on it). Since the experience is a brain process, what would the relata be? Is the experience an experience of the brain process by the brain process? Or of one part by another? What's the difference between simply being that brain process and being an experience of that brain process? What kind of relation is signified by "(experience) of," and what sort of *physical* relation could make it intelligible?

Let's shift from the experience of an after-image to the perception of an external object—for instance, my visual experience of this book that's open in front of me. According to the materialist, my experience is nothing but a brain process or a set of such processes. Unlike the after-image, the book is "out there," a part of the public world. The brain processes that are the visual experience must be "of" or "directed upon" the book. Noting the direction of the eyes' focus won't explain this "direction" because no one thinks that the visual experience takes place in the eyes. We can certainly find direction in the sequence of events that begins with the reflecting of certain frequencies of light from the surface of the book to the retinas, and in the chain of neural events by which signals leave the retinas and reach the visual cortices of each hemisphere. And we can also find direction in the behavior occasioned by the visible presence of the book (I reach toward it, adjust its position, and so on). Yet, to many philosophers this neuro-scientific or behavioral narrative seems only to be about causal antecedents and behavioral effects of the visual experience. To Colin McGinn, for instance (see the fifth passage quoted above), these narratives seem not to describe the "of" or intentional relation at all. His description of this relation echoes that of Aristotle in the first passage, and those of a succession of philosophers influenced by Aristotle on this issue. Three of these are quoted in the intervening passages.

What McGinn calls the "primitive notion," the one addressed by the Aristotelian analysis, is something like this: As I shift my gaze from the book in front of me to other objects nearby, the book drops from my field of vision and other objects enter it. The *somatosensory* equivalent occurs as I move my hand from one thing to another. Things "enter" and then "leave" my awareness. These "entries" and "departures" happen without any physical change of place on the part of the external objects involved. My perceptual life seems to consist of a succession of non-physical inclusions and exclusions of the items in my physical environment. These items become "part" of me as a conscious being, ingredients of my life as a perceiver. Being me is not limited to being the body or organism that I am. Other things become ingredients of that being even while remaining themselves "out there." The range of such things is limitless, as Aristotle says: "The soul is in a way all existing things."

Aristotle is saying that "You are what you perceive," but in a way that is very different from what is meant by the diet-conscious slogan "You are what you eat." What we eat enters physically into us and, after undergoing various transformations, becomes part of our bodies, and has effects that dieters monitor anxiously. But what we eat ceases thereby to exist as the external object(s) it was before consumption, whereas the book I'm perceiving remains where and what it was. Brentano's term, in the fourth passage, for the "indwelling" or *presence* of an object within our consciousness of it is "intentional inexistence." This expression signifies a mode of being or degree of reality somewhere between nonbeing and the being which the object has "out there" or that food has after it literally becomes part of you.

As you would quickly discover by reading the book from which the passage came, McGinn argues that our minds are essentially incapable of an adequate theoretical analysis of consciousness and intentionality, even though (he is sure) they are as much a part of nature as electricity and gravitation, and could probably be understood better by minds more advanced than we humans possess.

Like Aristotle, Thomas Aquinas and John of St. Thomas thought they could get a theoretical handle on intentionality. As we see in the quoted passages, they followed Aristotle in using the terminology of "form" and "matter" to analyze the structure and behavior of bodies as well as what takes place in perception and thought. These two philosophers belong to a tradition often called Aristotelian Scholasticism, which adapted and developed the philosophy of Aristotle over many centuries into an instrument for expressing and analyzing a Christian world-view both in philosophy and theology. Franz Brentano, though not himself an adherent of this philosophical school, was introduced to it in the course of his seminary education for the Catholic priesthood. He borrowed his notion of "intentional inexistence" from Aristotelian scholastic textbooks.

To attempt to explain in any depth the concepts of form and matter in Aristotle and his scholastic followers would be a distraction here. We'll have to settle instead for the minimum necessary to make sense of the passages where the terms occur. We can begin with an example Aristotle often employed: the shaping of a sculpture. It's easy here to distinguish between the material receiving the shape (wood, for instance) and the shape it receives (a human figure). The shape is to the wood as form is to matter. In fact, Aristotle's usual Greek terms for form and matter are *morphē* (form or shape) and *hylē* (wood, or matter), and a philosophical theory that gives central place to these concepts is called *hylomorphic*. Notice that the human shape which this particular wooden statue has could, in principle, be given to indefinitely many other pieces of wood of the right size. This possibility suggests the idea that there is some identical ingredient in all those possible statues, an ingredient that can't be identified with the wood in this statue, because that wood is limited to being in this statue. Furthermore, just as the wood can come to have this shape, it can also lose it (by being damaged or given another shape). This shape, while the wood has it, is what makes the piece of wood recognizable as a statue of a certain kind. The wood's acquisition of this shape or form is the actualization of a potentiality of that wood. The shape is what gives unity and intelligibility to the statue. If we take all these aspects of the shape in relation to the statue and make a sweeping generalization of them, we get the hylomorphic analysis of the structure of individual things or *substances:* Every concrete individual or substance is a composite of matter and form. A form can be embodied in indefinitely many substances by coming to actualize the matter in each, and all the various sorts of changes taking place in the world are cases of substances acquiring or losing certain forms. Whenever I recognize something as being of a certain kind—something white or heavy or human—my mind is apprehending the relevant form embodied in what I'm perceiving.

Here is where the hylomorphic account tries to dissect the intentional relation, the "of" that binds a perception to its object in the external world. If the perceiver is to *become* or *be* the object perceived, then the perceiver must, in hylomorphic terms, acquire the *form* of that object, since it is form that makes something to *be* the kind of thing it is. (The mechanics of *how* this acquisition takes place via sense organs was not very clear.) However, if the perceiver acquires that form the way that *matter* in a substance does, then the perceiver, a human let's say, will physically become the kind of being that he or she is perceiving (e.g., to use Aristotle's example, become a stone by looking at one). So the perceiver must receive the form in an *immaterial* way, i.e., without physically becoming the kind of being that the form would induce in matter. Aquinas, in the original Latin of the passage quoted, refers to the form as it exists in the perceiver by the Latin word *species,* which could be translated as form, appearance, idea, or (what I chose) representation. In his commentary on that passage, John of St. Thomas focuses on this immaterial presence of form as what distinguishes beings capable of perception from those that are not: A perceiver acquires the form of another being in such a way that the form presents the other being. The other being is "intentionally inexistent" in the perceiver. That is how the being of a perceiver is of a higher order than that of a plant, for instance. The plant is limited to being whatever it can materially incorporate within its body. Thus did scholastic hylomorphism use its central concepts in an attempt to explain (in the words of McGinn) "the way consciousness *arcs out* into the world."

Because there was a poor fit between hylomorphic ideas and the **corpuscularian** analysis of bodies in the new mathematical science of the seventeenth century, Aristotelian scholasticism was largely displaced in European universities by philosophical doctrines more congenial to the perspective of the **scientific revolution.** However, the scholastic doctrine of intentional inexistence raised an important issue that played a crucial role in the philosophies of the seventeenth and eighteenth centuries long after the hylomorphic terminology fell into disuse (until resurrected by Brentano). We can get at this issue by asking whether the intentional *species* or form that is present in the perception of an object is the *content* of that perception. Is it, in other words, what the perceiver is directly or immediately aware of, or is it only something that makes the perception directly *of* the external object itself? Each alternative has its problems. Aquinas opted for the second. He spoke of the *species* as a that-by-which (*id quo*) the perceiver is aware of the external object, and not as that-which (*id quod*) the perceiver is aware of. However, one could object that the Thomistic account displaces the problem instead of solving it. Being unable to figure out how the external object could remain itself and still become an ingredient of the inner process of perception, we have the *form* of the external object become the ingredient and let the external object stay where it is, then we proclaim that once that happens, the external object comes to have a nonphysical or immaterial existence in the perceiver. Are we any further ahead by saying this than we were to start with, when we just "knew" that the external object *somehow* enters our consciousness? Have we violated Occam's razor by adding a third entity in addition to the perceiver and the external object without any progress in understanding the mysterious "of" in perception?

Philosophers such as Descartes and Locke in the era of the scientific revolution opted for the first alternative—that what the scholastics called the *species* was the *object,* the *id quod* or content of perception. Their usual term for this content was "idea." For example, here is how Locke distinguishes "quality" and "idea" in his discussion of primary and secondary qualities:

> Whatsoever the mind perceives in itself, or is the immediate object of perception, thought, or understanding, that I call *idea;* and the power to produce any *idea* in our mind, I call *quality* of the subject wherein that power is.[5]

Locke has substituted *quality-of-the-object* and *idea* for the Thomistic pair of *form-of-the-object* and *species* and made the *idea/species* that which, rather than that *by* which, one perceives. One of the reasons why Locke and Descartes wanted to say that the immediate object of perception is an idea is that we seemed to perceive objects as having properties (such as color) that did not belong to the true scientific description of those objects. Since we were not aware of objects as they really were, it seemed to follow that we must be directly aware of something that existed only in the mind— an idea. That we are directly aware only of ideas and not things in themselves is the assumption of the entirety of Descartes' *Meditations.* What his six meditations try to establish with the premise of a truthful God is that we are not alone with our ideas, that God has created a world outside our minds that corresponds to what we (clearly and distinctly) perceive within us in the form of ideas. However, as later philosophers were to point out, if all we are directly aware of is ideas, then it would make no difference to what we *experience* as the world "out there" if there really weren't any world outside the mind. The world that is supposed to exist independently of our

---

[5] See Reading 6, note 22.

perception of it becomes a metaphysical fifth wheel. The way is then open to meta-physical *idealism*—the opposite of physicalism—which asserts that there is nothing but the mental.

It should be clear from this capsule history of the notion of intentionality as it ap-plies to perception, that the problem of the intentional relation between perceiver and perceived is strongly interwoven with the problem of the relation between the mental and physical or between consciousness and brain events. Intentionality is a special problem for materialism, not because other metaphysical views have dealt suc-cessfully with intentionality whereas materialism has not; but because materialism commits itself to the principle that the only fundamental kinds of entities, relations and properties are those belonging to the domain of physical science. As Jerry Fodor has said:

> I suppose that sooner or later the physicists will complete the catalogue they've been compiling of the ultimate and irreducible properties of things. When they do, the likes of *spin, charm* [a property of quarks], and *charge* will perhaps appear on their list. But *aboutness* surely won't; intentionality simply doesn't go that deep. (1987, 97)

19

Brentano on Descriptive
Psychology and the Intentional

Roderick M. Chisholm

Roderick Chisholm is Professor Emeritus of Philosophy at Brown University where he has taught since 1947. His books and other publications cover a wide variety of philosophical areas, including the history of philosophy, ethics, theory of knowledge, and philosophy of perception. *Franz Brentano* (1838–1917) was a German philosopher who taught at the University of Vienna. His best known work is *Psychologie vom empirischen Standpunkt* [*Psychology from an Empirical Point of View*] which was first published in 1874, and then in expanded form in 1911, with a final edition in 1925–28.

In this reading Chisholm explains with exceptional clarity Brentano's thesis that intentional inexistence is the characteristic that distinguishes the mental from the physical, and discusses some of the reasons for and against holding such a metaphysical or "ontological" doctrine. He concludes by arguing not for an ontological, but rather for a "logical" criterion of the mental, one that distinguishes intentional from nonintentional *sentences*. Insofar as we can define the mental as what must be described with intentional sentences, the criterion for such sentences amounts to a criterion for what is mental.

3

Now we may turn to Brentano's conception of the intentional, beginning with the doctrine of intentional inexistence which he propounded in 1874 and was subsequently to abandon.

In his *Psychologie vom empirischen Standpunkt,* first published in 1874, Brentano proposed the doctrine of intentional inexistence as a means of distin-

guishing the mental or psychical from the physical. The familiar passage follows:

Every mental phenomemon is characterized by what the scholastics of the middle ages called the intentional (and also mental) inexistence of an object, and what we would call, although not in entirely unambiguous terms, the reference to a content, a direction upon an object (by which we are not to understand a reality), or an immanent objectivity. Each one includes something as an object within itself, although not always in the same way. In presentation something is presented, in judgment something is affirmed or denied, in love something is loved, in hate something is hated, in desire something is desired, etc. This intentional inexistence is exclusively characteristic of

From: Roderick M. Chisholm, "Brentano on Descriptive Psychology and the Intentional," in *Phenomenology and Existentialism,* eds. Edward N. Lee and Maurice Mandelbaum (Baltimore: The Johns Hopkins Press, 1967) pp. 6–23. Reprinted by permission of the Johns Hopkins University Press.

mental phenomena. No physical phenomenon manifests anything similar. Consequently, we can define mental phenomena by saying that they are such phenomena as include an object intentionally within themselves.[1]

We have here an ontological[2] thesis concerning "intentional inexistence," which Brentano was later to abandon, and a psychological thesis,[3] implying that reference to an object is what distinguishes the mental from the physical. Each of these theses seems to me to be important. The ontological thesis seems to me to be problematic and not, as Brentano subsequently thought, to be obviously false. And the psychological thesis seems to me to be true. Let us consider them in order.

We are readily led to the ontological doctrine of intentional inexistence, though not, of course, to the particular terminology that Brentano used, if we ask ourselves what is involved in having thoughts, beliefs, desires, purposes, and other intentional attitudes that are directed upon objects that do not exist. There is a distinction between a man who is thinking about a horse and a man who is thinking about a unicorn. The distinction lies in the *objects* of their respective thoughts. It does *not* lie in the fact that where the first man has an object the second man does not, for this is not a fact. There is a distinction between a man who is thinking about a unicorn and a man who is thinking about nothing at all; *this* distinction lies in the fact that where one man has an object of thought the other man does not.[4] What, then, is the ontological sta-

tus[5] of the object that the man is intentionally related to when he is thinking about a unicorn?

One is tempted to say that although the man's thought quite obviously has an object, this object—also quite obviously—cannot be a unicorn. For one might reason as follows: If the man's thought is directed upon *something* and if there are no unicorns, then his thought must be directed upon something other than a unicorn. But what could this something possibly be? Moreover, if the man is thinking about something that is *not* a unicorn, how, then, can we say that he is thinking about a unicorn?

The doctrine of intentional inexistence may seem, at first consideration, to provide us with answers to our questions. It seems to tell us three different things. It tells us, first, that the object of the man's thought *is* a unicorn. It tells us, secondly, that this unicorn is not an actual unicorn (for there are no actual unicorns). And it tells us, thirdly, that this unicorn has a certain mode of being other than actuality. Whatever has this mode of being—called "intentional inexistence" or "immanent objectivity"—is an entity that is mind-dependent and therefore appropriately called an *ens rationis*,[6] in the traditional sense of this term. The intentionally inexistent unicorn is an entity that is *produced* by the mind or intellect; it comes into being as soon as the man starts to think about a unicorn and it ceases to be as soon as he stops.[7]

---

[1] The passage may be found on pp. 124–125 of Volume I of the Second Edition of the *Psychologie vom empirischen Standpunkt* (Leipzig: 1924). The present version is from D. B. Terrell's translation of the chapter in which it appeared ("The Distinction between Mental and Physical Phenomena"), in *Realism and the Background of Phenomenology,* ed. Roderick M. Chisholm (Glencoe, Illinois: 1960); the passage appears on pp. 50–51.

[2] An "ontological" thesis is one that asserts the existence of something, especially the existence of a certain kind or category of being. Ed.

[3] In this context the thesis is said to be psychological in the sense that it defines or delimits the subject matter or domain of psychology. Ed.

[4] Compare Plato's *Theaetetus* 189a–b:

> Soc. And does not he who thinks, think some one thing?
> Theaet. Certainly.
> Soc. And does not he who thinks some one thing, think something which is?
> Theaet. I agree.
> Soc. Then he who thinks of that which is not, thinks of nothing?
> Theaet. Clearly.
> Soc. And he who thinks of nothing, does not think at all?
> Theaet. Obviously.

> Soc. Then no one can think that which is not, either as a self-existent substance or as a predicate of something else?
> Theaet. Clearly not.

[5] In other words, what sort of being or reality does the unicorn have as object of thought? Ed.

[6] *Ens rationis,* literally translated, means "a being of reason." Ed.

[7] This doctrine is at the basis of St. Anselm's ontological argument; for St. Anselm takes it to be self-evident that if God is thought about then God does "exist in the understanding." William of Ockham contrasted the "intentional existence" (he did not use "inexistence") of the object of thought with the "subjective existence" of the thinking itself. "Objective existence" (meaning existence as an object of thought) came to be a synonym for "intentional (in)existence." Thus Descartes contrasted the *formale esse* of actual objects with the *objective in intellectu esse* of objects that are merely thought about. In the present century, the late Professor A. O. Lovejoy of Johns Hopkins appealed to those entities that are objects merely of thought (unicorns, as well as many of the objects of dreams and hallucinations) in order to defend what he called "psychophysical dualism"—the view that there is, in addition to the world of physical things, a world of nonphysical, mental things, "a second world to which could be allocated all experienced objects which do not appear to satisfy the rules of membership in the physical system." See A. O. Lovejoy, *The Revolt against Dualism* (New York: 1930), pp. 28–29.

Are there, then, certain objects such as intentionally inexistent unicorns which are produced by the mind? In *The True and the Evident,* we find this interesting passage, which was written sometime prior to 1903. Brentano asks us to consider a person whose thought is directed upon a certain object A and, in this case, an A that happens also to be actual:

> The concept of this object A, like that of the person who is thinking, is the concept of a thing. We may also say of this thing A that it is an object which is thought about. It is just as true that this A is a contemplated A [ein gedachtes A] as it is that this A is an actual A, existing in reality. A can cease to be actual and yet continue to be thought about—so long as the thinking person does in fact think about it. And conversely it can cease to be thought about—if the person stops thinking about it—and yet continue to be actual.
>
> In contrasting the A which is contemplated or thought about with the A which is actual, are we saying that *the contemplated A* is itself nothing actual or true? By no means! *The contemplated A* can be something actual and true without being an actual A. It is an actual contemplated A and therefore—since this comes to the same thing—it is an actual contemplated A [ein wirkliches gedachtes A] which may be contrasted with what is a mere *contemplated* contemplated A [ein gedachtes gedachtes A]. (One may *think* that someone is thinking about A.)
>
> There cannot be anyone who contemplates an A unless there is a contemplated A; and conversely. But we must not infer from this fact that the one who is thinking about the A is identical with the A which he is thinking about. The two concepts[8] are not identical but they are correlative. Neither can correspond to anything in reality unless the other does as well. But only one of these is the concept of a thing—the concept of something which can act and be acted upon. The second is the concept of a being which is only a sort of accompaniment to the first; when the first thing comes into being, and when it ceases to be, then so does the second.[9]

Brentano took these considerations to show that there *are* certain entities that are not concrete individual things. For, he says, the situation that he has described involves an actual thinker and an *actual contemplated A* (just as the situation he refers to parenthetically involves an actual, contemplated contemplated A). The contemplated A and the contemplated contemplated A are *entia rationis* that are *produced* by the mind.

According to Brentano's earlier doctrine, then, as soon as a man starts to think about a unicorn there comes into being an actual contemplated unicorn. This actual contemplated unicorn is an *ens rationis* that depends upon the thinker for its existence and that ceases to be as soon as the man ceases to think about a unicorn.

In the fourteenth century, Walter Burleigh[10] had appealed to a slightly different aspect of the phenomenon of intentionality in order to make out a case for still another type of entity—an entity that, like the merely contemplated A, is not a concrete individual thing, but that, unlike the merely contemplated A, exists "outside the mind." It will be useful at this point to recall Burleigh's argument, for, as we shall see, it will throw light upon Brentano's thought and upon the subsequent fate of the doctrine of intentionality. Burleigh argued in this way:

> Something about which real promises and contracts are made, such as buying and selling, donations, pledges, etc., exists outside the soul. But contracts are not always made about individual things. Therefore something exists outside the soul that is other than an individual nature. The major[11] is obvious. The proof of the minor is that in the statement "I promise you an ox," something outside the soul is being promised to you, and yet no individual thing is being promised to you because you cannot lay claim to this or that particular ox on the strength of this promise.

Therefore something outside the soul that is other than an individual thing is being promised to you.[12]

---

[8] The two concepts are *the contemplator of A* and *the contemplated A.* ED.

[9] *The True and the Evident,* p. 27; the passage appears on page 31 of *Wahrheit und Evidenz.* Compare also *The True and the Evident,* p. 64: "There is nothing universal in the things; the so-called universal, as such, is only in the one who is thinking." (*Wahrheit und Evidenz,* p. 74.)

[10] Walter Burleigh (or Burley) (1275–1343) was a prominent teacher of philosophy at Oxford during the early fourteenth century. ED.

[11] The major premise is the first sentence and the minor is the second sentence. ED.

[12] Walter Burleigh, "On the Existence of Universals," in *Philosophy in the West: Readings in Ancient and Medieval Philosophy,* ed. Hiseog Jatz and R. H. Weingartner (New York: 1965), pp. 563–569. The passage appears on p. 564. For an account of Jean Buridan's treatment of the same problem, see Peter Geach, "A Medieval Discussion of Intentionality," *Proceedings of the 1964 International Congress for Logic, Methodology and Philosophy of Science,* Jerusalem, August 26–September 2, 1964 (Amsterdam: 1965), pp. 425–433.

Since the entities with which Burleigh is here concerned are not produced by the mind and are not in any way dependent upon the mind,[13] they are not properly called "*entia rationis.*" Hence we need a more general term to cover non-things in general, non-things that may or may not be *entia rationis.* Brentano proposed the expressions "*entia non realia,*" "*entia irrealia,*" or simply "*irrealia.*"[14]

For the present, let us restrict ourselves to those *irrealia* that are also *entia rationis* and consider some of the difficulties involved in the concept of intentional inexistence.

4

The doctrine of intentional inexistence may seem at least to have this advantage: It provides us with a literal interpretation for the traditional dictum, "Veritas est adaequatio intellectus rei."[15] One could say that an affirmative judgment is true provided only that the properties of the intentional object are the same as those of the actual object.

But the very statement of this advantage betrays the fact that what the true affirmative judgment is directed upon is the actual object and not the intentional object.

To be sure, our intentional attitudes *may* be directed upon objects that do not exist. But they may also be directed upon objects that *do* exist: I may think of a golden mountain, but I may also think about Mt. Monadnock. Diogenes looked for an honest man and perhaps there was none; but there *are* many dishonest men who are also objects of quests, as the police files will indicate. And these objects are not things having mere intentional inexistence.

And even in those cases where the objects of our intentional attitudes do *not* exist, our attitudes are not normally directed upon an immanent, intentionally inexisting object. Whether or not there are honest men, Diogenes in his quest was looking for an *actual* honest man, not for an intentionally

inexisting honest man. If the doctrine of intentional inexistence is true, the very fact that Diogenes was looking for an honest man implies that he already had the immanent object; hence it could not be the object of his quest. Thus Brentano was later to say that "what we think about is *the object* or *thing* and not the 'object of thought {vorgestelltes Objekt}.'"[16]

The ontological use of the word "intentional," therefore, seems to undermine its psychological use. Intentionally inexistent objects were posited in the attempt to understand intentional reference, but the attempt did not succeed—precisely because the objects so posited *were* intentionally inexistent. Thus Husserl[17] said, with the later Brentano, that the objects of our "intentional experiences" are never objects that exist merely in the understanding; they are always something "transcendent."[18]

There are still other difficulties in the ontological doctrine of intentionally inexisting objects, actual intentionally inexisting objects, as Brentano was later to emphasize. "If there are such objects, in the strict and proper sense of the term *are,* then, whenever anyone thinks of anything that is contradictory, there comes into being an object that is contradictory."[19]

---

[13] To carry out my promise to you of an ox, I need to give you an ox, and what I give you is not something depending on my mind for its existence. I can't promise you a unicorn. Ed.

[14] Compare *The True and the Evident,* pp. 80f. [Neuter plural expressions in Latin such as these are hard to translate literally into English. Roughly, they mean *entities (that are) not real, unreal entities, unreal (things).* Ed.]

[15] "Truth is the equation of intellect and thing." Ed.

[16] *The True and the Evident,* p. 77. In this passage, Brentano also seems to deny ever having held the doctrine of intentional inexistence, as I have formulated it. Kraus believes, however, that by the time Brentano wrote the passage (March 17, 1905), the older doctrine (which, Kraus believes, Brentano had in fact held) "had become so foreign to him that he questioned whether he had ever enunciated it" (*op. cit.,* p. 154). One might try to reconcile this passage with what seems to have been Brentano's earlier doctrine by taking the earlier doctrine to be this: (1) an actual intentionally inexistent unicorn is *produced* when one thinks about a unicorn; (2) one's thought, however, is *not* directed upon this actual intentionally inexistent unicorn; and yet (3) it is *in virtue of* the existence of the intentionally inexistent unicorn that one's thought may be said to be directed upon a unicorn. But in this case, what point would there be in supposing that there *is* the inexistent unicorn? Compare Brentano's further remarks, *op. cit.,* pp. 77–79, and the notes by Oskar Kraus, *ibid.,* pp. 165–170. Compare also Jan Srzednicki, *Franz Brentano's Analysis of Truth* (The Hague: 1965), Chapter II.

[17] Edmund Husserl (1859–1938) was a German philosopher who studied under Brentano and taught at various German universities. He is the originator of the philosophical method called *phenomenology.* This method involved analyzing the contents of mental acts as far as possible without any preconceptions about their causes and effects or about the existence of these objects outside the mind. Ed.

[18] Husserl, *Logische Untersuchungen* (4th ed.: Halle: 1928), Vol. II, Part I, p. 425; compare pp. 373–374.

[19] Franz Brentano, *Kategorienlehre,* ed. Alfred Kastil (Leipzig: 1933). [That is not a very cogent objection. One could interpret "thinking about a square circle" as *attempting* (in vain) to think about a single two-

Almost all intentionally inexisting objects, moreover, violate the law of excluded middle.[20] Consider, for example, the promised ox that was the object of *our* thought a while back. It may have been brown and presumably it had four legs, a head, and a tail. Presumably also it was heavy. But was it such that it weighed 817 pounds, or was it such that it did not weigh 817 pounds? Evidently we must answer both of these questions in the negative. In this case, the actual intentionally inexisting ox was what Meinong[21] called an incomplete object."[22] Whatever the status of such objects in Meinong's realm of *Aussersein*[23], Brentano was certain, in his later thoughts, that there are *no* such objects, whether "in" or "outside" the mind. (This incompleteness of the immanent object would seem to insure disaster for the attempt to construe truth as a relation of correspondence or adequacy holding between the immanent object and the actual object. For, since all actual objects are complete and no immanent objects or complete, no immanent object can be adequate to any actual object.)

And what, finally, of Walter Burleigh's *ens irreale*—the promised ox that is not identical with any individual ox? Brentano, in a letter to Kraus, had considered a slightly different example. You might promise to marry and yet not promise with respect to any particular person, to marry *that* particular person. But what happens if you keep the promise? "It would be paradoxical to the highest degree," Brentano said, "to suppose that you could promise to marry an *ens rationis* and then to keep the promise by marrying an actual, concrete particular."[24]

---

dimensional figure that is both square and circular. Similarly, I can think about the solution I haven't yet arrived at. ED.]

[20] This law, like the principles of identity and contradiction, has traditionally been regarded as a law governing all thought. Let *p* stand for a statement or proposition. The law states that "Either it is the case that *p* or it is not the case that *p*." ED.

[21] Alexius Meinong (1853–1920) was an Austrian philosopher who studied under Brentano and wrote extensively about intentionality. ED.

[22] See A. Meinong, *Über Möglichkeit und Wahrscheinlichkeit* (Leipzig: 1915), pp. 168–181.

[23] This is the realm of objects that don't have *Sein* (being or existence) but do have *Sosein* (being thus or such). To say that such objects have *Sosein* without *Sein* is to say that there can be true statements about them even though they don't exist. Meinong allows incomplete objects and even contradictory ones such as square circles into his *Aussersein*. ED.

[24] Quoted by Oskar Kraus in his Introduction to *Psychologie vom empirischen Standpunkt* (2nd ed.; Leipzig: 1924), p. xlix. Presumably Brentano should have written "*ens irreale*" instead of "*ens rationis*."

But it is much easier to ridicule the doctrine of *entia non realia* than it is to find a way of getting along without them. Let us consider, then, how Brentano himself made out in his subsequent attempts to get along without the ontology of intentionally inexistent objects.

5

Brentano's later thought was what Kotarbinski has called "reistic." The only things that can be said to *be,* in the strict and proper sense of the expression "to be," are particular, individual things. (But Brentano's reism, unlike that of Kotarbinski, is not also a "somatism."[25] For Brentano held that there are concrete individual things that are not material things—for example, human souls and God.) Brentano thus repudiated all *entia rationis* and *entia irrealia*.

Our language contains a multiplicity of terms, purporting to refer to non-things, or *entia irrealia*. Brentano says that such terms are convenient fictions, comparable to such expressions as "negative quantities," "irrational numbers," "imaginary numbers," and the like.[26] When we find a true sentence, ostensibly referring to a non-thing, then, according to Brentano, we can "form an equivalent in which the subject and predicate are replaced by expressions referring only to things."[27]

For example, the sentence "There is a dearth of bread in the larder" may seem to affirm the existence of a *privativum*—that non-thing which is the absence of bread. But actually, according to Brentano, it is concerned with the denial or rejection of a *thing:* namely bread in the larder. Again, "There is redness" and "Red is a color" may seem to pertain to *abstracta*[28] and thus, once again, to non-things. But "There is redness," Brentano says, is just another way of saying "There are red things"; and what "Red is a color" tells us is simply that red things, *as such,* are colored.[29]

---

[25] *Soma* is Greek for body. ED.

[26] *The True and the Evident,* p. 83.

[27] *Psychologie vom empirischen Standpunkt,* 2nd ed., II, 163.

[28] Chisholm is using the Latin term *abstracta* in much the same sense as the English term "abstraction." It refers to a general concept, something that lacks all the particular specifications something would need in order to exist, e.g., *red(ness)* as opposed to *the shade of red on this wall.* ED.

[29] Brentano's reism is set forth in detail in *Kategorienlehre* and *The True and the Evident.* Compare the exposition in Srzednicki, *op. cit.,* pp. 42–49.

In a similar way, Brentano attempts to translate away all ostensible reference to propositional objects. Thus, in the second edition of the *Psychologie* and in *The True and the Evident,* he defends a non-propositional theory of judgment. Language suggests that judgment involves a relation between a man and a proposition (or content, state of affairs, or objective). We say, "He believes that there are horses," thus seeming to describe a relation between the believer and that non-thing named by the propositional clause "that there are horses." But actually, Brentano says, what "He believes that there are horses" tells us is simply that the believer accepts or affirms (*anerkennt*) horses. And if we say, "He believes that there are no unicorns," we are simply saying that he rejects or denies (*leugnet*) unicorns. "He believes that some horses are red" tells us that he accepts red horses, and "He believes that no horses are green" tells us that he rejects green horses. Brentano's theory becomes complex, after this point.[30] But what it is that he is attempting to do is clear throughout: he wishes to translate those true sentences that seem to refer to non-things into sentences that refer only to things. In this way, he thinks, he will eliminate one of the most fundamental sources of error and confusion in philosophy. Philosophers go wrong and fall into confusion "when they take some word to be a name when in fact the word is not a name at all, and then look for the concept which this ostensible name designated."[31] Brentano's reism thus led him to revise his original doctrine of the intentional in two ways. First, he gave up the doctrine that our intentional attitudes are sometimes directed upon non-things or *entia irrealia.* Whatever language we may use for the description of our intentional attitudes— whether we use words ostensibly referring to *abstracta, privativa, negativa,* whether we use clauses ostensibly referring to propositions or what Meinong called "Objektive"—our attitudes are in fact always directed upon *things.* Second, Brentano gave up the doctrine that our intentional attitudes, whatever they may be directed upon, do somehow involve actual intentionally inexistent objects.

What, then, is the reistic replacement for the actual intentionally inexistent object?

6

The following passage, dictated in 1914, may be found in the *Kategorienlehre* (p. 8):

> Instead of saying that a person is thinking about a thing, one may also say that there is something which is the object of his thought. But this is not the strict or proper sense of *is.* For the thinker may in fact deny that there is any such object as the object he is thinking about. Moreover, one can think about what is contradictory, but nothing that is contradictory can possibly be said to be. We said above that roundness cannot be said to *be,* in the strict and proper sense of the term; that which is round, but not roundness, may be said to be. And so too, in the present case. What there is in the strict and proper sense is not the round thing that is thought about; what there *is* is the person who is thinking about it. The thing "as object of thought" is a fiction which, in many contexts, is perfectly harmless. But if we do not see that it is a fiction, then we will be led to the most blatant of absurdities. We are not dealing here with a type of being, in the strict sense of the term. What we say can be expressed in such a way that we do refer to a being in the strict sense of the term— namely, the thinker who has the thought. And what holds generally for that which is thought about also holds more particularly, for that which is accepted, that which is rejected, that which is loved, that which is hated, that which is hoped for, that which is feared, that which is willed, and so on.

Saying that there *is* an immanent object, then, is just another way of saying that there *is* an actual person who is thinking about that object. "*Es gibt ein Gedachtes*" says no more nor less than "*Es gibt ein Denkendes.*"[32] Hence if we continue to say, as Brentano had said earlier, that there is an *actual* intentionally inexistent unicorn when an actual man is thinking about a unicorn, we are using the first "actual" in its loose and improper sense and the second "actual" in its strict and proper sense. And where Brentano had said earlier that our thought *produces* an entity, he now denies that our thought thus produces any entity at all.

---

[30] See *Psychologie,* II, 158–172; part of this passage is translated by D. B. Terrell in *Realism and the Background of Phenomenology,* ed. by Roderick M. Chisholm, pp. 62–70.

[31] Franz Brentano, *Die Lehre vom richtigen Urteil,* ed. F. Mayer-Hillebrand (Bern: 1956), pp. 45–46.

[32] *Wahrheit und Evidenz,* p. 79; compare *The True and the Evident,* p. 68. [The two sentences in English are "There is something thought about" and "There is a thinker." ED.]

There are four possible views here that are easily confused with each other. There is what I have taken to be Brentano's original view; there is the later reistic view; and then there seem to be two different ways of combining the first two views. Let us consider these possibilities more explicitly.

i. According to what I have taken to be Brentano's view of 1874, when a man thinks about a unicorn there is *produced* an immanent or intentionally inexistent unicorn. This immanent or intentionally inexistent unicorn is an actual immanent or intentionally inexistent unicorn. And therefore it is an entity *in addition to* the man who is thinking.

ii. According to Brentano's later, reistic view, when a man thinks about a unicorn no intentionally inexistent unicorn is produced and therefore the situation involves no actual entity other than the man who is thinking.

iii. Suarez,[33] in his *Metaphysicae Disputationes,* seems to combine these two views in the following way. He seems to suggest that when a man thinks about a unicorn, the act of thought *produces* an immanent or intentionally inexistent unicorn; hence we have an element of Brentano's first view. But Suarez adds that the unicorn that is thus *produced* is *not* an *actual* immanent or intentionally inexistent unicorn and therefore it is not an entity in addition to the thinker himself; hence we have an element of Brentano's second view.[34] Now if this immanent or intentionally inexistent unicorn is produced, or (to use the terms that Suarez used) if this *ens rationis* that has only "objective being in the mind" had an efficient cause, then, one would think, the entity must be actual. If there *is* production or causation, then there must *be* that which is caused[35] or produced.[36]

iv. There is, finally, still another way of combining the first and second views of Brentano; this final view is suggested by one passage in G. E. Moore.[37] We could say (a) that when a man thinks about a unicorn, there is involved an *actual* intentionally inexistent unicorn; hence we have an element of Brentano's first view. And then we could add (b) that to say that there is such an actual intentionally inexistent unicorn is to say no more nor less than that the man is thinking about a unicorn.[38]

Do we have, then, a clear alternative to the original doctrine of intentional inexistence?

7

It seems to me that these alternatives to the doctrine of intentional inexistence involve a serious difficulty, and I am not at all sure that I know how it ought to be treated. The difficulty may be seen if we try to give a positive answer to the question "How are we using the word 'unicorn' when we say, 'John is thinking about a unicorn'?"

---

[33] Francisco Suarez (1548–1617) was a Spanish Jesuit philosopher and theologian. Next to Aquinas, he was probably the most prominent and influential thinker in the scholastic tradition. His textbook, *Metaphysicae Disputationes,* was a commonly employed textbook in seventeenth-century European universities. ED.

[34] See disputation LIV ("De Ente Rationis"), Section 1. It is quite obvious that Brentano was influenced by this discussion in Suarez; compare the *Psychologie*, II, 272. I am indebted to the late Professor Ralph M. Blake for calling my attention to the importance of this and other discussions in the *Metaphysicae Disputationes*.

[35] A cause, in this sense, is typically understood as that which brings into *being* something else—the effect. ED.

[36] It should be noted that Suarez is fully aware of the difficulty (which he attributes to one Bernardinus Mirandulus) and that he attempts to resolve it. We *could* so interpret the view of Suarez that it becomes identical with Brentano's second view above. Where Brentano had distinguished a strict and proper sense and a loose and improper sense of "is," we might read into Suarez a distinction between a strict and proper sense and a loose and improper sense of "produce" or "cause." He could then be interpreted as saying that it is only in the latter sense of "cause" that an *ens rationis* may be said to have an efficient cause.

[37] G. E. Moore (1873–1958) was a prominent British philosopher best known for his ethical theory. ED.

[38] ". . . if it should happen that at the present moment two different people are having an hallucination of a different tame tiger, it will follow there are at the present moment two different imaginary tigers. . . . The sentence 'There are some tame tigers which do not exist' is, therefore, certainly significant, if it means only that there are some imaginary tigers. . . . But what it means is that either some real people have written stories about imaginary tigers, or are having or have recently had hallucinations of tame tigers, or, perhaps, are dreaming or have dreamed of particular tame tigers. If nothing of this sort has happened or is happening to anybody, then there are no imaginary tame tigers." G. E. Moore, *Philosophical Papers* (London: 1959), p. 120.

Brentano in his later view gives the question a negative answer. That is to say, he tells us how we are *not* using the word "unicorn" when we say, "John is thinking about a unicorn." But he formulates this negative answer affirmatively—in very much the way in which, according to him, "There is a dearth of bread in the larder" expresses a negative belief affirmatively. He tells us that in the sentence "John is thinking about a unicorn," the word "unicorn" is being used syncategorematically or synsemantically.[39] And this may be said to be a negative answer to our question, for to say that a word is being used syncategorematically or synsemantically is to say, negatively, that the word is *not* being used referentially—that the word is *not* being used to designate or to refer to an object. Thus our question now becomes, more positively: If the word is not being used to designate or refer to an object, how *is* it being used?

We may say, as Brentano suggests, that in "John is thinking about a unicorn" the word "unicorn" is being used to contribute to the description of John. But *how* does it contribute to the description of John? We are *not* saying, obviously, that John is a unicorn. We are saying that John is *thinking* about a unicorn, and so one might be tempted to say the word "unicorn" is being used to describe John's thought. But *how* does the word "unicorn" contribute to the description of John's thought? We are not saying, obviously, that John's *thought* is a unicorn. We are saying—again, obviously—that the *object* of John's thought is a unicorn. But, Brentano tells us, statements ostensibly about the object of John's thought are actually statements about John. And so we have completed a kind of circle. For now we can ask, once again: what does this use of "unicorn" tell us about John?

One may be tempted to say that the use of "unicorn" in such sentences as "John is thinking about a unicorn" and "John believes that there are unicorns" has no connection at all with what would be its designative or referential use. What we have

here, one is tempted to continue, are simply two different predicates of John—predicates that might be written as "thinking-about-a-unicorn" and "believing-that-there-are-unicorns." Better still, the hyphens could be removed, thereby making it clear that the predicates have no more to do with unicorns than they have to do with, say, ink, or with hats, or with corn, or with her, or with any of the other objects whose names happen to be imbedded in our intentional predicates.

That this suggestion will not do, however, is indicated by the fact that "John believes that there are unicorns" (or "John believesthatthereareunicorns") and "All of John's beliefs are true" together imply "There are unicorns"—a mode of inference that would not be valid if "unicorn" functioned here as an equivocal middle term.[40]

Alonzo Church has suggested that the English sentence "Schliemann sought the site of Troy" tells us that a certain relation obtains between Schliemann and the *concept* of the site of Troy, suggesting therefore that seeking is a relation between a person and an *abstractum*. But *what* relation is asserted to obtain between Schliemann and the concept of the site of Troy? He was not *seeking* the concept, since he already had it when he set out on his quest. Church says, negatively, that the relation that Schliemann bore to the concept of the site of Troy

---

[39] See *The True and the Evident*, p. 68. [As Brentano uses "synsemantic," it has in this context roughly the same meaning as "syncategorematic": A syncategorematic term is one, like "all," "and," or "some," that needs to be with a *categorematic* term in order to form a meaningful unit in a sentence or proposition. Categorematic terms are ones that designate or refer to something. For instance, "*all* women" and "Tom *and* Bill" combine both sorts of terms. ED.]

[40] "One may have the feeling that in the sentence 'I expect he is coming' one is using the words 'he is coming' in a different sense from the one they have in the assertion 'He is coming.' But if it were so how could I say that my expectation had been fulfilled? If I wanted to explain the words 'he' and 'is coming,' say by means of ostensive definitions, the same definitions of these words would go for both sentences." Ludwig Wittgenstein, *Philosophical Investigations* (Oxford: 1953), p. 130e. The following passage occurs on this same page: "'The report was not so loud as I had expected.'—'Then there was a louder bang in your expectation?'"

[In the traditional analysis of a categorical syllogism, there are three and only three terms: the major, minor and middle terms. The minor term is the subject of the conclusion, and the major term is the predicate of the conclusion. The middle term doesn't occur in the conclusion, but occurs in both premises in such a way as to justify predicating the major term of the minor term in the conclusion. For instance, in

All humans are *mortal* (major)
Socrates is a human (minor)
Socrates is *mortal* (conclusion)

"human" is the middle term. Obviously for this sort of argument to work (be valid), the middle term must be univocal; it must have the same meaning in both premises. Is Chisholm correct in calling "unicorn" the middle term in the argument he is discussing? Try putting the argument into the syllogistic form just exemplified in the argument for Socrates' mortality. ED.]

is "not quite like that of having sought," but he does not tell us more positively what it is.[41]

Rudolf Carnap[42] once suggested that *words* or other linguistic entities are the objects of our intentional attitudes. "Charles thinks (asserts, believes, wonders about) A," he said, might be translated as "Charles thinks 'A.'"[43] But when we say that Charles wonders whether there are unicorns, we do not mean to say that Charles wonders whether there is the word "unicorn." And when we make the semantic statement, "The word 'unicorn' in English designates unicorn," we cannot replace the last word in our statement with the expression "the word 'unicorn.'"[44]

One way out, if we are to avoid *entia irrealia* and at the same time do justice to the phenomenon of intentionality, is to follow Meinong's suggestion: There are certain truths which hold of objects that do not exist. There are no unicorns; yet there are certain truths that hold of unicorns; hence unicorns have certain properties, among them that of being the object, on occasion, of our intentional attitudes. But this suggestion was anathema to Brentano, as it is to most contemporary logicians.[45]

8

Brentano's doctrine of intentional inexistence was proposed as a way of distinguishing mental or psychical phenomena from physical phenomena: mental phenomena are distinguished by the fact that they contain objects immanently within themselves.

If we give up the doctrine of intentional inexistence, how are we to make the distinction between the mental and the physical?

In the *Klassifikation der psychischen Phänomene,* published in 1911 and included in the second edition of the *Psychologie vom empirischen Standpunkt,* Brentano said that, since every psychical phenomenon involves a relation to something as object, psychical activity may be described as being essentially relational. But psychical relations, he said, are distinguished from other relations in the following way:

> In the case of other relations, the Fundament as well as the Terminus must be an actual thing. . . . If one house is larger than another house, then the second house as well as the first house must exist and have a certain size. . . . But this is not at all the case with psychical relations. If a person thinks about something, the thinker must exist but the objects of his thought need not exist at all. Indeed, if the thinker is denying or rejecting something, and if he is right in so doing, then the object of his thinking must not exist. Hence the thinker is the only thing that needs to exist if a psychical relation is to obtain. The Terminus of this so-called relation need not exist in reality. One may well ask, therefore, whether we are dealing with what is really a relation at all. One could say instead that we are dealing with something which is in a certain respect similar to a relation, and which, therefore, we might describe as being something that is "relation-like" [*etwas "relativliches"*].[46]

This passage suggests the possibility of a logical distinction between the mental and the physical. We might say that the language we use in characterizing the mental has certain logical properties that are not shared by the language we use in characterizing the physical. We could say, for example, that in characterizing the mental we must use "intentional terms" and that we do not need to use such terms when we characterize the physical; and we might then attempt to characterize intentional terms logically. The following definition of "intentional sentence," which is suggested by the passage from Brentano above, may be found in *Webster's Third New International Dictionary:* A simple categorical statement (for example, "Parsifal sought the Holy Grail") is intentional if it uses a substantial

---

[41] Alonzo Church, *Introduction to Mathematical Logic* (Princeton: 1955), p. 8n.

[42] Rudolph Carnap (1891–1970) was a German-born American philosopher who taught at the University of Chicago after fleeing Nazi Germany. He is one of the founders of the philosophical movement called Logical Positivism. ED.

[43] Rudolf Carnap, *The Logical Syntax of Language* (New York: 1937), p. 248.

[44] Israel Scheffler's "inscriptionalism" might be interpreted as saying that linguistic entities constitute the objects of our intentional attitudes. But if we do interpret it in this way, it becomes very difficult to ascertain just what relation is being asserted to hold between a man and an inscription when we say of him that he is thinking, wondering, desiring, loving, and the like. See Israel Scheffler, *The Anatomy of Inquiry* (New York: 1963), pp. 57ff.

[45] See A. Meinong, "The Theory of Objects," in *Realism and the Background of Phenomenology,* ed. Roderick M. Chisholm. I have attempted to defend Meinong in "*Jenseits vom sein und Nichtsein,*" in *Dichtung und Deutung,* ed. Karl S. Guthke (Bern and Munich: 1961).

[46] *Psychologie vom empirischen Standpunkt,* II, 133–134.

expression (in this sentence "the Holy Grail") without implying either that there is or that there isn't anything to which the expression truly applies.

But this characterization of "intentional sentence," as it stands, is too broad. The following sentences, none of them concerned with what is mental, satisfy the conditions of the criterion: "The site of Troy is not New Zealand"; "That lady has a profile like the profile of Satan"; "It is possible that the Loch Ness monster exists."

We will be more faithful to Brentano's intention if we look for a peculiar characteristic of the expressions we use to designate "intentional relations." And possibly we will find one if we remind ourselves of the type of situation involved in Walter Burleigh's promise: The man promised to deliver an ox, but there was no particular ox that he promised to deliver. Expressions for intentional relations may exhibit a unique type of behavior when they are found in contexts of quantification.[47] An example involving believing will illustrate the point; similar examples may be constructed which will hold of knowing, desiring, doubting, being pleased, being displeased, hoping, fearing, and still other intentional attitudes.

Consider the two formulae[48]

(1)   (Ex) (Ey) (y = a & xRa).
(2)   (Ex) (Ey) (y = a & xRy).

Let us here restrict the values of variables to concrete entities. An expression which may occupy the place of "R" in such formulae could be said to be intentional if there is an individual term that may occupy the place of "a" with the results that (1) does not imply (2); (2) does not imply (1); and no well-formed sentence that is part of (1) is non-contingent.[49]

We find an example of such an intentional expression if we replace "a" by "the next President" and "R" by "believes that the Mayor of New York is." Let us now suppose that Senator Robert Kennedy is the next President and that one of Mayor Lindsay's supporters believes that he, the Mayor of New York, is the next President. In this case (1) will be true. But (1) is consistent with the negation of (2). That is to say, affirming (1) is consistent with denying that there is anyone who mistakes Kennedy for the Mayor, i.e., with denying that there is anyone who supposes with respect to Kennedy that the Mayor of New York is he. But let us assume that there is, in fact, a man who mistakes Kennedy for the Mayor (expecting the Mayor on a certain occasion and then seeing the Senator in a conspicuous position, he takes it for granted that the man he sees, *viz.*, the Senator, is the Mayor). In this case (2) will be true. But (2) is consistent with the negation of (1). That is to say, affirming (2) is consistent with denying that there is anyone who believes that the Mayor of New York is the next President.

We might say, then, that a well-formed sentence is intentional if it contains an intentional expression (e.g., "believes that the Mayor of New York is") and in addition to that only individual terms or quantifiers and variables. We could also say that a well-formed sentence is intentional if it is consistent and implies a sentence that is intentional. The psychological thesis of intentionality could then be put by saying, "All intentional sentences pertain to what is psychological."

If I am not mistaken, no expressions designating nonpsychological phenomena have the logical properties that the expression "R" has just been described as having. And if this is so, then we may say with Brentano that what distinguishes the psychological from the physical is "*etwas 'relativliches.'*"[50]

---

[47] In "Notes on the Logic of Believing," *Philosophy and Phenomenological Research* XXIV (1963), 195–201, I described one such possibility, somewhat different from the one referred to here.

[48] The symbol *E* in front of a variable such as *x* means "for some *x*," or "There exists an *x*." (The symbol ∀ in front of *x* would mean "For all *x*'s.") *E* and ∀ are called *quantifiers*. (1) Translates as "There exists an *x* and a *y* such that *y* is identical with *a*, and *x* is R-related to *a*." (2) Translates as "There exists an *x* and a *y* such that *y* is identical with *a* and *x* is R-related to *y*." If R were a nonintentional relation such as *resides near,* (1) would imply (2) and (2) would imply (1). However, these implications don't hold when R is an intentional relation. See for yourself by substituting "is aware of residing near" for "resides near." ED.

[49] In other words, neither "y = a" nor "xRa" is necessarily true. ED.

[50] [I.e., "something relation-like." ED.]

Since the writing of this essay, the following work has appeared: Franz Brentano, *Die Abkehr vom Nichtrealen,* ed. Franziska Mayer-Hillebrand (Bern: 1966). This book is composed of selections, taken from Brentano's correspondence and hitherto unpublished manuscripts, concerning the repudiation of *entia irrealia*. It also contains a useful discussion of Brentano's reism by Professor Mayer-Hillebrand.

There is a curiously dangling quality about the outcome of Chisholm's arguments. He first explains why he believes that the ontological thesis of intentional inexistence is "not obviously false" but nevertheless open to what he regards as serious objections. He then drops the ontological issue and moves on to argue for a "logical" criterion of intentional sentences, and thereby, of the mental or psychological domain constituted by such sentences or the intentional expressions within them. Granted that the logic of intentional sentences is strikingly different from that of ordinary sentences describing states of affairs, what are we to make of that linguistic fact? That the kind of *relation* designated by intentional expressions is importantly different from other sorts of relations, especially those that obtain between concrete things in the public world? But that was already well known, and was the reason why the Scholastics and Brentano concluded that intentional relations have intentional inexistents as relata. Many philosophers would argue that the important question about intentionality is not what makes intentional *sentences* special, but what is special about the intentional relation *in mental events,* and whether and how we can make this relation intelligible in terms of relations among or within brain events and/or other physical events.

REVIEW QUESTIONS

1. In explaining Brentano's *later* position ("reism") on the status of intentional objects, Chisholm says that "Where Brentano had said earlier that our thought *produces* an entity, he now denies that our thought thus produces any entity at all" (p. 284 above). Could we plausibly say that about dreams? If no entity was produced in a nightmare, how could Brentano answer the question "What were you afraid of?"

2. Can a materialist theory of mind allow for any sort of intentional inexistence? Why?

20

Intentional Systems [1]

Daniel C. Dennett

Daniel C. Dennett teaches philosophy at Tufts University. He is the author of several influential works in the philosophy of mind, including *The Intentional Stance* (1987) and *Consciousness Explained* (1991).

Dennett is among the best known and most vigorous proponents of a materialist theory of mind today. One of the purposes of his essay is to do justice to the intentional aspect of mental phenomena and yet still leave the world safe for materialism. A physicalist universe seems to be just as closed to intentionally inexistent objects as it is to really occurring appearances or **phenomenal properties.** So we are not surprised at Dennett's declaration in note 2 that for him "as for many recent authors, Intentionality is to be viewed as a feature of linguistic entities" rather than as a relation internal to the mind or brain. He notes that there are some major differences between intentional and nonintentional sentences, and that the task of defining these differences is important and ongoing, although it is not the task he will undertake in this essay. Instead, he argues

(1) that in both our theoretical and practical dealings with our fellow humans and with other things (such as organisms and computers) we often cannot predict their behavior except by regarding them as having perceptions, beliefs, desires, and other intentional attributes;

(2) that treating a thing or system in this way (taking the "intentional stance" toward them) is (like the topic-neutrality of the Causal Theory) noncommittal about what is really going on inside the system; and

(3) that the occurrence of phenomena that we must initially characterize as intentional (e.g., social interaction or a computer's chess playing), like those that we must initially characterize as having design or being structured for a purpose (e.g., an animal's fur or its withdrawal reflex) can all be explained, at least in principle, as the outcome of purely physical processes such as those at work in **natural selection.**

I wish to examine the concept of a system whose behavior can be (at least sometimes) explained and predicted by relying on ascriptions to the system of beliefs and desires (and hopes, fears, intentions, hunches, . . .). I will call such systems Intentional systems and such explanations and predictions Intentional explanations and predictions in virtue of the Intentionality of the idioms of belief and desire (and hope, fear, intention, hunch, . . .).[2]

From Daniel C. Dennett, "Intentional Systems," *The Journal of Philosophy* LXVIII, 4 (Feb. 25, 1971), 87–106. Reprinted by permission of the journal and author.

[1] I am indebted to Peter Woodruff for making extensive improvements in this paper.—D. C. D

[2] I capitalize the terms derived from Brentano's notion of *intentionality* in order to distinguish them from the narrower notion of intentional action, meaning what one intends to do. For me, as far many recent authors, Intentionality is to be viewed as a feature of linguistic entities—idioms, contexts—and for my purposes here we can be satisfied that an

I

The first point to make about Intentional systems as I have just defined them is that a particular thing is an Intentional system only in relation to the strategies of someone who is trying to explain and predict its behavior. What this amounts to can best be brought out by example. Consider the case of a chess-playing computer, and the different strategies or stances one might adopt as its opponent in trying to predict its moves. There are three different stances of interest to us. First there is the *design stance*. If one knows exactly how the computer is designed (including the impermanent part of its design: its program[3]), one can predict its designed response to any move one makes by following the computation instructions of the program. One's prediction will come true provided only that the computer performs as designed—that is, without breakdown. Different varieties of design-stance predictions can be discerned, but all of them are alike in relying on the notion of *function* which is purpose-relative or teleological.[4] That is, a design of a system breaks it up into larger or smaller functional parts, and design-stance predictions are generated by assuming that each functional part will function properly. For instance, the radio engineer's schematic wiring diagrams have symbols for each

resistor, capacitor, transistor, etc.—*each with its task to perform*—and he can give a design-stance prediction of the behavior of a circuit by assuming that each element performs its task. Thus one can make design-stance predictions of the computer's response at several different levels of abstraction, depending on whether one's design treats as smallest functional elements strategy-generators and consequence-testers, multipliers and dividers, or transistors and switches. (It should be noted that not all diagrams or pictures are designs in this sense, for a diagram may carry no information about the functions—intended or observed—of the elements it depicts.)

We generally adopt the design stance when making predictions about the behavior of mechanical objects, e.g., "As the typewriter carriage approaches the margin, a bell will ring (provided the machine is in working order)," and more simply "Strike the match and it will light." We also often adopt this stance in predictions involving natural objects: "Heavy pruning will stimulate denser foliage and stronger limbs." The essential feature of the design stance is that we make predictions solely from knowledge or assumptions about the system's functional design, irrespective of the physical constitution or condition of the innards of the particular object.[5]

Second, there is what we may call the *physical stance*. From this stance our predictions are based on the actual physical state of the particular object, and are worked out by applying whatever knowledge we have of the laws of nature. It is from this stance alone that we can predict the malfunction of systems (unless, as sometimes happens these days, a system is *designed* to malfunction after a certain time, in which case malfunctioning in one sense becomes a part of its proper functioning). Instances of predictions from the physical stance are common enough: "If you turn on the switch you'll get a nasty shock," and "When the snows come that branch will break right off." One seldom adopts the

---

idiom is Intentional if substitution of codesignative terms does not preserve truth or if the "objects" of the idiom are not capturable in the usual way by quantifiers. I defend this apparently slapdash approach to the knotty problem of defining the Intentional because on the one hand I want to press on to points that seem to me to be independent of these interesting and important difficulties, and on the other hand experience seems to show that a general consensus about the Intentionality of particular cases can be relied upon in the absence of any agreement about formal criteria. I discuss the matter in more detail in *Content and Consciousness* (London: Routledge & Kegan Paul; New York: Humanities Press, 1969), ch. II.

[3] When you run a program on your computer, you introduce a temporary physical change in the computer's circuitry such that its outputs will be of a desired kind given specific inputs. ED.

[4] The word "teleological" means "pertaining to purpose or design." The functional design of a system involves the notion of what the system is structured *for*, i.e., what a rational designer *would* have in mind as the *end* for which the system is to be constructed as a *means*. That is how we would think of the differences among breeds of dogs (created by human breeders) as well as of the "design" of organs in naturally occurring animals. We understand the breeds and the organs as existing because they served certain purposes. From that perspective, the "design stance" and the "intentional stance" (which Dennett explains below) overlap, and the principal contrast is between them and the "physical stance" which, as he explains next, doesn't invoke rationality as an explanatory factor or predictive device. ED.

[5] It isn't clear why Dennett gives as examples of the design stance the typewriter, match, and pruning cases. In each of these, one's prediction can be grounded in simple generalization of past experience, without invoking the functions of the systems involved. It's unclear why the prediction "Strike the match and it will light" is significantly different from "Bend the match and it will break." Both seem consistent with the "physical stance." ED.

physical stance in dealing with a computer just because the number of critical variables in the physical constitution of a computer would overwhelm the most prodigious calculator. Significantly, the physical stance is generally reserved for instances of breakdown, where the condition preventing normal operation is generalized and easily locatable, e.g., "Nothing will happen when you type in your questions, because it isn't plugged in" or "It won't work with all that flood water in it." Attempting to give a physical account or prediction of the chess-playing computer would be a pointless and herculean labor, but it would work in principle. One could predict the response it would make in a chess game by tracing out the effects of the input energies all the way through the computer until once more type was pressed against paper and a response was printed. (Because of the digital nature of computers, quantum-level indeterminacies, if such there be, would cancel out rather than accumulate, unless of course a radium "randomizer" or other amplifier of quantum effects were built into the computer.)[6]

The best chess-playing computers these days are practically inaccessible to prediction from either the design stance or the physical stance; they have become too complex for even their own designers to view from the design stance. A man's best hope of defeating such a machine in a chess match is to predict its responses by figuring out as best he can what the best or most rational move would be, given the rules and goals of chess. That is, one assumes not only (1) that the machine will function as designed, but (2) that the design is optimal as well, that the computer will "choose" the most rational move. Predictions made on these assumptions may well fail if either assumption proves unwarranted in the particular case, but still this *means* of prediction may impress us as the most fruitful one to adopt in dealing with a particular system. Put another way, when one can no longer hope to beat the machine by utilizing one's knowledge of physics or programming to anticipate its responses, one may still be able to avoid defeat by treating the machine rather like an intelligent human opponent.[7]

We must look more closely at this strategy. A prediction relying on the assumption of the system's rationality is relative to a number of things. First, rationality here so far means nothing more than optimal design relative to a goal or optimally weighted hierarchy of goals (checkmate, winning pieces, defense, etc., in the case of chess) and a set of constraints (the rules and starting position).[8] Prediction itself is, moreover, relative to the nature and extent of the information the system has at the time about the field of endeavor. The question one asks in framing a prediction of this sort is: What is the most rational thing for the computer to do, given goals $x,y,x, \ldots$, constraints $a,b,c, \ldots$ and information (including misinformation, if any) about the present state of affairs $p,q,r, \ldots$? In predicting the computer's response to my chess move my assessment of the computer's most rational move may depend, for instance, not only on my assumption that the computer has information about the present disposition of all the pieces, but also on whether I believe the computer has information about my inability to see four moves ahead, the relative powers of knights and bishops, and my weakness for knight-bishop exchanges. In the end I may not be able to frame a very good prediction, if I am unable to determine with any accuracy what information and goals the computer has, or if the information and goals I take to be given do not dictate any one best move, or if I simply am not so good as the computer is at generating an optimal move from this given. Such predictions then are very precarious; not only are they relative to a set of postulates about goals, constraints, and information, and not only do they hinge on determining an optimal response in situations where we may have no clear criteria for what is optimal, but also they are vulnerable to short-circuit falsifications that are in

---

sociated Press report, Kasparov asked for a draw "and the computer named 'Deep Blue' agreed in the 39th move that the game could be advanced no further. . . ." Kasparov's aggressive play gave him an advantage through the early part of this game, but then Deep Blue made a series of unorthodox moves that stymied him. "'It played what no human would have played, but it was right,' Ashley [a commentator] said. 'It looked and said "You can't win"—that's scary.'" The concerns and anxieties associated with the Kasparov-Deep Blue match are the topic of Reading 14. ED.

[8]Notions such as *optimal, set of constraints* and especially *optimal weighting of goals* have fairly clear applications in a game like chess, but they become complex without limit in proportion to the complexity of the environments to which they are applied. Imagine using them to restructure the political and economic organization of a society. ED.

---

[6]You don't need to understand this parenthetical sentence in order to understand Dennett's argument here. ED.

[7]At the time of this writing, Garry Kasparov, the reigning world chess champion, is playing a six-game match with the current best chess-playing computer. In their third game, according to Wayne Woolley's As-

principle unpredictable from this stance. Just as design-stance predictions are vulnerable to malfunctions (by depending on the assumption of no malfunction), so these predictions are vulnerable to design weaknesses and lapses (by depending on the assumption of optimal design). It is a measure of the success of contemporary program designers that these precarious predictions turn out true with enough regularity to make the method useful.

The dénouement of the extended example should now be obvious: this third stance, with its assumption of rationality, is the *Intentional stance;* the predictions one makes from it are Intentional predictions; one is viewing the computer as an Intentional system. One predicts behavior in such a case by ascribing to the system *the possession of certain information* and by supposing it to be *directed by certain goals,* and then by working out the most reasonable or appropriate action on the basis of these ascriptions and suppositions. It is a small step to calling the information possessed the computer's *beliefs,* its goals and subgoals its *desires.* What I mean by saying this is a small step is that the notion of possession of information or misinformation is just as Intentional a notion as that of belief. The "possession" at issue is hardly the bland and innocent notion of storage one might suppose; it is, and must be, "epistemic possession"—an analogue of belief. (Consider: the Arabian sheik who possesses the *Encyclopedia Britannica* but knows no English might be said to possess the information in it, but if there is such a sense of possession, it is not strong enough to serve as the sort of possession the computer must be supposed to enjoy relative to the information it *uses* in "choosing" a chess move.) In a similar way, the goals of a goal-directed computer must be specified Intentionally, just like desires.

Lingering doubts about whether the chess-playing computer *really* has beliefs and desires are misplaced; for the definition of Intentional systems I have given does not say that Intentional systems *really* have beliefs and desires, but that one can explain and predict their behavior by *ascribing* beliefs and desires to them, and whether one calls what one ascribes to the computer beliefs or belief-analogues or information complexes or Intentional whatnots makes no difference to the nature of the calculation one makes on the basis of the ascriptions. One will arrive at the same predictions whether one forthrightly thinks in terms of

the computer's beliefs and desires, or in terms of the computer's information-store and goal-specifications. The inescapable and interesting fact is that, for the best chess-playing computers of today, Intentional explanation and prediction of their behavior is not only common but works when no other sort of prediction of their behavior is manageable. We do quite successfully treat these computers as Intentional systems, and we do this independently of any considerations about what substance they are composed of, their origin, their position or lack of position in the community of moral agents, their consciousness or self-consciousness, or the determinacy or indeterminacy of their operations. The decision to adopt the strategy is pragmatic, and is not intrinsically right or wrong. One can always refuse to adopt the Intentional stance toward the computer, and accept its checkmates. One can switch stances at will without involving oneself in any inconsistencies or inhumanities, adopting the Intentional stance in one's role as opponent, the design stance in one's role as redesigner, and the physical stance in one's role as repairman.[9]

This celebration of our chess-playing computer is not intended to imply that it is a completely adequate model or simulation of Mind or intelligent human or animal activity; nor am I saying that the attitude we adopt toward this computer is precisely the same that we adopt toward a creature we deem to be conscious and rational. All that has been claimed is that on occasion a purely physical system can be so complex, and yet so organized, that we find it convenient, explanatory, pragmatically necessary for prediction, to treat it as if it had beliefs and desires and was rational. The chess-playing computer is just that, a machine for playing chess, which no man or animal is; and hence its "rationality" is pinched and artificial.

Perhaps we could straightforwardly expand the chess-playing computer into a more faithful model of human rationality, and perhaps not. I prefer to pursue a more fundamental line of inquiry first.

When should we expect the tactic of adopting the Intentional stance to pay off? Whenever we have reason to suppose the assumption of optimal design is warranted, and doubt the practicality of

---

[9] I discuss the moral dimension of Intentional systems and stances in some detail in "Mechanism and Responsibility," in T. Honderich, ed. *Essays on Freedom of Action* (London: Routledge and Kegan Paul).

prediction from the design or physical stance. Suppose we travel to a distant planet and find it inhabited by things moving about its surface, multiplying, decaying, apparently reacting to events in the environment, but otherwise as unlike human beings as you please. Can we make Intentional predictions and explanations of their behavior? If we have reason to suppose that a process of natural selection has been in effect, then we can be assured that the populations we observe have been selected in virtue of their design: they will respond to at least some of the more common event-types in this environment in ways that are normally appropriate—that is, conducive to propagation of the species.[10] Once we have (tentatively) identified the perils and succors of the environment (relative to the constitution of the inhabitants, not ours) we shall be able to estimate which goals and which weighting of goals would be optimal relative to the creatures' *needs* (for survival and propagation), which sorts of information about the environment will be *useful* in guiding goal-directed activity, and which activities will be appropriate given the environmental circumstances. Having doped out these conditions (which will always be subject to revision) we can proceed at once to ascribe beliefs and desires to the creatures. Their behavior will "manifest" their beliefs by being seen as the actions which, given the creatures' desires, would be appropriate to such beliefs as would be appropriate to the environmental stimulation. Desires, in turn, will be "manifested" in behavior as those appropriate desires (given the needs of the creature) to which the actions of the creature would be appropriate, given the creature's beliefs. The circularity of these interlocking specifications is no accident. Ascriptions of beliefs and desires must be interdependent, and the only points of anchorage are the demonstrable needs for survival, the regularities of behavior, and the assumption, grounded in faith in natural selection, of optimal design.[11] Once one has ascribed beliefs and desires, however, one can at once set about predicting be-

havior on their basis, and if evolution has done its job—as it must over the long run—our predictions will be reliable enough to be useful.

It might at first seem that this tactic unjustifiably imposes human categories and attributes (belief, desire, and so forth) on these alien entities. It is a sort of anthropomorphizing, to be sure, but it is conceptually innocent anthropomorphizing. We do not have to suppose these creatures share with us any peculiarly human inclinations, attitudes, hopes, foibles, pleasures, or outlooks; their actions may not include running, jumping, hiding, eating, sleeping, listening, or copulating. All we transport from our world to theirs are the categories of rationality, perception (information input by some "sense" modality or modalities—perhaps radar or cosmic radiation), and action. The question of whether we can expect them to share any of our beliefs or desires is tricky, but there are a few points that can be made at this time; in virtue of their rationality they can be supposed to share our belief in logical truths,[12] and we cannot suppose that they normally desire their own destruction, for instance.

II

When one deals with a system—be it man, machine, or alien creature—by explaining and predicting its behavior by citing its beliefs and desires,

---

[10] Note that what is *directly* selected, the gene, is a diagram and not a design; it is selected, however, because it happens to ensure that its bearer has a certain (functional) design. (This was pointed out to me by Woodruff.)

[11] "Satisficing" has become a "buzz word" lately in many circles. It means *being good enough* to accomplish a goal or good enough to survive or even win in a competitive situation. Let's take an example from the marketplace. At this time it seems that the combination of IBM-style computer hardware and Microsoft software is winning the market battle with Apple. Many analysts claim that the IBM-Microsoft software is still not as good as that of Apple. However, for complicated reasons, the superiority of Apple software is not enough to make users of IBM-compatible software accept the inconvenience and cost of switching to Apple. To put it another way, IBM-style software is *good enough* for the actual competitive situation. Economic competition does not inevitably bring about optimal design in the products of the computer industry, at least not relative to the *function* of a computer. Instead, it brings about a *satisficing* of the design relative to the function of computers, to the corresponding goals and purchasing power of consumers, and to the designs of competing products.

Something similar happens in the kind of competition we call "natural selection." Victory in this competition is reproductive success. Organisms need not have an optimal (in the sense of "best") design relative to their needs. They need only have a design that is *good enough* to prevail against such obstacles to reproductive success as competition within their species for mates, or competition against other species within their ecological niches for such necessities as territory and food. In sufficiently favorable environments, very little may be more than enough. ED.

[12] Cf. Quine's argument about the necessity of "discovering" our logical connectives in any language we can translate [*Word and Object* (Cambridge, Mass.: MIT, 1960), § 13]. More will be said in defense of this below.

one has what might be called a "theory of behavior" for the system. Let us see how such Intentional theories of behavior relate to other putative theories of behavior.

One fact so obvious that it is easily overlooked is that our "common-sense" explanations and predictions of the behavior of both men and animals are Intentional. We start by assuming rationality. We do not *expect* new acquaintances to react irrationally to particular topics or eventualities, but when they do we learn to adjust our strategies accordingly, just as, with a chess-playing computer, one sets out with a high regard for its rationality and adjusts one's estimate downward wherever performance reveals flaws. The presumption of rationality is so strongly entrenched in our inference habits that when our predictions prove false we at first cast about for adjustments in the information-possession conditions (he must not have heard, he must not know English, he must not have seen *x,* been aware that *y,* etc.) or goal weightings before questioning the rationality of the system as a whole. In extreme cases personalities may prove to be so unpredictable from the Intentional stance that we abandon it, and if we have accumulated a lot of evidence in the meanwhile about the nature of response patterns in the individual, we may find that a species of design stance can be effectively adopted. This is the fundamentally different attitude we occasionally adopt toward the insane. To watch an asylum attendant manipulate an obsessively countersuggestive patient, for instance, is to watch something radically unlike normal interpersonal relations.[13]

Our prediction of animal behavior by "common sense" is also Intentional. Whether or not sentimental folk go overboard when they talk to their dogs or fill their cats' heads with schemes and worries, even the most hardboiled among us predict animals' behavior Intentionally. If we observe a mouse in a situation where it can see a cat waiting at one mousehole and cheese at another, we know which way the mouse will go (providing it is not deranged); our prediction is not based on our familiarity with maze-experiments or any assumptions about the sort of special training the mouse has been through. We suppose the mouse can see the cat and the cheese, and hence has beliefs (belief-analogues, Intentional whatnots) to the effect that there is a cat to the left, cheese to the right, and we ascribe to the mouse also the desire to eat the cheese and the desire to avoid the cat (subsumed, appropriately enough, under the more general desires to eat and to avoid peril); so we predict that the mouse will do what is appropriate to such beliefs and desires, namely, go to the right in order to get the cheese and avoid the cat. Whatever academic allegiances or theoretical predilections we may have, we would be astonished if, in the general run, mice and other animals falsified such Intentional predictions of their behavior. Indeed, experimental psychologists of every school would have a hard time devising experimental situations to support their various theories without the help of their Intentional expectations of how the test animals will respond to circumstances.

Earlier I alleged that even creatures from another planet would share with us our beliefs in logical truths; light can be shed on this claim by asking whether mice and other animals, in virtue of being Intentional systems, also believe the truths of logic. There is something bizarre in the picture of a dog or mouse cogitating a list of tautologies,[14] but we can avoid that picture. The assumption that something is an Intentional system is the assumption that it is rational; that is, one gets nowhere with the

---

[13] The behavior of persons with passive-aggressive personality disorder is often countersuggestive. These persons express their chronic and inappropriate hostility indirectly, by stubbornness and procrastination in response to suggestions. This syndrome is a species of a more general one known as Personality Disorder, which also includes the psychopathic or sociopathic personality. Personality Disorder is, in the words of the Encyclopedia Britannica, "marked by deeply ingrained and lasting patterns of inflexible, maladaptive, or antisocial behavior." Persons with PD, as well as those with more serious afflictions that we call "insane," behave in ways that may be predictable but nevertheless "don't make sense" because these behaviors interfere with one's ability to function in society in a way that is generally important to one's well-being. For this reason, Dennett says, we sometimes give up the Intentional stance in their regard. It may be just too difficult for us to figure out what such people want or believe, and thereby interpret or predict their behavior as rationally ordered to intelligible goals. ED.

[14] A tautology (e.g., *No unmarried woman is married*) is a necessarily true proposition the negation of which is self-contradictory. Tautologies are often called logical truths because we can ascertain their truth solely by the interpretation of the syncategorematic or nondesignating terms in the proposition (such as *no* and *un-* in the preceding example). The statement of the truth or rule of logic known as *modus ponens* (see fn. 17 below) is a tautology or logical truth in just this sense. ED.

assumption that entity x has beliefs $p,q,r, \ldots$ unless one supposes that x believes what follows from $p,q,r, \ldots$; otherwise there is no way of ruling out the prediction that x will, in the face of its beliefs $p,q,r, \ldots$ do something utterly stupid, and, if we cannot rule out *that* prediction, we will have acquired no predictive power at all. So whether or not the animal is said to *believe* the *truths* of logic, it must be supposed to *follow* the *rules* of logic. Surely our mouse follows or believes in *modus ponens*[15] for we ascribed to it the beliefs: (a) *there is a cat to the left,* and (b) *if there is a cat to the left, I had better not go left,* and our prediction relied on the mouse's ability to get to the conclusion. In general there is a trade-off between rules and truths; we can suppose x to have an inference rule taking A to B or we can give x the belief in the "theorem": if A then B. As far as our predictions are concerned, we are free to ascribe to the mouse either a few inference rules and belief in many logical propositions or many inference rules and few if any logical beliefs.[16] We can even take a patently nonlogical belief like (b) and recast it as an inference rule taking (a) directly to the desired conclusion.

Will all logical truths appear among the beliefs of an Intentional system? If the system were ideally or perfectly rational, all logical truths would appear, but any actual Intentional system will be imperfect, and so not all logical truths must be ascribed as beliefs to any system. Moreover, not all the inference rules of an actual Intentional system may be valid;

not all its inference-licensing beliefs may be truths of logic. Experience may indicate where the shortcomings lie in any particular system. If we found an imperfectly rational creature whose allegiance to *modus ponens,* say, varied with the subject matter, we could characterize that by excluding *modus ponens* as a rule and ascribing in its stead a set of nonlogical inference rules covering the *modus ponens* step for each subject matter where the rule was followed. Not surprisingly, as we discover more and more imperfections (as we banish more and more logical truths from the creature's beliefs), our efforts at Intentional prediction become more and more cumbersome and undecidable, for we can no longer count on the beliefs, desires, and actions going together that *ought* to go together. Eventually we end up, following this process, by predicting from the design stance; we end up, that is, dropping the assumption of rationality.[17,18]

This migration from common-sense Intentional explanations and predictions to more reliable design-stance explanations and predictions that is forced on us when we discover that our subjects are imperfectly rational is, independently of any such discovery, the proper direction for theory builders to take whenever possible. In the end, we want to be able to explain the intelligence of man (or beast) in terms of his design, and this in turn in terms of the natural selection of this design;[19] so when-

---

[15]If p and q are variables for propositions, the *modus ponens* rule may be stated as follows:

1. If p, then q
2. p (is the case)
3. q (is the case)

Dennett is saying that in order to treat a system as intentional, one must give it the capacity and proclivity to infer one belief from another and act accordingly. Otherwise we could not make predictions about its behavior, since we make those predictions by making inferences to what follows (in the way of beliefs and conduct) from the beliefs we have attributed to the system. So the intentional system must be thought of as *following* the rules of logic one way or another—either by believing in such abstract logical truths as *modus ponens,* or by believing indefinitely many "inference rules" such as that it (the mouse) is to infer, from the combination of its belief that a cat is now present and its belief that it should get away when cats are present, that it should now get away. ED.

[16]Accepting the argument of Lewis Carroll, in "What the Tortoise Said to Achilles," *Mind,* 1895, reprinted in I. M. Copi and J. A. Gould, *Readings on Logic* (New York: MacMillan, 1964), we cannot allow all the rules for a system to be replaced by beliefs, for this would generate an infinite and unproductive nesting of distinct beliefs about what can be inferred from what.

[17]We drop the assumption of rationality in the sense of belief in or compliance with the rules of logic. However, as I pointed out in footnote 5, the teleological aspect of *function* and *design* does invoke rationality in the ordering of means (such as structure and behavior) to ends. ED.

[18]This paragraph owes much to discussion with John Vickers, whose paper "Judgment and Belief," in K. Lambert, *The Logical Way of Doing Things* (New Haven, Conn.: Yale, 1969), goes beyond the remarks here by considering the problems of the relative strength or weighting of beliefs and desires.

[19]There are two reductions (transitions from higher to lower levels) called for here by Dennett: *First,* to show what biological functions were served by the evolution of intelligence or rationality in human organisms, bringing us to the "design stance" with its recourse to purpose; and *second,* to show how intelligence or rationality, because of the purposes it served, would have been promoted by *natural selection,* which brings us to the "physical stance." In *natural selection* genes for traits which are adaptive (i.e., contribute to reproductive success) get "selected" over those that are not. We may even use the notion of a rational designer to predict the sorts of traits that get selected. But we don't regard *natural selection* as an Intentional system. We understand it instead as a mechanism or system of physical causes that simulates to some degree the operation of an Intentional system by having an optimizing or satisficing effect on the design of organisms. With natural selection we have made the occurrence of functional design and intentionality intelligible from the physical stance, something Dennett considers important for a physicalist theory of mind to do. ED.

ever we stop in our explanations at the Intentional level we have left an unexplained instance of intelligence or rationality. This comes out vividly if we look at theory building from the vantage point of economics.

Any time a theory builder proposes to call any event, state, structure, etc., in any system (say the brain of an organism) a *signal* or *message* or *command* (or otherwise endows it with content) he *takes out a loan* of intelligence. He implicitly posits along with his signals, messages, or commands, something that can serve as a signal-*reader,* message-*understander,* or *commander* (else his "signals" will be for naught, will decay unreceived, uncomprehended). This loan must be repaid eventually by finding and analyzing away these readers or comprehenders; for, failing this, the theory will have among its elements unanalyzed man-analogues endowed with enough intelligence to read the signals, etc., and thus the theory will *postpone* answering the major question: what makes for intelligence? The Intentionality of all such talk of signals and commands reminds us that rationality is being taken for granted, and in this way shows us where a theory is incomplete. It is this feature that, to my mind, puts a premium on the yet unfinished task of devising a rigorous definition of Intentionality, for if we can lay claim to a purely formal criterion of Intentional discourse, we will have what amounts to a medium of exchange for assessing theories of behavior.[20] Intentionality *abstracts* from the inessential details of the various forms intelligence-loans can take (e.g., signal-readers, volition-emitters, librarians in the corridors of memory, egos and superegos) and serves as a reliable means of detecting exactly where a theory is *in the red* relative to the task of explaining intelligence; wherever a theory relies on a formulation bearing the logical marks of Intentionality, there a little man is concealed.

This insufficiency of Intentional explanation from the point of view of psychology has been widely felt and as widely misconceived. The most influential misgivings, expressed in the behaviorism

of Skinner[21] and Quine,[22] can be succinctly characterized in terms of our economic metaphor. Skinner's and Quine's adamant prohibition of Intentional idioms at all levels of theory is the analogue of rock-ribbed New England conservatism: no deficit spending when building a theory! In Quine's case the abhorrence of loans is due mainly to his fear that they can never be repaid, whereas Skinner stresses rather that what is borrowed is worthless to begin with. Skinner's suspicion is that Intentionally couched claims are empirically vacuous in the sense that they are altogether too easy to accommodate to the data, like the *virtus dormativa* Molière's doctor ascribes to the sleeping powder.[23] Questions can be begged on a temporary basis, however, permitting a mode of prediction and explanation not totally vacuous. Consider the following Intentional prediction: if I were to ask a thousand American mathematicians how much seven times five is, more than nine hundred would respond by saying that it was thirty-five.[24] (I have allowed for a few to mis-hear my question, a few others to be obstreperous, a few to make slips of the tongue.) If you doubt the prediction, you can test it; I would bet good money on it. It seems to have empirical content because it can, in a fashion, be tested, and yet it is unsatisfactory as a prediction of an empirical theory of psychology. It works, of course, because of the contingent, empirical (but evolution-guaranteed) fact that men in general are well enough designed both to get the answer right and to want to get it right. It will hold with as few exceptions for any group of Martians with whom we are able to converse, for it is not a

---

[20]Chisholm, in the previous reading, concludes by attempting to provide just such a criterion. By isolating what is common to all manifestations of intentionality, the criterion prevents us from being distracted by the detailed differences among these manifestations; it serves as a "medium of exchange" or a measure of how much unreduced, higher-level content remains in a theory of behavior. ED.

[21]B. F. Skinner (1904–1990) was one of the most influential proponents of behaviorism in American psychology. ED.

[22]Willard V. Quine (1908–) is many philosophers' candidate for most influential American philosopher of the second half of the twentieth century. ED.

[23]"Virtus dormativa" means sleep-inducing power. To say that a sleeping powder has a sleep-inducing power is just about as trivial as saying that a sleeping powder is a sleeping powder. There is no advance in understanding when you attribute to an object that has a predictable effect the power (*virtus*) for such an effect. It is a common parody of scholastic philosophy that it engaged in such pseudo-explanation. Having a character in a play use the phrase was a way to show the character as spouting nonsense. ED.

[24]The mathematicians are regarded as Intentional systems with not only a capacity for computation but also perceptions of what is occurring in their environment, beliefs about when and how to respond to questions of this sort and about the purpose of the questioner in asking, and so on. If your prediction was merely about the vocalized output of a calculator whose input is "7 × 5 =", you would be adopting the design rather than the intentional stance. ED.

prediction just of *human* psychology, but of the "psychology" of Intentional systems generally.

Deciding on the basis of available empirical evidence that something is a piece of copper or a lichen permits one to make predictions based on the empirical theories dealing with copper and lichens, but deciding on the basis of available evidence that something is (to be treated as) an Intentional system permits predictions having a normative or logical basis [25] rather than an empirical one, and hence the success of an Intentional prediction, based as it is on no particular picture of the system's design, cannot be construed to confirm or disconfirm any particular pictures of the system's design.

Skinner's reaction to this has been to try to frame predictions purely in non-Intentional language, by predicting bodily responses to physical stimuli, but to date this has not provided him with the alternative mode of prediction and explanation he has sought, as perhaps an extremely cursory review can indicate. To provide a setting for non-Intentional prediction of behavior, he invented the Skinner box, in which the rewarded behavior of the occupant—say, a rat—is a highly restricted and stereotypic bodily motion—usually pressing a bar with the front paws.

The claim that is then made is that, once the animal has been trained, a law-like relationship is discovered to hold between non-Intentionally characterized events: controlling stimuli and bar-pressing responses. A regularity is discovered to hold, to be sure, but the fact that it is a regularity that can be held to hold between non-Intentionally defined events is due to a property of the Skinner box and not of the occupant. For let us turn our prediction about mathematicians into a Skinnerian prediction: strap a mathematician in a Skinner box so he can move only his head; display in front of him a card on which appear the marks: "How much is seven times five?", move into the range of his head-motions two buttons, over one of which is the mark "35" and over the other "34"; place electrodes on the soles of his feet and give him a few quick shocks; the controlling stimulus is then to be

the sound: "Answer now!" I predict that in a statistically significant number of cases, even *before* training trials to condition the man to press button "35" with his forehead, he will do this when given the controlling stimulus. Is this a satisfactory scientific prediction just because it eschews the Intentional vocabulary? No, it is an Intentional prediction disguised by so restricting the environment that only one bodily motion is available to fulfill the Intentional *action* that anyone would prescribe as appropriate to the circumstances of perception, belief, desire.[26] That it is action, not merely motion, that is predicted can also be seen in the case of subjects less intelligent than mathematicians. Suppose a mouse were trained, in a Skinner box with a food reward, to take exactly four steps forward and press a bar with its nose; if Skinner's laws truly held between stimuli and responses defined in terms of bodily motion, were we to move the bar an inch farther away, so four steps did not reach it, Skinner would have to predict that the mouse would jab its nose into the empty air rather than take a fifth step.

A variation of Skinnerian theory designed to meet this objection acknowledges that the trained response one predicts is not truly captured in a description of skeletal motion alone, but rather in a description of an environmental effect achieved: the bar going down, the "35" button being depressed. This will also not do. Suppose we could in fact train a man or animal to achieve an environmental effect, as this theory proposes. Suppose, for instance, we train a man to push a button under the longer of two displays (such as drawings or simple designs). That is, we reward him when he pushes the button under the longer of two pictures of pencils, or cigars, etc. The miraculous consequence of this theory, were it correct, would be that if, after training him on simple views, we were to present him with the Müller-Lyer arrow-head illusion,[27] he

---

[25] If an organism is treated as an Intentional system, one can infer that it will do certain things because they ought to be done or because they are consequences of beliefs attributable to the organism. A merely empirical basis for the prediction would rely entirely on empirical generalizations based on the organism's past behavior. ED.

[26] The *action* that any rational being under those circumstances would choose is to obey the command. Since there is only one way to do so, the rational decision leads to one and the same head motion each time, as if it were being mechanically induced by the stimulus. In this way the intentionality of perception, belief, and decision is masked. ED.

[27] In the Müller-Lyer illusion at right, two lines of the same length *appear* otherwise because the lines drawn away from the endpoints of each are at acute angles to the first and obtuse angles to the second. The "trained" man would *perceive* the line at the right as longer even though it is not. Therefore, according to Dennett, what would happen *could not be described without intentional language.* ED.

The Müller-Lyer Illusion

would be immune to it, for *ex hypothesi* he has been trained to achieve an actual environmental effect (choosing the display that *is* longer) not a *perceived* or *believed* environmental effect (choosing the display that *seems* longer). The reliable prediction, again, is the Intentional one.

Skinner's experimental design is supposed to eliminate the Intentional, but it merely masks it. Skinner's non-Intentional predictions work to the extent they do, not because Skinner has truly found non-Intentional behavioral laws, but because the highly reliable Intentional predictions underlying his experimental situations (the rat desires food and believes it will get food by pressing the bar—so it will press the bar) are disguised by leaving virtually no room in the environment for more than one bodily motion to be the appropriate action and by leaving virtually no room in the environment for discrepancy to arise between the subject's beliefs and the reality.

Where, then, should we look for a satisfactory theory of behavior? Intentional theory is vacuous as psychology because it presupposes and does not explain rationality or intelligence. The apparent successes of Skinnerian behaviorism, however, rely on hidden Intentional predictions. Skinner is right in recognizing that Intentionality can be no *foundation* for psychology, and right also to look for purely mechanistic regularities in the activities of his subjects, but there is little reason to suppose they will lie on the surface in gross behavior (except, as we have seen, when we put an artificial straitjacket on an Intentional regularity). Rather, we will find whatever mechanistic regularities there are in the functioning of internal systems whose design approaches the optimal (relative to some ends). In seeking knowledge of internal design our most promising tactic is to take out intelligence-loans, endow peripheral and internal events with content, and then look for mechanisms that will function appropriately with such "messages" so we can pay back the loans. This tactic is hardly untried. Research in artificial intelligence (which has produced, among other things, the chess-playing computer) proceeds by working from an Intentionally characterized problem (how to get the computer to consider the right sorts of information, make the right decisions) to a design-stance solution—an approximation of optimal design. Psychophysicists and neurophysiologists who routinely describe

events in terms of the transmission of information within the nervous system are similarly borrowing Intentional capital—even if they are often inclined to ignore or disavow their debts.

Finally, it should not be supposed that, just because Intentional theory is vacuous as psychology, in virtue of its assumption of rationality, it is vacuous from all points of view. Game theory, for example, is inescapably Intentional,[28] but as a formal normative theory[29] and not a psychology this is nothing amiss. Game-theoretical predictions applied to human subjects achieve their accuracy in virtue of the evolutionary guarantee that man is well designed as a game player,[30] a special case of rationality. Similarly, economics, the social science of greatest predictive power today, is not a psychological theory and presupposes what psychology must explain. Economic explanation and prediction is Intentional (although some is disguised) and succeeds to the extent that it does because individual men are in general good approximations of the optimal operator in the marketplace.

III

The concept of an Intentional system is a relatively uncluttered and unmetaphysical notion, abstracted as it is from questions of the composition, constitution, consciousness, morality, or divinity of the entities falling under it. Thus, for example, it is much easier to decide whether a machine can be an Intentional system than it is to decide whether a machine can *really* think, or be conscious, or morally responsible. This simplicity makes it ideal as a source

---

[28] Hintikka notes in passing that game theory is like his epistemic logic in assuming rationality, in *Knowledge and Belief* (Ithaca, N.Y.: Cornell, 1962), p. 38.

[29] Game theory is a kind of applied mathematics designed to analyze interactions between or among decision-makers who need to take into account each other's reasoning. It is therefore essentially intentional because it must ascribe beliefs, perceptions, and other intentional states and acts to the participants, as well as rationality in the sense used by Dennett. It is also "normative" in the sense that it is used to predict what rational participants in a "game" *ought* to do. The notion of a "game" is very broad, covering everything from a literal game such as chess or poker to economic and political interactions. ED.

[30] Not everyone would agree that humans are that well designed as rational game players. The conduct of individuals and communities regularly exhibits something far less than enlightened self-interest. All that evolution and natural selection really "guarantee" is that our rationality "satisfied," was *good enough* to get us where we are today—enjoying all too much reproductive success. ED.

of order and organization in philosophical analyses of "mental" concepts. Whatever else a person might be—embodied mind or soul, self-conscious moral agent, "emergent" form of intelligence—he is an Intentional system, and whatever follows just from being an Intentional system thus is true of a person. It is interesting to see just how much of what we hold to be the case about persons or their minds follows directly from their being Intentional systems. To revert for a moment to the economic metaphor, the guiding or challenging question that defines work in the philosophy of mind is this: are there mental treasures that cannot be purchased with Intentional coin? If not, a considerable unification of science can be foreseen in outline. Of special importance for such an examination is the subclass of Intentional systems that have language, that can communicate; for these provide a framework for a theory of consciousness. Elsewhere[31] I have attempted to elaborate such a theory; here I would like to consider its implications for the analysis of the concept of belief. What will be true of human believers just in virtue of their being Intentional systems with the capacity to communicate?

Just as not all Intentional systems currently known to us can fly or swim, so not all Intentional systems can talk, but those which can do this raise special problems and opportunities when we come to ascribe beliefs and desires to them. That is a massive understatement; without the talking Intentional systems, of course, there would be no ascribing beliefs, no theorizing, no assuming rationality, no predicting. The capacity for language is without doubt the crowning achievement of evolution, an achievement that feeds on itself to produce ever more versatile and subtle rational systems, but still it can be looked at as an adaptation which is subject to the same conditions of environmental utility as any other behavioral talent. When it is looked at in this way several striking facts emerge. One of the most pervasive features of evolutionary histories is the interdependence of distinct organs and capacities in a species. Advanced eyes and other distance receptors are of no utility to an organism unless it develops advanced means of locomotion; the talents of a predator will not accrue to a species that does not evolve a carnivore's digestive system. The capacities of belief and communication have prereq-

uisites of their own. We have already seen that there is no point in ascribing beliefs to a system unless the beliefs ascribed are in general appropriate to the environment, and the system responds appropriately to the beliefs. An eccentric expression of this would be: the capacity to believe would have no survival value unless it were a capacity to believe truths. What is eccentric and potentially misleading about this is that it hints at the picture of a species "trying on" a faculty giving rise to beliefs most of which were false, having its inutility demonstrated, and abandoning it.[32] A species might "experiment" by mutation in any number of inefficacious systems, but none of these systems would deserve to be called belief systems precisely because of their defects, their nonrationality, and hence a false belief system is a conceptual impossibility. To borrow an example from a short story by MacDonald Harris, a soluble fish is an evolutionary impossibility, but a system for false beliefs cannot even be given a coherent description. The same evolutionary bias in favor of truth prunes the capacity to communicate as it develops; a capacity for false communication would not be a capacity for communication at all, but just an emission proclivity of no systematic value to the species. The faculty of communication would not gain ground in evolution unless it was by and large the faculty of transmitting true beliefs, which means only: the faculty of altering other members of the species in the direction of more optimal design.[33]

---

[31] *Content and Consciousness*, part II.

[32] As Dennett suggests by quotation marks around "trying on," we must avoid such misconceptions as imagining organisms developing physical and behavioral modifications simply as a response to environmental needs or stresses. Generally, alterations of physical and behavioral traits (including permanent central nervous system modifications) in nonhuman organisms arise from genetic mutations that are random rather than responsive to environmental conditions. In the small percentage of cases where the genetically induced modifications are adaptive, there is a greater likelihood that the mutant organism will survive to reproduce. In that way the advantageous mutation is *selected*. ED.

[33] The acquisition and communication of beliefs can be understood as a kind of programming of oneself and others—altering neural circuitry in the reversible way that inputting a program into a computer temporarily alters its circuitry and thereby the kind of output there will be for a given input. We need to keep in mind the strong connection between belief and action in us Intentional systems. In even the simplest judgments I make about the world around me, I am *orienting* myself (and others to whom I communicate) behaviorally toward the world. For instance, if I believe that *this is a chair*, I enter a state of readiness to rest my weight on it in a sitting position. In this context, Dennett is putting forward a kind of pragmatic conception of truth as that attribute of a belief by which it *adaptively* modifies a believer with respect to what the belief is about. ED.

This provides a foundation for explaining a feature of belief that philosophers have recently been at some pains to account for.[34] The concept of belief seems to have a normative cast to it that is most difficult to capture. One way of putting it might be that an avowal like "I believe that p" seems to imply in some fashion: "One ought to believe that p." This way of putting it has flaws, however, for we must then account for the fact that "I believe that p" seems to have normative force that "He believes that p" said of me, does not. Moreover, saying that one ought to believe this or that suggests that belief is voluntary, a view with notorious difficulties.[35] So long as one tries to capture the normative element by expressing it in the form of moral or pragmatic injunctions to believers, such as "One ought to believe the truth" and "One ought to act in accordance with one's beliefs," dilemmas arise. How, for instance, is one to follow the advice to believe the truth? Could one abandon one's sloppy habit of believing falsehoods? If the advice is taken to mean: believe only what you have convincing evidence for, it is the vacuous advice: believe only what you believe to be true. If alternatively it is taken to mean: believe only what is in fact the truth, it is an injunction we are powerless to obey.

The normative element of belief finds its home not in such injunctions but in the preconditions for the ascription of belief, what Phillips Griffiths calls "the general conditions for the possibility of application of the concept." For the concept of belief to find application, two conditions, we have seen, must be met: (1) In general, normally, more often that not, if x believes p, p is true. (2) In general, normally, more often than not, if x avows that p, he believes p [and, by (1), p is true]. Were these conditions not met, we would not have rational, communicating systems; we would not have believers or belief-avowers. The norm for belief is evidential well-foundedness (assuring truth in the long run), and the norm for avowal of belief is accuracy (which includes sincerity). These two norms determine pragmatic implications of our utterances. If I assert that p (or that I believe that p—it makes no difference), I assume the burden of defending my assertion on two fronts: I can be asked for evidence for the truth of p, and I can be asked for behavioral evidence that I do in fact believe p.[36] I do not need to examine my own behavior in order to be in a position to avow my belief that p, but if my sincerity or self-knowledge is challenged this is where I must turn to defend my assertion. But again, challenges on either point must be the exception rather than the rule if belief is to have a place among our concepts.

Another way of looking at the importance of this predominance of the normal is to consider the well-known circle of implications between beliefs and desires (or intentions) that prevent non-Intentional behavioral definitions of Intentional terms. A man's standing under a tree is a behavioral indicator of his belief that it is raining, but only on the assumption that he desires to stay dry, and if we then look for evidence that he wants to stay dry, his standing under the tree will do, but only on the assumption that he believes the tree will shelter him; if we ask him if he believes the tree will shelter him, his positive response is confirming evidence only on the assumption that he desires to tell us the truth, and so forth *ad infinitum*. It is this apparently vicious circle that turned Quine against the Intentional (and foiled Tolman's efforts at operational definition[37] of Intentional terms), but if it is true that in any particular case a man's saying that p is evidence of his belief only conditionally, we can be assured that in the long run and in general the circle is broken; a man's assertions are, unconditionally, indicative of his beliefs, as are his actions in general. We get around the "privacy" of beliefs and desires by recognizing that in general anyone's beliefs and desires must be those he "ought to have" given the circumstances.

These two interdependent norms of belief, one favoring the truth and rationality of belief, the other favoring accuracy of avowal, normally complement each other, but on occasion can give rise to conflict. This is the "problem of incorrigibility."

---

[34] I have in mind especially A. Phillips Griffiths' penetrating discussion "On Belief," *Proceedings of the Aristotelian Society* LXIII (1962/3): 167–186; and Bernard Mayo's "Belief and Constraint," *ibid.*, LXIV (1964): 139–156, both reprinted in Phillips Griffiths, ed., *Knowledge and Belief* (New York: Oxford, 1967).

[35] See, e.g., H. H. Price, "Belief and Will," *Proceedings of the Aristotelian Society,* suppl. vol. XXVIII (1954), reprinted in S. Hampshire, ed., *Philosophy of Mind* (New York: Harper & Row, 1966).

[36] Cf. A. W. Collins, "Unconscious Belief," [*The Journal of Philosophy*] LXVI 20 (Oct. 16, 1969): 667–680.

[37] An *operational definition* of a concept such as *belief* would identify the concept with the scientific operations (measurements of behavior) used to study belief. ED.

If rationality is the mother of Intention, we still must wean Intentional systems from the criteria that give them life, and set them up on their own. Less figuratively, if we are to make use of the concept of an Intentional system in particular instances, at some point we must cease *testing* the assumption of the system's rationality, adopt the Intentional stance, and grant without further ado that the system is qualified for beliefs and desires. For mute animals (and chess-playing computers) this manifests itself in a tolerance for less than optimal performance. We continue to ascribe beliefs to the mouse, and explain its actions in terms of them, after we have tricked it into some stupid belief. This tolerance has its limits of course, and the less felicitous the behavior—especially the less adaptable the behavior—the more hedged are our ascriptions. For instance, we are inclined to say of the duckling that "imprints" on the first moving thing it sees upon emerging from its shell that it "believes" the thing is its mother, whom it follows around, but we emphasize the scare-quotes around 'believes'. For Intentional systems that can communicate—persons for instance—the tolerance takes the form of the convention that a man is incorrigible or a special authority about his own beliefs. This conception is "justified" by the fact that evolution does guarantee that our second norm is followed. What better source could there be of a system's beliefs than its avowals? Conflict arises, however, whenever a person falls short of perfect rationality, and avows beliefs that either are strongly disconfirmed by the available empirical evidence or are self-contradictory or contradict other avowals he has made. If we lean on the myth that a man is perfectly rational, we must find his avowals less than authoritative ("You *can't* mean—understand—what you're saying!"); if we lean on his "right" as a speaking Intentional system to have his word accepted, we grant him an irrational set of beliefs. Neither position provides a stable resting place; for, as we saw earlier, Intentional explanation and prediction cannot be accommodated either to breakdown or to less than optimal design, so there is no coherent Intentional description of such an impasse.[38]

Can any other considerations be brought to bear in such an instance to provide us with justification for one ascription of beliefs rather than another? Where should one look for such considerations? The Phenomenologist[39] will be inclined to suppose that individual introspection will provide us a sort of data not available to the outsider adopting the Intentional stance; but how would such data get used? Let the introspector amass as much inside information as you please; he must then communicate it to us, and what are we to make of his communications? We can suppose that they are incorrigible (barring corrigible verbal errors, slips of the tongue, and so forth), but we do not need Phenomenology to give us that option, for it amounts to the decision to lean on the accuracy-of-avowal norm at the expense of the rationality norm. If, alternatively, we demand certain standards of consistency and rationality of his utterances before we accept them as authoritative, what standards will we adopt? If we demand perfect rationality, we have simply flown to the other norm at the expense of the norm of accuracy of avowal. If we try to fix minimum standards at something less than perfection, what will guide our choice? Not Phenomenological data, for the choice we make will determine what is to count as Phenomenological data.[40] Not neurophysiological data either, for whether we interpret a bit of neural structure to be endowed with a particular belief content hinges on our having granted that the neural system under examination has met the standards of rationality for being an Intentional system, an assumption jeopardized by the impasse we are trying to resolve. That is, one might have a theory about an individual's neurology that permitted one to "read off" or predict the propositions to which he would assent, but whether one's theory had uncovered his *beliefs* or

---

of persons would have to go by the board. Thus his rule **ACBB** ([op. cit.], pp. 24–26), roughly that if one believes *p* one believes that one believes *p*, cannot be understood, as it is tempting to suppose, as a version of the incorrigibility thesis.

[39] Dennett is using "phenomenologist" here in the loose sense of someone willing to accept as data what subjects report as privately or introspectively available to their consciousness. ED.

[40] If we give predominance to the accuracy-of-avowal standard, we will be open to introspective reports of beliefs that we would reject as insincere or false if we emphasize that such reports must be "rational"—consistent with certain norms such as "common sense" or reasonableness. Rorty's discussion of privacy toward the end of Reading 8 is relevant here. ED.

---

[38] Hintikka takes this bull by the horns. His epistemic logic is acknowledged to hold only for the ideally rational believer; were we to apply this logic to persons in the actual world in other than a normative way, thus making its implications *authoritative* about actual belief, the authority

merely a set of assent-inducers would depend on how consistent, reasonable, true we found the set of propositions.

John Vickers has suggested to me a way of looking at this question. Consider a set T of transformations that take beliefs into beliefs. The problem is to determine the set T_8 for each Intentional system S, so that if we know that S believes p, we will be able to determine other things that S believes by seeing what the transformations of p are for T_8; S would believe every logical consequence of every belief (and, ideally, S would have no false beliefs). Now we know that no actual Intentional system will be ideally rational; so we must suppose any actual system will have a T with less in it. But we also know that, to qualify as an Intentional system at all, S must have a T with some integrity; T cannot be empty. What rationale could we have, however, for fixing some set between the extremes and calling it *the* set for belief (for S, for earthlings, or for ten-year-old girls)? This is another way of asking whether we could replace Hintikka's normative theory of belief[41] with an empirical theory of belief, and, if so, what evidence we would use. "Actually," one is tempted to say, "people do believe contradictions on occasion, as their utterances demonstrate; so any adequate logic of belief or analysis of the concept of belief must accommodate this fact." But any attempt to *legitimize* human fallibility in a theory of belief by fixing a permissible level of error would be like adding one more rule to chess: an Official Tolerance Rule to the effect that any game of chess containing no more than k moves that are illegal relative to the other rules of the game is a legal game of chess. Suppose we discovered that, in a particular large population of poor chess-players, each game on average contained three illegal moves undetected by either opponent. Would we claim that these people *actually* play with k fixed at 3? This would be to confuse the norm they follow with what gets by in their world. We could claim in a similar vein that people *actually* believe, say, all synonymous or intentionally isomorphic consequences of their beliefs, but not all their logical consequences,[42] but of course the occasions

when a man resists assenting to a logical consequence of some avowal of his are unstable cases; he comes in for criticism and cannot appeal in his own defense to any canon absolving him from believing nonsynonymous consequences. If one wants to get away from norms and predict and explain the "actual, empirical" behavior of the poor chess-players, one stops talking of their *chess moves* and starts talking of their proclivities to move pieces of wood or ivory about on checkered boards; if one wants to predict and explain the "actual, empirical" behavior of believers, one must similarly cease talking of belief and descend to the design stance or physical stance for one's account.[43]

The concept of an Intentional system explicated in these pages is made to bear a heavy load. It has been used here to form a bridge connecting the Intentional domain (which includes our "common-sense" world of persons and actions, game theory, and the "neural signals" of the biologist) to the non-Intentional domain of the physical sciences. That is a lot to expect of one concept, but nothing less than Brentano himself expected when, in a day of less fragmented science, he proposed Intentionality as the mark that sunders the universe in the most fundamental way: dividing the mental from the physical.

---

[41] This theory assumes ideal rationality in the believer. ED.

[42] Roughly speaking, synonymous beliefs would be expressed by differently worded sentences having the same meaning. There is ongoing controversy among philosophers over the precise definition of synonymy or synonymity. "Intentional isomorphism" is one of the candidate theories of synonymy. The case that Dennett appears to be considering here is one in which a person is said to believe what is asserted by any sentence that is synonymous with the sentence in which she expresses a belief, but does not always believe what is said by sentences that are the logical consequences of what she believes. She might, for instance, believe that *all animals are mortal* (and that *all animals die* and other synonymous statements) and that *humans are animals,* while being unwilling to believe that *all humans die.* ED.

[43] Making illegitimate moves in chess is not playing chess but rather *failing to play* it while in the midst of a game, even though chess is being played before and after the illegitimate move. Similarly, you may learn to predict that someone will avow, or act according to, certain unreasonable "beliefs." You may understand why this happens—because someone is depressed or aggrieved, for instance. You may even have a theory about why people in general arrive at certain kinds of unreasonable or inconsistent "beliefs." But then, says Dennett, you're no longer operating from the Intentional stance, because that stance assumes rationality in the fixation of beliefs. Your theory isn't an Intentional theory. Dennett goes further, however, by saying that a "belief" that isn't rationally fixed should no more be called a belief than an illegitimate "chess move" should be called a chess move (in the sense of a move in *the* game of chess properly so called). He seems to be suggesting a reform of our vocabulary, restricting "belief" to its normative sense of rationally fixed belief. ED.

I selected the quotations at the beginning of the Introduction to Part VI in order to sample the Aristotelian-Scholastic tradition out of which Brentano drew his notion of intentional inexistence. I added the passage from McGinn as a rare instance of a current philosopher writing in English who explicitly adverts to an aspect of perception that struck Aristotle and his scholastic successors. This aspect is the nonphysical presence or inclusion within consciousness of something that continues to exist in the external environment. Perception is perhaps the paradigm case for this relation of *aboutness* that Brentano attributes to all mental events, whether they are about an existing object of perception or about something that does not actually exist. In either case it is very difficult to do justice to the intentional relation in terms of physical relations.

In his initial reference and in his final paragraph Dennett locates his essay in the tradition of theorizing about intentionality that goes back to Brentano. He even calls intentionality "Brentano's notion." Despite this declaration, once we enter Dennett's discussion of Intentional systems, it is as if we had gotten onto a fast moving walkway that takes us, within a few steps, far along in a different direction. There was some anticipation of this turn in the previous reading when Chisholm moved from the early Brentano's ontological thesis of intentional inexistence to establishing a criterion for intentional *sentences.* However, Chisholm seemed not to lose sight of the connection between intentional sentences and the mental events they supposedly express. He noted that intentional expressions have in common with their mental correlates that they are *relational,* and he then explained how their logic is strikingly different from that of other relational expressions.

For Dennett Intentionality is a feature of linguistic entities, of *sentences* with distinctive logical properties such as the one formulated by Chisholm. The concept of an Intentional system "abstracted as it is from questions of the composition, constitution, consciousness, morality, or divinity of the entities falling under it" has little to do with minds or mental events as these have usually been understood. Can we even conceptualize the mental in abstraction from *consciousness?* Treating something as an Intentional system is merely to adopt a "stance" or method for predicting its behavior from premises expressing beliefs, goals, and perceptual information. The concept of an Intentional system is the concept of a rational being understood entirely from the outside or third-party viewpoint, the viewpoint of scientific analysis. From that viewpoint you never get started down the road that leads to Aristotle talking about the soul being potentially all existing things and Brentano talking about intentional inexistence. In his *The Rediscovery of the Mind* (1992) John Searle has this to say about the kind of theory presented by Dennett:

> The way that the third-person point of view is applied in practice makes it difficult for us to see the difference between something really having a mind, such as a human being, and something behaving *as if* it had a mind, such as a computer. And once you have lost the distinction between a system's really having mental states and merely acting as if it had mental states, then you lose sight of an essential feature of the mental, namely that its ontology is essentially a first-person ontology. Beliefs, desires, etc., are always *somebody's* beliefs and desires, and they are always potentially conscious, even in cases where they are actually unconscious. (16–17)

REVIEW QUESTIONS

1. "Suppose we travel to a distant planet and find it inhabited by things moving about its surface, multiplying, decaying, apparently reacting to events in the environment, but otherwise as unlike human beings as you please. Can we make Intentional predictions and explanations of their behavior?" Dennett gives an affirmative answer to his question. Go back to p. 294 and see why he thinks so, and whether you agree with him. What sorts of terrestrial creatures would satisfy his description? Would you treat them as Intentional systems?

2. According to Dennett, "One fact so obvious that it is easily overlooked is that our 'common-sense' explanations and predictions of the behavior of both men and animals are Intentional" (p. 295). Thus, he tells us, we common-sensically attribute to the mouse a *belief* that there is a cat in one direction and piece of cheese in the other, and "desires" to eat cheese and escape cats. From these we infer that the feline Intentional system will decide to go one way and not the other. Do you find this fact "so obvious"? Do you literally attribute beliefs to your pets? If someone said to you that "they don't really have beliefs (after all, they can't talk), but they do behave as if they had beliefs," would you regard this statement as a violation of "common sense"?

21

If You Can't Make One, You Don't Know How It Works

Fred Dretske

Fred Dretske is a professor of philosophy at Stanford University. His publications have been mainly in epistemology and philosophy of mind. Among his recent books are *Explaining Behavior: Reasons in a World of Causes* (1991) and *Naturalizing the Mind* (1995).

Unlike Dennett, Dretske believes that there really are Intentional systems, and that the minds of humans and other animals are more or less complex versions of this sort of system. Dretske's treatment of the mind is *naturalistic* in the philosophical sense—he holds that intentional and mental phenomena can be understood by means of the concepts and methods of science. However, he thinks that reductive accounts of intentional phenomena in terms of entities that have *no* intentional properties are failures that give naturalism a bad name. So he looks for intentionality in systems at a much lower level than minds, in order to get scientifically respectable ingredients into his "recipe" for higher-level mental intentionality.

There are things I believe that I cannot say—at least not in such a way that they come out true. The title of this essay is a case in point. I really do believe that, in the relevant sense of all the relevant words, if you can't make one, you don't know how it works. The trouble is I do not know how to specify the relevant sense of all the relevant words.

I know, for instance, that you can understand how something works and, for a variety of reasons, still not be able to build one. The raw materials are not available. You cannot afford them. You are too clumsy or not strong enough. The police will not let you.

I also know that you may be able to make one and still not know how it works. You do not know how the parts work. I can solder a snaggle to a radzak, and this is all it takes to make a gizmo, but if I do not know what snaggles and radzaks are, or how they work, making one is not going to tell me much about what a gizmo is. My son once assembled a television set from a kit by carefully following the instruction manual. Understanding next to nothing about electricity, though, assembling one gave him no idea of how television worked.

From: Fred Dretske, "If You Can't Make One, You Don't Know How It Works," *Midwest Studies in Philosophy* XIX(1994)—*Philosophical Naturalism,* ed. P. A. French, Theodore E. Uehling, Jr., and Howard K. Wettstein. © 1994 by the University of Notre Dame Press. Reprinted with permission of the publisher.

I am not, however, suggesting that being able to build one is sufficient for knowing how it works. Only necessary. And I do not much care about whether you can *actually* put one together. It is enough if you *know how* one is put together. But, as I said, I do not know how to make all the right qualifications. So I will not try. All I mean to be suggesting by my provocative title is something about the spirit of philosophical naturalism. It is motivated by a constructivist's model of understanding. It embodies something like an engineer's ideal, a designer's vision, of what it takes to really know how something works. You need a blueprint, a recipe, an instruction manual, a program. This goes for the mind as well as any other contraption. If you want to know what intelligence is, or what it takes to have a thought, you need a recipe for creating intelligence or assembling a thought (or a thinker of thoughts) out of parts you already understand.

INFORMATION AND INTENTIONALITY

In speaking of parts one *already* understands, I mean, of course, parts that do not already possess the capacity or feature one follows the recipe to create. One cannot have a recipe for cake that lists a cake, not even a small cake, as an ingredient. One can, I suppose, make a big cake out of small cakes, but recipes of this sort will not help one understand what a cake is (though it might help one understand what a *big* cake is). As a boy, I once tried to make fudge by melting fudge in a frying pan. All I succeeded in doing was ruining the pan. Don't ask me what I was trying to do—change the *shape* of the candy, I suppose. There are perfectly respectable recipes for cookies that list candy (e.g., gumdrops) as an ingredient, but one cannot have a recipe for *candy* that lists candy as an ingredient. At least it will not be a recipe that tells you how to make candy or helps you understand what candy is. The same is true of minds. That is why a recipe for thought cannot have interpretive attitudes or explanatory stances among the eligible ingredients—not even the attitudes and stances of *others*. That is like making candy out of candy—in this case, one person's candy out of another person's candy. You can do it, but you still will not know how to make candy or what candy is.

In comparing a mind to candy and television sets I do not mean to suggest that minds are the sort of thing that can be assembled in your basement or in the kitchen. There are things, including things one fully understands, things one knows how to make, that cannot be assembled that way. Try making Rembrandts or $100 bills in your basement. What you produce may look genuine, it may pass as authentic, but it will not be the real thing. You have to be the right person, occupy the right office, or possess the appropriate legal authority in order to make certain things. There are recipes for making money and Rembrandts[1], and knowing these recipes is part of understanding what money and Rembrandts are, but these are not recipes you and I can use. Some recipes require a special cook.

This is one (but only one) of the reasons it is wrong to say, as I did in the title, that if you cannot make one, you do not know how it works. It would be better to say, as I did earlier, that if you do not know how to make one, or know how one is made, you do not really understand how it works.

Some objects are constituted, in part, by their relationships to other objects. Rembrandts and $100 bills are like that. So are cousins and mothers-in-law. That is why you could not have built my cousin in your basement while my aunt and uncle could. There is a recipe in this case, just not one you can use. The mind, I think, is also like that, and I will return to this important point in a moment.

It is customary to think of naturalistic recipes for the mind as starting with extensional[2] ingredients and, through some magical blending process, producing an intentional product: a thought, an experience, or a purpose. The idea behind this proscription of intentional ingredients seems to be that since what we are trying to build—a thought—is an intentional product, our recipe cannot use intentional ingredients.

This, it seems to me, is a mistake, a mistake that has led some philosophers to despair of ever finding a naturalistic recipe for the mind. It has given naturalism an undeserved bad name. The mistake is the same as if we proscribed using, say, copper wire in our instruction manual for building amplifiers

---

[1] Is it so obvious that there are "recipes" for making objects that are great works of art? ED.

[2] *Extensional*, in this context, means what can be described *without* using *intentional* terms. ED.

because copper wire conducts electricity—exactly what the amplifiers we are trying to build do. This, though, is silly. It is perfectly acceptable to use copper wire in one's recipe for building amplifiers. Amplifier recipes are supposed to help you understand how something amplifies electricity, not how something conducts electricity. So you get to use conductors of electricity, and in particular copper wire, as a part in one's amplifier kit. Conductors are eligible components in recipes for building amplifiers even if one does not know how they manage to conduct. An eligible part, once again, is an ingredient, a part, a component, that does not already have the capacity or power one uses the recipe to create. That is why one can know what gumdrop cookies are, know how to make them, without knowing how to make gumdrops or what, exactly, gumdrops are.

The same is true for mental recipes. As long as there is no mystery—not, at least, the *same* mystery—about how the parts work as how the whole is supposed to work, it is perfectly acceptable to use intentional ingredients in a recipe for thought, purpose, and intelligence. What we are trying to understand, after all, is not intentionality, *per se,* but the mind. Thought may be intentional, but that is not the property we are seeking a recipe to understand. As long as the intentionality we use is not itself mental, then we are as free to use intentionality in our recipe for making a mind as we are in using electrical conductors in building amplifiers and gumdrops in making cookies.

Consider a simple artifact—a compass. If it was manufactured properly (do not buy a cheap one), and if it is used in the correct circumstances (the good ones come with directions), it will tell you the direction of the arctic pole (I here ignore differences between magnetic and geographic poles). That is what the pointer indicates. But though the pointer indicates the direction of the arctic pole, it does not indicate the whereabouts of polar bears even though polar bears live in the arctic. If you happen to know this fact about polar bears, that they live in the arctic (not the antarctic), you could, of course, figure out where the polar bears are by using a compass. But this fact about what you could figure out *if you knew* does not mean that the compass pointer is sensitive to the location of polar bears—thus indicating *their* whereabouts—in the

way it indicates the location of the arctic. The pointer on this instrument does not track the bears; it tracks the pole. If there is any doubt about this, try using Mill's Methods: move the bears around while keeping the pole fixed. The pointer on your compass will not so much as quiver.

Talking about what a compass indicates is a way of talking about what it tracks, what information it carries, what its pointer movements are dependent on, and a compass, just like any other measuring instrument, can track one condition without tracking another even though these conditions co-occur. Talk about what instruments and gauges indicate or measure creates the same kind of intensional (with an 's') context as does talk about what a person knows or believes.[3] Knowing or believing that *that* is the north pole is not the same as knowing or believing that that is the habitat of polar bears even though the north pole is the habitat of polar bears. If we regard intensional (with an 's') discourse, referentially opaque contexts, as our guide to intentional (with a 't') phenomena, then we have, in a cheap compass, something we can buy at the local hardware store, intentionality. Describing what such an instrument indicates is describing it in intensional terms. What one is describing is, therefore, in this sense, an intentional state of the instrument.

It is worth emphasizing that this is not derived or in any way second-class intentionality. This is the genuine article—*original* intentionality as some philosophers (including this one) like to say. The intentional states a compass occupies do not depend on our explanatory purposes, attitudes, or stances. To say that the compass (in certain conditions C) indicates the direction of the arctic pole is to

---

[3] The *extension* of a predicate is the class of objects to which it applies, whereas the *intension* of a predicate is the respect or aspect under which the predicate picks out the objects in the class. For instance, *mammalian featherless biped* and *human* have the same extension, but differ intensionally. A sentence places a predicate in an *extensional context* when that predicate is used in such a way that any other predicate with the same extension can be substituted for it without affecting the truth of the sentence. For instance, from "There are five humans in that room" it follows that "There are five mammalian featherless bipeds in that room." In an *intensional context* such a substitution does not preserve the truth of the sentence. For instance, it does *not* follow from "Tom believes that there are five humans in that room" that "Tom believes there are five mammalian featherless bipeds in that room." Thus there is a link between the intensional (with an 's') and the intentional (with a 't'). *Intentional* verbs typically generate intensional contexts (see fn. 48 in Reading 19). Ed.

say that, in these conditions, the direction of the pointer depends in some lawlike way on the whereabouts of the pole. This dependency exists whether or not we know it exists, whether or not anyone ever exploits this fact to build and use compasses. The intentionality of the device is not, like the intentionality of words and maps, *borrowed* or *derived* from the intentionality (purposes, attitudes, knowledge) of its users. The power of this instrument to indicate north *to* or *for* us may depend on our taking it to be a reliable indicator (and, thus, on what we believe or know about it), but its *being* a reliable indicator does not itself depend on us.

Intentionality is a much abused word and it means a variety of different things. But one thing it has been used to pick out are states, conditions, and activities having a propositional content the verbal expression of which does not allow the substitution, *salva veritate,* of co-referring expressions[4]. This is Chisholm's third mark of intentionality.[5] Anything exhibiting this mark is about something else under an aspect. It has, in this sense, an aspectual shape.[6] Compass needles are about geographical regions or directions under one aspect (as, say, the direction of the pole) and not others (as the habitat of polar bears). This is the same way our thoughts are about a place under one aspect (as where I was born) but not another (as where you were born). If having this kind of profile is, indeed, one thing that is meant by speaking of a state, condition, or activity as intentional, then it seems clear that there is no need to naturalize intentionality. It is already a familiar part of our physical world. It exists wherever you find clouds, smoke, tree rings, shadows, tracks, light, sound, pressure, and countless other natural phenomena that carry information about how other parts of the world are arranged and constituted.

Intentional systems[7], then, are not the problem. They can be picked up for a few dollars at your lo-

cal hardware store. We can, therefore, include them on our list of ingredients in our recipe for building a mind without fear that we are merely changing the shape of the candy or the size of the cake. What we are trying to build when we speak of a recipe for building a mind is not merely a system that exhibits intentionality. We already have that in systems and their information-carrying states that are in no way mental. Rather, what we are trying to build is a system that exhibits that peculiar array of properties that characterizes thought. We are, among other things, trying to build something that exhibits what Chisholm describes as the first mark of intentionality, the power to say that something is so when it is not so, the power to misrepresent how things stand in the world. Unlike information-providing powers, the capacity to misrepresent is *not* to be found on the shelves of hardware stores. For that we need a recipe.

MISREPRESENTATION

Let us be clear about what we seek a recipe to create. If we are trying to build a thought, we are looking for something that cannot only say that x is F without saying x is G despite the co-extensionality of 'F' and 'G',[8] thus being about x under an aspect, we are looking for something that can say this, like a thought can say it, even [if] x is not F. Unless we have a recipe for this, we have no naturalistic understanding of *what it is* that we think, no theory of meaning or content. Meaning or content, the what-it-is that we think, is like intelligence and rationality, independent of truth. So a recipe for thought, where this is understood to include what one thinks, is, of necessity, a recipe for building systems that can misrepresent the world they are about. Without the capacity to misrepresent, we

---

[4] I.e., they create *intensional contexts,* in the sense explained in fn. 3. ED.

[5] Roderick M. Chisholm, *Perceiving: A Philosophical Study* (Ithaca, N.Y., 1957), chap. 11.

[6] This is John Searle's way of putting it; see his *The Rediscovery of Mind* (Cambridge, Mass., 1992), 131, 156. I think Searle is wrong when he says (p. 161) that there are no aspectual shapes at the level of neurons. Indicators in the brain, those in the sensory pathways, are as much about the perceived world under an aspect as is the compass about the arctic under an aspect.

[7] Dretske's use of "intentional system" is obviously much broader than Dennett's use of "Intentional system" in Reading 20. ED.

[8] Despite even the *necessary* co-extensionality of "F" and "G". A thought that x is F is different than a thought that x is G even if F-ness and G-ness are related in such a way that nothing *can* be F without being G. This, too, is an aspect of intentionality. In *Knowledge and the Flow of Information* (Cambridge, Mass., 1981), 173, I called this the second (for nomic necessity) and third (for logical necessity) orders of intentionality. Although measuring instruments exhibit first-order intentionality (they can indicate that x is F without indicating that x is G even when "F" and "G" happen to be coextensional), they do not exhibit higher levels of intentionality. If (in virtue of a natural law between F-ness and G-ness) Fs *must* be G, then anything carrying information that x is F will thereby carry the information that it is G. Unlike thoughts, compasses cannot distinguish between nomically equivalent properties.

have no capacity for the kind of representation which is the stuff of intelligence and reason.

Jerry Fodor focused attention on what he calls the disjunction problem[9] for naturalistic theories of representation.[10] The problem is one of explaining how, in broadly causal terms, a structure in the head, call it R, could represent, say, or mean that something was F even though (if misrepresentation is to be possible) non-F-ish things are capable of causing it. How, in roughly causal terms, can R mean that something is F (the way a thought can be the thought that something is F) when something's being F is (at best[11]) only one of the things capable of causing R? For someone trying to formulate an information[12]-based recipe for thought, this is, indeed, a vexing problem. But I mention the problem here only to point out that this problem is merely another way of describing the problem (for naturalistic theories) of misrepresentation. For if one could concoct a recipe for building systems capable of misrepresentation—capable, that is, of saying of something that was not F that it was F—then one would have a recipe for meaning, for constructing structures having a content that was independent of causes in the desired sense. This is so because if R can misrepresent something as being F, then R is, of necessity, something whose meaning is independent of its causes, something that can mean cow even when it is caused by a distant buffalo or a horse on a dark night. It is, therefore, something whose meaning is less than the disjunction of situations capable of causing it. In the words of Antony and Levine it is something whose meaning has been "detached" from its causes.[13] A naturalistic recipe for misrepresentation, therefore, is a recipe for solving the disjunction problem.[14] One

way of solving problems is to show that two problems are really, at bottom, the same problem. We are making progress.

For this problem artifacts are of no help. Although clocks, compasses, thermometers, and fire alarms—all readily available at the corner hardware store—can misrepresent the conditions they are designed to deliver information about, they need our help to do it. Their representational successes and failures are underwritten by—and, therefore, depend on—our purposes and attitudes, the purposes and attitudes of their designers and users. *As representational devices, as devices exhibiting a causally detached meaning, such instruments are not therefore eligible ingredients in a recipe for making thought.*

The reason the representational powers of instruments are not, like their indicative (information-carrying) powers, an available ingredient in mental recipes is, I think, obvious enough. I will, however, take a moment to expand on the point in order to set the stage for what follows.

Consider the thermometer. Since the volume of a metal varies lawfully with the temperature, both the mercury in the glass tube and the paper clips in my desk drawer carry information about the local temperature. Both are intentional systems in that minimal, that first, sense already discussed. Their behavior depends on a certain aspect of their environment (on the temperature, not the color or size, of their neighbors) in the same way the orientation of a compass needle depends on one aspect of its environment, not another. The only difference between thermometers and paper clips is that we have given the one volume of metal, the mercury in the glass tube, the job, the function, of telling us about temperature. The paper clips have been given a different job. Since it is the thermometer's job to provide information about temperature, it (we say) misrepresents the temperature when it fails to do its assigned job just as (we say) a book or a map might misrepresent the matters of which they (purport to) inform us about. What such artifacts say or mean is what we have given them the job of indicating or informing us about, and since they do not lose their

---

[9] Dretske gives a clearer definition of what he understands as the "disjunction problem" below, in the section titled "The Disjunction Problem." ED.

[10] Jerry Fodor, *A Theory of Content and Other Essays* (Cambridge, Mass., 1990) and, earlier, *Psychosemantics* (Cambridge, Mass., 1987).

[11] "At best" because, with certain "F"s ("unicorn," "miracle," "angel," etc.) something's being F will not even be *among* the things that cause R.

[12] "Information" seems to be used here to designate the kind of "intentional state" exemplified in the compass as it *indicates* the direction of the pole. ED.

[13] Louise Antony and Joseph Levine, "The Nomic and the Robust," in *Meaning in Mind: Fodor and His Critics* (Oxford, 1991), 1–16.

[14] Fodor puts it a bit differently, but the point, I think, is the same: "Solving the disjunction problem and making clear how a symbol's mean-

ing could be so insensitive to variability in the causes of its tokenings are really two ways of describing the same undertaking" (*A Theory of Content and Other Essays,* 91).

job—at least not immediately—merely by failing to satisfactorily perform their job, these instruments continue to mean that a certain condition exists even when that condition fails to exist, even when some other condition (a condition other than the one they have the job of informing about) is responsible for their behavior. For such measuring instruments, meanings are causally detached from causes for the same reason that functions are causally detached from (actual) performance. This is why thermometers can, while paper clips cannot, misrepresent the temperature. When things go wrong, when nothing is really 98°, a paper clip fails to say, while the broken thermometer goes right on saying, that it is 98°.

But, as I said, thermometers cannot do this by themselves. They need our help.[15] We are the source of the job, the function, without which the thermometer could not say something that was false. Take us away and all you have is a tube full of mercury being caused to expand and contract by changes in the temperature—a column of metal doing exactly what paper clips, thumb tacks, and flag poles do. Once we change our attitude, once we (as it were) stop investing informational trust in the instrument, it loses its capacity to misrepresent. Its meaning ceases to be detached. It becomes, like every other piece of metal, a mere purveyor of information.

NATURAL FUNCTIONS

Though representational artifacts are thus not available as eligible ingredients in our recipe for the mind, their derived (from us) power to misrepresent is suggestive. If an information-carrying element in a system could somehow acquire the function of carrying information, and acquire this function in a way that did not depend on our intentions, purposes, and attitudes, then it would thereby acquire (just as a thermometer or a compass acquires) the power to misrepresent the conditions it had the function of informing about. Such

functions would bring about a detachment of meaning from cause. Furthermore, since the functions would not be derived from us, the meanings (unlike the meaning of thermometers and compasses) would be original, underived, meanings. Instead of [our] just being able to build an instrument that could, because of the job we give it, fool *us,* the thing we build with these functions could, quite literally, *itself* be fooled.

If, then, we could find naturalistically acceptable functions, we could combine these with natural indicators (the sort used in the manufacture of compasses, thermometers, pressure gauges, and electric eyes) in a naturalistic recipe for thought. If the word 'thought' sounds too exalted for the mechanical contraption I am assembling, we can describe the results in more modest terms. What we would have is a naturalistic recipe for representation, a way of building something that would have, quite apart from its creator's (or anyone else's) purposes or thoughts, a propositional content that could be either true or false. If that is not quite a recipe for mental bernaise sauce, it is at least a recipe for a passable gravy. I will come back to the bernaise sauce in a moment.

What we need in the way of another ingredient, then, is some natural process whereby elements can acquire, on their own, apart from us, an information-carrying function. Where are these natural processes, these candyless functions, that will let us make our mental confections?[16]

As I see it, there are two retail suppliers for the required natural functions: one phylogenetic, the other ontogenetic.

If the heart and kidneys have a natural function, something they are *supposed* to be doing independently of our knowledge or understanding of what it is, then it presumably comes from their evolutionary, their selectional, history. If the heart has the function of pumping blood, if (following Larry Wright[17]) that is why the heart is there, then, by

---

[15] For instance, in addition to the surrounding air, a heat source in the wall unknown to us may be contributing to the expansion of the mercury. The mercury, like the paper clip, is still expanding in a lawlike way that indicates the degree of heat in its environment, but it is not doing this in the way it was designed by us. We assume that the thermometer is "working" (functioning), but it is not. ED.

[16] For the purpose of this essay, I ignore skeptics about functions—those who think, for example, that the heart only has the function of pumping blood because this is an effect in which we have (for whatever reason) a special interest. See, for example, John Searle, *The Rediscovery of Mind,* p. 238, and Dan Dennett's "Evolution, Error and Intentionality," in *The Intentional Stance* (Cambridge, Mass., 1987).

[17] Larry Wright, "Functions," *Philosophical Review* 82 (1973): 139–68, and *Teleological Explanations* (Berkeley, 1976).

parity of reasoning, and depending on actual selectional history, the senses would have an information-providing function, the job of "telling" the animal in whom they occur what it needs to know about the world in which it lives. If this were so the *natural* function of sensory systems would be to provide information about an organism's optical, acoustic, and chemical surroundings. There would thus exist, inside the animal, representations of its environment, elements capable of saying what is false. Though I have put it crudely, this, I take it, is the sort of thinking that inspires biologically oriented approaches to mental representation.[18]

There is, however, a second, an ontogenetic, source of natural functions. Think of a system with certain needs, certain things it must have in order to survive.[19] In order to satisfy those needs it has to do A in conditions C. Nature has not equipped it with an automatic A-response to conditions C. There is, in other words, no hard-wired, heritable, instinct to A in circumstances C. Think of C as a mushroom that has recently appeared in the animal's natural habitat. Though attractive (to this kind of animal)[20], the mushroom is, in fact, poisonous. The animal can see the mushrooms. It has the perceptual resources for picking up information about (i.e., registering) the presence of C (it looks distinctive), but it does not yet have an appropriate A response (in this particular case, A = avoidance) to C.

We could wait for natural selection, and a little bit of luck, to solve this problem for the species, for the descendants of this animal, but if the problem—basically a coordination problem—is to be solved at the individual level, by *this* animal, learning must occur. If *this* animal is to survive, what must happen is that the internal sign or indicator of C—something inside this animal that constitutes its perception of C—must be made into a cause of A (avoidance). Control circuits must be reconfigured by inserting the internal indicators of C (the internal sensory effects of C) into the behavioral chain of command. Short of a miracle—the fortuitous occurrence of A whenever C is encountered—this is the only way the coordination problem essential for survival can be solved. Internal indicators must be harnessed to effector mechanisms so as to coordinate output A to the conditions, C, they carry information about. Learning of this kind achieves the same result as do longer-term evolutionary solutions: internal elements that supply needed information acquire the function of supplying it by being drafted (in this case, through a learning process) into the control loop because they supply it. A supplier of information acquires the function of supplying information by being recruited for control duties because it supplies it.[21]

Obviously this ingredient, this source of natural functions, whether it be phylogenetic or ontogenetic, cannot be ordered from a Sears catalog. There is nothing that comes in a bottle that we can squirt on thermally sensitive tissue that will give this tissue the natural function of indicating temperature, nothing we can rub on a photo-sensitive pigment that will give it the job of detecting light. If something is going to get the function, the job, the purpose, of carrying information in this natural way, it has to get it on its own. We cannot "assign" these functions although we can (by artificial selection or appropriate training) encourage their development. If the only natural functions are those provided by evolutionary history and individual learning, then, no one is going to build thinkers of thoughts, much less a mind, in the laboratory. This would be like building a heart, a real one, in your basement. If hearts are essentially organs of the body having the biological function of pumping blood, you cannot build them. You can wait for

---

[18] E.g., Ruth Millikan, *Language, Thought, and Other Biological Categories: New Foundations for Realism* (Cambridge, Mass., 1984) and "Biosemantics," *Journal of Philosophy* 86, no. 6, (1989); David Papineau, *Reality and Representation* (New York, 1987) and "Representation and Explanation," *Philosophy of Science* 51, no. 4 (1984): 550–73; Mohan Matthen, "Biological Functions and Perceptual Content," *Journal of Philosophy* 85, no. 1 (1988): 5–27; and Peter Godfrey-Smith, "Misinformation," *Canadian Journal of Philosophy* 19, no. 4 (December 1989): 533–50 and "Signal, Decision, Action," *Journal of Philosophy* 88, no. 12 (December 1991): 709–22.

[19] This may sound as though we are smuggling in the back door what we are not allowing in the front; a tainted ingredient, the idea of a *needful* system, a system that, given its needs, has a use for information. I think not. All that is here meant by a need (for system of type S) is some condition or result without which the system could (or would) not exist as a system of type S. Needs, in this minimal sense, are merely necessary conditions for existence. Even plants have needs in this sense. Plants cannot exist (*as* plants) without water and sunlight.

[20] Its looking attractive to that kind of animal (without the needed learning) constitutes a *misrepresentation* because the sensory input is causally linked to seeking or feeding rather than to aversive behavior. ED.

[21] This is a short and fast version of the story I tell in *Explaining Behavior* (Cambridge, Mass., 1988).

them to develop, maybe even hurry things along a bit by timely assists, but you cannot assemble them out of ready-made parts. These functions are the result of the right kind of history, and you cannot—not *now*—give a thing the right kind of history. It has to have it. Though there is a recipe for building internal representations, structures having natural indicator functions, it is not a recipe you or I, or anyone else, can use to build one.

THE DISJUNCTION PROBLEM

There are, I know, doubts about whether a recipe consisting of information and natural teleology (derived from natural functions—either phylogenetic or ontogenetic) is capable of yielding a mental product—something with an original power to misrepresent. The doubts exist even with those who share the naturalistic impulse. Jerry Fodor, for instance, does not think Darwin (or Skinner, for that matter) can rescue Brentano's chestnuts from the fire.[22] He does not think teleological theories of intentionality will solve the disjunction problem. Given the equivalence of the disjunction problem and the problem of misrepresentation, this is a denial, not just a doubt, that evolutionary or learning-theoretic accounts of functions are up to the task of detaching meaning from cause, of making something say cow when it can be caused by horses on a dark night.

I tend to agree with Fodor about the irrelevance of Darwin for understanding *mental* representation. I agree, however, not (like Fodor) out of the general skepticism about teleological accounts of meaning, but because I think Darwin is the wrong place to look for the teleology, for the functions, underlying *mental* representations (beliefs, thoughts, judgments, preferences, and their ilk). *Mental* representations have their place in explaining deliberate pieces of behavior, intentional acts for which the agent has reasons. This is exactly the sort of behavior which evolutionary histories are unequipped to explain. We might reasonably expect Darwin to tell us why people blink, reflexively, when someone pokes a finger at their eye, but not why they deliberately wink at a friend, the kind of behavior we invoke beliefs and desires (*mental* rep-

resentations) to explain. I do not doubt that the processes responsible for blink (and a great many other) reflexes are controlled by elements having an information-providing function (derived from natural selection). After all, if the reflex is to achieve its (presumed) purpose, that of protecting the eye, there must be something in there with the job of telling (informing) the muscles controlling the eyelids that there is an object approaching. But the representations derived from these phylogenetic functions are not mental representations. We do not blink because we believe a finger is being jabbed at our eye. And even if we do believe it, we blink, reflexively, *before* we believe it and independent of believing it. So even if there are representations whose underlying functions are phylogenetic, these are not the representations we would expect to identify with *mental* representations, the representations that serve to explain intentional behavior. For that, I submit, one needs to look to the representations whose underlying functions are ontogenetic.

Nonetheless, wherever we get the teleology, Fodor thinks it is powerless to solve the disjunction problem and, hence, hopeless as an account of thought content. I disagree. There are, to be sure, some problems for which teleology is of no help. But there are, or so I believe, some aspects of the naturalization project for which functions are indispensable. Whether teleology helps specifically with the disjunction problem depends on what one identifies as the disjunction problem. Since I have heard various things singled out as *the* disjunction problem, I offer the following two problems. Both have some claim to be called the disjunction problem. I will indicate, briefly, the kind of solution I favor to each. Teleology only helps with one.[23]

1. If a token of type R indicates (carries the information that) A, it also indicates that A or B (for any B). If it carries the information that x is a jersey cow, for instance, it carries the information that x is either a jersey cow or a holstein cow (or a can opener, for that matter). It also carries the information that x is, simply, a cow—either a jersey cow, a holstein cow, etc. This being so, how does an information-based approach to meaning get a token

---

[22] Fodor, *A Theory of Content*, 70.

[23] I was helped in my thinking about these problems by Peter Godfrey-Smith's "Misinformation."

of type R to mean that A rather than A or B? How can an event have the content JERSEY COW rather than, say, COW when any event that carries the first piece of information also carries the second? To this problem functions provide an elegant answer. A token of type R can carry information that it does not have the function of carrying—that it does not, therefore, mean (in the sense of "mean" in which a thing can mean that P when P is false). Altimeters, for instance, carry information about air pressure (that is *how* they tell the altitude), but it is not their function to indicate air pressure. Their function is to indicate altitude. That is why they represent (and can misrepresent) altitude and not air pressure.

2. If tokens of type R can be caused by both A and B, how can tokens of this type mean that A (and not A or B)? If R is a type of structure tokens of which can be caused by both cows and, say, horses on a dark night, how can any particular token of R mean COW rather than COW OR HORSE ON A DARK NIGHT? For this problem I think Fodor is right: a teleology is of no help. What we need, instead, is a better understanding of information, how tokens of a type R can carry information (that x is a cow, for instance) even though, in different circumstances and on other occasions, tokens of this same type fail to carry this information (because x is not a cow; it is a horse on a dark night). The solution to this problem requires understanding the way information is relativized to circumstances, the way tokens of type R that occur in broad daylight at ten feet, say, can carry information that tokens of this same type, in *other* circumstances, in the dark or at two-hundred feet, fail to carry.[24]

The problem of detaching meaning from causes—and thus solving the problem of misrepresentation—occurs at two distinct levels, at the level of types and the level of tokens. At the token level the problem is: how can tokens of a type all have the same meaning or content, F, when they have different causes (hence, carry different information)? Answer: each token, whatever information it happens to carry, whatever its particular cause, has the same information-carrying function, a function it derives from the type of which it is a token. Since

meaning is identified with information-carrying function, each token, whatever its cause, has the same meaning, the job of indicating F.[25] Teleology plays a crucial role here—at the level of tokens. The problem at the type level is: how can a *type* of event have, or acquire, the function of carrying information F when tokens of this type occur, or *can* occur (if misrepresentation is to be possible), without F? Answer: certain tokens, those that occur in circumstances C, depend on F. *They* would not occur unless F existed. These tokens carry the information that F. It is from them that the type acquires its information-carrying function.[26] At the type level, then, teleology is of no help. Information carries the load. Both are needed to detach meaning from causes.

There is a third problem, sometimes not clearly distinguished from the above two problems, that has still a different solution (why should different problems have the same solution?). How can R represent something as F without representing it as G when the properties F and G are equivalent in some strong way (nomically, metaphysically, or logically)? How, for instance, can R have the function (especially if this is understood as a *natural* function) of indicating that something is water without having the function of indicating that it is H_2O? If it cannot, then, since we can obviously believe that something is water and not believe that it is H_2O, a theory of representation that equates content with what a structure has the natural function of indicating is too feeble to qualify as a theory of belief. It does not cut the intentional pie into thin enough slices.

I mention this problem here (I also alluded to it in note 8), not for the purpose of suggesting an an-

---

[24] In *Knowledge and the Flow of Information* I called these circumstances, the ones to which the informational content of a signal was relative, 'channel conditions'.

[25] Take, for instance, Descartes' discussion of pain sensation of the foot in *Meditation 6* (Reading 1). The nerves that are normally stimulated at their terminals in the foot may also be stimulated upstream, for instance at an injured knee joint. This leads to the brain misrepresenting the stimulus event as occurring in the foot rather than (e.g.) at the knee. The misrepresentation in this case or "token" is *natural* but dysfunctional, since the job of that neural pathway is to monitor the condition of the foot and engage the organism in foot-related behavior. ED.

[26] Consider again the example in the previous footnote. Given the structure of the human body, under *normal* circumstances ("C") there is a regular causal link between stimuli at various points in the foot and the corresponding brain events that are associated with the perception of pain in the foot. This "informational" feature is the basis for natural selection as a function even thought there *can* be cases or tokens of this neural pathway being active apart from the normal foot stimuli. ED.

swer to it,[27] but merely to set it apart as requiring special treatment.[28] The problem of distinguishing representational contents that are equivalent in some strong way is surely a problem for naturalistic theories of content, but it is not a problem that teleology (at least not a naturalistic teleology) can be expected to solve. To discredit a teleological approach to representation because it fails to solve this problem, then, is like criticizing it because it fails to solve Zeno's Paradoxes.

THE RECIPE

We have, then, the following recipe for making a thought-like entity. It does not give us a very fancy thought—certainly nothing like the thoughts we have every day: that tomorrow is my birthday, for example, or that I left my umbrella in the car. But one thing at a time. The recipe will do its job if it yields *something*—call it a proto-thought—that has belief-like features. I, personally, would be happy with a crude *de re*[29] belief about a perceived object that it was, say, moving.

Recipe: Take a system that has a need for the information that F, a system whose survival or well-being depends on its doing A in conditions F. Add an element, or a detector system that produces elements, that carries information about condition F. Now, stir in a natural process, one capable of conferring on the F-indicator the *function* of carrying this piece of information.[30] One does not quite "stir" these processes in (the metaphor is getting a bit strained at this point). Once you have got the right system, adding functions is more like *waiting*

for the dough to rise. There is nothing more one can do. You sit back and hope that natural processes will take a favorable turn. Just as one cannot expect everything in which one puts yeast to rise (it does not work in sand), one cannot expect to get representational "bread" from everything in which needed indicators are placed. You need a reasonably sophisticated system, one with a capacity to reorganize control circuits so as to exploit information in coordinating its behavior to the conditions it gets information about. You need a system, in other words, capable of the right kind of learning.[31] These are special systems, yes, but they are *not* systems that must already possess representational powers. We are not, in requiring such systems in our recipe, smuggling in tainted ingredients.

If all goes well, when the process is complete, the result will be a system with internal resources for representing—and, equally important from the point of view of modeling the mind, *mis*representing—its surroundings. Furthermore, that this system represents, as well as what it represents, will be independent of what we know or believe about it. For we, the cooks, are not essential parts of this process. The entire process can happen "spontaneously" and, when it does, the system will have its own cache of *original* intentionality.

RATIONALITY: THE FUNCTIONAL ROLE OF THOUGHT

Whether this is really *enough* to have supplied a recipe for thought depends, of course, on just what one demands of thought. What does it take to *be* a thought? If all it takes is possession of content, then, perhaps, we have supplied a recipe of sorts for making a thought. But the product is pretty disappointing, a mere shadow of what we know (in ourselves and others) to be the fullest and richest expression of the mind. What I have described might be realized in a snail. What we want (I expect to hear) is something more, something exhibiting the complex dynamics, both inferential and explanatory, that our thoughts have. To have a cow thought it is not

---

[27] I tackled that in *Knowledge and the Flow of Information*, 215ff.

[28] In note 27 Dretske refers to his discussion of this point in *Knowledge and the Flow of Information*, pp. 215ff. This analysis is too complex to summarize adequately here, but it rests on a distinction between *simple* and *complex* concepts (the latter being composed of simple concepts). The concepts *square* and *equilateral rectangle* are logically equivalent, but one can have the first concept (in the sense of being able unerringly to distinguish squares from other figures), while not understanding the second concept. The second concept is composed of at least three simpler concepts, one of which someone might not even have, or else someone may have them all, but not grasp their combination. His theory requires that the link between *simple* concepts and their objects rest on a natural function, but complex concepts composed of these simple ones need not have their own natural function. ED.

[29] *De re* beliefs are about particular things. ED.

[30] It gets this function insofar as the F-indicator becomes part of the loop between the external stimulus and an adaptive response. ED.

[31] You need, for instance, a system in which an external stimulus (e.g., the feel and sight of a ripe fruit) occurring together with a reinforcer (a rewarding stimulus such as sweet taste) generates a link between a representation and adaptive behavior (such as seeking or eating). ED.

enough to have an internal, isolated, cow representation. To be a cow thought, this representation must actually *do* what cow thoughts do. It must be involved in reasoning and inference about cows. It must, together with cow-directed desires, explain cow-directed behavior and rationalize cow-related attitudes and intentions.

There is validity to this complaint. If we are going to make a thought, we want the product to both look and behave like a thought. What we have so far devised may (to be generous) look a bit like a thought. At least it has representational content of the sort we associate with thought. Nonetheless, there is nothing to suggest that our product will behave like a thought. Why, then, advertise the recipe as a recipe for thought? I have, after all, already conceded that there may be representations of this sort, mechanisms in the body having an indicator function, which are not mental representations at all. When the underlying functions are phylogenetic (e.g., in the processes controlling various reflexes), the representations are not thoughts. They have a content, yes, but they do not *behave* like thoughts. They do not, for instance, interact with desires and other beliefs to produce intelligent and purposeful action. Why, then, suppose that when the functions are ontogenetic, when they develop in learning, the results are any better qualified to be classified as mental?

Since I have addressed this issue elsewhere[32] I will merely sketch an answer. A system that acquires, in accordance with the above recipe, and in its own lifetime, the power to represent the objects in its immediate environment will also, automatically, be an intelligent system, one capable of behaving (at least insofar as these representations are concerned) in a rational way. To see why this is so, consider a process by means of which an indicator of F might acquire the function of carrying information about the F-ness of things—becoming, thereby, a representation (possibly, on occasion, a misrepresentation) that something is F. In order to acquire this status, the element must acquire the job of supplying information about the F-ness of things. The only way an element can acquire this job description, I submit, is by being recruited to

perform control-related services *because* it supplies this needed information. If R is drafted to shape output because it supplies needed information about when and where that output is appropriate, then, no matter what further services may be required of R, part of R's job, its function, is to supply this needed information. That is why it is there, directing traffic, in the way that it is.

In achieving its representational status, then, R becomes a determinant of need-related behavior, behavior that satisfies needs when R carries the information it is its function to carry. Since R represents the conditions (F) in which the behavior it is called upon to cause is need-satisfying, R must, when it is doing its job, produce intelligent (i.e., need-satisfying) output. Even when it is not doing its job, even when it misrepresents, the behavior it helps produce will be behavior that is rationalized by the f-facts that R (mis)represents as existing. According to this recipe for thought, then, something becomes the thought that F by assisting in the production of an intelligent response to F.

Something not only becomes the thought that F by assisting in the production of an intelligent response to F, it assists in the intelligent response *because* it signifies what it does. When the capacity for thought emerges in accordance with the above recipe, not only do thoughts (together with needs and desires) conspire to produce intelligent behavior, they produce this behavior because they are the thoughts they are, because they have *that* particular content. It is their content, the fact that they are thoughts that F, not thoughts that G, that explains why they were recruited to help in the production of those particular responses to F. This, it seems to me, vindicates, in one fell swoop, both the explanatory and rationalizing role of content. We do not need "rationality constraints" in our theory of content. Rationality emerges as a by-product from the process in which representational states are created.

Our recipe yields a product having the following properties:

1. The product has a propositional content that represents the world in an aspectual way (as, say, F rather than G even when Fs are always G).

2. This content can be either true or false.

---

[32] *Explaining Behavior,* chaps. 4 and 5.

3. The product is a "player" in the determination of system output (thus helping to explain system behavior).

4. The propositional content of this product is
the property that explains the product's role
in determining system output. The system
not only does what it does because it has
this product, but what it is about this product that explains why the system does what
it does is its propositional content.

5. Though the system *can* behave stupidly, the
normal role of this product (the role it will

play when it is doing the job for which it
was created) will be in the production of
intelligent (need and desire satisfaction)
behavior.

This, it seems to me, is about all one could ask
of a naturalistic recipe for thought.[33]

---

[33] I read an early version of this essay at the annual meeting of the Society for Philosophy and Psychology, Montreal, 1992. I used an enlarged
form of it at the NEH Summer Institute on the Nature of Meaning, co-
directed by Jerry Fodor and Ernie LePore, at Rutgers University in the
summer of 1993. There were many people at these meetings [who] gave
me useful feedback and helpful suggestions. I am grateful to them.

Dretske's principal task in this paper is to find a proto-intentionality in low-level systems out of
which he can "build" an intentional system at the much higher, *mental* level. There are two
important steps in his argument: (1) He argues that when the state changes in one system (e.g.,
the direction of a compass) "track" the state changes in another system (location of the pole)
by covarying in a lawlike way because of a causal link between the two systems, then the first
system is an "indicator" for the second one. In such cases the first system is, objectively, in an
"intentional state," and this fact is independent of us. (2) He then attempts to make this proto-
intentionality more like the mental sort by giving it the capacity to *misrepresent,* just as we do
when we believe that something is an apple when it's a red rubber ball. He concedes that artifacts such as compasses will not have this capacity independently of us. It is because *we* humans have assigned a direction-indicating *function* to the compass that misrepresentation will
occur, e.g., in cases where the compass is (without our knowing it) affected by some magnetic
field other than the north pole. In such a context, *we* misrepresent what is going on, but the
compass is "correctly" indicating what the laws of nature have it indicate. A naturalist account
of misrepresentation must be able to present us with *naturally occurring misrepresentation.*
And this in turn calls for systems with *natural functions* (not ones that are assigned by us).

So Dretske has to move up to the biological level to locate natural misrepresentation. Living systems are self-maintaining. What is distinctive about them is that they are incessantly responding to changes in their environments, and these responses are functional to the extent
that they are self-maintaining or adaptive. To the extent that responses fail to address situations
that harm the organism, they are objectively or naturally dysfunctional. The sensory systems of
organisms are among its most important "indicator" systems. Since the states of these systems
are indicators of potentially dangerous and beneficial events in the environment, it is essential
to the survival of the organism that sensory input become causally linked to the initiation of
adaptive responses to the events. To some extent these links are "hard-wired" as reflexes. But
the evolutionary trend is toward an increasing role for learning, for links between sensory input
and behavioral output forged by the negative or positive outcomes of trial behaviors. For instance, the visual system of a lion cub has been selected by evolution because, among other
things, it precisely locates prey. Prey location is, in other words, among its *natural* functions.
The cub's visual system may represent a porcupine as prey, in the sense that sighting the porcupine elicits predatory behavior. The cub will soon learn that this was a *misrepresentation.*
The cub's attack is a case of its *mis-taking* the porcupine as prey—a *naturally occurring
misrepresentation.*

REVIEW QUESTION

Has Dretske succeeded in naturalizing intentionality? Let's look again at the compass. He tells us that describing "what such an instrument indicates is describing it in intensional terms [i.e., the needle relates to only one aspect of the pole—its location relative to the observer]. What one is describing is, therefore, in this sense, an intentional state of the instrument" (p. 308). The key word here is "indicates." This word, in Dretske's analysis, is carrying the burden of *aboutness*—that aspect of intentionality that seems so hard to understand in physical terms. The direction of the compass needle is *about* something else in the physical world. Far from being mysterious or perplexing, this aboutness is everywhere in the physical world:

> It exists wherever you find clouds, smoke, tree rings, shadows, tracks, light, sound, pressure, and countless other natural phenomena that carry information about how other parts of the world are arranged and constituted. (p. 309)

Is Dretske painting with too broad a brush here? Is he saying, and do you want to say, that a cookie, in virtue of its shape, is in an *intentional* state with respect to the cutter? Has he kept his promise (p. 307) to avoid "starting with extensional ingredients and, through some magical blending process, producing an intentional product: a thought, an experience, or a purpose"?

PART VII

CONSCIOUSNESS AND QUALIA

22

"What Is It Like to Be a Bat?"

Thomas Nagel

> Philosophy is . . . infected by a broader tendency of contemporary intellectual life: **scientism.** Scientism is actually a special form of **idealism,** for it puts one type of human understanding in charge of the universe and what can be said about it. At its most myopic it assumes that everything there is must be understandable by the employment of scientific theories like those we have developed to date—physics and evolutionary biology are the current paradigms—as if the present age were not just one in the series.—*Thomas Nagel (1986)*

> My intuitions about what "cannot be adequately understood" and what is "patently real" do not match Nagel's. Our tastes are very different. Nagel, for instance, is oppressed by the desire to develop an evolutionary explanation of the human intellect; I am exhilarated by the prospect. My sense that philosophy is allied with, and indeed continuous with, the physical sciences grounds both my modesty about philosophical method and my optimism about philosophical progress. To Nagel, this is mere scientism.—*Daniel Dennett (1984)*

Thomas Nagel is a professor of philosophy and law at New York University. He has written extensively on topics in ethics and the philosophy of mind. His book *The View from Nowhere* (1986), this reading, and Reading 32 (also by Nagel) have been the focus of much discussion in the philosophy of mind. Although this reading differs from Reading 32 in topic, they both (like Colin McGinn in Reading 26) emphasize the limitations of anything like our current concepts and theories for understanding human consciousness.

In this reading Nagel will argue that there is something very fundamental about the human mind and minds in general which scientifically inspired philosophy of mind inevitably and perhaps wilfully ignores. He uses various words for that something—"consciousness," "subjectivity," "point of view," and "what it is like to be (this sort of subject)." The last expression is in the title of his paper and seems to fit his argument most precisely. It refers to what most people have in mind when they line up in amusement parks to get on wild and scary roller-coaster rides. Unless they're anthropologists or reporters at work, they aren't trying to *learn* anything. Nor are they trying to *accomplish* anything—they're paying to let something intense happen to them. They want an *experience,* a thrill; they want *what it's like to be in that kind of motion.* The meanings of the other expressions overlap with the last but also include other things.

For instance, "conscious(ness)" can signify simple perception or attention ("She became conscious of a noise in the room"), awareness in general ("He regained consciousness"), and self-awareness or voluntariness ("Did you do it consciously?"). "Point of view" has a more cognitive overtone. We think of points of view as shaped by values, beliefs, education, and other social and psychological factors. These factors may possibly play a role in what it's like to be on a roller-coaster, but they have little bearing on what we mean when we say a blind person doesn't know what it's like to see, and when we wonder what it's like to be a bat. "Subjectivity" is fairly close in meaning, but it can also signify something you *can* and should avoid—a stance that gets in the way of objectivity and fairness; yet you *can't* stop being a *human subject* with a human type of subjectivity. You're stuck with the experience of what it's like to be a human being.

Consciousness is what makes the mind-body problem really intractable. Perhaps that is why current discussions of the problem give it little attention or get it obviously wrong. The recent wave of reductionist euphoria has produced several analyses of mental phenomena and mental concepts designed to explain the possibility of some variety of materialism, psychophysical identification, or reduction.[1] But the problems dealt with are those common to this type of reduction and other types, and what makes the mind-body problem unique, and unlike the water-H_2O problem or the Turing machine-IBM machine problem or the lightning-electrical discharge problem or the gene-DNA problem or the oak tree-hydrocarbon problem, is ignored.[2]

Every reductionist has his favorite analogy from modern science. It is most unlikely that any of these unrelated examples of successful reduction will shed light on the relation of mind to brain. But philosophers share the general human weakness for explanations of what is incomprehensible in terms suited for what is familiar and well understood, though entirely different. This has led to the acceptance of implausible accounts of the mental largely because they would permit familiar kinds of reduction. I shall try to explain why the usual examples do not help us to understand the relation between the mind and body—why, indeed, we have at present no conception of what an explanation of the physical nature of a mental phenomenon would be. Without consciousness the mind-body problem would be much less interesting. With consciousness it seems hopeless. The most important and characteristic feature of conscious mental phenomena is very poorly understood. Most reductionist theories do not even try to explain it. And careful examination will show that no currently available concept of reduction is applicable to it. Perhaps a new theoretical form can be devised for the purpose, but such a solution, if it exists, lies in the distant intellectual future.

Conscious experience is a widespread phenomenon. It occurs at many levels of animal life, though we cannot be sure of its presence in the simpler organisms, and it is very difficult to say in general what provides evidence of it. (Some extremists have been prepared to deny it even of mammals other than man.)[3] No doubt it occurs in countless forms

Reprinted from *The Philosophical Review* 83 (1974): 435–50. © 1974 Cornell University. Reprinted by permission.

[1] Examples are J. J. C. Smart, *Philosophy and Scientific Realism* (London, 1963); David K. Lewis, "An Argument for the Identity Theory," *Journal of Philosophy* LXIII (1966 reprinted with addenda in David M. Rosenthal, *Materialism & the Mind-Body Problem* (Englewood Cliffs, N. J., 1971); Hilary Putnam, "Psychological Predicates," in Capitan and Merril, *Art, Mind, & Religion* (Pittsburgh, 1967), reprinted in Rosenthal, *op. cit.,* as "The Nature of Mental States"; D. M. Armstrong, *A Materialist Theory of the Mind* (London, 1968); D. C. Dennett, *Content and Consciousness* (London, 1969). I have expressed earlier doubts in "Armstrong on the Mind," *Philosophical Review* LXXIX (1970), 394–403; "Brain Bisection and the Unity of Consciousness," *Synthèse* 22 (1971); and a review of Dennett, *Journal of Philosophy* LXIX (1972). See also Saul Kripke, "Naming and Necessity" in Davidson and Harman, *Semantics of Natural Language* (Dordrecht, 1972), esp. pp. 334–342; and M. T. Thornton, "Ostensive Terms and Materialism," *The Monist* 56 (1972).

[2] This list contains two very different types of relations: (1) Of the macro-perceptible to the micro-imperceptible (water, lightning, oak) and (2) of function to embodiment (Turing machine and gene). ED.

[3] Tissues, organs, and organ systems of a multicellular organism are successively higher levels of functional organization among cells. The various organ systems consist of large populations of cells that have evolved to specialize in one or other of the vital functions carried out by unicellular organisms as they maintain and replicate themselves. For instance, the digestive system specializes in what a bacterium does when it selectively permits various molecules to cross its membrane and uses them as reactants in **metabolic** processes. Similarly, the central nervous system specializes in generically the same adaptive control function exercised by bacterial DNA as it regulates the cell's metabolic activity. There is a fairly smooth progression of nervous systems from the very primitive to the great complexity of the mammalian and human systems. Unless we take

totally unimaginable to us, on other planets in other solar systems throughout the universe. But no matter how the form may vary, the fact that an organism has conscious experience *at all* means, basically, that there is something it is like to *be* that organism. There may be further implications about the form of the experience; there may even (though I doubt it) be implications about the behavior of the organism. But fundamentally an organism has conscious mental states if and only if there is something that it is like to *be* that organism—something it is like *for* the organism.

We may call this the subjective character of experience. It is not captured by any of the familiar, recently devised reductive analyses of the mental, for all of them are logically compatible with its absence.[4] It is not analyzable in terms of any explanatory system of functional states, or intentional states, since these could be ascribed to robots or automata that behaved like people though they experienced nothing.[5] It is not analyzable in terms of the causal role of experiences in relation to typical human behavior—for similar reasons.[6] I do not deny that conscious mental states and events cause behavior, nor that they may be given functional characterizations. I deny only that this kind of thing exhausts their analysis. Any reductionist program has to be based on an analysis of what is to be reduced. If the analysis leaves something out, the problem will be falsely posed. It is useless to base the defense of materialism on any analysis of mental phenomena that fails to deal explicitly with their subjective character. For there is no reason to suppose that a reduction which seems plausible when no attempt is made to account for consciousness can be extended to include consciousness. Without some idea, therefore, of what the subjective charac-

ter of experience is, we cannot know what is required of a physicalist theory.

While an account of the physical basis of mind must explain many things, this appears to be the most difficult. It is impossible to exclude the phenomenological[7] features of experience from a reduction in the same way that one excludes the phenomenal features of an ordinary substance from a physical or chemical reduction of it—namely, by explaining them as effects on the minds[8] of human observers.[9] If physicalism is to be defended, the phenomenological features must themselves be given a physical account.[10] But when we examine their subjective character it seems that such a result is impossible. The reason is that every subjective phenomenon is essentially connected with a single point of view, and it seems inevitable that an objective, physical theory will abandon that point of view.

Let me first try to state the issue somewhat more fully than by referring to the relation between the subjective and the objective, or between the *pour-soi* and the *en-soi*.[11] This is far from easy. Facts about what it is like to be an *X* are very peculiar, so peculiar that some may be inclined to doubt their reality, or the significance of claims about them. To illustrate the connection between subjectivity and a point of view, and to make evident the importance of subjective features, it will help to explore the matter in relation to an example that brings out clearly the divergence between the two types of conception, subjective and objective.

I assume we all believe that bats have experience. After all, they are mammals, and there is no more doubt that they have experience than that

---

the radical step of denying "consciousness" or the what-it-is-like-to-be dimension to nonhuman mammals (or mammals without language), we may be looking down a smoothly graded slope that levels off with unicellular organisms. ED.

[4]For instance, the description of Campbell's Imitation Man in Reading 23 omits this feature. ED.

[5]Perhaps there could not actually be such robots. Perhaps anything complex enough to behave like a person would have experiences. But that, if true, is a fact which cannot be discovered merely by analyzing the concept of experience.

[6]It is not equivalent to that about which we are incorrigible, both because we are not incorrigible about experience and because experience is present in animals lacking language and thought, who have no beliefs at all about their experiences.

[7]"Phenomenological" signifies in this context the way that an object appears, is experienced or perceived; the way something is *for* a conscious subject. ED.

[8]As an example of such an explanation, see Smart's discussion of lightning in his reply to objection one in Reading 6. ED.

[9]Cf. Richard Rorty, "Mind-Body Identify, Privacy, and Categories," *The Review of Metaphysics* XIX (1965), esp. 37–38.

[10]We can separate the yellowness of the flash of lightning from the physical science description of lightning by calling it a mere appearance, an effect in the mind. But this is only to postpone an accounting, in physical terms, of the appearance as such. The materialist account of the *mind* must make such features as the yellowness intelligible. ED.

[11]These two French expressions translate as "for itself" and "in itself" respectively. A subject is *for itself* because it is present to itself and is that to which objects are present, whereas an object is there *for the subject* and not for itself. It is the *in itself*. ED.

mice or pigeons or whales have experience. I have chosen bats instead of wasps or flounders because if one travels too far down the phylogenetic tree, people gradually shed their faith that there is experience there at all. Bats, although more closely related to us than those other species, nevertheless present a range of activity and a sensory apparatus so different from ours that the problem I want to pose is exceptionally vivid (though it certainly could be raised with other species). Even without the benefit of philosophical reflection, anyone who has spent some time in an enclosed space with an excited bat knows what it is to encounter a fundamentally *alien* form of life.

I have said that the essence of the belief that bats have experience is that there is something that it is like to be a bat. Now we know that most bats (the microchiroptera, to be precise) perceive the external world primarily by sonar, or echolocation, detecting the reflections, from objects within range, of their own rapid, subtly modulated, high-frequency shrieks. Their brains are designed to correlate the outgoing impulses with the subsequent echoes, and the information thus acquired enables bats to make precise discriminations of distance, size, shape, motion, and texture comparable to those we make by vision. But bat sonar, though clearly a form of perception, is not similar in its operation to any sense that we possess, and there is no reason to suppose that it is subjectively like anything we can experience or imagine. This appears to create difficulties for the notion of what it is like to be a bat. We must consider whether any method will permit us to extrapolate to the inner life of the bat from our own case,[12] and if not, what alternative methods there may be for understanding the notion.

Our own experience provides the basic material for our imagination, whose range is therefore limited. It will not help to try to imagine that one has webbing on one's arms, which enables one to fly around at dusk and dawn catching insects in one's mouth; that one has very poor vision, and perceives the surrounding world by a system of reflected high-frequency sound signals; and that one spends the day hanging upside down by one's feet in an attic. In so far as I can imagine this (which is not very far), it tells me only what it would be like for *me* to behave as a bat behaves. But that is not the question. I want to know what it is like for a *bat* to be a bat. Yet if I try to imagine this, I am restricted to the resources of my own mind, and those resources are inadequate to the task. I cannot perform it either by imagining additions to my present experience, or by imagining segments gradually subtracted from it, or by imagining some combination of additions, subtractions, and modifications.

To the extent that I could look and behave like a wasp or a bat without changing my fundamental structure, my experiences would not be anything like the experiences of those animals. On the other hand, it is doubtful that any meaning can be attached to the supposition that I should possess the internal neurophysiological constitution of a bat. Even if I could by gradual degrees be transformed into a bat, nothing in my present constitution enables me to imagine what the experiences of such a future stage of myself thus metamorphosed would be like. The best evidence would come from the experiences of bats, if we only knew what they were like.

So if extrapolation from our own case is involved in the idea of what it is like to be a bat, the extrapolation must be incompletable. We cannot form more than a schematic conception of what is *is* like. For example, we may ascribe general *types* of experience on the basis of the animal's structure and behavior. Thus we describe bat sonar as a form of three-dimensional forward perception; we believe that bats feel some versions of pain, fear, hunger, and lust, and that they have other, more familiar types of perception besides sonar. But we believe that these experiences also have in each case a specific subjective character, which it is beyond our ability to conceive. And if there is conscious life elsewhere in the universe, it is likely that some of it will not be describable even in the most general experiential terms available to us.[13] (The problem is not confined to exotic cases, however, for it exists between one person and another. The subjective

---

[12] By "our own case" I do not mean just "my own case," but rather the mentalistic ideas that we apply unproblematically to ourselves and other human beings.

[13] Therefore the analogical form of the English expression "what it is *like*" is misleading. It does not mean "what (in our experience) it *resembles*," but rather "how it is for the subject himself."

character of the experience of a person deaf and blind from birth is not accessible to me, for example, nor presumably is mine to him. This does not prevent us each from believing that the other's experience has such a subjective character.)

If anyone is inclined to deny that we can believe in the existence of facts like this whose exact nature we cannot possibly conceive, he should reflect that in contemplating the bats we are in much the same position that intelligent bats or Martians[14] would occupy if they tried to form a conception of what it was like to be us. The structure of their own minds might make it impossible for them to succeed, but we know they would be wrong to conclude that there is not anything precise that it is like to be us: that only certain general types of mental state could be ascribed to us (perhaps perception and appetite would be concepts common to us both; perhaps not). We know they would be wrong to draw such a skeptical conclusion because we know what it is like to be us. And we know that while it includes an enormous amount of variation and complexity, and while we do not possess the vocabulary to describe it adequately, its subjective character is highly specific, and in some respects describable in terms that can be understood only by creatures like us. The fact that we cannot expect ever to accommodate in our language a detailed description of Martian or bat phenomenology[15] should not lead us to dismiss as meaningless the claim that bats and Martians have experiences fully comparable in richness of detail to our own. It would be fine if someone were to develop concepts and a theory that enabled us to think about those things; but such an understanding may be permanently denied to us by the limits of our nature. And to deny the reality or logical significance of what we can never describe or understand is the crudest form of cognitive dissonance.

This brings us to the edge of a topic that requires much more discussion than I can give it here: namely, the relation between facts on the one hand and conceptual schemes or systems of representation on the other. My **realism** about the subjective domain in all its forms implies a belief in the existence of facts beyond the reach of human concepts. Certainly it is possible for a human being to believe that there are facts which humans never *will* possess the requisite concepts to represent or comprehend. Indeed, it would be foolish to doubt this, given the finiteness of humanity's expectations. After all, there would have been transfinite numbers even if everyone had been wiped out by the Black Death before Cantor discovered them. But one might also believe that there are facts which *could* not ever be represented or comprehended by human beings, even if the species lasted forever—simply because our structure does not permit us to operate with concepts of the requisite type. This impossibility might even be observed by other beings, but it is not clear that the existence of such beings, or the possibility of their existence, is a precondition of the significance of the hypothesis that there are humanly inaccessible facts. (After all, the nature of beings with access to humanly inaccessible facts is presumably itself a humanly inaccessible fact.) Reflection on what it is like to be a bat seems to lead us, therefore, to the conclusion that there are facts that do not consist in the truth of propositions expressible in a human language. We can be compelled to recognize the existence of such facts without being able to state or comprehend them.

I shall not pursue this subject, however. Its bearing on the topic before us (namely, the mind-body problem) is that it enables us to make a general observation about the subjective character of experience. Whatever may be the status of facts about what it is like to be a human being, or a bat, or a Martian, these appear to be facts that embody a particular point of view.

I am not adverting here to the alleged privacy of experience to its possessor. The point of view in question is not one accessible only to a single individual. Rather it is a *type*. It is often possible to take up a point of view other than one's own, so the comprehension of such facts is not limited to one's own case. There is a sense in which phenomenological facts are perfectly objective: one person can know or say of another what the quality of the other's experience is. They are subjective, however, in the sense that even this objective ascription of experience is possible only for someone sufficiently similar to the object of ascription to be able to adopt his point of view—to understand the ascription in

---

[14] Any intelligent extraterrestrial beings totally different from us.

[15] The term "phenomenology" is used both for the *study* or analysis of objects as they appear to a subject, and also for the *content* of experience. ED.

the first person as well as in the third, so to speak. The more different from oneself the other experiencer is, the less success one can expect with this enterprise. In our own case we occupy the relevant point of view, but we will have as much difficulty understanding our own experience properly if we approach it from another point of view as we would if we tried to understand the experience of another species without taking up *its* point of view.[16]

This bears directly on the mind-body problem. For if the facts of experience—facts about what it is like *for* the experiencing organism—are accessible only from one point of view, then it is a mystery how the true character of experiences could be revealed in the physical operation of that organism. The latter is a domain of objective facts *par excellence*—the kind that can be observed and understood from many points of view and by individuals with differing perceptual systems.[17] There are no comparable imaginative obstacles to the acquisition of knowledge about bat neurophysiology by human scientists, and intelligent bats or Martians might learn more about the human brain than we ever will.

This is not by itself an argument against reduction. A Martian scientist with no understanding of visual perception could understand the rainbow, or lightning, or clouds as physical phenomena, though he would never be able to understand the human concepts of rainbow, lightning, or cloud, or the place these things occupy in our phenomenal world. The objective nature of the things picked out by these concepts could be apprehended by him because, although the concepts themselves are connected with a particular point of view and a particular visual phenomenology, the things apprehended from that point of view are not: they are observable from the point of view but external to it; hence they can be comprehended from other points of view also, either by the same organisms or by others. Lightning has an objective character that is not exhausted by its visual appearance, and this can be investigated by a Martian without vision. To be precise, it has a *more* objective character than is revealed in its visual appearance. In speaking of the move from subjective to objective characterization, I wish to remain noncommittal about the existence of an end point, the completely objective intrinsic nature of the thing, which one might or might not be able to reach. It may be more accurate to think of objectivity as a direction in which the understanding can travel.[18] And in understanding a phenomenon like lightning, it is legitimate to go as far away as one can from a strictly human viewpoint.[19]

In the case of experience, on the other hand, the connection with a particular point of view seems much closer. It is difficult to understand what could be meant by the *objective* character of an experience, apart from the particular point of view from which its subject apprehends it. After all, what would be left of what it was like to be a bat if one removed the viewpoint of the bat? But if experience does not have, in addition to its subjective character, an objective nature that can be apprehended from many different points of view, then how can it be supposed that a Martian investigating my brain might be observing physical processes which were my mental processes (as he might observe physical processes which were bolts of lightning), only from a different point of view? How,

---

[16] It may be easier than I suppose to transcend inter-species barriers with the aid of the imagination. For example, blind people are able to detect objects near them by a form of sonar, using vocal clicks or taps of a cane. Perhaps if one knew what that was like, one could by extension imagine roughly what it was like to possess the much more refined sonar of a bat. The distance between oneself and other persons and other species can fall anywhere on a continuum. Even for other persons the understanding of what it is like to be them is only partial, and when one moves to species very different from oneself, a lesser degree of partial understanding may still be available. The imagination is remarkably flexible. My point, however, is not that we cannot *know* what it is like to be a bat. I am not raising that epistemological problem. My point is rather that even to form a *conception* of what it is like to be a bat (and a fortiori to know what it is like to be a bat) one must take up the bat's point of view. If one can take it up roughly, or partially, then one's conception will also be rough or partial. Or so it seems in our present state of understanding.

[17] A blind neuroscientist may possess all the scientific knowledge about human vision that any sighted neuroscientist can possess, and much more about it than most sighted people. What escapes reduction by scientific explanation is what the blind scientist *doesn't* know about human vision. Reading 24 addresses this point. ED.

[18] The ideal of completely objective understanding is referred to in the title of Nagel's 1986 book *The View from Nowhere*. If a particular point of view is always a view from *somewhere,* then full objectivity would be a view without that limitation. ED.

[19] The problem I am going to raise can therefore be posed even if the distinction between more subjective and more objective descriptions or viewpoints can itself be made only within a larger human point of view. I do not accept this kind of conceptual relativism, but it need not be refuted to make the point that psychophysical reduction cannot be accommodated by the subjective-to-objective model familiar from other cases.

for that matter, could a human physiologist observe them from another point of view?[20]

We appear to be faced with a general difficulty about psychophysical reduction. In other areas the process of reduction is a move in the direction of greater objectivity, toward a more accurate view of the real nature of things. This is accomplished by reducing our dependence on individual or species-specific points of view toward the object of investigation. We describe it not in terms of the impressions it makes on our senses, but in terms of its more general effects and of properties detectable by means other than the human senses. The less it depends on a specifically human viewpoint, the more objective is our description. It is possible to follow this path because although the concepts and ideas we employ in thinking about the external world are initially applied from a point of view that involves our perceptual apparatus, they are used by us to refer to things beyond themselves—toward which we *have* the phenomenal point of view. Therefore we can abandon it in favor of another, and still be thinking about the same things.[21]

Experience itself, however, does not seem to fit the pattern. The idea of moving from appearance to reality seems to make no sense here. What is the analogue in this case to pursuing a more objective understanding of the same phenomena by abandoning the initial subjective viewpoint toward them in favor of another that is more objective but concerns the same thing? Certainly it *appears* unlikely that we will get closer to the real nature of human experience by leaving behind the particularity of our human point of view and striving for a description in terms accessible to beings that could not imagine what it was like to be us. If the subjective character of experience is fully comprehensible only from one point of view, then any shift to greater objectivity—that is, less attachment to a specific viewpoint—does not take us nearer to the

real nature of the phenomenon: it takes us farther away from it.

In a sense, the seeds of this objection to the reducibility of experience are already detectable in successful cases of reduction; for in discovering sound to be, in reality, a wave phenomenon in air or other media, we leave behind one viewpoint to take up another, and the auditory, human or animal viewpoint that we leave behind remains un-reduced. Members of radically different species may both understand the same physical events in objective terms, and this does not require that they understand the phenomenal forms in which those events appear to the senses of members of the other species. Thus it is a condition of their referring to a common reality that their more particular viewpoints are not part of the common reality that they both apprehend. The reduction can succeed only if the species-specific viewpoint is omitted from what is to be reduced.

But while we are right to leave this point of view aside in seeking a fuller understanding of the external world, we cannot ignore it permanently, since it is the essence of the internal world, and not merely a point of view on it. Most of the neo-behaviorism[22] of recent philosophical psychology results from the effort to substitute an objective concept of mind for the real thing, in order to have nothing left over which cannot be reduced. If we acknowledge that a physical theory of mind must account for the subjective character of experience, we must admit that no presently available conception gives us a clue how this could be done. The problem is unique. If mental processes are indeed physical processes, then there is something it is like, intrinsically,[23] to undergo certain physical processes.

---

[20] The problem is not just that when I look at the "Mona Lisa," my visual experience has a certain quality, no trace of which is to be found by someone looking into my brain. For even if he did observe there a tiny image of the "Mona Lisa," he would have no reason to identify it with the experience.

[21] Nagel is referring here, of course, to the scientific description of the world exclusively in mathematically analyzable or primary qualities (see section 1 of the Introduction, "Descartes and the Scientific Revolution," for a discussion of these ideas). Ed.

[22] The causal theory and its successor, functionalism, can be seen as developing from behaviorism because all three are third-person points of view that emphasize the connection between mind and behavior. Ed.

[23] The relation would therefore not be a contingent one, like that of a cause and its distinct effect. It would be necessarily true that a certain physical state is felt a certain way. Saul Kripke (*op. cit.*) argues that causal behaviorism and related analyses of the mental fail because they construe, e.g., "pain" as a merely contingent name of pains. The subjective character of an experience ("its immediate phenomenological quality" Kripke calls it [p. 340]) is the essential property left out by such analyses, and the one in virtue of which it is, necessarily, the experience it is. My view is closely related to his. Like Kripke, I find the hypothesis that a certain brain state should *necessarily* have a certain subjective character incomprehensible without further explanation. No such explanation emerges from

What it is for such a thing to be the case remains a mystery.

What moral should be drawn from these reflections, and what should be done next? It would be a mistake to conclude that physicalism must be false. Nothing is proved by the inadequacy of physicalist hypotheses that assume a faulty objective analysis of mind. It would be truer to say that physicalism is a position we cannot understand because we do not at present have any conception of how it might be true. Perhaps it will be thought unreasonable to require such a conception as a condition of understanding. After all, it might be said, the meaning of physicalism is clear enough: mental states are states of the body; mental events are physical events. We do not know *which* physical states and events they are, but that should not prevent us from understanding the hypothesis. What could be clearer than the words "is" and "are"?

But I believe it is precisely this apparent clarity of the word "is" that is deceptive. Usually, when we are told that *X* is *Y* we know *how* it is supposed to be true, but that depends on a conceptual or theoretical background and is not conveyed by the "is" alone. We know how both "*X*" and "*Y*" refer, and the kinds of things to which they refer, and we have a rough idea how the two referential paths might converge on a single thing, be it an object, a person, a process, an event, or whatever.[24] But when the two terms of the identification are very disparate it may not be so clear how it could be true. We may not have even a rough idea of how the two referential paths could converge, or what kind of things they might converge on, and a theoretical framework may have to be supplied to enable us to understand this. Without the framework, an air of mysticism surrounds the identification.

This explains the magical flavor of popular presentations of fundamental scientific discoveries, given out as propositions to which one must subscribe without really understanding them. For example, people are now told at an early age that all matter is really energy. But despite the fact that they know what "is" means, most of them never form a conception of what makes this claim true, because they lack the theoretical background.

At the present time the status of physicalism is similar to that which the hypothesis that matter is energy would have had if uttered by a pre-Socratic philosopher. We do not have the beginnings of a conception of how it might be true. In order to understand the hypothesis that a mental event is a physical event, we require more than an understanding of the word "is." The idea of how a mental and a physical term might refer to the same thing is lacking, and the usual analogies with theoretical identification in other fields fail to supply it. They fail because if we construe the reference of mental terms to physical events on the usual model, we either get a reappearance of separate subjective events as the effects through which mental reference to physical events is secured, or else we get a false account of how mental terms refer (for example, a causal behaviorist one).[25]

---

theories which view the mind-brain relation as contingent, but perhaps there are other alternatives, not yet discovered.

A theory that explained how the mind-brain relation was necessary would still leave us with Kripke's problem of explaining why it nevertheless appears contingent. That difficulty seems to me surmountable, in the following way. We may imagine something by representing it to ourselves either perceptually, sympathetically, or symbolically. I shall not try to say how symbolic imagination works, but part of what happens in the other two cases is this. To imagine something perceptually, we put ourselves in a conscious state resembling the thing itself. (This method can be used only to imagine mental events and states—our own or another's.) When we try to imagine a mental state occurring without its associated brain state, we first sympathetically imagine the occurrence of the mental state: that is, we put ourselves into a state that resembles it mentally. At the same time, we attempt to perceptually imagine the non-occurrence of the associated physical state, by putting ourselves into another state unconnected with the first: one resembling that which we would be in if we perceived the non-occurrence of the physical state. Where the imagination of physical features is perceptual and the imagination of mental features is sympathetic, it appears to us that we can imagine any experience occurring without its associated brain state, and vice versa. The relation between them will appear contingent even if it is necessary, because of the independence of the disparate types of imagination. (Solipsism, incidentally, results if one misinterprets sympathetic imagination as if it worked like perceptual imagination: it then seems impossible to imagine any experience that is not one's own.)

[24] "The morning star is the evening star" is a good example here. The referents of both expressions are bright objects in their respective skies. The right sort of orbit puts the one where the other is at a later time for a convergence of their "referential paths." Place discusses this issue in section 4 of Reading 5. ED.

[25] Suppose, for instance, that you're a neuroscientist who's been successful in discovering exactly what goes on where in the brain when a certain kind of painful sensation is felt. You've established a reliable correlation between the having of that kind of pain and the occurrence of a specific set of neural events. Unless that set had been correlated with your pain sensation and with reports of that sensation by other humans, there would have been no reason to single it out over any other collection. If you regard the pain sensation as an *effect* of the neural events, then it is distinct from them and not identical with them. If you argue, with the

Strangely enough, we may have evidence for the truth of something we cannot really understand. Suppose a caterpillar is locked in a sterile safe by someone unfamiliar with insect metamorphosis, and weeks later the safe is reopened, revealing a butterfly. If the person knows that the safe has been shut the whole time, he has reason to believe that the butterfly is or was once the caterpillar, without having any idea in what sense this might be so. (One possibility is that the caterpillar contained a tiny winged parasite that devoured it and grew into the butterfly.)

It is conceivable that we are in such a position with regard to physicalism. Donald Davidson has argued that if mental events have physical causes and effects, they must have physical descriptions.[26] He holds that we have reason to believe this even though we do not—and in fact *could* not—have a general psychophysical theory.[27] His argument applies to intentional mental events, but I think we also have some reason to believe that sensations are physical processes, without being in a position to understand how. Davidson's position is that certain physical events have irreducibly mental properties, and perhaps some view describable in this way is correct. But nothing of which we can now form a conception corresponds to it; nor have we any idea

what a theory would be like that enabled us to conceive of it.[28]

Very little work has been done on the basic question (from which mention of the brain can be entirely omitted) whether any sense can be made of experiences having an objective character at all. Does it make sense, in other words, to ask what my experiences are *really* like, as opposed to how they appear to me? We cannot genuinely understand the hypothesis that their nature is captured in a physical description unless we understand the more fundamental idea that they *have* an objective nature (or that objective processes can have a subjective nature).[29]

I should like to close with a speculative proposal. It may be possible to approach the gap between subjective and objective from another direction. Setting aside temporarily the relation between the mind and the brain, we can pursue a more objective understanding of the mental in its own right. At present we are completely unequipped to think about the subjective character of experience without relying on the imagination—without taking up the point of view of the experiential subject. This should be regarded as a challenge to form new concepts and devise a new method—an objective phenomenology not dependent on empathy or the imagination. Though presumably it would not capture everything, its goal would be to describe, at least in part, the subjective character of experiences in a form comprehensible to beings incapable of having those experiences.

We would have to develop such a phenomenology to describe the sonar experiences of bats; but it would also be possible to begin with humans. One might try, for example, to develop concepts that could be used to explain to a person blind from birth what it was like to see. One would reach a blank wall eventually, but it should be possible to devise a method of expressing in objective terms much more than we can at present, and with much

---

Churchlands in Reading 25, that it is nonessential to the type-identity of pain as a mental event, then Nagel would say that you're omitting from pain the very aspect that makes it a *mental* event in the first place—the what-it-is-like-to-be-in-that-state, the subjectivity. ED.

[26] Nagel is referring to Davidson's argument in his widely discussed essay "Mental Events" (1970). Davidson claims that mental events cause physical events. However, for two events to be related as cause and effect, the first must be a type of event that is related to the second by a scientific law. He further argues that there cannot be lawlike connections between physical events and mental events inolving **propositional attitudes;** for instance, there cannot be a strict correlation between a certain type of brain event and the belief that the economy is improving. Exactly which belief a person has can never be inferred from the isolated fact that she is in a certain brain state. The specification of beliefs requires a much broader, social context. Since there cannot be *psychophysical correlations,* there cannot be *type-identities* between mental and physical events. The former are irreducible. Nevertheless, since mental events do cause physical events, there must be a token identity between any particular mental event and some physical event since only physical events can be causes since only they can be lawfully correlated with physical events. Thus, Davidson is a materialist who maintains that mental events are physical events with some property that is irreducibly mental and cannot be incorporated into scientific laws. The mental is a lawless or anomalous domain. For this reason, his position is known as "anomalous monism." ED.

[27] See "Mental Events" in Forster and Swanson, *Experience and Theory* (Amherst, 1970); though I don't understand the argument against psychophysical laws.

---

[28] Similar remarks apply to my paper "Physicalism," *Philosophical Review* LXXIV (1965), 339–356, reprinted with postscript in John O'Connor, *Modern Materialism* (New York, 1969).

[29] This question also lies at the heart of the problem of other minds, whose close connection with the mind-body problem is often overlooked. If one understood how subjective experience could have an objective nature, one would understand the existence of subjects other than oneself.

greater precision. The loose intermodal analogies— for example, "Red is like the sound of a trumpet"—which crop up in discussions of this subject are of little use. That should be clear to anyone who has both heard a trumpet and seen red. But structural features of perception might be more accessible to objective description, even though something would be left out. And concepts alternative to those we learn in the first person may enable us to arrive at a kind of understanding even of our own experience which is denied us by the very ease of description and lack of distance that subjective concepts afford.

Apart from its own interest, a phenomenology that is in this sense objective may permit questions about the physical[30] basis of experience to assume a more intelligible form. Aspects of subjective experience that admitted this kind of objective description might be better candidates for objective explanations of a more familiar sort. But whether or not this guess is correct, it seems unlikely that any physical theory of mind can be contemplated until more thought has been given to the general problem of subjective and objective. Otherwise we cannot even pose the mind-body problem without sidestepping it.[31]

---

[30] I have not defined the term "physical." Obviously it does not apply just to what can be described by the concepts of contemporary physics, since we expect further developments. Some may think there is nothing to prevent mental phenomena from eventually being recognized as physical in their own right. But whatever else may be said of the physical, it has to be objective. So if our idea of the physical ever expands to include mental phenomena, it will have to assign them an objective character—whether or not this is done by analyzing them in terms of other phenomena already regarded as physical. It seems to me more likely, however, that mental-physical relations will eventually be expressed in a theory whose fundamental terms cannot be placed clearly in either category.

[31] I have read versions of this paper to a number of audiences, and am indebted to many people for their comments.

Nagel's "speculative proposal" in the last three paragraphs of his paper is difficult to understand. He asks us to contemplate the possibility of an account of the subjective that would be objective and about "the mental in its own right" rather than trying to understand the mental in terms of the physical. This account would have as its goal to "develop concepts that could be used to explain to a person blind from birth what it was like to see" and presumably help us non-bats get a conceptual access to what it is like to be a bat. He admits that we would eventually "reach a blank wall." However, if we are talking simply about the *sensuous* differentiation of one kind of subjectivity from another, bats from those without a sonar modality, sighted humans from ones that are blind at birth, it's hard to see how the blank wall isn't there from the start and forever. What blocks access to these alternate subjectivities is not that the differentiation can't be expressed in neurochemical or other physical terms, but that it can't be expressed at all. A materialist might say the following to Nagel: "Look, I don't deny that there are sensuous ingredients in our experience, and that they are ineffable or even unintelligible. I'm *not* claiming that experience includes *only* what is scientifically intelligible. All I'm saying is that what *is* intelligible about the mental and the world in general is what can be understood scientifically."

An anti-materialist (not necessarily a dualist, just a philosopher dissatisfied with the status quo in philosophy of mind) might make the following complaint to Nagel: "You reduce subjectivity to a single aspect (the what-it-is-like) that you contrast with the objective; and that aspect is one that makes subjectivities incommensurable with one another insofar as they are based on qualitatively different sensuous content. But subjectivity is really much more complex, including not only the ineffably sensuous, but also psychosocial determinants such as culture and language, and intentionality—the *presence* of an object to a subject, of an external world within a self. Intentionality is not an appearance of something else, it's not a what-it-is-like sort of thing, but rather the *structure* of what I am as a conscious being, and what any nonhuman consciousness *would* be. By focusing so heavily on the sensuously ineffable, you've made yourself an easy target for hylophiles who want to call you a "New Mysterian.""

REVIEW QUESTION

Here is a short, and inconclusive exchange between two characters—a materialist and a dualist (M and D), talking about qualia (aspects of the world as it *appears* to a being with my sort of sensory receptors and brain):

D: You don't deny, do you, that appearances *occur*, and that among these appearances are qualia?

M: Of course not. How could I?

D: And these are not part of the public, measurable world of physical science.

M: Correct.

D: Then, since appearances do occur and they don't belong to the world as described by physical science, there must be more to reality than what is physical. And that "more" is the mind, in which appearances occur.

M: Not so. From the fact that the sun actually appears to move across the sky, it does not follow that there is some actual domain in which the sun really moves that way. In general, it does not follow from the fact that something appears to happen or be in a certain way, that there is some place or part of reality in which it really occurs.

D: You're missing the point.

M: That's what *I* was going to say.

Comment on this exchange from Nagel's point of view.

23

A Critique of Central-State Materialism

Keith Campbell

Keith Campbell is a native of New Zealand who has been teaching philosophy at the University of Sydney in Australia since 1966. The reading that follows consists of excerpts from his popular textbook *Body and Mind* in which he provides in clear and accessible prose some powerful objections to the sort of causal theory presented by Armstrong, objections which are also relevant to the functionalist theories discussed in Part VII. He also focuses on the problem posed for materialism by qualia. The reading concludes with a brief statement of his own view—what he calls "new epiphenomenalism."

THE CAUSAL THEORY OF MIND EXAMINED

There are two strands in Central-State Materialism, the doctrine that the mind is the cause of behavior, and the doctrine that the central nervous system, being the cause of behavior, is the mind. Survival, freedom, and paranormal powers are threats to the second strand,[1] but do not touch the first.

The Causal Theory of mind states that descriptions of mental events, states, and processes are descriptions of inner conditions insofar as they are, directly or indirectly, causally efficacious in the behavior of an organism. This is a simplified statement of the view. Some states, for example, having dream images, are described not as themselves causally efficacious, but as resembling other mental states, perceptual ones, which do have a real role in governing behavior. But images are exceptional; the simplified formula captures the heart of the mind. Whatever else the mind is, matter or spirit, electric or chemical, it is a field of causes, and all its distinctively mental properties prove to be causal ones.

There seems to me no doubt that there is a conceptual connection, a connection of meaning, between mental and behavioral descriptions. It also seems plain enough that mental descriptions cannot in general be dissolved into statements of behavior

---

From Keith Campbell, *Body and Mind,* 2nd ed. (Notre Dame: University of Notre Dame Press, 1984), pp. 97–109 and 124–127. Reprinted with permission of the author and of Macmillan Press (UK).

[1] "Survival" refers to survival after death. The freedom that would threaten materialism is the one that is defined as *being able to act otherwise because one can choose otherwise.* Such a definition appears to exclude the possibility that the sum of causally relevant physical events (including brain processes) *determines* the event we call "choosing," and thereby the ensuing behavior. Many philosophers would prefer an alternative definition that is more compatible with materialism: an act is free when it is brought about by *unimpeded rational choice.* This formula seems consistent with the claim that the choice is determined by the sum of causally relevant events (including those brain processes that embody what we call reasoning). "Paranormal" occurrences (such as telepathy) are those which, if certifiable, science can't explain, and for which there does not seem to be a possible scientific explanation. They threaten materialism to the extent that the materialist thesis about what is real is restricted to the kinds of entities and events recognized by *current* physical science. ED.

and behavioral disposition[2] without leaving something essential out. Further, we constantly employ mental categories in expounding the causes of human behavior. The Causal Theory of mind retains the vital conceptual link with behavior, gives to mind an independent existence as an inner something whose states are typically causes of that behavior, and so accounts for our natural employment of mental terms in causal explanations.

A doctrine with which it is hard to quarrel is that in our very understanding of what a mind is there proves to be an idea of the inner causation of behavior. The mental states, whether states of a spirit or states of a brain, will of course have many properties, of location, extent, physics, and chemistry (or mayhap spiritual machinery) in virtue of which they are causes. A state cannot be a cause and have *no* other properties; such a "pure cause" is just magic. But the Causal Theory of mind maintains that none of these other properties are mental. They do not enter into what we mean in any description of a state of mind as a state of mind. It is like a political description of an electorate. The electors are described by eligibility to vote, number, division into districts and wards, party affiliation, and so on. The electors are also men and women, short and tall, slim and stout. But sex and size do not enter into the political descriptions of these people. Similarly, only as causes of behavior do properties of inner states count as mental. The mental description, according to the Causal Theory of mind, encompasses only description as cause.

The crucial question, therefore, is: Is the mind, insofar as it is mental, nothing but a field of causes? Are the only genuinely mental properties of inner states causal properties, or similarities to states with causal powers?

Pains Again

In urging the deficiencies of Behaviorism, we argued that the theory could not cope satisfactorily with the fact that pains hurt. How does the Causal Theory of mind fare in dealing with this question?

Being in pain is a complex condition. Suppose my finger is burned, and is painful in consequence.

In my mental state there are at least two components: awareness that my finger has been overheated, as a result of which it is still damaged, and a peremptory desire that this awareness should cease forthwith. In this present discussion, both the awareness and the desire must naturally be given a causal analysis.

"I am aware that my finger has been burned" is analyzed as "As a result of having been burned on the finger, I have entered a new inner state apt to produce behavior wherein I discriminate the burned finger from others which are not burned." In the discriminating behavior I not only favor the correct finger, I favor it in the burn-soothing way. That is, I give verbal and active expression to the belief that my finger has been burned.

So far so good. But the hurtfulness of the burn has not yet been captured. All that has so far been said would be true even if burns did not hurt but throbbed. Instead of the whole range of bodily sensations we in fact enjoy or endure, tingles, tickles, itches, searing pain, jabbing pains, aches, feelings of numbness, etc., suppose we only ever felt throbs. The frequency of the throbs could differentiate different bodily conditions. One throb per second in the finger would signal a burn, two a cut, three an itchy mosquito bite, three and a half a tickling feather, and so on.[3] Then in our case of the burned finger, the whole of the above analysis of "I am aware that my finger has been burned" would be true, and the episode would not be one which hurt in the slightest.

Or again, suppose a being very like us except that instead of feeling a pain when he burns his finger or breaks his toe, he has no locatable sensations at all. He just spontaneously gains a new belief, it just "pops into his head" that he has burned his finger or broken his toe, as the case may be. Call this being an *imitation man*. His awareness of his own body would be like our awareness that the car we are driving in is getting a flat tire. Some change in our body, of which we are not conscious, has as a result that it just pops into our heads that the tire is going flat.

---

[2] See Armstrong's objection, on pp. 138–139 above, to the behaviorist notion of mental states as dispositions (mere likelihoods) rather than actual states or processes within the subject of the behavior. ED.

[3] One has to suppose here that being in a particular throb state causes me to enter the state that produces the pain behavior even though throbs aren't hurtful. ED.

Awareness of the kind we have, that our finger is burned, ceases at the end of successful soothing operations. The bare belief of the imitation man that his finger has been burned could just disappear in the same way, as our belief that the tire is flat evaporates when we change the wheel.

The imitation man satisfies the analysis given above of "I am aware that I have burned my finger." But his pains do not hurt. There is nothing essentially hurtful, indeed no element which can be hurtful, in awareness of damage or malfunction as that awareness is analyzed by the Causal Theory. So the hurtfulness of pain must lie elsewhere.

Does it perhaps lie in the desire that the awareness should cease? Pains are unpleasant. We prefer not to have them. We often think that we prefer not to have them *because* they are hurtful. But perhaps this is a mistake. Perhaps their hurtfulness is precisely that we desire to be rid of them. Consider in the following how desire appears in a causal analysis.

"I desire to be rid of this condition of finger-burned awareness" is glossed as "I have entered an inner condition driving me toward (apt to produce) general expressions of pain, such as grimacing, together with whatever behavior I likely believe likely to minimize or eliminate another inner condition, my awareness of my burned finger." In everyone, this condition leads to wringing the hand and trying to cool it. In sophisticates like us, it leads us further to searching out the burn cream, the analgesics, and even the doctor.

The strength of my drive to minimize awareness of my burned finger is the extent to which this purpose excludes or overrides all my other inner causes of behavior, and this varies directly with the intensity of the hurt. This is a point in favor of the idea that the desire is the hurtful element in pain. If conditions A and B increase and decrease together, then perhaps A and B are the same condition. If they vary inversely, or independently, then they must be different conditions.

Nevertheless, there seems to be something wrong with the idea that a desire, understood as a cause, could be the very thing which is hurtful. What is hurtful must be something felt, and we can see that a causally understood desire is not something felt by considering other cases.

An urgent desire, causally understood, is an inner condition which, temporarily suppressing other causes of behavior, generates a pattern of bodily activity. A condition of this kind can be induced by hypnotic suggestion. A subject can be given an urgent desire, which is to say, an overmastering drive toward one particular behavior pattern, and it is clear from this case that such an inner cause is not something which, as cause, can be felt. So it is not something which can hurt.

We can also see that the causal analyses of awareness and desire in pain fail to capture the hurtfulness of pains by considering the possibility of the transposition of pains. Suppose a man for whom burning pains and crushing pains were transposed, so that when his finger is burned he feels as we do when our finger is crushed, and vice versa. The causal analyses of the elements in pain make his situation and ours exactly alike. He is aware that his finger has been burned, and so are we. He is gripped by the purpose to minimize the inner condition of awareness, and so are we. He works this purpose out in grimacing, handwringing, cream applying, etc., and so do we. On the causal analysis of mental states, his state and ours are identical. Yet he is being hurt in the feeling-crushed fashion, and we are not. Our mental states are not identical. So the causal analysis leaves something out, something which distinguishes burning from crushing pains even where a transposition of pains makes their causal properties identical.

We might try to save the causal analysis by further complicating the picture of pain. Neither the awareness that my finger is burned, nor my desire to be rid of this awareness, is itself anything hurtful. But in pain I am not only aware through bodily sense of the condition of my finger; I am also aware, by introspection, that I am aware of my finger's condition. So we might suppose the element of the pain situation which involves suffering is this inner awareness.

Or alternately, we could hold that the hurtful state is my introspective awareness of the desire that my bodily awareness of my burned finger should cease.

Neither of these strategies is successful. For the introspective awareness they invoke must itself be given a causal analysis. It is in its turn no more than the entering of a third new inner state enabling discriminative behavior—largely verbal behavior—toward the original states of bodily awareness and consequent desire. And once again, the description of this second, introspective, awareness as enabling discrimination leaves undescribed the hurtfulness which distinguishes us from the imitation man, who can perform this kind of introspection yet cannot suffer. So once again the hurtfulness of the burn in general, and its particular burning hurtfulness, elude a causal analysis of the mental concepts. Everything the causal doctrine can say about pains is true of the imitation man whose pains never hurt.

Although it is a very difficult matter, I believe the same general criticism holds in the case of the different perceptual states involved in seeing different colors, or smelling different smells, or, on the emotional side, undergoing different kinds of fear, fright, shock, and thrill. The causal doctrine covers well the description of mentality by one observing and explaining his fellow men. But the theory leaves out, to put it briefly, what waking life is like to him who is living it.

THE CAUSAL THEORY OF MIND AMENDED

The criticism leveled above at the Causal Theory of mind can be expressed in this way: The peculiarly "mental" features of mental states are not all of them causal properties respecting behavior or similarities to causal properties. There are, in addition, characteristics of some mental states which especially concern how those states seem to him who has them. Thus there are the burning, jabbing, throbbing, and aching sorts of pain; the salty, bitter, sweet, and avocado-like sorts of taste; the different experiences of seeing things as variously colored; the different feeling involved in different emotions.

Let us accept the existence of these additional, non-causal features of mental states, and let us call them *phenomenal* properties. What follows for Central-State Materialism from the existence of such phenomenal properties? The Causal Theory of mind is important for materialism because purely causal descriptions of a state are *ontically neutral*.[4]

That is to say, a purely causal description of a mental state begs no questions about what sort of state it is, claiming only that it is causally operative in producing an organism's behavior. So far as causal description goes, a mental state could be a state of a material thing, or a spiritual thing, or even a divine thing. The Causal Theory of mind leaves open, for scientific investigation to close, the question of what sort of thing a mind is.[5] Philosophers who adopt the Causal Theory and go on to say scientific investigations indicate that the brain, a material thing, is the object whose states are causes of behavior are of course Central-State Materialists.

But Central-State Materialism is not automatically refuted if the Causal Theory is inadequate. If any property is ontically neutral, it is of course possible for a material object to have that property. So the mind can be an entirely material object even if mental states have phenomenal properties, provided the phenomenal properties are ontically neutral. If phenomenal properties are ontically neutral, the Central-State Materialist is not embarrassed by their existence.

To see whether phenomenal properties are ontically neutral, let us return to the burning pain in my finger. The pain is a discrimination-enabling change in my mental state which sets up a desire for its own elimination. This change is in fact a change in the pattern and frequency of discharges of neurons in the cortex. But I am not aware of all this flurry of neuron firings *as a flurry of neuron firings*. Suppose, however, that I am aware of it as a condition which hurts. I do not grasp the brain-process clearly in its full reality, or in its reality at all. I grasp it, obscurely, in the guise of the painfulness of the pain. Nevertheless, it is this brain process, and not something else, which I grasp. To suffer is on this account, to introspect rather clumsily a process which is itself material.

The phenomenal properties are not, on this view, properties of things as they actually are. They

---

[4] This expression conveys the same idea as "topic neutral." ED.

[5] As the second Review Question for Reading 10 suggests, it's not obvious that the causal theory, in asserting a conceptual connection between the mental and *behavior*, is neutral with respect to dualism. The neutrality is even more questionable if we say, with Campbell, that the Causal Theory leaves open the question of the nature of mind "for scientific investigation to close." The choice between dualism and materialism is not a scientific issue. ED.

are how certain inner properties, which are both material and mental, appear to him who has them. They belong not to the reality, but to the appearance, of mental states.

Whatever belongs to appearance only is ontically neutral. It might have been some state of an indwelling spirit which, in suffering, I clumsily introspect. But it proves, so the argument runs, that the states set up in me by burning my finger, are brain states, and hurting is how these states seem to the organism enduring them.

The doctrine for hurting, that it is a merely apparent and not a real property, is then generalized to cover all phenomenal properties. So that they are all ontically neutral. And as a result, even if we amend the Causal Theory and admit phenomenal properties, Central-State Materialism survives intact.

For a considerable time, I found this view very attractive. But I no longer think it is acceptable. It is all very well to claim that hurtfulness is how activity of the C-fibers in the cortex appears, that the smell of onion is how the shape of onion molecules appears to a human with a normal nasal system, that scarlet is how a surface reflecting a certain pattern of photons appears to human vision. This deals with the pain, smell, or color apprehended and, relegating it to the category of appearance, renders it ontically neutral. But it leaves us with a set of *seemings,* acts of imperfect apprehension, in which the phenomenal properties are grasped. So that we must ask the new question: Is it possible that things can *seem to be* in a certain way to a merely material system? Is there a way in which acts of imperfect apprehension can be seen to be ontically neutral?

Consider a camera. A green tree can certainly be within the field the camera can photograph. And with color film, the camera produces a negative from which a photograph of a green tree can be made. We can say if we wish, although it is stretching words a bit, that the tree appears to the camera, and even appears to the camera as green. A fancy camera is made which develops and prints its own film once exposed, and we could say of this camera that at exposure it enters an inner state apt for the production of green tree photographs. Especially if the developing process varies with the color of the tree, this is a simulacrum of green tree-perceiving behavior. And it is stretching words

rather less to say that the tree appears as green to the fancy camera.

Even so, this is not the sort of *appearing to* that we are concerned with. We want to insist that the camera does not experience anything at all. For all its tricks, we do not think it makes a vast difference to the fancy camera whether its shutters are open or closed. We do not think this makes the world seem a very different place at all. With us it is different. Whether our eyelids are open or closed makes a great difference to how the world seems. It is this difference which is in question when we ask about the ontic neutrality of the awareness of phenomenal properties. Sensitivity to various environments and differential reaction to these environments do not suffice to account for the world's seeming thus and so.

Materialists sometimes argue at this point that the difference between an experiencing man and a non-experiencing self-developing camera lies in the simplicity of the one and the complexity of the other. The man is sensitive to a whole range of conditions whose variation makes no difference to the inner state of the camera. The man has memory, and purposes, and emotions, of which the camera is innocent. In the man, a whole host of feedback mechanisms monitor his activity. I do not find this appeal to complexity convincing. Think again of the imitation man, who duplicates all of a typical man's acquisition, processing, and retrieval of information, and all his activity, but for whom there are no phenomenal properties.

If the imitation man's finger is burned, he knows that something is going on in his finger. And he knows further that there is activity in him by which he knows this. The further activity is in fact activity of the C-fibers, but he does not know that that is what it is. He apprehends it imperfectly, as we do, but he does not apprehend it *by suffering,* as we do. He just knows it, as we just know when we are awake, for example, that whatever inner condition it is which marks off waking from sleep is present within us.

The imitation man can know sea and sky are alike in color, and even call them "blue". So can a blind man. Unlike a blind man, the imitation man can find it out for himself. When he looks at sea or sky he forms the belief that what he is looking at has the color which he has been taught to call "blue".

Yet the imitation man does not see the sea and sky as *blue*. He is not able to enjoy their color, for they do not appear as colored to him.[6] Similarly, he can tell when his finger is burned or crushed, and have a powerful drive[7] to eliminate the condition by which he knows this. Yet he cannot suffer.

So far as I can see, imperfect apprehension can be kept ontically neutral only so long as it is analyzed solely in terms of what is known. So long as it is given that sort of account, the imitation man's imperfect apprehension is no different from ours. The difference is not what is known but in how it is known. The materialist account of real men can find no place for the fact that our imperfect apprehension is by phenomenal property and not by, for example, beliefs just spontaneously arising.

I do not see how the ontically neutral descriptions available to the materialist can cover more than what is true of the imitation man. But I have not proved that this is impossible. Failing conclusive argument, we must just judge as best we can how adequate the materialist treatment of awareness by phenomenal properties can be.

* * *

A NEW EPIPHENOMENALISM

In [what precedes] we argued that although mental states are indeed inner causes apt to produce behavior, this is not all they are. Mental states have also, among their mental properties, phenomenal properties; and it was urged that awareness by phenomenal properties is incompatible with a purely materialist doctrine of the inner, mental causes of behavior.

So the position we reach is this: some bodily states, namely some states of the brain, are mental states. That is to say, they are the causes of particular forms of behavior. And provided that neurophysiology is in principle complete, the only properties of the brain relevant to their role in causing behavior will be physicochemical ones.[8] But these brain states have a complexity beyond their physical complexity, for some of them are also awarenesses of phenomenal properties. The grasping of such phenomenal properties resists material reduction, even though the causal role of such states does not.

To have a painfully burned finger is not just to encode burned finger information, to initiate burn-soothing behavior, and to encode in an imperfect apprehension that both these processes have occurred. It is also to suffer a burning hurtfulness. To be so suffering is a property of the man not reducible to his physics. As it occurs only when he is in a particular brain-state, it is best to hold that suffering pain is in the first place a property of his brain-state, and hence secondarily of the man as a whole.

The account given of awareness by phenomenal properties is the only point where the new **Epiphenomenalism** diverges from Central-State Materialism. Perhaps the new Epiphenomenalism could be called Central-State Materialism Plus.

If the brain's activities of a physical kind all occur in accordance with physical laws, suffering a burn, tasting the sweetness of sugar, or smelling the piquancy of cloves are processes in which the experience of the quality in question is inoperative in behavior, even the behavior in which such experiences are described. It is other aspects of the total state which play the operative part in setting the tongue in motion. The new Epiphenomenalism is therefore rather paradoxical in its account of the causation of behavior. To preserve the completeness of the physical accounts of human action, it must hold that, contrary to common belief, it is not

---

[6] We have to keep in mind what Campbell said two paragraphs above, that for the imitation man "there are no phenomenal properties." Examples of the latter are what the color is like for you as opposed to what physical science tells us about the absorption properties of the surface which "has" that color, or how you experience a sound as opposed to the frequency of the sound waves propagated in the air as medium. So for the imitation man nothing *appears* in the usual way at all, nothing has a look or feel, and there's no "what it's like for him to _____". When the imitation man "knows," or "forms the belief," that the sky is blue, we should avoid not only projecting into his humanoid head a visual image, but also any image of written or vocalized sentences with phenomenal color or sound. The imitation man's "knowledge" that the sky is blue is merely his being in a state of readiness to utter the relevant sentence or produce whatever behavior is relevant to the state of affairs signified by the sentence. ED.

[7] A "powerful drive" would consist of being in a behavior-producing state able and likely to override alternative states. ED.

[8] Recall that Descartes' dualism allowed for mind-body *inter*action. An interactionist dualism admits that some brain events (like the will-induced behavior of the pineal gland in Descartes' theory) are caused by something that is inaccessible to neuroscience—the acts of a nonphysical, unobservable mind. These brain events are in principle outside the scope of neuroscience, making that science forever incomplete. Campbell is taking care to avoid that position. ED.

the hurtfulness of pain which causes me to shun it nor the sweet taste of sugar which drives me to seek it. Strictly, it must be physical features of the processes in which awareness by phenomenal property is involved which have any effect on what I do. Whether we suffer or enjoy can be a sign that a given state is aversive or attractive for us, but cannot be a cause of aversion or attraction. To insist that it is a cause, in the present context, is to deny that the nervous system operates by purely physical principles. It is to turn from Epiphenomenalism back to some form of Dualism.[9,10]

The enjoying or enduring of phenomenal properties are called *epiphenomenal* characteristics for two reasons. They furnish the intrinsic content of sensibility. And although produced by what produces brain-states, they stand outside the causal chains linking stimulus to response.

The Old and New Epiphenomenalisms

The doctrine labeled *Epiphenomenalism* which flourished in the nineteenth century also held that the causation of behavior was an entirely physical affair. But it denied the title *mental* to any state of the body, reserving that title for spiritual objects, experiences, which came into being when bodily conditions were suitable. These experiences had no effect on the course of a man's activity. This doctrine makes the mind an impotent side show to the serious business of real events in the physical world. It denies that mental events can be causes of behavior. It robs us of any satisfactory way of specifying different mental states, for this must be done through the links with behavior which the theory denies. It makes the Mind-Body problem wholly insoluble and makes it impossible to know if anyone, besides ourselves, has a mind at all.

So it is a most unattractive view, and was indeed only embraced because it alone seemed to allow for the completeness of physical explanations of what occurs in the physical world.

The new Epiphenomenalism, by contrast, holds that some bodily states are also mental states, and that the causal mental properties are physical properties of these bodily states. It insists only that the enjoying or enduring of phenomenal properties is not a physical affair. The new view allows, indeed requires, that mental states be causes, and allows, indeed requires, that different mental states be distinguished by reference to their differing links with behavior.

In contrast with the old, the new view denies that an epiphenomenal character is essential to the concept of a mind. On the new view, but not on the old, the inner states of the imitation man, which never have an epiphenomenal side, are nevertheless states of mind.

---

[9] For reasons that are not clear, this sentence implies that Campbell's "new Epiphenomenalism" is *not* a dualism. However, epiphenomenalism usually is classified as a form of dualism since it asserts that there is something about the mind that is irreducible to the physical, and therefore that there is another or second kind of reality in addition to what is encompassed in physical science. ED.

[10] It may be a Dualism, not of things, body and mind, but of physical and mental properties of the same thing, the body. See, e.g., Ernest Nagel, "Are Naturalists Materialists?" in *Logic Without Metaphysics,* Glencoe, Ill., 1957.

In explaining the superiority of the new (NE) over the old Epiphenomenalism (OE) Campbell criticizes OE because it "makes the Mind-Body problem wholly insoluble and makes it impossible to know if anyone, besides ourselves, has a mind at all." Yet it is not clear how the relation between the physical characteristics of mental states and their nonphysical characteristics in NE is any more intelligible than the relation between brain and mental states or events was in OE. In both Epiphenomenalisms consciousness (or whatever term one may want to use for what differentiates us from the imitation man) does nothing, and therefore doesn't have any adaptive value that would allow it to be selected in the course of evolution. It can't be derived from the physical properties of brain processes, and "the new view denies that an epiphenomenal character is essential to the concept of a mind." Therefore consciousness, or the experiencing of phenomenal properties, is just a brute fact. Since the imitation man has all that is essential to a mind, she is presumably a person in the moral sense as well. What differentiates her from us doesn't add anything to our status as moral agents. Moreover, I am just as unable in the world of NE as in that of OE to know whether anyone else's mind has epiphenomenal characteristics. If the presence of epiphenomenal characteristics in the minds of *all* humans is a brute fact, would the fact be any less brute if these characteristics were present in only a very few humans, or in only one?

REVIEW QUESTIONS

1. If Campbell is right, and consciousness of phenomenal properties *does nothing,* then which would you prefer if given this choice: to continue as you or as an "imitation" you (the old you minus the experience of phenomenal properties)? Why?

2. If there are no phenomenal properties for the imitation man, is there still a sense in which external objects or events can be said to "appear" to him?

24

Epiphenomenal Qualia

Frank Jackson

Frank Jackson is a member of the Philosophy Program of the Research School of Social Sciences at the Australian National University. He also directs the university's Institute of Advanced Studies. His most recent publications include *The Philosophy of Mind and Cognition* (1996; with David Braddon-Mitchell) and his collected papers *Mind, Method, and Conditionals: Selected Essays* (1998).

Like Campbell in the previous reading, Jackson argues that qualia are epiphenomenal. He describes himself as a "qualia freak" who has a strong intuition that physicalism is false because it cannot accommodate qualia. He supports this intuition with what he calls the "knowledge argument," and gives reasons why this argument is better able to establish the inadequacy of physicalism than the kinds of arguments found in Nagel and Campbell. Finally, he responds to some standard objections against the epiphenomenalist account of qualia.

INTRODUCTION

It is undeniable that the physical, chemical and biological sciences have provided a great deal of information about the world we live in and about ourselves. I will use the label "physical information" for this kind of information, and also for information that automatically comes along with it. For example, if a medical scientist tells me enough about the processes that go on in my nervous system, and about how they relate to happenings in the world around me, to what has happened in the past and is likely to happen in the future, to what happens to other similar and dissimilar organisms, and the like, he or she tells me—if I am clever enough to fit it together appropriately—about what is often called the functional role of those states in me (and in organisms in general in similar cases). This information, and its kin, I also label "physical".

I do not mean these sketchy remarks to constitute a definition of "physical information", and of the correlative notions of physical property, process, and so on, but to indicate what I have in mind here. It is well known that there are problems with giving a precise definition of these notions, and so of the thesis of Physicalism that all (correct) information is physical information.[1] But—unlike some—I take the question of definition to cut across the central problems I want to discuss in this paper.

I am what is sometimes known as a "qualia freak." I think that there are certain features of the

From: Frank Jackson, "Epiphenomenal Qualia," *The Philosophical Quarterly* 32 (1982): 127–136. Reprinted with permission of the editors of *The Philosophical Quarterly*.

[1] See, e.g., D. H. Mellor, "Materialism and Phenomenal Qualities", *Aristotelian Society Supp. Vol.* 47 (1973), 107–19; and J. W. Cornman, *Materialism and Sensations* (New Haven and London, 1971).

bodily sensations especially, but also of certain perceptual experiences, which no amount of purely physical information includes. Tell me everything physical there is to tell about what is going on in a living brain, the kind of states, their functional role, their relation to what goes on at other times and in other brains, and so on and so forth, and be I as clever as I can be in fitting it all together, you won't have told me about the hurtfulness of pains, the itchiness of itches, pangs of jealousy, or about the characteristic experience of tasting a lemon, smelling a rose, hearing a loud noise or seeing the sky.

There are many qualia freaks, and some of them say that their rejection of Physicalism is an unargued intuition[2]. I think that they are being unfair to themselves. They have the following argument. Nothing you could tell of a physical sort captures the smell of a rose, for instance. Therefore, Physicalism is false. By our lights this is a perfectly good argument. It is obviously not to the point to question its validity, and the premise is intuitively obviously true both to them and to me.

I must, however, admit that it is weak from a polemical point of view. There are, unfortunately for us, many who do not find the premise intuitively obvious. The task then is to present an argument whose premises are obvious to all, or at least to as many as possible. This I try to do in Part I with what I will call "the Knowledge argument". In Part II I contrast the Knowledge argument with the Modal argument and in Part III with the "What is it like to be" argument. In Part IV I tackle the question of the causal role of qualia. The major factor in stopping people from admitting qualia is the belief that they should have to be given a causal role with respect to the physical world and especially the brain;[3] and it is hard to do this without sounding like someone who believes in fairies. I seek in Part IV to turn this objection by arguing that the view that qualia are epiphenomenal is a perfectly possible one.

I. THE KNOWLEDGE ARGUMENT FOR QUALIA

People vary considerably in their ability to discriminate colours. Suppose that in an experiment to catalogue this variation Fred is discovered. Fred has better color vision than anyone else on record; he makes every discrimination that anyone has ever made, and moreover he makes one that we cannot even begin to make. Show him a batch of ripe tomatoes and he sorts them into two roughly equal groups and does so with complete consistency. That is, if you blindfold him, shuffle the tomatoes up, and then remove the blindfold and ask him to sort them out again, he sorts them into exactly the same two groups.

We ask Fred how he does it. He explains that all ripe tomatoes do not look the same colour to him, and in fact that this is true of a great many objects that we classify together as red. He sees two colours where we see one, and he has in consequence developed for his own use two words "red1" and "red2" to mark the difference. Perhaps he tells us that he has often tried to teach the difference between red1 and red2 to his friends but has got nowhere and has concluded that the rest of the world is red1-red2 colour-blind — or perhaps he has had partial success with his children, it doesn't matter. In any case he explains to us that it would be quite wrong to think that because "red" appears in both "red1" and "red2" that the two colours are shades of the one colour. He only uses the common term "red" to fit more easily into our restricted usage. To him red1 and red2 are as different from each other and all the other colours as yellow is from blue. And his discriminatory behavior bears this out: he sorts red1 from red2 tomatoes with the greatest of ease in a wide variety of viewing circumstances. Moreover, an investigation of the physiological basis of Fred's exceptional ability reveals that Fred's optical system is able to separate out two groups of wavelengths in the red spectrum as sharply as we are able to sort out yellow from blue.[4]

I think that we should admit that Fred can see, really see, at least one more colour than we can;

---

[2]Particularly in discussion, but see, e.g., Keith Campbell, *Metaphysics* (Belmont 1976), p. 67.

[3]See, e.g., D. C. Dennett, "Current Issues in the Philosophy of Mind", *American Philosophical Quarterly,* 15 (1978), 249–61.

[4]Put this, and similar simplifications below, in terms of Land's theory if you prefer. See, e.g., Edwin H. Land, "Experiments in Color Vision", *Scientific American,* 200 (5 May 1959), 84–99.

red1 is a different colour from red2. We are to Fred as a totally red-green colour-blind person is to us. H. G. Wells' story "The Country of the Blind" is about a sighted person in a totally blind community.[5] This person never manages to convince them that he can see, that he has an extra sense. They ridicule this sense as quite inconceivable, and treat his capacity to avoid falling into ditches, to win fights and so on as precisely that capacity and nothing more. We would be making their mistake if we refused to allow that Fred can see one more colour than we can.

What kind of experience does Fred have when he sees red1 and red2? What is the new colour or colours like? We would dearly like to know but do not; and it seems that no amount of physical information about Fred's brain and optical system tells us. We find out perhaps that Fred's cones respond differently to certain light waves in the red section of the spectrum that make no difference to ours (or perhaps he has an extra cone) and that this leads in Fred to a wider range of those brain states responsible for visual discriminatory behavior. But none of this tells us what we really don't know. But we know, we may suppose, everything about Fred's body, his behavior and dispositions to behavior and about his internal physiology and everything about his history and relation to others that can be given in physical accounts of persons. We have all the physical information. Therefore, knowing all this is not knowing everything about Fred. It follows that Physicalism leaves something out.

To reinforce this conclusion, imagine that as a result of our investigations into the internal workings of Fred we find out how to make everyone's physiology like Fred's in the relevant respects; or perhaps Fred donates his body to science and on his death we are able to transplant his optical system into someone else—again the fine detail doesn't matter. The important point is that such a happening would create enormous interest. People would say, "At last we will know what it is like to see the extra colour, at last we will know how Fred has differed from us in the way he has struggled to tell us about for so long". Then it cannot be that we knew all along all about Fred. But ex hypothesi we did know all along everything about Fred that features

in the physicalist scheme; hence the physicalist scheme leaves something out.

Put it this way. After the operation, we will know more about Fred and especially about his colour experiences. But beforehand we had all the physical information we could desire about his body and brain, and indeed everything that has ever featured in physicalist accounts of mind and consciousness. Hence there is more to know than all that. Hence Physicalism is incomplete.

Fred and the new colour(s) are of course essentially rhetorical devices. The same point can be made with normal people and familiar colours. Mary was a brilliant scientist who is, for whatever reason, forced to investigate the world from a black and white room via a black and white television monitor. She specializes in the neurophysiology of vision and acquires, let us suppose, all the physical information there is to obtain about what goes on when we look at tomatoes, or the sky, and use terms like "red", "blue", and so on. She knows, for example, just which wave-length combinations from the sky stimulate the retina, and exactly how this produces via the central nervous system the contraction of the vocal chords and expulsion of air from the mouth that results in the uttering of the sentence "The sky is blue." (It can hardly be denied that it is in principle possible to obtain all this physical information from black and white television, otherwise the Open University would *of necessity* need to use colour television.)

What will happen when Mary is released from her black and white room or is given a colour television monitor? Will she *learn* anything or not? It seems just obvious that she will learn something about the world and our visual experience of it. But then it is inescapable that her previous knowledge was incomplete. But she had *all* the physical information. *Ergo* there is more to have than that, and Physicalism is false.

Clearly the same style of Knowledge argument could be deployed for taste, hearing, the bodily sensations and generally speaking for the various mental states which are said to have (as it is variously put) raw feels, phenomenal features or qualia. The conclusion in each case is that the qualia are left out of the physicalist story. And the polemical strength of the Knowledge argument is that it is so hard to deny the central claim that one can have all

---

[5] H. G. Wells, *The Country of the Blind and Other Stories* (London, n.d.).

the physical information without having all the information there is to have.

II. THE MODAL ARGUMENT

By the Modal[6] Argument I mean an argument of the following style.[7] Sceptics about other minds are not making a mistake in deductive logic, whatever else may be wrong with their position. No amount of physical information about another *logically entails* that he or she is conscious or feels anything at all. Consequently there is a possible world with organisms exactly like us in every physical respect (and remember that includes functional states, physical history, *et al.*) but which differ from us profoundly in that they have no conscious mental life at all. But then what is it that we have and they lack? Not anything physical *ex hypothesi*. In all physical regards we and they are exactly alike. Consequently there is more to us than the purely physical. Thus Physicalism is false.[8]

It is sometimes objected that the Modal argument misconceives Physicalism on the ground that that doctrine is advanced as a contingent truth.[9] But to say this is only to say that physicalists restrict their claim to some possible worlds, including especially ours; and the Modal argument is only directed against this lesser claim. If we in our world, let alone beings in any others, have features additional to those of our physical replicas in other possible worlds, then we have non-physical features of qualia.

The trouble with the Modal argument is that it rests on a disputable modal intuition. Disputable because it is disputed. Some sincerely deny that there can be physical replicas of us in other possible worlds which nevertheless lack consciousness. Moreover, at least one person who once had the intuition now has doubts.[10]

Head-counting may seem a poor approach to a discussion of the Modal argument. But frequently we can do no better when modal intuitions are in question, and remember our initial goal was to find the argument with the greatest polemical utility.

Of course, qua protagonists of the Knowledge argument we may well accept the modal intuition in question; but this will be a consequence of our already having an argument to the conclusion that qualia are left out of the physicalist story, not our ground for that conclusion. Moreover, the matter is complicated by the possibility that the connection between matters physical and qualia is like that sometimes held to obtain between aesthetic qualities and natural ones. Two possible worlds which agree in all "natural" respects (including the experiences of sentient creatures) must agree in all aesthetic qualities also, but it is plausibly held that the aesthetic qualities cannot be reduced to the natural.

III. THE "WHAT IS IT LIKE TO BE" ARGUMENT

In "What is it like to be a bat?"[11] Thomas Nagel argues that no amount of physical information can tell us what it is like to be a bat, and indeed that we, human beings, cannot imagine what it is like to be a bat.[12] His reason is that what this is like can only be understood from a bat's point of view, which is not our point of view and is not something capturable in physical terms which are essentially terms understandable equally from many points of view.

It is important to distinguish this argument from the Knowledge argument. When I complained that

---

[6] The *modality* of a claim has to do with the way in which it is true or false, especially with whether it is necessarily or contingently true. The argument here is "modal" in the sense that it focuses on the allegedly *contingent* fact that my, or our, neural hardware is associated with consciousness. Even in this actual world in which certain of my brain processes are correlated with consciousness, there seems to be no connection between the scientific description of them and the experiences with which they are associated. This is the sort of modal intuition behind Campbell's invocation of the imitation man in the previous reading. ED.

[7] See, e.g., Keith Campbell, *Body and Mind* (New York, 1970); and Robert Kirk, "Sentience and Behaviour", *Mind,* 83 (1974), 43–60.

[8] I have presented the argument in an inter-world rather than the more usual intra-world fashion to avoid inessential complications to do with supervenience, causal anomalies and the like

[9] See, e.g., W. G. Lycan, "A New Lilliputian Argument Against Machine Functionalism", *Philosophical Studies,* 35 (1979), 279–87, p. 280; and Don Locke, "Zombies, Schizophrenics and Purely Physical Objects", *Mind,* 85 (1976), 97–9.

[10] See R. Kirk, "From Physical Explicability to Full-Blooded Materialism", *The Philosophical Quarterly,* 29 (1979), 229–37. See also the arguments against the modal intuition in, e.g., Sydney Shoemaker, "Functionalism and Qualia", *Philosophical Studies,* 27 (1975), 291–315.

[11] Reading 22. ED.

[12] *The Philosophical Review,* 83 (1974), 435–50 Two things need to be said about this article. One is that, despite my dissociations to come, I am much indebted to it. The other is that the emphasis changes through the article, and by the end Nagel is objecting not so much to Physicalism as to all extant theories of mind for ignoring points of view, including those that admit (irreducible) qualia.

all the physical knowledge about Fred was not enough to tell us what his special colour experience was like, I was not complaining that we weren't finding out what it is like to *be* Fred. I was complaining that there is something *about* him. No amount of knowledge about Fred, be it physical or not, amounts to knowledge "from the inside" concerning Fred. We are not Fred. There is thus a whole set of items of knowledge expressed by forms of words like 'that it is *I myself* who is . . .' which Fred has and we simply cannot have because we are not him.[13]

When Fred sees the colour he alone can see, one thing he knows is the way his experience of it differs from his experience of seeing red and so on; *another* is that he himself is seeing it. Physicalist and qualia freaks alike should acknowledge that no amount of information of whatever kind that *others* have *about* Fred amounts to knowledge of the second. My complaint though concerned the first and was that the special quality of his experience is certainly a fact about it, and one which Physicalism leaves out because no amount of physical information told us what it is.

Nagel speaks as if the problem he is raising is one of extrapolating from knowledge of one experience to another, of imagining what an unfamiliar experience would be like on the basis of familiar ones. In terms of Hume's example, from knowledge of some shades of blue we can work out what it would be like to see other shades of blue.[14] Nagel argues that the trouble with bats *et al.* is that they are too unlike us. It is hard to see an objection to Physicalism here. Physicalism makes no special claims about the imaginative or extrapolative powers of human beings, and it is hard to see why it need do so.[15]

Anyway, our Knowledge argument makes no assumptions on this point. If Physicalism were true, enough physical information about Fred would obviate any need to extrapolate or to perform special feats of imagination or understanding in order to know all about his special colour experience. *The information would already be in our possession.* But it clearly isn't. That was the nub of the argument.

IV. THE BOGEY OF EPIPHENOMENALISM

Is there any really good reason for refusing to countenance the idea that qualia are causally impotent with respect to the physical world? I will argue for the answer no, but in doing this I will say nothing about two views associated with the classical epiphenomenalist position. The first is that mental states are inefficacious with respect to the physical world. All I will be concerned to defend is that it is possible to hold that certain properties of certain mental states, namely those I've called qualia, are such that their possession or absence makes no difference to the physical world. The second is that the mental is totally causally inefficacious. For all I will say it may be that you have to hold that the instantiation of qualia makes a difference to other mental states though not to anything physical. Indeed general considerations to do with how you could come to be aware of the instantiation of qualia suggest such a position.[16]

Three reasons are standardly given for holding that a quale like the hurtfulness of a pain must be causally efficacious in the physical world, and so, for instance, that its instantiation must sometimes make a difference to what happens in the brain. None, I will argue, has any real force. (I am much indebted to Alec Hyslop and John Lucas for convincing me of this.)

(i) It is supposed to be just obvious that the hurtfulness of pain is partly responsible for the subject seeking to avoid pain, saying "it hurts" and so on. But, to reverse Hume, anything can fail to cause anything.[17] No matter how often B follows A, and

---

[13] Knowledge *de se* in the terms of David Lewis, "Attitudes De Dicto and De Se", *The Philosophical Review,* 88 (1979), 513–43.

[14] David Hume (1711–1776) argued that all the content or perceptions of the mind consisted in either impressions or ideas. The ideas are no more than faint copies of impressions (cf. the difference between having a toothache and merely thinking of one). Thus we can't have an idea unless it is derivable from some antecedent sensory impression. In what sounded like an exception to an otherwise iron-clad principle, Hume conceded that if we had the impressions of all gradations of a color except for one, our minds were capable of supplying the idea in the absence of the relevant impression. ED.

[15] See Laurence Nemirow's comments on "What is it . . ." in his review of T. Nagel, *Mortal Questions,* in *The Philosophical Review,* 89 (1980), 473–7. I am indebted here in particular to a discussion with David Lewis.

[16] See my review of K. Campbell, *Body and Mind,* in *Australasian Journal of Philosophy,* 50 (1972), 77–80.

[17] Hume argued that there was never a necessary or intelligible connection between two events, one of which regularly precedes the

no matter how initially obvious the causality of the connection seems, the hypothesis that A causes B can be overturned by an over-arching theory which shows the two as distance effects of a common underlying causal process.[18]

To the untutored the image on the screen of Lee Marvin's first moving from left to right immediately followed by the image of John Wayne's head moving in the same general direction looks as causal as anything.[19] And of course throughout countless Westerns images similar to the first are followed by images similar to the second. All this counts for precisely nothing when we know the over-arching theory concerning how the relevant images are both effects of an underlying causal process involving the projector and the film. The epiphenomenalist can say exactly the same about the connection between, for example, hurtfulness and behavior. It is simply a consequence of the fact that certain happenings in the brain cause both.

(ii) The second objection relates to Darwin's Theory of Evolution. According to natural selection the traits that evolve over time are those conducive to physical survival. We may assume that qualia evolved over time—we have them, the earliest forms of life do not—and so we should expect qualia to be conducive to survival. The objection is that they could hardly help us to survive if they do nothing to the physical world.

The appeal of this argument is undeniable, but there is a good reply to it. Polar bears have particularly thick, warm coats. The Theory of Evolution explains this (we suppose) by pointing out that having a thick, warm coat is conducive to survival in the Arctic. But having a thick coat goes along with having a heavy coat, and having a heavy coat is *not* conducive to survival. It slows the animal down.

Does this mean that we have refuted Darwin because we have found an evolved trait—having a heavy coat—which is not conducive to survival? Clearly not. Having a heavy coat is an unavoidable concomitant of having a warm coat (in the context, modern insulation was not available), and the ad-

vantages for survival of having a warm coat outweighed the disadvantages of having a heavy one. The point is that all we can extract from Darwin's theory is that we should expect any evolved characteristic to be *either* conducive to survival *or* a by-product of one that is so conducive. The epiphenomenalist holds that qualia fall into the latter category. They are a by-product of certain brain processes that are highly conducive to survival.

(iii) The third objection is based on a point about how we come to know about other minds. We know about other minds by knowing about other behaviour, at least in part. The nature of the inference is a matter of some controversy, but it is not a matter of controversy that it proceeds from behaviour. That is why we think that stones do not feel and dogs do feel. But, runs the objection, how can a person's behaviour provide any reason for believing he has qualia like mine, or indeed any qualia at all, unless this behaviour can be regarded as the *outcome* of the qualia. Man Friday's footprint was evidence of Man Friday because footprints are causal outcomes of feet attached to people. And an epiphenomenalist cannot regard behaviour, or indeed anything physical, as an outcome of qualia.

But consider my reading in *The Times* that the Spurs won. This provides excellent evidence that *The Telegraph* has also reported that the Spurs won, despite the fact that (I trust) *The Telegraph* does not get the results from *The Times*. They each send their own reporters to the game. *The Telegraph*'s report is in no sense an outcome of *The Times*', but the latter provides good evidence for the former nevertheless.

The reasoning involved can be reconstructed thus. I read in *The Times* that Spurs won. This gives me reason to think that Spurs won because I know that Spurs' winning is the most likely candidate to be what caused the report in *The Times*. But I also know that Spurs' winning world have had many effects, including almost certainly a report in *The Telegraph*.

I am arguing from one effect back to its cause and out again to another effect. The fact that neither effect causes the other is irrelevant. Now the epiphenomenalist allows that qualia are effects of what goes on in the brain. Qualia cause nothing physical but are caused by something physical. Hence the epiphenomenalist can argue from the

---

other. The opposite of the usual sequence is always perfectly conceivable (i.e., the failure of the second event to follow the first). ED.

[18] The succession of day and night is an example of two effects of the same cause. ED.

[19] Cf. Jean Piaget, "The Child's Conception of Physical Causality", reprinted in *The Essential Piaget* (London, 1977).

behaviour of others to the qualia of others by arguing from the behaviour of others back to its causes in the brains of others and out again to their qualia.

You may well feel for one reason or another that this is a more dubious chain of reasoning than its model in the case of the newspaper reports. You are right. The problem of other minds is a major philosophical problem, the problem of other newspaper reports is not. But there is no special problem of Epiphenomenalism as opposed to, say, Interactionism here.

There is a very understandable response to the three replies I have just made. "All right, there is no knockdown refutation of the existence of epiphenomenal qualia. But the fact remains that they are an excrescence. They do nothing, they explain nothing, they serve merely to soothe the intuitions of dualists, and it is left a total mystery how they fit into the world view of science. In short we do not and cannot understand the how and why of them."

This is perfectly true; but is no objection to qualia, for it rests on an overly optimistic view of the human animal, and its powers. We are the products of Evolution. We understand and sense what we need to understand and sense in order to survive. Epiphenomenal qualia are totally irrelevant to survival. At no stage of our evolution did natural selection favour those who could make sense of how they are caused and the laws governing them, or in fact why they exist at all. And that is why we can't.

It is not sufficiently appreciated that Physicalism is an extremely optimistic view of our powers. If it is true, we have, in very broad outline admittedly, a grasp of our place in the scheme of things. Certain matters of sheer complexity defeat us—there are an awful lot of neurons—but in principle we have it all. But consider the antecedent probability that everything in the Universe be of a kind that is relevant in some way or other to the survival of homo sapiens. It is very low surely. But then one must admit that it is very likely that there is a part of the whole scheme of things, maybe a big part, which no amount of evolution will ever bring us near to knowledge about or understanding. For the simple reason that such knowledge and understanding is irrelevant to survival.

Physicalists typically emphasize that we are a part of nature on their view, which is fair enough.

But if we are a part of nature, we are as nature has left us after however many years of evolution it is, and each step in that evolutionary progression has been a matter of chance constrained just by the need to preserve or increase survival value. The wonder is that we understand as much as we do, and there is no wonder that there should be matters which fall quite outside our comprehension. Perhaps exactly how epiphenomenal qualia fit into the scheme of things is one such.

This may seem an unduly pessimistic view of our capacity to articulate a truly comprehensive picture of our world and our place in it. But suppose we discovered living on the bottom of the deepest oceans a sort of sea slug which manifested intelligence. Perhaps survival in the conditions required rational powers. Despite their intelligence, these sea slugs have only a very restricted conception of the world by comparison with ours, the explanation for this being the nature of their immediate environment. Nevertheless they have developed sciences which work surprisingly well in these restricted terms. They also have philosophers, called slugists. Some call themselves tough-minded slugists, others confess to being soft-minded slugists.

The tough-minded slugists hold that the restricted terms (or ones pretty much like them which may be introduced as their sciences progress) suffice in principle to describe everything without remainder. These tough-minded slugists admit in moments of weakness to a feeling that their theory leaves something out. They resist this feeling and their opponents, the soft-minded slugists, by pointing out—absolutely correctly—that no slugist has ever succeeded in spelling out how this mysterious residue fits into the highly successful view that their sciences have and are developing of how their world works.

Our sea slugs don't exist, but they might. And there might also exist super beings which stand to us as we stand to the sea slugs. We cannot adopt the perspective of these super beings, because we are not them, but the possibility of such a perspective is, I think, an antidote to excessive optimism.[20]

---

[20] I am indebted to Robert Pargetter for a number of comments and, despite his dissent, to (IV) of Paul E. Meehl, "The Compleat Autocerebroscopist" in *Mind, Matter and Method,* ed. Paul Feyerabend and Grover Maxwell (Minneapolis, 1966).

Jackson seems to mean what he says when he calls his argument the *Knowledge* Argument. The color that Fred sees and we can't is something about which we *lack knowledge,* even when we have learned what is physically different about Fred's visual system, and know all there is to know about what is physically going on when Fred sees this color. And when brilliant neuroscientist Mary leaves her black-and-white environment and begins seeing in color, she acquires *knowledge* that she lacked despite her comprehensive knowledge of human vision as a physical system. She *learns* "something about the world," a further fact over and above those facts that are available to physical science. Therefore physicalism is false.

A conversation between a Jacksonian epiphenomenalist (JE) and a physicalist (P) might go like this:

P: You say that knowing "what it is like to see the extra color" seen by Fred, and what Mary comes to know about color vision, *add* to the total of what was known before, when all and only the relevant physical scientific facts were known.

JE: Absolutely.

P: When you first learned about the H_2O chemical composition of the water you had seen, felt, and tasted all your life, did that *add* to the total of what you previously knew about water?

JE: Tricky question. My answer is yes and no, with a distinction. It did add to my previous knowledge of water as a physical object—that it comes in liquid and solid forms, flows downhill, and so on. However, the chemical knowledge was not an addition to my knowledge of what it is like to taste, feel, or see water. That is knowledge about what is going on when I have certain experiences.

P: Okay, so awareness of the phenomenal properties associated with physical objects gives you knowledge of what is going on as you *experience* those objects, knowledge in addition to the scientific knowledge of the concurrent brain processes. You're saying that neuroscience and awareness of phenomenal properties or qualia are two different kinds of knowledge about the same thing, namely, what is going on in experience, right?

JE: Yes, and that's why physicalism is false!

P: Not so fast! Part of the way you experience water is as a continuous, smooth stuff—it looks that way and it feels that way. But the physicochemical description of water makes it out to be mostly empty space populated by configurations of imperceptibly small particles rotating and vibrating more or less energetically. You can't perceive these particles, but you do perceive water, and you would admit that the water you perceive is nothing but these particles thus configured. Your perception of water as a continuous stuff is not a "knowledge" of water over and above what you know from its physicochemical description. Water is stuff that appears continuous (like macrobodies in general) but is *really* discontinuous. So with your inner awareness of some of your brain processes—they *appear* to have or contain qualia, but that doesn't give you a special, nonscientific "knowledge." They're *really* just as the neuroscientist describes them. That's what science is always doing for us, taking us from the appearances of things to their reality, from *ignorance* to *knowledge.*

REVIEW QUESTIONS

1. Join the above conversation and say what you think. Is *P* misrepresenting *JE's* position? Is *JE* defending herself adequately?

2. Jackson differentiates his argument from Nagel's this way:

It is important to distinguish this [Nagel's] argument from the Knowledge argument. When I complained that all the physical knowledge about Fred was not enough to tell us what his special colour experience was like, I was not complaining that we weren't finding out what it is like to *be* Fred. I was complaining that there is something *about* him. (pp. 343–344)

However, Nagel's title (Reading 22) is "What is it like to be a bat?" and not "What is it like to be one bat rather than another?" Nagel and Jackson both make prominent use of the phrase "what it is like." Are their arguments as different as Jackson claims?

3. Jackson puts to himself the following objection to granting epiphenomenal reality to qualia:

> They do nothing, they explain nothing, they serve merely to soothe the intuitions of dualists, and it is left a total mystery how they fit into the world view of science. In short we do not and cannot understand the how and why of them. (p. 346)

His reply is to agree that qualia are a mystery. However, he adds, we should not expect our human cognitive powers to be up to the task of explaining everything that we experience. After all, those powers were selected by evolution for their contribution to our species' survival, and we can survive without a philosophical understanding of qualia.

Is this a good answer? If our cognitive powers are too weak to explain qualia, how can we know they are *really* epiphenomenal rather than just apparently so (due to the weakness of our minds)?

25

Functionalism, Qualia,
and Intentionality

*Patricia Smith Churchland
and Paul M. Churchland*

Patricia Smith Churchland and *Paul M. Churchland* both teach philosophy at the University of
California, San Diego. Both have written a great deal about the philosophy of mind and cogni-
tive science. Patricia Smith Churchland is the author of *Neurophilosophy* (1986) and (with T. J.
Sejnowski) *The Computational Brain* (1992). Paul M. Churchland's books include *Matter and
Consciousness* (1988) and *The Engine of Reason, the Seat of the Soul* (1995).

In this reading the Churchlands defend functionalism against some of the most persistent
objections against it, including Searle's Chinese Room and arguments such as those of Campbell and Jackson concerning qualia.

Functionalism—construed broadly as the thesis
that the essence of our psychological states resides in the abstract causal roles they play in a complex economy of internal states mediating environmental inputs and behavioral outputs—seems
to us to be free from any fatal or essential shortcomings. Functionalism-on-the-hoof is another
matter. In various thinkers this core thesis is generally embellished with certain riders, interpretations,
and methodological lessons drawn therefrom. With
some of the more prominent of these articulations
we are in some disagreement, and we shall turn to
discuss them in the final section of this paper. Our
primary concern, however, is to *defend* functionalism from a battery of better-known objections
widely believed to pose serious or insurmountable

problems even for the core thesis outlined above. In
sections I and II we shall try to outline what form
functionalism should take in order to escape those
objections.

I. FOUR PROBLEMS
CONCERNING QUALIA

'Qualia' is a philosophers' term of art denoting
those intrinsic or monadic[1] properties of our sensations discriminated in **introspection**. The quale[2]
of sensation is typically contrasted with its causal,
relational, or functional features, and herein lies a
problem for functionalism. The quale of a given
sensation—pain, say—is at best contingently connected with the causal or functional properties of

From Paul M. Churchland and Patricia Smith Churchland, "Functionalism, Qualia, and Intentionality," *Philosophical Topics* 12 (Spring, 1981),
121–146. Reprinted with permission of the editor and authors.

[1] A *monadic* property is a one-place property, as opposed to relations,
which have two or more places. ED.
[2] "Quale" is the singular form of "qualia." ED.

that state; and yet common intuitions insist that said quale is an essential element of pain, on some views, the essential element. Functionalism, it is concluded, provides an inadequate account of our mental states.

Before addressing the issues in greater detail, let us be clear about what the functionalist need not deny. He need not and should not deny that our sensations have intrinsic[3] properties, and he should agree as well that those properties are the principal means of our introspective discrimination of one kind of sensation from another. What he is committed to denying is that any particular quale is essential to the identity of any particular type of mental state. Initially they may seem to be essential, but reflection will reveal that they do not have and should not be conceded that status. In what follows we address four distinct but not unrelated problems. Each problem is manageable on its own, but if they are permitted to band together for a collective assault, the result is rather confusing and formidable, in the fashion of the fabled Musicians of Bremen. With the problems separated, our strategy will be to explain and exploit the insight that intrinsic properties per se are not anathema to a functionalist theory of mental states.

A. The Problem of Inverted/Gerrymandered Qualia

This problem is just the most straightforward illustration of the general worry that functionalism leaves out something essential.[4] The recipe for concocting the appropriate intuitions runs thus. Suppose that the sensations having the quale typical of pain in you play the functional role of pleasure sensations in someone else,[5] and the quale typical of pleasure sensations in you are [sic] had instead by the sensations that have the functional role of pain in him. Functionally, we are to suppose, the two of you are indistinguishable, but his pleasure/pain qualia are simply inverted relative to their distribu-

tion among your own sensations, functionally identified. A variation on the recipe asks us to imagine someone with an inverted distribution of the color qualia that characterize your own visual sensations (functionally identified). He thus has (what you would introspectively identify as) a sensation of red in all and only those circumstances where you have a sensation of green, and so forth.

These cases are indeed imaginable, and the connection between quale and functional syndrome is indeed a contingent one.[6] Whether it is the quale or the functional syndrome that determines type-identity[7] qua psychological state, we must now address. The intuitions evoked above seem to confound functionalist pretensions. The objection to functionalism is that when the inversion victim has that sensation whose functional properties indicate pleasure, *he is in fact feeling pain,* functional properties notwithstanding; and that when the victim of a spectrum inversion says, "I have a sensation of green" in the presence of a green object, *he is in fact having a sensation of red,* functional properties notwithstanding. So far as type-identity of psychological states is concerned, the objection concludes, sameness of qualitative character dominates over sameness of functional role.

Now there is no point in trying to deny the possibilities just outlined. Rather, what the functionalist must argue is that they are better described as follows. "Your pains have a qualitative character rather different from that of his pains, and your sensations-of-green have a qualitative character rather different from that of his sensations-of-green. Such internal differences among the same psychological states are neither inconceivable, nor even perhaps very unusual." That is to say, the functionalist should concede the juggled qualia, while continuing to reckon type-identity in accordance with functional syndrome. This line has a certain intuitive appeal of its own, though rather less than the opposing story, at least initially. How shall we decide between these competing intuitions? By isolating the considerations that give rise to them, and examining their integrity.

---

[3] *Intrinsic* (monadic) properties are opposed, in this context, to the polyadic or n-adic *relational* (including causal) properties assigned to a mental state in a functional analysis. ED.

[4] The type of objection dealt with here is posed by Campbell's Imitation Man in Reading 23. ED.

[5] The usual pain quale in others causes you, for instance, to smile and to want to persevere in whatever condition or activity you associate with the sensation. ED.

[6] I.e., there is no essential connection between your sensation having the intrinsic quality it has and the role it plays within the network of causal relations making up the functional system that is your mind. ED.

[7] The *type-identity* of a sensation is its being a sensation of a certain type, such as pain or thirst. ED.

The "pro-qualia" intuitions, we suggest, derive from two main sources. To begin with, all of us have a strong and entirely understandable tendency to think of each type of psychological state as constituting a **natural kind.** After all, these states do play a vigorous explanatory and predictive role in everyday commerce, and the common-sense conceptual framework that comprehends them has all the features and functions of a sophisticated empirical theory (see Wilfrid Sellars, 1956; and Paul Churchland, 1979). To think of pains, for example, as constituting a natural kind is to think of them as sharing an *intrinsic nature* that is common and essential to every instance of pain. It is understandable then, that the qualitative character of a sensation, the only non-relational feature to which we have access, should present itself as being that essential element.

Our inclination to such a view is further encouraged by the fact that one's introspective discrimination of a sensation's qualitative character is far and away the most immediate, most automatic, most deeply entrenched, and (in isolation) most authoritative measure of what sensations one has. In one's own case, at least, the functional features of one's sensations play a minor role in one's recognition of them. It is as if one had a special access to the intrinsic nature of any given type of sensation, an access that is independent of the purely contingent and causal features that constitute its functional role.

Taken conjointly, these considerations will fund very strong intuitions in favor of qualia as *the* determinants of type-identity for psychological states. But though natural enough, the rationale is exceptionally feeble on both points.

Take the first. However accustomed or inclined we are to think of our psychological states as constituting natural kinds, it is vital to see that it is not a semantic or conceptual matter, but an objective *empirical* matter, whether or not they do. Either there is an objective intrinsic nature common to all cases of, e.g., pain, as it occurs in humans, chimpanzees, dogs, snakes, and octopi, or there is not. And the fact is, the functionalist can point to some rather persuasive considerations in support of the view that there is not. Given the physiological and chemical variety we find in the nervous systems of the many animals that feel pain, it appears very unlikely that their pain states have a common physical nature underlying their common functional nature (see Hilary Putnam, 1971). It remains possible that they all have some intrinsic *non*-physical nature in common, but dualism is profoundly implausible on sheer evolutionary grounds. (The evolutionary process just is the diachronic[8] articulation of matter and energy. If we accept an evolutionary origin for ourselves, then our special capacities must be construed as the capacities of one particular articulation of matter and energy. This conclusion is confirmed by our increasing understanding of the nervous system, both of its past evolution and its current regulation of behavior.) In sum, the empirical presumption *against* natural-kind status for psychological states is substantial. We should not place much trust, therefore, in intuitions born of an uncritical prejudice to the contrary. Such intuitions may reflect ordinary language more or less faithfully, but they beg the question against functionalism.

The facts of introspection provide no better grounds for thinking sensations to constitute natural kinds, or for reckoning qualia as their constituting essences. That the qualitative character Q of a psychological state S should serve as the standard ground of S's introspective discrimination is entirely consistent with Q's being a non-essential feature of S. The black and yellow stripes of a tiger serve as the standard ground on which tigers are visually discriminated from other big cats, but the stripes are hardly an essential element of tigerhood: there are albino tigers, as well as the very pale Himalayan tigers. The telling question here is this: why should the qualia of our familiar psychological states be thought any different? We learn to pick out those qualia in the first place, from the teeming chaos of our inner lives, only because the states thus discriminated are also the nexus of various generalizations connecting them to other inner states, to environmental circumstances, and to overt behaviors of interest and importance to us. Had our current taxonomy of introspectible qualia been unsuccessful in this regard, we would most certainly have thrown it over, centered our attention on different aspects of the teeming chaos within, and recarved it into a different set of similarity classes—a set that *did* display its objective integrity by its many nomic[9]

---

[8] "Diachronic" means "over time." ED.

[9] "Nomic" here means "exhibiting law-like regularity." ED.

connections, both internal and external. In short, the internal world comes pre-carved into observational kinds no more than does the external world,[10] and it is evident that the introspective taxonomies into which we eventually settle are no less shaped by considerations of explanatory and causal coherence than are the taxonomies of external observation.

It is therefore a great irony, it seems to us, that anyone should subsequently point to whatever qualia our introspective mechanisms have managed tenuously to fix upon as more-or-less usable indicators of nomologically interesting states, and claim *them* as constituting the *essence* of such states. It is of course distantly possible that our mechanisms of introspective discrimination have lucked onto the constituting essences of our psychological states (assuming, contrary to our earlier discussion, that each type *has* a uniform natural essence), but a priori that seems about as likely as that the visual system lucked onto the constituting essence of tigerhood when it made black-on-yellow stripes salient for distinguishing tigers.

Therefore, it seems very doubtful that the type-identity of any psychological state derives from its sharing in any uniform natural essence. Moreover, even if it does so share, it seems entirely unlikely that introspection provides any special access to that essence. Consequently, this beggars the intuition which sustains the inverted-qualia objections.

The preceding investigation into the weight and significance of factors determining type-identity of psychological states does more than that, however. It also enriches the competing intuition, namely, that the type-identity of psychological states is determined by functional characteristics. To repeat the point made earlier, since the taxonomy of observational qualia constructed by the questing child *follows* the discovered taxonomy of states as determined by interesting causal roles, it is evident that sameness of functional role dominates over differences in qualitative character, so far as the type-identity of psychological states is concerned. That a single category, unified by functional considerations, can embrace diverse and disparate qualitative characters has a ready illustration, ironically enough, in the case of pain.

Consider the wide variety of qualia wilfully lumped together in common practice under the heading of pain. Compare the qualitative character of a severe electric shock with that of a sharp blow to the kneecap; compare the character of hands dully aching from making too many snowballs with the piercing sensation of a jet engine heard at very close range; compare the character of a frontal headache with the sensation of a scalding pot grasped firmly. It is evident that what unites sensations of such diverse characters is the similarity in their functional roles. The sudden onset of any of them prompts an involuntary withdrawal of some sort. Our reaction to all of them is immediate dislike, and the violence of the dislike increases with the intensity and duration of the sensation. All of them are indicators of physical trauma of some kind, actual or potential. All of them tend to produce shock, impatience, distraction, and vocal reactions of familiar kinds. Plainly, these collected causal features are what unite the class of painful sensations, not some uniform quale, invariant across cases. (For a general account of the intentionality of our sensations, in which qualia also retreat into the background, see Paul Churchland, 1979: ch. 2.)

The converse illustration is formed by states having a uniform or indistinguishable qualitative character, states which are nevertheless distinguished by us according to differences in their functional roles. For example, our emotions have a certain qualitative character, but it is often insufficient to distinguish which emotion should be ascribed. On a particular occasion, the felt knot in one's soul might be mild sorrow, severe disappointment, or gathering despair, and which of these it is—really is—would depend on the circumstances of its production, the rest of one's psychological state, and the consequences to which it tends to give rise. Its type-identity need not be a mystery to its possessor—he has introspective access to some of the context which embeds it—but the identification remains unmakeable on qualitative grounds alone. Similarly, a therapist may be needed, or a thought-

---

[10] For instance, the way we divide up the visual field into separate things does have some connection with the contrasts in color and brightness that we detect there, but it doesn't come close to coinciding with those contrasts. Motion, resistance to acceleration, and other relationships among items in the visual field are just as important, allowing us, for example, to distinguish colored markings on a surface from colored objects lying on that surface. We perceive such features through our interactions with our environments. Ed.

ful friend, to help you distinguish your decided un-ease about some person as your hatred for him, envy of him, or simple fear of him. The felt quality of your unease may be the same for each of these cases, but its causes and effects would be significantly different for each. Here again, functional role is the dominant factor in the type-identity of psychological states.

The reason that functional role dominates introspectible qualitative differences and similarities is not that the collected laws descriptive of a state's functional relations are analytically true,[11] or that they exhaust the essence of the state in question (though withal, they may). The reason is that the common-sense conceptual framework in which our psychological terms are semantically embedded is an *empirical theory*. As with theoretical terms generally, their changeable position in semantic space[12] is fixed by the set of theoretical laws in which they figure. In the case of folk psychology, those laws express the causal relations that connect psychological states with one another, with environmental circumstances, and with behavior. Such laws need not be seen, at any given stage in our growing understanding, as *exhausting* the essence of the states at issue, but at any given stage they constitute the best-founded and most authoritative criterion available for identifying those states.

We conclude against the view that qualia constitute an essential element in the type-identity of psychological states. Variations within a single type are both conceivable and actual. The imagined cases of qualia inversion are of interest only because they place directly at odds intuitions that normally coincide: the non-inferential impulse of observational habit against the ponderous background of theoretical understanding. However, the qualitative character of a sensation is a relevant mark of its type-identity only insofar as that character is the uniform concomitant of a certain repeatable causal

syndrome. In the qualia-inversion thought experiments, that uniformity is broken, and so, in consequence, is the relevance of those qualia for type-identity, at least insofar as they can claim a *uniform* relevance across people and across times.

B. The Problem of Absent Qualia

The preceding arguments may settle the qualia-inversion problem, but the position we have defended is thought to raise in turn an even more serious problem for functionalism (see Ned Block and Jerry Fodor, 1972; and Block, 1978). If the particular quale a sensation has contributes nothing to its type-identity, what of a "psychological" system functionally isomorphic with us, whose functional states have no qualia whatever? Surely such systems are possible (nomically as well as logically), runs the objection.[13] Surely functionalism entails that such a system feels pain, warmth, and so on. But since its functional states have no qualitative character whatever, surely such a system *feels nothing at all*. Functionalism, accordingly, must be false.

This argument is much too glib in the contrast it assumes between functional features (which supposedly matter to functionalism) and qualitative character (which supposedly does not). As the functionalist should be the first to admit, our various sensations are introspectively discriminated by us on the basis of their qualitative character, and any adequate psychological theory must take this fact into account. How might functionalism do this? Straightforwardly. It must require of any state that is functionally equivalent to the sensation-of-warmth, say, that it have some intrinsic property or other whose presence is detectable by (= is causally sufficient for affecting) our mechanisms of introspective discrimination in such a way as to cause, in conceptually competent creatures, belief-states such as the belief that I have a sensation-of-warmth. If these sorts of causal relations are not part of a given state's functional identity, then it fails to be a sensation-of-warmth on purely functional grounds. (Sydney Shoemaker makes much the same point in Shoemaker, 1975. We do not know if he will agree with the points that follow.)

So functionalism *does* require that sensations have an intrinsic property that plays a certain causal

---

[11] I.e., we don't discover these laws simply by analyzing the concept of the mental state in question. ED.

[12] Think of terms as forming a spatial network in which the position of any one term is a function of its definitional relationships to other terms (such as those that would be used in a dictionary definition of the term). As our understanding of the world around us changes, so, to a degree, would the positions of terms in such a network. Consider the semantic shifts in the terms Sun and Earth as humans have learned new and important things about them. ED.

[13] This objection is what Jackson, in the previous reading, called the Modal Argument. ED.

role. But it is admittedly indifferent as to precisely what that intrinsic property might happen to be for any given type of sensation in any given person. So far as functionalism is concerned, that intrinsic property might be the spiking frequency of the signal in some neural pathway, the voltage across a polarized membrane, the temporary deficit of some neurochemical, or the binary configuration of a set of DC pulses. So long as it is one of these properties to which the mechanisms of introspective discrimination happen to be keyed, the property fills the bill.

"But *these* are not qualia!" chorus the outraged objectors. Are they not indeed. Recall the characterization of qualia given on the first page of this paper: ". . . those intrinsic or monadic properties of our sensations discriminated in introspection." Our sensations are anyway **token-identical** with the physical states that realize them, so there is no problem in construing a spiking frequency of 60 hertz as an intrinsic property of a certain sensation. And why should such a property, or any of the others listed, *not* be at the objective focus of introspective discrimination? To be sure, they would be opaquely discriminated,[14] at least by creatures with a primitive self-conception like our own. That is to say, the spiking frequency of the impulses in a certain neural pathway need not prompt the non-inferential belief, "My pain has a spiking frequency of 60 Hz"; it may prompt only the belief, "My pain has a searing quality." But withal, the property you opaquely distinguish as "searingness" may be precisely the property of having 60 Hz as a spiking frequency.

There are many precedents for this sort of thing in the case of the intrinsic properties of material objects standardly discriminable in observation. The redness of an object turns out to be a specific reflectance triplet for three critical wavelengths in the EM spectrum. The pitch of a singer's note turns out to be its frequency qua oscillation in air pressure. The warmth of a coffee cup turns out to be the vibrational energy of its molecules. The tartness of one's lemonade turns out to be its high relative concentration of H+ ions. And so forth.

These chemical, electromagnetic, and micromechanical properties have been briskly discriminated by us for many millennia, but only opaquely. The reason is that we have not possessed the concepts necessary to make more penetrating judgments, and our mechanisms of sensory discrimination are of insufficient resolution to reveal on their own the intricacies uncovered by other means. Unambiguous perception of molecular KE,[15] for example, would require sensory apparatus capable of resolving down to about 10^{-10} metres, and of tracking particles having the velocity of rifle bullets, millions of them, simultaneously. Our sensory apparatus for detecting and measuring molecular KE is rather more humble, but even so it connects us reliably with the parameter at issue. Mean molecular kinetic energy may not seem like an observable property of material objects, but most assuredly it is. (For a working-out of these themes in detail see Paul Churchland, 1979.)

Similarly, spiking frequency may not seem like an introspectible property of sensations, but there is no reason why it should not be, and no reason why the epistemological story for the faculty of inner sense should be significantly different from the story told for outer sense. Qualia, therefore, are not an ineffable mystery, any more than colors or temperatures are. They are physical features of our psychological states, and we may expect qualia of some sort or other in any physical system that is sufficiently complex to be functionally isomorphic with our own psychology. The qualia of such a robot's states are not "absent." They are merely *unrecognized* by us under their physical/electronic description, or as discriminated by the modalities of outer rather than inner sense.

---

[14] The corresponding term in Campbell is "imperfect apprehension." He has a very different take on this issue. See pp. 336–337 above. It should be noted that the term "opaque" also has a related but different meaning in current philosophical discourse. The expression in which a term occurs may give that term a (referentially) *opaque* context—a context in which a second term that designates what is identical to the referent of the first term cannot be substituted for the first term without changing the truth value of the enclosing sentence. For instance, if we say that "Tom believes there is water in the glass," it is invalid to infer that Tom believes there is H_2O in the glass, even though H_2O and water are identical. (Moreover, if we add the premise that Tom is ignorant of the chemical formula for water, we could even infer that it is not the case that Tom believes there is H_2O in the glass.) Insofar as introspective awareness of what it is like to be aware of one or other kind of qualia is expressed in a sentence with a propositional attitude such as belief, the term for the quale will be in a (referentially) opaque context and therefore substitution of the relevant functional term will always be invalid, even if it is true that the functional term correctly describes what the qualitative term designates. ED.

[15] KE = kinetic energy. Molecules have it by being in motion in various ways. ED.

We may summarize all of this by saying that the functionalist need not and perhaps should not attempt to deny the existence of qualia. Rather, he should be a realist[16] about qualia—in particular, he should be a *scientific* realist.[17]

It is important to appreciate that one can be reductionistic about qualia, as outlined above, without being the least bit reductionistic about the taxonomy of states appropriate to psychological theory. Once qualia have been denied a role in the type-identity of psychological states, the path described is open. If this line on qualia is correct, then it vindicates Ned Block's prophecy (1978: p. 309) that the explication of the nature of qualia does not reside in the domain of psychology. On the view argued here, the nature of specific qualia will be revealed by neurophysiology, neurochemistry, and neurophysics.[18]

C. The Problem of Distinguishing States With Qualia From States Without

One could distinguish many differences between the sensations and the propositional attitudes,[19] but one particular difference is of special interest here. A sensation-of-warmth, for example, has a distinct qualitative character, whereas the belief-that-Tom-is-tall does not. Can functionalism account for the difference?

Yes it can. The picture to be avoided here depicts sensations as dabbed with metaphysical paint, while beliefs remain undabbed and colorless. The real difference, we suggest, lies less in the objective nature of sensations and beliefs themselves, than in the nature of the introspective mechanisms used to discriminate and identify the states of each class. This hypothesis requires explanation.

How many different types of sensation are there? One hundred? One thousand? Ten thousand? It is difficult to make an estimate, since most sensations are arrayed on a qualitative continuum of some sort, and it is to some extent arbitrary where and how finely the lines between different kinds are drawn. It is plain, however, that the number of distinct continua we recognize, and the number of significant distinctions we draw within each, is sufficiently small that the brain can use the following strategy for making non-inferential identifications of sensations.

Consider the various physical properties which in you are characteristic of the repeatable brain state that realizes a given sensation. Simply exploit whichever of those physical properties is accessible to your innate discriminatory mechanisms, and contrive a standard habit of conceptual response ("lo, a sensation of warmth") to the property-evoked activation of those mechanisms. While this strategy will work nicely for the relatively small class of sensations, it will not work at all well for the class of beliefs, or for any of the other propositional attitudes.[20] The reason is not that the brain state that realizes a certain belief *lacks* intrinsic properties characteristic of it alone. Rather, the reason is that there are far too many beliefs, actual and possible, for us to have any hope of being able to discriminate and identify all of them on such a one-by-one basis. The number of possible beliefs is at least a denumerable infinity, and the number of possible beliefs expressible in an English sentence of ten words or less is still stupendous. Assuming a vocabulary of 10^5 words for English, the number of distinct strings of ten words or less is 10^{50}. Assuming conservatively that only one string in every trillion trillion is grammatically and semantically well-formed, this still leaves us over 10^{25} distinct sentences. Even if there were a distinct and accessible monadic property for each distinct belief-state, therefore, the capacity of memory is insufficient to file all of them. Evidently the brain must use some more systematic strategy for discriminating and identifying

---

[16] Roughly speaking, a *realist* (about human perception and knowledge) holds that the object exists independently of our ways of perceiving, conceptualizing, or talking about the object. An *idealist* would deny this, saying instead that the object exists only in relation to a human and/or other type of subject. ED.

[17] A scientific realist is one who holds that the world as described scientifically exists independently of us. ED.

[18] The authors say this because they believe that there is a strong parallel between such cases as "Heat is molecular kinetic energy" and "Quale X is a certain pattern of neural activity." Both are scientific claims about the nature of what we "opaquely" discriminate as a specific qualitative feature. ED.

[19] Propositional attitudes are the relations that one can take toward a particular proposition. For instance, I could believe, doubt, deny, or hope *that it will rain*. ED.

[20] We should avoid confusion here between *belief* as propositional attitude and *belief* as proposition which is believed. The class of propositional attitudes is limited like the class of types of sensation. But the class of beliefs (propositions toward which one could have the propositional attitude of belief) is limitless. ED.

beliefs—a strategy that exploits in some way any belief's unique combinatorial structure.

But this is a very complex and sophisticated matter, requiring the resources of our higher cognitive capacities, capacities tuned to the complex relational, structural, and combinatorial features of the domain in which the discriminations are made. Unlike the sensation case, no narrow range of stimulus/response connections will begin to characterize the mechanisms at work here.

Sensations and beliefs, accordingly, must be introspectively discriminated by entirely distinct cognitive mechanisms, mechanisms facing quite different problems and using different strategies for their solutions. Sensations are identified by way of their intrinsic properties; beliefs are identified by way of their highly abstract structural features. It should not be wondered at then, that there is a subjective contrast in the nature of our awareness of each.

D. The Differentiation Problem

This problem arises because we are occasionally able to discriminate between qualitatively distinct sensations where we are ignorant of any corresponding functional differences between them, and even where we are wholly ignorant of the causal properties of both of them, as when they are new to us, for example. These cases are thought to constitute a problem in that functional considerations should bid us count the states as type-identical, whereas by hypothesis, they are type-distinct (see Block, 1978: p. 300).

The objection has two defects. First, sheer ignorance of functional differences need not bind us to counting the sensations as functionally identical. The functionalist can and should be a realist about functional properties. Functional identities are not determined by what we know or do not know, but by what is actually out there in the world (or, *in* there, in the world). Second, the objection begs the question against functionalism by assuming that a discriminable qualitative difference between two sensations entails that they are type-distinct qua psychological states. We have already seen that this inference is wrong in any case: pains display a variety of qualitative characters, but because of their functional similarities, they still count as pains.

In short, we can and do make discriminations among our sensations in advance of functional understanding. But whether the discriminations thus made mark a difference of any importance for the taxonomy of psychological theory is another question. In some cases they will; in other cases they will not. What decides the matter is whether those qualitative differences mark any causal or functional differences relevant to the explanation of psychological activity and overt behavior.

So long as introspectible qualia were thought to be ineffable, or epiphenomenal, or dualistic, or essential for type-identity, one can understand the functionalist's reluctance to have anything to do with them. But once we have seen how the functionalist can acknowledge them and their epistemic role, within a naturalistic framework, the reluctance should disappear. For the taxonomy of states appropriate for psychological theory remains dictated entirely by causal and explanatory factors. Qualia are just accidental hooks of opportunity for the introspective discrimination of dynamically significant states.

II. THE PROBLEM OF NON-STANDARD REALIZATIONS

Some of the issues arising here have already been broached in the section concerning absent qualia. However, novel problems arise as well, and organization is best served by a separate section. All of the problems here begin with the functionalist's central contention that the functional organization necessary and sufficient for personhood is an abstract one, an organization realizable in principle in an indefinite variety of physical systems. Such liberalism seems innocent enough when we contemplate the prospect of humanoid aliens, biomechanical androids, and electromechanical robots whose physical constitutions are at least rough parallels of our own. Who could deny that C3PO and R2D2 are persons? But our liberal intuitions are quickly flummoxed when we consider bizarre physical systems which might nevertheless realize the abstract causal organization at issue, and such cases move one to reconsider one's generosity in the more familiar cases as well.

The following discussion will explore but two of these non-standard "persons": Ned Block's "Chinese Nation" (Block, 1978), and John Searle's

"Chinese-speaking room" with the monolingual anglophone locked inside it (Searle, 1980). Block is concerned with the absence of *qualia* from states posing as sensations, and Searle is concerned with the absence of *intentionality* from states posing as prepositional attitudes.

Block's example will be examined first. He has us imagine a certain Turing machine[21] T_m, which is realized in the population of China, as follows. Each citizen enjoys a two-way radio link to a certain robotic device with *sensory transducers* and motor effectors. This robot is the body of the simulated person, and it interacts with its collective brain thus: it sends a sensory input message I_j to every citizen and subsequently receives a motor output message O_i from exactly one citizen. Which citizen sends what output is determined as follows. Overhead from a satellite some state letter S_k is displayed in lights for all to see. For each possible state letter S_k there is assigned a distinct subset of the population. In the rare event when S_k is displayed *and* input I_j is received, one person in the S_k group to whom I_j has been assigned performs this preassigned task: she sends to the robot the unique output message O_i antecedently assigned to her, and then subsides, waiting for the next opportunity to do exactly the same thing in exactly the same circumstances.

As organized above, each citizen realizes exactly one square of the machine table that specifies T_m. (A machine table is a matrix or checkerboard with state letters heading the columns and input letters heading the rows. Any square is the intersection of some S_k and I_j, and it specifies an output O_i and a shift to some state S_p, where possibly $p = k$.) Block asks us to assume that T_m adequately simulates your own functional organization. One is likely to grant him this, since any input-output function can in principle be simulated by a suitable Turing machine. In pondering an apparently fussy detail, Block wonders, "How many homunculi are required?" and answers, "perhaps a billion are enough; after all, there are only about a billion neurons in the brain" (p. 278). Hence his choice of China as the potential artificial brain.

Finally, Block finds it starkly implausible to suppose that this realization of T_m has states with a qualitative character like pains, tastes, and so on. It is difficult not to agree with him. His homunculi do not even interact with one another, save indirectly through the satellite state letter, and, even less directly, through the adventures of the robot body itself. The shimmering intricacies of one's inner life are not to be found here.

The way to avoid this criticism is just to insist that any subject of beliefs and sensations must not only be "Turing-equivalent"[22] to us (that is, produce identical outputs given identical inputs), it must be computationally equivalent to us as well. That is, it must have a system of inner states whose causal interconnections mirror those in our own case. This is not an arbitrary restriction. Folk psychology is, and scientific psychology should be, realistic[23] about our mental states, and mere parity of gross behavior does not guarantee parity of causal organization among the states that produce it. The computational organization displayed in the Chinese Turing machine is not even distantly analogous to our own. If it were analogous to our own, worries about absent qualia could be handled as outlined in section I, part B, above.

There is a further reason why it is not arbitrary to demand a computational organization more along the lines of our own, and we may illustrate it by examining a further defect in Block's example. It is demonstrable that no T_m realized as described in the population of China could possibly simulate your input-output relations. There are not nearly enough Chinese—not *remotely* enough. In fact, a spherical volume of space centered on the Sun and ending at Pluto's orbit packed solidly with cheek-to-cheek Chinese (roughly 10^{36} homunculi) would still not be remotely enough, as we shall show.

Being realized on a one-man/one-square basis, the Chinese T_m can have at most 10^9 distinct possible outputs, and at most $10^9/S$ distinct possible inputs, where S is the total number of distinct state letters. That is, T_m has rather less than 10^9 possible inputs.

---

[21] For an explanation of Turing machines, see Reading 15, sections 3 and 5. ED.

[22] This term means the same as "functionally equivalent." ED.

[23] "Realistic" here means that the mental states in question are really "in there" and have a reality independent of our ways of talking or theorizing. ED.

How many distinct possible inputs characterize your own functional organization? Since the present argument requires only a lower limit, let us consider just one of your retinas. The surface of your retina contains roughly 10^8 light sensitive cells, which we shall assume (conservatively) to be capable of only two states: stimulated or unstimulated. Good eyesight has a resolution limit of about one foot at a distance of a mile, or slightly less than one arc-minute, and this angle struck out from the lens of the eye subtends about six microns at the retina.[24] This is roughly the distance between the individual cells to be found there, so it is evident that individual cells, and not just groups, can serve as discriminative atoms, functionally speaking.

If we take distinct stimulation patterns in the set of retinal cells as distinct inputs to the brain, it is evident that we are here dealing with 2 to the (10^8) power distinct inputs. This is an appallingly large number. Since $2^{332} \approx 10^{100}$ (a googol), $2^{10^8} \approx 10^{30,000,000}$ distinct possible inputs[25] from a single retina! Since a one-man/one-square Turing machine must have at least as many homunculi as possible inputs, any such realization adequate to the inputs from a single retina would require no less than $10^{30,000,000}$ distinct homunculi. However, there are only about 10^{80} distinct atoms in the accessible universe. Small wonder the Chinese nation makes an unconvincing simulation of our inner lives, but we should never have acquiesced in the premise that a Turing machine thus realized could even begin to simulate your overall functional organization. The Chinese robot body can have at most a mere 30 binary input sensors, since $2^{30} \approx 10^9$, and the number of inputs[26] cannot exceed 10^9.

This argument does not depend on inflated estimates concerning the retina or its input to the brain. (It might be objected that retinal cell stimulation is not independent of the state of its immediate neighbor cells, or that the optic nerve has only 800,000 axons.) If your retina contained only 332 discriminatory units, instead of 10^8, the number of distinct inputs would still be 2^{332}, or roughly 10^{100}: ninety-one orders of magnitude beyond the atoms in the universe. Nor have we even begun to consider the other dimension of the required machine table: the range of states, S, of the brain which receives these inputs, a brain which has at least 10^{10} distinct cells in its own right, each with about 10^3 connections with cells. Our estimate of the number of distinct states of the brain must be substantially in excess of $10^{30,000,000}$, our number for the retina.

Our conclusion is that *no* brute-force one-device/one-square realization of a Turing machine constructible in this universe could even begin to simulate your input-output organization. Even the humblest of creatures are beyond such simulation. An unprepossessing gastropod like the sea slug *Aplysia Califonica* has well in excess of 332 distinct sensory cells, and thus is clearly beyond the reach of the crude methods at issue. This does not mean that the human input/output relations cannot be represented by an abstract Turing machine T_m. What it does mean is that any *physical* machine adequate to such simulation *must* have its computational architecture and executive hardware organized along lines vastly different from, and much more unified and efficient than, those displayed in Block's example. That example, therefore, is not even remotely close to being a fair test of our intuitions. Quite aside from the question of qualia, the Chinese Turing machine couldn't simulate an earthworm.

This weakness in the example is not adequately made up by allowing, as Block does at one point

---

[24] For a description of the eye as visual receptor, see section 3.3 of Reading 4. The authors are telling us that a person with good eyesight can distinguish from a mile away an object no smaller than one foot in diameter. Suppose points A and B in the drawing on the right to be one foot apart on the edge of an object one foot in diameter and one mile away. Light from each point converges at the lens, forming an angle of one arc-minute (1/60 of a degree), and diverging

from the lens to the retina a distance of six microns (CD = six millionths of a meter). This distance is, approximately, the space taken up by a rod or cone cell. This arithmetic suggests that individual retinal cells may be distinct sources of visual input. However, as the authors point out, one has to qualify this suggestion by taking into account the convergences of signals as they cross the network of the retina before being channeled to the brain. ED.

[25] We don't need to follow the authors' number play here to get their point. However one individuates and counts visual sensory inputs, their very plausible claim is that it says something relevant about the world in general and vision in particular that no human population is large enough (or fast enough, for that matter) to serve as the functional equivalent of the brain's internal workings. ED.

---

[26] Each binary sensor contributes one of two elements to the pattern created by the elements from all the sensors combined. E.g., each sensor is on or off. Thus there are 2^n possible patterns of on's and off's for n sensors. ED.

(p. 284), that each homunculus might be responsible for a wide range of inputs, each with corresponding outputs. On this modification, each homunculus would thus realize, dispositionally, many machine-table squares simultaneously. Suppose then that we make each Chinese citizen responsible for one billion squares peculiar to him. This raises the number of distinct inputs processable by the system to 10^9 citizens $\times$ 10^9 squares $=$ 10^{18} possible inputs, still well short of the $10^{30,000,000}$ we are striving for. Well, how many squares must each citizen realize if the nation as a whole is to instantiate some Turing machine adequate to handle the required input? The answer is, of course, $10^{(30,000,000 - 9)}$ squares each. But how will each citizen/homunculus handle this awesome load? *Not* by being a simple one-device/one-square Turing machine in turn, as we have already seen. No physical simulation adequate to your input-output relations, therefore, can avoid having the more unified and efficient modes of computational organization alluded to in the last paragraph, even if they only show up as modes of organization of its various subunits. Any successful simulation of you, that is, must somewhere display a computational/executive organization that is a much more plausible home for qualitative states than Block's example would suggest.[27]

But can a number of distinct persons or near-persons collectively constitute a further person? Apparently so, since the system consisting of your right hemisphere and left hemisphere (and your cerebellum and thalamus and limbic system, etc.) seems to do precisely that.[28] Further attempts to construct homunculi-headed counter-examples to functionalism should perhaps bear this fact in mind.

The argument of the preceding pages does not, of course, show that the specific details of *our* computational organization are essential to achieving the informational capacity required. And this raises a question we might have asked anyway: if we do require of any subject of sensations, beliefs, and so forth, that it be functionally equivalent to us in the strong sense of "computationally equivalent," do we not then run the opposite danger of allowing too few things to count as sites of mentality? (See

again Block, p. 310ff.) If we restrict the application of the term 'mentality' to creatures having sensations, beliefs, intentions, etc., we will indeed have become too restrictive. Yet the functionalist need not pretend that our internal functional organization exhausts the possible kinds of mentality. He needs only claim that our kind of internal functional organization is what constitutes a psychology of *beliefs, desires, sensations,* and so forth. He is free to suggest that an alien functional organization, comparable only in sophistication to our own, could constitute an alien psychology of quite different internal states. We could then speak of Martian mentality, for example, as well as of human mentality.

Still, it might be wondered, what is the shared essence that makes both of us instances of the now more general term, 'mentality'? There need be none, beyond the general ideas of a sophisticated control center for complex behavior.[29] One of the functionalist's principal theses, after all, is that there are no natural essences to be found in this domain. If he is right, it is folly to seek them. In any case, it is question-begging to demand that he find them.

On the other hand, there may yet prove to be some interesting natural kind, of which both we and the Martians are variant instances: some highly abstract thermodynamic kind, perhaps. In this case, orthodox functionalism would be mistaken in one of its purely negative theses. On this matter, see the final section of this paper.

Let us now turn to John Searle's worries about meaning and intentionality.[30] The states at issue here are beliefs, thoughts, desires, and the rest of the propositional attitudes. On the functionalist's

---

[27] The increased plausibility depends, of course, on our granting that the more the description of the inner functioning of a system approximates some description of our brain's functions, the more plausible it will seem, intuitively, that qualia are happening. ED.

[28] This reflects the issues raised in Reading 32. ED.

[29] One wonders whether the wonderfully complex regulation of metabolism within any cell would have enough of this "sophistication" to count as an instance of "mentality" at work. And if not, then is there a difference in kind, rather than just degree, of sophistication? ED.

[30] As this term figures in the ensuing discussion, it appears to mean that property of mental states whereby they are *about* something (an object). Moreover, the intentional aboutness is not just the object's being present somehow, but also that the object is always perceived or thought of in a certain way. I am never just presented with a combination of sensory qualities which I subsequently label. Instead, I am always thinking of or regarding the object as being of a certain kind, standing in various relations, possible and actual, to me and to its physical and social environment. For Searle, only mental states have this intentionality *intrinsically.* We can talk about other things *as if* they had it—for instance, we can say that *words* are *about* things, but the aboutness in words is derived from the intentionality in us as we use them about things. ED.

view, the type-identity of any of these states is determined by the network of relations it bears to the other states, and to external circumstances and behavior. In the case of the propositional attitudes, those relations characteristically reflect a variety of logical and computational relations among the propositions they "contain." We can thus at least imagine a computer of sufficient capacity programmed so as to display an economy of internal states whose interconnections mirror those in our own case. The simulation would create the required relational order by exploiting the logical and computational relations defined over the formal/structural/combinatorial features of the individual prepositional states.

Searle has no doubt that such a simulation could, in principle, be constructed. His objection to functionalism is that the states of such a system would nevertheless lack meaning and intentionality: ". . . no purely formal model will ever be sufficient by itself for intentionality" (Searle, 1980: p. 422). His reasons for holding this position are illustrated in the following thought-experiment.

Imagine a monolingual anglophone locked in a room with (a) a substantial store of sequences of Chinese symbols, and (b) a set of complex transformation rules, written in English, for performing operations on sets and sequences of Chinese symbols. The occupant periodically receives a new sequence of Chinese symbols through a postal slot. He applies his transformation rules dutifully to the ordered pair (new sequence, old store of sequences), and they tell him to write out a further sequence of Chinese symbols, which he sends back out through the postal slot.

Now, unknown to the occupant, the large store of sequences embodies a rich store of information on some one or more topics, all written in Chinese. The new sequences sent through the door are questions and comments on those topics. The transformation rules are a cunningly devised program designed to simulate the thought processes and conversational behavior of a native speaker of Chinese. The symbol-sequences the occupant sends out are "responses" to the queries and comments received. We are to suppose that the transformation rules are well-devised, and that the simulation is as convincing as you please, considered from the outside.

However convincing it is, says Searle, it remains plain that the room's occupant does not understand Chinese: he applies transformation rules, and he understands those rules, but the sequences of Chinese symbols are meaningless to him. Equally clear, claims Searle, is that the system of the room-and-its-contents does not understand Chinese either. Nothing here understands Chinese, save those sending and receiving the messages, and those who wrote the program. No computational state or output of that system has any meaning or intentionality save as it is interpretively imposed from without by those who interact with it.

However, concludes Searle, this system already contains everything relevant to be found in the physical realization of any purely formal program. If meaning and intentionality are missing here, they will be missing in any such attempt to simulate human mental activity. Instantiating a program could not be a sufficient condition of understanding,

> Because the formal symbol manipulations by themselves don't have any intentionality; they are quite meaningless; they aren't even *symbol* manipulations, since the symbols don't symbolize anything. In the linguistic jargon, they have only a syntax but no semantics. Such intentionality as computers appear to have is solely in the minds of those who program them, those who send in the input and those who interpret the output. {Ibid., p. 422}

The set of commentaries published in the same issue provides many useful and interesting criticisms of Searle's argument, and of his conclusion as well. The critical consensus is roughly as follows. If the system of the room-plus-contents is upgraded so that its conversational skills extend beyond a handful of topics to include the entire range of topics a normal human could be expected to know; and if the system were supplied with the same inductive capacities we enjoy; and if the "belief store" were integrated in the normal fashion with some appropriately complex goal structure; and if the room were causally connected to a body in such a fashion that its inputs reflected appropriate sensory discriminations and its outputs produced appropriate behavior; then the system of the room-plus-contents jolly well would understand Chinese, and its various computational states—beliefs that *p*, desires that *q*—would indeed have meaning and intentionality, in the same way as with a normal Chinese speaker.[31]

Searle is quite willing to consider upgradings of the kind described—he attempts to anticipate them in his paper—but he is convinced they change nothing relevant to his case. As it emerges clearly in his "Author's Response" (pp. 450–56), of central importance to his argument is the distinction between

> . . . cases of what I will call *intrinsic intentionality,* which are cases of actual mental states, and what I will call *observer-relative* ascriptions of intentionality, which are ways that people have of speaking about entities figuring in our activities but lacking intrinsic intentionality. [p. 451] [The latter] are always dependent on the intrinsic intentionality of the observers. [p. 452]

Examples of the latter would be the words and sentences of one's native tongue. These have meanings and intentionality, allows Searle, but only insofar as they bear certain relations to our beliefs, thoughts, and intentions—states with intrinsic intentionality. And since they lack a feature essential to genuine mental states, they cannot be genuine mental states, and to that extent the simulation must be a failure.

As we see it, this criticism of functionalism is profoundly in error. It is a mistake to try to meet it, however, by continuing with the strategy of trying to upgrade the imagined simulation in hopes of finally winning Searle's concession that at last its states have achieved intrinsic intentionality. The correct strategy is to argue that our own mental states are just as innocent of "intrinsic intentionality" as are the states of any machine simulation. On our view, all ascriptions of meaning or propositional content are relative—in senses to be explained. The notion of "intrinsic intentionality" makes no more empirical sense than does the notion of position in absolute space.[32] We shall try to explain these claims.

There are basically just two ways in which one can assign propositional content to the representational states[33] of another organism. An example of the first is the translation of a foreign language. An example of the second is the calibration of an instrument of measurement or detection.

In the case of translation, one assigns specific propositional contents to the alien representations because one has found a general mapping between the alien representations and our own such that the network of formal and material inferences holding among the alien representations closely mirrors that same network holding among our own representations. Briefly, their collected representations display an *intensional structure* that matches the intensional structure displayed by our own.[34]

The story is essentially the same when we are assigning propositional content to an alien's thoughts, beliefs, etc. It matters naught whether the alien's representation is overt, as with a sentence, or covert, as with a belief. We assign a specific content, *p,* to one of the alien's representations, on the strength of whatever assurances we have that his representation plays the same abstract inferential role in his intellectual (computational) economy that the belief-that-*p* plays in ours. And what goes for aliens goes also for one's brothers and sisters.

This is not to say that the representational states of other humans have content only insofar as others interpret them in some way. After all, the set of abstract inferential relations holding among the representations in someone's intellectual economy is

---

[31] See my remarks at the end of the first selection in Reading 18, pp. 252–253. Ed.

[32] According to Isaac Newton, *absolute* space was the totality of all spaces standing in eternal and immutable relations to each other, irrespective of any bodies that may be in them or moving through them. He contrasted absolute with *relative* space, a space constituted by a set of perceptible objects serving as a frame of reference. For instance, if I remain perfectly still inside a moving car, I am not moving in the relative space framed by the structure of the car, but I am moving in the relative space

framed by the highway markers and scenery I pass. Since any such framework or relative space may itself be moving or at rest, the question of whether I am moving in *absolute* space, and at what velocity, is hard to answer since absolute space is not itself perceptible. Many philosophers believe that the notion of absolute space makes no sense, and that space is essentially relative. The authors are drawing a parallel between absolute space and "intrinsic intentionality," arguing that intentionality is essentially observer-relative. Ed.

[33] *Representational states* are supposedly *about* objects or facts. Ascribing to them "propositional content" specifies what state of affairs the representational states represent. As the authors use this phrase, it seems to apply both to sentences and to the mental states that generate the sentences. Ed.

[34] For example, French "maps" onto English in ways such as these: when I translate "The sky is blue" and "The sky is not overcast" into French, one can make an inference from the French translation of the first sentence to the French translation of the second sentence similar to the inference in English; there are corresponding genus-species relationships in both languages (e.g., in the classifications of animal species); and there are parallel contrarieties such as *froid/chaud* and *cold/hot.*

an objective, non-relational feature of that person.[35] But it does mean that the content, call it the *translational content,* of any specific representation of his *is a matter of the inferential/computational relations it bears to all the rest of his representations.* There can be no question of an isolated state or token possessing an intrinsic translation content; it will have a specific translational content only if, and only insofar as, it enjoys a specific set of relations to the other elements in a *system* of representations.[36]

Contrast translational content with what is naturally termed *calibrational content.* The repeatable states of certain physical systems are more-or-less reliable indicators of certain features of their environment, and we may assign content (e.g., "The temperature is 0 degree C.") to such states (e.g., a certain height in a column of red alcohol) on the strength of such empirical connections. This goes for the human system as well. The various states we call 'perceptual beliefs' can be assigned contents in this manner, as a function of which type of environmental circumstance standardly triggers their occurrence.[37] In fact, if a system has any systematic responses to its environment at all, then calibration can take place even where translation cannot—either because the system simply lacks the internal economy necessary for translational content, or because the intensional structure of that economy is incommensurable with our own.[38] Furthermore, calibrational content may regularly *diverge* from translational content, even where translation is possible. Consider an utterance which calibrates as 'There is thunder', but which translates as 'God is

shouting'; or one which calibrates as 'This man has a bacterial infection', but which translates as 'This man is possessed by a pink demon'.

Accordingly, Searle is right to resist the suggestion that merely hooking up the room-system, via some sensors, to the outside world, would supply a unique meaning or content to the room's representational states. Genuine mental states do indeed have a content or intentionality that is independent of, and possibly quite different from, their calibrational content. (The reader will notice that this entails that it is just possible that all or most of our beliefs are false—that their translational contents may be systematically out of agreement with their actual calibrational contents. For an extended exploration of this real possibility, see Paul Churchland, 1979: ch. 2. On this matter see also Stephen Stich, this issue.[39]) That independent intentionality is their *translational content.* But this content falls well short of being the "intrinsic intentionality" Searle imagines our states to have. Translational content is not environmentally determined, nor is it observed-relative, but it is most certainly a *relational* matter, a matter of the state's inferential/computational relations within a system of other states. Accordingly, it is entirely possible for translational content to be possessed by the states of a machine—the realization of a purely formal program.

What more than this Searle imagines as fixing the content of our mental states, we are unable to surmise. He floats the distinction between intrinsic intentionality and other kinds by means of illustrative examples (p. 451); he hazards no palpable account of what intrinsic intentionality consists in; and the intuitions to which he appeals can be explained in less mysterious ways, as outlined above. To conclude, there is simply no such thing as intrinsic intentionality, at least as Searle conceives it. Functionalists need not be concerned then that computer simulations of human mentality fail to display it.

We complete this section by underscoring a contrast. In the first half of this section we conceded to the critic of functionalism that our mental states have qualia, but we argued that the states of a machine simulation could have them as well. In this

---

[35] In other words, the fact that "The sky is not overcast" commands the assent of an English speaker who believes that "The sky is blue" is not an observer-relative fact, not something due to my interpretation of that person's thoughts or sentences. ED.

[36] The authors are asserting the view mentioned by Searle (on pp. 255–256 of Reading 18) about proof theory showing that syntactic relations mirror semantic relations. See fn. 14 of Reading 18. ED.

[37] For instance, if a dog begins to cross back and forth with frequent sniffing over a patch of ground, you can reliably infer that some other animal has recently been there and that the dog "believes" or "perceives" that this animal has been there. ED.

[38] Imagine observing extra-terrestrial beings that seem to be communicating with each other using a complex symbol system. After prolonged observation, you still can't begin to hazard a translation of any of their utterances, perhaps because their technology and ways of classifying things are wildly different from ours. Nevertheless, you may find their behavior sufficiently intelligible and predictable to begin attributing certain perceptual beliefs to them such as that they recognize each other as individuals and can tell when they are agreed on something. ED.

---

[39] Stephen Stich, "Dennett on Intentional Systems," *Philosophical Topics* 12 (Spring, 1981). ED.

second half we have conceded to the critic of functionalism that the states of certain machine simulations must lack intrinsic intentionality. But we insist that our own states are devoid of it as well.

III. FUNCTIONALISM AND METHODOLOGY

Despite the defenses offered above, we do wish to direct certain criticisms against functionalism. The criticisms are mainly methodological rather than substantive, however, and we shall here provide only a brief summary, since they have been explained at length elsewhere.

A. Conceptual Conservatism

No functionalist will suppose that the functional organization recognized in the collected lore of folk psychology exhausts the functional intricacies that make up our internal economy. All will agree that folk psychology represents only a partial, and in some respects even a superficial, grasp of the more complex organization that empirical psychology will eventually unravel. Even so, there is a decided tendency on all sides to suppose that, so far as it goes, folk psychology is essentially correct in the picture it paints, at least in basic outlines. Empirical psychology will add to it, and explain its principles, most expect, but almost no one expects it to be overthrown or transmogrified by such research.

This sanguine outlook is not unique to functionalists, but they are especially vulnerable to it. Since the type-identity of mental states is held to reside, not in any shared physical or other natural essences, but in the structure of their causal relations, there is a tendency to construe the generalizations connecting them as collectively stipulating what it is to be a belief, a desire, a pain, and so forth. Folk psychology is thus removed from the arena of empirical criticism.[40] This is unfortunate, since the "denaturing" of folk psychology does not change its **epistemic** status as a speculative account of our

internal workings. Like any other theory, it may be radically false; and like any other deeply entrenched theory, its falsity is unlikely to be revealed without a vigorous exploration of that possibility.

A functionalist can of course accept these points without danger to what is basic in his position. Nevertheless, they are worth making for two reasons. First, eliminative materialism[41] is not a very widespread opinion among adherents of functionalism, despite being entirely consistent with their view. And second, there are very good reasons for doubting the integrity of folk psychology in its central structures as well as in its peripheral details (see Paul Churchland, 1979: ch. 5; 1981a; also, Patricia Churchland, 1980a; 1980b; and Stephen Stich, *From Folk Psychology to Cognitive Science: The Case Against Belief,* 1983).

B. Top-Down Versus Bottom-Up

Given that the essence of our psychological states resides in the set of causal relations they bear to one another, etc., and given that this abstract functional organization can be realized in a nomically heterogeneous variety of substrates, it is fair enough that the functionalist should be more interested in that abstract organization than in the machinery that realizes it. With the science of psychology, it is understanding the "program" that counts; an understanding of such hardwares as may execute it is secondary and inessential.

This much is fair enough, but so long as we are so profoundly ignorant of our functional organization as we are at present, and ignorant of where to draw the line between "hardware" and "program" in organisms, we cannot afford to be so casual about or indifferent to the neurosciences as the preceding rationale might suggest. If we wish to unravel the functional intricacies of our internal economy, one obvious way to go about it is to unravel the intricacies of the physical system that executes it. This

---

[40] In other words, if one assumes that there really are such things as beliefs, hopes, the other kinds of mental entities, and states referred to in our everyday language about the mind, this assumption will shape psychological research into the task of establishing functional analyses of those kinds of entities. It would be better if categorization of the mental were subject to revision in light of the empirical data of psychological research. ED.

[41] Like Richard Rorty in Reading 8, the authors are proponents of this variant of materialism, according to which a sufficiently developed neuroscience would make distinctively psychological terms dispensable, or perhaps even render psychology (as a distinct science) obsolete. Many functionalists would not agree that eliminative materialism is consistent with functionalism because they include in their theory the claim that scientific psychology is irreducible to neuroscience because the latter does not deal with functional systems *as such,* and that the mind (or mentality) understood as a functional system, is a valid subject of scientific investigation. Paul Churchland argues for this view in Reading 9. ED.

"bottom–up" approach is not the only approach we might follow, but it does boast a number of advantages: it is very strongly empirical; it is not constrained by the preconceptions of folk psychology; it has the capacity to force surprises on us;[42] it permits a non–behavioral comparison of cognitive differences across species; it enjoys direct connections with evolutionary ethology; and at least in principle it can reveal the functional organization we are looking for.

Neuroscience is an awkward and difficult pursuit, however, and there is an overwhelming preference among philosophers, psychologists, and artificial intelligence researchers for a more "top–down" approach: hypothesize functional systems ("programs") and test them against our molar behavior, as conceived within common sense. This is entirely legitimate, but if the functionalist is moved by the argument from abstraction to ignore or devalue the bottom–up approach, his methodology is dangerously conservative and one–sided. (We have discussed these shortcomings at length in Patricia Churchland, 1980a, 1980c; and in Paul Churchland, 1981a, 1981b, 1980.)

C. Reductionism

Thanks to the argument from abstraction, functionalists tend to be strongly anti–reductionist. They deny that there can be any general characterization of what makes something a *thinker* that is expressible in the language of any of the physical sciences. Given the variety of possible substrates (biological, chemical, electromechanical) that could realize a thinking system, it is difficult not to agree

with them. But it does not follow, from multiple instantiability *per se,* that no such general characterization is possible. It follows only that the required characterization cannot be expressed in the theoretical vocabulary peculiar to any one of the available substrates. It remains entirely possible that there is a level of physical description sufficiently abstract to encompass all of them, and yet sufficiently powerful to fund the characterization required.[43]

As it happens, there is indeed a physical theory of sufficient generality to encompass the activity of all of these substrates, and any others one might think of. The theory is thermodynamics—the general theory of energy and entropy. It has already supplied us with a profoundly illuminating characterization of what the nineteenth century called "vital activity," that is, of the phenomenon of life. And it is far from unthinkable that it might do the same for what this century calls "mental activity." (For a brief exploration of these ideas, see Paul Churchland, 1981b.)[44] The theoretical articulation

---

[42] There are many things about the way that our brains carry out cognitive functions that we would never have guessed from our common-sense or "folk-psychological" conceptions of those functions. For instance, our common–sense conception of vision makes it a contradiction to assert that we can both see something and be blind. Yet this happens in certain cases where individuals who are totally blind in the usual sense are nevertheless able to point to a moving object in what would be their field of vision, even while denying they see anything. The neuroscientific explanation for this phenomenon is that there is a separate pathway from the eye to the brain dedicated to location and motion of objects, distinct from the pathway which terminates in the visual cortex and specializes in color, shape, and pattern. Furthermore, as we will see in Reading 33, the brain's hemispheric duality of structure and function severely challenges our ordinary intuition of the unity of consciousness.

Knowing such facts about brain-based deficits in mental functions at the very least keeps us more honest and realistic about what it is that we are trying to do when we run computer-simulations of *human* mental operations. ED.

[43] The description must be abstract enough to be applicable to all the very different physical systems that might embody mentality yet specific enough to distinguish a thinking system from other complex systems. ED.

[44] From the perspective of thermodynamics, the energy in a system can be loosely understood as its capacity to produce an effect or to do work. Energy comes in various forms such as heat, light, electricity and magnetism; and it can be converted from one form to another as in a wood fire that turns into heat and light the energy sustaining the chemical bonds of carbon compounds. The *first* law of thermodynamics states that in all transformations, the quantity of energy is conserved (energy is neither created nor destroyed). In the case of the wood fire, the net increase in heat and light caused by the fire equals the quantity of energy released from chemical bonds in the fuel. However, the resulting energy is not available to produce an effect of this magnitude again; it has been used up. If we think of the wood and the immediate environment of the fire as a single system, the fire has brought about an increase in the *entropy* of that system, the quantity of its unusable energy.

In general, the quantity of the work that a system's energy can do is a function of the orderliness of that energy, as we can see more easily in this example. Suppose you have a box with an internal wall dividing it into two equal chambers. All the walls of the box are highly insulated and waterproof and each chamber is nearly full of water. You heat the water in one chamber to the boiling point, and before the boiling water ruptures the box you do one of two things: (1) Allow the vapor from the boiling water to escape into a spout on the external wall, so that it emits a high-pitched whistle (call this the tea-kettle effect); or (2) Remove the internal wall separating boiling from cool water. You know what will happen in the second case. The combined water will quickly reach a temperature somewhere between the temperatures of the separate chambers, and it will then remain there (at what is called the *equilibrium* temperature). As long as the box system remains closed to external energy inputs, it is incapable of any major change in temperature anywhere within its boundaries, and incapable of producing a whistle in a spout or any other perceptible (macro) effect.

of such a characterization would be a very great achievement. It would be unfortunate if the search for it were impeded by the general conviction that it is impossible, a conviction born of the anti-reductionist urgings of a false orthodoxy among functionalists.

REFERENCES

Block, Ned. "Troubles with Functionalism." *Minnesota Studies in the Philosophy of Science,* Vol. IX: pp. 261–325. Edited by C. Wade Savage. Minneapolis: University of Minnesota Press, 1978.

Block, Ned and Fodor, Jerry. "What Mental States Are Not." *The Philosophical Review,* LXXXI (1972): 159–81.

Churchland, Patricia Smith. (1980a). "A Perspective on Mind-Brain Research." *The Journal of Philosophy,* LXXVII, 4 (April, 1980): 185–207.

———. (1980b). "Language, Thought, and Information Processing." *Nous* 14 (1980): 147–69.

———. (1980c). "Neuroscience and Psychology: Should the Labor Be Divided?" *The Behavioral and Brain Sciences,* III, 1 (March, 1980): 133.

Churchland, Paul M. (1979). *Scientific Realism and the Plasticity of Mind.* Cambridge: Cambridge University Press, 1979.

———. (1980). "Plasticity: Conceptual and Neuronal." *The Behavioral and Brain Sciences,* III, 1 (March, 1980): 133–34.

———. (1981a). "Eliminative Materialism and the Propositional Attitudes." *The Journal of Philosophy* (LXXVII, 2 February, 1981): 67–90.

———. (1981b). "Is Thinker a Natural Kind?" *Dialogue.*

Putnam, Hilary. "The Nature of Mental States." *Materialism and the Mind-Body Problem,* pp. 150–61. Edited by David Rosenthal. New Jersey: Prentice-Hall, 1971.

Searle, John. "Minds, Brains, and Programs." *The Behavioral and Brain Sciences,* III, 3 (September, 1980): 417–57.

Sellars, Wilfrid. "Empiricism and the Philosophy of Mind." *Minnesota Studies in the Philosophy of Science,* Vol. 1 Edited by Herbert Feign and Michael Shriven. Minneapolis: University of Minnesota Press, 1956. Reprinted in Sellars, *Science, Perception, and Reality.* London: Routledge & Keegan Paul, 1963: 127–96.

Shoemaker, Sydney. "Functionalism and Qualia." *Philosophical Studies* 27 (1975): 291–315.

Stich, Stephen. *From Folk Psychology to Cognitive Science: The Case Against Belief.* Cambridge, MA: MIT Press, 1983.

When you were heating the water in one chamber, the water molecules in that chamber began to move around and vibrate ever faster. In other words, their average kinetic energy was increasing. (It is this increase that you sense as the water "getting hot.") Before you lifted the internal wall, nearly all the more rapidly moving molecules were in one chamber, and the slower ones in the other. When the waters merged, slower and faster molecules became randomly distributed throughout the system. The initial distribution of fast and slow molecules was much more orderly than the subsequent one (like a deck of cards sorted by suit and then shuffled). Whenever something happens within a system other than minor fluctuations, the *second* law of thermodynamics states that the entropy will increase within that system—the energy involved becomes disordered, unavailable to do again what it did, so that what happened is irreversible (wood doesn't "unburn" and cream poured into coffee doesn't gather itself together again).

The second law of thermodynamics makes the existence of living systems seem almost miraculous. As a rule organisms are incessantly active. *Inanimate* bodies such as rocks stay whole and entire by being rigidly inert or flexible enough that they are pretty much unchanged by the normal events in their immediate environments. However, *living* bodies are constantly interacting with their environments, using up ordered, usable energy (sometimes called *negentropy*) which the organism must constantly restore. A living body does life-long battle against entropy until the terminal disorder of death. To *go on,* an organism must be able to extract and take in from its environment the negentropy it loses through incessant activity. However, uncontrolled energetic input can be just as deadly as running out of energy (remember what would have happened if we just kept on heating the sealed water chamber). The organism must take in measured amounts of specific energies, and either store them, change them into usable form (as we do when we digest our food), and/or channel them into some vital, adaptive activity. This energy management is part of the function of a living body's *adaptive control system,* as explained in Reading 4, section 2. In general, this system enables an organism to respond to events in its environment in such a way as to maintain its capacity to respond in the same ways to the same sorts of events.

The nervous system (including the brain) is an evolutionary specialization in the function of adaptive control. And a nervous system with a symbolic and thinking capacity is a further evolutionary development of this same generic function. In the paper to which the authors refer in parentheses, Churchland argued that because the activity of what I have called adaptive control systems can be described in the language of thermodynamics—a branch of natural science—such a system is a *natural kind,* and because *thinking* is an evolutionary adaptation of this general sort of activity, *thinker* may also be a *natural kind.* ED.

In the first part of their essay, the authors undertake to defend functionalism against objections based on the presence of *qualia* within our sensory experience. They define *qualia* as "intrinsic or monadic properties of our sensations discriminated in introspection" (p. 349), and argue very plausibly that functionalists should not be afraid to admit the existence of qualia because they can be given a perfectly good role within the network of causal relations into which a functionalist would analyze perception. When qualia such as those occurring with pain (e.g., a toothache) or temperature perception (e.g., feeling hot) are regular enough to be reliable indicators of an objective situation calling for a specific kind of response on our part (e.g., seeing a dentist or removing one's hand from a surface), they play a useful, adaptive role in our lives. Descartes too gives this kind of functional analysis of sensations in *Meditation 6* (see Reading 1) to explain why a truthful and all-powerful God would give us pain, hunger, thirst and other such "confused" ideas of certain kinds of physical events in our bodies and environments. Like Descartes, the Churchlands regard these qualia as fuzzy or cognitively deficient: "To be sure, they would be opaquely discriminated. . ." (p. 354). The reason for this opaqueness is, they tell us, the same as the reason why we don't perceive color or temperature as what they *really* are (according to physical science):

> . . . our mechanisms of sensory discrimination are of insufficient resolution to reveal on their own the intricacies discovered by other means. Unambiguous perception of molecular KE [the kinetic energy of molecules that causes us to have temperature sensation] would require sensory apparatus capable of resolving down to about 10^{-10} metres, and of tracking particles having the velocity of rifle bullets, millions of them, simultaneously. . . . [There is] no reason why the epistemological story told for the faculty of inner sense [introspection] should be significantly different from the story told for outer sense. Qualia, therefore, are not an ineffable mystery, any more than colors or temperatures are. (p. 354)

This way of reducing the sensuous, qualitative aspect of the world around us to its mathematically analyzable and (therefore) scientifically intelligible aspect has a venerable pedigree going back at least to John Locke's *An Essay Concerning Human Understanding* (1690):

> Had we senses acute enough to discern the minute particles of bodies and the real constitution on which their sensible qualities depends, I doubt not but they would produce quite different *ideas* in us; and that which is now the yellow colour of gold would then disappear, and instead of it we should see an admirable texture of parts, of a certain size and figure. This microscopes plainly discover to us. . . . (II, XXIII, 11)

The authors argue very plausibly that qualia, despite the causal role they do play in our perceptual systems, are *not* essential to the type-identity of such things as pain and sensations of warmth. The qualitative distinctness of toothaches from burning sensations shows that what ties together all the inner states labeled *pain* is the functional role they have in common. Because qualia are "opaque," it is good for functionalism to be able to exclude them from an account of the type-identity of inner states because such an account would be muddied by their opaqueness.

The Churchlands may have served *functionalism* well by enabling it to claim that qualia are both real and functional yet don't belong in a functionalist account of the type-identity of inner states. However, it's unclear whether the Churchlands' explanation about the opaqueness of qualia works as well for their professed *materialism*. Recall Keith Campbell's question about the ontological status of the fuzzy content of our low-grade awareness of what *appears* to us as a searing pain but is *really* a 60 Hz spiking frequency in some set of neurons:

> It leaves us with a set of *seemings,* acts of imperfect apprehension, in which the phenomenal properties are grasped. So that we must ask the new question: Is it possible that things can *seem to be* in a certain way to a merely material system? Is there a way in which acts of imperfect apprehension can be seen to be ontically neutral? (Reading 23, pp. 336–337)

From Campbell's perspective, the Churchlands seem to say that appearances *really happen* in a materialist universe that *excludes* them.

REVIEW QUESTION

Look at the argument in the section of Reading 23 titled "The Causal Theory of Mind Amended," in which Campbell argues against the kind of position taken by the Churchlands regarding the perception of phenomenal parties. What do you think, and why?

26

Can We Solve the
Mind-Body Problem?

Colin McGinn

> How it is that anything so remarkable as a state of consciousness comes about as a result of initiating nerve tissue, is just as unaccountable as the appearance of the Djin, where Aladdin rubbed his lamp in the story.—T. H. Huxley

Colin McGinn teaches philosophy at Rutgers University. His recent publications include *Minds and Bodies: Philosophers and Their Ideas* (1997) and *The Problem of Consciousness: Essays Towards a Resolution* (1993).

As he acknowledges in his final note, McGinn is pursuing the problem of consciousness from a perspective he inherited from Thomas Nagel (see Reading 22). He and Nagel share a kind of "realism" according to which there is more to the world than what our human cognitive capacities may ever be able to apprehend. They agree that current physicalist philosophy of mind has been unable to make intelligible "consciousness," the what-it-is-like aspect of experience, including awareness of qualia. However, where Nagel leaves the door open (by a crack at least) to future progress in understanding how consciousness can be an aspect of brain processes, McGinn will argue that human cognitive capacities are *essentially* incapable of understanding what he calls the "psychophysical nexus." Because of these limitations, McGinn argues, we should be agnostic about consciousness and avoid taking metaphysical positions about qualia such as physicalism or Jackson's epiphenomenalism.

We have been trying for a long time to solve the mind–body problem. It has stubbornly resisted our best efforts. The mystery persists. I think the time has come to admit candidly that we cannot resolve the mystery. But I also think that this very insolubility—or the reason for it—removes the philosophical problem. In this paper I explain why I say these outrageous things.

The specific problem I want to discuss concerns consciousness, the hard nut of the mind-body problem. How is it possible for conscious states to depend upon brain states? How can [T]echnicolor **phenomenology** arise from soggy grey matter? What makes the bodily organ we call the brain so radically different from other bodily organs, say the kidneys—the body parts without a trace of con-

From: Colin McGinn, "Can We Solve the Mind-Body Problem?", *Mind* V, xcviii, no. 391 (July, 1989): 349–366. © Oxford University Press 1989. Reprinted with permission of the publisher.

sciousness? How could the aggregation of millions of individually insentient neurons generate subjective awareness? We know that brains are the *de facto* causal basis of consciousness, but we have, it seems, no understanding whatever of how this can be so. It strikes us as miraculous, eerie, even faintly comic. Somehow, we feel, the water of the physical brain is turned into the wine of consciousness, but we draw a total blank on the nature of this conversion. Neural transmissions just seem like the wrong kind of materials with which to bring consciousness into the world, but it appears that in some way they perform this mysterious feat. The mind-body problem is the problem of understanding how the miracle is wrought, thus removing the sense of deep mystery. We want to take the magic out of the link between consciousness and the brain.[1]

Purported solutions to the problem have tended to assume one of two forms. One form, which we may call constructive, attempts to specify some natural property of the brain (or body) which explains how consciousness can be elicited from it. Thus functionalism, for example, suggests a property—namely, causal role—which is held to be satisfied by both brain states and mental states; this property is supposed to explain how conscious states can come from brain states.[2] The other form, which

has been historically dominant,[3] frankly admits that nothing merely natural could do the job, and suggests instead that we invoke supernatural entities or divine interventions. Thus we have Cartesian dualism and Leibnizian pre-established harmony. These "solutions" at least recognize that something pretty remarkable is needed if the mind-body relation is to be made sense of; they are as extreme as the problem. The approach I favor is naturalistic but not constructive: I do not believe we can ever specify what it is about the brain that is responsible for consciousness, but I am sure that whatever it is it is not inherently miraculous. The problem arises, I want to suggest, because we are cut off by our very cognitive constitution from achieving a conception of that natural property of the brain (or of consciousness) that accounts for the psychophysical link. This is a kind of causal nexus that we are precluded from ever understanding, given the way we have to form our concepts and develop our theories. No wonder we find the problem so difficult!

Before I can hope to make this view plausible, I need to sketch the general conception of cognitive competence that underlies my position. Let me introduce the idea of *cognitive closure*. A type of mind M is cognitively closed with respect to a property P (or theory T) if and only if the concept-forming procedures at M's disposal cannot extend to a grasp of P (or an understanding of T). Conceiving minds come in different kinds, equipped with varying powers and limitations, biases and blindspots, so that properties (or theories) may be accessible to some minds but not to others. What is closed to the mind of a rat may be open to the mind of a monkey, and what is open to us may be closed to the monkey. Representational power is not all or nothing. Minds are biological products like bodies, and like bodies they come in different shapes and sizes, more or less capacious, more or less suited to certain cognitive tasks.[4] This is particularly clear for

---

[1] One of the peculiarities of the mind-body problem is the difficulty of formulating it in a rigorous way. We have a sense of the problem that outruns our capacity to articulate it clearly. Thus we quickly find ourselves resorting to invitations to look inward, instead of specifying precisely *what* it is about consciousness that makes it inexplicable in terms of ordinary physical properties. And this can make it seem that the problem is spurious. A creature without consciousness would not properly appreciate the problem (assuming such a creature could appreciate other problems). I think an adequate treatment of the mind-body problem should explain why it is so hard to state the problem explicitly. My treatment locates our difficulty in our inadequate conceptions of the nature of the brain and consciousness. In fact, if we knew their natures fully we would already have solved the problem. This should become clear later.

[2] I would also classify panpsychism as a constructive solution, since it attempts to explain consciousness in terms of properties of the brain that are as natural as consciousness itself. Attributing specks of proto-consciousness to the constituents of matter is not supernatural in the way postulating immaterial substances or divine interventions is; it is merely extravagant. I shall here be assuming that panpsychism, like all other extant constructive solutions, is inadequate as an answer to the mind-body problem, as (of course) are the supernatural "solutions." I am speaking to those who still feel perplexed (almost everyone, I would think, at least in his heart).

---

[3] Dualism of the Cartesian or interactionist sort has been dominant over the past two millennia, but certainly not in the twentieth century. ED.

[4] This kind of view of cognitive capacity is forcefully advocated by Noam Chomsky (1975) in *Reflections on Language* and by Jerry Fodor (1983) in *The Modularity of Mind*. Chomsky distinguishes between "problems," which human minds are in principle equipped to solve, and "mysteries," which systematically elude our understanding; and he envisages a study of our cognitive systems that would chart these powers and

perceptual faculties, of course: perceptual closure is hardly to be denied. Different species are capable of perceiving different properties of the world, and no species can perceive every property things may instantiate (without artificial instrumentation anyway). But such closure does not reflect adversely on the reality of the properties that lie outside the representational capacities in question; a property is no less real for not being reachable from a certain kind of perceiving and conceiving mind. The invisible parts of the electromagnetic spectrum are just as real as the visible parts, and whether a specific kind of creature can form conceptual representations of these imperceptible parts does not determine whether they exist. Thus cognitive closure with respect to P does not imply irrealism about P. That P is (as we might say) *noumenal*[5] for M does not show that P does not occur in some naturalistic scientific theory T. It shows only that T is not cognitively accessible to M. Presumably monkey minds and the property of being an electron illustrate this possibility. And the question must arise as to whether human minds are closed with respect to certain true explanatory theories. Nothing, at least, in the concept of reality shows that everything real is open to the human concept-forming faculty—if, that is, we are realists[6] about reality.[7]

Consider a mind constructed according to the principles of classical empiricism, a Humean mind. Hume mistakenly thought that human minds were Humean, but we can at least conceive of such a mind (perhaps dogs and monkeys have Humean minds). A Humean mind is such that perceptual closure determines cognitive closure, since "ideas" must always be copies of "impressions"; therefore

the concept-forming system cannot transcend what can be perceptually presented to the subject. Such a mind will be closed with respect to unobservables; the properties of atoms, say, will not be representable by a mind constructed in this way. This implies that explanatory theories in which these properties are essentially mentioned will not be accessible to a Humean mind.[8] And hence the observable phenomena that are explained by allusion to unobservables will be inexplicable by a mind thus limited. But notice: the incapacity to explain certain phenomena does not carry with it a lack of recognition of the theoretical problems the phenomena pose. You might be able to appreciate a problem without being able to formulate (even in principle) the solution to that problem (I suppose human children are often in this position, at least for a while). A Humean mind cannot solve the problems that our physics solves, yet it might be able to have an inkling of what needs to be explained. We would expect, then, that a moderately intelligent inquiring Humean mind will feel permanently perplexed and mystified by the physical world, since the correct science is forever beyond its cognitive reach. Indeed, something like this was precisely the view of Locke. He thought that our ideas of matter are quite sharply constrained by our perceptions and so concluded that the true science of matter is eternally beyond us, that we could never remove our perplexities about (say) what solidity ultimately is.[9] But it does not follow for Locke that nature is itself inherently mysterious; the felt mystery comes from our own cognitive limitations, not from any objective eeriness in the world. It looks today as if Locke was wrong about our capacity to fathom the nature of the physical world, but we can still learn from his fundamental thought: the insistence that our cognitive faculties may not be up to solving every problem that con-

---

limitations. I am here engaged in such a study, citing the mind-body problem as falling on the side of the mysteries.

[5] This term was used by Immanuel Kant (1724–1804) to refer to objects that we can think about and assume the existence of, but which the limitations of our cognitive powers prevent us from coming to know. ED.

[6] To be a realist about reality is to think of reality as what exists independently of the human mind. ED.

[7] See Thomas Nagel's discussion of realism in *The View From Nowhere* (1986, ch. 6). He argues there for the possibility of properties we can never grasp. Combining Nagel's realism with Chomsky-Fodor cognitive closure gives a position looking very much like Locke's in the *Essay Concerning Human Understanding*: the idea that our God-given faculties do not equip us to fathom the deep truth about reality. In fact, Locke held precisely this about the relation between mind and brain: only divine revelation could enable us to understand how "perceptions" are produced in our minds by material objects.

[8] Hume, of course, argued, in effect, that no theory essentially employing a notion of objective causal necessitation could be grasped by our minds—and likewise for the notion of objective persistence. We might compare the frustrations of the Humean mind to the conceptual travails of the pure sound beings discussed in ch. 2 of P. F. Strawson's *Individuals* (1959); both are types of mind whose constitution puts various concepts beyond them. We can do a lot better than these truncated minds, but we also have our constitutional limitations.

[9] See the *Essay*, Book II, ch. IV. Locke compares the project of saying what solidity ultimately is to trying to clear up a blind man's vision by talking to him.

fronts us. To put the point more generally: the human mind may not conform to empiricist principles, but it must conform to *some* principles, and it is a substantive claim that these principles permit the solution of every problem we can formulate or sense. Total cognitive openness is not guaranteed for human beings and it should not be expected. Yet what is noumenal for us may not be miraculous in itself. We should therefore be alert to the possibility that a problem that strikes us as deeply intractable, as utterly baffling, may arise from an area of cognitive closure in our ways of representing the world.[10] That is what I now want to argue is the case with our sense of the mysterious nature of the connection between consciousness and the brain. We are biased away from arriving at the correct explanatory theory of the psychophysical nexus. And this makes us prone to an illusion of objective mystery. Appreciating this should remove the philosophical problem: consciousness does not, in reality, arise from the brain in the miraculous way in which the djin arises from the lamp.

I now need to establish three things: (1) there exists some property of the brain that accounts naturalistically for consciousness; (2) we are cognitively closed with respect to that property; but (3) there is no philosophical (as opposed to scientific) mind-body problem. Most of the work will go into establishing (2).

Resolutely shunning the supernatural, I think it is undeniable that it must be in virtue of *some* natural property of the brain that organisms are conscious. There just *has* to be some explanation for how brains subserve minds. If we are not to be eliminativists about consciousness, then some theory must exist which accounts for the psychophysical correlations we observe. It is implausible to take these correlations as ultimate and inexplicable facts, as simply brute[11]. And we do not want to ac-

knowledge radical **emergence** of the conscious with respect to the cerebral: that is too much like accepting miracles *de re*. Brain states cause conscious states, we know, and this causal nexus must proceed through necessary connections of some kind, the kind that would make the nexus intelligible *if* they were understood.[12] Consciousness is like life in this respect. We know that life evolved from inorganic matter, so we expect there to be some explanation of this process. We cannot plausibly take the arrival of life as a primitive brute fact, nor can we accept that life arose by some form of miraculous emergence. Rather, there must be some natural account of how life comes from matter, whether or not we can know it. Eschewing vitalism and the magic touch of God's finger, we rightly insist that it must be in virtue of some natural property of (organized) matter that parcels of it get to be alive. But consciousness itself is just a further biological development, and so it too must be susceptible of some natural explanation—whether or not human beings are capable of arriving at this explanation. Presumably there exist objective natural laws that somehow account for the upsurge of consciousness. Consciousness, in short, must be a natural phenomenon, naturally arising from certain organizations of matter. Let us then say that there exists some property P, instantiated by the brain, in virtue of which the brain is the basis of consciousness. Equivalently, there exists some theory T, referring to P, which fully explains the dependence of conscious states on brain states. If we knew T, then we would have a constructive solution to the mind-body problem. The question then is whether we can ever come to know T and grasp the nature of P.

Let me first observe that it is surely *possible* that we could never arrive at a grasp of P; there is, as I said, no guarantee that our cognitive powers permit the solution of every problem we can recognize. Only a misplaced idealism about the natural world could warrant the dogmatic claim that everything is knowable by the human species at this stage of its evolutionary development (consider the same claim made on behalf of the intellect of Cro-Magnon man). It *may* be that every property for which we

---

[10] Some of the more arcane aspects of cosmology and quantum theory might be thought to lie just within the bounds of human intelligibility. Chomsky suggests that the causation of behavior might be necessarily mysterious to human investigators (see Chomsky [*Reflections on Language*], 1975, p. 156). I myself believe that the mind-body problem exhibits a qualitatively different level of mystery from this case (unless it is taken as an aspect of that problem).

[11] Some might see this as a very fine distinction: for McGinn the key word seems to be "ultimately." Psychophysical correlations are not ultimately brute or absolutely inexplicable (some more powerful mind might understand them), but human cognitive closure leaves them unintelligible to *us*. ED.

[12] Cf. Nagel's discussion of emergence in "Panpsychism," in *Mortal Questions* (1979). I agree with him that the apparent radical emergence of mind from matter has to be epistemic only, on pain of accepting inexplicable miracles in the world.

can form a concept is such that *it* could never solve the mind-body problem. We *could* be like 5-year-old children trying to understand Relativity Theory. Still, so far this is just a possibility claim: what reason do we have for asserting, positively, that our minds are closed with respect to P?

Longstanding historical failure is suggestive, but scarcely conclusive. Maybe, it will be said, the solution is just around the corner, or it has to wait upon the completion of the physical sciences? Perhaps we simply have yet to produce the Einstein-like genius who will restructure the problem in some clever way and then present an astonished world with the solution?[13] However, I think that our deep bafflement about the problem, amounting to a vertiginous sense of ultimate mystery, which resists even articulate formulation, should at least encourage us to explore the idea that there is something terminal about our perplexity. Rather as traditional theologians found themselves conceding cognitive closure with respect to certain of the properties of God, so we should look seriously at the idea that the mind-body problem brings us bang up against the limits of our capacity to understand the world. That is what I shall do now.

There seems to be two possible avenues open to us in our aspiration to identify P: we could try to get to P by investigating consciousness directly, or we could look to the study of the brain for P. Let us consider these in turn, starting with consciousness. Our acquaintance with consciousness could hardly be more direct; phenomenological description thus comes (relatively) easily. "Introspection" is the name of the faculty through which we catch consciousness in all its vivid nakedness. By virtue of possessing this cognitive faculty we ascribe concepts of consciousness to ourselves; we thus have "immediate access" to the properties of consciousness. But does the introspective faculty reveal property P? Can we tell just by introspecting what the solution to the mind-body problem is? Clearly not. We have direct cognitive access to one term of the mind-

brain relation, but we do not have such access to the nature of the link. Introspection does not present conscious states *as* depending upon the brain in some intelligible way. We cannot therefore introspect P. Moreover, it seems impossible that we should ever augment our stock of introspectively ascribed concepts with the concept P, that is, we could not acquire this concept simply on the basis of sustained and careful introspection. Pure phenomenology will never provide the solution to the mind-body problem. Neither does it seem feasible to try to extract P from the concepts of consciousness we now have by some procedure of conceptual analysis—any more than we could solve the life-matter problem simply by reflecting on the concept *life*.[14] P has to lie outside the field of the introspectable, and it is not implicitly contained in the concepts we bring to bear in our first-person ascriptions. Thus the faculty of introspection, as a concept-forming capacity, is cognitively closed with respect to P; which is not surprising in view of its highly limited domain of operation (*most* properties of the world are closed to introspection).

But there is a further point to be made about P and consciousness, which concerns our restricted access to the concepts of consciousness themselves. It is a familiar point that the range of concepts of consciousness attainable by a mind M is constrained by the specific forms of consciousness possessed by M. Crudely, you cannot form concepts of conscious properties unless you yourself instantiate those properties. The man born blind cannot grasp the concept of a visual experience of red, and human beings cannot conceive of the echolocatory experiences of bats.[15] These are cases of cognitive

---

[13] Despite his reputation for pessimism over the mind-body problem, a careful reading of Nagel reveals an optimistic strain in his thought (by the standards of the present paper): see, in particular, the closing remarks of "What is it like to be a bat?" (Nagel, 1979). Nagel speculates that we might be able to devise an "objective phenomenology" that made conscious states more amenable to physical analysis. Unlike me, he does not regard the problem as inherently beyond us.

[14] This is perhaps the most remarkably optimistic view of all—the expectation that reflecting on the ordinary concept of pain (say) will reveal the manner of pain's dependence on the brain. If I am not mistaken, this is in effect the view of commonsense functionalists: they think that P consists in causal role, and that this can be inferred analytically from the concepts of conscious states. This would make it truly amazing that we should ever have felt there to be a mind-body problem at all, since the solution is already contained in our mental concepts. What optimism!

[15] See "What is it like to be a bat?" (Nagel, 1979). [Reading 22—ED.] Notice that the fugitive character of such properties with respect to our concepts has nothing to do with their "complexity"; like fugitive color properties, such experiential properties are "simple.' Note too that such properties provide counterexamples to the claim the (somehow) rationality is a faculty that, once possessed, can be extended to encompass all concepts, so that if *any* concept can be possessed then *every* concept can.

closure within the class of conscious properties. But now this kind of closure will, it seems, affect our hopes of access to P. For suppose that we were cognitively open with respect to P; suppose, that is, that we had the solution to the problem of how specific forms of consciousness depend upon different kinds of physiological structure. Then, of course, we would understand how the brain of a bat subserves the subjective experiences of bats. Call this type of experience B, and call the explanatory property that links B to the bat's brain PI. By grasping PI it would be perfectly intelligible to us how the bat's brain generates B-experiences; we would have an explanatory theory of the causal nexus in question. We would be in possession of the same kind of understanding we would have of our own experiences if we had the correct psychophysical theory of them. But then it seems to follow that grasp of the theory that explains B-experiences would *confer* a grasp of the nature of those experiences: for how could we understand that theory without understanding the concept B that occurs in it? How could we grasp the *nature* of B-experiences without grasping the *character* of those experiences? The true psychophysical theory would seem to provide a route to a grasp of the subjective form of the bat's experiences. But now we face a dilemma, a dilemma which threatens to become a reductio: either we *can* grasp this theory, in which case the property B becomes open to us; or we *cannot* grasp the theory, simply because property B is *not* open to us. It seems to me that the looming reductio here is compelling: our concepts of consciousness just *are* inherently constrained by our own form of consciousness, so that any theory the understanding of which required us to transcend these constraints would *ipso facto* be inaccessible to us. Similarly, I think, any theory that required us to transcend the finiteness of our cognitive capacities would *ipso facto* be a theory we could not grasp, and this despite the fact that it might be needed to explain something we can see needs explaining. We cannot simply stipulate that our concept-forming abilities are indefinitely plastic and unlimited just because they would have to be to enable us to grasp the truth about the world. We constitutionally lack the concept-forming capacity to encompass all possible types of conscious state, and this obstructs our path to a general solution to the mind-body prob-

lem.[16] Even if we could solve it for our own case, we could not solve it for bats and Martians. P is, as it were, too close to the different forms of subjectivity for it to be accessible to all such forms, given that one's form of subjectivity restricts one's concepts of subjectivity.[17]

I suspect that most optimists about constructively solving the mind-body problem will prefer to place their bets on the brain side of the relation. Neuroscience is the place to look for property P, they will say. My question then is whether there is any conceivable way in which we might come to introduce P in the course of our empirical investigations of the brain. New concepts have been introduced in the effort to understand the workings of the brain, certainly; could not P then occur in conceivable extensions of this manner of introduction? So far, indeed, the theoretical concepts we ascribe to the brain seem as remote from consciousness as any ordinary physical properties are, but perhaps we might reach P by diligent application of essentially the same procedures: so it is tempting to think. I want to suggest, to the contrary, that such procedures are inherently closed with respect to P. The fundamental reason for this, I think, is the role of *perception* in shaping our understanding of the brain—the way that our perception of the brain constrains the concepts we can apply to it. A point whose significance it would be hard to overstress here is this: the property of consciousness itself (or specific conscious states) is not an observable or

---

[16] Imagine a species of organisms that had language, and could reliably discern the various geometrical figures such as triangles and rectangles, but could not do geometry, or could understand only a few of the most basic theorems. We would want to say that their *concepts* of these figures were inferior to ours, since they don't enable these organisms to derive much that is true about those concepts. Perhaps our self-based concept of consciousness is like that. ED.

[17] It might be suggested that we borrow Nagel's idea of "objective phenomenology" in order to get around this problem. Instead of representing experiences under subjective descriptions, we should describe them in entirely objective terms, thus bringing them within our conceptual ken. My problem with this is that, even allowing that there could be such a form of description, it would not permit us to understand how the subjective aspects of experience depend upon the brain, which is really the problem we are trying to solve. In fact, I doubt that the notion of objective phenomenology is any more coherent than the notion of subjective physiology. Both involve trying to bridge the psychophysical gap by a sort of stipulation. The lesson here is that the gap cannot be bridged just by applying concepts drawn from one side to items that belong on the other side; and this is because neither sort of concept could ever do what is needed.

perceptible property of the brain. You can stare into a living conscious brain, your own or someone else's, and see there a wide variety of instantiated properties—its shape, colour, texture, etc.—but you will not thereby *see* what the subject is experiencing, the conscious state itself. Conscious states are simply not potential objects of perception: they depend upon the brain but they cannot be observed by directing the senses on to the brain. In other words, consciousness is noumenal with respect to perception of the brain.[18] I take it this is obvious. So we know there *are* properties of the brain that are necessarily closed to perception of the brain; the question now is whether P is likewise closed to perception.

My argument will proceed as follows. I shall first argue that P is indeed perceptually closed; then I shall complete the argument to full cognitive closure by insisting that no form of *inference* from what is perceived can lead us to P. The argument for perceptual closure starts from the thought that nothing we can imagine perceiving in the brain would ever convince us that we have located the intelligible nexus we seek. No matter what recondite property we could see to be instantiated in the brain we would always be baffled about how it could give rise to consciousness. I hereby invite you to try to conceive of a perceptible property of the brain that might allay the feeling of mystery that attends our contemplation of the brain-mind link: I do not think you will be able to do it. It is like trying to conceive of a perceptible property of a rock that would render it perspicuous that the rock was conscious. In fact, I think it is the very impossibility of this that lies at the root of the mind-body problem. But why is this? Basically, I think, it is because the senses are geared to representing a spatial world; they essentially present things in space with spatially defined properties. But it is precisely *such* properties that seem inherently incapable of resolving the mind-body problem: we cannot link consciousness to the brain in virtue of spatial properties of the

brain. There the brain is, an object of perception, laid out in space, containing spatially distributed processes; but consciousness defies explanation in such terms.[19] Consciousness does not seem made up out of smaller spatial processes; yet perception of the brain seems limited to revealing such processes.[20] The senses are responsive to certain *kinds* of properties—those that are essentially bound up with space—but these properties are of the wrong sort (the wrong *category*) to constitute P. Kant was right, the form of outer sensibility is spatial; but if so, then P will be noumenal with respect to the senses, since no spatial property will ever deliver a satisfying answer to the mind-body problem. We simply do not understand the idea that conscious states might intelligibly arise from spatial configurations of the kind disclosed by perception of the world.

I take it this claim will not seem terribly controversial. After all, we do not generally expect that every property referred to in our theories should be a potential object of human perception: consider quantum theory and cosmology. Unrestricted perceptual openness is a dogma of empiricism if ever there was one. And there is no compelling reason to suppose that the property needed to explain the mind-brain relation should be in principle perceptible; it might be essentially "theoretical," an object of thought, not sensory experience. Looking harder at nature is not the only way of discovering its theoretically significant properties. Perceptual closure does not entail cognitive closure, since we have available the procedure of hypothesis formation, in which *un*observables come to be conceptualized.

I readily agree with these sentiments, but I think there are reasons for believing that no coher-

---

[18] We should distinguish two claims about the imperceptibility of consciousness: (1) consciousness is not perceivable by directing the senses onto the brain; (2) consciousness is not perceivable by directing the senses anywhere, even towards the behavior that "expresses" conscious states. I believe both theses, but my present point requires only (1). I am assuming, of course, that perception cannot be unrestrictedly theory-laden; or that if it can, the infusions of theory cannot have been originally derived simply by looking at things or tasting them or touching them or . . .

[19] In these sentences McGinn sounds very much like Descartes in the *Sixth Meditation* (Reading 1): "It is true that I may have (or, to anticipate, that I certainly have) a body that is very closely joined to me. But nevertheless, on the one hand I have a clear and distinct idea of myself, in so far as I am simply a thinking, non-extended thing; and on the other hand I have a distinct idea of body, in so far as this is simply an extended, non-thinking thing. And accordingly, it is certain that I am really distinct from my body, and can exist without it." ED.

[20] Nagel discusses the difficulty of thinking of conscious processes in the spatial terms that apply to the brain in *The View From Nowhere* (1986, pp. 50–1), but he does not draw my despairing conclusion. The case is exactly *unlike* (say) the dependence of liquidity on the properties of molecules, since here we do think of both terms of the relation as spatial in character; so we can simply employ the idea of spatial composition.

ent method of concept introduction will ever lead us to P. This is because a certain principle of *homogeneity* operates in our introduction of theoretical concepts on the basis of observation. Let me first note that consciousness itself could not be introduced simply on the basis of what we observe about the brain and its physical effects. If our data, arrived at by perception of the brain, do not include anything that brings in conscious states, then the theoretical properties we need to explain these data will not include conscious states either. Inference to the best explanation of purely physical data will never take us outside the realm of the physical, forcing us to introduce concepts of consciousness.[21] Everything physical has a purely physical explanation. So the property of consciousness is cognitively closed with respect to the introduction of concepts by means of inference to the best explanation of perceptual data about the brain.

Now the question is whether P could ever be arrived at by this kind of inference. Here we must be careful to guard against a form of magical *emergentism* with respect to concept formation. Suppose we try out a relatively clear theory of how theoretical concepts are formed; we get them by a sort of analogical extension of what we observe. Thus, for example, we arrive at the concept of a molecule by taking our perceptual representations of macroscopic objects and conceiving of smaller scale objects of the same general kind. This method seems to work well enough for unobservable material objects, but it will not help in arriving at P, since analogical extensions of the entities we observe in the brain are precisely as hopeless as the original entities were as solutions to the mind-body problem. We would need a method that left the base of observational properties behind in a much more radical way. But it seems to me that even a more unconstrained conception of inference to the best explanation would still not do what is required; it would no more serve to introduce P than it serves to introduce the property of consciousness itself. To explain the observed physical data we need only such theoretical properties as bear upon those data, not the property that explains consciousness, which

does not occur in the data. Since we do not need consciousness to explain those data, we do not need the property that explains consciousness. We will never get as far away from the perceptual data in our explanations of those data as we need to get in order to connect up explanatorily with consciousness. This is, indeed, why it seems that consciousness is theoretically *epiphenomenal* in the task of accounting for physical events. No concept needed to explain the workings of the physical world will suffice to explain how the physical world produces consciousness. So if P is perceptually noumenal, then it will be noumenal with respect to perception-based explanatory inferences. Accordingly, I do not think that P could be arrived at by empirical studies of the brain alone. Nevertheless, the brain *has* this property, as it has the property of consciousness. Only a magical idea of how we come by concepts could lead one to think that we can reach P by first perceiving the brain and then asking what is needed to explain what we perceive.[22] (The mind-body problem tempts us to magic in more ways than one.)

It will help elucidate the position I am driving towards if I contrast it with another view of the source of the perplexity we feel about the mind-brain nexus. I have argued that we cannot know which property of the brain accounts for consciousness, and so we find the mind-brain link unintelligible. But, it may be said, there is another account of our sense of irremediable mystery, which does not require positing properties our minds cannot represent. This alternative view claims that, even if we *now* had a grasp of P, we would *still* feel that there is something mysterious about the link, because of a special epistemological feature of the situation. Namely this: our acquaintance with the brain and our acquaintance with consciousness are necessarily mediated by distinct cognitive faculties, namely perception and introspection. Thus the faculty through which we apprehend one term of

---

[21] Cf. Nagel: 'it will never be legitimate to infer, as a theoretical explanation of physical phenomena alone, a property that includes or implies the consciousness of its subject,' 'Panpsychism,' in *Mortal Questions* (Nagel, 1979, p. 183).

[22] It is surely a striking fact that the microprocesses that have been discovered in the brain by the usual methods seem no nearer to consciousness than the gross properties of the brain open to casual inspection. Neither do more abstract "holistic" features of brain function seem to be on the right lines to tell us the nature of consciousness. The deeper science probes into the brain the more remote it seems to get from consciousness. Greater knowledge of the brain thus destroys our illusions about the kinds of properties that might be discovered by traveling along this path. Advanced neurophysiological theory seems only to deepen the miracle.

the relation is necessarily distinct from the faculty through which we apprehend the other. In consequence, it is not possible for us to use one of these faculties to apprehend the nature of the psychophysical nexus. No single faculty will enable us ever to apprehend the fact that consciousness depends upon the brain in virtue of property P. Neither perception alone nor introspection alone will ever enable us to witness the dependence. And this, my objector insists, is the real reason we find the link baffling: we cannot make sense of it in terms of the deliverances of a single cognitive faculty. So, even if we now had concepts for the properties of the brain that explain consciousness, we would still feel a residual sense of unintelligibility; we would still take there to be something mysterious going on. The necessity to shift from one faculty to the other produces in us an illusion of inexplicability. We might in fact have the explanation right now but be under the illusion that we do not. The right diagnosis, then, is that we should recognize the peculiarity of the epistemological situation and stop trying to make sense of the psychophysical nexus in the way we make sense of other sorts of nexus. It only *seems* to us that we can never discover a property that will render the nexus intelligible.[23]

I think this line of thought deserves to be taken seriously, but I doubt that it correctly diagnoses our predicament. It is true enough that the problematic nexus is essentially apprehended by distinct faculties, so that it will never reveal its secrets to a single faculty; but I doubt that our intuitive sense of intelligibility is so rigidly governed by the "single-faculty condition." Why *should* facts only seem intelligible to us if we can conceive of apprehending them by one (sort of) cognitive faculty? Why not allow that we can recognize intelligible connections between concepts (or properties) even when those concepts (or properties) are necessarily ascribed using different faculties? Is it not suspiciously empiricist to insist that a causal nexus can only be made sense of by us if we can conceive of its being an object of a single faculty of apprehension? Would we think this of a nexus that called for touch and sight

to apprehend each term of the relation[24] Suppose (*per impossible*) that we were offered P on a plate, as a gift from God: would we still shake our heads and wonder how that could resolve the mystery, being still the victims of the illusion of mystery generated by the epistemological duality in question? No, I think this suggestion is not enough to account for the miraculous appearance of the link: it is better to suppose that we are permanently blocked from forming a concept of what accounts for that link.

How strong is the thesis I am urging? Let me distinguish *absolute* from *relative* claims of cognitive closure. A problem is absolutely cognitively closed if no possible mind could resolve it; a problem is relatively closed if minds of some sorts can in principle solve it while minds of other sorts cannot. Most problems, we may safely suppose, are only relatively closed; armadillo minds cannot solve problems of elementary arithmetic but human minds can. Should we say that the mind-body problem is only relatively closed or is the closure absolute? This depends on what we allow as a possible concept-forming mind, which is not an easy question. If we allow for minds that form their concepts of the brain and consciousness in ways that are quite independent of perception and introspection, then there may be room for the idea that there are possible minds for which the mind-body problem is soluble, and easily so. But if we suppose that *all* concept formation is tied to perception and introspection, however loosely, then *no* mind will be capable of understanding how it relates to its own body; the insolubility will be absolute. I think we can just about make sense of the former kind of mind, by exploiting our own faculty of a priori reasoning. Our mathematical concepts (say) do not seem tied either to perception or to introspection, so there does seem to be a mode of concept formation that operates without the constraints I identified earlier. The suggestion might then be that a mind that formed all of its concepts in this way—including its concepts of the brain and consciousness—would be free of the biases that prevent *us* from coming up with the right theory of how the two connect. Such a mind would have to be able to

---

[23] A materialist functionalist could take that position, claiming that the sought-for property *P* is accessible to research in psychology, that it will be a functional property embodied in brain processes whose causal operations will, of course, never seem like what we are introspectively aware of while they are occurring. ED.

[24] Is this an adequate analogy? Or are the differences between perception and introspection much greater than those between two modalities of perception? ED.

think of the brain and consciousness in ways that utterly prescind from the perceptual and the introspective, in somewhat the way we now (it seems) think about numbers. This mind would conceive of the psychophysical link in totally a priori terms. Perhaps this is how we should think of God's mind, and God's understanding of the mind-body relation. At any rate, something pretty radical is going to be needed if we are to devise a mind that can escape the kinds of closure that make the problem insoluble for us—if I am right in my diagnosis of our difficulty. *If* the problem is only relatively insoluble, then the type of mind that can solve it is going to be very different from ours and the kinds of mind we can readily make sense of (there may, of course, be cognitive closure here too[25]). It certainly seems to me to be at least an open question whether the problem is absolutely insoluble; I would not be surprised if it were.[26]

My position is both pessimistic and optimistic at the same time. It is pessimistic about the prospects for arriving at a constructive solution to the mind-body problem, but it is optimistic about our hopes of removing the philosophical perplexity. The central point here is that I do not think we need to do the former in order to achieve the latter. This depends on a rather special understanding of what the philosophical problem consists in. What I want to suggest is that the nature of the psychophysical connection has a full and non-mysterious explanation in a certain science, but that this science is inaccessible to us as a matter of principle. Call this explanatory scientific theory T: T is as natural and prosaic and devoid of miracle as any theory of nature; it describes the link between consciousness and the brain in a way that is no more remarkable (or alarming) than the way we now describe the link between the liver and bile.[27] According to T, there is nothing eerie going on in the world when an event in my visual cortex causes me to have an experience of yellow, however much it seems to *us* that there is. In other words, there is no intrinsic conceptual or metaphysical difficulty about how consciousness depends on the brain. It is not that the correct science is compelled to postulate miracles *de re;* it is rather that the correct science lies in the dark part of the world for us. We confuse our own cognitive limitations with objective eeriness. We are like a Humean mind trying to understand the physical world, or a creature without spatial concepts trying to understand the possibility of motion. This removes the philosophical problem because it assures us that the entities *themselves* pose no inherent philosophical difficulty. The case is unlike, for example, the problem of how the abstract world of numbers might be intelligibly related to the world of concrete knowing subjects: here the mystery seems intrinsic to the entities, not a mere artifact of our cognitive limitations or biases in trying to understand the relation.[28] It would not be plausible to suggest that there exists a science, whose theoretical concepts we cannot grasp, which completely resolves any sense of mystery that surrounds the question how the abstract becomes an object of knowledge for us. In this case, then, eliminativism[29] seems a live option. The *philosophical* problem about consciousness and the brain arises from a sense that we are compelled to accept that nature contains miracles, as if the merely metallic lamp of the brain could really spirit into existence the Djin

---

[25]I.e., our sort of mind may, because of its characteristic limitations, be unable even to conceive of the kind of mind that could understand the mind-body nexus. ED.

[26]The kind of limitation I have identified is therefore not the kind that could be remedied simply by a large increase in general intelligence. No matter how large the frontal lobes of our biological descendants may become, they will still be stumped by the mind-body problem, so long as they form their (empirical) concepts on the basis of perception and introspection.

[27]Or again, no more miraculous than the theory of evolution. Creationism is an understandable response to the theoretical problem posed by the existence of complex organisms; fortunately, we now have a theory that renders this response unnecessary, and so undermines the theism

required by the creationist thesis. In the case of consciousness, the appearance of miracle might also tempt us in a "creationist" direction, with God required to perform the alchemy necessary to transform matter into experience. Thus the mind-body problem might similarly be used to prove the existence of God (no miracle without a miracle-maker). We cannot, I think, refute this argument in the way we can the original creationist argument, namely by actually producing a non-miraculous explanatory theory, but we can refute it by arguing that such a naturalistic theory must *exist.* (It is a condition of adequacy upon any account of the mind-body relation that it avoid assuming theism.)

[28]See Paul Benacerraf (1973) [Mathematical Truth] for a statement of this problem about abstract entities. Another problem that seems to me to differ from the mind-body problem is the problem of free will. I do not believe that there is some unknowable property Q which reconciles free will with determinism (or indeterminism); rather, the concept of free will contains internal incoherencies, as the concept of consciousness does not. This is why it is much more reasonable to be an eliminativist about free will than about consciousness.

[29]McGinn is saying that in the case of numbers there is good reason to consider an ontology that excludes numbers as real entities. ED.

of consciousness. But we do not need to accept this: we can rest secure in the knowledge that some (unknowable) property of the brain makes everything fall into place. What creates the philosophical puzzlement is the assumption that the problem must somehow be scientific but that any science *we* can come up with will represent things as utterly miraculous. And the solution is to recognize that the sense of miracle comes from us and not from the world. There is, in reality, nothing mysterious about how the brain generates consciousness. There is no *metaphysical* problem.[30]

So far that deflationary claim has been justified by a general naturalism and certain considerations about cognitive closure and the illusions it can give rise to. Now I want to marshall some reasons for thinking that consciousness is actually a rather simple natural fact; objectively, consciousness is nothing very special. We should now be comfortable with the idea that our own sense of difficulty is a fallible guide to objective complexity; what is hard for us to grasp may not be very fancy in itself. The grain of our thinking is not a mirror held up to the facts of nature.[31] In particular, it may be that the extent of our understanding of facts about the mind is not commensurate with some objective estimate of their intrinsic complexity: we may be good at understanding the mind in some of its aspects but hopeless with respect to others, in a way that cuts across objective differences in what the aspects involve. Thus we are adept at understanding action in terms of the folk psychology of belief and desire, and we seem not entirely out of our depth when it comes to devising theories of language. But our understanding of how consciousness develops from

the organization of matter is nonexistent. But now, think of these various aspects of mind from the point of view of evolutionary biology. Surely language and the propositional attitudes are more complex and advanced evolutionary achievements than the mere possession of consciousness by a physical organism. Thus it seems that we are better at understanding some of the more complex aspects of mind than the simpler ones. Consciousness arises early in evolutionary history and is found right across the animal kingdom. In some respects it seems that the biological engineering required for consciousness is less fancy than that needed for certain kinds of complex motor behavior. Yet we can come to understand the latter while drawing a total blank with respect to the former. Conscious states seem biologically quite primitive, comparatively speaking. So the theory T that explains the occurrence of consciousness in a physical world is very probably less objectively complex (by some standard) than a range of other theories that do not defy our intellects. If only we could know the psychophysical mechanism it might surprise us with its simplicity, its utter naturalness. In the manual that God consulted when he made the earth and all the beasts that dwell thereon the chapter about how to engineer consciousness from matter occurs fairly early on, well before the really difficult later chapters on mammalian reproduction and speech. It is not the *size* of the problem but its *type* that makes the mind-body problem so hard for us. This reflection should make us receptive to the idea that it is something about the tracks of our thought that prevents us from achieving a science that relates consciousness to its physical basis: the enemy lies within the gates.[32]

The position I have reached has implications for a tangle of intuitions it is natural to have regarding the mind-body relation. On the one hand, there are intuitions, pressed from Descartes to Kripke, to the effect that the relation between conscious states and bodily states is fundamentally contingent.[33] It

---

[30] A test of whether a proposed solution to the mind-body problem is adequate is whether it relieves the pressure towards eliminativism. If the data can only be explained by postulating a miracle (i.e., not explained), then we must repudiate the data; this is the principle behind the impulse to deny that conscious states exist. My proposal passes this test because it allows us to resist the postulation of miracles; it interprets the eeriness as merely epistemic, though deeply so. Constructive solutions are not the only way to relieve the pressure.

[31] Chomsky suggests that the very faculties of mind that make us good at some cognitive tasks may make us poor at others (see Chomsky [*Reflections on Language*], 1975, pp. 155–6). It seems to me possible that what makes us good at the science of the purely physical world is what skews us away from developing a science of consciousness. Our faculties bias us towards understanding matter in motion, but it is precisely this kind of understanding that is inapplicable to the mind-body problem. Perhaps, then, the price of being good at understanding matter is that we cannot understand mind. Certainly our notorious tendency to think of everything in spatial terms does not help us in understanding the mind.

[32] I get this phrase from Fodor [The Modularity of Mind,] (1983, p. 121). The intended contrast is with kinds of cognitive closure that stem from exogenous factors—as, say, in astronomy. Our problem with P is not that it is too distant or too small or too large or too complex; rather, the very structure of our concept-forming apparatus points us away from P.

[33] Saul Kripke, [Naming and Necessity,] (1980). Of course, Descartes explicitly argued from (what he took to be) the essential natures of the body and mind to the contingency of their connection. If we abandon the

can easily seem to us that there is no necessitation involved in the dependence of the mind on the brain. But, on the other hand, it looks absurd to try to dissociate the two entirely, to let the mind float completely free of the body. Disembodiment is a dubious possibility at best, and some kind of necessary supervenience of the mental on the physical has seemed undeniable to many. It is not my aim here to adjudicate this longstanding dispute; I want simply to offer a diagnosis of what is going on when one finds oneself assailed with this flurry of conflicting intuitions. The reason we feel the tug of contingency, pulling consciousness loose from its physical moorings, may be that we do not and cannot grasp the nature of the property that intelligibly links them. The brain has physical properties we can grasp, and variations in these correlate with changes in consciousness, but we cannot draw the veil that conceals the manner of their connection. Not grasping the nature of the connection, it strikes us as deeply contingent; we cannot make the assertion of a necessary connection intelligible to ourselves. There *may* then be a real necessary connection; it is just that it will always strike us as curiously brute and unperspicuous. We may thus, as upholders of intrinsic contingency, be the dupes of our own cognitive blindness. On the other hand, we are scarcely in a position to assert that there is a necessary connection between the properties of the brain we can grasp and states of consciousness, since we are so ignorant (and irremediably so) about the character of the connection. For all we know, the connection may be contingent, as access to P would reveal if we could have such access. The link between consciousness and property P is not, to be sure, contingent—virtually by definition—but we are not in a position to say exactly how P is related to the "ordinary" properties of the brain. It may be necessary or it may be contingent. Thus it is that we tend to vacillate between contingency and necessity; for we lack the conceptual resources to decide the question, or to understand the answer we are inclined to give. The indicated conclusion appears to be that we can never really know whether disembodiment is metaphysically possible, or whether necessary supervenience is the case, or whether **spectrum inversion** could occur. For these all involve claims about the **modal** connections between properties of consciousness and the ordinary properties of the body and brain that we can conceptualize; and the real nature of these connections is not accessible to us. Perhaps P makes the relation between C-fiber firing and pain necessary or perhaps it does not: we are simply not equipped to know. We are like a Humean mind wondering whether the observed link between the temperature of a gas and its pressure (at a constant volume) is necessary or contingent. To know the answer to that you need to grasp atomic (or molecular) theory, and a Humean mind just is not up to attaining the requisite theoretical understanding. Similarly, we are constitutionally ignorant at precisely the spot where the answer exists.

I predict that many readers of this paper will find its main thesis utterly incredible, even ludicrous. Let me remark that I sympathize with such readers: the thesis is not easily digestible. But I would say this: if the thesis is actually true, it will still strike us as hard to believe. For the idea of an explanatory property (or set of properties) that is noumenal for us, yet is essential for the (constructive) solution of a problem we face, offends a kind of natural idealism that tends to dominate our thinking. We find it taxing to conceive of the existence of a real property, under our noses as it were, which we are built not to grasp—a property that is responsible for phenomena that we observe in the most direct way possible. This kind of realism, which brings cognitive closure so close to home, is apt to seem both an affront to our intellects and impossible to get our minds around. We try to think of this unthinkable property and understandably fail in the effort; so we rush to infer that the very supposition of such a property is nonsensical. Realism of the kind I am presupposing thus seems difficult to hold in focus, and any philosophical theory that depends upon it will also seem to rest on something systematically elusive.[34] My response to such misgivings, however, is unconcessive: the limits of our

---

[34] This is the kind of realism defended by Nagel (1986) in ch. 6 of *The View From Nowhere*: to be is not to be conceivable by us. I would say that the mind-body problem provides a demonstration that there *are* such concept-transcending properties, not merely that there *could* be. I would also say that realism of this kind should be accepted precisely because it helps solve the mind-body problem; it is a metaphysical thesis that pulls its weight in coping with a problem that looks hopeless otherwise. There is thus nothing "epiphenomenal" about such radical realism: the existence of a reality we cannot know can yet have intellectual significance for us.

---

assumption that we know these natures, then agnosticism about the modality of the connection seems the indicated conclusion.

minds are just not the limits of reality. It is deplorably anthropocentric to insist that reality be constrained by what the human mind can conceive. We need to cultivate a vision of reality (a metaphysics) that makes it truly independent of our given cognitive powers, a conception that includes these powers as a proper part. It is just that, in the case of the mind-body problem, the bit of reality that systematically eludes our cognitive grasp is an aspect of our own nature. Indeed, it is an aspect that makes it possible for us to have minds at all and to think about how they are related to our bodies. This particular transcendent tract of reality happens to lie within our own heads. A deep fact about our own nature as a form of embodied consciousness is thus necessarily hidden from us. Yet there is nothing inherently eerie or bizarre about this embodiment. We are much more straightforward than we seem. Our weirdness lies in the eye of the beholder.

The answer to the question that forms my title is therefore "No and Yes."[35]

---

[35] Discussions with the following people have helped me work out the ideas of this paper: Anita Avramides, Jerry Katz, Ernie LePore, Michael Levin, Thomas Nagel, Galen Strawson, Peter Unger. My large debt to Nagel's work should be obvious throughout the paper: I would not have tried to face the mind-body problem down had he not first faced up to it.

REFERENCES

Benacerraf, P. (1973) "Mathematical truth," *Journal of Philosophy* 70, pp. 661–79.

Chomsky, N. (1975) *Reflections on Language,* New York: Pantheon Press.

Fodor, J. (1983) *The Modularity of Mind: an Essay on Faculty Psychology,* Cambridge, Mass.: Bradford Books/MIT Press.

Kripke, S. (1980) *Naming and Necessity,* Oxford: Blackwell.

McGinn, C. (1991) *The Problem of Consciousness: Essays Towards Resolution,* Oxford: Blackwell.

McGinn, C. (1993) *Problems in Philosophy,* Oxford: Blackwell.

Nagel, T. (1979) *Mortal Questions,* Cambridge: Cambridge University Press.

Nagel, T. (1986) *The View from Nowhere,* Oxford and New York: Oxford University Press.

Strawson, P. F. (1959) *Individuals: an Essay in Descriptive Metaphysics,* London: Methuen.

Like Nagel, McGinn regards *consciousness* as the core or "hard nut" of the perennial mind-body problem. Both regard consciousness as a widespread phenomenon, present in humans, bats, snakes, bees, and perhaps in any animal with a nervous system. After delivering his message that our human cognitive powers aren't up to the task of understanding consciousness, McGinn consoles us with the thought that "consciousness is actually a rather simple natural fact; objectively, consciousness is nothing very special" (p. 378) It developed rather early in evolution, long before such sophisticated mental capacities as those involved in producing language or doing science. Within the totality of what constitutes the human mind, then, McGinn says that the intractability of the mind-body problem is due only to a relatively simple component that human minds have in common with the minds of far more primitive creatures. Presumably cognitive science and related disciplines are well launched on their quest for an explanation of the rest of human mentality (philosophers such as Searle [Reading 18] would disagree, of course), and need only reconcile themselves to the human inability to understand consciousness.

How plausible is this picture? It invites many questions: What is the basis for ascribing consciousness to non-human animals? Since we don't have access to the subjectivity of animals, and, according to McGinn's own thesis, we don't have any idea what properties of the brain or any other physical system give rise to consciousness, how can we know that nonhuman animals are conscious at all? Descartes (see his Letter to More in Reading 1) argued that animals are no more than unconscious machines to which we mistakenly attribute consciousness because of the similarities between their sensory organs and ours: since "thought is included in our mode of sensation, similar thought seems to be attributable to them." For Descartes the inner self-awareness that we call consciousness is *essentially* connected with our higher cognitive powers, and occurs in sensation only because the mind happens to be united with a body. We needn't accept Cartesian dualism in order to raise the following question: Is human consciousness (the only sort that we are acquainted with) intelligible apart from the conceptual and other cognitive capacities of the human mind? Perhaps it is, but should we not establish this first?

REVIEW QUESTIONS

1. According to McGinn, the apparent mystery and magic of consciousness arising from the brain is due to the limitations of our human cognitive powers (what he calls "cognitive closure") and not to anything objectively and intrinsically weird or "eerie" about the world itself. In more prosaic terms, McGinn tells us that his thesis removes the "perplexity" of the mind-body problem by showing that "there is no philosophical (as opposed to scientific) mind-body problem." Is it any less eerie or perplexing to accept that the weakness of the human mind forever prevents you from understanding consciousness (which pervades your every waking moment) instead of accepting that consciousness is just an intrinsically brute fact that has no explanation? Is eeriness in the eye of the beholder?

2. If McGinn is correct in asserting cognitive closure with respect to consciousness and its relation to the brain, is he entitled to claim that, despite this bad news, the good news is that

> the nature of the psychophysical connection has a full and non-mysterious explanation in a certain science, but that this science is inaccessible to us as a matter of principle. Call this explanatory scientific theory T: T is as natural and prosaic and devoid of miracle as any theory of nature; it describes the link between consciousness and the brain in a way that is no more remarkable (or alarming) than the way we now describe the link between the liver and bile. (p. 377)

In a more general form, the question is this: If the limitations of human cognition deny us epistemic access to certain features of the world, can we be confident that *everything* is intrinsically intelligible or that there is a theory for everything even if we could never grasp the theory?

27

Facing Up to the Problem of Consciousness

David J. Chalmers

David Chalmers is Professor of Philosophy and Associate Director of the Center for Consciousness Studies at the University of Arizona. Among his most recent publications are *The Conscious Mind: In Search of a Fundamental Theory* (1996) and a reprinting of the paper included as this reading in *Explaining Consciousness: The Hard Problem* (1997)—an anthology of papers by various philosophers discussing the ideas in his 1996 book. *Explaining Consciousness* ends with Chalmer's response to the papers in the book.

Like Nagel, Campbell and Jackson in previous readings, Chalmers focuses in on consciousness—the what-it-is-like aspect of human (and presumably other) minds. A term he frequently uses for this subjective aspect is "experience." He urges us not to make the common mistake of confusing the "hard" and seemingly intractable problem of consciousness with "easier" topics such as perception, awareness, and attention, all of which he is confident are susceptible to functionalist analyses. However, his approach to the "hard" problem is quite different from Campbell's and Jackson's epiphenomenalism or McGinn's cognitive closure. He argues that, instead of trying to reduce consciousness, we should rank it as a primitive fact about the world, as *fundamental* and *underived* in its own way as are mass, energy, and time, none of which we try to derive from anything else. Our theorizing about consciousness would then rest on psychophysical laws as basic as those expressing relations between the fundamental entities in physical science. Chalmers calls his position "naturalistic dualism."

I: INTRODUCTION

Consciousness poses the most baffling problems in the science of the mind. There is nothing that we know more intimately than conscious experience, but there is nothing that is harder to explain. All sorts of mental phenomena have yielded to scientific investigation in recent years, but consciousness has stubbornly resisted. Many have tried to explain it, but the explanations always seem to fall short of the target. Some have been led to suppose that the problem is intractable, and that no good explanation can be given.

To make progress on the problem of consciousness, we have to confront it directly. In this paper, I first isolate the truly hard part of the problem, separating it from more tractable parts and giving an account of why it is so difficult to explain. I critique some recent work that uses reductive methods to address consciousness, and argue that these methods inevitably fail to come to grips with the hardest part

From: David J. Chalmers, "Facing up to the Problem of Consciousness," *Journal of Consciousness Studies,* vol. 2, no. 3 (1995): 200–219. Reprinted with permission of the publisher.

of the problem. Once this failure is recognized, the door to further progress is opened. In the second half of the paper, I argue that if we move to a new kind of nonreductive explanation, a **naturalistic** account of consciousness can be given. I put forward my own candidate for such an account: a nonreductive theory based on principles of structural coherence and organizational invariance and a double-aspect view of information.

II: THE EASY PROBLEMS AND THE HARD PROBLEM

There is not just one problem of consciousness. 'Consciousness' is an ambiguous term, referring to many different phenomena. Each of these phenomena needs to be explained, but some are easier to explain than others. At the start, it is useful to divide the associated problems of consciousness into 'hard' and 'easy' problems. The easy problems of consciousness are those that seem directly susceptible to the standard methods of cognitive science, whereby a phenomenon is explained in terms of computational or neural mechanisms. The hard problems are those that seem to resist those methods.

The easy problems of consciousness include those of explaining the following phenomena:

- the ability to discriminate, categorize, and react to environmental stimuli;
- the integration of information by a cognitive system;
- the reportability of mental states;
- the ability of a system to access its own internal states;
- the focus of attention;
- the deliberate control of behaviour;
- the difference between wakefulness and sleep.

All of these phenomena are associated with the notion of consciousness. For example, one sometimes says that a mental state is conscious when it is verbally reportable, or when it is internally accessible. Sometimes a system is said to be conscious of some information when it has the ability to react on the basis of that information, or, more strongly, when

it attends to that information, or when it can integrate that information and exploit it in the sophisticated control of behaviour. We sometimes say that an action is conscious precisely when it is deliberate. Often, we say that an organism is conscious as another way of saying that it is awake.

There is no real issue about whether *these* phenomena can be explained scientifically. All of them are straightforwardly vulnerable to explanation in terms of computational or neural mechanisms. To explain access and reportability, for example, we need only specify the mechanism by which information about internal states is retrieved and made available for verbal report. To explain the integration of information, we need only exhibit mechanisms by which information is brought together and exploited by later processes. For an account of sleep and wakefulness, an appropriate neurophysiological account of the processes responsible for organisms' contrasting behaviour in those states will suffice. In each case, an appropriate cognitive or neurophysiological model can clearly do the explanatory work.

If these phenomena were all there was to consciousness, then consciousness would not be much of a problem. Although we do not yet have anything close to a complete explanation of these phenomena, we have a clear idea of how we might go about explaining them. This is why I call these problems the easy problems. Of course, 'easy' is a relative term. Getting the details right will probably take a century or two of difficult empirical work. Still, there is every reason to believe that the methods of cognitive science and neuroscience will succeed.

The really hard problem of consciousness is the problem of *experience*. When we think and perceive, there is a whir of information-processing, but there is also a subjective aspect. As Nagel (1974)[1] has put it, there is *something it is like* to be a conscious organism. This subjective aspect is experience. When we see, for example, we *experience* visual sensations: the felt quality of redness, the experience of dark and light, the quality of depth in a visual field. Other experiences go along with perception in different modalities: the sound of a clarinet, the smell of mothballs. Then there are bodily sensations,

---

[1] Reading 22. ED.

from pains to orgasms; mental images that are conjured up internally; the felt quality of emotion, and the experience of a stream of conscious thought. What unites all of these states is that there is something it is like to be in them. All of them are states of experience.

It is undeniable that some organisms are subjects of experience. But the question of how it is that these systems are subjects of experience is perplexing. Why is it that when our cognitive systems engage in visual and auditory information-processing, we have visual or auditory experience: the quality of deep blue, the sensation of middle C? How can we explain why there is something it is like to entertain a mental image, or to experience an emotion? It is widely agreed that experience arises from a physical basis, but we have no good explanation of why and how it so arises. Why should physical processing give rise to a rich inner life at all? It seems objectively unreasonable that it should, and yet it does.

If any problem qualifies as *the* problem of consciousness, it is this one. In this central sense of 'consciousness,' an organism is conscious if there is something it is like to be that organism, and a mental state is conscious if there is something it is like to be in that state. Sometimes terms such as 'phenomenal consciousness' and 'qualia' are also used here, but I find it more natural to speak of 'conscious experience' or simply 'experience'. Another useful way to avoid confusion (used by e.g. Newell 1990, Chalmers 1996) is to reserve the term 'consciousness' for the phenomena of experience, using the less loaded term 'awareness' for the more straightforward phenomena described earlier. If such a convention were widely adopted, communication would be much easier. As things stand, those who talk about 'consciousness' are frequently talking past each other.

The ambiguity of the term 'consciousness' is often exploited by both philosophers and scientists writing on the subject. It is common to see a paper on consciousness begin with an invocation of the mystery of consciousness, noting the strange intangibility and ineffability of subjectivity, and worrying that so far we have no theory of the phenomenon. Here, the topic is clearly the hard problem—the problem of experience. In the second half of the paper, the tone becomes more optimistic, and the author's own theory of consciousness is outlined. Upon examination, this theory turns out to be a theory of one of the more straightforward phenomena—of reportability, of introspective access, or whatever. At the close, the author declares that consciousness has turned out to be tractable after all, but the reader is left feeling like the victim of a bait-and-switch. The hard problem remains untouched.

III: FUNCTIONAL EXPLANATION

Why are the easy problems easy, and why is the hard problem hard? The easy problems are easy precisely because they concern the explanation of cognitive *abilities* and *functions*. To explain a cognitive function, we need only specify a mechanism that can perform the function. The methods of cognitive science are well-suited for this sort of explanation, and so are well-suited to the easy problems of consciousness. By contrast, the hard problem is hard precisely because it is not a problem about the performance of functions. The problem persists even when the performance of all the relevant functions is explained.[2]

To explain reportability, for instance, is just to explain how a system could perform the function of producing reports on internal states. To explain internal access, we need to explain how a system could be appropriately affected by its internal states and use information[3] about those states in directing later processes. To explain integration and control, we need to explain how a system's central processes can bring information contents together and use them in the facilitation of various behaviours. These are all problems about the explanation of functions.

---

[2] Here 'function' is not used in the narrow teleological sense of something that a system is designed to do, but in the broader sense of any causal role in the production of behaviour that a system might perform.

[3] The phrase "use information" is rather vague without a definition of "information." In this context it means something pretty straightforward, as in the following simplified scheme: the occurrence of a specific internal state (e.g., in an organism's sensory system) reliably produces a specific change of state in a linked system (call it a modulator). What the modulator does is to initiate from a range of behaviors the particular behavior that is regularly caused by the specific state change induced in it by the sensory system. In this situation we can speak clearly of a *signal* going from the first system to the second, a signal that constitutes *information* which is *used* by the second system in executing its function of generating behavior. ED.

How do we explain the performance of a function? By specifying a *mechanism* that performs the function. Here, neurophysiological and cognitive modelling are perfect for the task. If we want a detailed low-level explanation, we can specify the neural mechanism that is responsible for the function. If we want a more abstract explanation, we can specify a mechanism in computational terms. Either way, a full and satisfying explanation will result. Once we have specified the neural or computational mechanism that performs the function of verbal report, for example, the bulk of our work in explaining reportability is over.

In a way, the point is trivial. It is a *conceptual* fact about these phenomena that their explanation only involves the explanation of various functions, as the phenomena are *functionally definable*. All it *means* for reportability to be instantiated in a system is that the system has the capacity for verbal reports of internal information. All it means for a system to be awake is for it to be appropriately receptive to information from the environment and for it to be able to use this information in directing behaviour in an appropriate way. To see that this sort of thing is a conceptual fact, note that someone who says 'you have explained the performance of the verbal report function, but you have not explained reportability' is making a trivial conceptual mistake about reportability. All it could *possibly* take to explain reportability is an explanation of how the relevant function is performed; the same goes for the other phenomena in question.

Throughout the higher-level sciences, reductive explanation works in just this way. To explain the gene, for instance, we needed to specify the mechanism that stores and transmits hereditary information from one generation to the next. It turns out that DNA performs this function; once we explain how the function is performed, we have explained the gene. To explain life, we ultimately need to explain how a system can reproduce, adapt to its environment, metabolize, and so on. All of these are questions about the performance of functions, and so are well-suited to reductive explanation.[4] The same holds for most problems in cognitive science. To explain learning, we need to explain the way in which a system's behavioural capacities are modified in light of environmental information, and the way in which new information can be brought to bear in adapting a system's actions to its environment. If we show how a neural or computational mechanism does the job, we have explained learning. We can say the same for other cognitive phenomena, such as perception, memory, and language. Sometimes the relevant functions need to be characterized quite subtly, but it is clear that insofar as cognitive science explains these phenomena at all, it does so by explaining the performance of functions.

When it comes to conscious experience, this sort of explanation fails. What makes the hard problem hard and almost unique is that it *goes beyond* problems about the performance of functions. To see this, note that even when we have explained the performance of all the cognitive and behavioural functions in the vicinity of experience—perceptual discrimination, categorization, internal access, verbal report—there may still remain a further unanswered question: *Why is the performance of these functions accompanied by experience?* A simple explanation of the functions leaves this question open.

There is no analogous further question in the explanation of genes, or of life, or of learning. If someone says 'I can see that you have explained how DNA stores and transmits hereditary information from one generation to the next, but you have not explained how it is a *gene*,' then they are making a conceptual mistake. All it means to be a gene is to be an entity that performs the relevant storage and transmission function. But if someone says 'I can see that you have explained how information is discriminated, integrated, and reported, but you have not explained how it is *experienced*,' they are not making a conceptual mistake. This is a nontrivial further question.

This further question is the key question in the problem of consciousness. Why doesn't all this information-processing go on 'in the dark,' free of any inner feel? Why is it that when electromagnetic waveforms impinge on a retina and are discriminated and categorized by a visual system, this discrimination and categorization is experienced as a sensation of vivid red? We know that conscious experience *does* arise when these functions are performed, but the very fact that it arises is the central

---

[4]Jaegwon Kim goes into much greater detail about this functionalizing conception of *reductive* explanation in Reading 13. ED.

mystery. There is an *explanatory gap* (a term due to Levine 1983) between the functions and experience, and we need an explanatory bridge to cross it. A mere account of the functions stays on one side of the gap, so the materials for the bridge must be found elsewhere.

This is not to say that experience *has* no function. Perhaps it will turn out to play an important cognitive role. But for any role it might play, there will be more to the explanation of experience than a simple explanation of the function. Perhaps it will even turn out that in the course of explaining a function, we will be led to the key insight that allows an explanation of experience. If this happens, though, the discovery will be an *extra* explanatory reward. There is no cognitive function such that we can say in advance that explanation of that function will *automatically* explain experience.

To explain experience, we need a new approach. The usual explanatory methods of cognitive science and neuroscience do not suffice. These methods have been developed precisely to explain the performance of cognitive functions, and they do a good job of it. But as these methods stand, they are *only* equipped to explain the performance of functions. When it comes to the hard problem, the standard approach has nothing to say.

IV: SOME CASE-STUDIES

In the last few years, a number of works have addressed the problems of consciousness within the framework of cognitive science and neuroscience. This might suggest that the analysis above is faulty, but in fact a close examination of the relevant work only lends the analysis further support. When we investigate just which aspects of consciousness these studies are aimed at, and which aspects they end up explaining, we find that the ultimate target of explanation is always one of the easy problems. I will illustrate this with two representative examples.

The first is the 'neurobiological theory of consciousness' outlined by Francis Crick and Christof Koch (1990; see also Crick 1994). This theory centers on certain 35–75 hertz neural oscillations in the cerebral cortex; Crick and Koch hypothesize that these oscillations are the basis of consciousness. This is partly because the oscillations seem to be correlated with awareness in a number of different

modalities—within the visual and olfactory systems, for example—and also because they suggest a mechanism by which the *binding* of information contents might be achieved. Binding is the process whereby separately represented pieces of information about a single entity are brought together to be used by later processing, as when information about the colour and shape of a perceived object is integrated from separate visual pathways.[5] Following others (e.g. Eckhorn *et al.* 1988), Crick and Koch hypothesize that binding may be achieved by the synchronized oscillations of neuronal groups representing the relevant contents. When two pieces of information are to be bound together, the relevant neural groups will oscillate with the same frequency and phase.

The details of how this binding might be achieved are still poorly understood, but suppose that they can be worked out. What might the resulting theory explain? Clearly it might explain the binding of information contents[6], and perhaps it might yield a more general account of the integration of information in the brain. Crick and Koch also suggest that these oscillations activate the mechanisms of working memory, so that there may be an account of this and perhaps other forms of memory in the distance. The theory might eventually lead to a general account of how perceived information is bound and stored in memory, for use by later processing.

Such a theory would be valuable, but it would tell us nothing about why the relevant contents are experienced. Crick and Koch suggest that these oscillations are the neural *correlates* of experience. This

---

[5] See section 3.3 and section 4 of Reading 4 for a description of these neural functions. ED.

[6] Chalmer's use of "contents" in the phrase "information contents" is not clear. But the kinds of brain events he envisions can be roughly described this way: As we saw in Reading 4, there is a massive degree of **parallel processing** occurring in the brain's reception of signals from sensory receptors. There is parallel processing of input *within* modalities, such as color and shape within vision; and parallel processing *across* modalities, as in the pain that I feel from the cut that I see in my finger. From a biological point of view, the brain functions as a modulator which selects and initiates adaptive behavior in response to events in the organism's internal or external environment as these events are signaled by sensory input along numbers of discrete channels. To make these responses possible, the various kinds of sensory signals relevant to the same event must be "tagged" as such, must all get used in elaborating a coordinated response to the event in questions. This mechanism of integration of related but discrete sensory input is the "binding" to which Chalmers is referring. ED.

claim is arguable—does not binding also take place in the processing of unconscious information?[7]—but even if it is accepted, the *explanatory* question remains: Why do the oscillations give rise to experience? The only basis for an explanatory connection is the role they play in binding and storage, but the question of why binding and storage should themselves be accompanied by experience is never addressed. If we do not know why binding and storage should give rise to experience, telling a story about the oscillations cannot help us. Conversely, if we *knew* why binding and storage gave rise to experience, the neurophysiological details would be just the icing on the cake. Crick and Koch's theory gains its purchase by *assuming* a connection between binding and experience, and so can do nothing to explain that link.

I do not think that Crick and Koch are ultimately claiming to address the hard problem, although some have interpreted them otherwise. A published interview with Koch gives a clear statement of the limitations on the theory's ambitions.

> Well, let's first forget about the really difficult aspects, like subjective feelings, for they may not have a scientific solution. The subjective state of play, of pain, of pleasure, of seeing blue, of smelling a rose—there seems to be a huge jump between the materialistic level, of explaining molecules and neurons, and the subjective level. Let's focus on things that are easier to study—like visual awareness. You're now talking to me, but you're not looking at me, you're looking at the cappuccino, and so you are aware of it. You can say, 'It's a cup and there's some liquid in it.' If I give it to you, you'll move your arm and you'll take it—you'll respond in a meaningful manner. That's what I call awareness. ('What is Consciousness?', *Discover*, November 1992, p. 96.)

The second example is an approach at the level of cognitive psychology. This is Bernard Baars' global workspace theory of consciousness, presented in his book *A Cognitive Theory of Consciousness* (1988). According to this theory, the contents of consciousness are contained in a *global workspace,* a central processor used to mediate communication between a host of specialized nonconscious processors. When

these specialized processors need to broadcast information to the rest of the system, they do so by sending this information to the workspace, which acts as a kind of communal blackboard for the rest of the system, accessible to all the other processors.

Baars uses this model to address many aspects of human cognition, and to explain a number of contrasts between conscious and unconscious cognitive functioning. Ultimately, however, it is a theory of *cognitive accessibility,* explaining how it is that certain information contents are widely accessible within a system, as well as a theory of informational integration and reportability. The theory shows promise as a theory of awareness, the functional correlate of conscious experience, but an explanation of experience itself is not on offer.

One might suppose that according to this theory, the contents of experience are precisely the contents of the workspace. But even if this is so, nothing internal to the theory *explains* why the information within the global workspace is experienced. The best the theory can do is to say that the information is experienced because it is *globally accessible*. But now the question arises in a different form: why should global accessibility give rise to conscious experience? As always, this bridging question is unanswered.

Almost all work taking a cognitive or neuroscientific approach to consciousness in recent years could be subjected to a similar critique. The 'Neural Darwinism' model of Edelman (1989), for instance, addressed questions about perceptual awareness and the self-concept, but says nothing about why there should also be experience. The 'multiple drafts' model of Dennett (1991) is largely directed at explaining the reportability of certain mental contents. The 'intermediate level' theory of Jackendoff (1987) provides an account of some computational processes that underlie consciousness, but Jackendoff stresses that the question of how these 'project' into conscious experience remains mysterious.

Researchers using these methods are often inexplicit about their attitudes to the problem of conscious experience, although sometimes they take a clear stand. Even among those who are clear about it, attitudes differ widely. In placing this sort of work with respect to the problem of experience, a

---

[7] This is an important point. A good deal of sensory input is integrated in the execution of reflexes at the spinal level, or in brain components such as the cerebellum, where sensory input does not register in our consciousness. ED.

number of different strategies are available. It would be useful if these strategic choices were more often made explicit.

The first strategy is simply to *explain something else*. Some researchers are explicit that the problem of experience is too difficult for now, and perhaps even outside the domain of science altogether. These researchers instead choose to address one of the more tractable problems such as reportability or the self-concept. Although I have called these problems the 'easy' problems, they are among the most interesting unsolved problems in cognitive science, so this work is certainly worthwhile. The worst that can be said of this choice is that in the context of research on consciousness it is relatively unambitious, and the work can sometimes be misinterpreted.

The second choice is to take a harder line and *deny the phenomenon*. (Variations on this approach are taken by Allport 1988; Dennett 1991; Wilkes 1988.) According to this line, once we have explained the functions such as accessibility, reportability, and the like, there is no further phenomenon called 'experience' to explain. Some explicitly deny the phenomenon, holding for example that what is not externally verifiable cannot be real. Others achieve the same effect by allowing that experience exists, but only if we equate 'experience' with something like the capacity to discriminate and report. These approaches lead to a simpler theory, but are ultimately unsatisfactory. Experience is the most central and manifest aspect of our mental lives, and indeed is perhaps the key explanandum[8] in the science of the mind. Because of this status as an explanandum, experience cannot be discarded like the vital spirit when a new theory comes along.[9] Rather, it is the central fact that any theory of consciousness must explain. A theory that denies the phenomenon 'solves' the problem by ducking the question.

In a third option, some researchers *claim to be explaining experience* in the full sense. These researchers (unlike those above) wish to take experience very seriously; they lay out their functional model or theory, and claim that it explains the full subjective quality of experience (e.g. Flohr 1992; Humphrey 1992). The relevant step in the explanation is usually passed over quickly, however, and usually ends up looking something like magic. After some details about information processing are given, experience suddenly enters the picture, but it is left obscure *how* these processes should suddenly give rise to experience. Perhaps it is simply taken for granted that it does, but then we have an incomplete explanation and a version of the fifth strategy below.

A fourth, more promising approach appeals to these methods to *explain the structure of experience*. For example, it is arguable that an account of the discriminations made by the visual system can account for the structural relations between different colour experiences, as well as for the geometric structure of the visual field (see e.g. Clark 1992; Hardin 1992). In general, certain facts about structures found in processing will correspond to and arguably explain facts about the structure of experience. This strategy is plausible but limited. At best, it takes the existence of experience for granted and accounts for some facts about its structure, providing a sort of nonreductive explanation of the structural aspects of experience (I will say more on this later). This is useful for many purposes, but it tells us nothing about why there should be experience in the first place.

A fifth and reasonable strategy is to *isolate the substrate of experience*. After all, almost everyone allows that experience *arises* one way or another from brain processes, and it makes sense to identify the sort of process from which it arises. Crick and Koch put their work forward as isolating the neural correlate of consciousness, for example, and Edelman (1989) and Jackendoff (1987) make related claims. Justification of these claims requires a careful theoretical analysis, especially as experience is not directly observable in experimental contexts, but when applied judiciously this strategy can shed indirect light on the problem of experience. Nevertheless, the strategy is clearly incomplete. For a satisfactory theory, we need to know more than *which* processes give rise to experience; we need an account of why and how. A full theory of consciousness must build an explanatory bridge.

---

[8] An *explanandum* is that which is in need of explanation. ED.

[9] The "vital spirit" was understood as an irreducibly biological ingredient of living systems with causal powers that could not be explained in merely chemical terms. With the advent of reductive explanations, in the new science of molecular biology, of metabolism, heredity, and other higher-level biological functions, the notion of a "vital spirit" lost its relevance. ED.

V. THE EXTRA INGREDIENT

We have seen that there are systematic reasons why the usual methods of cognitive science and neuroscience fail to account for conscious experience. These are simply the wrong sort of methods; nothing that they give to us can yield an explanation. To account for conscious experience, we need an *extra ingredient* in the explanation. This makes for a challenge to those who are serious about the hard problem of consciousness. What is your extra ingredient, and why should *that* account for conscious experience?

There is no shortage of extra ingredients to be had. Some propose an injection of chaos and nonlinear dynamics. Some think that the key lies in nonalgorithmic processing. Some appeal to future discoveries in neurophysiology. Some suppose that the key to the mystery will lie at the level of quantum mechanics. It is easy to see why all these suggestions are put forward. None of the old methods work, so the solution must lie with *something* new. Unfortunately, these suggestions all suffer from the same old problems.

Nonalgorithmic[10] processing, for example, is put forward by Penrose (1989; 1994) because of the role it might play in the process of conscious-mathematical insight. The arguments about mathematics are controversial, but even if they succeed and an account of nonalgorithmic processing in the human brain is given, it will still only be an account of the *functions* involved in mathematical reasoning and the like. For a nonalgorithmic process as much as an algorithmic process, the question is left unanswered: why should this process give rise to experience? In answering *this* question, there is no special role for nonalgorithmic processing.

The same goes for nonlinear and chaotic dynamics.[11] These might provide a novel account of the dynamics of cognitive functioning, quite different from that given by standard methods in cognitive science. But from dynamics, one only gets more dynamics. The question about experience here is as mysterious as ever. The point is even clearer for new discoveries in neurophysiology. These new discoveries may help us make significant progress in understanding brain function, but for any neural process we isolate, the same question will always arise. It is difficult to imagine what a proponent of new neurophysiology expects to happen, over and above the explanation of further cognitive functions.

Perhaps the most popular 'extra ingredient' of all is quantum mechanics (e.g. Hameroff 1994). The attractiveness of quantum theories of consciousness may stem from a Law of Minimization of Mystery: consciousness is mysterious and quantum mechanics is mysterious, so maybe the two mysteries have a common source. Nevertheless, quantum theories of consciousness suffer from the same difficulties as neural or computational theories. Quantum phenomena have some remarkable functional properties, such as nondeterminism and nonlocality.[12] It is natural to speculate that these properties

---

[10] For an explanation of the term *algorithm,* see section 4 of Reading 15. ED.

[11] *Dynamics* is the study of the effects on the motions of bodies by forces applied to them. In classical dynamics the equations (e.g., $f = ma$) expressing the relationship between force as input and change of motion as output are *linear*—they would plot as straight lines on graphs, because there is a direct proportion between input and output. However, in various unstable or *chaotic* systems the dynamics seem to be *nonlinear*—output is often greatly disproportionate to input in a seemingly unpredictable way. Weather systems and economies are examples of this sort of instability. The mathematical theory being developed to deal with such systems is often called *chaos* or *chaos theory,* and has been applied with sometimes controversial results in many fields.

An interneuron's transition from resting to action potential (see Reading 4, section 3.1) is an example of nonlinear dynamics. The action potential is the neuron's functional output, and its inputs are the gradual raising and lowering of the potential inside the neuron as a result of large numbers of synaptic transmissions from other neurons. Nothing happens as a result of these inputs unless they cause the interior potential to reach a certain threshold. If the threshold depolarization occurs at the axon hillock, the output along the axon is always the same (all-or-nothing). Thus its quantity is not directly proportional to the number or values of synaptic inputs. Such threshold effects can be incorporated into computer modeling of cognitive processes. ED.

[12] Quantum theory deals with particles at extremely small levels of magnitude at which the quantum nature of energy has important effects. Quantum theory rests on the discovery that energy of all sorts is not continuously variable, but moves from one level to another in leaps (from one quantum to another). According to quantum theory there is a certain randomness or *indeterminacy* in the events within its domain, so that we can predict only the *probability* of an outcome. Take the case of an assembly of identical nuclei undergoing atomic decay by emissions of alpha particles. According to quantum theory, given any two of those nuclei in identical conditions at a particular time, one may emit an alpha particle while the other does not. The usual interpretation of this quantum indeterminacy is that it is intrinsic to the entities in question rather than a function of our ignorance of other variables that actually determine the outcome.

In quantum theory it is recognized that particles such as electrons behave sometimes as particles and other times as waves. Depending on

may play some role in the explanation of cognitive functions, such as random choice and the integration of information, and this hypothesis cannot be ruled out *a priori*. But when it comes to the explanation of experience, quantum processes are in the same boat as any other. The question of why these processes should give rise to experience is entirely unanswered.[13]

At the end of the day, the same criticism applies to *any* purely physical account of consciousness. For any physical process we specify there will be an unanswered question: Why should this process give rise to experience? Given any such process, it is conceptually coherent that it could be instantiated in the absence of experience. It follows that no mere account of the physical process will tell us why experience arises. The emergence of experience goes beyond what can be derived from physical theory.

Purely physical explanation is well-suited to the explanation of physical *structures,* explaining macroscopic structures in terms of detailed microstructural constituents; and it provides a satisfying explanation of the performance of *functions,* accounting for these functions in terms of the physical mechanisms that perform them. This is because a physical account can *entail* the facts about structures and functions; once the internal details of the physical account are given, the structural and functional properties fall out as an automatic consequence. But the structure and dynamics of physical processes yield only more structure and dynamics, so structures and functions are all we can expect these processes to explain. The facts about experience cannot be an automatic consequence of any physical account, as it is conceptually coherent that any

given process could exist without experience. Experience may *arise* from the physical, but it is not *entailed* by the physical.

The moral of all this is that *you can't explain conscious experience on the cheap.* It is a remarkable fact that reductive methods—methods that explain a high-level phenomenon wholly in terms of more basic physical processes—work well in so many domains. In a sense, one *can* explain most biological and cognitive phenomena on the cheap, in that these phenomena are seen as automatic consequences of more fundamental processes. It would be wonderful if reductive methods could explain experience, too; I hoped for a long time that they might. Unfortunately, there are systematic reasons why these methods must fail. Reductive methods are successful in most domains because what needs explaining in those domains are structures and functions, and these are the kind of things that a physical account can entail. When it comes to a problem over and above the explanation of structures and functions, these methods are impotent.

This might seem reminiscent of the vitalist claim that no physical account could explain life, but the cases are disanalogous. What drove vitalist scepticism was doubt about whether physical mechanisms could perform the many remarkable functions associated with life, such as complex adaptive behavior and reproduction. The conceptual claim that explanation of functions is what is needed was implicitly accepted, but lacking detailed knowledge of biochemical mechanisms, vitalists doubted whether any physical process could do the job and put forward the hypothesis of the vital spirit as an alternative explanation. Once it turned out that physical processes could perform the relevant functions, vitalist doubts melted away.

With experience, on the other hand, physical explanation of the functions is not in question. The key is instead the *conceptual* point that the explanation of functions does not suffice for the explanation of experience. This basic conceptual point is not something that further neuroscientific investigation will affect. In a similar way, experience is disanalogous to the *elan vital.* The vital spirit was put forward as an explanatory posit, in order to explain the relevant functions, and could therefore be discarded when those functions were explained without it. Experience is not an explanatory posit

---

initial conditions, an electron seems to pass through two slits at once (like a wave) or only one slit (like a particle). Insofar as it is a particle, it seems, under certain conditions, to be located in two places at once.

   This kind of indeterminacy is not what we associate with matter at the level of magnitude at which it is observable to us. It seems to some thinkers to be enough unlike matter that it may be the basis for certain mental attributes such as freedom of will. ED.

   [13] One special attraction of quantum theories is the fact that on some interpretations of quantum mechanics, consciousness plays an active role in 'collapsing' the quantum wave function. Such interpretations are controversial, but in any case they offer no hope of *explaining* consciousness in terms of quantum processes. Rather, these theories *assume* the existence of consciousness, and use it in the explanation of quantum processes. At best, these theories tell us something about a physical role that consciousness may play. They tell us nothing about how it arises.

but an explanandum in its own right, and so is not a candidate for this sort of elimination.

It is tempting to note that all sorts of puzzling phenomena have eventually turned out to be explainable in physical terms. But each of these were problems about the observable behaviour of physical objects, coming down to problems in the explanation of structures and functions. Because of this, these phenomena have always been the kind of thing that a physical account *might* explain, even if at some points there have been good reasons to suspect that no such explanation would be forthcoming. The tempting induction from these cases fails in the case of consciousness, which is not a problem about physical structures and functions. The problem of consciousness is puzzling in an entirely different way. An analysis of the problem shows us that conscious experience is just not the kind of thing that a wholly reductive account could succeed in explaining.

VI: NONREDUCTIVE EXPLANATION

At this point some are tempted to give up, holding that we will never have a theory of conscious experience. McGinn (1989),[14] for example, argues that the problem is too hard for our limited minds; we are 'cognitively closed' with respect to the phenomenon. Others have argued that conscious experience lies outside the domain of scientific theory altogether.

I think this pessimism is premature. This is not the place to give up; it is the place where things get interesting. When simple methods of explanation are ruled out, we need to investigate the alternatives. Given that reductive explanation fails, *nonreductive* explanation is the natural choice.

Although a remarkable number of phenomena have turned out to be explicable wholly in terms of entities simpler than themselves, this is not universal. In physics, it occasionally happens that an entity has to be taken as *fundamental*. Fundamental entities are not explained in terms of anything simpler. Instead, one takes them as basic, and gives a theory of how they relate to everything else in the world. For

example, in the nineteenth century it turned out that electromagnetic processes could not be explained in terms of the wholly mechanical processes that previous physical theories appealed to, so Maxwell and others introduced electromagnetic charge and electromagnetic forces as new fundamental components of a physical theory. To explain electromagnetism, the ontology of physics had to be expanded. New basic properties and basic laws were needed to give a satisfactory account of the phenomena.

Other features that physical theory takes as fundamental include mass and space-time. No attempt is made to explain these features in terms of anything simpler. But this does not rule out the possibility of a theory of mass or of space-time. There is an intricate theory of how these features interrelate, and of the basic laws they enter into. These basic principles are used to explain many familiar phenomena concerning mass, space, and time at a higher level.

I suggest that a theory of consciousness should take experience as fundamental. We know that a theory of consciousness requires the addition of *something* fundamental to our ontology, as everything in physical theory is compatible with the absence of consciousness. We might add some entirely new nonphysical feature, from which experience can be derived, but it is hard to see what such a feature would be like. More likely, we will take experience itself as a fundamental feature of the world, alongside mass, charge, and space-time. If we take experience as fundamental, then we can go about the business of constructing a theory of experience.

Where there is a fundamental property, there are fundamental laws. A nonreductive theory of experience will add new principles to the furniture of the basic laws of nature. These basic principles will ultimately carry the explanatory burden in a theory of consciousness. Just as we explain familiar high-level phenomena involving mass in terms of more basic principles involving mass and other entities, we might explain familiar phenomena involving experience in terms of more basic principles involving experience and other entities.

In particular, a nonreductive theory of experience will specify basic principles telling us how experience depends on physical features of the world.

---

[14]Reading 26. Ed.

These *psychophysical* principles will not interfere with physical laws, as it seems that physical laws already form a closed system. Rather, they will be a supplement to a physical theory. A physical theory gives a theory of physical processes, and a psychophysical theory tells us how those processes give rise to experience. We know that experience depends on physical processes, but we also know that this dependence cannot be derived from physical laws alone. The new basic principles postulated by a nonreductive theory give us the extra ingredient that we need to build an explanatory bridge.

Of course, by taking experience as fundamental, there is a sense in which this approach does not tell us why there is experience in the first place. But this is the same for any fundamental theory. Nothing in physics tells us why there is matter in the first place, but we do not count this against theories of matter. Certain features of the world need to be taken as fundamental by any scientific theory. A theory of matter can still explain all sorts of facts about matter, by showing how they are consequences of the basic laws. The same goes for a theory of experience.

This position qualifies as a variety of dualism, as it postulates basic properties over and above the properties invoked by physics. But it is an innocent version of dualism, entirely compatible with the scientific view of the world. Nothing in this approach contradicts anything in physical theory; we simply need to add further *bridging* principles to explain how experience arises from[15] physical processes. There is nothing particularly spiritual or mystical about this theory—its overall shape is like that of a physical theory, with a few fundamental entities connected by fundamental laws. It expands the ontology slightly, to be sure, but Maxwell did the same thing. Indeed, the overall structure of this position is entirely naturalistic, allowing that ultimately the universe comes down to a network of basic entities obeying simple laws, and allowing that there may ultimately be a theory of consciousness cast in terms of such laws. If the position is

to have a name, a good choice might be *naturalistic dualism*.

If this view is right, then in some ways a theory of consciousness will have more in common with a theory in physics than a theory in biology. Biological theories involve no principles that are fundamental in this way, so biological theory has a certain complexity and messiness to it; but theories in physics, insofar as they deal with fundamental principles, aspire to simplicity and elegance. The fundamental laws of nature are part of the basic furniture of the world, and physical theories are telling us that this basic furniture is remarkably simple. If a theory of consciousness also involves fundamental principles, then we should expect the same. The principles of simplicity, elegance, and even beauty that drive physicists' search for a fundamental theory will also apply to a theory of consciousness.[16]

VII: TOWARD OF A THEORY OF CONSCIOUSNESS

It is not too soon to begin work on a theory. We are already in a position to understand some key facts about the relationship between physical processes and experience, and about the regularities that connect them. Once reductive explanation is set aside, we can lay those facts on the table so that they can play their proper role as the initial pieces in a nonreductive theory of consciousness, and as constraints on the basic laws that constitute an ultimate theory.

There is an obvious problem that plagues the development of a theory of consciousness, and that is the paucity of objective data. Conscious experi-

---

[15]"Arises from" may not be the best choice of words here. If consciousness is to be treated as fundamental, then it no more arises from anything else than do mass or space-time from each other. A phrase such as "correlates with" or "varies with" might be more appropriate, just as we would say that in relativity theory mass varies with velocity (greatly increasing as a body approaches the speed of light). Ed.

[16]Some philosophers argue that even though there is a *conceptual* gap between physical processes and experience, there need be no metaphysical gap, so that experience might in a certain sense still be physical (e.g. Hill 1991; Levine 1983; Loar 1990). Usually this line of argument is supported by an appeal to the notion of a *posteriori* necessity (Kripke 1980). I think that this position rests on a misunderstanding of a *posteriori* necessity, however, or else requires an entirely new sort of necessity that we have no reason to believe in; see Chalmers 1996 (also Jackson 1994; Lewis 1994) for details. In any case, this position still concedes an *explanatory* gap between physical processes and experience. For example, the principles connecting the physical and the experiential will not be derivable from the laws of physics, so such principles must be taken as *explanatorily* fundamental. So even on this sort of view, the explanatory structure of a theory of consciousness will be much as I have described.

ence is not directly observable in an experimental context, so we cannot generate data about the relationship between physical processes and experience at will. Nevertheless, we all have access to a rich source of data in our own case.[17] Many important regularities between experience and processing can be inferred from considerations about one's own experience. There are also good indirect sources of data from observable cases, as when one relies on the verbal report of a subject as an indication of experience. These methods have their limitations, but we have more than enough data to get a theory off the ground.

Philosophical analysis is also useful in getting value for money out of the data we have. This sort of analysis can yield a number of principles relating consciousness and cognition, thereby strongly constraining the shape of an ultimate theory. The method of thought-experimentation can also yield significant rewards, as we will see. Finally, the fact that we are searching for a *fundamental* theory means that we can appeal to such nonempirical constraints as simplicity, homogeneity, and the like in developing a theory. We must seek to systematize the information we have, to extend it as far as possible by careful analysis, and then make the inference to the simplest possible theory that explains the data while remaining a plausible candidate to be part of the fundamental furniture of the world.

Such theories will always retain an element of speculation that is not present in other scientific theories, because of the impossibility of conclusive intersubjective experimental tests. Still, we can certainly construct theories that are compatible with the data that we have, and evaluate them in comparison to each other. Even in the absence of intersubjective observation, there are numerous criteria available for the evaluation of such theories: simplicity, internal coherence, coherence with theories in other domains, the ability to reproduce the properties of experience that are familiar from our own case, and even an overall fit with the dictates of common sense. Perhaps there will be significant indeterminacies remaining even when all these constraints are applied, but we can at least develop

plausible candidates. Only when candidate theories have been developed will we be able to evaluate them.

A nonreductive theory of consciousness will consist of a number of *psychophysical principles,* principles connecting the properties of physical processes to the properties of experience. We can think of these principles as encapsulating the way in which experience arises from the physical. Ultimately, these principles should tell us what sort of physical systems will have associated experiences, and for the systems that do, they should tell us what sort of physical properties are relevant to the emergence of experience, and just what sort of experience we should expect any given physical system to yield. This is a tall order, but there is no reason why we should not get started.

In what follows, I present my own candidates for the psychophysical principles that might go into a theory of consciousness. The first two of these are *nonbasic principles*—systematic connections between processing and experience at a relatively high level. These principles can play a significant role in developing and constraining a theory of consciousness, but they are not cast at a sufficiently fundamental level to qualify as truly basic laws. The final principle is a candidate for a *basic principle* that might form the cornerstone of a fundamental theory of consciousness. This principle is particularly speculative, but it is the kind of speculation that is required if we are ever to have a satisfying theory of consciousness. I can present these principles only briefly here; I argue for them at much greater length in Chalmers 1996.

1. The Principle of Structural Coherence

This is a principle of coherence between the *structure of consciousness* and the *structure of awareness*. Recall that 'awareness' was used earlier to refer to the various functional phenomena that are associated with consciousness. I am now using it to refer to a somewhat more specific process in the cognitive underpinnings of experience. In particular, the contents of awareness are to be understood as those information contents that are accessible to central systems, and brought to bear in a widespread way in the control of behaviour. Briefly put, we can think of awareness as *direct availability for*

---

[17] See Norman Malcolm's discussion of the problems with the notion of knowing about consciousness "from one's own case" in Reading 3, pp. 46–47. ED.

global control. To a first approximation, the contents of awareness are the contents that are directly accessible and potentially reportable, at least in a language-using system.

Awareness is a purely functional notion, but it is nevertheless intimately linked to conscious experience. In familiar cases, wherever we find consciousness, we find awareness. Wherever there is conscious experience, there is some corresponding information in the cognitive system that is available in the control of behaviour, and available for verbal report. Conversely, it seems that whenever information is available for report and for global control, there is a corresponding conscious experience. Thus, there is a direct correspondence between consciousness and awareness.

The correspondence can be taken further. It is a central fact about experience that it has a complex structure. The visual field[18] has a complex geometry, for instance. There are also relations of similarity and difference between experiences, and relations in such things as relative intensity. Every subject's experience can be at least partly characterized and decomposed in terms of these structural properties: similarity and difference relations, perceived location, relative intensity, geometric structure, and so on. It is also a central fact that to each of these structural features, there is a corresponding feature in the information-processing structure of awareness.

Take colour sensations as an example. For every distinction between colour experiences, there is a corresponding distinction in processing. The different phenomenal colours that we experience form a complex three-dimensional space, varying in hue, saturation, and intensity. The properties of this space can be recovered from information-processing considerations: examination of the visual systems shows that waveforms of light are discriminated and analysed along three different axes, and it is this three-dimensional information that is relevant to later processing.[19] The three-dimensional

structure of phenomenal colour space therefore corresponds directly to the three-dimensional structure of visual awareness. This is precisely what we would expect. After all, every colour distinction corresponds to some reportable information, and therefore to a distinction that is represented in the structure of processing.

In a more straightforward way, the geometric structure of the visual field is directly reflected in a structure that can be recovered from visual processing.[20] Every geometric relation corresponds to something that can be reported and is therefore cognitively represented. If we were given only the story about information-processing in an agent's visual and cognitive system, we could not *directly* observe that agent's visual experiences, but we could nevertheless infer those experiences' structural properties.

In general, any information that is consciously experienced will also be cognitively represented. The fine-grained structure of the visual field will correspond to some fine-grained structure in visual processing. The same goes for experiences in other modalities, and even for nonsensory experiences. Internal mental images have geometric properties that are represented in processing. Even emotions have structural properties, such as relative intensity, that correspond directly to a structural property of processing; where there is greater intensity, we find a greater effect on later processes. In general, precisely because the structural properties of experience are accessible and reportable, those properties will be directly represented in the structure of awareness.

It is this **isomorphism** between the structures of consciousness and awareness that constitutes the principle of structural coherence. This principle reflects the central fact that even though cognitive processes do not conceptually entail facts about conscious experience, consciousness and cognition do not float free of one another but cohere in an intimate way.

---

[18] Keep in mind the difference between the phenomenal space of the *visual field* and the physical space that is being monitored by the visual system. The blur of a rapidly spinning wheel has a precise location in one's visual field, but there is no blur in the physical space in which the spinning wheel is located as a physical object. ED.

[19] *Hue* is that property of a color by which we distinguish it as red, brown, etc., and is associated with variations in the wavelengths of light impinging on the retina. *Saturation* is the purity of the color, which varies

with the amount of white light mixed with the color. *Intensity* or brightness is the vividness of a color, which decreases with shadowing. The brain's visual system is able to detect differences in three aspects or dimensions of the incoming pattern of visual sensory signals related to a visible surface, aspects that co-vary with the subjective experience of the hue, saturation, and intensity of the color. ED.

[20] See section 3.3 and section 4 of Reading 4 for a description of the mapping of geometrical features from retina to cortical sensory areas. ED.

This information has its limits. It allows us to recover structural properties of experience from information-processing properties, but not all properties of experience are structural properties. There are properties of experience, such as the intrinsic nature of a sensation of red, that cannot be fully captured in a structural description. The very intelligibility of inverted spectrum scenarios[21], where experiences of red and green are inverted but all structural properties remain the same, shows that structural properties constrain experience without exhausting it. Nevertheless, the very fact that we feel compelled to leave structural properties unaltered when we imagine experiences inverted between functionally identical systems shows how central the principle of structural coherence is to our conception of our mental lives. It is not a *logically* necessary principle, as after all we can imagine all the information processing occurring without any experience at all, but it is nevertheless a strong and familiar constraint on the psychophysical connection.

The principle of structural coherence allows for a very useful kind of indirect explanation of experience in terms of physical processes. For example, we can use facts about neural processing of visual information to indirectly explain the structure of colour space. The facts about neural processing can entail and explain the structure of awareness; if we take the coherence principle for granted, the structure of experience will also be explained. Empirical investigation might even lead us to better understand the structure of awareness within animals, shedding indirect light on Nagel's vexing question of what it is like to be a bat. This principle provides a natural interpretation of much existing work on the explanation of consciousness (e.g. Clark 1992, Hardin 1992 on colours; Akins 1993 on bats), although it is often appealed to inexplicitly. It is so familiar that it is taken for granted by almost everybody, and is a central plank in the cognitive explanation of consciousness.

The coherence between consciousness and awareness also allows a natural interpretation of work in neuroscience directed at isolating the *substrate* (or the *neural correlate*) of consciousness. Various specific hypotheses have been put forward. For example, Crick and Koch (1990) suggest that 40-hertz oscillations may be the neural correlate of consciousness, whereas Libet (1993) suggests that temporally-extended neural activity is central. If we accept the principle of coherence, the most *direct* physical correlate of consciousness is awareness: the process whereby information is made directly available for global control. The different specific hypotheses can be interpreted as empirical suggestions about how awareness might be achieved. For example, Crick and Koch suggest that 40-Hz oscillations are the gateway by which information is integrated into working memory and thereby made available to later processes. Similarly, it is natural to suppose that Libet's temporally extended activity is relevant precisely because only that sort of activity achieves global availability. The same applies to other suggested correlates such as the 'global workspace' of Baars (1988), the 'high-quality representations' of Farah (1994), and the 'selector inputs to action systems' of Shallice (1972). All these can be seen as hypotheses about the *mechanisms of awareness:* the mechanisms that perform the function of making information directly available for global control.

Given the coherence between consciousness and awareness, it follows that a mechanism of awareness will itself be a correlate of conscious experience. The question of just *which* mechanisms in the brain govern global availability is an empirical one; perhaps there are many such mechanisms. But if we accept the coherence principle, we have reason to believe that the processes that *explain* awareness will at the same time be part of the *basis* of consciousness.

2. The Principle of Organizational Invariance

This principle states that any two systems with the same fine-grained *functional organization* will have qualitatively identical experiences. If the causal

---

[21] Such a scenario is a special case of the inversion of qualia scenario which the Churchlands have described in Reading 25:

Suppose that the sensations having the quale typical of pain in you play the functional role of pleasure sensations in someone else, and the quale typical of pleasure sensations in you are [sic] had instead by the sensations that have the functional role of pain in him. Functionally, we are to suppose, the two of you are indistinguishable, but his pleasure/pain qualia are simply inverted relative to their distribution among your own sensations, functionally identified. A variation on the recipe asks us to imagine someone with an inverted distribution of the color qualia that characterize your own visual sensations (functionally identified). He thus has (what you would introspectively identify as) a sensation of red in all and only those circumstances where you have a sensation of green, and so forth (p. 350).

patterns of neural organization were duplicated in silicon, for example, with a silicon chip for every neuron and the same patterns of interaction, then the same experiences would arise. According to this principle, what matters for the emergence of experience is not the specific physical makeup of a system, but the abstract pattern of causal interaction between its components. This principle is controversial, of course. Some (e.g. Searle 1980) have thought that consciousness is tied to a specific biology, so that a silicon isomorph of a human need not be conscious. I believe that the principle can be given significant support by the analysis of thought-experiments, however.

Very briefly: suppose (for the purposes of a *reductio ad absurdum*) that the principle is false, and that there could be two functionally isomorphic systems with different experiences. Perhaps only one of the systems is conscious, or perhaps both are conscious but they have different experiences. For the purposes of illustration, let us say that one system is made of neurons and the other of silicon, and that one experiences red where the other experiences blue. The two systems have the same organization, so we can imagine gradually transforming one into the other, perhaps replacing neurons one at a time by silicon chips with the same local function. We thus gain a spectrum of intermediate cases, each with the same organization, but with slightly different physical makeup and slightly different experiences. Along this spectrum, there must be two systems A and B between which we replace less than one tenth of the system, but whose experiences differ. These two systems are physically identical, except that a small neural circuit in A has been replaced by a silicon circuit in B.

The key step in the thought-experiment is to take the relevant neural circuit in A, and install alongside it a causally isomorphic silicon circuit, with a switch between the two. What happens when we flip the switch? By hypothesis, the system's conscious experiences will change; from red to blue, say, for the purposes of illustration. This follows from the fact that the system after the change is essentially a version of B, whereas before the change it is just A.

But given the assumptions, there is no way for the system to *notice* the changes! Its causal organization stays constant, so that all of its functional states and behavioural dispositions stay fixed. As far as the system is concerned, nothing unusual has happened. There is no room for the thought, 'Hmm! Something strange just happened!' In general, the structure of any such thought must be reflected in processing, but the structure of processing remains constant here. If there were to be such a thought it must float entirely free of the system and would be utterly impotent to affect later processing. (If it affected later processing, the systems would be functionally distinct, contrary to hypothesis.) We might even flip the switch a number of times, so that experiences of red and blue dance back and forth before the system's 'inner eye'. According to hypothesis, the system can never notice these 'dancing qualia'.

This I take to be a *reductio* of the original assumption. It is a central fact about experience, very familiar from our own case, that whenever experiences change significantly and we are paying attention, we can notice the change; if this were not to be the case, we would be led to the skeptical possibility that our experiences are dancing before our eyes all the time. This hypothesis has the same status as the possibility that the world was created five minutes ago: perhaps it is logically coherent, but it is not plausible. Given the extremely plausible assumption that changes in experience correspond to changes in processing, we are led to the conclusion that the original hypothesis is impossible, and that any two functionally isomorphic systems must have the same sort of experiences. To put it in technical terms, the philosophical hypotheses of 'absent qualia' and 'inverted qualia', while logically possible, are empirically and nomologically impossible.[22]

There is more to be said here, but this gives the basic flavour. Once again, this thought experiment draws on familiar facts about the coherence between consciousness and cognitive processing to yield a strong conclusion about the relation between physical structure and experience. If the argument goes through, we know that the only

---

[22] Some may worry that a silicon isomorph of a neural system might be impossible for technical reasons. That question is open. The invariance principle says only that *if* an isomorph is possible, then it will have the same sort of conscious experience.

physical properties directly relevant to the emergence of experience are *organizational* [23] properties. This acts as a further strong constraint on a theory of consciousness.

3. The Double-Aspect Theory of Information

The two preceding principles have been *nonbasic* principles. They involve high-level notions such as 'awareness' and 'organization', and therefore lie at the wrong level to constitute the fundamental laws in a theory of consciousness. Nevertheless, they act as strong constraints. What is further needed are *basic* principles that fit these constraints and that might ultimately explain them.

The basic principle that I suggest centrally involves the notion of *information*. I understand information in more or less the sense of Shannon (1948). Where there is information, there are *information states* embedded in an *information space*. [24] An information space has a basic structure of *difference* relations between its elements, characterizing the ways in which different elements in a space are similar or different, possibly in complex ways. An information space is an abstract object, but following Shannon we can see information as *physically embodied* when there is a space of distinct physical states, the differences between which can be transmitted down some causal pathway. The states that are transmitted can be seen as themselves constituting an information space. To borrow a phrase from Bateson

(1972), physical information is a *difference that makes a difference*. [25]

The double-aspect principle stems from the observation that there is a direct isomorphism between certain physically embodied information spaces and certain *phenomenal* (or experiential) information spaces. From the same sort of observations that went into the principle of structural coherence, we can note that the differences between phenomenal states have a structure that corresponds directly to the differences embedded in physical processes; in particular, to those differences that make a difference down certain causal pathways implicated in global availability and control. That is, we can find the *same* abstract information space embedded in physical processing and in conscious experience.

This leads to a natural hypothesis: that information (or at least some information) has two basic aspects, a physical aspect and a phenomenal aspect. This has the status of a basic principle that might underlie and explain the emergence of experience from the physical. Experience arises by virtue of its status as one aspect of information, when the other aspect is found embodied in physical processing.

This principle is lent support by a number of considerations, which I can only outline briefly here. First, consideration of the sort of physical changes that correspond to changes in conscious experience suggests that such changes are always relevant by virtue of their role in constituting *informational changes*—differences within an abstract space of states that are divided up precisely according to their causal differences along certain causal

---

[23] We should bear in mind that for Chalmers, as for Kim (Reading 13), *organizational* (i.e., functional) properties are always reducible to the *physical* properties or causal powers that embody the relevant function(s). He would also be able to accept the Churchlands' requirement (in section II of Reading 25) of detailed "computational equivalence" for systems that are to be called functionally equivalent. ED.

[24] Take as an example a beach cottage which, the rental brochure tells us, "sleeps eight." We know only that it is currently occupied by one or more renters. Assume, for simplicity, that it is equally likely that the cottage is occupied by any number of persons from one to eight. This cottage scenario contains an amount of *uncertainty* which is greater or lesser depending on the *number* that the cottage sleeps. If it slept more than eight, more possibilities would need to be eliminated for me to know exactly how many occupants there were. *Information*, in the sense alluded to by Chalmers, is the negative of the quantifiable uncertainty in the situation. The greater the number that the cottage "sleeps," the more information we need in order to know how many occupants. This is the sense of "information" as the term occurs in *information theory*, a mathematical discipline of which C. E. Shannon was one of the founders. The cottage-that-sleeps-eight is a physically embodied *information space* with eight possible information states (nine, if you count being unoccupied). ED.

[25] The measurable information constituted by the presence of one to eight occupants of the beach house is an objective feature of that embodied information space. For someone standing outside the cottage at 3 AM, that information would, however, be unavailable unless it could be *communicated*. Communication involves the sending and receiving of information. There must be another embodied information space (a *receiver*) with states that co-vary with the states of the house (the *sender*), and there must be a causal link (a *channel*) whereby a specific occupancy level brings about a specific state in the receiver. Suppose that there are sensors in each bed, and these send electronic signals to a display screen on the outside wall of the house. The sensors are wired to the screen in such a way that n bodies in beds registers as N on the screen. If we can reliably assume that everyone in the house will be tucked away by 3 AM, then an information state has been sent from one information space to another. The differences in occupancy states make corresponding differences in the display states. ED.

pathways[26]. Second, if the principle of organizational invariance is to hold, then we need to find some fundamental *organizational* property for experience to be linked to, and information is an organizational property *par excellence*. Third, this principle offers some hope of explaining the principle of structural coherence in terms of the structure present within information spaces. Fourth, analysis of the cognitive explanation of our *judgments* and *claims* about conscious experience[27]—judgments that are functionally explainable but nevertheless deeply tied to experience itself—suggests that explanation centrally involves the information states embedded in cognitive processing. It follows that a theory based on information allows a deep coherence between the explanation of experience and the explanation of our judgments and claims about it.

Wheeler (1990) has suggested that information is fundamental to the physics of the universe. According to this 'it from bit' doctrine, the laws of physics can be cast in terms of information, postulating different states that give rise to different effects without actually saying what those states *are*. It is only their position in an information space that counts. If so, then information is a natural candidate to also play a role in a fundamental theory of consciousness. We are led to a conception of the world on which information is truly fundamental, and on which it has two basic aspects, corresponding to the physical and the phenomenal features of the world.

Of course, the double-aspect principle is extremely speculative and is also underdetermined, leaving a number of key questions unanswered. An obvious question is whether *all* information has a phenomenal aspect. One possibility is that we need a further constraint on the fundamental theory, indicating just what *sort* of information has a phenomenal aspect. The other possibility is that there is no such constraint. If not, then experience is much more widespread than we might have believed, as information is everywhere. This is counterintuitive at first, but on reflection I think the position gains

a certain plausibility and elegance. Where there is simple information-processing, there is simple experience, and where there is complex information processing, there is complex experience. A mouse has a simpler information-processing structure than a human, and has correspondingly simpler experience; perhaps a thermostat, a maximally simple information-processing structure, might have maximally simple experience? Indeed, if experience is truly a fundamental property, it would be surprising for it to arise only every now and then; most fundamental properties are more evenly spread. In any case, this is very much an open question, but I believe that the position is not as implausible as it is often thought to be.

Once a fundamental link between information and experience is on the table, the door is opened to some grander metaphysical speculation concerning the nature of the world. For example, it is often noted that physics characterizes its basic entities only *extrinsically,* in terms of their relations to other entities, which are themselves characterized extrinsically, and so on. The intrinsic nature of physical entities is left aside.[28] Some argue that no such intrinsic properties exist, but then one is left with a world that is pure causal flux (a pure flow of information) with no properties for the causation to relate. If one allows that intrinsic properties exist, a natural speculation given the above is that the intrinsic properties of the physical—the properties that causation ultimately relates—are themselves phenomenal properties. We might say that phenomenal properties are the internal aspect of information. This could answer a concern about the causal relevance of experience—a natural worry, given a picture on which the physical domain is causally closed, and on which experience is supplementary to the physical. The informational view allows us to understand how experience might have a subtle kind of causal relevance in virtue of its status as the intrinsic aspect of the physical. This metaphysical speculation is probably best ignored for the purposes of developing a scientific theory, but in addressing some philosophical issues it is quite suggestive.

---

[26] In general, the causal pathways are ones from perception to behavior. Changes in experiential content tend to be related to environmental events of the sort that call for adaptive responses, as Descartes noticed in *Meditation Six*. ED.

[27] E.g., judgments such as "This feels cold." ED.

[28] This issue is discussed in the commentary following Reading 13. The question of whether all or just some physical properties are relational is a speculation beyond the scope of this book. ED.

VIII: CONCLUSION

The theory I have presented is speculative, but it is a candidate theory. I suspect that the principles of structural coherence and organizational invariance will be planks in any satisfactory theory of consciousness; the status of the double-aspect theory of information is much less certain. Indeed, right now it is more of an idea than a theory. To have any hope of eventual explanatory success, it will have to be specified more fully and fleshed out into a more powerful form. Still, reflection on just what is plausible and implausible about it, on where it works and where it fails, can only lead to a better theory.

Most existing theories of consciousness either deny the phenomenon, explain something else, or elevate the problem to an eternal mystery. I hope to have shown that it is possible to make progress on the problem even while taking it seriously. To make further progress, we will need further investigation, more refined theories, and more careful analysis. The hard problem is a hard problem, but there is no reason to believe that it will remain permanently unsolved.

FURTHER READING

The problems of consciousness have been widely discussed in the recent philosophical literature. For some conceptual clarification of the various problems of consciousness, see Block 1995, Nelkin 1993 and Tye 1995. Those who have stressed the difficulties of explaining experience in physical terms include Hodgson 1988, Jackson 1982, Levine 1983, Lockwood 1989, McGinn 1989, Nagel 1974, Seager 1991, Searle 1992, Strawson 1994 and Velmans 1991, among others. Those who take a reductive approach include Churchland 1995, Clark 1992, Dennett 1991, Dretske 1995, Kirk 1994, Rosenthal 1996 and Tye 1995. There have not been many attempts to build detailed nonreductive theories in the literature, but see Hodgson 1988 and Lockwood 1989 for some thoughts in that direction. Two excellent collections of recent articles on consciousness are Block, Flanagan and Güzeldere 1996 and Metzinger 1995.

REFERENCES

Akins, K. (1993), "What is it like to be boring and myopic?" in *Dennett and his Critics,* ed. B. Dahlbom (Oxford: Blackwell).

Allport, A. (1988), "What concept of consciousness?" in *Consciousness in Contemporary Science,* ed. A. Marcel and E. Bisiach (Oxford: Oxford University Press).

Baars, B. J. (1988), *A Cognitive Theory of Consciousness* (Cambridge: Cambridge University Press).

Bateson, G. (1972), *Steps to an Ecology of Mind* (Chandler Publishing).

Block, N. (1995), 'On a confusion about the function of consciousness', *Behavioral and Brain Sciences* 18: 227–2247.

Block, N., Flanagan, O., and Güzeldere, G. (eds. 1996), *The Nature of Consciousness: Philosophical and Scientific Debates* (Cambridge, MA: MIT Press).

Chalmers, D. J. (1996), *The Conscious Mind* (New York: Oxford University Press).

Churchland, P. M. (1995), *The Engine of Reason, The Seat of the Soul: A Philosophical Journey into the Brain* (Cambridge, MA: MIT Press).

Clark, A. (1992), *Sensory Qualities* (Oxford: Oxford University Press).

Crick, F. and Koch, C. (1990), 'Toward a neurobiological theory of consciousness', *Seminars in the Neurosciences,* 2, pp. 263–75.

Crick, F. (1994), *The Astonishing Hypothesis: The Scientific Search for the Soul* (New York: Scribners).

Dennett, D. C. (1991), *Consciousness Explained* (Boston: Little, Brown).

Dretske, F. I. (1995), *Naturalizing the Mind* (Cambridge, MA: MIT Press).

Eckhorn, R., Bauer, R., Jordan, W., Brosch, M., Kruse, W., Munk, M. & Reitbock, H. J. (1988). *Coherent Oscillations: A Mechanism for Feature Linking in the Visual Cortex Biological Cybernetics* 60: 121–30.

Edelman, G. (1989), *The Remembered Present: A Biological Theory of Consciousness* (New York: Basic Books).

Farah, M. J. (1994), 'Visual perception and visual awareness after brain damage: a tutorial overview', in *Consciousness and Unconscious Information Processing: Attention and Performance* 15, ed. C. Umilta and M. Moscovitch (Cambridge, MA: MIT Press).

Flohr, H. (1992), 'Qualia and brain processes', in *Emergence or Reduction?: Prospects for Nonreductive Physicalism,* ed. A. Beckermann, H. Flohr, and J. Kim (Berlin: De Gruyter).

Hameroff, S. R. (1994), 'Quantum coherence in microtubules: a neural basis for emergent consciousness?', *Journal of Consciousness Studies,* 1, pp. 91–118.

Hardin, C. L. (1992), 'Physiology, phenomenology, and Spinoza's true colors', in *Emergence or Reduction?: Prospects for Nonreductive Physicalism,* ed. A. Beckermann, H. Flohr, and J. Kim (Berlin: De Gruyter).

Hill, C. S. (1991), *Sensations: A Defense of Type Materialism* (Cambridge: Cambridge University Press).

Hodgson, D. (1922), *The Mind Matters: Consciousness and Choice in a Quantum World* (Oxford: Oxford University Press).

Humphrey, N. (1992), *A History of the Mind* (New York: Simon and Schuster).

Jackendoff, R. (1987), *Consciousness and the Computational Mind* (Cambridge, MA: MIT Press).

Jackson, F. (1982), 'Epiphenomenal qualia', *Philosophical Quarterly,* 32, pp. 127–36.

—— (1994), 'Finding the mind in the natural world', in *Philosophy and the Cognitive Sciences,* ed. R. Casati, B. Smith, and S. White (Vienna: Hölder-Pichler-Tempsky).

Kirk, R. (1994), *Raw Feeling: A Philosophical Account of the Essence of Consciousness* (Oxford: Oxford University Press).

Kripke, S. (1980), *Naming and Necessity* (Cambridge, MA: Harvard University Press).

Levine, J. (1983), 'Materialism and qualia: the explanatory gap', *Pacific Philosophical Quarterly,* 64, pp. 354–61.

Lewis, D. (1994), 'Reduction of mind', in *A Companion to the Philosophy of Mind,* ed. S. Guttenplan (Oxford: Blackwell).

Libet, B. (1993), 'The neural time factor in conscious and unconscious events', in *Experimental and Theoretical Studies of Consciousness* (Ciba Foundation Symposium 174), ed. G. R. Block and J. Marsh (Chichester: John Wiley and Sons).

Loar, B. (1990), 'Phenomenal states', *Philosophical Perspectives,* 4, pp. 81–108.

Lockwood, M. (1989), *Mind, Brain, and the Quantum* (Oxford: Blackwell).

McGinn, C. (1989), 'Can we solve the mind-body problem?', *Mind,* 98, pp. 349–66.

Metzinger, T. (ed. 1995), *Conscious Experience* (Exeter: Imprint Academic).

Nagel, T. (1974), 'What is it like to be a bat?', *Philosophical Review,* 4, pp. 435–50.

Nelkin, N. (1993), 'What is consciousness?', *Philosophy of Science,* 60, pp. 419–34.

Newell, A. (1990), *Unified Theories of Cognition* (Cambridge, MA: Harvard University Press).

Penrose, R. (1989), *The Emperor's New Mind* (Oxford: Oxford University Press).

—— (1994), *Shadows of the Mind* (Oxford: Oxford University Press).

Rosenthal, D. M. (1996), 'A theory of consciousness', in *The Nature of Consciousness,* ed. N. Block, O. Flanagan, and G. Güzeldere (Cambridge, MA: MIT Press).

Seager, W. E. (1991), *Metaphysics of Consciousness* (London: Routledge).

Searle, J. R. (1980), 'Minds, brains and programs', *Behavioral and Brain Sciences,* 3, pp. 417–57.

—— (1992), *The Rediscovery of the Mind* (Cambridge, MA: MIT Press).

Shallice, T. (1972), 'Dual functions of consciousness', *Psychological Review,* 79, pp. 383–93.

Shannon, C. E. (1948), 'A mathematical theory of communication', *Bell Systems Technical Journal,* 27, pp. 379–423.

Strawson, G. (1994), *Mental Reality* (Cambridge, MA: MIT Press).

Tye, M. (1995), *Ten Problems of Consciousness* (Cambridge, MA: MIT Press).

Velmans, M. (1991), 'Is human information-processing conscious?' *Behavioral and Brain Sciences,* 14, pp. 651ff.

Wheeler, J. A. (1990), 'Information, physics, quantum: the search for links', in *Complexity, Entropy, and the Physics of Information,* ed. W. Zurek (Redwood City, CA: Addison-Wesley).

Wilkes, KV. (1988), '——, Yishi, Duh, Um and consciousness', in *Consciousness in Contemporary Science,* ed. A. Marcel and E. Bisiach (Oxford: Oxford University Press).

Chalmers wants to show that a nonreductive *explanation* of consciousness is possible. He rejects epiphenomenalism of the sort espoused by Campbell and Jackson because it leaves consciousness as an unintelligible remainder in a universe that is otherwise amenable to scientific theory. Yet he argues that the kinds of reductive, functionalist explanations that seem to apply to other aspects of the mind cannot work with consciousness. The only alternative, he concludes, is to give to consciousness an ontological status as fundamental as that of basic physical items such as space-time, energy, and mass. These entities are not reductively explained, yet we don't regard their occurrence as a mystery. So let's treat consciousness that way, and look for psychophysical laws that will relate it to other basic entities, in a fundamental theory even more inclusive than physical science.

In section VII ("Toward a Theory of Consciousness") Chalmers boldly announces that it "is not too soon to begin work on a theory." What he gives us next are three "psychophysical principles" that are candidates for a future theory. The *first* is a principle of "structural coherence" which asserts a general correspondence between structural features of *consciousness* and structural features of the physical processes that embody *awareness* (understood in the functional sense of direct availability for global control). For example, experienced differences in colors correspond to different input values detectable by the neural processes that enable us to report color differences. The *second* principle ("organizational invariance") asserts that wherever there is the same "fine-grained" functional organization, there will be qualitatively the same experience. Here he introduces his "dancing qualia" argument for the claim that a silicon functional equivalent of our neural wetware would give rise to the same qualia. From Chalmers' point of view, the trouble with these two otherwise promising principles is that they are nonbasic: they deal with *higher-level* physical processes of the sort found in organisms with a central nervous system. They don't interrelate *basic* entities. Chalmers believes that consciousness can't be made intelligible unless it can be understood as a fundamental entity. His third principle is supposed to do that.

The *third* principle is his "double-aspect theory of information." As Chalmers himself admits, this principle is highly speculative and in great need of elaboration. It seems to ride on a theory of the physicist J. A. Wheeler that *information* is a fundamental entity in the domain of physical science, and that the properties studied in physical science can be understood as extrinsic and informational. The phenomenal aspect of the world could then be understood as constituting the inner aspect or *intrinsic* nature of what is characterized *extrinsically* in physical science.

Quite apart from the very speculative and sketchy nature of his claims about the domain of physical science, there is a further problem with Chalmers' attempt to treat consciousness as a fundamental entity: The only consciousness we have any access to is our own, and (as his first two principles emphasize) this consciousness has a strong degree of structural coherence with the highly evolved neural processes of our brains. What could we mean by "experience" that coheres with, or is the inner aspect of, processes at a fundamental physical level?

REVIEW QUESTIONS

1. As he describes what a future theory of consciousness might be like, Chalmers acknowledges a possible objection which he regards as nonfatal:

> There is an obvious problem that plagues the development of a theory of consciousness, and that is the paucity of objective data. Conscious experience is not directly observable in an experimental context, so we cannot generate data about the relationship between physical processes and experience at will. Nevertheless, we all have access to a rich source of data in our own case. Many important regularities between experience and processing

can be inferred from considerations about one's own experience. There are also good indirect sources of data from observable cases, as when one relies on the verbal report of a subject as an indication of experience. These methods have their limitations, but we have more than enough data to get a theory off the ground. (pp. 392–393)

From what he says in Reading 3, it seems that Norman Malcolm would disagree:

One supposes that one inwardly picks out something as thinking or pain and thereafter identifies it whenever it presents itself in the soul. But the question to be pressed is, Does one make *correct* identifications? . . . Suppose that he identified the emotion of anxiety as the sensation of pain? Neither he nor anyone else could know about this "mistake." Perhaps he makes a mistake *every* time! Perhaps all of us do! We ought to see now that we are talking nonsense. We do not know what a *mistake* would be. We have no standard, no examples, no customary practice, with which to compare our inner recognitions. The inward identification cannot hit the bull's-eye, or miss it either, because there is no bull's-eye. When we see that the ideas of correct and incorrect have no application to the supposed inner identification, the latter notion loses its appearance of sense. (pp. 46–47)

What could Chalmers say to this?

2. Chalmers also has this to say about a future theory of consciousness:

Ultimately, these principles should tell us what sort of physical systems will have associated experiences, and for the systems that do, they should tell us what sort of physical properties are relevant to the emergence of experience, and just what sort of experience we should expect any given physical system to yield. (p. 393)

Comment on this claim from the perspective of Nagel in Reading 22.

28

Phenomenal States

Brian Loar

Brian Loar is a professor of philosophy at Rutgers University. He has published extensively in the philosophy of mind and philosophy of language.

Loar mounts a defense of physicalist-functionalism against objections of the sort raised by Kripke, Nagel, Jackson, and Chalmers. He begins by accepting what he calls the "antiphysicalist intuition" that phenomenal concepts (concepts of phenomenal qualities, i.e., of what it is like to have one or another kind of experience) are *irreducibly different* from any physicochemical or functional concepts we may have or come to have of associated brain states. His central thesis is that even if one agrees with this intuition, one can still be a physicalist—one can still claim that the phenomenal qualities (qualia) which phenomenal concepts designate are identical with "physical-functional properties of the sort envisaged by contemporary brain science." He supports this thesis by analyzing phenomenal concepts as a special sort of *recognitional* concept, a sort that picks out physical-functional properties of the brain directly, but opaquely.

On a natural view of ourselves, we introspectively discriminate our own experiences and thereby form conceptions of their qualities, both salient and subtle. These discriminations are of various degrees of generality, from small differences in tactual and color experience to broad differences of sensory modality, for example, those among smell, hearing, and pain. What we apparently discern are ways experiences differ and resemble each other with respect to *what it is like to have them*. Following common usage, I will call these experiential resemblances *phenomenal qualities,* and the conceptions we have of them, *phenomenal concepts*. Phenomenal concepts are formed "from one's own case." They are *type-demonstratives* that derive their reference

from a first-person perspective: 'that type of sensation', 'that feature of visual experience'. And so third-person ascriptions of phenomenal qualities are projective ascriptions of what one has grasped in one's own case: 'she has an experience of that type.'

'Phenomenal quality' can have a different sense, namely, how the *object* of a perceptual experience appears. In this sense, a phenomenal quality is ascribed to an object and not directly to an experience. Some have argued that all we discern phenomenologically are phenomenal qualities in this sense; they deny that experiences themselves have introspectible qualities that are not ascribed primarily to their objects (Harman 1990; Block 1990). I will not pursue the issue here, but will assume a certain view of it. For the present objective is to engage antiphysicalist arguments and entrenched intuitions to the effect that conscious mental qualities cannot be identical with ordinary physical properties, or at least that it is problematic to suppose that

"Phenomenal States," by Brian Loar appeared in *Philosophical Perspectives, 4, Action Theory and Philosophy of Mind, 1990* edited by James E. Tomberlin (copyright by Ridgeview Publishing Co., Atascadero, CA). Reprinted by permission of Ridgeview Publishing Company.

they are so. Antiphysicalists typically suppose that such mental properties are not relational—that is, that they present themselves as not intrinsically involving relations to things outside the mind. They may allow that, say, visual experiences are in some sense intrinsically representational. That is hard to deny because, as regards ordinary visual experiences, we cannot apparently conceive them phenomenally in a way that abstracts from their *purporting* to represent things in a certain way. The antiphysicalist intuition is compatible with visual experiences' having (some sort of) internally determined intentional structure, so that it is an introspectable and nonrelational feature of a visual experience that it represents things visually as being thus and so. Antiphysicalists suppose that we have conceptions of how visual experiences differ and resemble each other with respect to what it is like to have those experiences. These conceptions then are of qualities of experiences, whatever allowances one may also make for the apparent qualities of the intrinsic objects of those experiences. I will assume that the antiphysicalists' phenomenological and internalist intuitions are correct. The idea is to engage them over the central point, that is, whether those aspects of the mental that we both count as phenomenologically compelling raise substantive difficulties for the thesis that phenomenal qualities (thus understood) are physical properties of the brain that lie within the scope of current science.

We have to distinguish between *concepts* and *properties,* and this chapter turns on that distinction. Antiphysicalist arguments and intuitions take off from a sound intuition about concepts. Phenomenal concepts are conceptually irreducible in this sense: they neither a priori imply, nor are implied by, physical-functional concepts. Although that is denied by analytical functionalists[1] (Levin 1983, 1986), many other physicalists, including me, find it intuitively appealing. The antiphysicalist takes this conceptual intuition a good deal further, to the

conclusion that phenomenal qualities are themselves irreducible, are not physical-functional properties, at least not of the ordinary sort. The upshot is a range of antireductionist views: that consciousness and phenomenal qualities are unreal because irreducible,[2] that they are irreducibly non-physical-functional facts,[3] that they are forever mysterious, or pose an intellectual problem different from other empirical problems, or require new conceptions of the physical.[4]

It is my view that we can have it both ways. We may take the phenomenological intuition at face value, accepting introspective concepts and their conceptual irreducibility, and at the same time take phenomenal qualities to be identical with physical-functional properties of the sort envisaged by contemporary brain science. As I see it, there is no persuasive philosophically articulated argument to the contrary.

This is not to deny the power of raw metaphysical intuition. Thoughtful people compare phenomenal qualities and kinds of physical-functional property, say the activation of neural assemblies. It appears to them to be an evident and unmediated truth, independent of further premises, that phenomenal qualities cannot be identical with properties of those types or perhaps of any physical-functional type. This intuition is so compelling that it is tempting to regard antiphysicalist arguments as rationalizations of an intuition whose independent force masks their tendentiousness. It is the point of this chapter to consider the arguments. But I will also present a positive account of the relation between phenomenal concepts and physical properties that may provide some relief, or at least some distance, from the illusory metaphysical intuition.

In recent years the central problem with physicalism has been thought by many to be "the explanatory gap."[5] This is the idea that we cannot *explain,* in terms of physical-functional properties, what makes a certain experience 'feel like this', in the way we can explain what makes a certain substance a liquid, say. It is concluded that physicalism is defective in some respect, that there cannot be a

---

[1] An *analytical functionalist* is one who maintains that there is a *necessary connection* between the concept of a mental state and the concept of a function which that state plays in the system we call the mind, or in the more broadly conceived system that links the mind with the environment as a source of input and a domain of behavioral output for the mind. Such a connection is notoriously difficult to find in the case of what Loar is calling phenomenal concepts (see, for example, Campbell's discussion of the varieties of pain sensation and the imitation man in Reading 23). ED.

[2] Cf. Rey (forthcoming) and Dennett (1991).
[3] Jackson (1982, 1986). [This is Jackson's thesis in Reading 24. ED.]
[4] Nagel (1974, 1986); McGinn (1993). [See Reading 22 by Nagel, and Reading 26 by McGinn. ED.]
[5] Chalmers discusses this term in section III of Reading 27. ED.

(proper) reduction of the mental to the physical. Before we consider this explanatory gap, we must first examine, in some detail, a more basic antiphysicalist line of reasoning that goes back to Leibniz and beyond, a leading version of which is now called the knowledge argument. Answering this argument will generate a framework in which to address antiphysicalist concerns in general.

1. THE KNOWLEDGE ARGUMENT AND ITS SEMANTIC PREMISE

The knowledge argument is straightforward on the face of it. Consider any phenomenal quality and any physical property however complex. We can know that a person has the physical property without knowing that she experiences the phenomenal quality. And no amount of a priori reasoning or construction can bridge this conceptual gap. That is the intuitive premise. The conclusion is drawn that the phenomenal quality cannot be identical with the physical property. The argument is equivalent to this: since physical and phenomenal conceptions can be connected only a posteriori, physical properties must be distinct from phenomenal properties.

The best known and liveliest version of the knowledge argument is Frank Jackson's,[6] which features the physiologically omniscient Mary, who has never seen color and so does not know what it is like for us to see red, despite her knowing all the physical-functional facts about us.[7] She later sees colors, and thus learns what is has been like all along for us to see red. She learns a new fact about us. Jackson concludes that this fact is not among the physical facts, since Mary already knew them. It is not difficult to see that this argument depends on a more or less technical premise.

In my view, the physicalist should accept Jackson's intuitive description of Mary: she fails to know that we have certain color experiences even though she knows all relevant physical facts about us. And when she acquires color experience, she does learn something new about us—if you like, learns a new fact or truth. But this is to be granted, of course, only on an **opaque** reading of 'Mary

learns that we have such and such color experiences', and on corresponding readings of 'learns a new fact or truth about us'. For as regards the **transparent** versions of those ascriptions of what Mary did not know and then learned, they would beg the question, amounting to this: 'as for the property of having such and such color experiences, Mary did not know, but then learned, *of that property that we have it*'. Physicalists reject this, for according to us those experiential properties are physical properties, and Mary already knew of all our physical properties that we have them—under their physical descriptions. What she lacked and then acquired, rather, was knowledge of certain such properties couched in experiential terms.

Drawing metaphysical conclusions from opaque contexts is risky. And in fact inferences of Jackson's form, without additional premises, are open to straightforward counter examples of a familiar sort. Let me describe two cases.

(1) Max learns that the bottle before him contains CH_3CH_2OH. But he does not know that the bottle contains alcohol. This holds on an opaque reading: he would not assert that there's stuff called alcohol in the bottle, or that the bottle contains the intoxicating component of beer and wine. Let sheltered Max even lack the ordinary concept 'alcohol'. After he acquires that ordinary concept, he learns something new—that the bottle contained alcohol. If the knowledge argument has a generally valid form, we could then infer from Max's epistemic situation that alcohol is not identical with CH_3CH_2OH. Evidently this does not follow.

(2) Margot learns about the element Au and reads that people decorate themselves with alloys of Au. But she has never seen gold and cannot visually identify it: she lacks an adequate visual conception. She later is shown some gold and forms a visual conception of it, "that stuff," and she acquires a new piece of information—individuated opaquely—to the effect that those previously read-about embellishments are made of that stuff. Again, if the knowledge argument were unrestrictedly valid, it would follow that that stuff is not identical with Au. This case differs from the case of Max by involving not a descriptive mode[8] of presentation

---

[6]See Reading 24. ED.
[7]Jackson (1982, 1986).

[8]I.e., the stuff in beer and wine that makes people get drunk. ED.

but (as we might say) a perceptual mode[9] of presentation.

It is not difficult to find a difference between both these cases and the case of Mary. Max lacks knowledge of the bottle's contents under a contingent description of it—"ingredient of wine and beer that makes you intoxicated." What Margot lacks is a certain visual conception of Au, which is to say gold. This typically would not be a descriptive conception; it would not self-consciously take the form "the stuff that occasions this type of visual experience." Still on the face of it such a concept implicates a visual-experience type. For it picks out the kind it picks out by virtue of that kind's occasioning experiences of that type. And that is a crucial *contingency* in how the concept that Margot lacks is related to its reference. I hope I will be understood, then, if I say that the visual take on Au that Margot lacks would have conceived Au 'under a contingent mode of presentation'.

This brings us back to Mary, whose acquired conception of what it is like to see red does not conceive it under a contingent mode of presentation. She is not conceiving of a property that presents itself *contingently* thus: it is like such and such to experience *P*. Being experienced like that is essential to the property Mary conceives. She conceives it directly. When Mary later acquires new information about us (construed opaquely), the novelty of this information cannot be explained— as in the case of Margot—as her acquiring a new contingent mode of presentation of something she has otherwise known of all along. She has a *direct* grasp of the property involved in the new information; she conceives of it somehow, but not under a contingent mode of presentation. Proponents of the knowledge argument will say that is why it is valid on an opaque reading: there is no contingency in Mary's conception of the new phenomenal information that explains it as a novel take on old facts. She learns new facts *simpliciter* and not new conceptions of old facts.

Notice how close this comes to Saul Kripke's well-known antiphysicalist argument (1980).[10] Kripke assumes that a phenomenal concept such as

'pain' cannot be a priori linked with a physical concept such as that of the stimulation of C-fibers. The case of Mary is a vivid way of making the same point. Kripke points out that property identities can be true even if not a priori, for example, 'heat = such and such molecular property'. It seems fair to represent the next step in his argument as follows. 'Heat' has a contingent higher-order mode of presentation that connotes the property 'feeling like this'. That is what accounts for the a posteriori status of the identity. But, as Kripke points out, this cannot be how 'pain' works: the phenomenal concept 'pain' does not pick out its referent via a contingent mode of presentation; it conceives pain directly and essentially.[11] Kripke concludes that pain is not identical with a physical property.

The two arguments then turn on the same implicit assumption. The only way to account for the a posteriori status of a true property identity is this: one of the terms expresses a contingent mode of presentation. This ought to be given a place of prominence.

> (Semantic premise)   A statement of property identity that links conceptually independent concepts is true only if at least one concept picks out the property it refers to by connoting a contingent property of that property.

The knowledge argument and Kripke's argument then depend on two assumptions: the conceptual independence of phenomenal concepts and physical-functional concepts, which I accept, and the semantic premise, which I deny.

The antiphysicalist intuition that links concept-individuation and property-individuation (more closely than is in my view correct) is perhaps this. Phenomenal concepts and theoretical expressions of physical properties both conceive their references essentially. But if two concepts conceive a given property essentially, neither mediated by contingent modes of presentation, one ought to be able to see a priori—at least after optimal reflec-

---

[9] I.e., the visibly glittering stuff. ED.

[10] Reading 7. ED.

[11] It is not essential to heat (the average kinetic energy of the atomic constituents of matter) that it induce a certain kind of sensation in sentient creatures, whereas it belongs to the very nature of pain that it be a certain kind of sensation. It *does not just happen* to be the case that pain is felt. ED.

tion—that they pick out the same property. Such concepts' connections cannot be a posteriori; that they pick out the same property would have to be transparent.

But as against this, if a phenomenal concept can pick out a physical property directly or essentially, not via a contingent mode of presentation, and yet be *conceptually independent* of all physical-functional concepts, so that Mary's history is coherent, then Jackson's and Kripke's arguments are ineffectual. We could have two conceptually independent conceptions of a property, neither of which connote contingent modes of presentation, such that substituting one for the other in an opaquely interpreted epistemic context does not preserve truth. Even granting that our conception of phenomenal qualities is direct, physicalism would not entail that knowing the physical-functional facts implies knowing, on an opaque construal, the phenomenal facts; and so the failure of this implication would be quite compatible with physicalism. The next few sections give an account of phenomenal concepts and properties that would justify this claim.

2. RECOGNITIONAL CONCEPTS

Phenomenal concepts belong to a wide class of concepts that I will call recognitional concepts. They have the form 'x is one of *that* kind'; they are type-demonstratives. These type-demonstratives are grounded in dispositions to classify, by way of perceptual discriminations, certain objects, events, situations. Suppose you go into the California desert and spot a succulent never seen before. You become adept at recognizing instances, and gain a recognitional command of their kind, without a name for it; you are disposed to identify positive and negative instances and thereby pick out a kind. These dispositions are typically linked with capacities to form images, whose conceptual role seems to be to focus thoughts about an identifiable kind in the absence of currently perceived instances. An image is presumably 'of' a given kind by virtue of both past recognitions and current dispositions.

Recognitional concepts are generally formed against a further conceptual background. In identifying a thing as of a recognized kind, we almost always presuppose a more general type to which the kind belongs: four-legged animal, plant, physical

thing, perceptible event. A recognitional concept will then have the form 'physical thing of that (perceived) kind' or 'internal state of that kind,' and so forth.[12]

Here are some basic features of recognitional concepts that it will help to have in mind in connection with the account of phenomenal concepts that follows.

1. You can understand 'porcelain' from a technical description and only later learn visually, tactually, and aurally to recognize instances. By contrast, in the phenomenon I mean the concept is recognitional at its core; the original concept is recognitional.

2. A recognitional concept need involve no reference to a past instance, or have the form 'is of the same type as that (remembered) one'. You can forget particular instances and still judge 'another one of those'.

3. Recognitional abilities depend on no consciously accessible analysis into component features; they can be irreducibly gestalt.[13]

4. Recognitional concepts are perspectival. Suppose you see certain creatures up close and form a recognitional concept—'those creatures$_1$'; and suppose you see others at a distance, not being able to tell that they are of the same kind (even when they are), and form another recognitional concept—'those creatures$_2$'. These concepts will be a priori independent. Now the respect in which they differ is *perspectival,* in some intuitive sense. A recognitional concept is in part individuated by its constitutive perspective. Here is the important point: a recognitional concept can be ascribed

---

[12] How such background concepts themselves arise is not my topic; but we might think of them variously as deriving from more general recognitional capacities, or as functions of complex inferential roles, or as socially deferential; or they may be components of innate structures. Background concepts are not always presupposed. Someone may be extremely good at telling stars from other objects (e.g., lightning bugs, airplanes, comets, planets) without having any real idea of what they are.

[13] The *gestalt* theory of perception holds that interpretation or conceptualization is partly constitutive of the sensory experience as such. Thus, how one sees or recognizes a figure against its background alters the experience itself, as in the face-vase ambiguity illustrated in the review question at the end of Reading 8. It rejects the theory expounded by Locke, Hume, and others, that raw sensory contents can be "given" to our awareness, often in the form of simpler sensations compounded with each other, which the mind then interprets or classifies one way or the other. ED.

outside its constitutive perspective; 'that thing (seen at distance) is one of those creatures$_1$ (seen up close)' makes perfectly good sense. This plays a key role below in the account of third-person ascriptions of phenomenal concepts.

(This casual invoking of reference-determining dispositions will be a red flag for many who are aware of the vexing foundations of the theory of reference. Problems about referential scrutability[14], rule-following, naturalizing intentionality—however one wishes to put it—are as frustrating as any in contemporary philosophy. I do not propose to address them here. The idea rather is to appeal to unanalyzed common sense concerning a natural group of concepts and apparent conceptual abilities. The apparent irreducibility of phenomenal qualities itself arises from appeal to intuitions independent of the theory of reference; and it seems reasonable that we should, in resolving that issue, appeal to notions that arise at the same intuitive level. That we *appear* to have recognitional concepts and identifying dispositions[15] that are more or less determinate in their reference is hard to deny. My conception of 'those hedges' (seen around the neighborhood) may unambiguously pick out a variety of eugenia. An example closer to the present topic is this. We can imagine an experiment in which the experimenter tries to determine which internal property is the focus of her subject's identifications: 'again', . . . 'there it is again'. There seems no commonsensical implausibility—putting aside foundational worries about the inscrutability of reference—in the idea that there is a best possible answer to the experimenter's question, in the scientific long run.[16]

3. PHENOMENAL CONCEPTS AS RECOGNITIONAL CONCEPTS

Here is the view to be defended. Phenomenal concepts are recognitional concepts that pick out certain internal properties; these are physical-functional properties of the brain. They are the concepts we deploy in our phenomenological reflections; and there is no good philosophical reason to deny that, odd though it may sound, the properties these conceptions *phenomenologically reveal* are physical-functional properties—but not of course under physical-functional descriptions. Granted that brain research might discover that (what we take to be) our phenomenal concepts do not in fact discriminate unified physical-functional properties.[17] Failing that, it is quite coherent for a physicalist to take the phenomenology at face value: the property of *its being like this* to have a certain experience is nothing over and above a certain physical-functional property of the brain.

Phenomenal concepts are conceptually independent of physical-functional descriptions, and yet pairs of such concepts may converge on, pick out, the same properties. Rebutting the semantic premise of the knowledge argument requires making sense of the idea that phenomenal concepts conceive physical-functional properties 'directly', that is, not by way of contingent modes of presentation. The objective is to show that the knowledge argument fails for the same reason in the case of Mary as in the case of Max: both arguments require substitution in opaque contexts of terms that are conceptually independent. In the case of Max, the conceptual independence[18] appears to derive from 'alcohol''s connoting a contingent mode of presentation that is metaphysically independent of the property referred to by the chemical concept. In the case of Mary it has a different source.

What then accounts for the conceptual independence of phenomenal and physical-functional concepts? The simple answer is that recognitional concepts and theoretical concepts are in general conceptually independent. It is true that recognitional concepts other than phenomenal concepts connote contingent modes of presentation that are metaphysically independent of the natural kinds they pick out, and hence independent of the kind

---

[14] Quine and others have argued that reference is inscrutable or indeterminate, i.e., that there is no single reference for any given expression, because the assignment of a referent is always relative to one of many alternative ways of assigning referents. ED.

[15] I.e., dispositions to identify things around us. ED.

[16] For more on recognitional concepts and on the determinacy of reference, see Loar (1990; 1991; forthcoming).

[17] For instance, my phenomenal concept of a toothache (my concept of what it is like to have what I call a toothache) seems to be of a single, unitary quality or property of something going on in me, but brain research may disclose that what this concept picks out is really a complex set of functions widely dispersed in the brain. In general, we have no reason to expect strong correlations between folk-psychological typing of mental items and the kinds of brain processes at work. ED.

[18] I.e., between the concepts of CH_3CH_2OH and of alcohol. ED.

referred to by the theoretical term of the pair.[19] But we need not count this metaphysical independence as essential to the conceptual independence of co-referring recognitional and theoretical concepts. Concepts of the two sorts have quite different conceptual roles. It is hardly surprising that a recognitional conception of a physical property should discriminate it without analyzing it in scientific terms. Nor should it be surprising that, if there are recognitional concepts that pick out physical properties *not* via contingent modes of presentation, they do not discriminate their references by analyzing them (even implicitly) in scientific terms. Basic recognitional abilities do not depend on or get triggered by conscious scientific analysis. If phenomenal concepts reflect basic recognitions of internal physical-functional states, they *should* be conceptually independent of theoretical physical-functional descriptions. That is what you expect quite apart from issues concerning physicalism.

An antireductionist may reply that the physicalist view depends on an ad hoc assumption and that it is tendentious to suppose that phenomenal concepts differ from all other recognitional concepts in not having contingent modes of presentation.

But this is not fair. Even on the antiphysicalist view, phenomenal concepts are recognitional concepts, and we have 'direct' recognitional conceptions of phenomenal qualities, that is, conceptions unmediated by contingent modes of presentation.[20] Evidently it would be absurd to insist that the antiphysicalist hold that we conceive of a phenomenal quality of one kind via a phenomenal mode of presentation of a distinct kind. And why should the physicalist not agree that phenomenal recognitional concepts are structured in whatever simple way the antiphysicalist requires? That is after all the intuitive situation, and the physicalist simply claims that the intuitive facts about phenomenal qualities are compatible with physicalism. The physicalist makes the additional claim that the phenomenal quality thus directly conceived is a physical-functional property. On both metaphysical views, phenomenal concepts differ from other recognitional concepts; phenomenal concepts are a peculiar sort of recognitional concept on any account, and that can hardly count against physicalism. The two views agree about conceptual structure and disagree about the nature of phenomenal qualities. To insist that physicalism implies, absurdly, that phenomenal concepts could pick out physical properties only via metaphysically distinct phenomenal modes of presentation is unmotivated. There is, though, still more to be said about whether phenomenal concepts should be regarded as having modes of presentation of some sort.

Suppose this account of how phenomenal concepts refer is true. Here is a semantic consequence. The physicalist thesis implies that the judgments "the state *a* feels like that" and "the state *a* has physical-functional property *P*" can have the same truth condition even though their joint truth or falsity can be known only a posteriori. I mean, same condition of truth in a possible world. For truth conditions are determined in part by the possible world satisfaction conditions[21] of predicates; and if a phenomenal predicate directly refers to a physical property, that property constitutes its satisfaction condition.

On this account, a phenomenal concept **rigidly designates** the property it picks out. But then it rigidly designates the same property that some theoretical physical concept rigidly designates. This could seem problematic, for if a concept rigidly designates a property not via a contingent mode of presentation, must that concept not capture the *essence* of the designated property? And if two concepts capture the essence of the same property, must we not be able to know this a priori? These are equivocating uses of 'capture the essence of'. On one use, it expresses a referential notion that comes to no more than 'directly rigidly designate'. On the other, it means something like 'be conceptually interderivable with some theoretical predicate that reveals the internal structure of' the designated property. But the first does not imply

---

[19] For instance, as Loar pointed out above, recognitional concepts are *perspectival*. For example, one might have a recognitional concept of the dust-cloud-as-seen-from-(more or less of)-a-distance. It is metaphysically *contingent* that the cloud gets seen at all, but the recognitional concept does pick out, although opaquely, whatever are the scientifically described suspended particles making up the cloud. Here the *conceptual* independence between the recognitional concept and the scientific description is based on a *metaphysical* independence of the properties signified by the concepts. ED.

[20] It is *not* metaphysically contingent that pain is felt by someone. Even the antiphysicalist, then, admits that we have such phenomenal recognitional concepts as that of pain, and that such concepts *directly* pick out the intrinsic property of pain. ED.

[21] These are the facts that would have to obtain in a world in order for the predicate to be applied. ED.

the second. What is correct in the observation about rigid designation has no tendency to imply that the two concepts must be a priori interderivable.[22]

4. THE CONCEPT 'PHENOMENAL CONCEPT'

Not all self-directed recognitional concepts are phenomenal concepts, as may be seen in these two cases.

(1) Cramps have a characteristic feel, but they are not feelings. Cramps are certain muscle contractions, while feelings of cramp are, if physical, brain states. (Witness phantom-limb sufferers.) One has a recognitional concept that picks out certain muscle contractions in the having of them. This is not a phenomenal concept, for it does not purport to pick out a phenomenal quality. But of course, in exercising this concept, one often conceives its reference by way of a phenomenal mode of presentation, a cramp feeling or a cramp-feeling image.

(2) A more fanciful self-directed nonphenomenal concept can be conceived. To begin with, consider blindsight. Some cortically damaged people are phenomenally blind in restricted regions; and yet when a vertical or horizontal line (say) is presented to those regions, they can, when prompted, guess what is there with a somewhat high degree of correctness. We can extend the example by imagining a blindsight that is exercised spontaneously and accurately. At this point we shift the focus to internal properties and conceive of a self-directed recognitional ability, which is like the previous ability in being phenomenally blank and spontaneous but which discriminates an internal property of one's own. If this recognitional ability were suitably governed by the concept 'that state', the resulting concept would be a self-directed recognitional concept that is phenomenally blank.[23]

The two examples show that 'phenomenal concept' cannot mean 'self-directed recognitional concept'. This is compatible with my proposal. For it implies neither (a) that we can reductively explicate[24] the concept 'phenomenal quality' as 'property picked out by a self-directed discriminative ability', nor (b) that we can reductively explicate the concept 'phenomenal concept' as 'self-directed recognitional concept'. Phenomenal concepts are certain self-directed recognitional concepts. Our higher-order concept 'phenomenal concept' cannot be reductively explicated, any more than can our concept 'phenomenal quality'. The higher-order concept 'phenomenal concept' is as irreducibly demonstrative as phenomenal concepts themselves.

6. THIRD-PERSON ASCRIPTIONS

Ascriptions of phenomenal qualities to others ostensibly refer to properties that others may have independently of our ascribing them:[25] we have realist conceptions of the phenomenal states of others. But at the same time they are projections from one's own case; they have the form 'x has a state of this sort', where the demonstrative gets its reference from an actual or possible state of one's own.

Can phenomenal concepts as we predicate them of others be identified with the recognitional concepts we have characterized? A question naturally arises how essentially self-directed recognitional concepts can be applied in cases where it makes no sense to say that one can directly apply these concepts. This is a question that exercised Wittgensteinians.[26]

As we have already pointed out, recognitional concepts are perspectival, in the sense that their reference is determined from a certain constitutive perspective (depending on the concept). The above concept 'those creatures' (seen up close) picks out a creature-kind that one discriminates on close sightings. But nothing prevents ascribing the recognitional concept 'one of those creatures' to something

---

[22] What *is* correct about saying that the phenomenal concept and the coreferring physical concept rigidly designate the same physical property is that both concepts designate that property in all possible worlds. Loar is claiming that this common feature does *not* imply that the phenomenal concept has anything in it of the scientific analysis that yields the physical concept. ED.

[23] Loar seems to assume something here that not everyone would grant: that the absence of the usual *visually* phenomenal quality in blindsight implies that there is *no* phenomenal quality to the internal state in blindsight. ED.

[24] The explication would be reductive in the sense that it would reduce the *phenomenal* to the *behavioral*. ED.

[25] The earlier version of this chapter made heavy weather of third-person ascription of phenomenal concepts. General considerations about the perspectival nature of recognitional concepts permit a far neater account, which I here present.

[26] This issue "exercises" Norman Malcolm in Reading 3. ED.

observed from a different perspective, seen in the distance or heard in the dark. We have to distinguish the perspective from which reference is determined and the far broader range of contexts in which the referentially fixed concept can be ascribed. The former perspective hardly restricts the latter contexts. This holds also for phenomenal concepts. We acquire them from a first-person perspective, by discriminating a property in the having of it. Assuming that we successfully pick out a more or less determinate physical property, the extraperspectival ascription 'she is in a state of *this* kind' makes complete sense. And so it is not easy to see that Wittgensteinians succeeded in raising a philosophical problem that survives the observation that we can discriminate physical properties and so fix the reference of phenomenal concepts from a first-person perspective, and then go on to ascribe those concepts third-personally.

There is though a more up-to-date worry about the interpersonal ascribability of first-person concepts, however physical we suppose their references to be. Evidently there will be vagueness, and indeterminacy, concerning whether another person—whose neural assemblies will presumably always differ from mine in various respects—has a certain physical property that I discriminate phenomenally. And this on the face of it poses a problem, which may be framed as follows:

> The question whether another person's phenomenal states resemble yours can hardly consist in their neural assemblies' resembling yours. Any physical similarity you choose will be arbitrarily related to a given phenomenal similarity. Suppose there is a small physical difference between a neural state of yours and another person's state. What makes it the case that this small neural difference constitutes a small phenomenal difference or a large one or no phenomenal difference at all? It appears that there cannot be a fact of the matter.

But this objection appears to me to overlook a crucial element of the physicalist view we have presented—that phenomenal concepts are (type-) demonstrative concepts that pick out physical properties and relations. A first step in answering it is to consider the connection between interpersonal and intrapersonal phenomenal similarity. It appears that one's phenomenological conception of how others' phenomenal states resemble one's own has to be drawn from one's idea of how one's own phenomenal states resemble each other. A person's quality space of interpersonal similarity must derive from her quality space of intrapersonal similarity. How else is one to get a conceptual grip on interpersonal phenomenal similarity? This seems inevitable on any account—physicalist or antiphysicalist—on which phenomenal concepts are formed from one's own case.

But conceptions of phenomenal similarity relations are as much type-demonstrative concepts as those of phenomenal qualities. All one can apparently mean by "that spectrum of phenomenal similarity" is "*that ordering* among my phenomenal states." Physicalism implies that if such a type-demonstrative refers, it picks out a physical ordering. And there is no obvious philosophical difficulty (if we put aside scepticism in the theory of reference) in the idea that discriminations of resemblances and differences among one's own phenomenal properties pick out reasonably well defined physical relations.

Now I have to confess some uneasiness about extending this to interpersonal similarity without qualification; but the implications of the foregoing remarks are clear enough. If they are correct, whatever physical ordering relations are picked out by one's personal notions of phenomenal similarity must also constitute (what one thinks of as) interpersonal phenomenal similarity. It is easy to see that there still is room here for further trouble. But the difficulty the objection raises seems considerably diminished if one insists on the demonstrative nature of all phenomenal concepts, however relational and of whatever order. For the objection then becomes, "Suppose there is a small physical difference between a neural state of yours and another person's state. What makes it the case that this small neural difference constitutes a small difference of *that* type, or a large one, or no difference of *that* type at all?" If "that type" picks out a physical relation, then the question answers itself, and there seems no gloomy philosophical threat of phenomenal incommensurability.

Naturally there is the risk that physical investigation will not deliver the right physical properties and relations. Even if the risk is increased by bringing in interpersonal similarities, the nature of the risk is the same as in one's own case: the phenomenal might turn out to be not adequately embodied.

It goes without saying that one can coherently conceive that another person has *P,* conceived in physical-functional terms, and doubt that she has any given phenomenal quality; that has been central to this chapter. But one cannot coherently wonder whether another person in a *P* state has a state with *this* phenomenal quality if one acknowledges that one's concept 'this quality' refers to the property the concept discriminates in oneself (what else?) And that moreover it discriminates *P.*

Why then is there an apparent problem of other minds? It is as if one wishes to do to others as one does to oneself—namely, apply phenomenal concepts directly, apply phenomenal recognitional capacities to others from a first-person perspective. The impossibility of this can present itself as an epistemological barrier, as something that makes it impossible to know certain facts. Doubtless more can be said in explanation of the naturalness of the conflation of the innocuous conceptual fact with a severe epistemological disability. It is not easy to shake the grip of that conflation or therefore easy to dispel the problem of other minds. The cognitive remedy, the fortification against the illusion, is the idea of recognitional concepts that can be ascribed beyond their constitutive perspective, coupled with the reflection that there is no reason to doubt that it is physical-functional properties that those recognitional concepts discriminate.

7. KNOWING HOW VERSUS KNOWING THAT

Consider a different physicalist reply, to an antiphysicalist argument posed in this form: "knowledge of physical-functional facts does not yield knowledge of the phenomenal facts; therefore phenomenal facts are not physical-functional." Lawrence Nemirow and David Lewis have replied in effect that the premise is true only if you equivocate on "knowledge."[27] The first occurrence means theoretical knowledge, the second the ability to discriminate introspectively or to imagine certain properties. But theoretical knowledge of physical-functional properties that are identical with phenomenal qualities does not yield the other sort of knowledge of the same properties, that is, the ability to discriminate them in introspection or to imagine them. There are two epistemic relations to one class of properties.

Now this suggests something significantly different from my account. On the Nemirow-Lewis proposal, the only knowledge "that such and such" is knowledge couched in physical-functional terms, while what corresponds to (what we have been calling) phenomenal concepts is knowing how to identify or to imagine certain states. What I have proposed is evidently different. Knowing that a state feels a certain way is having distinctive information about it, couched in phenomenal conceptions. There is of course a central role for recognitional abilities, but that is in the constitution of phenomenal concepts. Antiphysicalists are right to count phenomenal knowledge as the possession of distinctive information, for it involves genuinely predicative components of judgment, whose association with physical-functional concepts is straightforwardly a posteriori.

Physicalists are forced into the Nemirow-Lewis reply if they individuate pieces of knowledge or cognitive information in terms of possible-world truth-conditions, that is, hold that "knowing that *p*' and 'knowing that *q*' ascribe distinct pieces of knowledge just in case 'that-*p*' and 'that-*q*' denote distinct sets of possible worlds. Then knowing that *x*'s phenomenal qualities are such and such will be distinct from knowing that *x*'s physical properties are so and so only if the former qualities are distinct from the latter properties. So then a physicalist who counts the basic antiphysicalist premise[28] as true on some interpretation must deny either that knowledge, cognitive information, is individuated in terms of possible-world-truth-conditions or deny that knowing the phenomenal facts (in the sense that makes the basic antiphysicalist premise true) is knowing that such and such or having distinctive information about it. Nemirow and Lewis deny the latter. Of course I deny the former; there are ample

---

[27] Nemirow (1980); Lewis (1983).

[28] The basic antiphysicalist premise here is that phenomenal concepts neither imply nor are implied by physical-functional concepts. ED.

independent reasons to deny it, and it seems otherwise unmotivated to deny the latter.

There are straightforward reasons to prefer the phenomenal concept view.[29]

1. A person can have thoughts not only of the form "coconuts have *this* taste" but also of the form "if coconuts did not have *this* taste, then Q." You may get away with saying that the former expresses (not a genuine judgment but) the mere possession of recognitional know-how. But there is no comparable way to account for the embedded occurrence of "coconuts have this taste"; it occurs as a predicate with a distinctive content.

2. We entertain thoughts about the phenomenal states of other people—"she has a state of that type"; this clearly calls for a predicative concept. It does of course involve a recognitional ability, but one that contributes to the formation of a distinctive concept.

3. For many conceptions of phenomenal qualities, there is no candidate for an independently mastered term[30] that one then learns how to apply: thinking of a peculiar way my left knee feels when I run (a conception that occurs predicatively in various judgments) is not knowing how to apply an independently understood term. I suppose a functionalist might say that, in such cases, one implicitly individuates the state in terms of some functional description that is fashioned on the spot, but this appears psychologically implausible.[31]

8. THE EXPLANATORY GAP

Can we *explain* how a certain phenomenal property might be identical with a certain physical-functional property? The answer is no, and then again, yes.

First, the no. When we explain, say, liquidity in physical-functional terms, the explanation is in crucial part a priori. You may find this surprising; but what we in effect do is analyze liquidity (or more precisely those aspects of liquidity that we count as

explained[32]) in terms of a functional description, and then show that the physical theory of water implies, a priori, that the functional description is realized.[33] But given the conceptual independence of phenomenal concepts and physical-functional concepts, we cannot have such an a priori explanation of phenomenal qualities in physical-functional terms.

Does this matter? The explanatory gap, as it appears to me, is an epistemic or conceptual phenomenon, without metaphysical consequences,[34] and it is predictable from the physicalist account we have proposed. But this may seem somewhat glib. As Georges Rey points out (Rey forthcoming), the mere fact of conceptual inequivalence for recognitional type-demonstratives and descriptive terms does not generate an explanatory gap. Many examples would make the point. We do not find a troubling explanatory gap in judgments of the form "that stuff is CH_3CH_2OH," even though this does not hold a priori.

Now what is it that needs accounting for? This seems to me to be it: how identity statements that connect phenomenal concepts and physical-functional concepts can be true despite our sense that, if true, they *ought to be* explanatory and yet are not. We can explain how such identity statements fail to be both explanatory (conceptual independence) and true; but this does not account for the

---

[29] I.e., the view that phenomenal concepts, although irreducible to physical *concepts,* nevertheless *opaquely* designate physical-functional properties. ED.

[30] E.g., the concept of the color red possessed by Jackson's scientist, Mary, and its application subsequent to her release (cf. Reading 24). ED.

[31] For instance, the ad hoc functional concept might be "the inner state that draws my attention to my left knee when I run." But why would I have or form such a concept apart from an attention-getting phenomenal awareness of how that knee feels? ED.

[32] This leaves open the possibility of twin-Earth cases in which the apparently defining properties of liquidity—those that are functionally explained—are kept constant across worlds even though the underlying kind changes. The defining properties then turn out to be merely reference fixing.

[33] Jaegwon Kim, in Reading 13, analyzes this kind of explanatory process in greater detail: "To reduce a property, or phenomenon, we first construe it—or reconstrue it—functionally, in terms of its causal/nomic relations to other properties and phenomena. To reduce temperature, for example, we must first construe it, not as an intrinsic property, but as an extrinsic property characterized relationally, in terms of causal/nomic relations, perhaps something like this: it is that magnitude of an object that is caused to increase when the object is in contact with another with a higher degree of it; that, when high, causes a ball of wax in the vicinity to melt; that causes the sensation of warmth or cold in humans; that, when extremely low, can make steel brittle; that, when extremely high, can turn steel into a molten state—well, you get the idea. The gene is construed as the mechanism in a biological organism that is causally responsible for the transmission of heritable characteristics from parents to offspring. To be transparent is to have the kind of molecular structure that causes light to pass through intact. And so on. We then find properties or mechanisms, often at the microlevel, that satisfy these causal/nomic specifications—that is, fill the specified causal roles" (p. 179). ED.

[34] For illuminating accounts of the explanatory gap and its significance see Levine (1983, 1993). Levine's diagnosis of the significance of the explanatory gap is different from mine.

thought that something that ought to be there is missing. We have to explain away the intuition that such identity statements ought to be explanatory.

There must be something special about phenomenal concepts that creates the expectation and the consequent puzzle. We have already seen a significant difference between phenomenal concepts and all other phenomenally mediated recognitional concepts. Might this make the difference here as well? That is what I will try to show.

Perhaps this is why we think that true phenomenal-physical identity judgments ought to be explanatory. It is natural to regard our conceptions of phenomenal qualities as conceiving them as they are in themselves, that is, to suppose we have a direct grasp of their essence. So in this respect there is a parallel with liquidity: the phenomenal concept and the concept 'liquid' both pick out properties directly, that is, not via contingent modes of presentation. And of course the physical-functional theoretical term of the identity, couched in fundamental theoretical terms, also reveals the essence of the property it picks out. Since both conceptions reveal this essence, then, if the psychophysical identity judgment is true, the sameness of that property, it might seem, ought to be evident from those conceptions, as in the liquidity case. The physical-functional concept structurally analyzes the property, and so we expect *it* to explain, asymmetrically, the phenomenal quality, much as physics explains liquidity, on the basis of an a priori analysis. The fact that this is not so makes it then difficult to understand how there can be just one property here.

If this is what makes the explanatory gap troubling, then the idea that phenomenal concepts are recognitional concepts of a certain sort does account for the explanatory gap in a way compatible with physicalism. Phenomenal concepts, as we have seen, do not conceive their reference via contingent modes of presentation. And so they can be counted as conceiving phenomenal qualities directly. Calling this a grasp of essence seems to me all right, for phenomenal concepts do not conceive their references by way of their accidental properties. But this is quite a different grasp of essence than we have in the term "liquid": for that term (or what there is in it that we count as functionally explained) is conceptually equivalent to some functional description that is entailed by the theoretical term of the identity.

The problem of the explanatory gap stems then from an illusion. What generates the problem is not appreciating that there can be two conceptually independent "direct grasps" of a single essence, that is, grasping it demonstratively by experiencing it, and grasping it in theoretical terms. The illusion is of *expected transparency:* a direct grasp of a property ought to reveal how it is internally constituted, and if it is not revealed as physically constituted, then it is not so. The mistake is the thought that a direct grasp of essence ought to be a transparent grasp, and it is a natural enough expectation.

The explanatory gap has led many philosophers of mind seriously astray into mistaken arguments for epiphenomenalism, for mystery, for eliminativism. At the root of almost all weird positions in the philosophy of mind lies this rather elementary and unremarkable conceptual fact, blown up into a metaphysical problem that appears to require an extreme solution. But it is a mistake to think that, if physicalism is true, consciousness as we conceive it at first hand needs explaining in the way that liquidity as we ordinarily conceive it gets explained.

There is another interpretation of "can we understand how physicalism might be true?", for which the answer is clearly yes. For we can explain, and indeed we have explained, how a given phenomenal concept can manage to pick out a particular physical-functional property without remainder: the concept discriminates the property but not via a contingent mode of presentation. This in its way closes the explanatory gap between the phenomenal and the physical. We understand how "such and such phenomenal quality" could pick out physical property P, even though "such and such phenomenal quality = P" does not provide an (a priori) explanation in physical terms of why a given phenomenal quality feels as it does. Since the former, when generalized, would entail that physicalism about phenomenal qualities is true, and since we understand both of these things, we thereby understand how physicalism can be true.

9. SUBJECTIVE CONCEPTS AND SUBJECTIVE PROPERTIES

You can ascribe an objective property—one completely expressable in the objective terms of natural science—under a subjective conception: '*x*'s state has *this* quality'. Thomas Nagel writes that mental facts are "accessible only from one point of view".[35] This does reflect something about phenomenal concepts; they are in some intuitive sense "from a point of view" and moreover subjective. Phenomenal concepts are subjective because they are essentially self-directed, involving capacities to discriminate certain states in the having of them and also involve imaginative capacities[36] anchored in such recognitional capacities. If that is it, then Nagel takes a correct observation about concepts and draws a wrong conclusion about facts and properties. For concepts can in that sense be "from a point of view" and subjective, and still introduce properties that are exhaustively captured in objective science.

But we can go further. Let us grant even that the *property* of experiencing such and such is aptly counted as subjective, as intrinsically involving a point of view. Why should this subjectivity not itself be identical with a physical-functional property, and therefore completely objectively conceivable under its physical-functional description? There is no contradiction in supposing that a property that is subjective—in the sense of being individuated in a way that invokes a relation to a mind—is also conceivable under an objective mode of presentation. There is no incoherence in the thought that the "subjectivity" of a phenomenal quality is identical with an objective physical-functional aspect of that property.

Does a fully objective description of reality not still leave something out, viz., the subjective conceptions? This is a play on 'leave something out'. A complete objective description leaves out subjective conceptions, not because it cannot fully characterize the properties they discriminate or fully account for the concepts themselves as psychological states but simply because it does not employ them.

10. PHENOMENAL STRUCTURE, AND EXOTIC OTHERS

Some functionalists might think this account ignores a major feature of our conceptions of the mental, namely, their systematic structure. We have conceptions of different sensory modalities, and of intramodality comparisons along various spectra, of pitch, timbre, hue, brightness, shape, size, texture, acidity, acridity, and so on. These could be seen as subsidiary functional organizations within a theory of the mental. Antiphysicalists may share something of the point, wanting to speak of phenomenological structures. My account could seem to imply that phenomenal concepts are atomistic, unstructured, unsystematic, for are these recognitional dispositions not in principle independent of each other?

We have phenomenal recognitional concepts of various degrees of generality. Some are of highly determinate qualities, and others are of phenomenal determinables: crimson, dark red, red, warm colored, colored, visual. The last is the recognitional conception of a whole sensory modality. And there is the most general of all, the recognitional concept *phenomenal* (state, quality), the highest-ranking phenomenal determinable. (This is a recognitional concept. One discriminates phenomenal states from nonphenomenal states, feeling a twinge from having a bruise, hearing a chirp from jerking a knee, and that highly general discriminative capacity is the basis of the concept of a phenomenal quality.)

There are also relational concepts: quality x is a determinate of quality y; quality x is more like quality y than like quality z; quality x is of a different modality from quality y. These are also recognitional concepts: dispositions to classify together, on phenomenal grounds, certain pairs and triples of phenomenal qualities. Combining them yields complex conceptions of abstract phenomenal structures, for example, of a structured sensory modality. One's general conception of such a structure is in effect one's ability to exercise in concert a group of such general phenomenal concepts.

Now it is important that our conceptions of such phenomenal structures, while abstract, are yet phenomenal conceptions. No purely functional conception of a complex structure, however isomorphic to a phenomenal-structure conception[37] it may be, will be cognitively equivalent to it; purely functional conceptions ignore that the structures

---

[35] Nagel (1974). [Reading 22. ED.]

[36] For instance, we can think about what it's like to see red or feel pain in the absence of actually having the relevant sensations. ED.

[37] Imagine, if you can, a deaf person with a perfect understanding of music theory. She *understands* all the complex relations symbolized on a sheet of music, but has never *heard* the notes, their durations, intervals, consonances, and dissonances. ED.

are of phenomenal similarity relations, of phenomenal determinateness, and so on.

But given the falsity of the semantic minor premise,[38] that is no impediment to holding that those abstract phenomenal conceptions can have purely functional or physical-functional structures as their references. For such structures may well be what these abstract phenomenal recognitional capacities in fact discriminate. Indeed we may go on to say that, if our phenomenal conceptions are to be fully vindicated by brain science, then the brain must have a certain functional structure; any possible totality of (as it were) semantic values for our phenomenal conceptions must have certain functional structures.[39] This perhaps explains the strong intuition of some commonsense functionalists that phenomenal concepts are functional concepts, without our having to accept that counterintuitive view.

"Can your projection analysis[40] accommodate the thought that a bat has highly specific, determinate, phenomenal states that are not like anything I can experience or imagine? It seems to me that your program will require you to bring in the bat's own recognitional-imaginative capacities, such as they are."[41]

When one thinks about a bat's sonar phenomenal states, one thinks about them as phenomenal, that is, as having in common with my phenomenal states what I discriminate them all as having in common, and that may be something physical-functional. One also thinks of them as of a distinctive phenomenal kind or modality, different from one's own states, of roughly that order of determinateness at which one's visual states are marked off from one's auditory states. One has such a general concept from one's own case, and one can project it. Again, that concept—'distinctive phenomenal modality'—may denote a physical-functional property, of sets of phenomenal states. And one thinks of the bat's sonar states as exhibiting phenomenal variation of different degrees of specificity. These conceptions of general phenomenal structure, determinable-determinate relations, resemblance relations, and so on, we have, as I have said, from our own case.

Now nothing in the foregoing requires that a necessary condition of having certain phenomenal qualities is having the capacity to discriminate them. (See, however, the discussion below of transparency.) We ascribe to bats not phenomenal concepts but phenomenal states; and we do that by projection, in the manner characterized above. Other-directed phenomenal conceptions are of others' states, and not as such of their conceptions.

Nagel proposes that we can achieve objectivity about the mental by abstracting from subjective conceptions of our own psychology, fashioning objective mental conceptions that are neither physical nor functional.[42] This would enable us to conceive abstractly of mental lives of which we have no subjective, projective, understanding whatever. Now that is evidentially at odds with my proposal. It appears to me that all mental concepts that are not functional concepts (where the latter include concepts of theoretical psychology) are subjective-projective concepts, however general and abstract they may be. The reason is simple: as far as I can determine, I have no objective nonfunctional mental concepts. If I try to conceive an alien mind in nonfunctional mental terms, I rely on concepts like 'sensory modality' and other general conceptions of phenomenalogical structure of the sort mentioned above, and I understand them from my own case. They are abstract conceptions; but, it appears to me, they are still recognitional concepts and hence as subjective as the highly specific phenomenal concept of having an itch in the left ankle.

11. TRANSPARENCY

The following could appear possible on my account: another person is in the state that in me amounts to feeling such and such but sincerely denies feeling anything relevant. It apparently has been left open that others have phenomenal states that are not introspectable at will, for no requirement of transparency has been mentioned. Then

---

[38] This is what Loar earlier called simply "the semantic premise" on p. 406 above. ED.

[39] Chalmers, in Reading 27, makes a similar point in much more detail, in explaining his "principle of structural coherence" (pp. 393–95).

[40] Nagel is referring here to Loar's explanation of how it is possible to ascribe to other subjects phenomenal states that we conceptualize from our first-person case. ED.

[41] Thomas Nagel, in a note commenting on an earlier draft.

[42] Nagel (1974). [See Nagel's discussion at the end of Reading 22. ED.]

the property that is the referent of my concept of feeling like *that* could, even if it occurs transparently in me, occur nontransparently in you. But (the objection continues) denying transparency is tantamount to allowing unconscious experiences; and it would not be unreasonable to say that the topic of phenomenal states is the topic of certain conscious states.

There really is no issue here. Suppose that any phenomenal quality must be essentially transparent, and that no property I correctly identify as phenomenal can be realized in another nontransparently. If cognitive integration is essential to the intuitive property of transparency, so be it; there is no reason to think that such integration itself is not a physical-functional property, as it were implicated by each phenomenal property.

But it is not obvious that phenomenal properties must be transparent in such a reflexive cognitive sense. What about infants and bats? There has always been a philosophical puzzle about how subtracting reflexive cognitive awareness from phenomenal or conscious states leaves something that is still phenomenal or conscious.[43] But that puzzle is independent of the present account. All that is implied here is that if I have a conception of a phenomenal quality that is shared by me and an infant, my conception of it involves a recognitional concept, and there is no reason why that phenomenal quality itself should not be a physical-functional property. Whatever indefinable, elusive aspect of phenomenal qualities might constitute their being conscious—transparent in some appropriately minimal sense—without requiring reflexive conceptualizability, there would be no reason to doubt it is a physical-functional property.

12. INCORRIGIBILITY

Physicalism, it may be said, cannot acknowledge the incorrigibility of phenomenal judgments of the form 'it feels like that'. For surely there is no guarantee that a capacity for recognizing a given physical property does not at times misfire; and per-

haps even more to the point, there can be no guarantee that to a given recognitional disposition there corresponds a repeatable physical property. Perhaps an antiphysicalist will grant that certain kinds of mistakes about phenomenal qualities are possible,[44] but the antiphysicalist will insist that we cannot be wrong in thinking that *there are* phenomenal qualities.

Now suppose it turns out that no system of physical-functional properties corresponds to the system of our phenomenal concepts. Would a physicalist not then have to say there are no phenomenal qualities? And is the fact that physicalism leaves this open not a serious problem?

But that very possibility ought to make us dubious about the incorrigibility of the judgment that there are real phenomenal repeatables. What reason have we to think that our phenomenal judgments discriminate real properties? Memory, one might say, cannot be that mistaken: we can hardly deny that present inner states resemble past states in ways we would recognize again. Despite this conviction, however, if no system of physical-functional properties corresponded to one's putative phenomenal discriminations, an alternative to nonphysical qualities would be this: memory radically deceives us into thinking we discriminate internal features and nonrandomly classify our own states. Strong evidence that no suitable physical-functional properties exist might amaze and stagger one. It would then have emerged that we are subject to a powerful illusion, a cognitive rather than a phenomenal illusion; we would be judging falsely that we thereby discriminate real properties.

It does seem likely that we genuinely discriminate internal physical-functional states in introspection.[45] But with that said, positing nonphysical properties to forestall the *possibility* of radical error, however theoretically adventurous (even reckless) this may be, would in something like a moral sense still be rather faint-hearted. The whole point about

---

[43] This is perhaps the biggest question hovering over the question of (nonhuman) animal consciousness. What is it to have a feeling or sensation, *apart from* one's capacity to classify or conceptualize it to oneself and others? ED.

[44] See Warner (1986).

[45] When I see a ripe lemon in daylight and attend to my visual experience, I form the memory belief that what I introspect is what I introspected (phenomenologically inclined as I am) the last time I saw a ripe lemon in daylight. It seems a reasonable empirical inference that probably ripe lemons in such circumstances cause in me states that my memory accurately records as the same. But this inference is, I take it, not reasonable on introspective grounds alone; it presupposes much about how the world works.

the phenomenal is how it appears. And that means there is no introspective guarantee of *anything* beyond mere appearance, even of discriminations of genuine repeatables. The dualist balks at the implications and invents a realm of properties to ensure that the appearances are facts, but this does not respect the truly phenomenal nature of what is revealed by introspection at its least theoretical.

I have to grant that, if it were to turn out that no brain properties are suitably correlated with our ascriptions of phenomenal qualities, one might well feel some justification in questioning physicalism. But that does not imply that one now has such a justification. There is no good reason for prophylactic dualism.

13. FUNCTIONALISM

There are two functionalist theses: that all concepts of mental states are functional concepts, and that all mental properties are functional properties. The first I rejected in accepting the antiphysicalist intuition. I agree with the antiphysicalist that phenomenal concepts cannot be captured in purely functional terms. But nothing in philosophy prevents phenomenal properties from being functional properties. There are two possibilities: they are commonsense-functional properties or they are psychofunctional, and I take the latter to be the interesting one.[46] Might the phenomenal quality of seeing red be identical with a property captured by a detailed psychological theory? This would be so if

the repeatable that triggers one's phenomenal concept 'seeing red' has psychofunctional rather than say biochemical identity conditions.[47] That this is possible has been denied by antifunctionalist physicalists on the grounds of inverted qualia and absent qualia possibilities, but I do not find these arguments persuasive.

The inverted qualia argument is commonly advanced against identifying phenomenal qualities with commonsense functional properties and also against the psychofunctional identification. The position I espouse is agnostic: for all philosophers know, phenomenal qualities are psychofunctional, neurofunctional, or some other fine-grained functional properties. The opposing argument is that it is possible that the functional role that seeing red has in me is had in you by, as I would think of it, seeing green. If this is, as they say, **metaphysically possible,** then of course phenomenal qualities are not functional properties.

But is seems the only argument for the possibility is the coherent conceivability of inverted qualia. One cannot presuppose that inverted qualia are **nomologically possible.** There seems to be no philosophical reason to assert that, apart from the coherent conceivability of inverted qualia. If there is empirical reason to assert that nomological possibility, then of course we should retreat from agnosticism. The present point is that nothing about the idea of inverted qualia provides philosophical reason to reject functionalism about qualia. For that would require another version of the antiphysicalist argument: it is conceivable that any given functional state can occur without the seeing of green and with the seeing of red, say; therefore the psychofunctional role and the phenomenal quality involve distinct properties. Clearly one cannot accept this argument against functionalism without also accepting the analogous argument against physicalism itself;[48] the philosophical antifunctionalist argument requires a premise that implies antiphysicalism.

---

[46]It is empirically unlikely that phenomenal qualities are identical with commonsense functional properties. Here is one way to see this. We know sensations can be produced by nonstandard means, that is by poking around in the brain; but this of course is no part of the commonsense functional role of the property of seeing red. Now suppose this property is produced in me by a brain probe. What constitutes its being a sensation of red? If it is its commonsense functional role, then that property would be the sensation of red by virtue of (something like) its *normally* having such and such causes and effects (it doesn't have them here). But this makes sense only if the property in question is itself a *distinct* lower-order property about which it is contingently true that normally it has such and such causes and effects although it lacks them here. That lower-order property would then be a far better candidate (than the commonsense functional property) for being the property one's phenomenal conception discriminates. For this reason, such brain probes turn out to be strong and perhaps even conclusive evidence that phenomenal qualities, the ones we discriminate in applying phenomenal concepts, are not identical with commonsense functional properties. There are other ways of reaching the same conclusion.

[47]I.e., assuming that psychological theories are *functional,* and not neurobiological, theories, then the objective property designated by the phenomenal concept would be a functional property rather than a property formulated in biochemical terms. ED.

[48]Loar seems to be referring to the argument that it is conceivable that any phenomenal state could occur without the physical state with which it is correlated, or indeed without the occurrence of any physical state whatsoever. ED.

There is a well-known absent qualia argument against functionalism by Ned Block (1978). Suppose the Chinese nation[49] were organized so as to realize the psychofunctional organization of a person seeing green. Evidently the Chinese nation would not collectively be seeing green or having any other sensation. Any psychofunctional property could in this way be realized without a given phenomenal quality and hence cannot be identical with one. Now this argument might appear dialectically more telling than the inverted qualia argument, for it apparently rests on more than a conceptual possibility. It seems a plain truth that the Chinese people would not thereby be having a collective sensation. Surely it is barmy to be agnostic about that. Block suggests a principle. "If a doctrine has an absurd conclusion which there is no independent reason to believe, and if there is no way of explaining away the absurdity or showing it to be misleading or irrelevant, and if there is no good reason to believe the doctrine that leads to the absurdity in the first place, then don't accept the doctrine."[50]

While we doubtless find an absurdity in ascribing phenomenal qualities to the Chinese nation as a whole, the matter is not so simple. It is hard to see how such a judgment of absurdity can be *justified* except by our having some intuitive knowledge of the nature of phenomenal qualities whereby we can say that the Chinese nation cannot have them collectively. Have I a special insight into my physical states whereby I can say: the repeatable that I reidentify whenever I attend to my seeing green is not a functional property? One feels skeptical that introspection can yield such knowledge. If the argument is not 'they do not collectively have, by virtue of their functional organization, however fine-grained, what I have when *this* occurs', then what is it? Is a further philosophical argument in the offing? It is difficult to see whence chest-beating to the contrary derives its credibility. Perhaps a dualist conception of Platonic insight into mental essences might help. But, on a naturalist view of human nature, one ought to find it puzzling that we have such a first-person insight into the nature of our mental properties. Perhaps there is reason to suppose that what one introspects and reidentifies is a categorical[51] and not a dispositional property. That has an intuitive ring to it, but it is not that easy to produce a decent argument for it. We are left with this question: how might we know short of detailed brain research that what we reidentify in ourselves when we see green is not a fine-grained functional property? But if we cannot know this by sheer insight into the essence of our own properties, or by philosophical argument, then we cannot know that the Chinese nation lacks what we have. Our ignorance concerns the nature of our own properties, and that ignorance would appear to prevent drawing substantive conclusions from thought experiments of this type.

There is no question that ordinary intuition counts strongly against applying phenomenal concepts to things that are not single organisms, and one cannot deny that the reply just given makes one uncomfortable, at the very least. And yet the alternative appears to be Platonism about mental essences,[52] and that sits awkwardly with naturalism. It is possible that phenomenal qualities are biochemical properties: and yet again it is difficult to see that philosophers know anything that implies that they are not fine-grained functional, or neurofunctional, properties.[53]

[49] This scenario is discussed in detail by the Churchlands in section II of Reading 25. ED.

[50] Block (1978).

[51] A *categorical* property is a property whereby something is a certain kind of thing (e.g., physicochemical), whereas a *dispositional* property is one whereby something will behave in a certain way under certain circumstances. This distinction in kinds of properties is not always applicable in a clear and nonarbitrary way. ED.

[52] Loar's phrase seems to designate the view that there is some separate domain of "forms" or essences of mental states, apart from the physical world, a domain to which the mind has direct access, like the soul of the philosopher in Plato's dialogues who is looking for the eternal truth about such things as justice and virtue by looking away from the world of the senses. ED.

[53] (Original version) For pointing out a substantial error in an ancestor of the paper, I am indebted to George Myro, whose correction put me on the right track as I now see it. I have learned much from conversations on phenomenal qualities with Janet Levin and Richard Warner. Stephen Schiffer made several valuable suggestions about the structure of the paper and got me to clarify certain arguments. I am also grateful for comments on the mentioned ancestor to Kent Bach, Hartry Field, Andreas Kemmerling, Dugald Owen, Thomas Ricketts, Hans Sluga, Stephen Stich, and Bruce Vermazen.

(Revised version) Many thanks to Ned Block for raising questions about modes of presentation and the blindsight case, to Georges Rey for making me see that more needed to be said about the explanatory gap, and to Kent Bach for helpful remarks on a number of points.

REFERENCES

Block, N. (1978). "Troubles with Functionalism," in C. Wade Savage, ed., *Perception and Cognition: Issues in the Foundations of Psychology.* Vol. 9, *Minnesota Studies in the Philosophy of Science,* Minneapolis: University of Minnesota Press.

———. (1990). "Inverted Earth." *Philosophical Perspectives* 4: 53–79.

Dennett, Daniel (1991). *Consciousness Explained.* Boston: Little Brown.

Harman, Gilbert (1990). "The Intrinsic Quality of Experience," *Philosophical Perspectives* 4: 31–52.

Jackson, Frank (1982). "Epiphenomenal Qualia," *Philosophical Quarterly,* 1982, 127–136.

———. (1986). "What Mary Didn't Know," *Journal of Philosophy* 83: 291–295.

———. (1994). "Armchair Metaphysics," in M. Michael ed., *Philosophy in Mind.* Norwell, MA: Kluwer.

Kripke, Saul (1980). *Naming and Necessity.* Cambridge, MA: Harvard University Press.

Levin, Janet (1983). "Functionalism and the Argument from Conceivability," *Canadian Journal of Philosophy,* Supplementary Volume 11.

———. (1986). "Could Love Be Like a Heatwave?" *Philosophical Studies,* 49: 245–261.

Levine, Joseph (1983). "Materialism and Qualia: the Explanatory Gap," *Pacific Philosophical Quarterly* 64: 354–61.

———. (1993). "On Leaving Out What It Is Like," in M. Davies and G. Humphreys, eds., *Consciousness.* Oxford: Blackwell.

Lewis, David (1983a). "Mad Pain and Martian Pain," in *Philosophical Papers,* Vol. 1. Oxford: Oxford University Press.

———. (1983b). "Postscript" to the foregoing.

Loar, Brian (1990). "Personal References," in E. Villanueva, ed., *Information, Semantics and Epistemology.* Oxford: Blackwell.

———. (1991). "Can We Explain Intentionality?," in G. Rey and B. Loewer, eds., *Meaning in Mind.* Oxford: Blackwell.

———. [   ]. "Reference from a First-Person Perspective," in *Philosophical Issues.*

McGinn, Colin (1930). "Consciousness and Cosmology: Hyperdualism Ventilated," in M. Davies and G. Humphreys, eds., *Consciousness.* Oxford: Blackwell.

Nagel, Thomas (1974). "What Is It Like To Be a Bat?," *Philosophical Review,* 1974: 435–450.

———. (1986). *The View From Nowhere.* Oxford: Oxford University Press.

Nemirow, Lawrence (1980). Review of Nagel's *Mortal Questions,* [in] *Philosophical Review,* July 1980.

Rey, Georges [1996]. "Towards a Projectivist Account of Conscious Experience," in T. Metzinger, ed., *Essays on Consciousness.*

Warner, Richard (1986). "A Challenge to Physicalism," *Australasian Journal of Philosophy* 64: 249–265.

———. (1993). "Incorrigibility," in H. Robinson, ed., *Objections to Physicalism.* Oxford: Oxford University Press.

Loar begins his elaborate defense of physicalism by accepting what he calls "the antiphysicalist intuition": that phenomenal *concepts* are irreducibly different from physical-functional *concepts.* Phenomenal concepts are irreducible in the sense that "they neither a priori imply, nor are implied by, physical-functional concepts" (p. 404) Loar's principal thesis is that we can accept this intuition and still hold that phenomenal *qualities* are identical to physical-functional *properties* of the brain. His argument for this thesis is at the same time an argument *against* Kripke who, according to Loar, incorrectly derived antiphysicalist conclusions from this irreducibility.

Let's remind ourselves of what Kripke (Reading 7) had to say: He argued that the early identity theorists such as Place (Reading 5) and Smart (Reading 6) got it wrong when they assimilated the identity of sensations with brain processes to such physical-science paradigms as the identity of heat with the kinetic energy of molecules. To dualists who appealed to the conceptual independence of the concepts of consciousness and of a brain process Smart and Place thought they had developed an effective response: you find this same conceptual independence between the ordinary and scientific concepts of heat, yet heat *is,* as dualists admit, the kinetic energy of molecules. In both cases (heat and consciousness) the identity is *contingent;* it just *happens* to be the case that each is what science tells us it is. Kripke argued that identities such as that between heat and molecular motion are *necessary,* that 'heat' is a rigid designator (designating the same thing in all possible worlds). The fact that we learned about the nature of heat *a posteriori* does not imply that heat might not have had that nature. It *is a contingent* property of heat that it is part of a world in which there are beings with our sort of sensory apparatus, who experience a particular kind of sensation when affected by heat. In a world without such sensory apparatus heat would still be what it is—the kinetic energy of molecules. As Kripke put it, for heat to be felt the way we feel it is a "contingent mode of presentation," a contingent property of heat. Therefore, he argues, the model of physical-science identities cannot be used to assert an identity between brain processes and phenomenal qualities such as pain. While it is perfectly conceivable that the heat we identify with kinetic energy of molecules might not have been felt by anyone, it is *inconceivable* that the pain we want to identify with some brain process might never have been felt. Being felt is part of its essence, whereas being a brain process is not.

Loar accepts this conclusion: "On this [my] account, a phenomenal concept rigidly designates the property it picks out" (p. 409). And, he adds, the property it picks out is a physical-functional property of the brain. But how can this be? To say that the concept of heat is a rigid designator is to say that it is *inconceivable* that heat could be anything else but the kinetic energy of molecules; the scientific concept picks out the very nature or essence of heat. Similarly, if a phenomenal concept is a rigid designator of a physical-functional property, shouldn't it pick out at least something pertaining to the very nature of what it designates? However, Loar has stipulated that there is nothing physical-functional about the content of a phenomenal concept. How then can it designate what is essentially physical-functional?

To assess Loar's response to this difficulty, we need first to carefully distinguish the phenomenal from the physical concept of heat. The former is the concept of what it is like to experience heat, whereas the latter designates a macrophenomenon that induces the experience in us by acting on our thermal receptors. There are other things that physical heat does, such as getting conducted from one body to another, and causing some things to melt, burn, or vaporize. The concept of heat as kinetic energy of molecules enables us to explain in micro-terms the macrophenomenal behavior of heat. Thus, in identities such as the one between heat and the kinetic energy of molecules, we expect that one side of the identity (typically the micro) explains the other (usually macro) side. This doesn't happen in the alleged identity of a phenomenal quality with a physical-functional property—interacting arrays of brain neurons lack any intelligible causal relation to what it is like to have a certain feeling or sensation.

Within the context of the atomic theory of matter there is what Loar calls a "transparency" in the connection between the energy that atoms and molecules have by their various motions, and the macro-effect of melting that is part of the macrophysical behavior of heat. Thinking of little particles colliding helps to understand how the solid macrostructure of a body could be undone when the particles within it are shaken out of place by contact with the more energetic particles of a hotter body. We see how the melting might be "nothing but" the communication of motion among imperceptibly small particles. This is the kind of explanatory "transparency" that we then expect to find if we are to believe that a phenomenal quality such as pain is "nothing but" an array of neurons behaving in a certain way. But we don't find it. Instead, we experience an "explanatory gap." We think that if the physical-functional concept grasps the essence of a phenomenal quality, it ought to reveal how that quality is constituted, and ought to do so just as transparently as the kinetic theory of heat does for the macrophenomenon of heat.

According to Loar, this expectation is an *illusion* that is "the root of almost all weird positions in the philosophy of mind," one that has driven Nagel and McGinn into mysterianism, Jackson into epiphenomenalism, and (he might have added) Campbell into his "new epiphenomenalism". We're now at the core of Loar's complex defense of physicalism. To gain some perspective, let's set out the three correlates in the comparison between heat and pain:

1. *The macro-concept:* In the case of heat, it is the concept of what gives rise to observable behaviors such as conduction, melting, and combustion. In the case of pain, it is the concept of what gives rise to pain behavior.

2. *The micro-concept:* In the case of heat, this is the kinetic energy of molecules. For pain, it will be the neuro-functional explanation of the internal state that generates pain behavior.

3. *The phenomenal concept:* In the case of heat, this is the concept of what it is like to feel heat, and for pain, the concept of what it is like to feel pain.

In the case of heat, the rigid designators flanking the '=' are the macro-concept and the micro-concept. In the case of pain, according to Loar's analysis, the rigid designators are the phenomenal concept and the micro-concept. What Loar needs for his defense of physicalism is an account of how a phenomenal concept can rigidly designate what a micro-concept rigidly designates, without the micro-concept having any explanatory relation to the phenomenal concept. He has, in effect, conceded that psychophysical identities are *not* like the scientific identities that were invoked by Place, Smart *et al.* The risk he now runs is that identities of the sort between phenomenal pain and some neurofunctional property will be so unlike any plausible sort of identity that their very peculiarity makes them suspect.

To ward off this danger, Loar assimilates phenomenal concepts to *recognitional* concepts: "Here is the view to be defended. Phenomenal concepts are recognitional concepts that pick out certain internal properties; these are physical-functional properties of the brain" (p. 408).

REVIEW QUESTIONS

1. Summarize the way Loar uses the concept of a recognitional concept in order to make plausible the kind of identity that would hold between phenomenal qualities and physical-functional properties of the brain.

2. According to Loar, phenomenal concepts differ from other recognitional concepts insofar as they *rigidly* designate the properties they pick out—other recognitional concepts are based on contingent modes of presentation. Does this exceptional feature of phenomenal-recognitional concepts weaken Loar's position by being suspiciously ad hoc? In other words, has he simply *traded* the problem of how a phenomenal quality can *be* a neurofunctional property for the problem of how a recognitional concept could rigidly designate something?

PART VIII

SELVES

Metaphysics is an area of philosophy that deals with the most common attribute of all: *being*. It asks not only what is meant by words such as *being* and *existence* in their various uses, but also what (very general) kinds of being there are. It also deals with terms that are closely related to *being* such as *unity* (since every being is in some way *one*). We can ask, for instance, what kind of unity the world or universe has, whether it has the kind and degree of unity that an animal has, or just the loose unity characteristic of a heap of stones. Since each of us is a part of the universe and of various other wholes such as families, political communities, and cultures, how we understand the unity of these wholes will strongly affect how we conceive of ourselves.

If there is such a thing as a "common-sense" metaphysics of the western world, it would probably include the belief that the world is made up of *individuals* that are not just collections of things, and not just parts or aspects of other things, but beings that, in some hard-to-define way, exist on their own or in their own right. Common-sense metaphysicians, especially those in western industrialized democracies, would surely classify *themselves* as individuals in this strong sense, along with dogs and cats, oak trees, and perhaps some inanimate entities such as rocks or tables. These individuals appear to be paradigm cases of being and unity—their distinctness from their environments overrides whatever connectedness and dependency they may have, and their unity seems stronger than their internal multiplicity. Aristotle was the earliest, and probably the greatest, expositor of this common-sense scheme of things. His Greek word for the kind of *individual* I've been talking about is *ousia,* which is usually translated into English as *substance.* According to Aristotle, the other categories of being (such as quality, quantity, and action) exist only *in,* or as aspects of, substance. For instance, *brown, large,* and *running* can exist only in a substance (a horse, perhaps). The categories of being other than substance are generically referred to as *accidents* in the philosophical tradition deriving from Aristotle.

Like so much that seems obvious and commonsensical, the notion of substance quickly gets complicated and even murky when we attempt a careful analysis of it. Take us humans, for instance. We're composed of hundreds of billions of cells. There are also single-celled organisms (such as bacteria) that live on their own, and therefore seem to be substances in Aristotle's sense. Is a human a single, individual substance or a collection such as a community? It's true that the cells making up the tissues in a human body usually can't live outside it. But neither can separate unicellular organisms exist apart from some specific kind of environment. All organisms have such a dependency. What, then, makes a human to be more of a *one* than a *many?* Is a rock one individual rather than a tightly bonded collection? And what about a single member of a beehive or ant colony, as rigidly and facelessly contributing to the life of the whole as any neuron or skin cell in us?

The notion of substance is closely related to that of a *subject of change*. The unity of a substance encompasses not only the three-dimensional space of a body at a single moment, but also its duration or fourth dimension. A substance is one over a period of time. Since all bodies are subject to change as they interact with their environments, the temporal unity or *identity* of a substance must allow for the *differences* that change brings to that substance over time. Somehow a substance, as a subject of change, must have a *sameness* in and through these *differences*. However, when we try to identify or characterize the subject of change in concrete instances, we encounter problems such as these: Exactly what is the subject of change that persists through the transitions whereby an acorn becomes an oak or a zygote becomes an adult human? In both cases there isn't a single cell that is there throughout.

What I have called the common-sense metaphysics of substances with spatiotemporal unity reflects a fundamental structure of our thought and language about things in the world. Descartes, looking at what happened when he applied a flame to his piece of beeswax, could have summed up what he saw in this way: "It liquefied." The verb signifies a process over time, and the pronoun subject implies a single entity present throughout that process—a subject of change. Moreover, this sentence is also an example of what logicians would call the subject-predicate relation: We always think of things around us as *particulars* with *universal* predicates. *Liquefied* is like *large, red,* or *running:* a universal applicable to indefinitely many particulars. A particular, in this sense, is a *logical subject*—that about which we say or predicate something but which is never itself said or predicated of anything. *This* oak is not *that* oak, although both are of the same kind. Particulars are often referred to metaphorically as "bearers" of predicates or universals. This suggests that *particulars,* in themselves, are "bare" of characteristics, featureless because all features are *universal.*

We have to distinguish between the logical and grammatical relations of subject and predicate in order to discern the logical subject. In "This oak is tall" the *grammatical* subject is "this oak," but the *logical* subject is more properly designated by "this," as we see when we reformulate the sentence to bring out its logical structure: "This (particular) is an oak (universal) and tall (universal)." As this sentence also suggests, not all predicates are equal. If I said "This is tall," you could ask what sort of thing I'm talking about. But your question usually wouldn't arise if I said "This is an oak." *Tall* doesn't signify a type of being that can exist on its own (a substance), whereas *oak* does. Substances, then, are the ultimate particulars insofar as they are bearers of predicates that enable them to exist on their own and be the bearers of "accidental" predicates of quality, quantity, and so on. In the philosophical tradition we have been discussing, a substance as ultimate particular and as ultimate subject of change (in which predicates come and go) is often referred to as a *substratum* or *substrate.* However, a substance can't be only a substrate since it is always a *kind* of thing, whereas an ultimate particular as such is a featureless entity left over once we try to think away all that is universal or predicable in our notion of a substance.

According to philosophers such as Descartes, among the predicates that designate something *as* a substance are special ones that capture precisely the nature of the thing. In Descartes' dualist metaphysics there are, of course, only two such predicates: extension and thinking. Insofar as each is supposed to be a feature without which a body or a mind, respectively, would not be the kind of thing it is, and in virtue of which a body or a mind is enabled to have all the other features it has, extension and thinking are each the *essence* or essential attribute of their respective substances.

We have seen that there are serious problems with the notion of substance. Perhaps the single strongest support for this beleaguered notion is our intuition of our-*selves* as independent existents and unique, incommunicable (i.e., ultimately particular) subjects of the constant change both in our bodies and in the flux of our experience. Some philosophers have even argued that the common-sense metaphysical view of the world as populated by substances of various kinds is a projection onto external things of the kind of substantial unity we seem to find through our self-awareness. However, this intuition about the unity of oneself is fragile and hard to reconcile with many facts of our mental lives. What happens to the temporal identity of my self when I go to sleep? Or when I more or less permanently forget segments of my past life, or change my values and habits so much that others say I am *not* myself? If I am really *one,* and self-transparently so, how can I be at odds with myself or have beliefs and feelings of which I seem to be unaware? Perhaps the substantial unities that we believe we *find* in ourselves and the world around us aren't really there, but are only useful fictions made plausible by the structure of our language and thought. These and other questions will be addressed by the readings that follow.

29

Of Identity and Diversity

John Locke

John Locke (1632–1704) lectured in philosophy at Oxford University from 1662 to 1684. His two best-known works are *An Essay Concerning Human Understanding* (first published in 1690), from which this reading is taken, and *Two Treatises of Government,* (1689–90) a defense of the ideas behind the Glorious Revolution of 1688.

As this reading will show, Locke is familiar with and strongly influenced by Descartes. Nevertheless there are major differences in their approaches to philosophical questions. Descartes was a *rationalist*—he claimed we get our knowledge not from the senses but only from purely intellectual ideas such as those of the mind as thinking thing and the body as extended. Locke, on the other hand, is an *empiricist;* for him the only two sources of knowledge are sensation and what he calls reflection—our awareness of our own mental states and operations. As Descartes said when he analyzed the melting beeswax, if you rely on the senses, it's hard to claim that you *understand* how a single thing can persist through the total change undergone by the wax. Locke is willing to rely on the senses, and to take the consequences. He concedes that we can't do without the notions of *substance* and *substratum* in organizing our experience. But apart from the ideas of the qualities which our senses reveal in bodies, and of the operations which reflection reveals in our minds, our idea of a material or mental substance is the same empty one of a something-that-supports, where "supports" is only an unclear metaphor like "bearing" or "underlying." So he can't even know for sure that mental substances are intrinsically different from material ones, though he is inclined to think so. He takes it as evident *that* there are thinking substances and extended ones, but he claims that we no more understand *how* we think than we understand what keeps the parts of matter or extension together. His skepticism about substance and about the essential difference between mental and material ones contributes to some vagueness and inconsistency in his use of the word "substance" in this reading. I will try to clarify where I can in footnotes.

Given his skepticism about substance, it's not surprising that Locke will argue that personal identity (the temporal identity of the self over time) does *not* depend on identity of *substance,* whether material or mental. Instead, what unites the present and past reality of my*self* is my recalling of past experience and action as *mine.*

3

... Let us suppose an atom,[1] i.e. a continued body under one immutable superficies, existing in a determined time and place; it is evident, that, considered in any instant of its existence, it is in that instant the same with itself. For, being at that instant what it is, and nothing else, it is the same, and so must continue as long as its existence is continued; for so long will it be the same, and no other. In like manner, if two or more atoms be joined together into the same mass, every one of those atoms will be the same, by the foregoing rule; and whilst they exist united together, the mass, consisting of the same atoms, must be the same mass, or the same body, let the parts be never so differently jumbled; but if one of these atoms be taken away, or one new one added, it is no longer the same mass or the same body. In the state of living creatures, their identity depends not on a mass of the same particles but on something else. For in them the variation of great parcels of matter alters not the identity: an oak growing from a plant to a great tree, and then lopped, is still the same oak; and a colt grown up to a horse, sometimes fat, sometimes lean, is all the while the same horse, though in both these cases there may be a manifest change of the parts, so that truly they are not either of them the same masses of matter, though they be truly one of them the same oak, and the other the same horse. The reason whereof is that, in these two cases of a mass of matter and a living body, *identity* is not applied to the same thing.

* * *

8

An animal is a living organized body; and consequently the same animal, as we have observed, is the same continued life communicated to different particles of matter as they happen successively to be united to that organized living body.[2] And what-

ever is talked of other definitions, ingenuous observation puts it past doubt that the *idea* in our minds of which the sound *man* in our mouths is the sign, is nothing else but of an animal of such a certain form: since I think I may be confident that whoever should see a creature of his own shape and make, though it had no more reason all its life than a *cat* or a *parrot,* would call him still a *man;* or whoever should hear a *cat* or a *parrot* discourse, reason, and philosophize would call or think it nothing but a *cat* or a *parrot* and say the one was a dull irrational *man,* and the other a very intelligent rational *parrot.*

* * *

9

This being premised, to find wherein *personal identity* consists, we must consider what *person* stands for; which, I think, is a thinking intelligent being that has reason and reflection and can consider itself as itself, the same thinking thing in different times and places; which it does only by the consciousness which is inseparable from thinking and, as it seems to me, essential to it; it being impossible for anyone to perceive without perceiving that he does perceive. When we see, hear, smell, taste, feel, meditate, or will anything, we know that we do so. Thus it is always as to our present sensations and perceptions, and by this everyone is to himself that which he calls *self:*[3] it not being considered in this case

---

From John Locke, *An Essay Concerning Human Understanding,* 5th ed. (London, 1706), vol. 1, bk. 2, c. 27.

[1] Locke is an advocate of *corpuscularianism:* the theory that matter ultimately consists of imperceptibly small indivisible particles of the same stuff, one type of particle differing from another only in shape and size. Since these particles or atoms are indivisible, they are incapable of change (i.e., immutable). ED.

[2] Like Hume in the next reading, Locke seems to think that there is a total turnover in the material components or "particles" of an organism. From the perspective of our current biology, this belief is mostly true, but

there are important exceptions. There is rapid turnover of entire cells (new ones replacing old ones) in many tissues such as skin and lung. However, in a minority of tissues there is no turnover—no regeneration of cells. For instance, throughout our adult lives we lose thousands of brain neurons per day without replacement. Fortunately we start out with so many billions of these cells that the surviving numbers are enough for a very long life. However, there is very rapid turnover in the molecular constituents of all cells, including long-lived neurons. Nearly all of a cell's components (except its genetic material) are disintegrated, flushed out, and replaced with new assemblies. So there is *nearly* total turnover of the material components of an organism.

Locke is claiming that as long as there is sameness of "form" or structure and physiological function over time, then the "same animal" or the "same life" continues to exist even if not a single particle of its original embodiment is still present and it now has a completely different "substance." Similarly, he will argue next that sameness of substance is not a necessary condition for sameness of person or self. ED.

[3] The influence of Descartes is very strong here. Like Descartes, Locke believes that mental events are inherently self-transparent. He even goes so far as to make the self-consciousness that accompanies all mental acts *explicit:* no one can perceive anything "without perceiving that he does perceive." An alternative that many philosophers would prefer is to say that self-awareness is most often only *implicit:* I *can* always take note of the fact that I am perceiving something, or later recall that I *perceived* it, even though I often do not. ED.

whether the same *self* be continued in the same or divers substances.[4] For since consciousness always accompanies thinking, and it is that that makes everyone to be what he calls *self,* and thereby distinguishes himself from all other thinking things: in this alone consists *personal identity,* i.e. the sameness of a rational being. And as far as this consciousness can be extended backwards to any past action or thought, so far reaches the identity of that *person:* it is the same *self* now it was then, and it is by the same *self* with this present one that now reflects on it, that that action was done.[5]

10

But it is further inquired whether it be the same identical substance? This, few would think they had reason to doubt of, if these perceptions, with their consciousness, always remained present in the mind whereby the same thinking thing would be always consciously present and, as would be thought, evidently the same to itself. But that which seems to make the difficulty is this: that this consciousness being interrupted always by forgetfulness, there being no moment of our lives wherein we have the whole train of all our past actions before our eyes in one view, but even the best memories losing the sight of one part whilst they are viewing another; and we sometimes, and that the greatest part of our lives, not reflecting on our past selves, being intent on our present thoughts, and in sound sleep having no thoughts at all, or at least none with that consciousness which remarks our waking thoughts; I say, in all these cases, our consciousness being interrupted, and we losing the sight of our past *selves,* doubts are raised whether we are the same thinking thing, i.e. the same substance, or no. Which, however reasonable or unreasonable, concerns not *personal identity* at all: the question being what makes the same *person,* and not whether it be the same identical substance, which always thinks in the same person; which, in this case, matters not at all; different substances, by the same consciousness (where they do partake in it) being united into one person, as well as different bodies by the same life are united into one animal, whose *identity* is preserved in that change of substances by the unity of one continued life. For, it being the same consciousness that makes a man be himself to himself, *personal identity* depends on that only, whether it be annexed only to one individual substance, or can be continued in a succession of several substances. For as far as any intelligent being can repeat the *idea* of any past action with the same consciousness it had of it at first, and with the same consciousness it has of any present action, so far it is the same *personal self.* For it is by the consciousness it has of its present thoughts and actions that it is *self* to *itself* now, and so will be the same *self* as far as the same consciousness can extend to actions past or to come, and would be by distance of time or change of substance no more two *persons* than a man be two men by wearing other clothes today than he did yesterday, with a long or short sleep between: the same consciousness uniting those distant actions into the same *person,* whatever substances contributed to their production.

11

That this is so, we have some kind of evidence in our very bodies, all whose particles, whilst vitally united to this same thinking conscious self so that we feel when they are touched and are affected

---

[4] Locke's use of the term "substance" is rather unclear. He is arguing that the temporal identity of animals (including human ones) as well as of persons or selves does *not* depend on identity of *substance*. In the case of animals, "substance" seems to designate either the compound body or its component particles. According to Locke, the continuing subject of all the changes undergone by an animal during its life is not its body or component particles, but rather its persisting structure and behavioral repertoire—its "life." If *same life* or *same animal* is not a case of *same substance,* then it seems that animals don't belong to the category of beings that exist on their own; they have only an "accidental" or inherent existence, like such entities as *brown* and *fleeing.* However, Locke is not explicit on this point.

He describes *persons* as "thinking things," which is Descartes' term for a mental *substance.* Yet he insists that a person's identity over time is *not* an identity of *substance.* If *same person* is not a case of *same substance,* then persons *as such* are not substances. He assumes that there is some substance or other serving as the **substratum** for a person at any particular time in its duration, but claims he doesn't know whether the substance is material or immaterial and whether or not there is a succession of substances in the duration of one person. But a "thinking thing" is a thing that thinks; and so is a substratum in which thinking inheres. So the combination of a person and its substance (substratum) seems to be a redundancy: a thing that thinks inhering in a thing that thinks. ED.

[5] Just as a multiplicity of items in one *present* experience is united by the singleness of our consciousness of all these items, and thereby is *my* experience rather than anyone else's, so with any multiplicity of items in past experiences. ED.

by and conscious of good or harm that happens to them, are a part of our *selves,* i.e. of our thinking conscious *self.*[6] Thus, the limbs of his body are to everyone a part of *himself;* he sympathizes and is concerned for them. Cut off a hand, and thereby separate it from that consciousness he had of its heat, cold, and other affections, and it is then no longer a part of that which is *himself,* any more than the remotest part of matter. Thus, we see the *substance* whereof *personal self* consisted[7] at one time may be varied at another, without the change of personal *identity:* there being no question about the same person, though the limbs, which but now were a part of it, be cut off.

* * *

13

But that which we call the *same consciousness* not being the same individual act, why one intellectual substance may not have represented to it, as done by itself, what it never did, and was perhaps done by some other agent:[8] why, I say, such a representation may not possibly be without reality of matter of fact, as well as several representations in dreams are, which yet whilst dreaming we take for true, will be difficult to conclude from the nature of things.[9] And that it never is so will by us, till we have clearer views of the nature of thinking substances, be best resolved into the goodness of God, who, as far as the happiness or misery of any of his sensible creatures is concerned in it, will not, by a fatal error of theirs, transfer from one to another that consciousness which draws reward or punishment to it.

* * *

15

And thus may we be able, without any difficulty, to conceive the same person at the resurrection, though in a body not exactly in make or parts the same which he had here, the same consciousness going along with the soul[10] that inhabits it. But yet the soul alone, in the change of bodies, would scarce, to anyone but to him that makes the soul the *man,* be enough to make the same *man.* For should the soul of a prince, carrying with it the consciousness of the prince's past life, enter and inform the body of a cobbler as soon as deserted by his own soul, everyone sees he would be the same person with the prince, accountable only for the prince's actions; but who would say it was the same man? The body too goes to the making the man and would, I guess, to everybody, determine the man in this case, wherein the soul, with all its princely thoughts about it, would not make another man: but he would be the same cobbler to everyone besides himself. I know that in the ordinary way of speaking, the same person and the same man stand for one and the same thing. And indeed, everyone will always have a liberty to speak as he pleases and to apply what articulate sounds to what *ideas* he thinks fit, and change them as often as he pleases. But yet when we will inquire what makes the same *spirit,*[11] *man,* or *person,* we must fix the *ideas* of *spirit, man,* or *person* in our minds; and having resolved with ourselves what we mean by them, it will not be hard to determine in either of them or the like when it is the *same* and when not.

16

But though the same immaterial substance or soul does not alone, wherever it be, and in whatsoever state, make the same man; yet, it is plain, consciousness, as far as ever it can be extended, should it be to ages past, unites existences and actions very

---

[6] This passage echoes the experience of mind-body union which Descartes discusses in connection with the sailor/ship simile in *Meditation 6.* When I experience sensations such as pain, hunger and thirst, I experience my body as my*self.* ED.

[7] Would Descartes accept as true Locke's description of the self as "consisting" of various body parts? ED.

[8] Since a voluntary act is not the same as the awareness of choosing and then executing an action, it is conceivable that this awareness, in the form of a memory, could be transferred from the doer of the act to someone else who would then (falsely) recall doing the deed. ED.

[9] Locke's prose is at its worst here. He seems to be saying that, because of our inadequate grasp of "the nature of things," we are unable to say that such mistaken memories never occur. These "memories" would be like dream experiences: While we are having them, they would seem completely real. ED.

[10] "Soul" in this context signifies an immaterial substance in a dualistic union with a human body. In this passage the soul is different from the body and from the backward-reaching consciousness that constitutes a person or self. A "man" is either the human animal understood exclusively as an appropriately structured and functioning body, or such a body along with an immaterial soul capable of thinking. In neither case is *same man* either sufficient or necessary for *same person.* ED.

[11] *Spirit = soul.* ED.

remote in time into the same person, as well as it does the existence and actions of the immediately preceding moment, so that whatever has the consciousness of present and past actions is the same person to whom they both belong. Had I the same consciousness that I saw the ark and *Noah's* flood as that I saw an overflowing of the *Thames* last winter, or as that I write now, I could no more doubt that I that write this now, that saw the *Thames* overflowed last winter, and that viewed the flood at the general deluge, was the same *self*, place that *self* in what substance you please, than I that write this am the same *myself* now whilst I write (whether I consist of all the same substance, material or immaterial, or no) that I was yesterday. For as to this point of being the same *self*, it matters not whether this present *self* be made up of the same or other substances, I being as much concerned and as justly accountable for any action that was done a thousand years since, appropriated to me now by this self-consciousness, as I am for what I did the last moment.

17

Self is that conscious thinking thing (whatever substance made up of, whether spiritual or material, simple or compounded, it matters not) which is sensible or conscious of pleasure and pain, capable of happiness or misery, and so is concerned for *itself*, as far as that consciousness extends. Thus everyone finds that, whilst comprehended under that consciousness, the little finger is as much as part of *itself* as what is most so. Upon separation of this little finger, should this consciousness go along with the little finger and leave the rest of the body, it is evident the little finger would be the *person, the same person;* and self then would have nothing to do with the rest of the body. As in this case it is the consciousness that goes along with the substance, when one part is separate from another, which makes the same *person* and constitutes this inseparable *self:* so it is in reference to substance remote in time. That with which the *consciousness* of this present thinking thing can join itself makes the same *person* and is one *self* with it, and with nothing else, and so attributes to *itself* and owns all the actions of that thing as its own, as far as that consciousness

reaches, and no further; as everyone who reflects will perceive.

18

In this *personal identity* is founded all the right and justice of reward and punishment: happiness and misery being that for which everyone is concerned for *himself*, not mattering what becomes of any substance not joined to or affected with that consciousness. For, as it is evident in the instance I gave but now, if the consciousness went along with the little finger when it was cut off, that would be the same *self* which was concerned for the whole body yesterday, as making part of *itself*, whose actions then it cannot but admit as its own now. Though, if the same body should still live and immediately from the separation of the little finger have its own peculiar consciousness, whereof the little finger knew nothing, it would not at all be concerned for it as part of *itself*, or could own any of its actions, or have any of them imputed to him.

19

This may show us wherein *personal identity* consists: not in the identity of substance but, as I have said, in the identity of *consciousness,* wherein, if *Socrates* and the present mayor of *Queensborough* agree, they are the same person; if the same *Socrates* working and sleeping do not partake of the same *consciousness,* *Socrates* waking and sleeping is not the same person. And to punish *Socrates* waking for what sleeping *Socrates* thought, and waking *Socrates* was never conscious of would be no more of right than to punish one twin for what his brother-twin did, whereof he knew nothing, because their outsides were so like that they could not be distinguished; for such twins have been seen.

20

But yet possibly it will still be objected, suppose I wholly lose the memory of some parts of my life beyond a possibility of retrieving them, so that perhaps I shall never be conscious of them again: yet am I not the same person that did those actions, had those thoughts that I once was conscious of, though I have now forgot them? To which I answer that we must here take notice what the word *I* is applied to, which, in this case, is the man only. And the same man being presumed to be the same person. But if it be possible for the same man to have distinct incommunicable consciousness at different times, it is past doubt the same man would at different times make different persons; which, we see, is the sense of mankind in the solemnest declaration of their opinions, human laws not punishing the *mad man* for the *sober man's* actions, nor the *sober man* for what the *mad man* did, thereby making them two persons: which is somewhat explained by our way of speaking in *English* when we say such an one *is not himself,* or is *beside himself;* in which phrases it is insinuated, as if those who now, or at least first used them, thought that *self* was changed, the *self*-same person was no longer in that man.

It is generally acknowledged that Locke's account of personal identity is seriously flawed. In asserting that I simply *am* the person whose deeds and thoughts I seem to remember, Locke disregards the possibility that a memory could be false. In such a case it would seem to me that it was I who had experienced or did something when in fact I did not. Having such a memory-experience no more establishes my personal identity than having a visual experience of a bent stick in the water proves that there is a bend in the stick.

Derek Parfit, in Reading 31, will present an amended version of Locke's account.

REVIEW QUESTIONS

1. Identity is a *transitive* relation: If x is identical to y, and y is identical to z, then x is identical to z. Suppose that at ten years of age I remember my first day on ice skates at age five, but that, at age twenty-five, I don't any longer remember that day. What's the problem here for Locke's theory?

2. Locke admits that, for all we know, it may be the case that human mental operations are actually carried out by a material substance—the body with its brain. Suppose that a Christian is convinced this is true but continues to believe in personal immortality and a final day of reckoning for one's good and bad deeds. Since the body evidently dies and disintegrates, resurrection would be a *replication* by God of a person's body, including all the neural connections that are the basis of that person's personality and memories. According to Locke's theory, this replica would recall and be responsible for all the deeds of the original person. Is there anything wrong with this picture? *Should* the replica be held responsible for the original's deeds? If you believe in an afterlife, does the prospect of replication after death satisfy the expectation that you will survive your death?

30

Of Personal Identity

David Hume

David Hume (1711–1776) was a Scottish historian, philosopher, and diplomat. His best known philosophical works are *A Treatise of Human Nature* (1739), from which this reading is taken, and *An Enquiry Concerning Human Understanding* (1748).

Hume was more consistent and therefore more radical than Locke in his application of the empiricist principle that all knowledge is derived from sense-perception. He divided all the contents of the mind (including those of what Locke called "reflection") into two classes: *impressions* and *ideas*. Ideas are no more than faint copies of impressions or collections of impressions. An impression is to an idea as the having of a toothache is to the thought of one. This reading is an example of a kind of criticism Hume frequently directs against traditional philosophical beliefs: that they appeal to ideas for which there is either no basis in experience (i.e., no impressions of which they could be copies) or a different basis than what philosophers have usually thought. As Descartes would have predicted, Hume fails to discover any impression from which the idea of an enduring self could have been copied. He concludes that our mistaken belief that we have such an idea is a likely by-product of the normal operations of the mind.

There are some philosophers who imagine we are every moment intimately conscious of what we call our *self;* that we feel its existence and its continuance in existence; and are certain, beyond the evidence of a demonstration, both of its perfect identity and simplicity. The strongest sensation, the most violent passion, say they, instead of distracting us from this view, only fix it the more intensely, and make us consider their influence on *self* either by their pain or pleasure. To attempt a further proof of this were to weaken its evidence; since no proof can be derived from any fact of which we are so intimately conscious; nor is there anything of which we can be certain if we doubt of this.

Unluckily all these positive assertions are contrary to that very experience which is pleaded for them; nor have we any idea of *self,* after the manner it is here explained. For, from what impression could this idea be derived? This question it is impossible to answer without a manifest contradiction and absurdity; and yet it is a question which must necessarily be answered, if we would have the idea of self pass for clear and intelligible. It must be some one impression that gives rise to every real idea. But self or person is not any one impression, but that to which our several impressions and ideas are supposed to have a reference.[1] If any impression gives rise to the idea of self, that impression must continue invariably the same, through the whole

These selections are from David Hume, *A Treatise of Human Nature*, Bk. 1, Pt. 4, Sec. 6; and from the Appendix to the *Treatise*.

[1] I.e., the self is supposed to be their *substratum.* ED.

course of our lives; since self is supposed to exist after that manner. But there is no impression constant and invariable. Pain and pleasure, grief and joy, passions and sensations succeed each other, and never all exist at the same time. It cannot therefore be from any of these impressions, or from any other, that the idea of self is derived; and consequently there is no such idea.

But further, what must become of all our particular perceptions upon this hypothesis? All these are different, and distinguishable, and separable from each other, and may be separately considered, and may exist separately, and have no need of anything to support their existence.[2] After what manner therefore do they belong to self, and how are they connected with it? For my part, when I enter most intimately into what I call *myself,* I always stumble on some particular perception or other, of heat or cold, light or shade, love or hatred, pain or pleasure. I never can catch *myself* at any time without a perception, and never can observe anything but the perception. When my perceptions are removed for any time, as by sound sleep, so long am I insensible of *myself,* and may truly be said not to exist. And were all my perceptions removed by death, and could I neither think, nor feel, nor see, nor love, nor hate, after the dissolution of my body, I should be entirely annihilated, nor do I conceive what is further requisite to make me a perfect nonentity. If any one, upon serious and unprejudiced reflection, thinks he has a different notion of *himself,* I must confess I can reason no longer with him. All I can allow him is, that he may be in the right as well as I, and that we are essentially differ-

ent in this particular. He may, perhaps, perceive something simple and continued, which he calls *himself;* though I am certain there is no such principle in me.

But setting aside some metaphysicians of this kind, I may venture to affirm of the rest of mankind, that they are nothing but a bundle or collection of different perceptions, which succeed each other with an inconceivable rapidity, and are in a perpetual flux and movement. Our eyes cannot turn in their sockets without varying our perceptions. Our thought is still more variable than our sight; and all our other senses and faculties contribute to this change; nor is there any single power of soul, which remains unalterably the same, perhaps for one moment. The mind is a kind of theater, where several perceptions successively make their appearance; pass, repass, glide away, and mingle in an infinite variety of postures and situations. There is properly no *simplicity* in it at one time, nor *identity* in different, whatever natural propension we may have to imagine that simplicity and identity. The comparison of the theater must not mislead us. They are the successive perceptions only, that constitute the mind; nor have we the most distant notion of the place where these scenes are represented, or of the materials of which it is composed.

What then gives us so great a propension to ascribe an identity to these successive perceptions, and to suppose ourselves possessed of an invariable and uninterrupted existence through the whole course of our lives? In order to answer this question we must distinguish betwixt personal identity, as it regards our thought or imagination, and as it regards our passions or the concern we take in ourselves. The first is our present subject; and to explain it perfectly we must take the matter pretty deep, and account for that identity, which we attribute to plants and animals; there being a great analogy betwixt it and the identity of a self or person.

We have a distinct idea of an object that remains invariable and uninterrupted through a supposed variation of time; and this idea we call that of *identity* or *sameness.* We have also a distinct idea of several different objects existing in succession, and connected together by a close relation; and this to an accurate view affords as perfect a notion of *diversity*

---

[2] Hume is calling into question the unity of the self *both* in the present *and* over time. Right now I'm having an experience which includes the sounds of nearby voices, the feeling of my body's joints and muscles configured in a sitting position, the sight of the room around me, and a vague feeling that I need to eat soon. Where Locke regards as obvious and essential a self-awareness that unifies all these contents of my present consciousness and links them to past experiences through memory, Hume brings a "show me" attitude to the discussion. He maintains that each of the contents could have occurred without the other (e.g., the sounds of voices without the sight of the room), so there's no "glue" binding one to the other, no intrinsic connection. Each content is a *conscious* one, so the separability of the contents implies the separability of the *consciousness* of each. There's no indivisible consciousness of them all. And the fact that you *and* I are discussing these contents suggests that there's nothing inherently *mine* rather than *yours* or *anyone else's* about the contents of "my" self. ED.

as if there was no manner of relation among the objects.[3] But though these two ideas of identity, and a succession of related objects, be in themselves perfectly distinct, and even contrary, yet it is certain that, in our common way of thinking, they are generally confounded with each other. That action of the imagination, by which we consider the uninterrupted and invariable object, and that by which we reflect on the succession of related objects, are almost the same to the feeling, nor is there much more effort of thought required in the latter case than in the former. The relation facilitates the transition of the mind from one object to another, and renders its passage as smooth as if it contemplated one continued object.[4] This resemblance is the cause of the confusion and mistake, and makes us substitute the notion of identity, instead of that of related objects. However at one instant we may consider the related succession as variable or interrupted, we are sure the next to ascribe to it a perfect identity, and regard it as invariable and uninterrupted. Our propensity to this mistake is so great from the resemblance above mentioned, that we fall into it before we are aware; and though we incessantly correct ourselves by reflection, and return to a more accurate method of thinking, yet we cannot long sustain our philosophy, or take off this bias from the imagination. Our last resource is to yield to it, and boldly assert that these different related objects are in effect the same, however interrupted and variable. In order to justify to ourselves this absurdity, we often feign some new and unintelligible principle, that connects the objects together, and prevents their interruption or variation. Thus we feign the continued existence of the perceptions of our senses, to remove the interruption; and run into the notion of a *soul,* and *self,* and *substance,* to disguise the variation[5]. But, we may further observe, that where we do not give rise to such a fiction, our propension to confound identity with relation is so great, that we are apt to imagine something unknown and mysterious, connecting the parts, beside their relation; and this I take to be the case with regard to the identity we ascribe to plants and vegetables. And even when this does not take place, we still feel a propensity to confound these ideas, though we are not able fully to satisfy ourselves in that particular, nor find anything invariable and uninterrupted to justify our notion of identity.

Thus the controversy concerning identity is not merely a dispute of words. For when we attribute identity, in an improper sense, to variable or interrupted objects, our mistake is not confined to the expression, but is commonly attended with a fiction, either of something invariable and uninterrupted, or of something mysterious and inexplicable, or at least with a propensity to such fictions. What will suffice to prove this hypothesis to the satisfaction of every fair inquirer, is to show, from daily experience and observation, that the objects

---

[3] The "object" here is a content of an impression or idea. If we were watching Descartes' wax changing shape and qualities as a flame is applied to it, we would perceive a succession of different contents or "objects" in Hume's sense. The cold wax *followed by* the warm wax is, for Hume, just as much a case of *two* different objects as a piece of cold wax and a piece of warm wax on the table *at the same time.* Just as one of two pieces of wax on the table is not the other, no matter what relations they may have to each other, so the hot wax I experience after applying the flame is not the cold wax I experienced before, even though the two are related to each other in various ways—one succeeds the other, both are part of an entirely familiar and predictable sequence, and so on. Only an uninterrupted awareness of something that is not changing at all would entitle me to call it the same then and now. ED.

[4] Think about reaching for and gripping the pen in front of you. Your mind immediately goes to the thought or image of how the pen feels and weighs in your hand. If you actually grasp the pen, what you experience next is what you anticipated; your mind has no trouble with the transition from one experience to the other. Suppose, however, that the pen were to collapse into a small puddle of liquid as soon as you grip it. You'd see and feel what happened just as clearly as in the normal sequence, but your mind's transition to the experience of a liquefied "pen" wouldn't be "smooth." In the first case, but not in the second, you would interpret your combined visual and tactile awareness of what's in your hand as a further experience of the *same* thing you saw lying on the table even though there are many differences in content. Such, according to Hume, is the illusion created by a sufficient degree of relatedness over time. ED.

[5] Hume's empiricism is at its most radical here: All that experience can tell us is that there are perceptions; they come in more or less permanent or transitory bundles. They aren't "in" anything, and they aren't intrinsically connected. *Material substance* is the fiction that a content of perception continues to exist "out there" in a nonconscious substratum when there's no perception of that content. Like the notions of a soul or self (mental substance), it is the attempt to think some unity and continuity into our experience.

Some terminology is in order here. *Dualism* (as in Descartes) is the doctrine that there are two irreducibly different kinds of being, mental and material; *materialism* holds that there is only one kind, roughly coinciding with the subject matter of physical science; and *idealism* claims that all being is mental or mind-dependent. Idealism comes in many forms; in his theory Hume regularly invokes the mind and its operation in explaining or criticizing philosophical views. But, as this reading makes clear, there is no room in Hume's universe for minds in the Cartesian sense, or even for selves in a fairly ordinary sense. Instead there exists nothing but perceptions in the form of ideas or impressions. Hume's sort of idealism is often called *phenomenalism.* ED.

which are variable or interrupted, and yet are supposed to continue the same, are such only as consist of a succession of parts, connected together by resemblance, contiguity,[6] or causation. For as such a succession answers evidently to our notion of diversity, it can only be by mistake we ascribe to it an identity; and as the relation of parts, which leads us into this mistake, is really nothing but a quality, which produces an association of ideas, and an easy transition of the imagination from one to another, it can only be from the resemblance, which this act of the mind bears to that by which we contemplate one continued object, that the error arises. Our chief business, then must be to prove, that all objects, to which we ascribe identity, without observing their invariableness and uninterruptedness, are such as consist of a succession of related objects.

In order to do this, suppose any mass of matter, of which the parts are contiguous and connected, to be placed before us; it is plain we must attribute a perfect identity to this mass, provided all the parts continue uninterruptedly and invariably the same, whatever motion or change of place we may observe either in the whole or in any of the parts. But supposing some very *small* or *inconsiderable* part to be added to the mass, or subtracted from it; though this absolutely destroys the identity of the whole, strictly speaking, yet as we seldom think so accurately, we scruple not to pronounce a mass of matter the same, where we find so trivial an alteration. The passage of the thought from the object before the change to the object after it, is so smooth and easy, that we scarce perceive the transition, and are apt to imagine, that it is nothing but a continued survey of the same object.

There is a very remarkable circumstance that attends this experiment; which is, that though the change of any considerable part in a mass of matter destroys the identity of the whole, yet we must measure the greatness of the part, not absolutely, but by its *proportion* to the whole. The addition or diminution of a mountain would not be sufficient to produce a diversity in a planet; though the change of a very few inches would be able to destroy the identity of some bodies. It will be impos-

sible to account for this, but by reflecting that objects operate upon the mind, and break or interrupt the continuity of its actions, not according to their real greatness, but according to their proportion to each other; and therefore, since this interruption makes an object cease to appear the same, it must be the uninterrupted progress of the thought which constitutes the imperfect identity.

This may be confirmed by another phenomenon. A change in any considerable part of a body destroys its identity; but it is remarkable, that where the change is produced *gradually* and *insensibly,* we are less apt to ascribe to it the same effect. The reason can plainly be no other, than that the mind, in following the successive changes of the body, feels an easy passage from the surveying its condition in one moment, to the viewing of it in another, and in no particular time perceives any interruption in its actions. From which continued perception, it ascribes a continued existence and identity to the object.

But whatever precaution we may use in introducing the changes gradually, and making them proportionable to the whole, it is certain, that where the changes are at last observed to become considerable, we make a scruple of ascribing identity to such different objects. There is, however, another artifice, by which we may induce the imagination to advance a step further; and that is, by producing a reference of the parts to each other, and a combination to some *common end* or purpose. A ship, of which a considerable part has been changed by frequent reparations, is still considered as the same; nor does the difference of the materials hinder us from ascribing an identity to it. The common end, in which the parts conspire, is the same under all their variations, and affords an easy transition of the imagination from one situation of the body to another.

But this is still more remarkable, when we add a *sympathy* of parts to their *common end,* and suppose that they bear to each other the reciprocal relation of cause and effect in all their actions and operations. This is the case with all animals and vegetables; where not only the several parts have a reference to some general purpose, but also a mutual dependence on, and connection with, each other. The effect of so strong a relation is, that though every one must allow, that in a very few years both vegetables

---

[6] "Contiguity" obtains between any two objects immediately adjacent to each other in space. ED.

and animals endure a *total* change,[7] yet we still attribute identity to them, while their form, size, and substance, are entirely altered. An oak that grows from a small plant to a large tree is still the same oak, though there be not one particle of matter or figure of its parts the same. An infant becomes a man, and is sometimes fat, sometimes lean, without any change in his identity.

We may also consider the two following phenomena, which are remarkable in their kind. The first is, that though we commonly be able to distinguish pretty exactly betwixt numerical and specific identity,[8] yet it sometimes happens that we confound them, and in our thinking and reasoning employ the one for the other. Thus, a man who hears a noise that is frequently interrupted and renewed, says it is still the same noise, though it is evident the sounds have only a specific identity or resemblance, and there is nothing numerically the same but the cause which produced them. In like manner it may well be said, without breach of the propriety of language, that such a church, which was formerly of brick, fell to ruin, and that the parish rebuilt the same church of freestone, and according to modern architecture. Here neither the form nor materials are the same, nor is there anything common to the two objects but their relation to the inhabitants of the parish; and yet this alone is sufficient to make us denominate them the same. But we must observe, that in these cases the first object is in a manner annihilated before the second comes into existence; by which means, we are never presented, in any one point of time, with the idea of difference and multiplicity; and for that reason are less scrupulous in calling them the same.

Secondly, we may remark, that though, in a succession of related objects, it be in a manner requisite that the change of parts be not sudden nor entire, in order to preserve the identity, yet where the objects are in their nature changeable and inconstant, we admit of a more sudden transition than would otherwise be consistent with that relation.

Thus, as the nature of a river consists in the motion and change of parts, though in less than four-and-twenty hours these be totally altered, this hinders not the river from continuing the same during several ages. What is natural and essential to anything is, in a manner, expected; and what is expected makes less impression, and appears of less moment than what is unusual and extraordinary. A considerable change of the former kind seems really less to the imagination than the most trivial alteration of the latter; and by breaking less the continuity of the thought, has less influence in destroying the identity.

We now proceed to explain the nature of *personal identity,* which has become so great a question in philosophy, especially of late years, in England, where all the abstruser sciences are studied with a peculiar ardor and application. And here it is evident the same method of reasoning must be continued which has so successfully explained the identity of plants, and animals, and ships, and houses, and of all compounded and changeable productions either of art or nature. The identity which we ascribe to the mind of man is only a fictitious one, and of a like kind with that which we ascribe to vegetable and animal bodies. It cannot therefore have a different origin, but must proceed from a like operation of the imagination upon like objects.

But lest this argument should not convince the reader, though in my opinion perfectly decisive, let him weigh the following reasoning, which is still closer and more immediate. It is evident that the identity which we attribute to the human mind, however perfect we may imagine it to be, is not able to run the several different perceptions into one, and make them lose their characters of distinction and difference, which are essential to them. It is still true that every distinct perception which enters into the composition of the mind, is a distinct existence, and is different, and distinguishable, and separable from every other perception, either contemporary or successive. But as, notwithstanding this distinction and separability, we suppose the whole train of perceptions to be united by identity, a question naturally arises concerning this relation of identity, whether it be something that really binds our several perceptions together, or only associates their ideas in the imagination; that is, in other words, whether, in pronouncing concerning the

---

[7] See footnote 2 of Reading 29. ED.

[8] Suppose there are two unopened cans of the same diet cola on the table. They are identical in every respect, except that one is not occupying the same space as the other, and so *is not* the other. The two cans would have what Hume calls "specific identity" or *qualitative identity,* but they would be *numerically different. Numerical identity* is what everything has to itself at any one time and (in Hume's theory) for as long as it is observed to be unchanged. ED.

identity of a person, we observe some real bond among his perceptions, or only feel one among the ideas we form of them. This question we might easily decide, if we would recollect what has been already proved at large, that the understanding never observes any real connection among objects, and that even the union of cause and effect, when strictly examined, resolves itself into a customary association of ideas.[9] For from thence it evidently follows, that identity is nothing really belonging to these different perceptions, and uniting them altogether, but is merely a quality which we attribute to them, because of the union of their ideas in the imagination when we reflect upon them. Now, the only qualities which can give ideas a union in the imagination, are these three relations above mentioned. These are the uniting principles in the ideal world, and without them every distinct object is separable by the mind, and may be separately considered, and appears not to have any more connection with any other object than if disjoined by the greatest difference and remoteness. It is therefore on some of these three relations of resemblance, contiguity, and causation, that identity depends; and as the very essence of these relations consists in their producing an easy transition of ideas, it follows that our notions of personal identity proceed entirely from the smooth and uninterrupted progress of the thought along a train of connected ideas, according to the principles above explained. The only question, therefore, which remains is, by what relations this uninterrupted progress of our thought is produced, when we consider existence of a mind or thinking person. And here it is evident we must confine ourselves to resemblance and causation, and must drop contiguity, which has little or no influence in the present case.

To begin with *resemblance;* suppose we could see clearly into the breast of another, and observe that succession of perceptions which constitutes his mind or thinking principle, and suppose that he always preserves the memory of a considerable part of past perceptions, it is evident that nothing could more contribute to the bestowing a relation on this succession amidst all its variations. For what is the memory but a faculty, by which we raise up the images of past perceptions? And as an image necessarily resembles its object, must not the frequent placing of these resembling perceptions in the chain of thought, convey the imagination more easily from one link to another, and make the whole seem like the continuance of one object? In this particular, then, the memory not only discovers the identity, but also contributes to its production, by producing the relation of resemblance among the perceptions. The case is the same, whether we consider ourselves or others.

As to *causation;* we may observe that the true idea of the human mind, is to consider it as a system of different perceptions or different existences, which are linked together by the relation of cause and effect, and mutually produce, destroy, influence, and modify each other. Our impressions give rise to their correspondent ideas; and these ideas, in their turn, produce other impressions. One thought chases another, and draws after it a third, by which it is expelled in its turn. In this respect, I cannot compare the soul more properly to anything than to a republic or commonwealth, in which the several members are united by the reciprocal ties of government and subordination, and give rise to other persons who propagate the same republic in the incessant changes of its parts. And as the same individual republic may not only change its members, but also its laws and constitutions; in like manner the same person may vary his character and disposition, as well as his impressions and ideas, without losing his identity. Whatever changes he endures, his several parts are still connected by the relation of causation. And in this view our identity with regard to the passions serves to corroborate that with regard to the imagination, by the making

---

[9] Hume's analysis of the cause-effect relation earlier in his *Treatise* is as skeptical as his treatment of personal identity. Hume would admit that we understand a *necessary connection* between something being triangular and its being three-sided. A four-sided triangle is contradictory and therefore as inconceivable as a square circle. But my book *not* falling when I hold it up and then release my grip on it *is conceivable;* I don't understand any necessary connection between the two events—my releasing the book and its falling. Hume is aware that we have a perfect confidence and certainty that the book will fall, but those are subjective feelings that don't give to what I expect any objective necessity. For all we *know,* an event of any one type could be followed by an event of any other type. What gives us our certainties about predictable sequences of events is that we have repeated experiences of similar sequences, and this repetition makes the mind's transition from one event to the other smooth and habitual or "customary," so that when we have the impression of the prior event occurring, we anticipate the subsequent event. And our impression of this irresistible mental transition gives rise to the idea of a *necessary* connection. However, "I can't help expecting *y* to happen after *x*" is not a warrant for claiming that *y* happens necessarily. ED.

our distant perceptions influence each other, and by giving us a present concern for our past or future pains or pleasures.

As memory alone acquaints us with the continuance and extent of this succession of perceptions, it is to be considered, upon that account chiefly, as the source of personal identity. Had we no memory, we never should have any notion of causation, nor consequently of that chain of causes and effects, which constitute our self or person. But having once acquired this notion of causation from the memory, we can extend the same chain of causes, and consequently the identity of our persons beyond our memory, and can comprehend times, and circumstances, and actions, which we have entirely forgot, but suppose in general to have existed. For how few of our past actions are there, of which we have any memory? Who can tell me, for instance, what were his thoughts and actions on the first of January 1715, the eleventh of March 1719, and the third of August 1733? Or will he affirm, because he has entirely forgot the incidents of these days, that the present self is not the same person with the self of that time; and by that means overturn all the most established notions of personal identity? In this view, therefore, memory does not so much *produce* as *discover* personal identity, by showing us the relation of cause and effect among our different perceptions.[10] It will be incumbent on those who affirm that memory produces entirely our personal identity, to give a reason why we can thus extend our identity beyond our memory.[11]

The whole of this doctrine leads us to a conclusion, which is of great importance in the present affair, viz. that all the nice and subtile questions concerning personal identity can never possibly be decided, and are to be regarded rather as grammatical

than as philosophical difficulties. Identity depends on the relations of ideas; and these relations produce identity, by means of that easy transition they occasion. But as the relations, and the easiness of the transition may diminish by insensible degrees, we have no just standard by which we can decide any dispute concerning the time when they acquire or lose a title to the name of identity. All the disputes concerning the identity of connected objects are merely verbal,[12] except so far as the relation of parts gives rise to some fiction or imaginary principle of union, as we have already observed.

What I have said concerning the first origin and uncertainty of our notion of identity, as applied to the human mind, may be extended with little or no variation to that of *simplicity*. An object, whose different coexistent parts are bound together by a close relation, operates upon the imagination after much the same manner as one perfectly simple and indivisible, and requires not a much greater stretch of thought in order to its conception. From this similarity of operation we attribute a simplicity to it, and feign a principle of union as the support of this simplicity, and the center of all the different parts and qualities of the object.[13]

---

[10] As the preceding analogy of the mind with a republic suggests, not just any old causal relation between perceptions will create the feeling of identity. The various, usually recurring, impressions and ideas will need to exhibit a good deal of causal *interaction*, like the parts of an organism. And, also like the parts of an organism or political community, they will need to have some discernible relation to long-range purposes and goals. Hume would have to agree that if a change in habits or belief were too sudden or total, one's feeling of personal identity and others' perception of one's identity would be weakened. ED.

[11] Among "those" is Locke in the previous reading. How do you think he would respond to Hume's challenge? (Section 20 of the Locke reading is especially relevant here.) ED.

[12] Imagine a preservationist conversing with the president of a college that has recently renovated a two-hundred-year-old building of great historical value. They disagree over whether the building is in its most important aspects still the *same* (whether it has been really *preserved*). The preservationist would have done things somewhat differently. She wishes, for instance, that more effort had been made to keep the original wood and other materials, and that the new lighting fixtures were less contemporary in look. The administrator points out how many features of the renovated building *are* faithful reproductions, and how much better the building can now serve its original purpose. Both agree on the *facts* about the building, but disagree over applying the word "same" to it. Theirs is what Hume would call a "merely verbal" dispute, even though it involves important values. Similarly, there might be important issues affected by the "merely verbal" distinction between being the same person or not. It might, for instance, determine how we are to treat someone who was a criminal during a much earlier period of his life. ED.

[13] What Hume is saying here about objects in general would also apply to the self at any point in time: The set of perceptions I now have includes familiar surroundings in which various items are interacting as usual and are spatially related in just the ways they usually are, so that my mind moves smoothly and habitually from one to the other in a way that mimics awareness of one unvarying content. For instance, my gaze wanders between the door and the differently colored surrounding wall in front of me as easily as it would scan an unbroken monochrome surface. Since my visual field is nevertheless visibly divided and varied, I tend to think of my*self* as an *un*divided and even indivisible or "simple" substratum for the array of distinct perceptions I'm now having. ED.

APPENDIX

I had entertained some hopes, that however deficient our theory of the intellectual world might be, it would be free from those contradictions and absurdities which seem to attend every explication that human reason can give of the material world. Upon a more strict review of the section concerning *personal identity*, I find myself involved in such a labyrinth that, I must confess, I neither know how to correct my former opinions, nor how to render them consistent. If this be not a good *general* reason for scepticism, it is at least a sufficient one (if I were not already abundantly supplied) for me to entertain a diffidence and modesty in all my decisions. I shall propose the arguments on both sides, beginning with those that induced me to deny the strict and proper identity and simplicity of a self or thinking being.

When we talk of *self* or *substance,* we must have an idea annexed to these terms, otherwise they are altogether unintelligible. Every idea is derived from preceding impressions; and we have no impression of self or substance, as something simple and individual. We have, therefore, no idea of them in that sense.

Whatever is distinct is distinguishable, and whatever is distinguishable is separable by the thought or imagination. All perceptions are distinct. They are, therefore, distinguishable, and separable, and may be conceived as separately existent, and may exist separately, without any contradiction or absurdity.

When I view this table and that chimney, nothing is present to me but particular perceptions, which are of a like nature with all the other perceptions. This is the doctrine of philosophers. But this table, which is present to me, and that chimney, may, and do exist separately. This is the doctrine of the vulgar, and implies no contradiction. There is no contradiction, therefore, in extending the same doctrine to all the perceptions.

In general, the following reasoning seems satisfactory. All ideas are borrowed from preceding perceptions. Our ideas of objects, therefore, are derived from that source. Consequently no proposition can be intelligible or consistent with regard to objects, which is not so with regard to perceptions.

But it is intelligible and consistent to say that objects exist distinct and independent, without any common *simple* substance or subject of inhesion.[14] This proposition, therefore, can never be absurd with regard to perceptions.

When I turn my reflection on *myself,* I never can perceive this *self* without some one or more perceptions; nor can I ever perceive anything but the perceptions. It is the composition of these, therefore, which forms the self.

We can conceive a thinking being to have either many or few perceptions. Suppose the mind to be reduced even below the life of an oyster. Suppose it to have only one perception, as of thirst or hunger. Consider it in that situation. Do you conceive anything but merely that perception? Have you any notion of *self* or *substance*? If not, the addition of other perceptions can never give you that notion.

The annihilation which some people suppose to follow upon death, and which entirely destroys this self, is nothing but an extinction of all particular perceptions; love and hatred, pain and pleasure, thought and sensation. These, therefore, must be the same with self, since the one cannot survive the other.

* * *

Philosophers begin to be reconciled to the principle, *that we have no idea of external substance, distinct from the ideas of particular qualities*. This must pave the way for a like principle with regard to the mind, *that we have no notion of it, distinct from the particular perception.*

So far I seem to be attended with sufficient evidence. But having thus loosened all our particular perceptions, when I proceed to explain the principle of connection, which binds them together, and makes us attribute to them a real simplicity and identity, I am sensible that my account is very defective, and that nothing but the seeming evidence of the precedent reasonings could have induced me to receive it. If perceptions are distinct existences, they form a whole only by being connected together. But no connections among distinct existences are ever discoverable by human understanding. We only *feel* a connection or determination of

---

[14] That is, objects (such as tables, trees and birds) exist without needing a *common* substratum. ED.

the thought to pass from one object to another. It follows, therefore, that the thought alone feels personal identity, when reflecting on the train of past perceptions that compose a mind, [and] the ideas of them are felt to be connected together, and naturally introduce each other. However extraordinary this conclusion may seem, it need not surprise us. Most philosophers seem inclined to think, that personal identity *arises* from consciousness, and consciousness is nothing but a reflected thought or perception. The present philosophy, therefore, has so far a promising aspect. But all my hopes vanish when I come to explain the principles that unite our successive perceptions in our thought or consciousness. I cannot discover any theory which gives me satisfaction on this head.

In short, there are two principles which I cannot render consistent, nor is it in my power to re-nounce either of them, viz. *that all our distinct perceptions are distinct existences,* and *that the mind never perceives any real connection among distinct existences.*[15] Did our perceptions either inhere in something simple and individual, or did the mind perceive some real connection among them, there would be no difficulty in the case. For my part, I must plead the privilege of a sceptic, and confess that this difficulty is too hard for my understanding. I pretend not, however, to pronounce it absolutely insuperable. Others, perhaps, or myself, upon more mature reflections, may discover some hypothesis that will reconcile those contradictions. . . .

---

[15] It isn't clear why Hume says that he "cannot render consistent" the two italicized "principles." They are not inconsistent with each other. However, they are inconsistent with our strong inclination, which Hume shares, to find *unity* in the world and/or ourselves. ED.

There is a degree of irony in Hume's writing that makes it difficult to judge how much real regret we should read into the last two paragraphs of the Appendix where he speaks of his "hopes vanish(ing)" and of his analysis as "defective" because it failed to find any *connections* among perceptions. For Hume's **phenomenalism** all that exists are perceptions; *self* and *world* are pretty much the same domains. The bodies around us, such as chairs, dogs, and humans, are wholes (perceptions) composed of parts (that are also perceptions). The unity of each whole can be nothing but a set of connections among its parts. Yet each of these parts is also a whole with its own parts. To say that there are no connections among perceptions amounts to denying there is any intelligible unity in the world or in oneself.

Of course, there has to be unity somewhere, and Hume knows this. If all that exists are perceptions, then there must be *many* of them, and there can't be *many* without there being many *ones*. To apply this principle to his world, Hume claimed that perceptions must ultimately be composed of perceptions that are *not* wholes, but simple, *indivisible* unities:

> The whole globe of the earth, nay the whole universe *may be considered as a unit*. That term of unity is merely a fictitious denomination, which the mind may apply to any quantity of objects it collects together. . . . But the unity which can exist alone, and whose existence is necessary to that of all number, is of another kind, and must be perfectly indivisible. . . . (Bk. 1, Pt. 2, Sec. 2)

These real unities are minimal sensibles, such as a dot of color just big enough to be visible: It is *indivisible* in the sense that a smaller dot would be *invisible*. Hume sometimes writes as if the grain of his visual field were apparent. For instance, he tells us that when he looks at a table, "*My senses convey to me only the impressions of colored points, disposed in a certain manner*" (Bk. 1, Pt. 2, Sec. 3).

It might be helpful to compare the self/world as he has described it to the image on a television screen. The screen is composed of more than 100,000 pictorial elements (usually shortened to "pixels"), each of which can at any moment be black, white, or one of several shades of gray or one of several colors. The moving image of, for example, several humans interacting in a room, consists of successions of "bundles" or configurations of 100,000 pixel states. That is why the picture loses its sharpness if we get too close to the television, and why smaller screens (other things being equal) have sharper pictures. What looks, from a distance, like a continuous line or surface is actually a set of dots. What looks like a single human body moving from one end of the room to another is nothing but a succession of different illumination states of different sets of pixels, beginning with those on one side of the screen and ending with those on the other. There is no "substratum" for this apparent motion, no subject that was in one place and then goes to another, no *it* for the sentence "It moved." To bring empiricism into the analogy, imagine that all you can ever observe is the television screen; you can't look behind it and you can't see yourself except as an image on that screen. You may be strongly inclined to think that the real you is more than a set of transitory dots, and that there must be some mechanism behind the screen generating the sequences of pixel states. But in neither case are you in a position to verify your belief or even understand what you could be talking about.

REVIEW QUESTIONS

1. Since "memory alone acquaints us with the continuance and extent of . . . [the] succession of perceptions," Hume claims that "it is to be considered, upon that account chiefly, as the source of personal identity" (p. 440). How, then, is his theory of personal identity different from that of Locke?

2. In diagnosing our mistaken belief in a continuing self, Hume speaks of the "imagination" or "thought" or "mind" making the transition from one closely related object to another in succession, and of how this "feels" the same as contemplating a single unchanging object. Some critics have argued that Hume is using, as part of his theory or diagnosis, the very idea (of a continuing mental subject) which he is attacking. What do you think?

31

Selections from
Reasons and Persons

Derek Parfit

Derek Parfit is a British philosopher who teaches at Oxford University. The selections in this reading are from his book *Reasons and Persons* (1984) which has been very influential in subsequent discussions of personal identity.

Parfit argues for what he calls "The Psychological Criterion" of personal identity, according to which the principal ingredient of identity, and the one that should matter most to a rational person, is "psychological continuity." Memories are a key ingredient of this relation, but so are beliefs, intentions, traits, and other psychological features. He presents cases in which one could be psychologically continuous with, but not identical with, one or more persons; and argues that we should regard such cases as being just as good as, or nearly as good as, survival. His account of personal identity has interesting implications for our attitude toward the prospect of death.

WHAT WE BELIEVE
OURSELVES TO BE

I enter the Teletransporter. I have been to Mars before, but only by the old method, a space-ship journey taking several weeks. This machine will send me at the speed of light. I merely have to press the green button. Like others, I am nervous. Will it work? I remind myself what I have been told to expect. When I press the button, I shall lose consciousness, and then wake up at what seems a moment later. In fact I shall have been unconscious for about an hour. The Scanner here on Earth will destroy my brain and body while recording the exact states of all of my cells. It will then transmit this information by radio. Travelling at the speed of light, the message will take three minutes to reach the Replicator on Mars. This will then create, out of new matter, a brain and body exactly like mine. It will be in this body that I shall wake up.

Though I believe that this is what will happen, I still hesitate. But then I remember seeing my wife grin when, at breakfast today, I revealed my nervousness. As she reminded me, she has been often teletransported, and there is nothing wrong with *her.* I press the button. As predicted, I lose and seem at once to regain consciousness, but in a different cubicle. Examining my new body, I find no change at all. Even the cut on my upper lip, from this morning's shave, is still there.

Several years pass, during which I am often Teletransported. I am now back in the cubicle, ready for another trip to Mars. But this time, when I press the green button, I do not lose consciousness. There is a whirring sound, then silence. I leave the cubicle, and say to the attendant: "It's not working. What did I do wrong?"

"It's working," he replies, handing me a printed card. This reads: "The New Scanner records your blueprint without destroying your brain and body. We hope that you will welcome the opportunities which this technical advance offers."

The attendant tells me that I am one of the first people to use the New Scanner. He adds that, if I stay for an hour, I can use the Intercom to see and talk to myself on Mars.

"Wait a minute", I reply, "If I'm here I can't *also* be on Mars."

Someone politely coughs, a white-coated man who asks to speak to me in private. We go to his office, where he tells me to sit down, and pauses. Then he says: "I'm afraid that we're having problems with the New Scanner. It records your blueprint just as accurately, as you will see when you talk to yourself on Mars. But it seems to be damaging the cardiac systems which it scans. Judging from the results so far, though you will be quite healthy on Mars, here on Earth you must expect cardiac failure within the next few days."

The attendant later calls me to the Intercom. On the screen I see myself just as I do in the mirror every morning. But there are two differences. On the screen I am not left-right reversed. And, while I stand here speechless, I can see and hear myself, in the studio on Mars, starting to speak.

* * *

In Simple Teletransportation, I do not co-exist with my Replica. This makes it easier to believe that this *is* a way of travelling—that my Replica *is* me. At the end of my story my life and that of my Replica overlap. Call this the *Branch-Line Case*. In this case, I cannot hope to travel on the *Main Line,* waking up on Mars with forty years of life ahead. I shall remain on the Branch-Line, on Earth, which ends a few days later. Since I can talk to my Replica, it seems clear that he is *not* me. Though he is exactly like me, he is one person, and I am another. When I pinch myself, he feels nothing. When I have my heart attack, he will again feel nothing. And when I am dead he will live for another forty years.

If we believe that my Replica is not me, it is natural to assume that my prospect, on the Branch Line, is almost as bad as ordinary death. I shall deny this assumption. As I shall argue later, I ought to regard having a Replica as being about as good as ordinary survival. I can best defend this claim, and the view that supports it, after briefly discussing part of the past debate about personal identity.

THE PSYCHOLOGICAL CRITERION

Some people believe in a kind of psychological continuity that resembles physical continuity. This involves the continued existence of a purely mental *entity,* or thing—a soul, or spiritual substance.[1] I shall return to this view. But I shall first explain another kind of psychological continuity. This is less like physical continuity, since it does not consist in the continued existence of some entity. But this other kind of psychological continuity involves only facts with which we are familiar.

What has been most discussed is the continuity of memory. This is because it is memory that makes most of us aware of our own continued existence over time. The exceptions are the people who are suffering from amnesia. Most amnesiacs lose only two sets of memories. They lose all of their memories of having particular past experiences—or, for short, their *experience memories*. They also lose some of their memories about facts, those that are about their own past lives. But they remember other facts, and they remember how to do different things, such as how to speak, or swim.

Locke suggested that experience-memory provides the criterion of personal identity. Though this is not, on its own, a plausible view, I believe that it can be part of such a view. I shall therefore try to answer Locke's critics.

Locke claimed that someone cannot have committed some crime unless he now remembers doing so.[2] We can understand a reluctance to punish people for crimes that they cannot remember. But, taken as a view about what is involved in a person's continued existence, Locke's claim is clearly false. If

---

[1] Examples of this belief are found in Descartes and persons who, like many Christians, believe that we survive the deaths of our bodies and continue to exist, at least for some time, without bodies. ED.

[2] See section 20 of Reading 29. ED.

it was true, it would not be possible for someone to forget any of the things that he once did, or any of the experiences that he once had. But this *is* possible. I cannot now remember putting on my shirt this morning.[3]

There are several ways to extend the experience-memory criterion so as to cover such cases. I shall appeal to the concept of an overlapping chain of experience-memories. Let us say that, between X today and Y twenty years ago, there are *direct memory connections* if X can now remember having some of the experiences that Y had twenty years ago. On Locke's view, this makes X and Y one and the same person. Even if there are *no* such direct memory connections, there may be *continuity of memory* between X now and Y twenty years ago. This would be so if between X now and Y at that time there has been an overlapping chain of direct memories. In the case of most people who are over twenty three, there would be such an overlapping chain. In each day within the last twenty years, most of these people remembered some of their experiences on the previous day. On the revised version of Locke's view, some present person X is the same as some past person Y if there is between them continuity of memory.

This revision meets one objection to Locke's view.[4] We should also revise the view so that it appeals to other facts. Besides direct memories, there are several other kinds of direct psychological connection. One such connection is that which holds between an intention and the later act in which this intention is carried out. Other such direct connections are those which hold when a belief, or a desire, or any other psychological feature, continues to be had.

I can now define two general relations:

Psychological connectedness is the holding of particular direct psychological connections.
Psychological continuity is the holding of overlapping chains of *strong* connectedness.

Of these two general relations, connectedness is more important both in theory and in practice.

Connectedness can hold to any degree. Between X today and Y yesterday there might be several thousand direct psychological connections, or only a single connection. If there was only a single connection, X and Y would not be, on the revised Lockean View, the same person[5]. For X and Y to be the same person, there must be over every day *enough* direct psychological connections. Since connectedness is a matter of degree, we cannot plausibly define precisely what counts as enough. But we can claim that there is enough connectedness if the number of connections, over any day, is *at least half* the number of direct connections that hold, over every day, in the lives of nearly every actual person.[6] When there are enough direct connections, there is what I call *strong* connectedness.

This relation cannot be the criterion of personal identity. A relation F is *transitive* if it is true that, if X is F-related to Y, and Y is F-related to Z, X and Z *must* be F-related. Personal identity is a transitive relation. If Bertie was one and the same person as the philosopher Russell, and Russell was one and the same person as the author of *Why I Am Not a Christian,* this author and Bertie must be one and the same person.

Strong connectedness is *not* a transitive relation. I am now strongly connected to myself yesterday, when I was strongly connected to myself two days ago, when I was strongly connected to myself three days ago, and so on. It does not follow that I am now strongly connected to myself twenty years ago. And this is not true. Between me now and myself twenty years ago there are many fewer than the number of direct psychological connections that hold over any day in the lives of nearly all adults. For example, while these adults have many memories of experiences that they had in the previous day, I have few memories of experiences that I had twenty years ago.

By "the criterion of personal identity over time" I mean what this identity *necessarily involves or consists in*. Because identity is a transitive relation,

---

[3] Does section 20 of Locke have an answer to this objection? ED.

[4] It addresses the objection against the memory criterion that I did not do what I can't remember doing. ED.

[5] On the *original* Lockean view, a *single* memory of doing something that Socrates did would make me the same person as Socrates. ED.

[6] This suggestion would need expanding, since there are many ways to count the number of direct connections. And some kinds of connections should be given more importance than others. As I suggest later, more weight should be given to those connections which are distinctive, or different in different people. (All English-speakers, for instance, share many undistinctive memories of how to speak English.)

the criterion of identity must be a transitive relation. Since strong connectedness is not transitive, it cannot be the criterion of identity. And I have just described a case in which this is shown. I am the same person as myself twenty years ago, though I am not now strongly connected to myself then.

Though a defender of Locke's view cannot appeal to psychological connectedness, he can appeal to psychological continuity, which *is* transitive. He can appeal to

> The Psychological Criterion: (1) There is *psychological continuity* if and only if there are overlapping chains of strong connectedness. X today is one and the same person as Y at some past time if and only if (2) X is psychologically continuous with Y, (3) this continuity has the right kind of cause, and (4) there does not exist a different person who is also psychologically continuous with Y. (5) Personal identity over time just consists in the holding of facts like (2) to (4).

* * *

Reductionists[7] admit that there is a difference between numerical identity and exact similarity. In some cases, there would be a real difference between some person's being me, and his being someone else who is merely exactly like me. Many people assume that there must *always* be such a difference. In the case of nations, or clubs, such an assumption is false. Two clubs could exist at the same time, and be, apart from their membership, exactly similar. If I am a member of one of these clubs, and you claim also to be a member, I might ask, "Are you a member of the very same club of which I am a member? Or are you merely a member of the other club, that is exactly similar?" This is not an empty question, since it describes two different possibilities.

Though there are two possibilities in a case in which the two clubs co-exist, there may not be two such possibilities when we are discussing the relation between some presently existing club and some past club. There were not two possibilities in the case that I described in Section 79.[8] In this case there was nothing that would justify either the claim that we have the very same club, or the claim that we have a new club that is merely exactly similar. In this case theses would *not* be two different possibilities.

In the same way, there are some cases where there is a real difference between someone's being me, and his being someone else who is exactly like me. This may be so in the Branch-Line Case, the version of Teletransportation where the Scanner does not destroy my brain and body. In the Branch-Line Case, my life overlaps with the life of my Replica on Mars. Given this overlap, we may conclude that we are two different people—that we are qualitatively but not numerically identical. If I am the person on Earth, and my Replica on Mars now exists, it makes a difference whether some pain will be felt by me, or will instead be felt by my Replica. This is a real difference in what will happen.

If we return to Simple Teletransportation, where there is no overlap between my life and that of my Replica, things are different. We could say here that my Replica will be me, or we could instead say that he will merely be someone else who is exactly like me. But we should not regard these as competing hypotheses about what will happen. For these to be competing hypotheses, my continued existence must involve a *further fact*. If my continued existence merely involves physical and psychological continuity, we know just what happens in this case. There will be some future person who will be physically exactly like me, and who will be fully psychologically continuous with me. This psychological continuity will have a reliable cause, the

---

[7] Parfit is not perfectly clear in his use of the term "reductionist" to characterize his theory. What *is* clear is that it excludes the dualist position that the mind exists, or could exist, separately from the body, so that personal identity would consist in, or depend on, the continued existence of a separable mind. His theory *reduces* personal identity by understanding it entirely in terms of the nonpersonal or *impersonal* facts "that there exists a particular brain and body, and a particular series of interrelated physical and mental events" (212). The only sense in which the existence of a person may be a "further fact" is the weak sense in which the existence of a nation is a further fact in relation to the existence and behavior of a population in a certain territory. ED.

[8] The case in section 79 is as follows. Suppose that a club stops meeting for several years, and then some of the original members form a club with the same name, rules, and activities. Suppose further that the original club had no rules concerning its status once it ceased to function, or concerning procedures for ending or reinstating the club. Is the later club the *same* club as the earlier one, or is it merely a different but exactly similar club? Parfit claims that this is an empty question, because knowing all the relevant facts doesn't yield an answer. Moreover, we aren't puzzled by the lack of an answer—it's perfectly intelligible. ED.

transmission of my blueprint. But this continuity will not have its normal cause, since this future person will not be physically continuous with me. This is a full description of the facts. There is no further fact about which we are ignorant. If personal identity does not involve a further fact, we should not believe that there are here two different possibilities: that my Replica will be me, or that he will be someone else who is merely like me. What could make these different possibilities? In what could the difference consist?

***

To simplify the case, I assume that I am one of three identical triplets. Consider

> *My Division.* My body is fatally injured, as are the brains of my two brothers. My brain is divided, and each half is successfully transplanted into the body of one of my brothers.[9] Each of the resulting people believes that he is me, seems to remember living my life, has my character, and is in every other way psychologically continuous with me and he has a body that is very like mine.

This case is likely to remain impossible. Though it is claimed that, in certain people, the two hemispheres may have the same full range of abilities, this claim might be false. I am here assuming that this claim is true when applied to me. I am also assuming that it would be possible to connect a transplanted half-brain with the nerves in its new body. And I am assuming that we could divide, not just the upper hemispheres, but also the lower brain.[10] My first two assumptions may be able to be made

true if there is enough progress in neurophysiology. But it seems likely that it would never be possible to divide the lower brain, in a way that did not impair its functioning.

Does it matter if, for this reason, this imagined case of complete division will always remain impossible? Given the aims of my discussion, this does not matter. This impossibility is merely technical. The one feature of the case that might be held to be *deeply* impossible—the division of a person's consciousness into two separate streams—is the feature that has actually happened.[11] It would have been important if this had been impossible, since this might have supported some claim about what we really are. It might have supported the claim that we are indivisible Cartesian Egos. It therefore matters that the division of a person's consciousness is in fact possible. There seems to be no similar connection between a particular view about what we really are and the impossibility of dividing and successfully transplanting the two halves of the lower brain. This impossibility thus provides no ground for refusing to consider the imagined case in which we suppose that this can be done. And considering this case may help us to decide both what we believe ourselves to be, and what in fact we are. As Einstein's example showed, it can be useful to consider impossible thought-experiments.[12]

It may help to state, in advance, what I believe this case to show. It provides a further argument against the view that we are separately existing entities. But the main conclusion to be drawn is that *personal identity is not what matters.*

It is natural to believe that our identity is what matters. Reconsider the Branch-Line Case, where I

---

[9] Like the rest of the human body (and the bodies of vertebrates generally) the brain and spine are bilaterally symmetrical. Just as we have two arms, two legs and two lungs, so the brain consists of two hemispheres. As we will see in more detail in the next reading, there is considerable overlap or redundancy in the functions of each hemisphere, but there is some specialization. For instance, usually in adults just one hemisphere is mostly responsible for our linguistic capacity. So the dual transplant scenario sketched here by Parfit is rather unlikely with anything like our current medical knowledge and technology. But lest the scenario seem too far-fetched, we should keep in mind that hemispheric specialization doesn't become permanent until puberty. As a way to treat severe and otherwise intractable epilepsy in very young children, surgeons have performed hemispherectomies, removing an entire hemisphere. The human brain at that age is so plastic that these children have been able to lead normal lives. ED.

[10] Most of the "lower" or subcortical brain is also bilaterally symmetrical. It's not clear why Parfit makes this qualification. ED.

[11] What Parfit is talking about here will be the subject of the next reading. For now it's enough to note the following: Sensory input from the left side of the visual field and the left side of the body is *contralateral*—it goes to the right hemisphere first (and vice versa). Olfactory input is *ipsilateral;* sensory input from each nostril goes to the hemisphere on the same side. Each hemisphere shares sensory input with the other via large bundles of fibers (*commissures*). The most prominent bundle is the *corpus callosum.* Some humans were born without it or have had it surgically severed to treat epilepsy. If you insert an unpleasant scent into only the right nostril of such persons, most will be unable to say (using the left hemisphere's linguistic capacity) whether they are smelling anything, even as their right hemisphere causes them to register facially the unpleasant odor. This seems to be a case in which having two hemispheres causes a human to have two consciousnesses or selves for a brief time at least. ED.

[12] For instance, Einstein drew a useful conclusion from imagining what someone would see who was traveling at the front of a beam of light. ED.

have talked to my Replica on Mars, and am about to die. Suppose we believe that I and my Replica are different people. It is then natural to assume that my prospect is almost as bad as ordinary death. In a few days, there will be no one living who will be me. It is natural to assume that *this* is what matters. In discussing My Division, I shall start by making this assumption. In this case, each half of my brain will be successfully transplanted into the very similar body of one of my two brothers. Both of the resulting people will be fully psychologically continuous with me, as I am now. What happens to me?

There are only four possibilities: (1) I do not survive; (2) I survive as one of the two people; (3) I survive as the other; (4) I survive as both.

The objection to (1) is this. I would survive if my brain was successfully transplanted.[13] And people have in fact survived with half their brains destroyed. Given these facts, it seems clear that I would survive if half my brain was successfully transplanted, and the other half was destroyed. So how could I fail to survive if the other half was also successfully transplanted? How could a double success be a failure?

Consider the next two possibilities. Perhaps one success is the maximum score. Perhaps I shall be one of the two resulting people. The objection here is that, in this case, each half of my brain is exactly similar, and so, to start with, is each resulting person. Given these facts, how can I survive as only one of the two people? What can make me one of them rather than the other?[14]

These first three possibilities cannot be dismissed as incoherent. We can understand them. But, while we assume that identity is what matters, (1) is not plausible. It is not plausible that My Division is equivalent to death. Nor are (2) and (3) plausible. There remains the fourth possibility: that I survive as both of the resulting people.

* * *

WHAT MATTERS WHEN I DIVIDE?

Some people would regard division as being as bad, or nearly as bad, as ordinary death. This reaction is irrational. We ought to regard division as being about as good as ordinary survival. As I have argued, the two "products" of this operation would

be two different people. Consider my relation to each of these people. Does this relation fail to contain some vital element that is contained in ordinary survival? It seems clear that it does not. I would survive if I stood in this very same relation to only one of the resulting people. It is a fact that someone can survive even if half his brain is destroyed. And on reflection it was clear that I would survive if my whole brain was successfully transplanted into my brother's body. It was therefore clear that I would survive if half my brain was destroyed, and the other half was successfully transplanted into my brother's body. In the case that we are now considering, my relation to each of the resulting people thus contains everything that would be needed for me to survive as that person. It cannot be the *nature* of my relation to each of the resulting people that, in this case, causes it to fail to be survival. Nothing is *missing*. What is wrong can only be the duplication.

Suppose that I accept this, but still regard division as being nearly as bad as death. My reaction is now indefensible. I would be like someone who, when told of a drug that could double his years of life, regarded the taking of this drug as death. The only difference in the case of division is that the extra years are to run concurrently. This is an interesting difference. But it cannot mean that there are *no* years to run. We might say "You will lose your identity. But there are at least two ways of doing this. Dying is one, dividing is another. To regard these as the same is to confuse two with zero. Double survival is not the same as ordinary survival. But this does not make it death. It is further away from death than ordinary survival."

The problem with double survival is that it does not fit the logic of identity. Like certain other Reductionists, I claim

> *Relation R* is what matters. R is psychological connectedness and/or psychological continuity, with the right kind of cause.[15]

I also claim

> The right kind of cause could be any cause.

Other Reductionists might require that R have a reliable cause, or have its normal cause. To postpone this disagreement, consider only cases where R would have its normal cause. In these cases, these Reductionists would all accept the following claim. A future person will be me if he will be R-related to me as I am now, and no different person will be R-related to me. If there is no such different person, the fact that this future person will be me just consists in the fact that relation R holds between us. There is nothing more to personal identity than the holding of relation R. In nearly all of the actual cases, R takes a one-one form. It holds between one presently existing person and one future person. When R takes a one-one form, we can use the language of identity. We can claim that this future person will be this present person.

In the imagined case where I divide, R takes a "branching" form. But personal identity cannot take a branching form. I and the other two resulting people cannot be one and the same person. Since I cannot be identical with two different people, and it would be arbitrary to call one of these people me, we can best describe the case by saying neither of these people will be me.

Which is the relation that is important? Is what matters personal identity, or relation R? In ordinary cases we need not decide which of these is what matters, since these relations coincide. In the case of My Division these relations do not coincide. We must therefore decide which of the two is what matters.

If we believe that we are separately existing entities, we could plausibly claim that identity is what matters. On this view, personal identity is a deep further fact. But we have sufficient evidence to reject this view. If we are Reductionists, we *cannot* plausibly claim that, of these two relations, it is identity that matters. On our view, the fact of personal identity just consists in the holding of relation R, when it takes a non-branching form. If personal identity just consists in this other relation, this other relation must be what matters.

It may be objected: "You are wrong to claim that there is nothing more to identity than relation R. As you have said, personal identity has one extra feature, not contained in relation R. Personal identity consists in R holding *uniquely*—holding between one present person and *only one* future person. Since there is something more to personal

identity than to relation R, we can rationally claim that, of the two, it is identity which is what matters."

In answering this objection, it will help to use some abbreviations. Call personal identity *PI*. When some relation holds uniquely, or in a one-one form, call this fact U. The view that I accept can be stated with this formula:

$$PI = R + U.$$

Most of us are convinced that PI matters, or has value. Assume that R may also have value. There are then four possibilities:

(1) R without U has no value.
(2) U enhances the value of R, but R has value even without U.
(3) U makes no difference to the value of R.
(4) U reduces the value of R (but not enough to eliminate this value, since R + U = PI, which has value).

Can the presence or absence of U make a great difference to the value of R? As I shall argue, this is not plausible. If I will be R-related to some future person, the presence or absence of U makes no difference to the intrinsic nature of my relation to this person. And what matters most must be the intrinsic nature of this relation.

Since this is so, R without U would still have most of its value. Adding U makes R = PI. If adding U does not greatly increase the value of R, R must be what fundamentally matters, and PI mostly matters just because of the presence of R. If U makes no difference to the value of R, PI matters only because of the presence of R. Since U can be plausibly claimed to make a small difference, PI may, compared with R, have some extra value. But this value would be much less than the intrinsic value of R. The extra value of PI is much less than the value that R would have in the absence of PI, when U fails to hold.

If it was put forward on its own, it would be difficult to accept the view that personal identity is not what matters. But I believe that, when we consider the case of division, this difficulty disappears. When we see *why* neither resulting person will be me, I believe that, on reflection, we can also see that this does not matter, or matters only a little.

* * *

LIBERATION FROM THE SELF

The truth is very different from what we are inclined to believe. Even if we are not aware of this, most of us are Non-Reductionists. If we considered my imagined cases, we would be strongly inclined to believe that our continued existence is a deep further fact, distinct from physical and psychological continuity, and a fact that must be all-or-nothing. This belief is not true.

Is the truth depressing? Some may find it so. But I find it liberating, and consoling. When I believed that my existence was a such a further fact, I seemed imprisoned in myself. My life seemed like a glass tunnel, through which I was moving faster every year, and at the end of which there was darkness. When I changed my view, the walls of my glass tunnel disappeared. I now live in the open air. There is still a difference between my life and the lives of other people. But the difference is less. Other people are closer. I am less concerned about the rest of my own life, and more concerned about the lives of others.

When I believed the Non-Reductionist View, I also cared more about my inevitable death. After my death, there will [be] no one living who will be me. I can now redescribe this fact. Though there will later be many experiences, none of these experiences will be connected to my present experiences by chains of such direct connections as those involved in experience-memory, or in the carrying out of an earlier intention. Some of these future experiences may be related to my present experiences in less direct ways. There will later be some memories about my life. And there may later be

thoughts that are influenced by mine, or things done as the result of my advice. My death will break the more direct relations between my present experiences and future experiences, but it will not break various other relations. This is all there is to the fact that there will be no one living who will be me. Now that I have seen this, my death seems to me less bad.

Instead of saying, "I shall be dead," I should say, "There will be no future experiences that will be related, in certain ways, to these present experiences." Because it reminds me what this fact involves, this redescription makes this fact less depressing. Suppose next that I must undergo some ordeal. Instead of saying, "The person suffering will be me," I should say, "There will be suffering that will be related, in certain ways, to these present experiences." Once again, the redescribed fact seems to me less bad.

* * *

After Hume thought hard about his arguments, he was thrown into "the most deplorable condition imaginable, environed with the deepest darkness."[16] The cure was to dine and play backgammon with his friends. Hume's arguments supported total scepticism. This is why they brought darkness and utter loneliness. The arguments for Reductionism have on me the opposite effect. Thinking hard about these arguments removes the glass wall between me and others. And, as I have said, I care less about my death. This is merely the fact that, after a certain time, none of the experiences that will occur will be related, in certain ways, to my present experiences. Can this matter all that much?

---

[16] *Treatise*, Bk. 1, pt. 4, sec. 7

Although Parfit presents his theory as a modification of Locke's, one could argue that it is much more like Hume's theory.

In section 9 of Reading 29 we saw Locke treating personal identity as the backward extension, through memory, of our present self-awareness or "consciousness." He says that it is this consciousness that makes each of us a *self* different from any other self. The self is a single consciousness uniting all its present contents with whatever past contents it remembers. My *self* is both the single *perceiver* of various experiences and the single *doer* of various deeds that I call mine. Hume and Parfit are reductionists: They analyze the self and its identity as nothing but a set of relations among psychological items such as experiences, beliefs, and intentions. Locke clearly seems to be what Parfit would call a *non*-reductionist; he treats the self and its identity over time as a "further fact" in a strong but unclear sense. The sense is unclear because Locke repeatedly argues that personal identity is *not* a sameness of substance. Yet he doesn't tell us to what **category** the self belongs if it is not a substance. He refers to the self with terms such as *person* and *rational/thinking being* that were used in his day to designate substances. But he also acknowledges that consciousness is an intermittent process or activity regularly interrupted by sleep among other things. It's hard to understand how an activity or process can *be,* or constitute, a person. Making such a claim sounds like what Ryle would call a "category mistake."

Instead of focusing, like Locke, on the self that *does* the remembering, Hume treats the self as a complex *object* largely constituted by relations of resemblance and causality among perceptions that are *remembered.* Yet the Lockean self is also present and functioning in Hume's theory, despite his repeated claims that we have no idea of such a thing. It is what Hume refers to as the "mind" or "imagination" or "we" and which he needs for perceiving the relation *between* two perceptions or feeling the ease of *its* transition from one closely related idea to another and "mistaking" that for identity. Although each of his perceptions is a distinct bit of consciousness, Hume can't avoid speaking of his consciousness of the relations among these bits, a consciousness that has to be distinct from, and inclusive of, these bits. In short, it would seem that the ongoing presence of a Lockean self is a necessary condition of the *interrelated* perceptions that constitute the Humean self.

Hume calls himself a skeptic for concluding that we have no idea of a continuing self distinct from transient perceptions and their relations. He seems to accept that there is something more to be understood about the self, but that our minds are limited to the superficial aspects of things revealed to our senses. Sincerely or not, he professes regret that we cannot understand how the world can be as we are inclined to think of it—according to what I have called the "common-sense" metaphysical conviction that the world contains individuals that are not just aspects or parts or collections of something else, individuals existing on their own and as subjects of change. Selves or persons were supposedly paradigm cases of such individuality. It was this commonsense conviction that the traditional notion of *substance* attempted to articulate. The term is now unfashionable and doesn't occur in the Parfit reading, but the metaphysical questions that the term tried to address are still there.

In the final paragraph of this reading, Parfit notes the similarity between his account of the self and that of Hume, but he tells us that he doesn't share Hume's regret over the results. In fact, his reductionist analysis "liberates" him from a "glass tunnel" from which he could see everything going on outside but could never be a part of it. Parfit seems to be saying that if the self is *not* a "deep further fact" over and above the relations among one's experiences, intentions and beliefs, then there is no one on the "inside" of these, unable to get out into the "open air" of the public world.

Let's suppose, for the reasons I gave in discussing Hume, that a "deep further fact" something like a Lockean self *is* a necessary condition of psychological continuity and personal identity. We can easily understand why this self would not be a *sufficient condition* of personal identity and why it would not be what "matters" in personal identity: What makes me *who* I am is a set of strongly interrelated items including memories, intentions, habits, and beliefs— the ingredients of what is usually called *personality* and *character.* That is the set of items that both Hume and Parfit consider the real stuff of personal identity. It is that which makes me, in the more important sense, a uniquely different person. There is also a more trivial sense in which I am not anyone else: my *numerical* difference. Every person is *this* person rather than *that* person. There is nothing distinctive and nothing to prefer or value in mere numerical identity and difference, in being *this* rather than *that* person. Yet that is the only identity that a Lockean self has, and that's why Locke says that if I remember doing something that was done by someone living a thousand years ago, then I am the one, the self, that did the thousand-year-old deed, despite the nearly total psychological discontinuity between me and the other human from a millennium ago. The Lockean self is qualitatively identical in all persons, whatever their experiences. That is why this self is open, in principle, to having *any* memory-experience of any other person. This self is the basis for our *community* with one another, our ability to adopt another's point of view and to share experiences. Its value, in that sense, is beyond measure. But it is not what matters in personal identity, if what matters is the survival of what is distinctive about oneself.

Let's go back to Parfit's branch-line scenario: For simplicity's sake, suppose that I know that I will die painlessly in a few minutes while my replica, with whom I'm conversing, will live on. The difference between him and me, between *my* living on and my replica living on is, in every respect that matters, merely numerical. To see what will happen as equivalent to death in the usual sense would be as groundless as agonizing over which of two identical cans of soda I should drink. A numerically different (Lockean) self in a numerically different body will be who I am now, and there will be no discernible or intelligible difference between *his* being me and *my* being me. I would mourn the extinction of my current moribund self only if it took with it *who-I-am*.

REVIEW QUESTIONS

1. Parfit says that "For X and Y to be the same person, there must be over every day *enough* direct psychological connections." Since this sort of connectedness varies in degree from day to day and person to person, Parfit admits that "enough" can't be precisely defined. So he settles for "*at least half* the number of connections that hold, over every day, in the lives of nearly every actual person." Is he being arbitrary here? If there is an average of *n* connections in the day-to-day lives of most persons, why is .5*n* "enough"? Is Parfit's claim an example of what Hume meant when he said that all disputes over the temporal identity of things that change are "merely verbal, except so far as the relation of parts gives rise to some fiction or imaginary principle of union. . . ."?

2. Suppose that the technician operating the teletransporter mistakenly replicates you twice. Since there are now two of you, neither can be regarded as *identical* to your original prior to teletransportation. Nevertheless, this *loss* of personal identity with your original is not a great one according to Parfit's account, since both of you have everything that mattered in the personal identity of your original: You both are psychologically continuous with her. Should you then both accept responsibility for what your original did? Should you both be punished for a crime she committed that is detected only after the teletransportation?

32

Brain Bisection and the Unity of Consciousness

Thomas Nagel

(For information on *Thomas Nagel,* see Reading 22.)

Whereas the three prior readings have dealt mostly with the unity of the self over time (its *diachronic* unity), Nagel's essay focuses on its unity at a single time (its *synchronic* unity). I am inclined to think of myself as a single, undivided subject of a variety of mental contents at any one time. My current awareness, for instance, combines auditory, visual, *somatosensory* and other kinds of sensation and feeling into a single experience with a pervasive and strong unity (one that extends back in time in ways we have just examined). I understand that I could have experienced many of these contents independently of each other. But I don't see how my current awareness of them all could be divisible into anything like parts. This is the intuition Descartes expressed when he contrasted the *in*divisibility of mind with the divisibility of body. However, this intuition isn't easy to reconcile with a major structural feature of the central nervous system: its bilateral symmetry.

There is a striking symmetry on either side of the vertical midline of the human body seen from the front, including paired eyes, ears, nostrils, ribs, arms, hands, legs, and feet. Where we have arms most land animals have a front pair of legs, and the head that rests on top of human bodies is these animals' frontmost body part, the one that first enters the space into which the animal is moving. Ask yourself why natural selection would have favored such a configuration for nearly all land animals needing to move about safely and efficiently.

The nervous system also exhibits bilateral symmetry, with right and left halves of each segment of the spinal cord sending out motor fibers and receiving sensory fibers from corresponding body parts on the right and left sides of the body. The brain stem continues this right-left segregation of fibers, and each cerebral hemisphere is, to a striking degree, a semi-detached brain receiving sensory input from, and sending motor signals to, one or other side of the body. There is cross-signaling that coordinates the functions of the two hemispheres so that they normally function as one. Nagel is going to discuss what happens with those persons whose interhemispheric links are for various reasons inoperative, and what implications these cases have for us "normals."

I

There has been considerable optimism recently, among philosophers and neuroscientists, concerning the prospect for major discoveries about the neuropsychological basis of mind. The support for this optimism has been extremely abstract and general. I wish to present some grounds for pessimism. That type of self-understanding may encounter limits which have not been generally foreseen: the personal, mentalist idea of human beings may resist the sort of coordination with an understanding of humans as physical systems, that would be necessary to yield anything describable as an understanding of the physical basis of mind. I shall not consider what alternatives will be open to us if we should encounter such limits. I shall try to present grounds for believing that the limits may exist—grounds derived from extensive data now available about the interaction between the two halves of the cerebral cortex, and about what happens when they are disconnected. The feature of the mentalist conception of persons which may be recalcitrant to integration with these data is not a trivial or peripheral one, that might easily be abandoned. It is the idea of a *single* person, a single subject of experience and action, that is in difficulties. The difficulties may be surmountable in ways I have not foreseen. On the other hand, this may be only the first of many dead ends that will emerge as we seek a physiological understanding of the mind.

To seek the physical basis or realization of features of the phenomenal world is in many areas a profitable first line of inquiry, and it is the line encouraged, for the case of mental phenomena, by those who look forward to some variety of empirical reduction of mind to brain, through an identity theory, a functionalist theory, or some other device. When physical reductionism is attempted for a phenomenal feature of the external world, the results are sometimes very successful, and can be pushed to deeper and deeper levels.[1] If, on the other

hand, they are not entirely successful, and certain features of the phenomenal picture remain unexplained by a physical reduction, then we can set those features aside as *purely* phenomenal, and postpone our understanding of them to the time when our knowledge of the physical basis of mind and perception will have advanced sufficiently to supply it. (An example of this might be the moon illusion, or other sensory illusions which have no discoverable basis in the objects perceived.)[2]

However, if we encounter the same kind of difficulty in exploring the physical basis of the phenomena of the mind itself, we cannot adopt the same line of retreat. That is, if a phenomenal feature of mind is left unaccounted for by the physical theory, we cannot postpone the understanding of it to the time when we study the mind itself—for that is exactly what we are supposed to be doing. To defer to an understanding of the basis of mind which lies beyond the study of the physical realization of certain aspects of it is to admit the irreducibility of the mental to the physical. A clear-cut version of this admission would be some kind of dualism.[3] But if

---

ample, there are certain readily observable features which people (and other animals) seem to inherit from their parents. The complete set of these features is what biologists call an organism's *phenotype* (the prefix *pheno-* is the same as in *phenomenal*). Biologists discovered that an organism's phenotype is the effect and manifestation of its *genotype,* the complete set of its genes. And genes are understood in terms of the structure and function of strands of DNA. Something apparent at a macrolevel (the *phenomenon* of inherited traits) has thus been *reduced* to its non-apparent physicochemical base at the microlevel (self-replication of DNA). This sort of progression is typical of progress in our scientific understanding of the world. Ed.

[2] That the full moon low in the sky seems so large and just over the horizon, and then much smaller when it's higher in the sky can't be explained by reference to the physical properties of the moon alone, whereas the phenomenon of resembling traits of parents and children can be explained by the properties of DNA. The parents and children really have the traits they appear to have, and the traits really get transmitted; but the moon really *isn't* where and as big as it seems. The apparent position and size are "purely phenomenal." The explanation for the phenomenal properties of the moon must be sought in the causal relationship between the physical object (the moon) and the behavior of the mind (or brain and nervous system) being affected by it. Ed.

[3] In the case of the moon illusion, there is one physical system—the moon—acting on another—the brain, which is the physical realization of what we call mind in humans. However, if the mind itself has a phenomenal property (as it appears to itself in self-awareness or introspection) that cannot be grounded in the physical properties of the brain alone, then we cannot do what we did for the moon's apparent position and size: we cannot look for an explanation in terms of the brain's relation to some other physical system. If we look instead to the brain's relation to a *non-*physical entity, then we embrace dualism.

From Thomas Nagel, "Brain Bisection and the Unity of Consciousness," *Synthese* 22 (1971) 396–413. Copyright © 1971 by D. Reidel Publishing Company, Dordrecht-Holland. Reprinted by permission of Kluwer Academic Publishers.

[1] In this context "phenomenal" seems to mean *as it appears,* especially to our senses or to our perception uninformed by the scientific theory that is supposed to explain the appearance or "phenomenon." For ex-

one is reluctant to take such a route, then it is not clear what one should do about central features of the mentalistic idea of persons which resist assimilation to an understanding of human beings as physical systems. It may be true of some of these features that we can neither find an objective basis for them, nor give them up. It may be impossible for us to abandon certain ways of conceiving and representing ourselves, no matter how little support they get from scientific research. This, I suspect, is true of the idea of the unity of a person: an idea whose validity may be called into question with the help of recent discoveries about the functional duality of the cerebral cortex. It will be useful to present those results here in outline.

II

The higher connections between the two cerebral hemispheres have been severed in men, monkeys, and cats, and the results have led some investigators to speak of the creation of two separate centers of consciousness in a single body. The facts are as follows.[4]

By and large, the left cerebral hemisphere is associated with the right side of the body and the right hemisphere is associated with the left side. Tactual stimuli from one side are transmitted to the opposite hemisphere—with the exception of the head and neck, which are connected to both sides. In addition, the left half of each retina, i.e. that which scans the right half of the visual field, sends impulses to the left hemisphere, and impulses from the left half of the visual field are transmitted by the right half of each retina to the right hemisphere.

[4] The literature on split brains is sizable. An excellent recent survey is Michael S. Gazzaniga, *The Bisected Brain*, New York, Appleton-Century-Crofts, 1970. Its nine-page list of references is not intended to be a complete bibliography of the subject, however. Gazzaniga has also written a brief popular exposition: 'The Split Brain in Man', *Scientific American* 217 (1967), p. 24. The best general treatment for philosophical purposes is to be found in several papers by R. W. Sperry, the leading investigator in the field: 'The Great Cerebral Commissure', *Scientific American* 210 (1964), p. 42; 'Brain Bisection and Mechanisms of Consciousness' in *Brain and Conscious Experience,* ed. by Eccles, J. C., Berlin, Springer-Verlag, 1966; 'Mental Unity Following Surgical Disconnections of the Cerebral Hemispheres', *The Harvey Lectures,* Series 62, New York, Academic Press, 1968, p. 293; 'Hemisphere Deconnection and Unity in Conscious Awareness,' *American Psychologist* 23 (1968), p. 723. Several interesting papers are to be found in *Functions of the Corpus Callosum: Ciba Foundation Study Group No. 20,* ed. by G. Ettlinger, London, J. and A. Churchill, 1965.

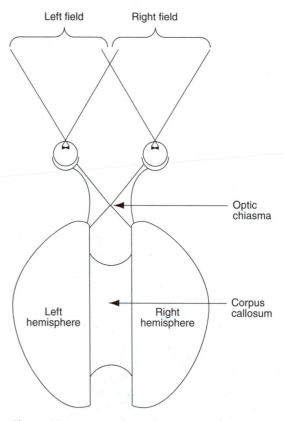

Figure 33.1 A very schematic top view of the eyes and cerebral cortex.

Auditory impulses from each ear are to some degree transmitted to both hemispheres. Smells, on the other hand, are transmitted ipsilaterally: the left nostril transmits to the left hemisphere and the right nostril to the right. Finally, the left hemisphere usually controls the production of speech.

Both hemispheres are linked to the spinal column and peripheral nerves through a common brain stem, but they also communicate directly with one another, by a large transverse band of nerve fibres called the corpus callosum, plus some smaller pathways. These direct cerebral commissures play an essential role in the ordinary integration of function between the hemispheres of normal persons. It is one of the striking features of the subject that this fact remained unknown, at least in the English-speaking world, until the late 1950's, even though a number of patients had had their

cerebral commissures surgically severed in operations for the treatment of **epilepsy** a decade earlier.
No significant behavioral or mental effects on these
patients could be observed, and it was conjectured
that the corpus callosum had no function whatever, except perhaps to keep the hemispheres from
sagging.

Then R. E. Myers and R. W. Sperry introduced a technique for dealing with the two hemispheres separately.[5] They sectioned the optic chiasma of cats, so that each eye sent direct information
(information about the opposite half of the visual
field) only to one side of the brain. It was then possible to train the cats in simple tasks using one eye,
and to see what happened when one made them
use the other eye instead. In cats whose callosum
was intact, there was very good transfer of learning.
But in some cats, they severed the corpus callosum
as well as the optic chiasma; and in these cases nothing was transmitted from one side to the other. In
fact the two severed sides could be taught conflicting discriminations simultaneously, by giving the
two eyes opposite stimuli during a single course of
reinforcement.[6] Nevertheless this capacity for independent function did not result in serious deficits
of behavior. Unless inputs to the two hemispheres
were artificially segregated, the animal seemed normal; (though if a split-brain monkey gets hold of a
peanut with both hands, the result is sometimes a
tug of war.)

Instead of summarizing all the data, I shall concentrate on the human cases, a reconsideration of
which was prompted by the findings with cats and
monkeys.[7] In the brain-splitting operation for epilepsy, the optic chiasma is left intact, so one cannot
get at the two hemispheres separately just through
two eyes. The solution to the problem of controlling visual input is to flash signals on a screen, on
one or other side of the midpoint of the patient's
gaze, long enough to be perceived but not long
enough to permit an eye movement which would
bring the signal to the opposite half of the visual
field[8] and hence to the opposite side of the brain.
This is known as tachistoscopic stimulation. Tactile
inputs through the hands are for the most part very
efficiently segregated, and so are smells through the
two nostrils. Some success has been achieved recently in segregating auditory input, since each ear
seems to signal more powerfully to the contralateral
than to the ipsilateral hemisphere. As for output,
the clearest distinction is provided by speech,
which is exclusively the product of the left hemisphere.[9] Writing is a less clear case: it can occasionally be produced in rudimentary form by the right
hemisphere, using the left hand. In general, motor
control is contralateral, i.e. by the opposite hemisphere, but a certain amount of ipsilateral control
sometimes occurs, particularly on the part of the
left hemisphere.

The results are as follows. What is flashed to the
right half of the visual field, or felt unseen by the
right hand, can be reported verbally. What is
flashed to the left half field or felt by the left hand
cannot be reported, though if the word hat is
flashed on the left, the left hand will retrieve a hat
from a group of concealed objects if the person is
told to pick out what he has seen. At the same time
he will insist verbally that he saw nothing. Or, if
two different words are flashed to the two half fields
(e.g. 'pencil' and 'toothbrush') and the individual is
told to retrieve the corresponding object from beneath a screen, with both hands, then the hands will

[5] Myers and Sperry, 'Interocular Transfer of a Visual Form Discrimination Habit in Cats after Section of the Optic Chiasm and Corpus Callosum', *Anatomical Record* 115 (1953), p. 351; Myers, 'Interocular Transfer of Pattern Discrimination in Cats Following Section of Crossed Optic
Fibers', *Journal of Comparative Physiological Psychology* 48 (1955), p. 470.

[6] For instance, a cat could receive a mild shock while a red light went
on in front of one uncovered eye, and it could be given food when the
red light goes on with the other eye uncovered. The result of this procedure would be a cat that becomes very conflicted when both eyes are uncovered and a red light goes on. ED.

[7] The first publication of these results was M. S. Gazzaniga, J. E. Bo-
gen, and R. W. Sperry, 'Some Functional Effects of Sectioning the Cerebral Commissures in Man', *Proceedings of the National Academy of Sciences*
48 (1962), Part 2, p. 1765. Interestingly, the same year saw publication of
a paper proposing the interpretation of a case of human brain *damage*
along similar lines, suggested by the earlier findings with animals. Cf. N.
Geschwind and E. Kaplan, 'A Human Cerebral Deconnection Syndrome', *Neurology* 12 (1962), p. 675. Also of interest is Geschwind's long

two-part survey of the field, which takes up some philosophical questions
explicitly: 'Disconnexion Syndromes in Animals and Man', *Brain* 88
(1965) 247–94, 585–644. Parts of it are reprinted, with other material,
in *Boston Studies in the Philosophy of Science,* Vol. IV (1969). See also his paper, 'The Organization of Language and the Brain', *Science* 170 (1970),
p. 940.

[8] This would happen as the midpoint of the patient's gaze crosses the
position of the light. ED.

[9] There are individual exceptions to this, as there are to most generalizations about cerebral function: left-handed people tend to have bilateral linguistic control, and it is common in early childhood. All the subjects of these experiments, however, were right handed, and displayed left
cerebral dominance.

search the collection of objects independently, the right hand picking up the pencil and discarding it while the left hand searches for it, and the left hand similarly rejecting the toothbrush which the right hand lights upon with satisfaction.

If a concealed object is placed in the left hand and the person is asked to guess what it is, wrong guesses will elicit an annoyed frown, since the right hemisphere, which receives the tactile information, also hears the answers. If the speaking hemisphere should guess correctly, the result is a smile. A smell fed to the right nostril (which stimulates the right hemisphere) will elicit a verbal denial that the subject smells anything, but if asked to point with the left hand at a corresponding object he will succeed in picking out e.g. a clove of garlic, protesting all the while that he smells absolutely nothing, so how can he possibly point to what he smells. If the smell is an unpleasant one like that of rotten eggs, these denials will be accompanied by wrinklings of the nose and mouth, and guttural exclamations of disgust.[10]

One particularly poignant example of conflict between the hemispheres is as follows. A pipe is placed out of sight in the patient's left hand, and he is then asked to write with his left hand what he was holding. Very laboriously and heavily, the left hand writes the letters P and I. Then suddenly the writing speeds up and becomes lighter, the I is converted to an E, and the word is completed as PENCIL. Evidently the left hemisphere has made a guess based on the appearance of the first two letters, and has interfered, with ipsilateral control. But then the right hemisphere takes over control of the hand again, heavily crosses out the letters ENCIL, and draws a crude picture of a pipe.[11]

There are many more data. The split brain patient cannot tell whether shapes flashed to the two half visual fields or held out of sight in the two hands are the same or different—even if he is asked to indicate the answer by nodding or shaking his head (responses available to both hemispheres). The subject cannot distinguish a continuous from a discontinuous line flashed across both halves of the visual field, if the break comes in the middle. Nor can he tell whether two lines meet at an angle, if the joint is in the middle. Nor can he tell whether two spots in opposite half-fields are the same or different in color—though he can do all these things if the images to be compared fall within a single half field. On the whole the right hemisphere does better at spatial relations tests, but is almost incapable of calculation. It appears susceptible to emotion, however. For example, if a photograph of a naked woman is flashed to the left half field of a male patient, he will grin broadly and perhaps blush, without being able to say what has pleased him, though he may say, "Wow, that's quite a machine you've got there".

All this combined with what appears to be complete normalcy in ordinary activities, when no segregation of input to the two hemispheres has been artificially created. Both sides fall asleep and wake up at the same time. The patients can play the piano, button their shirts, swim, and perform well in other activities requiring bilateral coordination. Moreover they do not report any sensation of division or reduction of the visual field. The most notable deviation in ordinary behavior was in a patient whose left hand appeared to be somewhat hostile to the patient's wife. But by and large the hemispheres cooperate admirably, and it requires subtle experimental techniques to get them to operate separately. If one is not careful, they will give each other peripheral cues, transmitting information by audible, visible, or otherwise sensorily perceptible signals which compensate for the lack of a direct commissural link. (One form of communication is particularly difficult to prevent, because it is so direct: both hemispheres can move the neck and facial muscles, and both can feel them move; so a response produced in the face or head by the right hemisphere can be detected by the left, and there is some evidence that they send signals to one another via this medium.)[12]

---

[10] H. W. Gordon and R. W. Sperry, 'Lateralization of Olfactory Perception in the Surgically Separated Hemispheres of Man', *Neuropsychologia* 7 (1969), p. 111. One patient, however, was able to say in these circumstances that he smelled something unpleasant, without being able to describe it further.

[11] Reported in Jerre Levy, *Information Processing and Higher Psychological Functions in the Disconnected Hemispheres of Human Commissurotomy Patients* (unpublished doctoral dissertation, California Institute of Technology, 1969).

---

[12] Moreover, the condition of radical disconnection may not be stable: there may be a tendency toward the formation of new interhemispheric pathways through the brain stem, with the lapse of time. This is supported partly by observation of commissurotomy patients, but more importantly by cases of agenesis of the callosum. People who have grown

III

What one naturally wants to know about these patients is how many minds they have. This immediately raises questions about the sense in which an ordinary person can be said to have one mind, and what the conditions are under which diverse experiences and activities can be ascribed to the same mind. We must have some idea what an ordinary person is one of in order to understand what we want to know whether there is *one or two* of, when we try to describe these extraordinary patients.

However, instead of beginning with an analysis of the unity of the mind, I am going to proceed by attempting to apply the ordinary, unanalyzed conception directly in the interpretation of these data, asking whether the patients have one mind, or two, or some more exotic configuration. My conclusion will be that the ordinary conception of a single, countable mind cannot be applied to them at all, and that there is no number of such minds that they possess, though they certainly engage in mental activity. A clearer understanding of the idea of an individual mind should emerge in the course of this discussion but the difficulties which stand in the way of its application to the split-brain cases will provide ground for more general doubts. The concept may not be applicable to ordinary human beings either, for it embodies too simple a conception of the way in which human beings function.

Nevertheless I shall imply the notion of an individual mind in discussing the cases initially, for I wish to consider systematically how they might be understood in terms of countable minds, and to argue that they cannot be. After having done this, I shall turn to ordinary people like you and me.

There appear to be five interpretations of the experimental data which utilize the concept of an individual mind.

(1) The patients have one fairly normal mind associated with the left hemisphere, and the responses emanating from the nonverbal right hemisphere are the responses of

an automaton, and are not produced by conscious mental processes.

(2) The patients have only one mind, associated with the left hemisphere, but there also occur (associated with the right hemisphere) isolated conscious mental phenomena, not integrated into a mind at all, though they can perhaps be ascribed to the organism.

(3) The patients have two minds, one which can talk and one which can't.

(4) They have one mind, whose contents derive from both hemispheres and are rather peculiar and dissociated.

(5) They have one normal mind most of the time, while the hemispheres are functioning in parallel, but two minds are elicited by the experimental situations which yield the interesting results. (Perhaps the single mind splits in two and reconvenes after the experiment is over.)

I shall argue that each of these interpretations is unacceptable for one reason or another.

IV

Let me first discuss hypotheses (1) and (2), which have in common the refusal to ascribe the activities of the right hemisphere to a mind, and then go on to treat hypotheses (3), (4), and (5), all of which associate a mind with the activities of the right hemisphere, though they differ on what mind it is.

The only support for hypothesis (1), which refuses to ascribe consciousness to the activities of the right hemisphere at all, is the fact that the subject consistently denies awareness of the activities of that hemisphere. But to take this as proof that the activities of the right hemisphere are unconscious is to beg the question, since the capacity to give testimony is the exclusive ability of the left hemisphere, and of course the left hemisphere is not conscious of what is going on in the right. If on the other hand we consider the manifestations of the right hemisphere itself, there seems no reason in principle to regard verbalizability as a *necessary* condition of consciousness. There may be other grounds for the ascription of conscious mental

up without one have learned to manage without it; their performance on the tests is much closer to normal than that of recently operated patients. (Cf. Saul and Sperry, 'Absence of Commissurotomy Symptoms with Agenesis of the Corpus Callosum,' *Neurology* 18 (1968).) This fact is very important, but for the present I shall put it aside to concentrate on the immediate results of disconnection.

states that are sufficient even without verbalization. And in fact, what the right hemisphere can do on its own is too elaborate, too intentionally directed and too psychologically intelligible to be regarded merely as a collection of unconscious automatic responses.

The right hemisphere is not very intelligent and it cannot talk; but it is able to respond to complex visual and auditory stimuli, including language, and it can control the performance of discriminatory and manipulative tasks requiring close attention—such as the spelling out of simple words with plastic letters. It can integrate auditory, visual, and tactile stimuli in order to follow the experimenter's instructions, and it can take certain aptitude tests. There is no doubt that if a person were deprived of his left hemisphere entirely, so that the only capacities remaining to him were those of the right, we should not on that account say that he had been converted into an automaton. Though speechless, he would remain conscious and active, with a diminished visual field and partial paralysis on the right side from which he would eventually recover to some extent. In view of this, it would seem arbitrary to deny that the activities of the right hemisphere are conscious, just because they occur side by side with those of the left hemisphere, about whose consciousness there is no question.

I do not wish to claim that the line between conscious and unconscious mental activity is a sharp one. It is even possible that the distinction is partly relative, in the sense that a given item of mental activity may be assignable to consciousness or not, depending on what other mental activities of the same person are going on at the same time, and whether it is connected with them in a suitable way. Even if this is true, however, the activities of the right hemisphere in split brain patients do not fall into the category of events whose inclusion in consciousness depends on what else is going on in the patient's mind. Their determinants include a full range of psychological factors, and they demand alertness. It is clear that attention, even concentration is demanded for the tasks of the concealed left hand and tachistoscopically stimulated left visual field. The subjects do not take their experimental tests in a dreamy fashion: they are obviously in contact with reality. The left hemisphere occasionally complains about being asked to perform tasks

which the right hemisphere can perform, because it does not know what is going on when the right hemisphere controls the response. But the right hemisphere displays enough awareness of what it is doing to justify that attribution of conscious control in the absence of verbal testimony. If the patients did not deny any awareness of those activities, no doubts about their consciousness would arise at all.

The considerations that make the first hypothesis untenable also serve to refute hypothesis (2), which suggests that the activities of the right hemisphere are conscious without belonging to a mind at all. There may be problems about the intelligibility of this proposal, but we need not consider them here, because it is rendered implausible by the high degree of organization and intermodal coherence[13] of the right hemisphere's mental activities. They are not free floating, and they are not organized in a fragmentary way. The right hemisphere follows instructions, integrates tactile, auditory and visual stimuli, and does most of the things a good mind should do. The data present us not merely with slivers of purposive behavior, but with a system capable of learning, reacting emotionally, following instructions, and carrying out tasks which require the integration of diverse psychological determinants. It seems clear that the right hemisphere's activities are not unconscious, and that they belong to something having a characteristically mental structure: a subject of experience and action.

V

Let me now turn to the three hypotheses according to which the conscious mental activities of the right hemisphere are ascribed to a mind. They have to be considered together, because the fundamental difficulty about each of them lies in the impossibility of deciding among them. The question, then, is whether the patients have two minds, one mind, or a mind that occasionally splits in two.

There is much to recommend the view that they have two minds, i.e. that the activities of the

---

[13] For instance, the left hand can feel and retrieve unseen the object signified by a word tachistoscopically flashed to the left half of the visual field, demonstrating an integration of vision with audible instruction and with somatosensory perception by the hand. ED.

right hemisphere belong to a mind of their own.[14] Each side of the brain seems to produce its own perceptions, beliefs, and actions, which are connected with one another in the usual way, but not to those of the opposite side. The two halves of the cortex share a common body, which they control through a common midbrain and spinal cord. But their higher functions are independent not only physically but psychologically. Functions of the right hemisphere are inaccessible not only to speech but to any direct combination with corresponding functions of the left hemisphere—i.e. with functions of a type that the right hemisphere finds easy on its home ground, like shape or color discrimination.[15]

One piece of testimony by the patients' left hemispheres may appear to argue against two minds. They report no diminution of the visual field, and little absence of sensation on the left side. Sperry dismisses this evidence on the ground that it is comparable to the testimony of victims of scotoma (partial destruction of the retina), that they notice no gaps in their visual field—although these gaps can be discovered by others observing their perceptual deficiencies. But we need not assume that an elaborate confabulatory mechanism is at work in the left hemisphere to account for such testimony. It is perfectly possible that although there are two minds, the mind associated with each hemisphere receives, through the common brain stem, a certain amount of crude ipsilateral stimulation, so that the speaking mind has a rudimentary and undifferentiated appendage to the left side of its visual field, and vice versa for the right hemisphere.[16]

The real difficulties for the two-minds hypothesis coincide with the reasons for thinking we are dealing with one mind—namely the highly integrated character of the patients' relations to the world in ordinary circumstances. When they are not in the experimental situation, their startling behavioral dissociation disappears, and they function normally. There is little doubt that information from the two sides of their brains can be pooled to yield integrated behavioral control. And although this is not accomplished by the usual methods, it is not clear that this settles the question against assigning the integrative functions to a single mind. After all, if the patient is permitted to touch things with both hands and smell them with both nostrils, he arrives at a unified idea of what is going on around him and what he is doing, without revealing any left-right inconsistencies in his behavior or attitudes. It seems strange to suggest that we are not in a position to ascribe all those experiences to the same person, just because of some peculiarities about how the integration is achieved.[17] The people who *know* these patients find it natural to relate to them as single individuals.

Nevertheless, if we ascribe the integration to a single mind, we must also ascribe the experimentally evoked dissociation to that mind, and that is not easy. The experimental situation reveals a variety of dissociation or conflict that is unusual not only because of the simplicity of its anatomical basis, but because such a wide *range* of functions is split into two noncommunicating branches. It is not as though two conflicting volitional centers shared a common perceptual and reasoning apparatus.[18] The split is much deeper than that. The one-mind hypothesis must therefore assert that the contents of the individual's single consciousness are produced by two independent control systems in the two hemispheres, each having a fairly complete mental structure. If this dual control were accomplished

---

[14] It is Sperry's view. He puts it as follows: "Instead of the normally unified single stream of consciousness, these patients behave in many ways as if they have two independent streams of conscious awareness, one in each hemisphere, each of which is cut off from and out of contact with the mental experiences of the other. In other words, each hemisphere seems to have its own separate and private sensations; its own perceptions; its own concepts; and its own impulses to act, with related volitional, cognitive, and learning experiences. Following the surgery, each hemisphere also has thereafter its own separate chain of memories that are rendered inaccessible to the recall process of the other." (*American Psychologist* 23, op. cit., p. 724.)

[15] For instance, although the right hemisphere is very good with spatial relations, the subject cannot tell whether two lines tachistoscopically flashed one into each half field meet at an angle. ED.

[16] There is some direct evidence for such primitive ipsilateral inputs, both visual and tactile; cf. Gazzaniga, *The Bisected Brain,* Chapter 3.

[17] This is an important point: *Even in normals* there is constant integration of sensory input initially received by one hemisphere or the other. The difference between normals and commissurotomy patients is entirely in the *pathways* for the input: the corpus callosum is not available to the latter, so they must compensate by using the other pathways (such as bilateral input from facial muscles) more heavily than normals. ED.

[18] That is how it seems when we want inconsistent things, such as having our cake and eating it, or when we have love-hate relationships to something or someone. ED.

during experimental situations by temporal alternation, it would be intelligible, though mysterious. But that is not the hypothesis, and the hypothesis as it stands does not supply us with understanding. For in these patients there appear to be things happening *simultaneously* which cannot fit into a single mind: simultaneous attention to two incompatible tasks, for example, without interaction between the purposes of the left and right hands.

This makes it difficult to conceive what it is like to be one of these people. Lack of interaction at the level of a preconscious control system would be comprehensible. But lack of interaction in the domain of visual experience and conscious intention threatens assumptions about the unity of consciousness which are basic to our understanding of another individual as a person. These assumptions are associated with our conception of ourselves, which to a considerable extent constrains our understanding of others. And it is just these assumptions, I believe, that make it impossible to arrive at an interpretation of the cases under discussion in terms of a countable number of minds.

Roughly, we assume that a single mind has sufficiently immediate access to its conscious states so that, for elements of experience or other mental events occurring simultaneously or in close temporal proximity, the mind which is their subject can also experience the simpler *relations* between them if it attends to the matter.[19] Thus, we assume that when a single person has two visual impressions, he can usually also experience the sameness or difference of their coloration, shape, size, the relation of their position and movement within his visual field, and so forth. The same can be said of cross-modal connections. The experiences of a single person are thought to take place in an *experientially* connected domain, so that the relations among experiences can be substantially captured in experiences of those relations.[20]

---

[19] This is the theoretical point that Hume seemed to neglect when he analyzed the contents of his mind into bundles of perceptions, with each perception being a discrete bit of consciousness. ED.

[20] The two can of course, diverge, and this fact underlies the classic philosophical problem of inverted spectra, which is only distantly related to the subject of this paper. A type of relation can hold between elements in the experience of a single person that cannot hold between elements of the experience of distinct persons: looking similar in color, for example. Insofar as our concept of similarity of experience in the case of a single person is dependent on his experience of similarity, the concept is not applicable between persons.

Split-brain patients fail dramatically to conform to these assumptions in experimental situations, and they fail over the simplest matters. Moreover the dissociation holds between two classes of conscious states each characterized by significant *internal* coherence: normal assumptions about the unity of consciousness hold intrahemispherically, although the requisite comparisons cannot be made across the interhemispheric gap.

These considerations lead us back to the hypothesis that the patients have two minds each. It at least has the advantage of enabling us to understand what it is like to *be* these individuals, so long as we do not try to imagine what it is like to be both of them at the same time. Yet the way to a comfortable acceptance of this conclusion is blocked by the compelling behavioral integration which the patients display in ordinary life, in comparison to which the dissociated symptoms evoked by the experimental situation seem peripheral and atypical. We are faced with diametrically conflicting bodies of evidence, in a case which does not admit of arbitrary decision. There is a powerful inclination to feel that there must be *some* whole number of minds in those heads, but the data prevent us from deciding how many.

This dilemma makes hypothesis (5) initially attractive, especially since the data which yield the conflict are to some extent gathered at different times. But the suggestion that a second mind is brought into existence only during experimental situations loses plausibility on reflection. First, it is entirely ad hoc: it proposes to explain one change in terms of another without suggesting any explanation of the second. There is nothing about the experimental situation that might be expected to produce a fundamental internal change in the patient. In fact it produces no anatomical changes and merely elicits a noteworthy set of symptoms. So unusual an event as a mind's popping in and out of existence would have to be explained by something more than its explanatory convenience.

But secondly, the behavioral evidence would not even be explained by this hypothesis, simply because the patients' integrated responses and their dissociated responses are not clearly separated in time. During the time of the experiments the patient is functioning largely as if he were a single individual: in his posture, in following instructions about where to focus his eyes, in the whole range of trivial behavioral control involved in situating himself in relation to the experimenter and the experimental apparatus. The two halves of his brain cooperate completely except in regard to those very special inputs that reach them separately and differently. For these reasons hypothesis (5) does not seem to be a real option; if two minds are operating in the experimental situation, they must be operating largely in harmony although partly at odds. And if there are two minds then, why can there not be two minds operating essentially in parallel the rest of the time?

Nevertheless the psychological integration displayed by the patients in ordinary life is so complete that I do not believe it is possible to accept that conclusion, nor any conclusion involving the ascription to them of a whole number of minds. These cases fall midway between ordinary persons with intact brains (between whose cerebral hemispheres there is also cooperation, though it works largely via the corpus callosum), and pairs of individuals engaged in a performance requiring exact behavioral coordination, like using a two-handed saw, or playing a duet. In the latter type of case we have two minds which communicate by subtle peripheral cues; in the former we have a single mind. Nothing taken from either of those cases can compel us to assimilate the split brain patient to one or the other of them. If we decided that they definitely had two minds, then it would be problematical why we didn't conclude on anatomical grounds that everyone has two minds, but that we didn't notice it except in these odd cases because most pairs of minds in a single body run in perfect parallel due to the direct communication between the hemispheres which provide their anatomical bases. The two minds each of us has running in harness would be much the same except that one could talk and other couldn't. But it is clear that this line of argument will get us nowhere. For if the idea of a single mind applies to anyone it applies to ordinary individuals with intact brains, and if it does not apply to them it ought to be scrapped, in which case there is point in asking whether those with split brains have one mind or two.[21]

VI

If I am right, and there is no whole number of individual minds that these patients can be said to have, then the attribution of conscious, significant mental activity does not require the existence of a single mental subject. This is extremely puzzling in itself, for it runs counter to our need to construe the mental states we ascribe to others on the model of our own. Something in the ordinary conception[22] of a person, or in the ordinary conception of experience, leads to the demand for an account of these cases which the same conception makes it impossible to provide. This may seem a problem not worth worrying about very much. It is not so surprising that, having begun with a phenomenon which is radically different from anything else previously known, we should come to the conclusion that it cannot be adequately described in ordinary terms. However, I believe that consideration of these very unusual cases should cause us to be skeptical about the concept of a single subject of consciousness as it applies to ourselves.

The fundamental problem in trying to understand these cases in mentalistic terms is that we take ourselves as paradigms of psychological unity, and are then unable to project ourselves into their mental lives, either once or twice. But in thus using ourselves as the touchstone of whether another organism can be said to house an individual subject of experience or not, we are subtly ignoring the possibility that our own unity may be nothing absolute, but merely another case of integration, more or less effective, in the control system of a complex organism. This system speaks in the first person singular through our mouths, and that makes it understandable that we should think of its unity as in some sense numerically absolute, rather than relative and a function of the integration of its contents.

But this is quite genuinely an illusion. The illusion consists in projecting inward to the center of the mind the very subject whose unity we are trying to explain: the individual person with all his

---

[21] In case anyone is inclined to embrace the conclusion that we all have two minds, let me suggest that the trouble will not end there. For the mental operations of a single hemisphere, such as vision, hearing, speech, writing, verbal comprehension, etc. can to a great extent be separated from one another by suitable cortical deconnections; why then should we not regard *each* hemisphere as inhabited by several cooperating minds with specialized capacities? Where is one to stop? If the decision on the number of minds associated with a brain is largely arbitrary, the original point of the question has disappeared.

[22] See the discussion of "common-sense" metaphysics in the introduction to Part VIII. ED.

complexities. The ultimate account of the unity of what we call a single mind consists of an enumeration of the types of functional integration that typify it. We know that these can be eroded in different ways, and to different degrees. The belief that even in their complete version they can be explained by the presence of a numerically single subject is an illusion. Either this subject contains the mental life, in which case it is complex and its unity must be accounted for in terms of the unified operation of its components and functions, or else it is an extensionless point, in which case it explains nothing.

An intact brain contains two cerebral hemispheres each of which possesses perceptual, memory, and control systems adequate to run the body without the assistance of the other. They cooperate in directing it with the aid of a constant two-way internal communication system. Memories, perceptions, desires and so forth therefore have duplicate physical bases on both sides of the brain, not just on account of similarities of initial input, but because of subsequent exchange. The cooperation of the undetached hemispheres in controlling the body is more efficient and direct than the cooperation of a pair of detached hemispheres, but it is co-operation nonetheless. Even if we analyze the idea of unity in terms of functional integration, therefore, the unity of our own consciousness may be less clear than we had supposed. The natural conception of a single person controlled by the mind possessing a single visual field, individual faculties for each of the other senses, unitary systems of memory, desire, belief, and so forth, may come into conflict with the physiological facts when it is applied to ourselves.

The concept of a person might possibly survive an application to cases which require us to speak of two or more persons in one body, but it seems strongly committed to some form of whole number countability. Since even this seems open to doubt, it is possible that the ordinary, simple idea of a single person will come to seem quaint some day, when the complexities of the human control system become clearer and we become less certain that there is anything very important that we are *one* of. But it is also possible that we shall be unable to abandon the idea no matter what we discover.[23]

----

[23] My research was supported in part by the National Science Foundation

One of Nagel's central claims is that our ordinary concept of a mind or person is deep into a dilemma: The behavior of a normal subject, and even of a split-brain subject, in normal circumstances displays too much coordination and integrity to attribute it to *two* minds. Yet we can readily infer from the case of split-brain patients that each of the two cerebral hemispheres in them *and in us normals* has its own stream of consciousness, and is unaware of the contents of the other hemisphere's consciousness. This reciprocal unawareness has no behavioral consequences because there is either duplication of contents in each hemisphere, or hemispheric dominance as in the case of language. So we seem unable to attribute either one or more than one mind to a human being. And yet the ordinary concept of a mind or person can be applied only to one or a whole number of instances.

It could be argued that Nagel's dilemma is false because it treats two distinct concepts of mind as if they were the same. The concept of *mind* according to which both normals and split-brain subjects have one mind is a *functional* concept based on behavior. Let's call this concept M_1. M_1 is the mind of another from a third-person point of view: the inner cause of a variety of types of behavior such as speech and discriminative responses to various kinds of sensory stimuli. Closely related to M_1 is the concept of *person*, which includes a broader range of psychological attributes, the configuration of which gives each of us an *identity* or *personality* or *character*. I can apply these third-person concepts to myself as well, in which case I am adopting an objective point-of-view toward myself. There is also a subjective, first-person concept of *mind* (M_2) as *self* or (ongoing) *consciousness*. This is the concept that I referred to in my discussion after the Parfit reading as the Lockean self, which there are good reasons to suppose is identical, except numerically, in each of us. The hemispheric structure of the human brain provides a reason for thinking that there is a redundancy not only in neural tissue analyzing visual, somatosensory, and auditory signals more or less the same way in each hemisphere, but also a redundancy in the *consciousness* generated by this duplicate neural activity. It could be argued that there is no inconsistency in attributing a single mind in the functional (M_1) sense *and* a dual mind in the subjective (M_2) sense to one and the same human being.

This attribution may seem "weird," but there is no escaping some weirdness in understanding the presence in us of two hemispheres, and no avoiding some shock to the ordinary concept of mind from neuroscientifc research in general. When we experience ourselves as *agents,* as doers of deeds mental and physical, we are consciously registering what our body parts do as we behave, just as we register what our mental processes achieve when we "find" the words for what we then go on to say. In each case we are aware of the *deed* rather than the *doing*—remembering is *not* a conscious process, whereas wanting to remember, and awareness of what we've just remembered, *is* conscious. We experience who and what we are in roughly the same way as others do, except that we are always around, and we have kinds of awareness of our body and feeling states that others cannot have. Although there is a degree of hemispheric asymmetry in motor control (e.g., in speech and handedness), it is not the actual *exercise* of motor control that enters consciousness, but only **feedback** (such as hearing oneself speak, or feeling one's muscles flex). So my awareness of who and what I am—my sense of personal identity—will be virtually identical in content in each hemisphere. The hemispheric duality of my awareness of that identity does not imply there are two of me or that there is a single awareness of two of me. It would imply only that there are two awarenesses of one me.

REVIEW QUESTION

If we accept Nagel's argument that the case of commissurotomy patients presents us with a dilemma about attributing one or two minds to them (and to normals), then, as Nagel points out, the fifth hypothesis becomes attractive: that these patients normally have one mind, but that a second mind is brought into existence by the experimental procedure. However, says Nagel, this hypothesis looks like nothing more than a device to escape the dilemma, because it has nothing else to recommend it: "There is nothing about the experimental situation that might be expected to produce a fundamental internal change in the patient. In fact it produces no anatomical changes and merely elicits a noteworthy set of symptoms." Is this a good argument?

In formulating your response consider what happens in hypnosis. The subject's anatomy isn't altered. Subjects fix their gaze on some object while the hypnotist gently makes suggestions, for example, that they will feel relaxed and it will be hard to open their eyes. In suitable subjects this minimal procedure has a profound effect. They become childlike in their suggestibility and exclusive focus on the hypnotist's instructions. On the suggestion of the hypnotist they can become blind, deaf, paralyzed, or impervious to pain. The hypnotist can also effectively command them to be amnesic about their experience under hypnosis. The hypnotic state is arguably just as profound a transformation of the subject's mind as what happens in experiments with split-brain patients. Both are cases of *dissociation* or psychological discontinuity, diachronic in the former and synchronic in the latter. There is no accepted theory of how hypnotism works, and no neurophysiological criterion (e.g., by some form of imaging of the brain) distinguishing hypnotic from normal states. Does this parallel case challenge Nagel's argument above?

33

Why Everyone
Is a Novelist

Daniel C. Dennett

(For information on *Daniel C. Dennett,* see Reading 20.)

In this reading Dennett argues that once we understand how the self is a fiction like a center of gravity in physical science or a character in a novel, we will see that there isn't any deep philosophical mystery in what happens to commissurotomy subjects and people with multiple personality disorder.

What is a self? I will try to answer this question by developing an analogy with something much simpler, something which is nowhere near as puzzling as a self, but has some properties in common with selves.

What I have in mind is *the centre of gravity*[1] of an object. This is a well-behaved concept in Newtonian physics. But a centre of gravity is not an atom or a subatomic particle or any other physical item in the world. It has no mass; it has no colour; it has no physical properties at all, except for spatio-temporal location. It is a fine example of what Hans Reichenbach[2] would call an *abstractum*.[3] It is a purely abstract object. It is, if you like, a theorist's fiction. It is not one of the real things in the universe in addition to the atoms. But it is a fiction that has a nicely defined, well-delineated and well-behaved role within physics.

From Daniel C. Dennett, "Why everyone is a novelist," *The Times Literary Supplement,* September 16–22, 1988, pp. 1016, 1028–1029. Reprinted with permission of the author and publisher. © Times Literary Supplements, London, Limited, 22 September 1988.

[1] A body in a gravitational field behaves as if all its weight or mass were at a single point. If the body is a sphere composed of evenly distributed matter, this point will roughly coincide with the body's geometrical center. On the other hand, the center of gravity of irregular bodies with uneven mass in their components will sometimes be external to the material of the bodies (e.g., at the center of a hollow ball or between the legs of a chair). ED.

[2] Hans Reichenbach (1891–1953) taught philosophy at several European universities before coming to the University of California, Los Angeles, where he taught from 1938–1953. He wrote extensively in the logic and philosophy of science. ED.

[3] In his *Experience and Prediction* (1938) Reichenbach gives as examples of *abstracta* the state, the spirit of a nation, the soul, and the character of a person. Abstracta contrast with *concreta,* objects in the middle dimension of the universe (macro, but not so large that we can't directly observe them with our sensory organs). We get an abstractum by treating as a single item similar predicates of a class of concreta. For instance, a person's character is what is common to all the particular attributes by which we predict morally relevant behavior in that individual and in others. Reichenbach says that it is a matter of convention whether we talk about abstracta as if they existed and had a spatial location. For instance, we don't usually talk as if the *average person* exists somewhere, but we do talk about a *state* occupying a certain territory. Abstracta are *reducible* to concreta in the sense that a claim about an abstractum can be translated into a claim or set of claims about concreta. For instance, a statement about a body's center of gravity is reducible to a set of statements about the masses of the body's components. ED.

Let me remind you how robust and familiar the idea of a centre of gravity is. Consider a chair. Like all other physical objects, it has a centre of gravity. If you start tipping it, you can tell more or less accurately whether it would start to fall over or fall back in place if you let go of it. We are all quite good at making predictions involving centres of gravity and devising explanations about when and why things fall over. Place a book on the chair. It, too, has a centre of gravity. If you start to push it over the edge, we know that at some point it will fall. It will fall when its centre of gravity is no longer directly over a point of its supporting base (the chair seat). Notice that that statement is itself virtually tautological.[4] The key terms in it are all interdefinable. And yet it can also figure in explanations that appear to be causal explanations of some sort. We ask "Why doesn't that lamp tip over?" We reply "Because its centre of gravity is so low." Is this a causal explanation? It can compete with explanations that are clearly causal, such as "Because it's nailed to the table", and "Because it's supported by wires".

We can manipulate centres of gravity. For instance, I change the centre of gravity of a water-pitcher easily, by pouring some of the water out. So, although a centre of gravity is a purely abstract object, it has a spatio-temporal career, which I can affect by my actions. It has a history, but its history can include some rather strange episodes. Although it moves around in space and time, its motion can be discontinuous. For instance, if I were to take a piece of bubble-gum and suddenly stick it on the pitcher's handle, that would shift the pitcher's centre of gravity from point A to point B. But the centre of gravity would not have to move through all the intervening positions. As an abstractum, it is not bound by all the constraints of physical travel.

Consider the centre of gravity of a slightly more complicated object. Suppose we wanted to keep track of the career of the centre of gravity of some complex machine with lots of turning-gears and camshafts and reciprocating rods—the engine of a steam-powered unicycle, perhaps. And suppose our theory of the machine's operation permitted

us to plot the complicated trajectory of the centre of gravity precisely. And suppose—most improbably—that in this particular machine the trajectory of the centre of gravity was precisely the same as the trajectory of a particular iron atom in the crankshaft. Even if this were discovered, we would be wrong even to *entertain* the hypothesis that the machine's centre of gravity was (identical with) that iron atom. That would be a category mistake.[5] A centre of gravity is *just* an abstractum. It's just a fictional object. But when I say it's a fictional object, I do not mean to disparage it; it's a wonderful fictional object, and it has a perfectly legitimate place within serious, sober, *echt* physical science.[6]

A self is also an abstract object, a theorist's fiction. The theory is not particle physics but what we might call a branch of people-physics; it is more soberly known as a phenomenology or hermeneutics,[7] or soul-science (*Geisteswissenschaft*). The physicist does an interpretation, if you like, of the chair and its behavior, and comes up with the theoretical abstraction of a centre of gravity, which is then very useful in characterizing the behaviour of the chair in the future, under a wide variety of conditions. The hermeneuticist or phenomenologist—or anthropologist—sees some rather more complicated things moving about in the world (human beings and animals) and is faced with a similar problem of interpretation. It turns out to be theoretically perspicuous to organize the interpretation around a central abstraction: each person has a self (in addition to a centre of gravity). In fact we have to posit selves for ourselves as well. The theoretical problem of self-interpretation is at least as difficult and important as the problem of other-interpretation.

Now how does a self differ from a centre of gravity? It is a much more complicated concept. I will try to elucidate it via an analogy with another

---

[4] The statement says, in effect, that the book will fall when nothing prevents it from falling. ED.

[5] For an explanation of the phrase "category mistake" see the introduction to Reading 2.

[6] Just as, presumably, the object we call a (political) state has a place in serious, sober political science. ED.

[7] Dennett is using the terms *phenomenology* and *hermeneutics* in a fairly loose but common way. The former means careful description of a phenomenon, of how it appears apart from theoretical preconceptions (insofar as this is possible). Phenomenology, in this sense, is often regarded as a first step on the path to a theoretical understanding of a phenomenon. A *hermeneutics* is a theory or method of interpretation. ED.

sort of fictional object: fictional characters in literature. Pick up *Moby Dick* and open it up to page one. It says, "Call me Ishmael." Call whom Ishmael? Call Melville Ishmael? No. Call Ishmael Ishmael. Melville has created a fictional character named Ishmael. As you read the book you learn about Ishmael, about his life, about his beliefs and desires, his acts and attitudes. You learn a lot more about Ishmael than Melville ever explicitly tells you. Some of it you can read in by implication. Some of it you can read in by extrapolation. But beyond the limits of such extrapolation fictional worlds are simply indeterminate. Thus, consider the following question (borrowed from David Lewis's "Truth and Fiction", *American Philosophical Quarterly,* 1978). Did Sherlock Holmes have three nostrils? The answer of course is no, but not because Conan Doyle ever says that he doesn't, or that he has two, but because we are entitled to make that extrapolation. In the absence of evidence to the contrary, Sherlock Holmes's nose can be supposed to be normal. Another question: Did Sherlock Holmes have a mole on his left shoulder-blade? The answer to this question is neither yes nor no. Nothing about the text or about the principles of extrapolation from the text permits an answer to that question. There is simply no fact of the matter. Why? Because Sherlock Holmes is merely a fictional character, created by, or constituted out of, the text and the culture in which that text resides.

This indeterminacy is a fundamental property of fictional objects which strongly distinguishes them from another sort of object scientists talk about: theoretical entities, or what Reichenbach called *illata*—inferred entities, such as atoms, molecules and neutrinos.[8] A logician might say that the "principle of bivalence" does not hold for fictional objects. That is to say, with regard to any actual man, living or dead, the question of whether or not he has or had a mole on his left shoulder-blade has an answer, yes or no. Did Aristotle have such a mole? There is a fact of the matter even if we can never discover it. But with regard to a fictional character, that question may have no answer at all.

We can imagine someone, a benighted literary critic, perhaps, who doesn't understand that fiction is fiction. This critic has a strange theory about how fiction works. He thinks that something literally magical happens when a novelist writes a novel. When a novelist sets down words on paper, this critic says (one often hears claims like this, but not meant to be taken completely literally), the novelist actually creates a world. A litmus test for this bizarre view is the principle of bivalence: when our imagined critic speaks of a fictional world he means a strange sort of real world, a world in which the principle of bivalence holds. Such a critic might seriously wonder whether Dr. Watson was really Moriarty's second cousin, or whether the conductor of the train that took Holmes and Watson to Aldershot was also the conductor of the train that brought them back to London. That sort of question can't properly arise if you understand fiction correctly, of course. Whereas analogous questions about historical personages have to have yes or no answers, even if we may never be able to dredge them up.

Centres of gravity, as fictional objects, exhibit the same feature. They have only the properties that the theory that constitutes them endowed them with[9]. If you scratch your head and say, "I wonder if maybe centres of gravity are really neutrinos!" you have misunderstood the theoretical status of a centre of gravity.

Now how can I make the claim that a self—your own real self, for instance—is rather like a fictional character? Are all fictional selves not de-

---

[8] "Illata" is the past participle of the Latin verb *infero* and means "inferred things." In Reichenbach's philosophy, illata are explanatory entities, usually causes or constituents, that are too small (e.g., molecules) to be detected by our sensory organs and/or are not, or don't have, the sort of energetic input for which we have sensory organs (e.g., radio waves). Although we can't directly observe illata, we infer their existence from that of concreta (which *are* directly observable). For instance, there is an observable increase in pressure on the cover of a pot when the water inside it is being brought to a boil. We have inferred from this and many other related phenomena that liquids and gases are composed of imperceptibly tiny particles (molecules) whose kinetic energy increases when a liquid is heated, so that the surface of the container is bombarded with increasing energy. Precisely because they are not directly observable, illata are for Reichenbach more *objective*. There is always a subjective ingredient in concreta. For instance: "We see the iron stove before us as a model of rigidity, solidity, immovability; but we know that its particles perform a violent dance, and that it resembles a swarm of dancing gnats more than the image of solidity we attribute to it" (Reichenbach, 1938, p. 219). Our inability to visualize objects below a certain magnitude causes us to see *as* smooth, continuous and stable what is in fact a swarm of irregularly moving bits of matter. ED.

[9] Similarly, Sherlock Holmes has only those attributes which the texts of Conan Doyle endowed him with. ED.

pendent for their very creation on the existence of real selves? It may seem so, but I will argue that this is an illusion. Let's go back to Ishmael. Ishmael is a fictional character, although we can certainly learn all about him. One might find him in many regards more real than many of one's friends.[10] But, one thinks, Ishmael was created by Melville, and Melville is a real character—was a real character. A real self. Does this not show that it takes a real self to create a fictional self? I think not, but if I am to convince you, I must push you through an exercise of the imagination.

First of all, I want to imagine something some of you may think incredible: a novel-writing machine. We can suppose it is a product of artificial intelligence research, a computer that has been designed or programmed to write novels. But it has not been designed to write any particular novel. We can suppose (if it helps) that it has been given a great stock of whatever information it might need, and some partially random and hence unpredictable ways of starting the seed of a story going, and building upon it. Now imagine that the designers are sitting back, wondering what kind of novel their creation is going to write. They turn the thing on and after a while the high-speed printer begins to go clickety-clack and out comes the first sentence. "Call me Gilbert", it says. What follows is the apparent autobiography of some fictional Gilbert. Now Gilbert is a fictional, created self but its creator is no self. Of course there were human designers who designed the machine, but they didn't design Gilbert. Gilbert is a product of a design or invention process in which there aren't any selves at all. That is, I am stipulating that this is not a conscious machine, not a "thinker". It is a dumb machine, but it does have the power to write a passable novel. (If you think this is strictly impossible I can only challenge you to show why you think this must be so, and invite you to read on; in the end you may not have an interest in defending such a precarious impossibility-claim.)

---

[10] If you aren't already acquainted with someone like this, imagine a person whose behavior in many important situations is unpredictable to you despite knowing her for years. This person might be very guarded and taciturn, or perhaps just not committed to any values, principles, or long-range goals—a person who acts on whim. You might find such a person far less intelligible or predictable than a well-defined character in a play or novel. The fictional character would have more of an identity for you; she would be more "real" than your friend in the real world. ED.

So we are to imagine that a passable story is emitted from the machine. Notice that we can perform the same sort of literary exegesis with regard to this novel as we can with any other. In fact if you were to pick up a novel at random out of a library, you could not tell with certainty that it wasn't written by something like this machine. (And if you're a New Critic you shouldn't care[11].) You've got a text and you can interpret it, and so you can learn the story, the life and adventures of Gilbert. Your expectations and predictions, as you read, and your interpretative reconstruction of what you have already read, will congeal around the central node of the fictional character, Gilbert.

But now I want to twiddle the knobs on this thought experiment. So far we've imagined the novel, *The Life and Times of Gilbert,* clanking out of a computer that is just a box, sitting in the corner of some lab. But now I want to change the story a little bit and suppose that the computer has arms and legs—or better: wheels. (I don't want to make it too anthropomorphic.) It has a television eye, and it moves around in the world. It also begins its tale with "Call me Gilbert", and tells a novel, but now we notice that if we do the trick that the New Critics say you should never do, and look outside the text, we discover that there's a truth-preserving interpretation of that text in the real world. The adventures of Gilbert, the fictional character, now bear a striking and presumably non-coincidental relationship to the adventures of this robot rolling around in the world. If you hit the robot with a baseball bat, very shortly thereafter the story of Gilbert includes his being hit with a baseball bat by somebody who looks like you. Every now and then the robot gets locked in the closet and then says "Help me!" Help whom? Well, help Gilbert, presumably. But who is Gilbert? Is Gilbert the robot, or merely the fictional self created by the robot? If we go and help the robot out of the closet, it sends us a note: "Thank you. Love, Gilbert."

At this point we will be unable to ignore the fact that the fictional career of the fictional Gilbert bears an interesting resemblance to the "career" of this mere robot moving through the world. We can

---

[11] Dennett is referring here to a viewpoint in literary criticism that has enjoyed wide acceptance since the 1930s: that the text is a self-contained artifact, the interpretation of which should not be determined by what we know of the author. ED.

still maintain that the robot's brain, the robot's computer, really knows nothing about the world; it's not a self. It's just a clanky computer. It doesn't know what it's doing. It doesn't even know that it's creating a fictional character. (The same is just as true of your brain; it doesn't know what it's doing either.) [12] Nevertheless, the patterns in the behaviour that is being controlled by the computer are interpretable, by us, as accreting biography—telling the narrative of a self. But we are not the only interpreters. The robot novelist is also, of course, an interpreter; a self-interpreter, providing its own account of its activities in the world.

I propose that we take this analogy seriously. "Where is the self?" a materialist philosopher or neuroscientist might ask. It is a category mistake to start looking around for the self in the brain. Unlike centres of gravity, whose sole property is their spatio-temporal position, selves have a spatio-temporal position that is only grossly defined. Roughly speaking, in the normal case if there are three human beings sitting on a park bench, there are three selves there, all in a row and roughly equidistant from the fountain they face. Or we might use a rather antique turn of phrase and talk about how many souls are located in the park. ("All twenty souls in the starboard lifeboat were saved, but those that remained on deck perished.")

Brain research may permit us to make some more fine-grained localizations, but the capacity to achieve *some* fine-grained localization does not give one grounds for supposing that the process of localization can continue indefinitely and that the day will finally come when we can say, "That cell there, right in the middle of the hippocampus (or wherever)—that's the self!"

There's a big difference, of course, between fictional characters and our own selves. One I would stress is that a fictional character is usually encoun-

tered as a *fait accompli*. After the novel has been written and published, you read it. At that point it is too late for the novelist to render determinate anything indeterminate that strikes your curiosity. Dostoevsky is dead; you can't ask him what else Raskolnikov thought while he sat in the police station. But novels don't have to be that way. John Updike has written three novels about Rabbit Angstrom: *Rabbit Run, Rabbit Redux* and *Rabbit is Rich*. Suppose that those of us who particularly like the first novel were to get together and compose a list of questions for Updike—things we wished he had talked about in that first novel, when Rabbit was a young former basketball star. We could send our questions to Updike and ask him to consider writing another novel in the series, only this time not continuing the chronological sequence. Like Lawrence Durrell's *Alexandria Quartet*,[13] the Rabbit series could include another novel about Rabbit's early days when he was still playing basketball, and this novel could answer our questions.

Notice what we would not be doing in such a case. We would not be saying to Updike, "Tell us the answers that you already know, the answers that are already fixed to those questions. Come on, let us know all those secrets you've been keeping from us." Nor would we be asking Updike to do research, as we might ask the author of a multi-volume biography of a real person, we would be asking him to write a new novel, to invent some more novel for us, on demand. And if he acceded, he would enlarge and make more determinate the character of Rabbit Angstrom in the process of writing the new novel. In this way matters which are indeterminate at one time can become determined later by a creative step.

I propose that this imagined exercise with Updike getting him to write more novels on demand to answer our questions, is actually a familiar exercise. That is the way we treat each other; that is the way we are. We cannot undo those parts of our pasts that are determinate, but our selves are constantly being made more determinate as we go along in response to the way the world impinges on

---

[12] This is an important and plausible claim. In his *Consciousness Explained* (1991) Dennett argues that, because of the lasting influence of Descartes' notion of the mental as essentially self-transparent, we fail to notice that the *doing* of even the higher mental acts we do is *not* itself conscious, that we are instead aware only of the *outcomes* of mental acts such as speaking, writing, remembering, and figuring out how to do something. If consciousness is not present in the *doing* of such things, then we must think of them as *mechanisms*. Thinking this way makes more plausible Dennett's thought-experiment of a novel-writing machine. Many writers would say that they discover what it was that they were trying to write only once they have managed to write it. ED.

[13] *The Alexandria Quartet* (1958–60) consists of three novels (*Justine, Balthazar, Mountolive*) that deal with the same characters and events in the same time period, seen from different perspectives and by different narrators. The fourth novel in the quartet (*Clea*) deals with the time after that of the first three. ED.

us. Of course it is also possible for a person to engage in auto-hermeneutics, interpretation of one's self, and in particular to go back and think about one's past, and one's memories, and to rethink them and rewrite them. This process does change the "fictional" character, the character that you are, in much the way that Rabbit Angstrom, after Updike writes the second novel about him as a young man, comes to be a rather different fictional character, determinate in ways he was never determinate before. This would be an utterly mysterious and magical prospect (and hence something no one should take seriously) if the self were anything but an abstractum.

I want to bring this out by extracting one more feature from the Updike thought experiment. Updike might take up our request but then he might prove to be forgetful. After all, it's been many years since he wrote *Rabbit Run*. He might not want to go back and re-read it carefully; and when he wrote the new novel it might end up being inconsistent with the first. He might have Rabbit being in two places at one time, for instance. If we wanted to settle what the true story was, we'd be falling into error; there is no true story. In such a circumstance there would simply be a failure of coherence of all the data that we had about Rabbit. And because Rabbit is a fictional character, we wouldn't smite our foreheads in wonder and declare "Oh my goodness! There's a rift in the universe; we've found a contradiction in nature!" Nothing is easier than contradiction when you're dealing with fiction; a fictional character can have contradictory properties because it's just a fictional character. We find such contradictions intolerable, however, when we are trying to interpret something or someone, even a fictional character, so we typically bifurcate the character to resolve the conflict.

Something like this seems to happen to real people on rare occasions.[14] Consider the putatively true case-histories recorded in Corbett H. Thigpen and Hervey Cleckly's *The Three Faces of Eve* (1957), and Flora Rheta Schreiber's *Sybil* (1973). Eve's three faces were the faces of three distinct personalities, it seems, and the woman portrayed in *Sybil* had many different selves, or so it seems. How can we make sense of this? Here is one way—a solemn, skeptical way favoured by some of the psychotherapists with whom I've talked about such cases: when Sybil went in to see her therapist the first time, she wasn't several different people rolled onto one body; she was a novel-writing machine that fell in with a very ingenious questioner, a very eager reader. And together they collaborated—innocently—to write many, many chapters of a new novel. And, of course, since Sybil was a sort of living novel, she went out and engaged in the world with these new selves, more or less created on demand, under the eager suggestion of a therapist.

I now believe that this is overly skeptical. The population explosion of new characters that typically follows the onset of psychotherapy for sufferers of Multiple Personality Disorder (MPD) is probably to be explained along just these lines, but there is quite compelling evidence in some cases that some multiplicity of selves (two or three or four, let us say) had already begun laying down biography before the therapist came along to do the "reading". And in any event, Sybil is only a strikingly pathological case of something quite normal, a behaviour pattern we can find in ourselves. We are all, at times, confabulators, telling and retelling ourselves the story of our own lives, with scant attention to the question of truth. Why, though, do we behave this way? Why are we all such inveterate and inventive autobiographical novelists? As Umberto Maturana has (uncontroversially) observed: "Everything said is said by a speaker to another speaker that may be himself." But why should one talk to oneself? Why isn't that an utterly idle activity, as systematically futile as trying to pick oneself up by one's own bootstraps?

A central clue comes from the sort of phenomena uncovered by Michael Gazzaniga's research on

---

[14] Dennett is talking about multiple personality disorder (MPD), a syndrome in which two or more personalities alternate in one human being. There is usually an amnesic barrier between the personalities. One of the most common of such cases involves a primary personality and one or more secondary ones. The latter may be aware of each other and share memories, but usually the primary personality is unaware of the secondary one(s). Primary personalities may conclude that they need therapy because they find themselves in situations they have no memory of getting into, and which *they* would never get into. A common cause for this rare condition appears to be some traumatic childhood incident or situation, such as sexual or physical abuse, which leaves these children in a seriously conflicted state, because, for instance, they cannot experience the traumatically induced emotions and still function in their daily lives. In such cases, a separate personality comes into being to cope with the unmanageable feelings. ED.

those rare individuals—the "split-brain subjects"—whose *corpus callosum* has been surgically severed, creating in them two largely independent cortical hemispheres that can, on occasion, be differently informed about the current scene. Does the operation split the self in two? After it, patients normally exhibit no signs of psychological splitting, appearing to be no less unified than you or I except under particularly contrived circumstances. But on Gazzaniga's view, this does not so much show that the patients have preserved their pre-surgical unity as that the unity of normal life is an illusion.

According to him, the normal mind is not beautifully unified, but rather a problematically yoked-together bundle of partly autonomous systems. All parts of the mind are not equally accessible to each other at all times. These modules or systems sometimes have internal communication problems which they solve by various ingenious and devious routes. If this is true (and I think it is), it may provide us with an answer to a most puzzling question about conscious thought: what good is it? Such a question begs for an evolutionary answer, but it will have to be speculative, of course. (It is not critical to my speculative answer, for the moment, where genetic evolution and transmission break off and cultural evolution and transmission take over.)

In the beginning—according to Julian Jaynes (*The Origins of Consciousness in the Breakdown of the Bicameral Mind,* 1976), whose account I am adapting—were speakers, our ancestors, who weren't really conscious. They spoke, but they just sort of blurted things out, more or less the way bees do bee dances, or the way computers talk to each other. That is not conscious communication, surely. When these ancestors had problems, sometimes they would "ask" for help (more or less like Gilbert saying "Help me!" when he was locked in the closet), and sometimes there would be somebody around to hear them. So they got into the habit of asking for assistance and, particularly, asking questions. Whenever they couldn't figure out how to solve some problem, they would ask a question, addressed to no one in particular, and sometimes whoever was standing around could answer them. And they also came to be designed to be provoked on many such occasions into answering questions like that—to the best of their ability—when asked.

Then one day one of our ancestors asked a question in what was apparently an inappropriate circumstance: there was nobody around to be the audience. Strangely enough, he heard his own question, and this stimulated him, cooperatively, to think of an answer, and sure enough the answer came to him. He had established, without realizing what he had done, a communication link between two parts of his brain, between which there was, for some deep biological reason, an accessibility problem. One component of the mind had confronted a problem that another component could solve; if only the problem could be posed for the latter component. Thanks to his habit of asking questions, our ancestor stumbled upon a route via the ears. What a discovery! Sometimes talking and listening to yourself can have wonderful effects, not otherwise obtainable. All that is needed to make sense of this idea is the hypothesis that the modules of the mind have different capacities and ways of doing things, and are not perfectly interaccessible. Under such circumstances it could be true that the way to get yourself to figure out a problem is to tickle your ear with it, to get that part of your brain which is best stimulated by hearing a question to work on the problem. Then sometimes you will find yourself with the answer you seek on the tip of your tongue.

This would be enough to establish the evolutionary endorsement (which might well be only culturally transmitted) of the behaviour of talking to yourself. But as many writers have observed, conscious thinking seems—much of it—to be a variety of a particularly efficient and private talking to oneself. The evolutionary transition to thought is then easy to conjure up. All we have to suppose is that the route, the circuit that at first went via mouth and ear, got shorter. People "realized" that the actual vocalization and audition was a rather inefficient part of the loop. Besides, if there were other people around who might overhear it, you might give away more information than you wanted. So what developed was a habit of subvocalization, and this in turn could be streamlined into conscious, verbal thought.

In his posthumous book *On Thinking* (1979), Gilbert Ryle asks: "What is *Le Penseur* doing?" For behaviourists like Ryle this is a real problem. One bit of chin-on-fist-with-knitted-brow looks pretty much like another bit, and yet some of it seems to arrive at good answers and some of it doesn't. What can be going on here? Ironically, Ryle, the arch-behaviourist, came up with some very sly suggestions about what might be going on. Conscious thought, Ryle claimed, should be understood on the model of self-teaching, or better, perhaps: self-schooling or training. He had little to say about how this self-schooling might actually work, but we can get some initial understanding of it on the supposition that we are not the captains of our ships; there is no conscious self that is unproblematically in command of the mind's resources. Rather, we are somewhat disunified. Our component modules have to act in opportunistic but amazingly resourceful ways to produce a modicum of behavioural unity, which is then enhanced by an illusion of greater unity.

What Gazzaniga's research reveals, sometimes in vivid detail, is how this must go on. Consider some of his evidence for the extraordinary resourcefulness exhibited by (something in) the right hemisphere when it is faced with a communication problem. In one group of experiments, split-brain subjects reach into a closed bag with the left hand to feel an object, which they then identify verbally. The sensory nerves in the left hand lead to the right hemisphere, whereas the control of speech is normally in the left hemisphere, but for most of us, this poses no problem. In a normal person, the left hand can know what the right hand is doing thanks to the *corpus callosum,* which keeps both hemispheres mutually informed. But in a split-brain subject, this unifying link has been removed; the right hemisphere gets the information about the touched object from the left hand, but the left, language-controlling, hemisphere must make the identification public. So the "part which can speak" is kept in the dark, while the "part which knows" cannot make public its knowledge.

There is a devious solution to this problem, however, and split-brain patients have been observed to discover it. Whereas ordinary tactile sensations are represented contralaterally—the signals go to the opposite hemisphere—pain signals are also represented ipsilaterally. That is, thanks to the way the nervous system is wired up, pain stimuli go to both hemispheres. Suppose the object in the bag is a pencil. The right hemisphere will sometimes hit upon a very clever tactic: hold the pencil in your left hand so its point is pressed hard into your palm; this creates pain, and lets the left hemisphere know there's something sharp in the bag, which is enough of a hint so that it can begin guessing; the right hemisphere will signal "getting warmer" and "got it" by smiling or other controllable signs, and in a very short time "the subject"—the apparently unified "sole inhabitant" of the body—will be able to announce the correct answer.

Now either the split-brain subjects have developed this extraordinarily devious talent as a reaction to the operation that landed them with such a radical accessibility problem, or the operation reveals—but does not create—a virtuoso talent to be found also in normal people. Surely, Gazzaniga claims, the latter hypothesis is the most likely one to investigate. That is, it does seem that we are all virtuoso novelists, who find ourselves engaged in all sorts of behaviour, more or less unified, but sometimes disunified, and we always put the best "faces" on if we can. We try to make all of our material cohere into a single good story. And that story is our autobiography.

The chief fictional character at the centre of that autobiography is one's self. And if you still want to know what the self really is, you're making a category mistake. After all, when a human being's behavioural control system becomes seriously impaired, it can turn out that the best hermeneutical story we can tell about that individual says that there is more than one character "inhabiting" that body. This is quite possible on the view of the self I have been presenting; it does not require any fancy metaphysical miracles. One can discover multiple selves in a person just as unproblematically as one could find Early Young Rabbit and Late Young Rabbit in the imagined Updike novels: all that has to be the case is that the story doesn't cohere around one self, one imaginary point, but coheres (coheres much better, in any case) around two different imaginary points.

We sometimes encounter psychological disorders, or surgically created disunities, where the only way to interpret or make sense of them is to posit in effect two centres of gravity, two selves. One isn't creating or discovering a little bit of ghost stuff in doing that. One is simply creating another abstraction. It is an abstraction one uses as part of a theoretical apparatus to understand, and predict, and make sense of, the behaviour of some very complicated things. The fact that these abstract selves seem so robust and real is not surprising. They are much more complicated theoretical entities than a centre of gravity. And remember that even a centre of gravity has a fairly robust presence, once we start playing around with it. But no one has ever seen or ever will see a centre of gravity. As David Hume noted, no one has ever seen a self, either.

For my part, when I enter most intimately into what I call *myself*, I always stumble on some particular perception or other, of heat or cold, light or shade, love or hatred, pain or pleasure. I never can catch *myself* at any time without a perception, and never can observe anything but the perception. . . . If anyone, upon serious and unprejudiced reflection, thinks he has a different notion of *himself*, I must confess I can reason no longer with him. All I can allow him is, that he may be in the right as well as I, and that we are essentially different in this particular. He may, perhaps, perceive something simple and continued, which he calls *himself*; though I am certain there is no such principle in me. [*Treatise on Human Nature*, I, IV, sec. 6.]

Dennett has argued that the self is in important respects like a centre of gravity. (In *Consciousness Explained*, Dennett even refers to the self as a "centre of narrative gravity.") He calls the centre of gravity a "fiction" because all the mass of a body is *not* really concentrated at a single point. The centre of gravity is a "theoretical fiction," and a good one, because it serves a theoretical purpose—it enables us to predict the behavior of a body in a gravitational field. A body really behaves *as if* all its mass were located at this point. Another way to put it is that for the purpose of certain calculations about the body's interactions with other bodies, it and they can be treated as points in space.

Similarly, Dennett seems to say, the self is a theoretical fiction useful in "hermeneutics" or "soul-science" for predicting the behavior of human organisms. Like a centre of gravity the self is an "imaginary point" with duration but no spatial dimension. Unlike a centre of gravity, it doesn't have an exact location with respect to the human body, although neuroscience inclines us to locate it in the brain. It is the nonspatial unity of the beliefs, habits, experiences, attitudes, and acts that we "hermeneutically" attribute to a person. A body has the same centre of gravity in the same location just as long as its parts stay together in the same configuration. If you remove one of those parts, you end up with two bodies and two centres of gravity, neither of which is the original one. There's nothing surprising about this because we're fully aware that a body isn't a point, that it is really a configuration of separable masses. Dennett wants us to note the parallel here with the human organism and its self: a human has one and the same self just as long as the physical components of its "behavioral control system" continue to act in harmony to produce coordinated behavior. The self as imaginary point is merely an abstract way of conceptualizing the unified operation of these components. If the components stop working together in the normal way, as in the case of commisurotomized subjects under experimental conditions or children who develop multiple personalities to cope with childhood trauma, the result is two or more "centres" just as when you break up a body. There's no "fancy metaphysical miracle" in either case, presumably because there's nothing "metaphysical" there to worry about in the first place; there's just a useful fiction or "abstractum." That is why Dennett quotes with approval at the end of his essay a passage in which Hume proclaims with certainty that he can't perceive within himself "something simple and continued" that would count as his self. Looking for oneself that way is, from Dennett's point of view, no more promising than taking a chair apart in a determined search for its centre of gravity.

Dennett's way of analyzing the two "centres" raises a very general and metaphysical question: Why isn't *every* body, from the largest to the smallest, a fictional center of this sort? It's important for Dennett's analysis that there be a clear answer to this question, because his thesis that the self is a fiction is meaningful only insofar as there is a clear contrast between "fictional" and "real." He implies such a contrast when, for instance, he says about a centre of

gravity that "It is not one of the real things in the universe in addition to the atoms." He's denying to selves and centres of gravity the reality that atoms have.

Let's look at the reality of atoms. They are internally complex systems near the bottom of
the hierarchy of components in an organism like the human: Beginning at the level of the organism itself, we descend in order of magnitude to organ systems, organs, tissues, cells, large
molecules such as proteins and DNA, smaller molecules such as sugar, *atoms* (the components
of molecules) such as carbon or hydrogen, sub-atomic particles such as the electrons, protons
and neutrons that make up each atom, and (?) finally quarks, the building blocks of protons
and neutrons.

"Atom" comes from a Greek term meaning "indivisible." Demokritos, a Greek philosopher
of the fifth century B.C.E., theorized that the world is composed of imperceptibly small particles
of a uniform stuff or matter (which he termed "being"). These particles, which Demokritos
called *atoms,* were supposed to be indivisible (and therefore immutable), internally undifferentiated, and different from one another only in shape and size. According to this theory, atoms
were the only true beings, the ultimate realities. Everything else was merely a temporary configuration of atoms which are forever coming together and separating in the void (which is
non-stuff or non-being). Each of these ultimate realities had an ultimate *unity*—it was not just
a part or aspect of something else, because it was unaffected by belonging to a body and could
exist entirely on its own. Because it was indivisible, it didn't have parts and therefore couldn't be
understood as just a collection of other things. Unlike bodies large enough for us to perceive,
an atom was a *one* that was not also a *many*. In Aristotle's language (see the introduction to
this part), atoms were *substances,* paradigm cases of *being* in the theory of Demokritos.

Philosophical atomism, as a metaphysical image of the world, has had a long and robust
career in the nearly two and a half millennia since Demokritos. It was especially influential
among philosophers and scientists in the era of the scientific revolution during the seventeenth
and eighteenth centuries. One major implication of philosophical atomism is that the "reality"
of those bodies that populate the macroworld of things large enough for us to see is derivative,
secondary to the reality of their microcomponents (such as atoms). Trees, rocks, and animals are
"nothing but" more or less complex configurations of lower-level particles. The unity of such
beings is not the industrial-strength unity of atoms; it is instead the much weaker unity of a
collection, a unity that is merely relational, constituted by spatial and other relations among
components.

Robert Boyle (1626–1691) is a good example of this mentality. One of his claims to fame is
as the discoverer of what we now call Boyle's law—that at a constant temperature the volume
of a gas is inversely proportional to the pressure. Boyle was a major contributor to the launch-
ing of chemistry as a science. His atomist image of nature made him confident that scientists
would succeed "in deducing all the phenomena of nature from matter and motion" (quoted
in Hall, 1965, p. 28). The matter in motion was, of course, that of particles. What then is the
metaphysical status of rocks, trees, and animals for Boyle? Here is what he has to say about
their formation or coming into being: "Not that there is, really, anything substantial produced,
but that those parts of matter, which, indeed, pre-existed in other dispositions, are now brought
together after a manner, requisite to entitle the body which results from them, to a new denomination. . . ." (*Works,* 1738, 3:211). A tree, then, is a collection of particles or corpuscles
arranged in a certain way, and everything about a tree is "deducible" from what we can know
about the properties and motions of its corpuscles. When this tree-configuration of particles
comes into being, there's no new "substance," only a collection with a "new denomination"
or name ("tree"). If you were to try to find in the tree "something simple and continued" (in
Hume's words) corresponding to the single word "tree," your error would be comparable to
taking apart a chair to find its centre of gravity.

Among those enthralled by the metaphysical image of atomism were scientists like Boyle
and Newton who were inspired by it to look for explanations of physical phenomena in terms
of the behavior of imperceptible particles. This research strategy has been enormously successful ever since. And the success of the strategy has given added lustre to the metaphysical

image. David Hume applied the atomist image to perceptions, which for him were the only objects of awareness. He argued (see p. 442 above) that *unity* is "merely a fictitious denomination" except for the indivisible minimal sensibles or perceptual atoms out of which all else is composed.

The atoms of physical science did not, of course, turn out to be indivisible. Far from it. They are composed of neutrons, positively charged protons, and negatively charged electrons. Over 99% of the mass of the atom is concentrated in the protons and neutrons making up the tiny core or *nucleus* of an atom. Most of the atom's "interior" beyond the nucleus is empty space. Its mass is the combined mass of its components. Its chemical properties are a function of the number and behavior of its electrons. The atom, then, is a *system.* If we grant that human minds or selves are nothing but human brains understood as functioning in certain ways, then we can say that states, ant colonies, organisms, selves, minds, molecules, and atoms are all systems consisting of lower-level interactive components. All these systems are aggregates that behave as units at some level of magnitude and in specific environments (e.g., nations or states in international relations). Why, then, is a self or mind *more* a "fiction" or "imaginary point" than an atom or a beehive? Why isn't Hume right in saying that *all* these unities are merely "fictitious denominations"? Just as there is no self that is distinct from sequences of closely related perceptions (Hume), or distinct from, and in command of, the interacting subsystems of the brain (Dennett), so there is no atom distinct from "its" sub-atomic components and sharing "its" electrons as "it" bonds with other atoms. However, if it's going to be meaningful to label all these systems as *fictions,* we need to know what is *real.* Quarks, perhaps. According to current theory, they are not divisible into further components; they have no structure.

Or perhaps there's something wrong with the atomist image of reality. According to this picture of the world, *relations* have no reality over and above that of the entities related (the *relata*). One of the most famous proponents of this principle was William of Ockham (1280–1349), for whom it was an application of a further principle he invoked so often that it is now called "Ockham's razor." The "razor" cuts this way: *Do not multiply entities without necessity.* Suppose you're looking at a couple of billiard balls on a table. Various relations obtain between the two, such as resemblance, difference, and distance. Put one ball in motion toward the other, and there will be a relation of causality between them on contact. For Ockham wielding his razor, there is no need to assert the existence of a further entity in addition to the two balls and their properties as individuals. For instance, in addition to the two resembling balls there doesn't exist a third, relational entity (their resemblance). And there is no relational entity (causality) over and above the motion of the first ball and the subsequent motions of both balls. Let's extrapolate this approach all the way up through the hierarchy of levels of magnitude in the composition of a human body. As we ascend from quarks, through all the levels up to that of the whole organism, we are moving from less to greater complexity of *relations* among whatever the foundational entities (the relata) are. All the way up the hierarchy there exists *nothing* but elementary particles. Dennett's addition to this perspective is that it may be theoretically useful to speak *as if* the higher-level, relational unities were themselves existents.

Both Dennett and Nagel speak of the mind or self as an imaginary *point.* Toward the end of his essay (see pp. 463–464 above), Nagel calls the traditional notion of a single self an "illusion," although he admits we may have a hard time getting by without it. "Either this subject contains the mental life, in which case it is complex and its unity must be accounted for in terms of the unified operation of its components and functions, or else it is an extensionless point, in which case it explains nothing." The language of "extensionless" or "imaginary points" refers to the same topic that was addressed by the traditional language of "substance" and "substrate." Quantity and extension were "accidents" inhering in a substance as its subject or substrate. If we try to think of the substrate *apart* from the quantitative features inhering in it, we do seem to be left with an "extensionless point" that "explains nothing." However, if we opt for a merely functional unity and discount the notion of a single subject as an "illusion," do we have to settle for a world populated only or mostly by useful "fictions"?

REVIEW QUESTIONS

1. Although both a centre of gravity and a character in a novel are fictions, does "fiction" mean the same thing in both cases? Is there enough similarity in meaning to allow the self to be a fiction in both senses?

2. Dennett presents an "evolutionary" hypothesis about the origin of conscious thought: In the beginning, humans "weren't really conscious. They spoke, but they just sort of blurted things out . . . the way computers talk to each other (p. 472)." They found it helpful to ask each other questions when they had problems they couldn't solve. This behavior enabled them to discover that they could sometimes answer their own questions—presumably one part of their brains could solve a problem posed by another part, and the spoken question broke a communications barrier between the two parts. "The evolutionary transition to thought is then easy to conjure up. All we have to suppose is that the route, the circuit that at first went via mouth and ear, got shorter." Natural selection and social selection would favor those who could most efficiently talk to themselves, and efficiency would be maximized if one's talk didn't need to be vocalized. "So what developed was a habit of subvocalization, and this in turn could be streamlined into conscious, verbal thought." Do you find this account plausible? Can conscious thought be understood as one part of the brain communicating with another like two computers (think about what happens when your computer "talks" to another "host" computer on the internet)?

34

Self and Substance

Sydney Shoemaker

Sydney Shoemaker is a professor of philosophy at Cornell University. His writings cover a variety of topics in metaphysics and the philosophy of mind. Among his most recent publications are *Identity, Cause and Mind: Philosophical Essays* (1984) and *The First-Person Perspective, and other Essays* (1996).

In this essay, Shoemaker attempts to synthesize what he regards as true or valuable in two traditionally opposed ways of understanding personal identity. The first ("conservative") way, associated with Descartes, Butler, and Reid, insists that the self or person to which we attribute identity is something more than the succession of interrelated psychological states. This something more is a subject or substance that endures through this succession. The second, or "reductionist" way, takes the contrary view, and is exemplified in Locke and Parfit. In formulating his position, Shoemaker presents an interesting interpretation of substances as "autonomous self-perpetuators," and gives this notion a functionalist analysis.

Nowadays the question whether the self is a substance[1], and whether the identity over time of a person requires the identity of a substance, has a musty smell to it. We recognize it as a question that played a central role in the intriguing discussions of personal identity in Locke[2], Butler[3], Hume[4] and Reid[5]; but it has not been the central question in contemporary discussions of personal identity, and in most such discussions it is simply not addressed.

Yet the question does have echoes in contemporary discussions. Contemporary "reductionists" about personal identity hark back to Locke and Hume, and contemporary antireductionists hark back to Butler and Reid. As I shall try to show, some of the intuitions of the antireductionists—e.g., their denial that the person who comes out at one end of a "teleportation" process can be the same as the person who went in at the other end—can be seen as expressions of the idea that in some good sense of "individual substance," a person must be an individual substance. And such a view seems at odds with the view of a reductionist like Derek Parfit,[6] who says that while we can allow that a person is a "subject" of experiences, since this is "the way we talk," it is nevertheless true that facts about

---

From: Sydney Shoemaker, "Self and Substance," in *Philosophical Perspectives* 11—*Mind, Causation and the World*, ed. James Tomberlin (Boston: Blackwell Publishers, 1997): 283–303. Reprinted with permission of the publisher.

[1] For a discussion of this notion in relation to the self, see the introduction to Part VIII. Ed.

[2] Reading 29. Ed.

[3] Joseph Butler (1692–1752) was an English theologian, philosopher, and Anglican Bishop. The relevant text is Dissertation I, "Of Personal Identity," at the end of *The Analogy of Religion, Natural and Revealed, to the Constitution and Course of Nature* (1736). Ed.

[4] Reading 30. Ed.

[5] Thomas Reid (1710–1796) was a noted critic of Hume and the founder of the influential school of "common-sense" philosophy. He discussed personal identity in Essay III of his *Essays on the Intellectual Powers of Man* (1785). Ed.

[6] Reading 31. Ed.

persons and their experiences admit of an impersonal description that reveals them to be nothing over and above facts about the relations of experiences to one another and to bodies.[7]

There is always a danger that framing a current philosophical issue in traditional metaphysical terms—here, in terms of the concepts of substance, inherence, etc.—will result in obfuscation rather than clarification. But that is a risk I shall take. I shall try to show that it is possible to combine some of the central intuitions that go with the claim that the self is a substance with some, although certainly not all, of the intuitions that go with reductionist views about personal identity. Among other things, I shall be developing the view, which I have presented elsewhere, that the psychological continuity view of personal identity, the contemporary heir to Locke's memory theory, can usefully be seen as complementary to—the "reverse side of the coin of"—a functionalist view about the nature of mental states.

* * *

Owing in large part to the work of Derek Parfit, the emphasis in recent literature on personal identity has shifted somewhat from the metaphysical issue of what constitutes such identity to questions about its importance—in particular, the question of whether it is identity "as such" that matters in "survival." My primary concern here will be with the metaphysical issue, not the issue of importance. But at the end I shall briefly discuss the relation between these.

II

As is well known, Locke denied that the identity of a person over an interval of time requires that it be one and the same substance that thinks "in" the person throughout that interval. As is also well known, Hume made the more radical denial that there is any substance at all involved in the existence of a person or self, unless our "perceptions" themselves count as substances.

Here Locke and Hume can be pitted against Joseph Butler and Thomas Reid, both of whom insisted that a self or person *is* a substance and that the identity over an interval of time of a self just *is* the

identity over that interval of the substance the person is. Butler and Reid were dualists, and took it for granted that the substance involved in personal identity is an immaterial one. Locke and Hume were committed to denying that a self or person is an immaterial substance. But they were equally committed to denying that it is a material substance. Hume, of course, rejected the notion of substance altogether. And Locke says that those "who place Thought in a purely material, animal Constitution, void of an immaterial Substance" plainly "conceive personal Identity preserved in something else than Identity of Substance; as animal Identity is preserved in Identity of Life, and not of Substance" (Locke 1975, p. 337).[8]

There is, as Butler and Reid both pointed out, a seeming contradiction involved in Locke's position. He defines "person" as meaning "a thinking intelligent Being, that has reason and reflection, and can consider itself as itself, the same thinking thing in different times and places" (p. 335). This seems to imply that a person is a Subject of a thought, and thereby a thinking substance, yet Locke denies the evident consequence of this, that the Identity of a person requires the identity of a thinking substance.

One might suggest, as I have done elsewhere[9], that Locke can be extricated from this apparent contradiction if we distinguish, as he (and Butler) did not, between two different senses of "substance." Call these the "subject of properties sense" (elsewhere I have called this the "Aristotelian sense") and the "parcel of stuff sense." What Locke's definition of "person" commits him to is that persons are substances in the subject of properties sense. This is compatible with the denial that a person is a substance in the parcel of stuff sense, and with the claim that one and the same person can at different times be constituted by different substances, in the latter sense.[10] Admittedly, this works better for the denial that a person is a material substance than for the denial that a person is an

---

[7] See Parfit 1984, pp. 223, 225, 226, 251, 341.

[8] For an explanation of Locke's doctrine here, see fn. 2 of Reading 29. ED.

[9] See my 1984.

[10] A parcel of stuff can be thought of as a "quantity" of stuff in Helen Cartwright's sense (see her 1970) that at no time is a scattered object. It must be composed of the same stuff at every moment of its existence. This is what Locke seems to take a "body" to be in *Essay, II, xxvii*, 3.

immaterial substance. Locke says that "those, who place thinking in an immaterial Substance only . . . must show why personal Identity cannot be preserved in the change of immaterial Substance, or variety of particular immaterial Substance, as well as animal Identity is preserved in the change of material Substances. . . ." (p. 337). To suppose that "substance" here means "parcel of stuff" is to invoke the notion immaterial stuff—which sounds disturbingly like immaterial matter. Yet *something* like that seems to be going on in Locke, given the comparison he is making between change of immaterial substance and change of material substance.

Hume presumably could have agreed with the Lockean definition of person as "a thinking, intelligent Being . . . etc." So why isn't he committed to persons being substances in the subject of properties sense? Here the obvious reply is that Hume thinks that a person's having a certain thought just consists in a certain bundle of perceptions having a perception of a certain sort as one of its members. So merely assenting to the truth of subject-predicate propositions about persons should not by itself commit one to persons being substances in the subject of properties sense. Following a suggestion of Paul Grice, in his classic 1941 paper on personal identity, let us say that a self is a substance in the subject of properties sense if and only if (1) statements of the form "S thinks, experiences, etc. such and such" are sometimes true, and (2) such statements are not analyzable in a certain way.[11] Bundle theorists *a la* Hume deny (2). The sort of analysis that would make (2) false would be one whose *analysans*[12] does not refer to or quantify over persons or subjects of mental properties.

The view that statements about persons are analyzable in a way that relieves us of commitment of mental subjects as constituents of the world seems at least akin to the "reductionist" view, championed by Derek Parfit and others, that personal identity is analyzable in terms of "psychological continuity and connectedness." And some proponents of the latter view have said things that seem at least in the spirit of the Humean denial that selves are substances. Parfit says that "because we

are not separately existing entities, we could fully describe our thoughts without claiming that they have thinkers" (Parfit 1984, p. 225). And he repeatedly says that it is "because of the way we talk" that it is true that persons are subjects. This strongly suggests that while condition (1) of the Gricean rendering of "Selves are substances" is satisfied, condition (2) is not.

III

Critics of reductionist views of personal identity are especially hostile to versions of reductionism that maintain that such imagined procedures as the teleportation of science fiction, and what I have called the "brain state transfer (BST) procedure," whereby the states of one brain are imposed on another without any transfer of matter, can be person-preserving.[13] To say that such a procedure is person-preserving means that a person A existing at time t_1 and a person B existing at a later time t_2 can be one and the same despite having different bodies and different brains, the identity holding in virtue of the mental states of A at t_1 and those of B at t_2 being linked by a chain of mental states exhibiting a certain sort of continuity and connectedness, which the procedure is sufficient to bring about.

The case against such versions of reductionism often rests on intuitions about what Parfit calls the "branch-line" case. In the branch-line case, two later persons stand in relations of psychological continuity and connectedness (psychological C&C) to one earlier person; in the case of one of these the body and brain are the same as those of the earlier person, and the chain of psychological C&C is carried in the normal way by physical processes in that body and brain, while in the case of the other the psychological C&C is due to an episode of teleportation or BST transfer. There are widespread intuitions that favor the former of these—the one having normal physical continuity with the original person—as being the original person. And these same intuitions are often seen as favoring the view that even where there is only one later person whose states are psychologically C&C with the states of an earlier one, the holding of the relation-

---

[11] See Grice 1941. Grice expresses (2) by saying that the self is not a logical construction.

[12] This Latin word means "analyzer." It refers to the expression(s) that the process of analysis produces. ED.

[13] See my 1984, section 10.

ship of psychological C&C is not sufficient for identity.[14]

One might think of such intuitions as rejecting one sort of reductionism, one that says that personal identity consists in psychological C&C, for another, one that says that it consists in physical continuity of a certain sort. But often those who are moved by such intuitions think of themselves as opposing reductionism generally. Such thinkers are in the tradition of Butler and Reid. And a natural way to express their view is by saying that persons have to be individual substances of a certain kind, and that if the conditions of personal identity were as the psychological C&C account claims—if they allowed teleportation and the BST-procedure to be person-preserving—persons could not be substances. In the branch-line case there is, intuitively, "substantial unity" between one of the candidates and the original person, and not between the other candidate and the original person.

What notion of substance is at work here? Proponents of the psychological C&C view can assent to the truism that persons are subjects of thought and experience; they think of themselves as giving the transtemporal identity conditions for such subjects. Are they committed to the denial that selves are substances in the Gricean version of the subject of properties sense, because they hold judgments of personal identity to be analyzable in a certain way?[15] But while some proponents of the psychological C&C view may be committed to the view that judgments about persons have an analysis of the sort ruled out by condition (2) of the Gricean rendering of "Selves are substances," others are not. Presumably philosophers who hold that the truth conditions for judgments of personal identity can be framed in terms of the notion of *physical* continuity are not thereby committed to the denial that

(2) is satisfied; so it is far from clear that those who hold that these truth conditions can be framed in terms of psychological C&C are committed to this denial, even if they think that these truth conditions allow teleportation and the like to be person-preserving.[16]

Could the notion of substance here be the parcel of stuff notion? It is true that in some versions of the branch-line example the preferred candidate for being the continuation of the original person is one that is composed of the same matter of the original person. But this will not in general be true. Everyone agrees that in normal, paradigmatic cases of persistence of persons over time there is constant interchange of matter with the environment. So the view cannot be that it is a requirement of personal identity that a person always be composed of the same parcel of matter. It could of course be held that it is a requirement of personal identity that there be a certain sort of continuity of material composition—one that requires that over very brief intervals the material composition remains nearly the same. But this would not of course imply that a person *is* a substance in the parcel of matter sense.

So proponents of the psychological C&C view of personal identity are not committed to the denial that selves are substances in the logical subject sense. And while they are committed to the denial that selves are substances in the parcel of matter sense, that is a denial they share with their opponents. So in what sense is it the latter, rather than the former, who are the proponents of the substantiality of the self?

IV

There is a strand in the traditional conception of substance that until now I have not mentioned. Substances are ontologically *independent* in ways in which other entities are not. What metaphysicians

---

[14]One way in which psychological continuity theorists attempt to handle such cases is by holding a "closest continuer view" which allows physical continuity to be the tiebreaker in cases in which two or more later persons are competitors for being identical with one earlier person, both being related to it to an equal degree by psychological C&C, but holds personal identity to consist in psychological C&C in cases where there is no such competition. See Nozick 1981, Chapter One.

[15]The question is whether adherents of the psychological C&C theory are *necessarily* committed to the view that transtemporal identity can be analyzed in such a way as to omit reference to *subjects* of mental properties (thus violating Grice's second condition for substance, as explained above). Ed.

[16]This is a difficult sentence, but here is what it seems to be saying: *Physical* reductionists can analyze the self in a way that refers to the *body,* or some part(s) thereof, as a continuing *subject* of mental states, thus satisfying Grice's second condition. Perhaps, Shoemaker goes on to suggest, one can be an adherent of *psychological* C&C and yet still satisfy Grice's second condition, insofar as the requisite psychological continuity necessarily involves a subject. This is the position Shoemaker intends to take, and his position will rule out person-preserving teleportation of the Parfit kind. Ed.

call "modes" and "affections," and what all of us call states, are entities whose existence is logically parasitic, or as C. D. Broad put it "adjectival," on the entities of which they are modes, affections, or states; their existence just consists in certain things being modified, affected, or qualified in certain ways. Entities on which other entities are dependent in these ways, and which are not themselves dependent in such ways on other entities, are individual substances.[17]

The independence criterion of substantiality is closely related to the conception of individual substances as subjects of properties, if that is understood as including condition (2) of the Gricean rendering of that conception. Suppose that the only tenable notion of mental particulars, such as thought, sensations, etc., is one on which these are modes or affections of—on which their existence is adjectival on—minds or selves that "have" them. In that case minds or selves will be independent relative to such mental particulars, and on that account will qualify as substances. And by the same token, there will be no possibility of a reductive analysis of judgments ascribing thoughts or experiences to minds or selves into judgments solely about mental particulars and their relations to one another—and no possibility of reduction of facts about minds or selves to facts about mental particulars. So minds and selves will count as substances by the Gricean criteria.

But I think that there is another way in which independence can function as a criterion of substantiality. As many have noted, it is a feature of the "continuants" that are paradigm individual substances that their persistence through time involves there being relations of causal and counterfactual dependence of their properties at later times on their properties at earlier times.[18] Other things equal, if this piece of wax had not had the shape it had an hour ago, it would not have the shape it has now; and it is, in part, *because* it had that shape then that it has its present shape now. This will be true if the shapes are the same. But it may also be true even

if the shapes are different; the piece of wax has a certain shape now because it had a certain other shape an hour ago and has been sitting in the sun for the last hour. (Of course, if the wax is left in the sun too long, the contribution of its earlier shape to its later shape may become negligible.) The causation involved here is largely what W. E. Johnson called "immanent" causation: causation that is internal to the thing's career, as contrasted with the "transeunt" causation involved in the action of one thing on another.[19] It is not always true that the resemblance between the later and earlier stages of a thing is due to immanent causation. If I take a watch to a jeweler to be repaired, its post-repair similarity to its pre-damage state is due in part to the intervention of the jeweler, which involves transeunt causation. But by and large, and especially in the case of those things (plants and animals) that are often taken as the paradigm individual substances, it is by immanent causation that things retain their properties over time and undergo those changes that are characteristic of the kinds of things they are.[20] In organisms, we now know, this immanent causation takes place in accordance with genetic "instructions" encoded in DNA molecules. (At the molecular and submolecular levels much of the causation involved here will of course be transeunt; it is only relative to the career of the organism as a whole that it is to be classified as immanent.)

We might sum all this up by saying that individual substances are autonomous self-perpetuators. Or, better, *relatively* autonomous self-perpetuators. Some things—e.g., images on movie screens—appear to be autonomous self-perpetuators when they are not; and to these we deny the status of being individual substances. In the case of inanimate objects like rocks, this self-perpetuation is a pretty boring

---

[17] The idea is not that substances can exist without having any states or affections at all, but that the existence of a substance does not require the existence of any particular state of affection. By contrast, each state or affection depends on its existence on the particular substance of which it is a state or affection.

[18] See my 1979.

[19] See Johnson 1964.

[20] This is a very important point. Living things continuously respond to changes in their environments, and they respond in such a way as to retain the capacity to respond in the same ways to the same kinds of events. Part of this repertoire of adaptive responses typically includes the maintenance of a boundary between organism and environment. Thus the spatial as well as the temporal extent of the organism is internally caused. In this way, a living system is a single thing independently of how *we* humans divide up the world around us by our concepts. An organism, by its adaptive behavior, is constantly bringing about the next instance of itself (as a kind of system with a certain repertoire). It is a self-instantiating system. ED.

affair—simply a matter of retaining the same properties over time, in the absence of influence of other things. In the case of organisms, and minds, it is a much more dynamic affair. Here there are characteristic kinds of change which something must undergo, or be apt to undergo, if it is to be a thing of the sort in question. Some of these are triggered by impacts of the environment, and involve transeunt causation. But there will always be a large element of immanent causation. And it is largely immanent causation which is responsible for the thing's continuing to exist as a thing of a certain kind, one embodying certain principles of change and unchange.

The existence of things that are autonomous self-perpetuators is not, of course, totally independent of other things. Organisms are sustained by nutrition derived from their environments, and even nonorganic things depend for their continued existence on things and conditions that lie outside their boundaries. But things can be said to be independent to the extent that the causation involved in their continued existence is immanent causation. The extent to which this is so varies from one sort of thing to another. At one extreme we have organisms, at the other we have images on movie screens. Among things between these extremes, self-regulating and self-repairing mechanisms have it to a greater extent than machines that need constant repair through human intervention. It seems plausible that it is to the extent that something is viewed as an autonomous self-perpetuator that we find it natural to regard it as an individual substance. It is a view that goes back to Aristotle that organisms have an edge over artifacts with respect to substantiality. It is also plausible to suppose that persons (or selves) have a high degree of this sort of independence—at least as high as that of organisms generally.[21] And my suggestion is that this is a

source of the view that persons are substances in a way they could not be if their identity conditions allowed teleportation and the BST-procedure to be person-preserving.

Here it is instructive to consider a thought experiment of Peter Unger's.[22] Unger describes a scenario, or rather a series of scenarios, in which a brain is "superfrozen," all of its matter is rapidly replaced in a way that preserves structure, and the resulting brain is then "superthawed," the result being a person psychologically indistinguishable from the owner of the original brain prior to the superfreezing. In one scenario, the replacement of the brain matter takes place in four stages, each involving the replacement of one quarter of the brain with an exactly similar chunk of brain matter. In another, the replacement has as many stages as there are atoms in the brain, and each stage involves the replacement of one atom. In both cases the whole process takes only a tenth of a second. Unger thinks that in the first case the person does not survive the procedure, while in the second case the person does survive. I think this is a natural view to take about these cases. And I think we can see it as a special case of the intuition that a person should be an autonomous self-perpetuator whose characteristic continuity over time is carried by immanent causation.

Both of Unger's procedures are of course radically invasive, involving a large dose of transeunt causation. But there is an important difference. In the first case, where the replacement takes place in four stages, it is essential to the success of the procedure that the replacement parts have the right psychologically relevant structure, namely that of the parts they replace. Miracles aside, this would require that the state of the original brain be somehow recorded, this providing a "blueprint" that can be used to construct replacement parts having the right structure. This means that if we regard the procedure as person-preserving, we will have to say that the process whereby the psychological traits of

---

[21] It should be noted, however, that the independence of persons, *qua* subjects of mental states, is compromised in one way in which that of other organisms is not. Assuming an "externalist" view about mental content, the content of a person's mental states is determined in part by her causal relations to things in her environment and, if Tyler Burge is right, by what linguistic practices exist in communities to which she belongs. To the extent that personal identity consists in a psychological continuity that involves the content of mental states, it requires a certain amount of constancy in the external factors that enter into the determination of such content. This is a further reason, beyond the dependence of persons, *qua* biological organisms, on an appropriate environment, for qualifying the

term "autonomous self-perpetuator" with the term "relatively." The independence of persons is compromised still further if, as Robert Wilson maintains in a recent paper (Wilson 1994), much of the computation involved in a person's mental life is "wide" rather than "narrow," i.e., involves systems lying outside the person's boundary.

[22] See his 1990, pp. 123–5. I have slightly altered the details of his examples.

the person are "perpetuated" is not one of *self-perpetuation*, and not one involving only immanent causation—it involves a large measure of transeunt causation, namely that involved in the recording and in the manufacture of duplicates on the basis of the recording.[23] By contrast, in the second procedure the replacement parts—the individual atoms—have no psychologically relevant structure.[24] No recording of psychologically relevant states need take place, and no construction of psychological duplicates need be involved. Here there seems much less reason to deny that the causation by which the psychological traits of the person are perpetuated is immanent causation.

The cases of teleportation and the BST-procedure resemble the first of Unger's replacement scenarios. In these it seems very natural to say that the causation involved in the perpetuation of mental states, and in bringing about psychological continuity over time, is transeunt rather than immanent causation. And insofar as that is true we cannot count these procedures as person-preserving without compromising the independence of persons, i.e., their status as autonomous self-perpetuators. It is in that sense that the view that such procedures can be person-preserving offends against the intuition that persons are individual substances.

Of course, if we are willing to be flexible enough about what count as the boundaries of a person, we can say in all of these cases that the psychological trait perpetuation takes place by immanent causation. In Unger's replacement example, let the recording mechanism and the duplicate-making mechanisms count, temporarily, as part of the person. Do the same with the mechanisms involved in teleportation and the BST procedure. But such gerrymandering is of course extremely unnatural. Moreover, it simply postpones the difficulty. For what explains how it is that a person at a certain time acquires these additional parts, and subsequently loses them? This—the person coming to be, and then ceasing to be, a certain sort of scat-

tered object—can hardly be due to the operation of immanent causation! To say the least, the view of these procedures as person-preserving cannot be made to fit comfortably with the view of persons as beings that are essentially autonomous self-perpetuators.

One aspect of the view that substances are autonomous self-perpetuators finds expression in an extreme form in Leibniz's theory of monads, according to which the future states of an individual substance are "contained in" its current state, and flow from it in accordance with a "rule of development" that is internal to its nature. The picture of the later states of a thing "flowing from" its previous ones of course requires that its history be temporally continuous. And if the substance is thought of as being a material thing (as of course Leibniz's monads are not), it seems to require a spatiotemporally continuous history. This does not mean only that the chains of causality involved in the thing's history should be spatiotemporally continuous. That much would presumably be true of the chains of causality involved in teleportation. What it requires in addition is that the thing's history should occupy a spatiotemporally continuous series of space-time locations, at each of which the thing exists with properties of the sort characteristic of that sort of thing, those properties "flowing" from the properties the thing has at earlier member of the series. And that will not be true in cases of teleportation and BST. On any such procedure, there will be short intervals in which there is nothing to the existence of the person but a series of radio signals, or a set of data stored in the memory of a computer. And of course it goes with this that, on the assumption that such procedures could be person-preserving, the causation involved in the perpetuation of the person's properties would in some cases have to be something other than immanent causation.

V

I have distinguished two parts of the claim that selves, or persons, must be such as to satisfy the "independence" criterion of substantiality. The first was that selves (persons, minds) are independent relative to mental particulars such as thoughts and sensations, the latter being "adjectival on" selves *qua*

---

[23] As Tamar Gendler pointed out to me, if brains naturally produced duplicates of their quadrants, and then stored them like spare tires somewhere in the body, then replacing the four quarters with *these* duplicates might seem more plausibly person-preserving.

[24] Of course, they have a structure that suits them to play various roles in the physical realization of mental states. What I mean is that their structure encodes no information about anyone's psychological makeup.

mental subjects. The second was that selves are (relatively) autonomous self-perpetuators. In this section I shall develop the first of these ideas further, relating it to certain general themes in the philosophy of mind, and in the next section I shall do the same with second.[25]

That certain mental particulars are adjectival on mental subjects can be read off (almost) from the expressions that designate them. Assuming that "S" designates anything at all, what is designated by such a gerundial phrase as "S's feeling pain at t" or "S's seeing red at t" will be an entity that is adjectival on what "S" refers to. By itself, this cuts no metaphysical ice. Suppose for a moment that selves are what Hume said they are, bundles of perceptions, and that it is such bundles that personal pronouns and names of persons refer to. It will be true even on such a Humean account that "S's seeing red at t" designates an entity that is adjectival on what "S" refers to. What this entity will be, on a Humean account, is something like: *the inclusion of a perception of red in S (a certain bundle of perceptions)*. But while that entity is adjectival on S, its existence clearly involves the existence of mental particulars whose existence is not (on the Humean view) adjectival on S, or in any way logically dependent on it, namely the perceptions that make up the bundle. Perceiv*ings*, as Hume conceives them, are adjectival on perceivers, but perceptions, as Hume conceives them, are not.

So to support the claim that mental particulars are adjectival on mental subjects it is not enough to argue on grammatical grounds that certain mental particulars, those designated by gerundial phrases, are adjectival on subjects. For one thing, not all of the mental particulars we speak of in everyday life are so designated; it takes some rather ruthless regimentation to construe talk of pains, for example, in such a way that the only entities referred to or quantified over are mental subjects and states of mental subjects.[26] For another, and this was the point of the preceding paragraph, it is compatible with a particular's being so designated that its existence involves the existence of mental particulars

that do not have this adjectival status—as is true on the Humean view.[27]

In part, the case for the dependent status of mental particulars is the case against the "act-object" conception of sensory states, and its close relative, the sense-datum theory of perception. On such a view, experiencing red and feeling pain (entities that are plainly adjectival) are given the relational analysis their superficial grammar suggests: being in such a state is held to consist in being related in a certain way (experiencing, or feeling) a mental particular of a certain kind (a red image, or a pain). And the mental particular to which one is thus related is not conceived of as being the sort of thing that could be designated by a gerundial phrase, or by any other designator that makes manifest that its existence is logically dependent on that of anything else. As it happens, proponents of the act-object conception and the sense-datum view have typically thought that these particulars *do* have a logically dependent status—that their *esse* is *percipi*.[28] It is one of the embarrassments of their view that they have no satisfactory account to give of this dependence—it is not the dependence of affections or states on their subjects, and it is not clear what else it can be. No doubt this is one source of bundle theories; having been committed to such particulars by the act-object/sense-datum mode of thinking, and being embarrassed by one's inability to explain their dependence, one drops the dependence claim and attempts to regard these mental particulars as the mental building blocks out of which the mind is built. But there are well-known objections to the act-object conception and the sense-datum theory, and I shall take it for granted that this way of thinking is mistaken.

---

[25] There are precursors of the discussions in these sections in, respectively, my 1985 and my 1984.

[26] For instance, we are perfectly comfortable using substantival rather than adjectival/gerundial expressions in talking about *pains*. "S's being in pain" is rather artificial. ED.

[27] In general, there is no necessary connection between the grammatical relations a word bears to other words in a sentence, and the relations between the referent of that word and the referents of other words in the sentence. ED.

[28] "Their *esse* is *percipi*" means that the existence of these objects consists in being perceived. George Berkeley (1685–1753) argued that this was true of all objects of sense perception. Berkeley understood this thesis as asserting that sensible objects existed "in" mental substances or subjects, since sensations can hardly exist *in* a nonmental or material substance. However, as Hume was to argue, there seems to be no clear sense to the word "in" when referring to objects "in" a mental substance. So Hume dropped substance altogether from his metaphysics, leaving perceptions as independent particulars, forming successive bundles in the history of what we mistakenly regard as a single, continuing mind. ED.

Even if one rejects the act-object conception and the sense-datum theory, and resolutely resists the reification of mental images and the like, one might think that a bundle theory is available to one. One allows that sensings and experiencings are entities whose existence is adjectival on mental subjects. But one thinks that a sensing or experiencing is just the inclusion of a sensation or experience in a bundle of suitably interrelated mental particulars, and takes sensations and experiences to be entities whose existence, unlike that of sense-data and the like, is unproblematical.

It is of course controversial whether we can distinguish, in the way this view must, between sensings and sensations, and between experiencings and experiences. But I think that there is a case against this view which does not depend at all on the claim that mental particulars can be shown to have a dependent status because of the gerund-like status of their designators (that claim being one that some will see as claiming the primacy of mental subjects on the basis of "the way we talk"). The more fundamental case rests on a consideration about the mental that has been put in a variety of different ways.

It is widely held, and not only by those who call themselves functionalists, that the identity of a mental state, e.g., its being a belief with a certain content, depends on what other states its subject has or is capable of having. Someone cannot have the belief that the cold war is over, or that the United States is in a state of political reaction, without believing and knowing a vast number of other things. The identity of beliefs is partly determined by their inferential connections—what beliefs they tend to give rise to when combined with other beliefs. And the identity of mental states generally is partly determined by the ways they combine with other states to influence behavior (as when a set of beliefs and desires produce a piece of behavior they jointly "rationalize") and to generate other mental states (as when new beliefs and desires arise from reasoning and deliberation). This remains true if we abstract from the status of these as "states," i.e., entities whose existence is adjectival, and speak of them simply as mental particulars. Insofar as these particulars have mental identities, as beliefs, desires, sensations, etc., of certain kinds, they are what they are

in virtue of their membership in a system of states (or if you like, particulars).

While in some cases having a certain mental state actually requires having others, as the belief that the cold war is over requires the belief that it occurred and the knowledge of what it was, this is not the most important point. The important point is that the existence of a mental state of a certain kind brings with it the truth of a vast number of conditional propositions about what other states would be apt to exist, or what behaviors would be apt to occur, were that state to be combined with—were it to be coinstantiated with—other states of certain kinds.

I think that the point can be clarified by reflecting on the notion of a "realization" of a mental state. Assuming physicalism and the supervenience of the mental on the physical, a mental state must be physically realized. Here I assume the functionalist view that the realization of a mental state is a physical state apt for playing a functional or causal role definitive of that mental state. So, it has been suggested, the firing of C-fibers may realize pain in human beings, because it is the neural state that has the characteristic causes and characteristic effects of pain. But, as I have insisted elsewhere, here it is essential to distinguish between the "core realization" and the "total realization" of a mental state.[29] C-fiber firing will not play the functional role of pain unless the brain as a whole is wired in such a way as to enable C-fiber firing to have those characteristic causes and effects. So C-fiber firing is at most the core realization of pain; the total realization will be C-fiber firing *plus* the brain's having that enabling wiring. In general, one can think of the total realization of a mental state as a realization of a sizable fragment of a psychology or psychological makeup, namely that part of it that serves as the categorical base—the truth-maker—for the conditional propositions that must be true of the core state if it is to be the core realization of that particular mental state. If we want to identify a token mental state with a physical state, and if we take it to belong to the essence of a token mental state that it is a state of a certain kind (a pain, or a hope or fear with a certain content), then we should identify it with the

---

[29] See my 1981.

total realization rather than the core realization. If we are willing to give up the claim that the mental identity of a token mental state is essential to it, we can perhaps identify a token mental state with a core realization. But in either case, it will be essential to the existence of a mental state of a certain kind that the core realization of it be embedded in a total realization which includes a fragment of a psychological makeup.

It is obvious that there will be a good deal of overlap between the total realizations of different mental states of the same individual. The realizations of both the belief that it is raining and the desire to keep dry will include the realization of the fragment of folk psychology which dictates that these states, in combination with others (e.g., certain beliefs about umbrellas), will lead to taking an umbrella if one goes outside. But to speak of what mental states will do when they are "combined" is just to speak of what they will do when they belong to the same subject—the same person, self, or mind. That notion, of what Bertrand Russell called the relation of co-personality and what we might call the psychological unity relation, will enter essentially into the characterization of any of the psychological makeup fragments that enter into the total realizations of mental states.

Now let us return to the status of mental particulars. Assuming physicalism, it is plausible to suppose that mental particulars are identical to physical particulars, these being token realizations of mental states and events. Insofar as they are token *states,* they already have an adjectival status. What in the first instance they are states of are brains and nervous systems, and their having this status doesn't automatically make them adjectival on persons or mental subjects. But if these token mental states are token total realizations, and if total realizations include fragments of psychological makeup whose characterization essentially involve the mental unity relation (the relation of *belonging to the same subject as*), then it seems that the existence of such a token state essentially involves its being the state of a subject having the psychological makeup in question.[30,31]

---

[30]Suppose that one believes in the possibility of person-preserving teleportation, or the like, and so denies that a person can be strictly identical to a particular brain or living human body. It might seem . . . that if

Here it is important to distinguish two components of reductionist views about the self. One is the claim that the unity relation between mental particulars—e.g., Russell's "co-personality" relation between experiences—can be characterized without explicit mention of any subject of which these particulars are affections, or on which their existence is adjectival. The other is the claim that the terms of the mental unity relation are entities that are not essentially affections of mental subjects—are entities that could, in principle, exist without their existence constituting some mental subjects's being in a certain mental state. The view I have sketched accepts the first claim but rejects the second. It accepts the first because it holds that the mental unity relation can be analysed in functional terms, in a way that does not involve explicit reference to mental subjects. It rejects the second, because it holds that the terms of this relation are

---

one is also a materialist one is committed to the absurdity that when one has a mental state, that mental state is realized in two different things—the brain or living human body, and the person that is temporarily constituted by that brain or living human body. But that is a mistake. The most that is shared by the person and brain/body on this view is the core realization. If, as this view holds, the identity conditions for persons and brains/bodies are different, then it is only the former that are capable of instantiating total realizations of mental states—and it is only when there is a total realization of the state that the state is realized. That persons and their brains share core realizations but not total realizations seems to me very plausible—most of us do not think that a person is identical with his or her brain, and do not think that one's brain is one's mental twin. The view that persons and living human bodies, or persons and human beings, share core realizations but not total realizations is intuitively much less plausible, but certainly not incoherent.

[31]It might be held that the most that has been established here is that there is a conceptual dependence of the existence of mental particulars of given kinds on their being a mental subject, and that this does not establish, by itself, that there is any ontological dependence of the particulars that are of these kinds on a mental subject. If we identify the token mental states and events with token *core* realizations rather than with token *total* realizations, then we can say that their existence does not depend on there being any mental subjects, although their having the status of being token core realizations of particular sorts of mental states or events does depend on this. The cost of adopting this view is that it requires us to give up the plausible view that a mental particular that is in fact of a given mental kind is essentially of that kind. But some are already prepared to give this up on the basis of externalist considerations about mental content—what is in fact a token thought about water, so they say, is only contingently so, since that same token event might have occurred on Twin Earth and been about twater instead. Of course, even those who say this typically allow that a token thought is essentially a thought, even though it is only accidentally a thought about water; whereas to avoid the view that token thoughts are ontologically dependent on minds one must hold that token thoughts are only accidentally thoughts.

entities whose very existence involves, in the way indicated above, their being related, or being disposed to be related, to other such entities in certain ways, this in turn constituting their being states of a mental subject.[32]

You cannot please everyone, and this view will not please advocates of an extreme version of the substance doctrine. It will not please those who think that the relation of subjects to affections is prior to the unity relation between affections, and that all that can be said about the latter is that it is the relation that holds between two affections when there is a single subject of which each of them is an affection. But I think that view is mistaken—and not just for the case of subjects and affections that are mental. Dents in fenders are a prime case of affections—entities whose existence is adjectival on other entities. But it is certainly not the case that nothing can be said about what it is for two dents to stand in the unity relation except that there is a single thing of which both are affections. Dents must be in surfaces, and to say what it is for there to be a surface on which there are two dents one must appeal to the unity relation whereby different bits of surface count as parts of the same surface. In general, as John Perry has brought out, the concept of a kind of objects essentially involves the unity relation whereby different events belong to the career of an object of that kind.[33]

VI

I turn now to the further development of the idea that individual substances are "relatively autonomous self-perpetuators," and its application to the case of personal identity. I want to show that this is compatible with, indeed finds natural expression in, a version of the psychological continuity view of personal identity. The version is closely connected

to the functionalist conception of mental states; as I have put it elsewhere, it sees the psychological continuity that is constitutive of personal identity as the "playing out over time" of the functional natures of the various sorts of mental states.[34] Since psychological continuity views of personal identity are commonly seen as "reductionist" views, one might expect them to be more in the spirit of the bundle theory of the self than of the view that the self is a substance. But I will be suggesting that a psychological continuity account of the sort indicated is not only compatible with the view that the self is a substance, in the sense elucidated earlier, but gives that view its best chance of being true.

Consider someone who at a given time has a typical set of mental states. The states include not only conscious mental states, but also all of the beliefs, desires, preferences, intentions, hopes, anxieties, etc., that are present only in dispositional form. Suppose that a functionalist account of mental states is true. It is a commonplace that an important part of the functional role of a mental state is to give rise, in combination with other mental states, to yet other mental states. This happens when people reason and deliberate. But it also happens in ways that involve no exercise of agency. The "cognitive dynamics" and "cognitive kinematics" of mental states is such that over time they change in certain ways depending on what other mental states accompany them. An expectation of something as being in the remote future evolves into an expectation of something immediately forthcoming, given normal awareness of the passage of time. And one need not engage in any deliberate reasoning or deliberation for one's understanding of a situation to mature over time, and for separate items of knowledge or belief to merge into a unified conception. One important way in which mental states give rise to later mental states is by laying down memories of themselves. And of course certain sorts of mental states have natural upshots which in the normal course of events they ultimately give rise to, as intentions give rise to decisions and decisions give rise to the initiation of courses of action. So given our person who starts at a particular time with a certain set of mental states, we expect there to be a series of mental states which

---

[32] One can give elaborate analyses of how one mental state causally interacts with others and/or with external events (in the case of sensations, for instance). Is Shoemaker claiming that one could adequately characterize these functional relations without characterizing the system as one whose function is that of a substance—"relatively autonomous self-perpetuation"? What do you think? ED.

[33] See his 1975. One example he uses is that of a baseball game; unless one knows how baseball events (pitches, hits, etc.) must be related in order to count as parts of the same game (as opposed, e.g., to being parts of different parts of a double-header), one doesn't have the concept of a baseball game.

[34] See my 1984.

develops from that set of mental states and which exhibits a kind of continuity.

It is the grossest oversimplification to characterize this continuity, as is commonly done, by saying that later stages of the series will contain memories of the contents of earlier stages, that temporally proximate stages of the series will have significant similarities, and that there will be relations of causal and counterfactual dependence of later stages of the series on earlier ones. All of that is true, but it vastly underdescribes what happens. A better description is that the later stages of the series are the consequences of the earlier stages in it playing the functional roles that are constitutive of their being the kinds of mental states they are.

That the mental histories of persons do in fact display this sort of continuity is not a controversial claim. But what the psychological continuity view says, in the version presented here, is that there being this sort of continuity in a series of mental states is constitutive of that series being the history of an individual person, or individual mental subject.

There is a threat of circularity here. Functional characterizations of mental states make free use of the notion of mental unity—of belonging to the same mental subject. What a functional definition tells us is that if a given state stands in this relation to other states of certain kinds (e.g., the belief that it is raining is accompanied by the desire to keep dry and certain beliefs about umbrellas), it will contribute to the production of another mental state (e.g., a decision to take an umbrella) which is related to it by this relation. Given this, it is *of course* the case that a series exhibiting the sort of functionally characterized continuity described above will be the mental career of an individual person or subject—for it follows from the description that successive stages of the series will be glued together by the mental unity relation. But that means that the account relies on the very notion, that of mental unity, which it purports to be defining.

The seeming circularity we confront here is akin to a seeming circularity that confronts functionalist accounts generally, and which is generally conceded to be avoidable. Functionalist accounts characterize particular kinds of mental states in terms of their relations to, among other things, other kinds of mental states. If all kinds of mental states are given such a characterization, the total set

of characterizations will apparently display a kind of circularity—state A is characterized (in part) in terms of a relation to state B, which is characterized (in part) in terms of a relation to state C . . . which is characterized (in part) in terms of a relation to state A.[35] The circle needn't even be very large; it belongs as much to the functional nature of a certain desire that in combination with a certain belief it gives rise to a certain action as it does to the functional nature of that belief that in combination with that desire it gives rise to that action. What all of this brings home is that functional definitions of mental states must be, in David Armstrong's words, "package deals"; and the Ramsey-Lewis technique for defining mental states is a way of giving such package-deal definitions[36] which ensures that no

---

[35] Shoemaker is talking about *two* kinds of circularity here. The *first* is a circularity connected with the word "mental." Functional analyses of specific kinds of *mental* states proceed by causally relating them to other kinds of *mental* states (as well as to sensory stimuli and behaviors). This procedure leaves unanswered the question "What is a mental state?" How for instance do we distinguish mental states intervening between stimulus and response from other intervening states that are *not* mental (such as states of the digestive or circulatory system), all of which can play important adaptive roles in an organism's response to events in its environment? What is the functional definition of the mental as such? Although Shoemaker raises this issue, his discussion of it trails off without a clear outcome. This much seems implicit in his discussion: a state is mental insofar as it belongs to a network of complexly interacting states of a system that plays a special role in the global function of self-perpetuation. But he does not spell out this role.

The *second* kind of circularity or infinite regression threatens to arise because the nature of any particular mental state is functionally defined in terms of a web of causal relations with a host of other mental states. Want to know what a mood is? It's something that stands in a certain relation to beliefs, memories, and sensations. What's a sensation? Something that stands in a certain relation to beliefs, memories, and moods. And so on. ED.

[36] The second kind of circularity mentioned in the preceding footnote is more apparent than real. It results from a forgetfulness of the core message in the functionalist account of mind—that mental states are relational in nature, that their identity consists precisely in their place within a complex set of input/output relations. The *intrinsic* nature of what happens to be a pain could be a pattern of neural activity, or something like the electrical activity in microcircuits of a silicon-based computational system. The Ramsey-Lewis technique for defining mental states makes their relational nature explicit by substituting variables for such intrinsic sounding expressions as *pain* or *sadness*. Suppose that one's "theory" of sadness consisted of the following generalizations:

1. If persons are sad, they move more slowly on average.
2. If persons are sad, they are less assertive than usual.
3. If persons are sad, they don't experience pleasure as much as usual.
4. If persons are sad, they usually believe that some major event in the recent past has been contrary to their interests.

If this absurdly simple "theory" were complete, then one could define sadness this way: First substitute variables m_1, m_2, and m_3 for the psychological states (sadness, pleasure, belief) in sentences 1–4. The theory then would assert that there exist states m_1, m_2, and m_3 such that when

vicious circularity is involved.[37] What we now see is that the "package" must include not only the individual mental states but also the mental unity relation. What we are talking about is a certain sort of relation between mental state instantiations, one such that token mental states related by that relation will tend to have certain joint consequences. This will be a multiply-realizable functional relation, in just the way that the mental states are multiply-realizable functional states. In a particular case it might be realized by the holding of certain neural connections between the neural states that realize particular mental states. But here we must remember the distinction drawn earlier between "core" and "total" realizations. What in the first instance the neural connections will connect are the neural states that are the core realizations of the mental states—e.g., of a particular belief and a particular desire. But these count as realizations of those mental states only because they are embedded in total realizations of them. And their being so embedded consists in the overall "wiring" of the brain being such that certain conditional propositions are true of states of these sorts. Part of what makes this true in a particular case might be that these two core states stand in a neural connection whereby they are apt to produce (in a relatively direct way) certain kinds of effects. But the holding of that neural connection will be only a core realization of the mental unity relation. The total realization will require this to be embedded in a realization of a fragment of a psychological makeup, one rich enough to make it true that the related states are indeed core realizations of mental states of the kinds in question, and that the consequence of their being so related is of the appropriate psychological kind.

VII

I have been arguing that certain conservative intuitions about personal identity, intuitions I have associated with the claim that the self is a substance, are compatible with a version of "reductionism," i.e., with a psychological continuity view of personal identity. These conservative intuitions are ones that I respect, and which—some of the time—I share. But they are, in me, at war with other intuitions. When I consider certain situations involving teleportation and BST-procedures, I am strongly inclined to say that these procedures are, in those situations, person-preserving. And that is incompatible with the view I have been presenting here.

What we see here is the introduction into the debate of the issue of "what matters." One can, without outright inconsistency, combine a conservative view about the metaphysics of personal identity with a Parfitian view about what matters. Consider, for example, the case in which people submit to the BST procedure every few years because, as they see it, this is the only way to survive in the face of radiation in their environment.[38] (Clones of their bodies are grown in radiation-proof vaults, and every few years the brain states of a person are transferred to one of his or her clones, by a procedure that destroys the original body.[39]) Here are

---

[37] See D. Lewis 1972.

[38] See [Parfit] 1984, section 10.

[39] In "Materialism and the Psychological Continuity Account of Personal Identity" ([*Philosophical Perspectives* 11—*Mind Causation and the World,* ed. James Tomberlin (Boston, 1997), 307]), Peter van Inwagen maintains that it is biological nonsense to suppose that cloning could result in a "blank brain" onto which a set of mental states could be imposed. No doubt he is right. Perhaps we should envisage instead something like Peter Unger's "informational taping" procedure, in which the molecular structure of a brain is recorded and a duplicate is constructed out of a stock of molecules. Judging from his remarks on teleportation, van Inwagen thinks that this would be physically impossible (given the time constraints). That could well be true. I think that the possibility that it is true can usefully be compared with the possibility that it is physically impossible for the functional organization that gives human beings their behavioral repertoire to be realized in an inanimate computer, or in aliens having a physical makeup radically different from that of ordinary human beings. Philosophers who suspect that the latter is so nevertheless take sides on the truth of the conditional "If (perhaps *per impossibile*) an electronic computer, or an alien with silicon based physiology, could pass the Super Turing Test (had a functional organization that made it behaviorally indistinguishable from a normal human being), it would have mental states of the sort we have." (For example, John Searle takes sides on this, because he denies the truth of the conditional.) To consider whether such conditionals are true is a useful way of probing our mental concepts. (Compare: it may be chemically impossible for there to be a substance other than the element with atomic number 79 that passes all of the layman's and jeweler's tests for being gold; certainly "fool's gold" [iron pyrites] doesn't pass them. That doesn't destroy the interest of the question of whether such a substance, were it to exist, would count as gold.) Similarly, philosophers who share van Inwagen's suspicion can take an interest in the truth or falsity of the conditional "If (perhaps *per impossibile*) there were psychological continuity via a BST procedure, the procedure would be person-preserving." Van Inwagen himself takes sides on the issue; he gives reasons (bad reasons, as we shall see) for thinking the conditional false.

---

a person is in m_1, he moves more slowly and is less assertive, and is also in m_2 and m_3. This assertion states what happens when one is in m_1. And sadness can then be defined as being in m_1. ED.

some possible views about this case. (1) It is false that these people survive the BST-procedure, and they are mistaken in thinking that it gets them what they want in wanting to survive (even though for thousands of years these people have lived happily—none of them for more than a year or two—with this mistaken belief.) (2) It is false that these people survive the BST-procedure, but identity is not what matters in survival; so it is perfectly reasonable for these people to believe that the BST-procedure gets them what they want in wanting to survive. (3) The BST-procedure is person-preserving, and for that reason it gets these people what they want in wanting to survive. It is view (2) that combines a conservative view about the metaphysics of personal identity with a Parfitian view about what matters.

Position (1) I regard as unacceptable. Perhaps these people could be making a metaphysical mistake in thinking that the BST-procedure as person-preserving—they are if selves are substances in the sense I have sketched. But suppose they don't think that, or are agnostic about the matter, but nevertheless think that the BST-procedure is "as good as" survival; given that they are under no illusions about the sorts of psychological continuity the BST-procedure will provide, it is not intelligible that their belief that the procedure gives them "what matters" could be mistaken. The same holds even if they have the mistaken belief that the procedure is person-preserving, as long as their belief that the procedure gives them what matters is not grounded on that mistaken belief.

Insofar as I am drawn to the version of the psychological continuity view that respects the conservative intuitions about personal identity, I am drawn to position (2). But while I think that there are possible cases in which identity and the proper object of special concern come apart, e.g., cases of "fission," I think that there is nevertheless a close conceptual link between these. I think that it is a constraint on the concept of a person that the truth conditions for judgments of personal identity should, so far as possible, make it true that persons are identical with the future persons for whom they rationally have a special sort of concern.[40] This conceptual link makes (2) an unstable position; the two parts of it, although not strictly inconsistent, do not

go comfortably together. If one starts with (2), but is more convinced of the conservative (self as substance) intuitions that make up its first part than of the Parfitian intuitions that make up its second part, one will be under pressure, because of the conceptual link, to revert to (1). If one starts with (2), and is more convinced of the Parfitian intuitions about what matters than of the conservative intuitions about the metaphysics of personal identity, one will be under pressure, again because of the conceptual link, to move to (3).

What I just said is right only on the assumption that the liberal version of the psychological continuity view, that on which the BST procedure and the like could be person-preserving, is at least coherent. And this has been questioned. Peter van Inwagen says that "if one is a materialist and if one believes that persons really exist, then one must concede that every person is strictly identical with *some* material being." He goes on to say "Someone who holds views like Shoemaker's [he has in mind a combination of materialism and the liberal version of the psychological continuity view] is therefore committed to the proposition that there could be two simultaneously existing material things such that one of them could become strictly identical with the other simply in virtue of a flow of information between them."[41] And this, he says, violates a well established modal principle, which earlier in the paper he expresses by saying "a thing and another thing cannot become a thing and itself."

This argument is mistaken, and it is instructive to see why. I fully agree that it is incoherent to hold that something could become strictly identical with another thing in virtue of a flow of information—or in any other way. But the combination of materialism and the liberal version of the psychological continuity view does not commit one to the

---

[40] See my 1967.

[41] "Materialism and the Psychological Continuity Account of Personal Identity," [op. cit.], p. 312.

[This implication would not hold for Parfit's analysis. If there were a BST between myself and a simultaneously existing clone, the post-BST situation would be comparable to what Parfit called the "branch-line case," in which, because of a malfunction in the teletransporter, I briefly overlap with my replica. According to Parfit, in such a case I am *not* identical with my replica, but, despite the imminence of my death, what *matters* about my survival is more or less intact–the R relation to my replica (what Shoemaker has referred to as "psychological C&C"). Parfit's formula for personal identity is $PI = R + U$, where "U" represents the one-to-one relation between predecessor and successor stages of a person. As soon as a bifurcation occurs in the succession of stages, the U-relation is lost, and with it, personal *identity*. Ed.]

possibility of this. What *does* commit one to the possibility of this is the combination of these views with the view that persons are substances in the sense I tried to elucidate earlier in this paper—in particular, the view that they are autonomous self-perpetuators.[42] But of course the clear-headed advocate of the liberal version of the psychological continuity view will deny this. And she can consistently do this without abandoning materialism. The claim that a person is a "material thing" might mean simply that a person is a thing whose existence consists in various of the material/physical components of the world standing in certain relations and having certain properties. A materialist is of course committed to persons being material things in that sense; she is also committed to baseball teams, corporations, religious sects, and so on being material things in that sense, assuming she agrees (as it is not clear van Inwagen does) that such things exist. From something's being a material thing in that sense, nothing much follows about its transtemporal identity conditions. But "material thing" is more likely to mean something like: something that is a material thing in the first sense *and* is a substance in the sense I have discussed. And being a materialist who believes in the existence of persons does not, by itself, commit one to persons being material things in this second sense. I have acknowledged that the view that persons are substances—and so, given materialism, are material things in this second sense—is a view that has a strong intuitive appeal. It is a view to which I am strongly drawn. But this view is not, I think, underwritten by any more general principle or theory which has an independent claim on our acceptance—independent, I mean, of the prima facie intuitive plausibility of this particular view. And if it conflicts, as I think it does, with other views that also have strong intuitive appeal, I know of no higher court of appeal that can be counted on to decide matters in its favor.

So I think that there are conflicting tendencies in our thinking. There are tendencies that might be summed up in the slogan that the self is a substance; these are what this paper has mainly been about. And there are tendencies that emerge when we think about certain possible situations, e.g., ones in which the "survival" afforded by teleportation or the BST-procedure is the only survival available, and put ourselves in the place of those in those situations. Now, of course, given the way the world actually is, we don't need to count teleportational and BST-procedures as persons-preserving in order to make it the case that personal identity is what matters. And it might be suggested that our concept of a person is made for the kinds of situations that actually exist—ones in which personal identity can matter in the right way *and* be the identity of an individual substance—and that we should not expect it to apply to imaginary situations radically different from these. But this seems too easy a way out of the difficulty. If the concept of a person does not apply to the imaginary community I have described, neither does the notion of being a subject of such mental states as belief, hope, fear, etc. And if that notion doesn't apply, neither do the notions of those mental states themselves. And that is too much to swallow. So there is a conflict here I do not know how to resolve.[43]

WORKS CITED

Cartwright, H. 1970: "Quantities." *The Philosophical Review,* 79, 25–42.

Grice, H. P. 1941: "Personal Identity." *Mind,* 50, 330–350.

Johnson, W. E. 1964: Logic Part III: *The Logical Foundations of Science.* New York: Dover.

Lewis, D. 1972: "Psychophysical and Theoretical Identifications." *Australasian Journal of Philosophy,* 50, 249–57.

Locke, J. 1975: *An Essay Concerning Human Understanding,* ed. By Peter H. Nidditch. Oxford: Oxford University Press.

Nozick, R. 1981: *Philosophical Explanations.* Cambridge MA: Harvard University Press.

Parfit, D. 1984: *Reasons and Persons.* Oxford: The Clarendon Press.

Perry, J. 1975: "The Problem of Personal Identity," in Perry, ed. *Personal Identity.* Berkeley, CA: University of California Press.

---

[42] I.e., if one holds the "liberal" view that a BST or other such information flow is person preserving, *and* the "conservative" or nonreductive view that a person is a physically embodied autonomous self-perpetuator, then one would be committed to the absurd implication that the information flow was a "substance flow." ED.

---

[43] I am grateful to Gail Fine, Tamar Gendler, Harold Langsam, Eleonore Stump, and Peter Unger for extremely helpful comments on an earlier draft of this paper.

Shoemaker, S. 1967: "Comments on Roderick Chisholm's "The Loose and Popular and the Strict and Philosophical Senses of Identity." In Norman S. Care and Robert H. Grimm, eds., *Perception and Personal Identity.* Cleveland: Case Western Reserve Press.

Shoemaker, S. 1979: "Identity Properties and Causality." *Midwest Studies in Philosophy,* 4, 321–342.

Shoemaker, S. 1981: "Some Varieties of Functionalism." In *Philosophical Topics,* 12, 1, 83–118.

Shoemaker, S. 1984: "Personal Identity, A Materialist's Account." In S. Shoemaker and R. Swinburne, *Personal Identity.* Oxford: Basil Blackwell.

Shoemaker, S. 1985: Critical Notice of Parfit, *Reasons and Persons. Mind* 44, 443–453.

Shoemaker, S. 1992: "Unger's Psychological Continuity Theory." *Philosophy and Phenomenological Research,* LII, 1, 139–143.

Unger, P. 1990: *Identity, Consciousness & Value.* New York: Oxford University Press.

Wilson, R. 1994: "Wide Computationalism." *Mind,* 103, 351–371.

Let's look closely at why Shoemaker thinks there is an "instability" to the position that he favors: a combination of a metaphysically "conservative" position about persons being substances or autonomous self-perpetuators, and a Parfitean position about what "matters" in survival (psychological continuity) in cases such as BSTs and teleportations. He thinks there should be a closer link between what matters in personal identity and the metaphysical base for personal identity. After all, a metaphysical base should not be a trivial matter. Yet he is convinced that it is inconsistent to claim (1) that persons are, or can exist only as, substances, and (2) that BST and teleportation preserve personal identity. Take the case of successful teleportation, as described in Parfit and depicted in the *Star Trek* television series. Why can't Shoemaker, in such a case, accept Parfit's formula, $PI = R + U$, while adding the metaphysically conservative proviso that R must hold between a single substance (materially embodied self-perpetuator) before, and a single substance after, teleportation? This hybrid position still maintains that personal identity requires temporal continuity of numerically the same body, in the sense that unless there were at least one such period of time, a person could not exist, since a person cannot function as such unless in a body that endures long enough to make possible the behavior that goes with being a person. Although there has to be at least one such duration, why couldn't there be a succession of them in the history of one person, punctuated by the kind of spatiotemporal discontinuities created by teleportation—an interval during which the person is replaced by information that enables replication?

REVIEW QUESTIONS

1. Shoemaker has a reply to the question just posed. What is it? Does it satisfy you?

2. Shoemaker claims a strong connection between self-perpetuation and immanent causation. One of his reasons for rejecting teleportation as person-preserving is that the replica is brought about by "transeunt" causation: "This—the person coming to be, and then ceasing to be, a certain sort of scattered object—can hardly be due to the operation of immanent causation!" (p. 484) From Shoemaker's discussion, it seems that self-perpetuation and self-preservation are closely related notions. Imagine an episode of *Star Trek* in which Captain Kirk, pursued by a would-be assassin, saves himself by running to the transporter room and *beaming himself* to the planet surface. Surely an act of self-preservation! According to Shoemaker's theory, does Kirk make it? What do you think?

Glossary

a posteriori / a priori a pair of terms that apply primarily to how propositions are known to be true or false. *A priori* propositions are those we can know to be true without experience or observation of facts that make them true (even though experience may be necessary to understand the meaning of the concepts involved in the proposition), and *a posteriori* propositions are those whose truth cannot be known in this way.

adaptive control system a *control system* which enables an enclosing system (such as an animal with a central nervous system) to respond to sensory stimuli in a way that promotes the enclosing system's continued existence.

algorithm a procedure in which every step, and each transition to a next step, is moronically simple, and the procedure invariably terminates in the sought-after or specified result (e.g., the procedure for summing integers).

analog(ue) the attribute of a procedure or process involving continuously variable quantities such as length, weight or distance (e.g., in a watch that tells time by the movement of hands); usually contrasted with **digital.**

aphasia a syndrome usually caused by damage to the speech "areas" of brain tissue, in which one or more aspects of the reception or production of language is defective even in the absence of any other kind of deficit (e.g., the subject cannot understand the spoken word even though her hearing is otherwise intact).

artificial intelligence (or AI) most commonly used to designate the interdisciplinary study of computational systems that have or **simulate** human cognitive, perceptual, theoretical and linguistic capacities.

behaviorism (1) as a doctrine about the methodology of psychology, it asserts that the proper domain of psychology is overt behavior (observable movements of the organism) and not inner, unobservable states or processes traditionally regarded as "mental" or "conscious." (2) as a philosophical doctrine, it asserts that there is nothing else than behavior (and dispositions to behavior) in the domain of the mental. Gilbert Ryle's analytical or logical behaviorism attempted to establish the truth of this philosophical doctrine by an analysis of ordinary mental language.

category categories are the most general kinds into which entities, or our concepts of entities, can be sorted, e.g., process, quantity, quality, and relation.

chromosomes long molecular strings of mostly DNA and protein, collections of genes, found in the nucleus of every plant or animal cell.

cognitive science an interdisciplinary study that strongly overlaps with **artificial intelligence** and the psychology of cognition. It is broader than AI insofar as it studies cognitive or intelligent activity in both artificial and living systems. Its research strategies rely strongly on computer **simulation.**

conditioning (operant or instrumental) the process by which a stimulus following a certain behavior alters the likelihood of that particular behavior being repeated by the organism affected. A stimulus which increases the likelihood is called a "reinforcer," and one that decreases it is a "punisher."

control system a system (e.g., a thermostatic climate control system) with the capacity to detect or sense the changing states of another system, measure their deviation from the norm or setting for that system, and respond to this sensory input in such a way as either to maintain that system in, or to cause it to return to, the condition specified by the setting.

corpuscularian(ism)   the doctrine (common in the seventeenth century) that all matter (gaseous, liquid, or solid) is composed of imperceptibly small particles of the same matter or stuff, differing only in shape and size.

cortical field   the set of cortical neurons that are excited or inhibited by stimulation of a specific **receptor** cell or sensory neuron.

digital   the attribute of a procedure or process involving discrete quantities or numbers (e.g., a watch that displays successive numbers rather than the continuously varying position of hands to indicate time); usually contrasted with **analog(ue).**

DNA   deoxyribonucleic acid, usually found in long strings configured as a double helix. Among its constituents are four kinds of bases, forming two complementary pairs; these bases project inward into the helix, and each bonds there with its complementary base. The order of these bases constitutes a code (the genetic code), in which any one triplet of bases specifies one kind of amino acid. Amino acids are the building blocks of proteins. The primary function of DNA is to serve as the **modulator** of a cell's **adaptive control system,** causing the production of specific proteins as the cell needs them for various chemical reactions inside its body, or for structural ingredients. A segment of DNA which codes for the sequence of amino acids making up a particular protein is called a gene. The double helix can also replicate itself as a cell divides, thereby transmitting a genetic code from one cell to a pair of successors.

effector   a component of a *control system,* it acts on the target system so as to maintain it in, or bring it back to, the condition specified by the setting in the **modulator.**

emergence   a term used in many related senses, some of which coincide with **supervenience.** It often applies to a property of a whole which is (a) not a property of the parts, and (b) cannot be defined or understood in terms of properties of the parts. In this sense, emergent properties are irreducible.

emergentism   the theory that there are emergent properties; see **emergence.**

empiricism   the doctrine that the domain of knowledge is limited to propositions whose truth or falsehood can be determined only through observations based on sense-perception. It is often contrasted with **rationalism.**

encoding   the correspondence between variations in aspects of the sensory stimulus as it occurs in a sensory **receptor,** and variations in aspects of the electrochemical activity induced in the sensory pathway by the stimulus; e.g., correspondence between the locus of a point of stimulation on the retinal surface and the locus of the neurons of the primary visual cortex affected by that stimulus.

entropy   a measure of the microscopic disorder of a system, and thereby of the system's capacity for work and the likelihood of anything but minor fluctuations occurring within the system as long as it is closed to further energetic input.

epilepsy   a pathological condition which makes the brain prone to seizures—abnormal electrochemical discharges usually originating in one part of the brain and spreading to other parts in a stereotypical progression with corresponding perceptual and behavioral effects.

epileptic seizure   see *epilepsy.*

epiphenomenalism   a variety of mind-body dualism which claims that mental events are caused by physical events but do not themselves have any effects.

epistemic   pertaining to knowledge; from the Greek word for knowledge, *epistēmē.*

feedback   the sensory input of a **control system** insofar as the input results from the action of the control system on the target system.

functional   see **functionalism.**

functionalism   the doctrine that mental states (as such) should be defined in a purely functional way, i.e., solely in terms of their causal relations to sensory input, other mental states, and behavioral output.

human chauvinism   the general type of mistake allegedly made by those who inappropriately limit the domain of terms such as "person" or "mind" by defining them in such a way as to restrict them to human beings.

idealism   the general claim that reality is mental in nature, or that all objects of knowledge exist only in relation to a knowing subject. **Phenomenalism** is a species of idealism.

inductive   deriving a general conclusion from particular instances.

intension   the aspect under which a predicate picks out an object; contrasts with the *extension* of a predicate—the class of objects that are picked out by the predicate.

intentionality   the "of" relation in awareness (relatedness to an object), a relation that seems to be an essential constituent of consciousness or awareness.

intertheoretic reduction   see **reductionism.**

introspect(ion)   each person's awareness of mental events or processes occurring within themselves; a kind of awareness which each person supposedly has only in their own case (privacy) and which is often said to be infallible or incorrigible (e.g., that I'm in pain).

inverted spectrum   the alleged possibility that two persons might have the same color vocabulary and discriminations even though their **qualia** might be systematically different—e.g., what it is like for one to see each color (as verbally reported) might be consistently different from what it is like for the other person.

ionic   pertaining to electrically charged atoms. An electrically neutral atom has an equal number of positively charged protons in its nucleus and negatively charged electrons in the space around the nucleus. A positive charge results from the atom having fewer electrons than protons, and a negative charge from its having more electrons than protons.

isomorphism   structural similarity; a relation that obtains between two systems when there is a one-to-one correspondence between elements of each, such that for each distinct element of one system there is one and only one element in the other.

logical behaviorism   see **behaviorism.**

materialism   the doctrine that there exist only those entities (a) such as particles and energies of various kinds, that are included in, or indispensable to, the description of the world in the language and theories of physical science, and (b) those entities which are **supervenient** upon the former.

metabolism   the sequences of chemical reactions occurring within a cell and regulated by the **adaptive control** function of **DNA** within the cell.

metaphysical possibility   what is conceivable or true in some possible world.

modal   pertaining to the notions of necessity and possibility.

modulator   a component of a **control system,** it embodies a norm or setting according to which it selects the control system's response to state variations detected in the target system.

natural kind   a kind or species that is in the world independently of our systems of classification.

natural selection   the process whereby randomly occurring mutations give some members of a breeding population traits that enable them to reproduce with greater success than members without those traits, often resulting in the gradual disappearance of members without those traits.

naturalism   a currently popular term in philosophy of mind, it is used in many senses, one common denominator of which is the view that all acceptable methods of research and justification are scientific in nature or consistent with scientific method; science-friendly without being as **ontologically** stringent as **materialism/physicalism.**

necessary condition   If p is a necessary condition of q, then q cannot be true unless p is true.

nomological   a generalization that is lawlike in its scope and necessity.

nomological possibility   also called natural, or physical possibility, it designates any fact or situation that is consistent with the laws of nature.

Occam's (or **Ockham's**) **razor**   a simplifying principle in theory construction, it tells us that we should not assert the existence of more entities (especially causes or constituents) than we need in order to explain something. The Latin version is: *Entia non multiplicanda sine necessitate* (Entities are not to be multiplied without necessity). The principle is named after the fourteenth-century philosopher William of Ockham.

ontology   a philosophical theory about what kinds (in a broad, categorial sense) of things exist (e.g., dualism, **materialism,** and **idealism**).

opaque   designates a context in which a referring expression occurs where another expression with the same reference cannot be substituted without affecting the truth of the enclosing sentence. A common sort of opaque context is created by expressions signifying **propositional attitudes.**

organelle   a part of a cell, a part with a persisting structure and function.

parallel processing   what goes on in a system capable of more than one distinct computation at the same time.

phenomenal properties   the properties an object appears to have as it is perceived by a subject, but which are not publicly observable and measurable; the content of our perception of *secondary qualities;* e.g., *green* as the content of our color awareness, as opposed to *green* as a measurable property of surfaces that selectively absorb electromagnetic radiation of certain frequencies within the visible spectrum.

phenomenal field   the totality of what a subject is experiencing insofar as it is being experienced; the world-as-it-appears, including *phenomenal properties* and a spatiotemporal structure that does not coincide with that of the public world.

phenomenalism   the doctrine that all objects of perception are nothing but sensations that exist only in relation to our perception. David Hume is the most famous proponent of this view.

phenomenology   (in the context of this book) an analysis of an object or phenomenon as it appears to consciousness, as in the attempt to describe the felt difference between two kinds of pain.

physicalism   a term that has, in philosophy of mind, the same meaning as **materialism.**

potential difference   the voltage between two points; a measure of the energy needed to move an electron or negatively charged *ion* away from a positively charged site or toward a negatively charged site; if there is a conducting medium between the two points, a current will flow between them.

primary qualities   as defined by John Locke, they are features of an object, such as its size, shape, or motion, that are like what they appear to be, that cause perceptions in us the contents of which resemble the qualities "out there." These qualities are directly measurable and subject to mathematical analysis, unlike **secondary qualities** or phenomenal properties such as color and taste.

propositional attitudes   the various relations a speaker or thinker can have toward a given proposition, such as believing, affirming, or doubting it.

qualia   (sing. **quale**) sometimes used with the same meaning as **phenomenal properties;** they are the qualities of what it is like to have a certain sensation or feeling.

rationalism   a family of views about the source or basis of knowledge, including the simple rejection of **empiricism** as well as stronger views about the primacy of reason over sense-perception.

realism   the doctrine that at least some of the objects of perception, or aspects of those objects, exist independently of their being perceived.

receptive field   The set of **receptor** cells that can influence the activity of a neuron downstream along a sensory pathway constitutes the receptive field for that neuron.

receptor   1. the component of a *control system* that detects or senses changes in the target system; 2. a type of neuron that **transduces** the energy in a sensory stimulus into the electro-chemical energy involved in neuronal interactions.

reductio ad absurdum   a method of indirect proof in which one deduces a contradiction from the negation of the proposition to be proven. If the negation of *P* leads to a contradiction, then not-*P* is false and, therefore, *P* is true.

reductionism   1. the doctrine that all sciences can be "reduced" to physical science by the device of identifying entities in a "higher-level" theory with entities or sets of entities in a "lower-level" theory (e.g., the identification of genes [entities in the domain of nineteenth-century genetics] with segments of DNA [entities in twentieth-century molecular biology]), so that laws governing the higher-level phenomena can be translated into laws of the lower-level phenomena in the domain of the "reducing" theory; 2. the doctrine that entities in one domain are "nothing but" entities in another domain; e.g., the claim that mental events are nothing but physical events of a certain sort. One can be a reductionist in the second sense without being a reductionist in the first sense.

rigid designator   a term that has the same reference in all possible worlds.

scientific revolution The period from the mid-sixteenth to the late seventeenth century, associated with the work of Copernicus, Kepler, and Galileo, and culminating in the publication of Newton's *Principia*. During this period a consensus arose that nature should be studied using the language of mathematics and the experimental method.

scientism the doctrine that only science, especially physical science, can yield a true, intelligible account of the world.

secondary qualities as defined by John Locke, they are those features of an object, such as odor or warmth, that are not in themselves what they appear to be, that cause perceptions in us the contents of which do not resemble the qualities in the object.

signals when there is a spatial interval between the **receptor** or effector and the **modulator** of a **control system,** signals are the intervening events making up the input from receptor to modulator; or the output from modulator to effector; e.g., sensory impulses reaching the brain from the eye or ear.

simulation imitating the function of one system by the functioning of another; with respect to computer simulation, Copeland (1993) gives the following definition: "To say that a computer can simulate another system is simply to say that the computer can be programmed so that it will generate correct symbolic descriptions of the system's outputs from descriptions of inputs into the system, for all possible outputs" (231).

somatosensory collective term for the sensory modalities served by receptors distributed throughout the body's surface and musculature, such as touch, temperature, and kinesthesia.

spectrum inversion see **inverted spectrum.**

substance a term derived from Aristotle, signifying the **category** of those entities that exist not as aspects or parts of something else, and not merely or primarily as collections; but are instead individuals existing on their own.

substratum an Aristotelian term signifying the subject of change, or that which "underlies" or is the subject of a **substance's** current attributes and persists through changes in those attributes.

sufficient condition In the formula 'If *a,* then *b*' (which is equivalent to 'Not *a* unless *b*') *a* is the sufficient condition of *b* and *b* is the **necessary condition** of *a*.

supervenience a dependence relation between properties or facts of one type (e.g. mental) and properties or facts of another type (e.g. physical).

token–token identity the doctrine that every particular mental event (token) is identical with (or nothing but) some physical event (token) or other. This position can be held without implying that there are any type-type identities between types of mental and types of physical events.

transduction the conversion of energy from one form to another.

transparent as a property of contexts of expressions, it designates a non-**opaque** context.

verificationism The doctrine that the meaning of a sentence or statement consists in its method of verification. Thus a sentence which cannot be verified is meaningless. An example of such a sentence for Ryle would be one which supposedly referred to unobservable, inner mental events.

weakly-coupled the attribute of two systems linked only by input-output relations.

Works Cited

Aristotle (1941). *The basic works of Aristotle*. Ed., McKeon, R. New York: Random House.

Armstrong, D. M. (1980). *The nature of mind*. St. Lucia, Queensland: University of Queensland Press.

Churchland, P. S. (1986). *Neurophilosophy: Toward a unified science of the mind/brain*. Cambridge, MA: MIT Press/A Bradford Book.

Chalmers, D. J. (1996). *The conscious mind: In search of a fundamental theory*. New York: Oxford University Press.

Copeland, J. (1993). *Artificial intelligence: A philosophical introduction*. Cambridge, MA: Blackwell.

Davidson, D. (1970). Mental events. In Foster, L. & Swanson, J. W. *Experience and theory*. Amherst: University of Massachusetts Press.

Dennett, D. (1978). Current issues in the philosophy of mind. *American Philosophical Quarterly* 15(4), 249–261.

——— (1987). *The intentional stance*. Cambridge, MA: MIT Press/A Bradford Book.

——— (1991). *Consciousness explained*. Boston: Little, Brown and Co.

Fodor, J. (1975). *The language of thought*. New York: Thomas Y. Crowell.

——— (1987). *Psychosemantics*. Cambridge, MA: MIT Press.

Hall, M. B. (1965). *Robert Boyle on natural philosophy: An essay with selections from his writings*. Bloomington: Indiana University Press.

Lenneberg, E. H. (1967). *Biological foundations of language*. New York: John Wiley and Sons.

Maréchal, J. (1949). *Le point de départ de la métaphysique*. Vol. 5—*Le thomisme devant la philosophie critique*. Paris: Desclée de Brouwer.

McGinn, C. (1991). *The problem of consciousness*. Oxford: Blackwell.

McKeon, R. (1941). *The basic works of Aristotle*. New York: Random House.

Nagel, T. (1986). *The view from nowhere*. New York: Oxford University Press.

Penfield, W. & Roberts, L. (1959). *Speech and brain mechanisms*. Princeton: Princeton University Press.

Penfield, W. (1975). *The mystery of the mind*. Princeton: Princeton University Press.

Plato (1981). *Five dialogues*. Indianapolis: Hackett Pub. Co.

Putnam, H. (1975). Philosophy and our mental life. In *Mind, language and reality: Philosophical Papers*, Vol. 2. Cambridge: Cambridge University Press.

Reichenbach, H. (1938). *Experience and prediction: An analysis of the foundations and structure of knowledge*. Chicago: University of Chicago Press.

Rumerlhart, C. E., & McClelland, J. L. (1986). On learning the past tenses of English verbs. In McClelland, J. L., Rumelhart, D. E., & The PDP Research Group. *Parallel distributed processing: Explorations in the microstructure of cognition.* Vol. 2: *Psychological and biological models.* Cambridge, MA: MIT Press.

Ryle, G. (1949). *The concept of mind.* London: Random House UK.

Searle, J. (1992). *The rediscovery of mind.* Cambridge, MA: MIT Press.